PARA LA CLASE

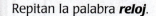

Repitan la palabra **reloj**.

reloj

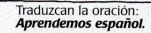

Traduzcan la oración: **Aprendemos español.**

We are learning Spanish.

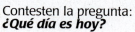

Contesten la pregunta: **¿Qué día es hoy?**

Es lunes.

Escuchen.

Vengan a la pizarra, por favor.

Levántense y vayan al laboratorio.

LABORATOR

PARA EL ESTUDIANTE

...hispanohablantes

Lo siento, pero no entiendo. Más despacio, por favor.

¿Cómo se escribe **lápiz** en español?

ele - a *con acento* - pe - i - zeta.

Do a mime activity, asking students to carry out the classroom directions. On an alternate day, play "Simon says". *Simón dice*: **Cierren el libro.** (Students all close books.) *Simón dice*: **Repitan la palabra "español".** (Students repeat "español".) **Abran el libro en la página 10.** (Students don't do anything, and students who open books are out!)

i

WileyPLUS

WileyPLUS is a research-based online environment for effective teaching and learning.

WileyPLUS builds students' confidence because it takes the guesswork out of studying by providing students with a clear roadmap:

- **what to do**
- **how to do it**
- **if they did it right**

It offers interactive resources along with a complete digital textbook that help students learn more. With *WileyPLUS*, students take more initiative so you'll have greater impact on their achievement in the classroom and beyond.

For more information, visit www.wileyplus.com

WileyPLUS

ALL THE HELP, RESOURCES, AND PERSONAL SUPPORT YOU AND YOUR STUDENTS NEED!

www.wileyplus.com/resources

1st DAY OF CLASS ... AND BEYOND!

2-Minute Tutorials and all of the resources you and your students need to get started

WileyPLUS
Student Partner Program

Student support from an experienced student user

Wiley Faculty Network

Collaborate with your colleagues, find a mentor, attend virtual and live events, and view resources
www.WhereFacultyConnect.com

WileyPLUS
Quick Start

Pre-loaded, ready-to-use assignments and presentations created by subject matter experts

Technical Support 24/7
FAQs, online chat, and phone support

© Courtney Keating/ iStockphoto

Your *WileyPLUS* Account Manager, providing personal training and support

¡Con brío!

Third Edition

Laila Dawson

María Concepción Lucas Murillo
Black Hawk College

Donna Shelton
Northeastern State University

Janet H. Sedlar
University of Chicago

WILEY

VICE PRESIDENT AND EXECUTIVE PUBLISHER	Jay O'Callaghan
DIRECTOR, WORLD LANGUAGES	Magali Iglesias
SENIOR DEVELOPMENTAL EDITOR	Elena Herrero
ASSOCIATE EDITOR	Maruja Malavé
ASSOCIATE CONTENT EDITOR	Christina Volpe
PROJECT ASSISTANT	Alejandra Barciela
SENIOR MARKETING MANAGER	Rolando Hernández
MARKET SPECIALISTS	Glenn Wilson and Dr. LeeAnn Stone
SENIOR PRODUCTION EDITOR	William A. Murray
SENIOR PHOTO EDITOR	Jennifer MacMillan
EDITORIAL OPERATIONS MANAGER	Lynn Cohen
SENIOR PRODUCT DESIGNER	Lydia Cheng
CREATIVE DIRECTOR	Harry Nolan
COVER DESIGN	Jason Vita/Maureen Eide
COVER PHOTOS	Joshua Blake/Vetta/Getty Images, Inc.

This book was set in ITC Legacy Serif Book by PreMediaGlobal and printed and bound by Courier/Kendallville.

Founded in 1807, John Wiley & Sons, Inc. has been a valued source of knowledge and understanding for more than 200 years, helping people around the world meet their needs and fulfill their aspirations. Our company is built on a foundation of principles that include responsibility to the communities we serve and where we live and work. In 2008, we launched a Corporate Citizenship Initiative, a global effort to address the environmental, social, economic, and ethical challenges we face in our business. Among the issues we are addressing are carbon impact, paper specifications and procurement, ethical conduct within our business and among our vendors, and community and charitable support. For more information, please visit our website: www.wiley.com/go/citizenship.

Evaluation copies are provided to qualified academics and professionals for review purposes only, for use in their courses during the next academic year. These copies are licensed and may not be sold or transferred to a third party. Upon completion of the review period, please return the evaluation copy to Wiley. Return instructions and a free of charge return shipping label are available at: www.wiley.com/go/returnlabel. If you have chosen to adopt this textbook for use in your course, please accept this book as your complimentary desk copy. Outside of the United States, please contact your local representative.

ISBN: 978-1-118-13062-9
BRV ISBN: 978-1-118-35927-3
AIE ISBN: 978-1-118-35179-6

Printed in the United States of America

10 9 8 7 6 5 4 3 2 1

About the Authors

A.C. Dawson

Laila Dawson

My love for Hispanic countries and cultures had its roots in Buenos Aires and Mexico City, where I spent my childhood. This foundation eventually led me to graduate studies at the University of Wisconsin and a teaching career, first at Virginia Union University and then at the University of Richmond, where, as director of the Intensive Spanish-Language Program I was able to help promote a communicative and truly student-centered approach to language learning, and also develop the department's first service-learning course. My passion for travel was shared with students through summer study and service programs in Spain, Venezuela, Ecuador, Costa Rica, and Honduras. I began writing Spanish textbooks for John Wiley & Sons in 1979. In my retirement, I work with Mexican immigrant women, teaching ESL and participating in community integration projects.

Dedico este libro a mis queridos nietos, Joel, Maya y Emmy.

I was born in Castile in the old university town of Salamanca, Spain. I spent my childhood in Galicia in the delightful city of Santiago de Compostela and thereafter, in the Basque Country, which greatly impacted my youth during the years I lived in Bilbao, and which continues to influence me as I spend every summer there.

Dale Haake

Conchita Lucas Murillo

I obtained a *Licenciatura* in German from the University of Deusto in Bilbao and a Master's degree in Spanish from the University of Iowa. I have also studied at the University of Saarbrücken in Germany and at the University of Perugia in Italy. After completing my studies in German, I moved to Madrid where I was hired to work as an interpreter at the Commission of the European Union in Brussels, Belgium. There I interpreted from German and French into Spanish. From Belgium I came to the United States.

The combination of those experiences, my studies abroad and teaching at Black Hawk College (25 years) inspired me to conceive and write the first edition of this book *together with Laila Dawson*. The fruits of this collaboration further deepened my commitment to **¡Con brío!**'s second and third editions.

En memoria de mi padre, Pablo Lucas Verdú.

Richard Wayne Shelton

Donna Shelton

I grew up in the Kansas City metropolitan area and began to study Spanish in junior high school. While I was an undergraduate at Baker University in Baldwin City, KS, a study-abroad experience in Guadalajara ignited my enduring fascination with the cultural richness of the Spanish-speaking world.

I specialized in Latin American literature, but I soon realized that my passion was working with students in the early years of language and culture study. I taught Spanish at Phillips University in Enid, OK, led summer study-abroad programs in Mexico, and mentored students preparing to become teachers. Then, at the University of Nebraska at Kearney, I directed a federal grant project that provided training to teachers in school districts with large Hispanic immigrant populations.

Since 2004 I have taught all levels of Spanish courses at Northeastern State University in Tahlequah, OK, and served as program coordinator. The students are from diverse backgrounds, and many will use the language in their work and personal lives in this region of the US. I enthusiastically agreed to contribute to **¡Con brío!** because it appreciates the needs of students of different ages and circumstances and it acknowledges the role of Hispanic culture in this country.

Quiero dedicar este trabajo a mi marido, Richard, por su apoyo; y a mis estudiantes, especialmente a aquellos que ahora están enseñando español.

Growing up in a small town in Pennsylvania, my experience with languages other than English was limited until I had the opportunity at age 12 to spend the summer in Belo Horizonte, Brazil . The experience opened my eyes to a completely different world and sparked what would become a lifelong passion for learning foreign languages and experiencing new cultures and perspectives on the world. I went on to earn a B.A. in Linguistics at the Université de Montréal, and then a Master's in Teaching French and English as Foreign Languages at McGill University. Upon graduation, I decided to move to Spain to continue studying Spanish and supported myself by teaching English in Madrid. I later completed an Advanced Certificate in Teaching Foreign Languages at New York University before moving to the Bay Area to pursue a Ph.D. in Romance Linguistics at the University of California, Berkeley. The challenges of teaching Spanish to undergraduates and mentoring graduate students in language teaching have inspired me to become a textbook author myself, in the hopes of making language learning more efficient and enjoyable for future generations of students and instructors.

Dr. Marie-Therese Ellis

Janet H. Sedlar

A la memoria de mi madre, Jean Whitenack Sedlar, sin cuyo apoyo constante nada de esto hubiera sido posible.

Acknowledgments

The *¡Con brío!* authors wish to express a very sincere and heartfelt thanks to the many individuals who were instrumental in making this third-edition project possible.

First, we gratefully acknowledge the indispensable contributions of members of the Wiley team: Elena Herrero, our Senior Developmental Editor and friend, for her on-going devotion and hands-on contributions to all aspects of the project, including her participation in the script-writing and on-site filming of the video; Magali Iglesias, for the expertise, vision, and *brío* she brings to the project; Alejandra Barciela, our Project Editor, for her dedication, attention to detail and extensive work in different aspects of the project. Maruja Malavé for her fine work with *¡Con brío!* En vivo Edition and Jay O'Callaghan for his attentive ear and constant encouragement and support.

We also want to thank Rolando Hernández, Glenn Wilson, and LeeAnn Stone for their enthusiasm, creativity, and brilliant work in developing a marketing program that conveys the *¡Con brío!* message to colleges and universities across the nation.

We are grateful to Jennifer MacMillan, Senior Photo Editor, for her excellent and efficient work in selecting magnificent photographs for *¡Con brío!*; to Lynn Cohen, Christina Volpe and Lydia Cheng, who are responsible for the text's highly innovative and technologically relevant media ancillaries; and to Bill Murray, Senior Production Editor, for coordinating all of the technical aspects of production.

We express our sincere gratitude to Katy Gabel, Senior Project Manager from PreMediaGlobal for her skillful management of the production stages of the project.

We also thank Hilary Grant for developing the excellent activities for the *¡Videos en acción!* sections, and for her work in writing the scripts for the video. And, we extend our sincere gratitude to Juan Calduch for his creative work in developing the characters and the story line for the *¡Con brío!* comic strips, and Christopher Hromalik for his careful work on the third edition of the Workbook and Lab Manual.

We acknowledge and applaud our splendid artists who so cleverly captured the spirit of *¡Con brío!* in their extraordinary illustrations.

Special gratitude is extended to Dorothy Beck, Professor emerita from Black Hawk College for her support, and to Professor Clara Camero from Oklahoma Northeastern State University. We also thank our colleagues, Julie Hanger, Keith Bonnstetter, María Eulalia Pulla and Brittany Kenney for their on-going use of *¡Con brío!*

For their contribution to *¡Diálogos en acción!*, we want to thank Izaskun Indacoechea, María Cecilia Lozada, Helena Mateos, Alejandro Maya, Verónica Moraga, Diego and Gladys Navarro and Briseida Pagador.

For their generous assistance in answering questions and providing photos and information, we acknowledge and thank Dr. Clara Camero, Bettina Díaz de Bolger, and Carlos Schwalb. Al Dawson, our in-house editor who answered countless questions and assisted in multiple other capacities, deserves a very special thank you.

For their critically important observations and comments, we wish to thank the following reviewers from across the nation:

Catalina Adams, *Winthrop University*

Jane Addeo, *Anne Arundel Community College*

Susana Alaiz Losada, *CUNY - Queensborough Community College*

M. Nieves Alonso-Almagro, *Suffolk County Community College*

Veronica Alvarez, *Golden West College*

Stacey Amling, *Des Moines Area Community College*

Guillermo Arango, *Otterbein University*

Corinne Arrieta, *American River College*

Maria Bauluz, *Santa Clara University*

Olga Bezhanova, *Southern Illinois University Edwardsville*

Marie Blair, *University of Nebraska - Lincoln*

Aymara Boggiano, *University of Houston*

Mayra Bonet, *Otterbein University*

Keith Bonnstetter, *Black Hawk College*

Aranzazu Borrachero, *CUNY - Queensborough Community College*

Alicia Bralove, *CUNY - Bronx Community College*

Cathy Briggs, *North Lake College*

Rosa Maria Brink, *DePaul University*

Daisy Bustio, *CUNY - La Guardia Community College*

Silvia Byer, *Park University*

Maria Cristina Campos Fuentes, *DeSales University*

Beth Cardon, *Georgia Perimeter College*

Oriol Casanas, *University of Denver*

Maria Castelo Millan, *Rutgers University*

Leon Chang Shik, *Claflin University*

Thomas Claerr, *Henry Ford Community College*

Marcos Contreras, University of California, *Santa Barbara*

Victoria Contreras, *University of Texas - Pan American*

Mayra Cortes-Torres, *Pima Community College - Northwest Campus*

Jose Cruz, *Fayetteville Technical Community College*

Stephanie Daffer, *University of Texas at El Paso*

Angeles Dam, *Norwalk Community College*

Ana Maria de Barling, *West Valley College*

Maria Teresa de Gordon, *Neumann University*

Ingrid de la Pena, *Chestnut Hill College*

Sandra Del Cueto, *Northampton Community College*

Anna Diakow, *Northwestern University*

Aida Diaz, *Valencia College*

Walberto Diaz, *Southwestern College*

Paula Ellister, *University of Oregon*

Luz Marina Escobar, *Tarrant County College - Southeast Campus*

Cindy Espinosa, *Central Michigan University*

Ronna Feit, *Nassau Community College*

Leah Fonder-Solano, *University of Southern Mississippi*

Sarah Fritz, *Madison Area Technical College*

Martha Gallegos, *Otterbein University*

Benjamin Garcia Egea, *Marshall University*

Ana Garcia, *City College of San Francisco*

Luisa Garcia-Conde, *CUNY - Queensborough Community College*

Claudia Geller, *CUNY - College of Staten Island*

Blanca Gill, *Cosumnes River College*

Yolanda Gonzalez, *Valencia College*

Diana Good, *Black Hawk College*

Marie Guiribitey, *Florida International University*

Bridgette Gunnels, *University of West Georgia*

Sergio Guzman, *College of Southern Nevada - Cheyenne Campus*

Josef Helebrandt, *Santa Clara University*

Marilyn Henry, *Bucks County Community College*

Milvia Hernández, *University of Maryland, Baltimore County*

Virginia Hojas, *Ohio University*

Eric Holt, *University of South Carolina - Columbia*

Silvana Hrepic, *Cuyahoga Community College - Metropolitan Campus*

Chris Hromalik, *Onandaga Community College*

Christine Huhn, *Marshall University*

Stacy Jazan, *University of California, Los Angeles*

David Julseth, *Belmont University*

Jorge Koochoi, *Central Piedmont Community College*

Luisa Kou, *University of Hawaii at Manoa*

Roxana Levin, *St. Petersburg College*

Leticia López-Jaurequi, *Santa Ana College*

José López-Marrón, *CUNY - Bronx Community College*

Nuria López-Ortega, *University of Cincinnati*

Francisco Martinez, *Northwestern Oklahoma State University*

Sergio Martinez, *Alamo Colleges - San Antonio College*

Alejandro Maya, *University of Chicago*

Kara McBride, *Saint Louis University*

CAPÍTULO 1

VOCABULARIO

GRAMÁTICA ¡MANOS A LA OBRA!

Primeros pasos, p. 1

Jack Hollingsworth/©Corbis

Paso I: Greetings, introductions, and saying good-bye, p. 2
Paso II: The verb *ser* to ask and answer questions about where you are from, p. 7
Paso III: Describing yourself and others using cognates, p. 11
Paso IV: Counting to 59, p. 14
Paso V: Telling time, p. 18
Paso VI: Indicating days of the week and dates, p. 20

1. Saying where you are from: *Ser* (to be) + *de* + place of origin, p. 7 (GH p. 3)
2. Expressing your nationality: Gender and number of adjectives to express nationality, p. 9 (GH p. 6)
3. Using cognates to describe yourself and others: Gender and number of adjectives, p. 11 (GH p. 8)

CAPÍTULO 2

La universidad y el trabajo, p. 33

Steve Hix/Fuse/Getty Images, Inc.

Escena 1: El campus universitario, p. 34

1. Identifying gender and number: Nouns and definite and indefinite articles, p. 39 (GH p. 4)
2. Saying where you are: The verb *estar* (to be) + location, p. 41 (GH p. 6)

Escena 2: En clase, p. 46

3. Describing people's current conditions: *Estar* + condition, p. 51 (GH p. 12)

Escena 3: Las profesiones y el trabajo, p. 56

4. Talking about going places: *Ir* (to go) + *a* + destination, p. 58 (GH p. 14)
5. Asking questions: Interrogative words, p. 61 (GH p. 15)

GRAMMAR HANDBOOK (GH) EXPANSIÓN:
· The present indicative of regular *–ar* verbs, GH p. 7
· Forming questions: *qué* vs. *cuál* and other interrogative words, GH p. 17
· Expressing reactions with *¡Qué!*, GH p. 22

GRAMÁTICA ... Y ALGO MÁS	TU MUNDO CULTURAL	TU MUNDO EN VIVO
Answering questions affirmatively and negatively, p. 13 (GH p. 9) Writing numbers, p. 14 (GH p. 13) Pluralizing nouns, p. 17 (GH p. 14) Indicating the days of the week, p. 20 (GH p. 15) *GRAMMAR HANDBOOK (GH)* EXPANSIÓN: · Tag questions, GH p. 10 · Word order in yes/no questions, GH p. 12	Breve historia del español, p. 25	¡Video en acción!: *¡Bienvenido al mundo hispano!*, p. 28 ¡Diálogos en acción!: *Informal and Formal Greetings and Introductions*, p. 28 ¡Lectura en acción!: *Skimming a Text for Cognates and Using Images to Understand Content*, p. 29 Vocabulario, p. 31
Asking at what time a class or event takes place, p. 38 (GH p. 2)	Dos universidades hispanas, p. 44	¡Videos en acción!: *Una visita a la UNAM; Ser bilingüe*, p. 66 ¡Diálogos en acción!: *Requesting Information; Greeting, Complaining, and Inviting*, p. 66
Colors, p. 48 (GH p. 11)	La influencia hispana en EE. UU., p. 54	¡Lectura en acción!: *Utilizing Your Background Knowledge*, p. 67
Que, cuando, porque, p. 61 (GH p. 20)	El español en el mundo laboral, p. 64	¡A conversar!: *Requesting Repetitions*, p. 68 ¡A escribir!: *Listing Information*, p. 68 ¡A investigar!: *Finding Spanish Language Sources*, p. 69 Vocabulario, p. 70

CAPÍTULO 3	VOCABULARIO	GRAMÁTICA ¡MANOS A LA OBRA!
La familia y los amigos, p. 71  Ariel Skelley/Taxi/Getty Images, Inc.	Escena 1: La familia, p. 72	1. Indicating possession: Possessive adjectives, p. 77 (GH p. 4) 2. Talking about the present: The present indicative of regular –ar verbs, p. 80 (GH p. 6)
	Escena 2: Los mejores amigos, p. 86	3. Describing people and things: *Ser* +descriptive adjectives, p. 89 (GH p. 11)
	Escena 3: Las relaciones humanas, p. 94	4. Describing people, places, and things: A summary of *ser* and *estar*, p. 97 (GH p. 15) *GRAMMAR HANDBOOK (GH)* EXPANSIÓN: · Expressing *to be: hay, ser, estar*, GH p. 17
CAPÍTULO 4		
El tiempo libre, p. 107 Oliver Furrer/Brand X Pictures/Getty Images	Escena 1: Actividades al aire libre, p. 108	1. Expressing likes and dislikes: The verb *gustar*, p. 112 (GH p. 3) 2. Talking about the present: Regular –er and -ir verbs, p. 115 (GH p. 7)
	Escena 2: Diversiones con la familia y amigos, p. 120	3. Talking about activities in the present: Verbs with an irregular *yo* form, p. 123 (GH p. 13)
	Escena 3: El clima y las estaciones, p. 128	4. Knowing facts, skills, people, and places: *Saber* and *conocer*, p. 131 (GH p. 19) 5. Talking about the future: *Ir + a +* infinitive, p. 134 (GH p. 20) *GRAMMAR HANDBOOK (GH)* EXPANSIÓN: · Other verbs like *gustar*, GH p. 5 · Let's (*nosotros*) commands with *Vamos a...*, GH p. 21

GRAMÁTICA ... Y ALGO MÁS	TU MUNDO CULTURAL	TU MUNDO EN VIVO
Tener to express ownership, p. 75 (GH p. 2) *Tener* to express age, p. 76 (GH p. 3) *Tú* affirmative commands for *–ar* verbs, p. 83 (GH p. 8)	La familia hispana, p. 84	¡Videos en acción!: *La familia hispana; Momentos importantes de la vida*, p. 102 ¡Diálogos en acción!: *Describing Physical and Personality Traits; Inquiring About and Describing Family Plans*, p. 102
The personal *a*, p. 87 (GH p. 9)	Diferencias culturales, p. 92	¡Lectura en acción!: *Guessing Meaning From Context*, p. 103
The adjectives *bueno/a, malo/a* and *grande*, p. 90 (GH p. 13)	Momentos importantes de la vida, p. 100	¡A conversar!: *Increasing Participation Through Questions*, p. 104 ¡A escribir!: *About Your Audience*, p. 104 ¡A investigar!: *Applying Reading Strategies to Research*, p. 105 Vocabulario, p. 106
The verb *encantar*, p. 113 (GH p. 3) Emphasizing who likes something: *A mí, a ti, a él*, etc., p. 113 (GH p. 3) *Tú* affirmative commands for *-er* and *-ir* verbs, p. 115 (GH p. 9) Uses of *creer, deber, aprender*, p. 116 (GH p. 10)	Dos deportes nacionales: el fútbol y el béisbol, p. 118	¡Videos en acción!: *El fútbol: pasión hispana; Fines de semana entre hispanos*, p. 140 ¡Diálogos en acción!: *Issuing and accepting invitations; Providing Information and Discussing Plans*, p. 140
Tú affirmative commands for *decir, hacer, poner, salir* and *venir*, p. 123 (GH p. 15)	Un sábado entre hispanos, p. 126	¡Lectura en acción!: *Scanning for Specific Information*, p. 141 ¡A conversar!: *Handling Unknown Words*, p. 142
	Lugares fascinantes para conocer, p. 138	¡A escribir!: *Gathering Information*, p. 142 ¡A investigar!: *Using Geography and Climate Resources Online*, p. 143 Vocabulario, p. 144
GRAMMAR HANDBOOK (GH) **EXPANSIÓN:** · **Verbs and prepositions to express direction or origin: *ir, venir,* and the prepositions *a, hacia, de, desde,* GH p. 16**		

CAPÍTULO 5	VOCABULARIO	GRAMÁTICA ¡MANOS A LA OBRA!
La comida, p. 145 Martin Jacobs/StockFood Creative/ Getty Images, Inc.	Escena 1: En el mercado, p. 146	1. Referring to people, places, and things: Direct object pronouns, p. 154 (GH p. 6)
	Escena 2: En el restaurante, p. 160	2. Talking about actions, desires, and preferences in the present: Stem-changing verbs, p. 164 (GH p. 11)
	Escena 3: Preparativos para una fiesta p. 170	3. Saying that an action is in progress: The present progressive, p. 173 (GH p. 15)

CAPÍTULO 6		
En casa, p. 183 Compassionate Eye Foundation/Getty Images, Inc.	Escena 1: Cuartos, muebles y otras cosas, p. 184	1. Expressing relationships in space and time: More about prepositions, p. 189 (GH p. 4) 2. Pointing out things and people: Demonstrative adjectives, p. 191 (GH p. 8)
	Escena 2: La vida diaria, p. 196	3. Talking about daily routines: Reflexive verbs, p. 199 (GH p. 13)
	Escena 3: Los quehaceres domésticos, p. 204	4. Giving orders and advice: Informal commands (*tú* affirmative and negative), p. 206–207 (GH p. 18)

GRAMMAR HANDBOOK (GH)
EXPANSIÓN:
· **Pronouns as objects of a preposition, GH p. 6**
· **Reflexive verbs in the present progressive, GH p. 15**
· **Reciprocal actions, GH p. 16**
· **Expressing obligation and duty:** *tener que, deber, necesitar, hay que, es necesario,* **GH p. 22**

GRAMÁTICA ... Y ALGO MÁS	TU MUNDO CULTURAL	TU MUNDO EN VIVO
The impersonal *se*, p. 149 (GH p. 2) Numbers from 200 to 999, p. 150 (GH p. 4) The suffix *–ísimo*, p. 156 (GH p. 9)	Los productos hispanos y su historia, p. 158	¡Videos en acción!: *En el supermercado; En el restaurante*, p. 178
Describing food, p. 161 (GH p. 10) Uses of *pensar*, p. 165 (GH p. 13)	Platos típicos de algunos países hispanos, p. 168	¡Diálogos en acción!: *Interacting with a Server in a Restaurant; Issuing and Accepting an Invitation, and Negotiating a Complication*, p. 178
	Dos recetas típicamente hispanas, p. 176	¡Lectura en acción!: *Summarizing*, p. 179
		¡A conversar!: *Using Descriptions to Avoid Lapses*, p. 180
GRAMMAR HANDBOOK (GH) EXPANSIÓN: · The impersonal and passive *se*, GH p. 3		¡A escribir!: *Let the First Draft Flow*, p. 180
		¡A investigar!: *Using Bilingual Dictionaries*, p. 181
		Vocabulario, p. 182
Affirmative and negative words: *alguien, nadie, algo, nada*, p. 186 (GH p. 2) Demonstrative pronouns, p. 192 (GH p. 10)	Las casas de estilo tradicional español, p. 194	¡Videos en acción!: *Mi vida aburrida; Los quehaceres*, p. 212
Adverbs ending in *–mente*, p. 198 (GH p. 12)	La vida diaria: costumbres y horarios, p. 202	¡Diálogos en acción!: *Answering and Inquiring about an Ad; Showing Someone Around and Negotiating Task-sharing*, p. 212
	Los quehaceres y el servicio doméstico, p. 210	¡Lectura en acción!: *Making Lists as you Read*, p. 213
		¡A conversar!: *Using Nonverbal Cues*, p. 214
		¡A escribir!: *Developing a Good Topic Sentence*, p. 214
		¡A investigar!: *Including Photo and Video Sources*, p. 215
		Vocabulario, p. 216

CAPÍTULO 7	VOCABULARIO	GRAMÁTICA ¡MANOS A LA OBRA!
La ciudad, p. 217  Robert Fried/Alamy	Escena 1: En la ciudad, p. 218	1. Giving orders and instructions: Formal commands (*Ud.* and *Uds.*), p. 222 (GH p. 2) 2. Talking about what happened: The preterit tense of regular *-ar* verbs, p. 226 (GH p. 9)
	Escena 2: La vida urbana, p. 232	3. Talking about what happened: The preterit tense of regular *-er* and *-ir* verbs, p. 234 (GH p. 11)
	Escena 3: En la carretera, p. 242	4. The preterit of four irregular verbs: *dar, ser, ir* and *hacer*, p. 237 (GH p. 13) 5. To whom? For whom?: Indirect object pronouns, p. 245 (GH p. 15) *GRAMMAR HANDBOOK (GH)* EXPANSIÓN: · Let's (*nosotros*) commands with imperative (opposite vowel) form, GH p. 5 · *Vosotros* commands, GH p. 7

CAPÍTULO 8		
De compras, p. 257  Gamma-Rapho/Getty Images, Inc.	Escena 1: En el centro comercial, p. 258	1. Talking about what happened: More irregular verbs in the preterit, p. 262 (GH p. 2)
	Escena 2: La ropa, p. 268	2. Making equal comparisons, p. 270 (GH p. 4) 3. Making unequal comparisons, p. 272 (GH p. 6)
	Escena 3: Los aparatos electrónicos, p. 278	4. Direct and indirect object pronouns together, p. 281 (GH p. 11) 5. Expressing possession: Emphatic possessive adjectives and pronouns, p. 283 (GH p. 14) *GRAMMAR HANDBOOK (GH)* EXPANSIÓN: · Possessive pronouns, GH p. 16

GRAMÁTICA ... Y ALGO MÁS	TU MUNDO CULTURAL	TU MUNDO EN VIVO
	La plaza: el corazón de la ciudad, p. 230	¡Videos en acción!: *La plaza: el centro de la ciudad hispana; El transporte público: el metro*, p. 252
	Un viaje a Machu Picchu, p. 240	¡Diálogos en acción!: *Formally Soliciting and Providing Advice and Directions; Inquiring about and Narrating Past Activities*, p. 252
For whom or to whom something happens: *Le* and *les*, p. 246 (GH p. 17)	El transporte público, p. 250	¡Lectura en acción!: *Identifying the Target Audience and Point of View*, p. 253
		¡A conversar!: *Using Strategic Pauses*, p. 254
		¡A escribir!: *Using Sequencing Words to Connect your Sentences*, p. 254
		¡A investigar!: *Exploring Cities Online*, p. 255
		Vocabulario, p. 256
Different meaning in the preterit, p. 262 (GH p. 2)	El estilo de los hispanos, p. 266	¡Videos en acción!: *De compras; La tecnología une a las familias*, p. 288
The superlatives, p. 274 (GH p. 9)	Diseñadores hispanos de fama internacional, p. 276	¡Diálogos en acción!: *Interacting with a Salesperson, Completing a Sales Transaction; Interacting with a Computer Repair Technician*, p. 288
	Los internautas hispanos, p. 286	¡Lectura en acción!: *Reading for the Main Idea*, p. 289
		¡A conversar!: *Active Listening*, p. 290
		¡A escribir!: *Providing Supporting Information*, p. 290
		¡A investigar!: *Participating in Language Communities*, p. 291
		Vocabulario, p. 292

	VOCABULARIO	GRAMÁTICA ¡MANOS A LA OBRA!
CAPÍTULO 9		
La salud y las emergencias, p. 293	**Escena 1: En el consultorio médico, p. 294**	1. Talking about what happened: The preterit of stem-changing verbs, p. 298 (GH p. 9)
Chris Ryan/OJO Images/Getty Images, Inc.	**Escena 2: El cuerpo humano, p. 304**	2. Describing in the past: The imperfect, p. 308 (GH p. 15)
	Escena 3: Situaciones de emergencia, p. 314	3. Piecing together the past: The preterit and the imperfect, p. 317 (GH p. 18)
		GRAMMAR HANDBOOK (GH) EXPANSIÓN: • The preterit and the imperfect: *saber, querer* and *poder*, GH p. 21
CAPÍTULO 10		
El barrio, p. 329	**Escena 1: La vida en el barrio, p. 330**	1. Expressing subjective reactions: The subjunctive mood and the formation of the present subjunctive, p. 334 (GH p. 3) 2. Expressing wishes and requests: The subjunctive with expressions of influence, p. 338 (GH p. 10)
Danita Delimont/Alamy	**Escena 2: Actividades del barrio, p. 344**	3. Expressing emotional reactions and feelings: The subjunctive with expressions of emotion, p. 346 (GH p. 13)
	Escena 3: Asuntos sociales, políticos y religiosos, p. 352	4. Expressing uncertainty or denial: The subjunctive with expressions of doubt or negation, p. 356 (GH p. 23) *GRAMMAR HANDBOOK (GH)* EXPANSIÓN: • *Ojalá que...*, GH p. 15 • The subjunctive with indefinite entities, GH p. 26 • The subjunctive with expressions of condition or purpose, GH p. 29

GRAMÁTICA ... Y ALGO MÁS	TU MUNDO CULTURAL	TU MUNDO EN VIVO
Some expressions with *tener*, p. 296 (GH p. 2) The verb *doler*, p. 296 (GH p. 7) *Hace. . .* to express "ago", p. 301 (GH p. 11)	La medicina natural en el mundo hispano, p. 302	¡Videos en acción!: *La medicina moderna y tradicional; ¿Qué significa ser hispano?*, p. 324
Irregular verbs in the imperfect, p. 309 (GH p. 15) The imperfect of *haber*, p. 309 (GH p. 15)	El lenguaje corporal, p. 312	¡Diálogos en acción!: *Narrating a Past Accident; Describing Habitual Past Activities*, p. 324
	La diversidad racial de los hispanos, p. 322	¡Lectura en acción!: *Read, Look up, Describe*, p. 325
		¡A conversar!: *Borrowing New Words*, p. 326
GRAMMAR HANDBOOK (GH) EXPANSIÓN: · Expressing plans and desires: *pensar, quisiera, me gustaría, tener ganas de*, GH p. 4 · Expressing the duration of an ongoing action, GH p. 13		¡A escribir!: *Drafting a Newspaper Article*, p. 325
		¡A investigar!: *Identifying Healthcare Sources*, p. 327
		Vocabulario, p. 328
Spelling changes in the *yo* form in the present subjunctive, p. 335 (GH p. 3) Wishes with *¡Qué* + present subjunctive!*, p. 335 (GH p. 5) Stem-changing verbs in the present subjunctive, p. 337 (GH p. 6) Six irregular verbs in the present subjunctive, p. 337 (GH p. 8)	El barrio en EE. UU., p. 342	¡Videos en acción!: *CLUES ayuda a inmigrantes hispanos; Un muralista con conciencia*, p. 362
		¡Diálogos en acción!: *Expressing Opinions and Disagreement; Requesting that Someone Change Behavior*, p. 362
		¡Lectura en acción!: *Recognizing Word Families*, p. 363
	Voluntarios dentro y fuera de EE. UU., p. 350	¡A conversar!: *Confirming Comprehension*, p. 364
Alguno/a/os/as and *ninguno/a*, p. 354 (GH p. 16)	Los murales de los barrios de EE. UU., p. 360	¡A escribir!: *Drafting a Persuasive Business Letter*, p. 364
		¡A investigar!: *Finding Opportunities for Service*, p. 365
GRAMMAR HANDBOOK (GH) EXPANSIÓN: · Expressing *either...or*, and *neither...nor*, GH p. 18 · *Pero vs. sino/sino que*, GH p. 20		Vocabulario, p. 366

CAPÍTULO 11	VOCABULARIO	GRAMÁTICA ¡MANOS A LA OBRA!
En el trabajo, p. 367  © Tom Merton/Age Fotostock America, Inc.	**Escena 1: En la oficina, p. 368**	**1. Talking about what has happened: The present perfect, p. 372** (GH p. 2)
	Escena 2: En la empresa, p. 378	**2. Talking about what will happen: The future tense, p. 382** (GH p. 14)
	Escena 3: En la fábrica, p. 388	**3.** *Por* and *para*, a summary, p. 390 (GH p. 25)
		GRAMMAR HANDBOOK (GH) **EXPANSIÓN:** · **Expressing condition with** *estar* + **past participle, GH p. 5** · **The past perfect, GH p. 6** · **The present perfect subjunctive, GH p. 9** · **The future perfect, GH p. 17**

CAPÍTULO 12		
Nuevos horizontes, p. 399 Travelstock44-Juergen Held/The Image Bank/Getty Images, Inc.	**Escena 1: De viaje por el mundo hispano, p. 400**	**1. Talking about what would happen: The conditional, p. 404** (GH p. 2)
	Escena 2: La ciencia y la tecnología, p. 412	**2. Reacting to past actions, conditions or events: The imperfect (past) subjunctive, p. 414** (GH p. 8)
	Escena 3: En busca de una vida mejor, p. 420	**3. Referring to people, objects, and situations: Relative pronouns, p. 422** (GH p. 17)
		GRAMMAR HANDBOOK (GH) **EXPANSIÓN:** · **The conditional of probability, GH p. 4** · **The conditional perfect, GH p. 6** · **Expressing wishes with** *Ojalá*, **GH p. 10** · **Past perfect subjunctive, GH p. 12** · *Lo que*, **GH p. 20** · *Lo* + adjective, GH p. 22

GRAMÁTICA ... Y ALGO MÁS	TU MUNDO CULTURAL	TU MUNDO EN VIVO
Verbs with irregular past participles, p. 373 (GH p. 2)	La etiqueta en los negocios, p. 376	**¡Videos en acción!:** *La jornada laboral en dos países diferentes; Fábrica que protege el medio ambiente,* p. 394
Ordinal numbers, p. 380 (GH p. 12) The future of *haber,* p. 383 (GH p. 14) The future of probability, p. 383 (GH p. 18) *Cuando* + present subjunctive, p. 384 (GH p. 20)	Dos empresas modelo de éxito, p. 386	**¡Diálogos en acción!:** *Interacting in an Interview; Describing a Future Situation,* p. 394
	Las maquiladoras de la frontera mexicana, p. 392	**¡Lectura en acción!:** *Making Predictions about a Text,* p. 395
		¡A conversar!: *Reformulating Your Speech,* p. 396
GRAMMAR HANDBOOK (GH) EXPANSIÓN: · The subjunctive with time expressions, GH p. 22		**¡A escribir!:** *Reviewing a Cover Letter,* p. 396
		¡A investigar!: *Using Business-Related Search Terms,* p. 397
		Vocabulario, p. 398
The conditional of *haber,* p. 405 (GH p. 2)	El ecoturismo, p. 410	**¡Videos en acción!:** *La contaminación: no todo está perdido; Inmigrantes: aprende de ellos,* p. 428
If clauses, p. 416 (GH p. 14)	Los desastres ecológicos, p. 418	**¡Diálogos en acción!:** *Requesting a favor; Expressing Reproach, Apologizing,* p. 428
	Inmigrantes en busca de una vida mejor, p. 426	**¡Lectura en acción!:** *Inferring Meaning from a Text,* p. 429
		¡A conversar!: *Asking Clarifying Questions,* p. 430
GRAMMAR HANDBOOK (GH) EXPANSIÓN: · Expressing *as if,* GH p. 15		**¡A escribir!:** *Reading Aloud,* p. 430
		¡A investigar!: *Following Current Events,* p. 431
		Vocabulario, p. 432

Apéndice 1: Diálogos en acción, Palabras útiles, Pasos 3 y 4, p. A-1
Apéndice 2: Transcripts for ¡Diálogos en acción!, p. A-14
Apéndice 3: Verbos, p. A-21

Glosario: español-inglés, p. G-1
Glosario: inglés-español, p. G-12
Índice, p. I-1

Preface

In language as in performance, a strong foundation is the basis for developing the core knowledge, strategies, and fluidity to speak Spanish with confidence and with brío! *¡Con brío!, Third Edition* prepares students with that strong foundation through the use of real, everyday situations that move the student from Spanish learner to Spanish speaker. With the confidence that students gain from the strong building blocks that *¡Con brío!, Third Edition* provides, they can take center stage in using Spanish to communicate with others both inside and outside the classroom walls.

This 12-chapter introductory program takes a highly **practical** approach with a simple chapter structure, activities in the core textbook that students find **relevant** and reflective of everyday conversations, easy access to media including new video segments, a wealth of teaching, learning, and practice resources in *WileyPLUS*, and brand new for the third edition, an online live language coaching option. ACTFL's recent release of its revised Proficiency Guidelines is a reminder of what beginning speakers can and will do with the language. This third edition of *¡Con brío!* is keenly focused on helping them do it with confidence and gusto.

WHY *¡CON BRÍO!* IS SUCCESSFUL

Equips students with vocabulary they will really use.

Illustrations that establish the context of each chapter's three *Escenas* present high-frequency, everyday vocabulary; these illustrations are keyed to a list of English equivalents right on the same page. Activities following these illustrations move students very quickly from identifying new vocabulary to using it in real conversations. Special effort has been made to select words that are standard among most Spanish speakers, with lexical variations presented in annotations to the instructor for presentation to the class as needed. Digital images with embedded audio, self-tests, and practice flashcards in *WileyPLUS* integrate the printed text seamlessly with online support and practice.

Focuses on the grammar beginning speakers need.

Grammar and other linguistic information are integrated according to their importance in creating the rock solid foundation that gives students learning with *¡Con brío!* the confidence to speak Spanish.

¡Manos a la obra!	Presents major grammar concepts important to laying a solid foundation.
...y algo más	Seals that foundation with aspects of mechanics and usage immediately relevant to the communicative tasks practiced in chapter activities.
De paso	Highlights simple mechanics and practical information like contractions and using *tú* versus *usted*.

Embedded grammar tutorials and self-tests in *WileyPLUS* extend the reach of grammar coverage to work with a variety of learning styles.

The Grammar Handbook

The Grammar Handbook, also found in *WileyPLUS*, further develops structures presented in *¡Manos a la obra!* and *...y algo más* with additional explanations and activities, and contains an *Expansión section,* which offers students and instructors deeper development of some of the concepts covered in the text, and the option to explore structures often outside the scope of beginning level courses. You can find a list of all the *Expansión* grammar points for each of the chapters in the Scope and Sequence (page xii). These appear in red.

Builds skills through a variety of engaging activities.

- *Sequencing*—Each *¡En acción!* activity set begins with one tightly-structured practice exercise which is designed to "ground" the student and build all-important self-confidence. This initial exercise is followed by carefully sequenced semi-controlled and then more open ended communicative activities.

- *Variety*—*¡Con brío!* includes both whole-class activities lead by the instructor, and a significant number of pair and small group activities. Activities are designed to be engaging, practical, and relevant.

Gets students thinking about culture.

- *Tu mundo cultural*—An attractive two-page spread at the end of each *Escena*, or module, provides insights into representative aspects of day to day life from varied Hispanic perspectives. There is special emphasis on traditions originating in Spanish-speaking countries that are also found in ever-growing Hispanic communities across the United States. Cultural topics selected are tightly tied to the *Escena* theme thus extending the opportunity for students to use the new language they're learning as they explore the cultures of its speakers.

- *¿Sabes que...?*—Brief culture notes throughout each chapter provide insights and information relevant to surrounding presentations or activities.

NEW FEATURES OF THE THIRD EDITION

We're grateful for the many good ideas and suggestions from instructors and reviewers at schools throughout the U.S. Changes for the third edition include the following:

- A more detailed Scope and Sequence lists all of the grammar concepts presented and practiced in each chapter and connects the textbook with the accompanying Grammar Handbook in *WileyPLUS*.

- We now introduce the affirmative *tú* commands beginning with *-ar* verbs in Capítulo 3 and conclude with a review and the presentation of negative *tú* commands in Capítulo 6. We also introduce relative pronouns in Capítulo 12.

- A completely revised *Tu mundo en vivo* section, at the end of each chapter, provides cultural input aimed at different learning styles (*¡Videos en acción!*, *¡Diálogos en acción!*, and *¡Lectura en acción!*) and a variety of output activities (*¡A conversar!*, *¡A escribir!*, *¡A investigar!*) that draw on all the language skills. The accompanying strategies in each of these sections give students the tools to express their own ideas in Spanish within a real-life context/environment.

  - *¡Videos en acción!* includes several new segments, and the *Mientras ves el video* activity can be now completed online in *WileyPLUS*.

  - *Trivia*, a new activity in each *Tu mundo en vivo* section that poses questions about the demographics, education and economy of countries referenced in the chapter and linked to the statistics appearing on the inside front cover.

- Each chapter now grabs students' attention with video right from the beginning to introduce its theme, encourage predictions about its content and motivate cultural discussions. Students can access the videos any time in *WileyPLUS*.

- Expanded instructors' annotations in the *Tu mundo cultural* and *Tu mundo en vivo* sections indicate the ACTFL standards met, and the modes of communication practiced through the various readings, realia, and activities.

- Comic strips provide a contextualized introduction for every major grammar point, and many of them are new or revised in the third edition. Example sentences of grammar in use drawn from the comic strip stories link grammar explanations right back to this illustration.
- Further revisions include updated *¿Sabes qué...?* information, revised PowerPoints, Workbook and Lab Manual, Grammar Handbook, and Testing Program. *Autoprueba y repaso* is now available in *WileyPLUS*.

A sharpened focus on 4-skills practice.

This third edition integrates practice of all the language skills in the textbook with extended practice opportunities in *WileyPLUS*. Conversation practice opportunity is even further extended with the brand new *En vivo* live language coaching option.

- A new *¡Diálogos en acción!* section uses short audio recordings of unscripted, spontaneous conversations between native speakers that incorporate both vocabulary and/or grammar structures from the chapter. One or more linguistic functions crucial for basic communicative competence such as issuing and accepting or declining an invitation. There are two *Diálogos* per chapter: one with activities in the core textbook, the other in *WileyPLUS*.
- *¡Lectura en acción!* readings have been updated or replaced with new realia.
- The new *¡A conversar!* section offers specific strategies for comprehension and self-expression. There is one *¡A conversar!* activity in the core textbook, and one additional activity in *WileyPLUS*.
- Theme-based writing activities in *¡A escribir!* section provide the students with corresponding strategies and process writing steps using the vocabulary and structures learned in the chapter.
- A new *¡A investigar!* section encourages students to explore the Spanish-speaking world around them through research tasks related to chapter themes and paired with strategies for finding and using appropriate sources. It develops digital literacy, encourages collaboration, and provides opportunities for presentational speaking and writing. *WileyPLUS* offers one additional *¡A investigar!* activity for each chapter.

The *En vivo* Option.

Through partnership with Linguameeting, students engage in a series of 30-minute live language coaching sessions designed to stimulate conversation around themes and topics from each chapter. A native-speaking language coach who is trained in maintaining a fully-in-Spanish environment meets with students in small groups, generally once per week, to engage and encourage them in conversation. The virtual meeting room provides video and voice connection, along with a shared space for collaboration. Instructors can find the special *En vivo* activities designed for use in the coaching sessions in *WileyPLUS*. Reports and recordings of each coaching session allow instructors to monitor student progress in developing their conversation skills in a relaxed setting and in real conversations.

Visual Walkthrough

Escenas

Each chapter is organized around three *Escenas*, or modules, which highlight various facets of the chapter theme. Each *Escena* begins with an illustration that presents the vocabulary of the scene.

Pronunciación

To reinforce and review the *La pronunciación* section found at the beginning of the book (P-1 → P-5), a small pronunciation section appears in the bottom right-hand corner of each opener scene, highlighting a particular point with examples taken from the scene vocabulary. Audio is available in the Book Companion Site and in *WileyPLUS*.

Vocabulario

New vocabulary in *¡Con brío!* is presented through images that present a visual and situational context. The vocabulary is recycled throughout the activities of each scene. A cumulative list of words is presented at the end of each chapter. These are included for oral practice in the Book Companion Site and in *WileyPLUS*.

¡A escuchar!

At the end of each vocabulary section, a listening selection, closely linked to the scene, provides practice that reflects everyday situations. These selections help students develop listening comprehension skills as they hear the new vocabulary and structures in a natural context. The Audio for *¡A escuchar!* is available in the BCS and in *WileyPLUS*.

¡A escuchar! Una cena especial

Paso 1. Los señores Alvar están en su restaurante favorito para celebrar el 23° aniversario de su matrimonio. Escucha la conversación entre ellos y el mesero.

PLUS Go to *WileyPLUS* to complete **Paso 2** of this listening activity.

¡Manos a la obra!

Grammar and structures are presented in the *¡Manos a la obra!* charts, which provides a strong foundation in basic structure and mechanics in a concise way needed for successful communication at the beginning level.

Historietas

Each *Escena* presents a comic strip illustrating an on-going story line with characters and situations that students can relate to. A comic strip precedes each *¡Manos a la obra!* to introduce a specific grammar point and provide practice for that structure within an authentic dialog. The conversations are available on audio in *WileyPLUS*, where you will also find a version without the bubble content, for students to write their own dialogs.

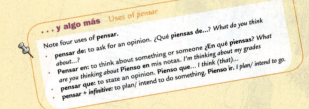

...y algo más

These boxes build on and reinforce the grammar in *¡Manos a la obra!* with aspects of everyday usage.

De paso

These boxes highlight details and exceptions in grammar, and present grammar topics of minor complexity.

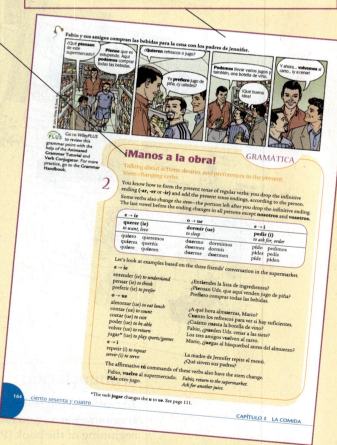

Grammar Handbook

The *Grammar Handbook* presents an alternate grammar explanation, additional examples and controlled practice for most of the grammar presented in the text. It also includes the *Expansión* sections which provides further grammar explanations and examples of concepts that are not fully developed in the textbook, accompanying with practice. The *Grammar Handbook* can be found in *WileyPLUS*, or sold on a print-on-demand basis.

¡En acción!

3-1 Mi familia y mis parientes

Can you identify the members of your family? Combine elements from each column to describe the ties.

Modelo

1f. Mi abuela es la madre de mi padre.

1. Mi abuela	es/son	a. la hija de mis padres
2. Mi tío		b. el esposo de mi hermana
3. Mis sobrinos		c. los padres de mi esposo/a
4. Mi hermana		d. el hermano de mi madre
5. Mi cuñado		e. los hijos de mi hermano/a
6. Mis nietos		f. la madre de mi padre
7. Mis primas		g. los hijos de mis hijos
8. Mis suegros		h. las hijas de mis tíos

De paso

The words **hijos, esposos, suegros, hermanos**, and so on, like the word **ellos**, represent both an all-male or a mixed-gender group.

3-2 La familia

Look at the wedding portrait and at the scene of the Roldán family seventeen years later (pages 72–73). Can you identify everyone? Take turns asking and answering the questions below.

La familia, el día del matrimonio

1. ¿Quién es la esposa de Damián? *Es...*
2. ¿Cómo se llaman los padres de Mª Luisa? ¿Y los de Damián?
3. ¿Quiénes son los suegros de Mª Luisa? ¿Y los de Damián? *Son...*
4. ¿Quiénes son los cuñados de Mª Luisa?
5. ¿Quiénes son los sobrinos de Mª Luisa y Damián?

La familia, diecisiete años más tarde

6. ¿Quién es la madre de los cinco hijos? ¿Y el padre?
7. ¿Cómo se llaman los hijos de Mª Luisa y Damián? ¿Quién es la bebé?
8. ¿Quién es el hermano menor de Ángel? ¿Y quiénes son las hermanas mayores de Anita?
9. ¿Cómo se llaman los abuelos? ¿Quiénes son sus nietos?
10. ¿Quiénes son Pedro y Teresa? ¿Y Clara y Lino?
11. ¿Cómo se llama el perro? ¿Y el gato?
12. ¿Quién es Nuria? ¿Y las personas que están en las fotos de la pared?

¡En acción!

The first activity in each grammar-related *¡En acción!* section is *¡Oye!*, an interactive listening activity where students hear the structure in context and give simple responses in the instructor-directed follow up. Each *¡Oye!* is then followed by a series of varied and often unique activities carefully sequenced for building communication skills. Instructors can find the recordings in *WileyPLUS* and BCS.

¿Sabes que...?

Located throughout each chapter, with topics that reflect the chapter theme, *¿Sabes que...?* provides interesting information related to Spanish culture within the USA and in Spanish-speaking countries.

Tu mundo cultural

Appearing in each *Escena*, this section presents a cultural topic related to the theme of the chapter. These carefully selected topics provide insights into the everyday life of various cultures of the Hispanic world. Special emphasis is given to traditions originating in Spanish-speaking countries that can also be found in Hispanic communities in the United States. The reading is followed by activities that ask students to compare with Hispanic cultures. *¿Qué aprendiste?* activity guides students in identifying the key points in the reading; the *Actividad cultural* provides a hands-on task for applying the cultural insights learned; and, finally, the *Contraste cultural* stimulates students to look at aspects of their own culture through different eyes by comparing them to what they have learned about aspects of the Hispanic world.

PLUS Go to *WileyPLUS* to see the video related to this reading.

Tu mundo cultural

La etiqueta en los negocios

Nunca se sabe. Quizás en un futuro próximo tengas que ir de viaje de negocios a un país hispano. Si eso ocurre, ¿estás preparado/a? Lee lo que sigue. Tal vez un día te pueda ser muy útil[1].

Hacer negocios en un país extranjero es siempre un reto[2] porque requiere conocer un idioma[3], una cultura y un sistema legal diferentes. Para tener éxito[4] en las relaciones comerciales con los países hispanos, conviene conocer la etiqueta o protocolo que siguen en los negocios. Es cuestión de estar preparado.

Las relaciones personales son la base del éxito en los negocios con los hispanos. Lo primero que hay que hacer es crear una relación personal y amistosa, y luego vienen los negocios.

En los negocios, como en el resto de la vida hispana, la proximidad física es algo normal, tanto en los saludos como durante la conversación y negociación.

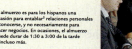

El almuerzo es para los hispanos una ocasión para entablar[5] relaciones personales y conocerse, no necesariamente para hacer negocios. En ocasiones, el almuerzo puede durar de la 1:30 a 3:00 de la tarde o incluso más.

[1]useful, [2]challenge, [3]language, [4]tener... to be successful, [5]to strike up

Tu mundo en vivo

This section provides authentic **linguistic input** (*¡Videos en acción!, ¡Diálogos en acción!*, and *¡Lectura en acción!*) and promotes **language prodution** (*¡A conversar!, ¡A escribir!, ¡A investigar!*).

¡Videos en acción!, two culturally thematic videos with unscripted interviews accompanying by pre-, while, and post-viewing activities.

¡Diálogos en acción!, two unscripted dialogue recordings modeling important linguistic functions with accompanying listening and speaking activities.

¡A conversar!, an interpersonal speaking activity related to the chapter theme and presented with a strategy to assist students in developing comprehension or self expression skills.

¡A escribir!, a presentational writing task paired with a prewriting, writing, or revising strategy and process writing steps.

¡Lectura en acción!, an excerpt of an authentic Spanish speaking source with accompanying comprehension and discussion questions; and reading strategies.

¡A investigar!, asks students to collaborate researching a theme-related topic using authentic materials and to present their findings in spoken or written form. The accompanying strategy guides students in finding online or community-based sources of information.

Trivia

This box consists of three questions related to the Spanish-speaking world. Instructors can use these trivia questions as a way to raise awareness about some geographical, demographic and socioeconomic aspects of these countries. Answers can be found consulting the map and data boxes provided in the map of the front inside cover of the book. Instructors can also use the trivia to organize contests in Spanish every four, five or six chapters.

The Complete Program

To receive a review or desk copy of any of these program components, please contact your local Wiley sales representative, call our Sales Office at 1-800-CALL-WILEY (1-800-225-5945), or contact us online at www.wiley.com/college/lucasmurillo.

Student Textbook
978-1-118-13062-9
The textbook is organized into twelve chapters, each of which is divided into three identically structured and thematically complementary *Escenas,* and culminates in the **Tu mundo en vivo**. An access code is required to download accompanying video and the audio from our Companion Site at www.wiley.com/college/lucasmurillo.

Annotated Instructor's Edition
978-1-118-35179-6
The Annotated Instructor's Edition contains side notes with suggestions for teaching, meaningful structural exercises, suggestions for varying or expanding communicative activities, transcripts of audio input for the *¡Oye!* listening activities. These annotations are especially helpful for first-time instructors.

Grammar Handbook
978-1-118-55088-5
The Grammar Handbook, also found in *WileyPLUS,* further develops structures presented in *¡Manos a la obra!* and *...y algo más* with additional explanations and activities, and contains an *Expansión section,* which offers students and instructors deeper development of some of the concepts covered in the text, and the option to explore structures often outside the scope of beginning level courses.

Activities Manual
978-1-118-35038-6
The Activities Manual is available in print or online in *WileyPLUS* or Quia™ and contains two components:

- A Workbook that links reading and writing, builds vocabulary, practices grammar, and helps students develop personal expression and composition skills. Some activities are self-correcting and the answer key appears at the end of the Activities Manual.

- A Lab Manual to be used with the Lab Manual Audio files available digitally on *WileyPLUS* and on the Instructor and Student Companion Sites (access codes are required). The Lab Manual includes a variety of contextualized listening comprehension activities. The Answer Key to the written responses in the Lab Manual and the audio scripts are available as an electronic file on the **¡Con brío!** Instructor Companion Site at www.wiley.com/college/lucasmurillo and in *WileyPLUS* as an Instructor Resource.

¡Con brío! *Video*
www.wileyplus.com
¡Con brío! has two videos per chapter (except for Chapter 1 which has one video). These text-specific and culturally-oriented segments are accompanied by activities in the **Tu mundo en vivo** section. Throughout the segments, students will watch real-life interactions between native speakers of Spanish in the U.S. and abroad, in professional or social settings, in order to explore cultural topics presented in the textbook. Video segments are available digitally in *WileyPLUS* and on the Instructor and Student Companion Sites. Access codes are required.

WileyFLEX
Students have more options than the traditional textbook. Consider an eBook, loose-leaf binder version or a custom publication. Learn more about our flexible pricing, flexible formats and flexible content at www.wiley.com/college/wileyflex.

WileyPLUS

www.wileyplus.com

WileyPLUS is an innovative, research-based, online teaching and learning environment that integrates relevant resources, including the entire digital textbook, in an easy-to-navigate framework that helps students study more effectively. Online Activities Manual available with our Premium version. *WileyPLUS* builds students' confidence because it takes the guesswork out of studying by providing a clear roadmap to academic success. With *WileyPLUS,* instructors and students receive 24/7 access to resources that promote positive learning outcomes. Throughout each study session, students can assess their progress and gain immediate feedback on their strengths and weaknesses so they can be confident they are spending their time effectively.

What do students receive with *WileyPLUS?*

WileyPLUS offers an innovative, research-based, online environment for effective teaching and learning that includes the following:

A Research-Based Design.   *WileyPLUS* provides an online environment that integrates relevant resources, including the entire digital textbook with audio and video hyperlinks, in an easy-to-navigate framework that helps students study more effectively.

- *WileyPLUS* adds structure by organizing textbook into a more manageable content.
- Related supplemental material reinforces the learning objectives.
- Innovative features such as self-evaluation tools improve time management and strengthen areas of weakness.

One-on-one Engagement.   With *WileyPLUS* for *¡Con brío!* students receive 24/7 access to resources that promote positive learning outcomes. Students engage with related activities (in various media) and sample practice items, including:

- **Live Learning Component:** Access to live learning materials and coaches
- **Blackboard IM functionality**: Student collaboration tool with IM, whiteboard, and desktop sharing capabilities
- **Wimba Voice Response Questions and Wimba VoiceBoards:** Recording functionality that allows instructors to test students' speaking skills.
- **Electronic Activities Manual:** Allows instructors to assign Workbook and Lab Manual activities which are then sent straight to the gradebook for automatic or manual grading. Available through Quia™ or in the assignment section of the Premium *WileyPLUS* course.
- **In-text activities:** Assignable electronic versions of select textbook activities that tests students' understanding of grammar and vocabulary
- **Animated Grammar Tutorials:** Animation series that reinforces key grammatical lessons
- **Videos with Activities:** Culture-based videos expose students to the various themes from the book, while the activities test their knowledge and understanding of those videos. Scripts in English and Spanish are also available to instructors.
- **Glossary:** Alphabetical listing of the key terms from the book; available in two versions: English-Spanish and Spanish-English
- **Map Quizzes:** Interactive study tool that tests students' geographical knowledge of Spanish-speaking countries and cities
- **Audio Flashcards:** Offers pronunciation, English/Spanish translations, and chapter quizzes
- **Verb Conjugator:** Supplemental guides and practice for conjugating verbs
- *Autopruebas* **Self-tests for additional practice:** Organized by *Escena* (or Paso in Chapter 1), these auto-graded exams allow students to test their understanding of the vocabulary and grammar points from each chapter; answers appear automatically upon submission
- **English Grammar Checkpoints:** Alphabetical listing of the major grammar points from the book that allow students to review their use in the English language
- **Grammar Handbook:** Presents an abbreviated grammar explanation, additional examples and controlled practice for most of the grammar presented in the text.
- *La pronunciación:* Guide that offers basic rules and practice for pronouncing the alphabet, diphthongs, accent marks and more

Measurable Outcomes. Throughout each study session, students can assess their progress and gain immediate feedback. *WileyPLUS* provides precise reporting of strengths and weaknesses, as well as individualized quizzes, so that students are confident they are spending their time on the right things. With *WileyPLUS*, students always know the exact outcome of their efforts.

What do instructors receive with *WileyPLUS*?

WileyPLUS provides reliable, customizable resources that reinforce course goals inside and outside of the classroom as well as visibility into individual student progress. Pre-created materials and activities help instructors optimize their time:

- **Syllabi:** Organized by semester and week
- **PowerPoint Presentations:** Broken down by *Escena,* instructors have the option to use:
  - Lecture: Presents explanations of the main grammatical and cultural points from each chapter, plus additional activities to reinforce students' understanding of the text
  - Media-Enriched: Includes the features of lecture PowerPoints, plus links to video and audio files
  - Take Note: PDF files that can be distributed in class to support the lecture presentation
- **Image Gallery:** Collection of the photographs, illustrations and artwork that are used in each chapter of the text
- **Pre-built Question Assignments:** Available in a variety of options, these pre-built electronic quizzes allow instructors to test students' understanding of vocabulary, grammar, and culture, as well as their reading, writing, listening and speaking skill levels
- **Test bank:** Collection of assignable questions that allow instructors to build custom exams; select Test bank questions are also available in Word documents
- **Printable exams with answer keys, audio files, and scripts:** All of the components that instructors need to distribute printed exams in class
- **Lab Manual audio script:** Organized by chapter, this offers the script for the Lab Manual audio files
- **Live Learning Lesson Plan and Suggest Assignment Guidelines:** Organized by semester and week, the Lesson Plans offer teaching guidance for the Coaches, while the Suggest Assignment Guidelines offer grading direction.
- ***Punto y coma*** create your own cultural Spanish Reader to accompany *¡Con brío!* through Wiley Custom Select. Visit http://mywiley.info/puntoycoma for more information.

Gradebook: *WileyPLUS* provides access to reports on trends in class performance, student use of course materials and progress towards learning objectives, helping inform decisions and drive classroom discussions.

WileyPLUS. Learn More.

www.wileyplus.com
Powered by proven technology and built on a foundation of cognitive research, *WileyPLUS* has enriched the education of millions of students, in over 20 countries around the world. If you are interested in a version that includes the electronic Activities Manual, please contact your sales representative for information about *WileyPLUS Premium*.

Student Companion Site

www.wiley.com/college/lucasmurillo
The Student Companion Site contains a link to an electronic Activities Manual offered by Quia™, complimentary self-tests, audio flashcards, the Verb Conjugator System with practice handouts, accompanying audio for the textbook and Lab Manual, map quizzes, videos, and access to *Panoramas Culturales* website (an access code is required).

Instructor Companion Site

www.wiley.com/college/lucasmurillo
The Instructor Companion Site includes the student resources mentioned above, plus chapter-level, mid-term, and final exams; computerized and Word versions of the Test Bank; and test audio files. It also includes the image gallery, answer keys for the exams and the Lab Manual, audio and video scripts, and various PowerPoint presentations.

LA PRONUNCIACIÓN

Learning to pronounce Spanish correctly is the first step in an exciting adventure with the Spanish language and Hispanic cultures. The information presented in this section will help you absorb the basic rules of pronunciation. Its content is recorded in www.wileyplus.com under Audio and in the Book Companion Site. Remember that you will only achieve correct pronunciation with regular practice from the very first day. *¡Con brío!* also offers you pronunciation guidance and practice in the opening scene of Chapters 2–12 and throughout the Laboratory Manual.

1. VOWELS

Unlike English vowels, each Spanish vowel has only one basic sound. Spanish vowels are short and clipped, never long and drawn out. Listen to and repeat each vowel sound and the corresponding examples.

Vowel	Sound	Examples
a	like the **a** in *spa*	banana, Amanda, Panamá
e	like the **e** in *Betty*	bebé, pelele, tema
i	like the **ee** in *tree* or the **ea** in *tea*	mi, sí, isla
o	like the **o** in *more*	oso, ocho, Rosa
u	like the **u** in *blue* or the **oo** in *too*	uno, único, Úrsula

A. Práctica

Read each of the following words, concentrating on the vowel sounds. The vowel in bold is the one to stress. Begin after you hear **¡Adelante!**[1] After you read each word, listen for confirmation.

alma	mamá	acampar	cama
Elena	entera	tema	meta
analista	misa	típica	ermita
no	dos	color	once
último	punto	Cuba	musa

---

[1]Go ahead! Begin!

2. DIPHTHONGS

In Spanish there are two types of vowels: strong (**a, e, o**) and weak (**i, u**). A diphthong is either a combination of two weak vowels or a combination of a weak vowel and a strong vowel. The consonant **y**, when it occurs at the end of a word, is pronounced like the vowel **i** and also forms a diphthong. Diphthongs constitute one unit of sound, and are thus pronounced as a single syllable. Listen to and repeat the following sounds and words.

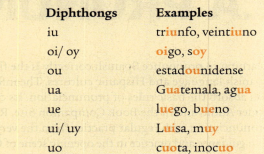

Diphthongs	Examples	Diphthongs	Examples
ai/ ay	**ai**re, ¡**ay**!	iu	tri**u**nfo, veint**iu**no
au	**au**la, **au**téntico	oi/ oy	**oi**go, s**oy**
ei/ ey	s**ei**s, r**ey**	ou	estad**ou**nidense
eu	**Eu**ropa, f**eu**do	ua	G**ua**temala, ag**ua**
ia	p**ia**no, d**ia**rio	ue	l**ue**go, b**ue**no
ie	s**ie**te, f**ie**sta	ui/ uy	L**ui**sa, m**uy**
io	id**io**ma, D**io**s	uo	c**uo**ta, inoc**uo**

B. Práctica

Read each of the following words, concentrating on the diphthong in bold. Begin after you hear **¡Adelante!** After you read each word, listen for confirmation.

estud**ia**nte   v**ei**nte   as**ie**nto   id**io**ma   v**iu**da   Ed**ua**rdo   esc**ue**la   d**úo**

b**ui**tre   car**ey**   b**ai**le   Bomb**ay**   **au**to   d**oy**   **eu**ro   **oi**ga   c**uy**

3. STRESS AND WRITTEN ACCENT

Listen to each of the following rules, then listen to and repeat each word, stressing the syllable in bold.

a. Words that end in a **vowel, n,** or **s** are stressed on the next-to-the-last syllable.

a-ma-**ri**-llo   **al**-ma   **gus**-to   re-**pi**-tan   **cla**-ses   do-**lo**-res

b. Words that do not end in a vowel, **n** or **s** are stressed on the last syllable.

pro-fe-**sor**   co-**lor**   doc-**tor**   u-ni-ver-si-**dad**   re-**loj**   es-pe-**cial**

c. Words that do not follow these rules carry a written accent to indicate where the stress falls.

ca-**fé**   te-**lé**-fo-no   **pá**-gi-na   mu-sul-**mán**   di-**fí**-cil   fi-lo-so-**fí**-a

Sometimes a written accent signals a different meaning in words with the same spelling. Examples: **tú** *you,* **tu** *your;* **él** *he,* **el** *the;* **sí** *yes,* **si** *if*

C. Práctica

Pronounce the following words, stressing the correct syllable. Begin after you hear **¡Adelante!** After you pronounce each word, listen for confirmation.

1. lu-nes
2. op-ti-mis-ta
3. có-mi-co
4. es-tu-dian
5. ac-tor
6. ca-li-dad
7. con-fir-mar
8. ge-ne-ral
9. brí-o
10. te-lé-fo-no
11. gra-tis
12. es-ta-dou-ni-den-se

4. THE ALPHABET AND PRONUNCIATION

As you have seen, the pronunciation of Spanish vowels is different from the pronunciation of their English counterparts. This is also true for certain Spanish consonants. In addition, pronunciation can vary in different regions of the Hispanic world.

Below, you will find the Spanish alphabet* with guidelines for pronouncing each letter. Note that every letter is pronounced except for **h**, which is always silent. Listen to and repeat the name of each letter (second column) and each example word (fourth column).

Letter	Name	Pronunciation	Examples
a	a	Like the **a** in *spa*.	ama, mapa
b	be	Like English **b**, but stronger at the beginning of a word or sentence and after **m**.	banco, nombre
		Softer in other positions (between vowels).	fábula, cabo
c	ce	Like English **c** in *cat*.	casa, coma, Cuba
		Like **s** before **e** or **i**.	cero, cita
		In some regions of Spain, like **th** in *thirst*.	cero, cita
		Ch is pronounced like **ch** in *chief*.	ocho, chévere
d	de	Like English **d**, but stronger at the beginning of a word or sentence and after **n** or **l**.	dama, disco banda, saldo
		Softer in other positions (between vowels; at the end of words)—like **th** in *though*.	todo, cada, Madrid
e	e	Like the **e** in *Betty*.	estéreo, mesero
f	efe	The same as in English.	feliz, Filipinas
g	ge	Like the **g** in *go*.	gasolina, golfo
		Like the **h** in *help* (before **e**) or in *hit* (before **i**).	general, Gibraltar
		In the combination **gue** and **gui**, the **u** is silent and the **g** is pronounced like the **g** in *game*.	guerra, guitarra
		When the **u** carries a *dieresis* (**ü**), **gü** is pronounced like the **gu** in *language*.	bilingüe, pingüino
h	hache	Always silent.	hola, hotel
i	i	Like the **ee** in *tree* or the **ea** in *tea*.	insecto, isla
j	jota	Like the **h** in *help*.	jefe, julio
k	ka	The same as in English. (Used only in words of foreign origin.)	kilómetro, karate

*In the past, two two-letter combinations—**ch** (che), **ll** (elle)—were part of the Spanish alphabet.

Letter	Name	Pronunciation	Examples
l	ele	The same as in English.	lunes, loco
		Double **l** (**ll**) is most often pronounced like the **y** in *yes*.	llama, calle
m	eme	Same as in English.	mandarina, mano
n	ene	Same as in English.	nada, nunca
ñ	eñe	Like **ni** in *onion*.	mañana, niño
o	o	Like the **o** in *more*.	oro, doctor
p	pe	Same as in English.	paso, piso
q	cu	Same as in English. (It occurs only in the combinations **que** and **qui**, where the **u** is silent.)	pequeño, arquitecto
r	ere, erre	Single **r** at the beginning of a word and double **r** (**rr**) in the middle of a word are trilled.	reloj, rojo perro, carro
		Otherwise, as **tt** and **dd** in *bitter* and *ladder*.	puro, caro
s	ese	Same as in English.	salsa, seis
t	te	Same as in English.	teléfono, tímido
u	u	Like the **u** in *true* or the **oo** in *too*.	único, usar
v	uve*	Spanish **b** and **v** are pronounced the same.	
		Like English **b**, but stronger at the beginning of a word or sentence and after **n**.	vista, vosotros enviar
		Softer in other positions (between vowels).	ceviche, aventura
w	doble uve*	Like Spanish **u**. (Used only in words of foreign origin.)	whisky, walkman
x	equis	Between vowels, like **ks** in *thanks*.	examen, boxeo
		Before a consonant or at the beginning of a word, like **s** or **ks**.	excelente, extraño xenofobia, xilófono
		(In words like **Texas** and **México**, pronounced like **j**.)	mexicano
y	ye*	Stronger than **y** in *yesterday*.	yo, yuca
		At the end of a word, pronounced like **i**.	muy, soy
z	zeta	Like **s**.	zapato, jerez
		In some regions of Spain, like **th** in *thanks*.	zapato, jerez

*In the last meeting of the members of the twenty-two Academies of the Spanish Language (November 2010) that is the way it was decided to call the letters "**v**", "**w**" and "**ye**".

D. Práctica

Read each of the following words, paying special attention to the consonants. Don't forget to stress each word on the right syllable. Begin after you hear **¡Adelante!** After you read each word, listen for confirmation.

casa	cero	costa	cinco	silencio
dedo	Dinamarca	nido	soldado	
gato	gente	gitano	guerra	guitarra	bilingüe
hotel	historia	Jalisco	Juan	
luna	llama	calle	llamar	
año	maña	niñera	dueño	
queso	quince	chiquito		
Ramón	risa	caro	carro	pero
violeta	brócoli	vestido	bicicleta	
zapato	Sandra	zumo	secreto	celestial

E. Práctica

Practice the alphabet by reading and spelling each of the following words. Read the word, spell it, then listen for confirmation. If the word has an accent, say the name of the letter, and then say **con acento.** Begin after you hear **¡Adelante!**

1. hora
2. lápiz
3. carro
4. ocho
5. amarillo
6. bueno
7. fugitivo
8. veinte
9. mañana

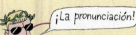
¡La pronunciación!

The pronunciation of **tr** is particularly difficult for native speakers of English. Observe your instructor and be sure to position your mouth and tongue properly in order to pronounce the sound correctly: **tres, cuatro, trabajo, triángulo, teatro, tronco, trucha, semestre.**

Correct pronunciation is the key to avoiding misunderstandings.
Examples: **pero** *but* / **perro** *dog*
   campaña *campaign* / **campana** *bell*

Also, be sure to stress the vowel with the written accent.
Examples: Est**u**dio. *I study* Estudi**ó**. *He studied*
   ¡H**a**ble! *Speak!*   Habl**é**. *I spoke.*

Hablo español

5. LINKING WORDS

Linking is a very important element of Spanish pronunciation.

a. A vowel sound at the end of a word is always linked to the vowel sound at the beginning of the next word. If the vowels are the same, they are pronounced as one long vowel. In linking, **y** acts like a vowel. Listen to and repeat each of the following sentences, paying special attention to the linked vowels.

No entiendo eso.

Va a hablar de ese estudiante.

Voy a almorzar.

b. A consonant sound at the end of a word is always linked to the vowel sound at the beginning of the next word. Listen to and repeat each of the following sentences, paying special attention to the linking of consonants and vowels.

Hablan español.

Están en un restaurante.

Nos encanta escribir y leer.

c. Two identical consonants, one at the end of a word and the other at the beginning of a word, sound like a single but longer consonant. Listen to and repeat each of the following sentences, paying special attention to the linking of consonants.

El borrador rojo no me gusta.

Es su restaurante favorito.

No trabajan nada.

F. Práctica

First mark all the links between words in the following sentences. Then read each of the sentences, paying special attention to the linking sounds. Begin after you hear **¡Adelante!** After you read each sentence, listen for confirmation.

1. ¿Cómo está usted?
2. Hoy es el ocho de enero.
3. Mi color favorito es el amarillo.
4. Es el día de su aniversario.
5. No hay examen en la clase de español.
6. ¿Qué hora es?

Capítulo 1

Primeros pasos*

Additional activities and **Autopruebas** for each **Escena** available online.

Jack Hollingsworth/©Corbis

Paso I
- Greetings, introductions and saying good-bye

Paso II
- GRAMÁTICA: The verb *ser* to ask and answer questions about where you are from

Paso III
- GRAMÁTICA: Gender and number of adjectives of nationality
- GRAMÁTICA: Gender and number of adjectives and use of cognates to describe yourself and others

Paso IV
- Counting to 59

Paso V
- Telling time

Paso VI
- Indicating days of the week and dates

CULTURA: Breve historia del español

TU MUNDO EN VIVO
¡Video en acción! ¡Bienvenido al mundo hispano!
¡Diálogos en acción! Informal and Formal Greetings and Introductions
¡Lectura en acción! Skimming a Text for Cognates and Using Images to Understand Content
¡A conversar! Confirming Comprehension
¡A escribir! Listing Information
¡A investigar! Including Photo and Video Sources

LEARNING OBJECTIVES
By the end of this chapter you will be able to:
- Meet and greet each other.
- State where you are from and ask where others are from.
- Describe yourself and others.
- Exchange phone numbers, e-mail addresses, and birthdays.
- Tell time and give the day of the week and the date.
- Describe the origin of Spanish.

*Primeros pasos *First steps*   *Note:* Before you begin this chapter, practice pronunciation of the text on pages P-1 through P-6 by going to the accompanying section called *La pronunciación* in WileyPLUS

Paso I

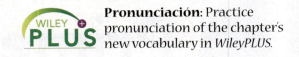
Greetings, introductions, and saying good-bye

Informal greetings and introductions

Note: Classroom directions in Spanish may be found on the pages that immediately follow the inside front cover of your book.

You may present the informal greetings and introductions using the PowerPoint slide of the scenes. Have students repeat each phrase, concentrating on pronunciation and intonation. Then have students read the conversations in groups of five playing the five characters. Finally, have students practice the dialogues again, using their own names.

©John Wiley & Sons, Inc.

1. Hello / Hi! How are you (doing)? 2. Fine, thanks, and you? 3. Fine, thanks. My name is Hugo. What is your name? 4. Rosa. 5. Good morning, Lupe. How are you? 6. I am very well, and you? 7. Okay. / So, so. (**Mal**. Not so well. Bad.) 8. Antonio, let me introduce you to Magdalena García. 9. Nice / Pleased to meet you. 10. I'm delighted to meet you. (Said by a female. If said by a male → **Encantado**.)

Vocabulary options that appear in bold face, such as 7. ... **Mal** and 10. ... **Encantado,** are active.

¡En acción!

¡Oye![1] El primer[2] día de clase

It is your first day on campus and you hear Spanish-speaking students meeting and greeting each other. On the basis of what you hear, determine whether the following people just met or already know each other.

1. Hugo and Rosa:
   - ☑ just met
   - ☐ already know each other

2. Antonio and Lupe:
   - ☐ just met
   - ☑ already know each other

3. Antonio and Magdalena:
   - ☑ just met
   - ☐ already know each other

De paso

In written Spanish, questions are preceded by an inverted question mark (¿), and exclamations are preceded by an inverted exclamation point (¡): **¡Hola! ¿Cómo estás?**

 For additional practice on this grammar point, see PowerPoint slides on BCS and in *WileyPLUS*.

1-1 ¡Hola!

Paso 1. You want to get to know your classmates. Walk around the classroom and say «**Hola**» to at least *six* of them, and ask their names. Follow the model.

MODELO

E (Estudiante) 1:	*¡Hola! ¿Cómo te llamas?*
E2:	*Me llamo María, ¿y tú?*
E1:	*Me llamo Juan. Mucho gusto.*
E2:	*Encantada.*

All art ©John Wiley & Sons, Inc.

Juan   María

Paso 2. Answering the instructor, students in the class will take turns raising their hands and saying the names of the persons they just met. Follow the model.

MODELO

Instructor:	(Pointing to a student in the class) **¿Cómo se llama[3]?**
E1:	(Pointing to the student he or she just met) **Se llama** *María.*

1-2 Presentaciones[4]

Some of your classmates want to meet your partner. Walk around the classroom in pairs and introduce your partner to at least *four* other classmates, following the model. Then switch roles.

MODELO

E1:	*Hola. ¿Qué tal? (o) ¿Cómo estás?*
E2:	*(Estoy) Muy bien. ¿Y tú?*
E1:	*Bien, gracias. Te presento a...*
E2:	*Mucho gusto.*
E3:	*Encantado/a.* (Shake hands.)

[1]Listen up!, [2]first, [3]**Se...** His/Her name is . . . , [4]Introductions

You may want to project the PowerPoint slide of the scenes. As you present each conversation, point to the people speaking.

Guión para ¡Oye!
1.—¡Hola! ¿Qué tal?
—Bien, gracias, ¿y tú?
—Bien, gracias.
—Me llamo Hugo. ¿Cómo te llamas?
—Rosa.
2.—Buenos días, Lupe. ¿Cómo estás?
—Estoy muy bien, ¿y tú?
—Regular.
3.—Antonio, te presento a Magdalena García.
—Mucho gusto.
—Encantada.

1-1 Remind students that **Me llamo** means *My name is. . .* and that it is incorrect to add **es** after **Me llamo**.

1-1, 1-2 "Walk around the classroom" activities encourage communication, keep students alert and motivated, and provide a change of pace. Each activity can generally be completed in five minutes. *Option:* Students complete the activities in groups of six.
1-2 Note that the question **¿Cómo estás?** can be answered in a complete sentence: **Estoy muy bien** or just **Muy bien** since **Estoy** is implied.

1-2 Review the **modelo** with students, having them repeat each phrase. Students provide their classmates' names in the ellipses [...].

1-2 ANOTHER STEP: First, review the alphabet with students. Then write **nombre** and **apellido** on the board, with an example of each. Finally, have students ask *four* classmates their names and how to spell them. E1: **¿Cómo te llamas?** E2: Peter. E1: **¿Y tu apellido?** E2: Johansen. E1: **¿Cómo se escribe?** E2: J-O-H-A-N-S-E-N. E1: **¿Así?** (Show spelling to classmate for confirmation.)

Formal greetings and introductions; saying good-bye

1. Professor Ruiz, let me introduce you to my friend David Smith. 2. I'm delighted to meet you. 3. Nice to meet you, David. 4. Good morning, ma'am. How are you? 5. Very well, thanks, and you? 6. Fine, thanks. My name is Kei Suzuki. What is your name? 7. Carmen López. Pleased to meet you! 8. I'm delighted to meet you! 9. Good afternoon, Mónica. How are you? 10. Very well. And you, professor? 11. I'm fine, thanks. 12. Good night, friends. 13. Good-bye! 14. See you later! 15. Bye! 16. See you tomorrow!

You may present the formal greetings, introductions, and saying good-bye, using the PowerPoint slide of the scenes. Have students repeat each phrase, concentrating on pronunciation and intonation. In pairs, students practice the conversations, playing the roles of the various characters.

De paso

In Spanish, there are formal and informal ways of addressing people. As a general rule for greetings, you use a formal greeting when speaking to someone you would address by his/her last name, and an informal greeting when you are on a first-name basis. Compare the following formal and informal greetings:

Formal	Informal
¿Cómo está (usted)*?	¿Cómo estás (tú)?
¿Cómo se llama (usted)?	¿Cómo te llamas (tú)?
Le presento a...	Te presento a...

PERSONAS Y TÍTULOS

masculino	femenino
(el) amigo	(la) amiga
(el) profesor	(la) profesora
(el) señor (Sr.)	(la) señora (Sra.)
	(la) señorita (Srta.)

¡Oye! Escenas

You will hear statements, each of which describes one of the scenes on page 4. Indicate which scene is being described by raising one, two, three, or four fingers, according to the number of the scene.

1-3 ¿Qué respondes?

Your instructor arrives on the first day of class. Match each of his/her greetings or inquiries with the corresponding response, completing the statements appropriately.

Tu profesor/a		Tú (*yourself*)
1. Buenos días, señor / señora / señorita.	c	a. Me llamo...
2. ¿Cómo está usted?	e	b. Mucho gusto.
3. ¿Cómo se llama usted?	a	c. Buenos días, profesor/a...
4. Le presento a...	b	d. Adiós.
5. Hasta luego.	d	e. Muy bien/ regular, gracias. ¿Y usted?

¡Chócala! es una expresión informal que se usa para celebrar un triunfo. ¿Cómo se dice ¡Chócala! en inglés?

©John Wiley & Sons, Inc.

*The parentheses around **(usted)** and **(tú)** indicate that these subjects are optional, and except for emphasis or clarification, are often dropped.

 For additional practice on this grammar point, see PowerPoint slides on BCS and in *WileyPLUS*.

ANOTHER STEP for De paso: First, review the alphabet with your students on page P-3. Then, write on the board @ = **arroba** and **¿Cuál es tu e-mail?** using your e-mail as an example. Finally, have students ask each other's e-mail addresses. Before they start, be the model by reading the question and telling the class your e-mail address **Mi e-mail es...**

¡Oye! Write on the board: **dice** *says*/**dicen** *say*. After students are familiar with the formal greetings, read the following statements to them. Be expressive! To confirm responses, you may use the appropriate PowerPoint illustration.

Guión para ¡Oye!
1. Dos (*hold up two fingers*) estudiantes conversan con la profesora. *1*
2. Mónica conversa con el profesor. *3*
3. Diego presenta a su amigo David Smith. *1*
4. La señora y la señorita están muy bien. *2*
5. Luis dice: «Buenas noches, amigos.» *4*
6. Una persona dice: «Buenos días.» *2*
7. Una persona dice: «Buenas tardes.» *3*
8. Dos estudiantes dicen: «¡Adiós!» «¡Hasta luego!» *4*

1-3 For each item, elicit responses from several students. For additional practice, students repeat the activity working in pairs, with one student playing the role of the instructor.

1-4 En una reunión

1-4 For **Paso 1,** ask two students to present their conversation to the class. For **Paso 2,** students walk around the classroom to make their four introductions. Encourage some of them to introduce their "colleagues" to you.

For additional vocabulary practice, see PowerPoint slides on BCS and in *WileyPLUS*.

Paso 1. You have just entered a business meeting that has not yet begun. You do not know the person sitting next to you. Speak with him/her following the outline in the chart.

Person 1:	Person 2:
· Greet the person (use **Sr., Sra., Srta.**) according to the time of day.	· Respond to the greeting.
· Introduce yourself giving your name, and ask the other person's name.	· Give your name.
· Shake the person's hand, and say that you are pleased to meet him/her.	· Shake the person's hand, and say that you are pleased to meet him/her.
· Say good-bye.	· Say good-bye.

Paso 2. Later you want to introduce your colleague to *four* of your business associates. On an individual basis, **(a)** greet them and **(b)** make your introductions. The people introduced **(c)** shake hands and say that they are pleased to meet each other.

In Latin America, women generally greet each other with a light kiss on the cheek, and in Spain, with a kiss on each cheek. Men and women greet each other with kisses, too.

Men greet other men with either a hug or a handshake. In formal job or business situations the handshake is the norm for both men and women.

Paso II

Asking and answering questions about where you are from

HUGO: ¿De dónde eres, Rosa?

ROSA: Soy de Nuevo México, ¿y tú?

De Chicago.

LA SRTA. SUZUKI: ¿De dónde es usted, señora?

De Japón.

LA SRA. LÓPEZ: Soy de Venezuela. ¿Y usted?

All art ©John Wiley & Sons, Inc.

WILEY PLUS Go to *WileyPLUS* to review this grammar point with the help of the **Animated Grammar Tutorial** and **Verb Conjugator**. For more practice, go to the **Grammar Handbook**.

GRAMÁTICA

¡Manos a la obra!

1

Saying where you are from: Ser (to be) + de + place of origin

The following chart presents subject pronouns and the verb **ser,** which has a number of uses in Spanish. In this section you will use it to say where people are from.

Subject pronouns		Ser *(to be)*	
yo	*I*	soy	*I am*
tú	*you, singular informal*	eres	*you are*
usted (Ud.)	*you, singular formal*	es	*you are*
él	*he*	es	*he/it is*
ella	*she*	es	*she/it is*
nosotros/as	*we*	somos	*we are*
vosotros/as	*you, plural informal*	sois	*you are*
ustedes (Uds.)	*you, plural formal/informal*	son	*you are*
ellos	*they, masculine*	son	*they are*
ellas	*they, feminine*	son	*they are*

- Spanish uses two different words to express *you, singular*. Although usage varies from region to region, **tú** is generally used when the relationship is informal (first-name basis); **usted** is used when the relationship is more distant (last-name basis). When in doubt, use **usted.**
- In Spain, **vosotros/as** is the informal way to address two or more people, while **ustedes** is the formal way. In Spanish America, **ustedes** is used to address two or more people, both informally and formally.
- Because Spanish verb forms almost always indicate the subject of a sentence, subject pronouns are usually omitted.

    Soy de Nueva York.   *I am from New York.*

- Subject pronouns *are* used, however, to clarify or contrast.

    Yo soy de México y **ella** es de Costa Rica.

- When a pair or group includes both males and females, the masculine forms are used: **nosotros, vosotros, ellos.**

For additional practice on this grammar point, see PowerPoint slides on BCS and in *WileyPLUS*.

Mention to your students that in some countries, the use of **tú** is very frequent (for example, Spain and the Caribbean), whereas in others (for example, Costa Rica, Honduras and Ecuador) the **Ud.** is more common, even between parents and children. When in doubt, students should use the **Ud.** form.

Also mention that there is no Spanish equivalent for the subject pronoun *it*. In Spanish, to say *It is from Perú* begin with the verb: **Es de Perú.**

¡En acción!

¡Oye! ¿De dónde son?

You will hear where your instructor and various people that he/she knows are from. Listen carefully. Then answer the questions, naming the place of origin of each person mentioned.

1-5 ¿Quién?[1]

In Spanish, using the correct form of address is important. How would you address or refer to the following people? Use **tú, usted, él, ella, nosotros/as, ustedes, ellos, ellas.**

You are talking to:		You are talking about:	
la profesora de biología →	*usted*	la Sra. López y la Srta. Suzuki →	*ellas*
dos profesores	ustedes	el profesor Blanco	él
David, un amigo	tú	Diego y David	ellos
dos amigos	ustedes	Magdalena	ella
un adolescente	tú	Rosa y tú (*yourself*)	nosotros/as
el rector[2] de la universidad	usted	tú (*yourself*)	yo

1-6 De orígenes diferentes

Paso 1. College and university students are often from cities and countries all over the world. Tell where the following students are from, matching the capital cities to the countries in the chart.

Países

Argentina	Japón
Egipto	Inglaterra
España	Italia
Francia	Rusia

1. Roger/ Londres → *Roger es de Londres, Inglaterra.*
2. Sergei y Anton/ Moscú — *Sergei y Anton son de Moscú, Rusia.*
3. Yuko y Sayaka/ Tokio — *Yuko y Sayaka son de Tokio, Japón.*
4. Giovanni/ Roma — *Giovanni es de Roma, Italia.*
5. Tania/ El Cairo — *Tania es de El Cairo, Egipto.*
6. Elena y María/ Madrid — *Elena y María son de Madrid, España.*
7. Ernesto/ Buenos Aires — *Ernesto es de Buenos Aires, Argentina.*
8. Monique/ París — *Monique es de París, Francia.*

Paso 2. If you or any members of your family are from countries other than the U.S.A., share the information with the class. Use the countries listed on the inside back cover of your textbook as needed.

MODELO

Yo… Mi mamá… Mi papá… Mis abuelos[3]…

1-7 ¿De dónde eres?

Paso 1. It is always interesting to find out the origin of your classmates. In groups of *five*, stand in a circle and tell each other where you are from. Listen carefully. Then take turns stating the origin of every person in the group. Use subject pronouns.

MODELO

E1: *Yo soy de…*

E1: *Tú eres de…*

E1: *Él/Ella es de…*

[1]Who/Whom, [2]president, [3]grandparents

¡Oye! On the board, draw the faces of some of your friends and relatives that come from different places. Write the person's name under each drawing. Then tell the class where you and they are from. Expand and personalize the list as you wish.

Guión para ¡Oye!
1. Yo soy de…
2. Mi amigo/a… es de…
3. Mis amigos… y… son de…
4. Mi mamá/papá es de…
5. …

Comprensión para ¡Oye!
1. ¿De dónde soy yo?
2. ¿De dónde es él/ella?
3. ¿De dónde son ellos/ellas?
4. ¿De dónde es mi mamá/papá?
5. ¿De dónde es…?

1-7 After students complete **Paso 1,** have several individuals tell the origin of everyone in their circle. Go over the expressions of courtesy on page 9 before students do **Paso 2.**

1-7 Students use their notes to report their findings to the class. **Linda y yo somos de Colorado. Tomás, Daniela y Carmen son de California.** Jot down the places of origin on the board; later ask for a show of hands to determine how many students are from each place mentioned.

EXPRESIONES DE CORTESÍA

Perdón.	*Pardon me/Excuse me (to get someone's attention or to seek forgiveness).*
Con permiso.	*Excuse me (to ask permission to pass by someone or to leave).*
Gracias.	*Thanks.*
De nada.	*You're welcome.*

 Paso 2. Ask approximately *ten* students **(tú)** and your instructor **(Ud.)** where they are from. Write down the information. Your goal is to try to find classmates that are from the same places. Be prepared to report to the class.

MODELO

E1: *Con permiso. / Perdón. ¿De dónde eres?* → **E2:** *Soy de...*

E1: *Gracias.* → **E2:** *De nada.*

PLUS For more practice, see **Grammar Handbook** found in *WileyPLUS*.

Have students practice the nationalities of the Hispanic countries in pairs looking at the maps on the inside front cover of their textbooks. One student calls out a country, and the other identifies the nationality. (Countries and nationalities for the rest of the world are listed on the inside back cover of the textbook.)

©John Wiley & Sons, Inc.

GRAMÁTICA

¡Manos a la obra!

Expressing your nationality: Gender and number of adjectives to express nationality

2

 Soy mexicana.

 Soy cubano.

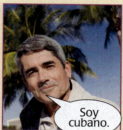 Soy costarricense.

 Soy español.

 Somos chilenos.

¿Cuál es tu nacionalidad?

- When you meet Hispanics in the United States, or travel to a Spanish-speaking country, you will frequently be asked **¿De dónde eres?** or **¿De dónde es usted?** If you are from the U.S. your response should be:
  Soy de Estados Unidos. (to refer to your country) or **Soy estadounidense.** (to refer to your nationality)

- Take a look at what the people in the photos are saying. Here is a summary of how nationalities are expressed in Spanish:
  - nationalities ending in **-o** refer to a male; **Soy cubano**.
  - nationalities ending in **-a** refer to a female; **Soy mexicana**.
  - nationalities ending in **-e** refer to either a male or a female: **Soy costarricense**.
  - nationalities ending in a **consonant** refer to a male: **Soy español**.
  - nationalities ending in a **consonant** add an **-a** to refer to a female: **Soy española.***

- Are nationalities capitalized? If you look carefully, you will see that nationality adjectives in Spanish are not capitalized, although countries are.

- Did you notice the **s** at the end of **chilenos** in the bubble above? That is the plural ending. To make adjectives plural add **-s** if the word ends in a vowel and **-es** if the word ends in a consonant.
  - Ellas son mexicana**s**, pero nosotros somos español**es**.

_____

*Other examples are: **francés francesa; inglés inglesa; alemán alemana; japonés japonesa**. Notice that the accent is dropped in the feminine form of these adjectives.

 For additional practice on this grammar point, see PowerPoint slides on BCS and in *WileyPLUS*.

Photos: L: Hola Images/Getty Images, Inc.; LC: Rick Gomez/Blend Images/ Getty Images, Inc.; C: Dave Nagel/Image Bank//Getty Images; RC: Jupiterimages/ Age Fotostock America, Inc.; R: Gabriela Medina/Blend Images/Getty Images, Inc.

1-8 ANOTHER STEP: Have pairs of students practice the nationalities by referring to the list on the inside back cover of their textbooks. Write the following on the board: **Dominique Rousseau (Francia); Natasha Kournikova (Rusia); David Johnson (Canadá); Birgit Hoffmann (Alemania); Luciano Antonioni (Italia).** Include additional items of your choice. One student names the person and the country of origin and the other says the nationality.

1-8 Entrevista intercultural

For your intercultural communications class, you and your classmate have been assigned to interview people from several Spanish-speaking countries. One of you asks if there is someone on campus from the assigned country **(Lista A)** and the other finds a person of that nationality on the Hispanic Student Association roster **(Lista B)**. Take turns. Use the nationalities chart on the inside-front-cover of your textbook as a guide.

MODELO

1. Argentina

E1: (Looking at Lista A) *¿Hay una persona de Argentina?*

E2: (Looking at Lista B) *Sí, Juan Silvestrini es* **argentino.**

> **Palabras útiles**
>
> Hay *There is / There are*

¿SABES QUE...?[1]

Puerto Rico is a self-governing commonwealth associated with the United States. Its official name is Commonwealth of Puerto Rico (**Estado Libre Asociado de Puerto Rico**). It has two legislative houses: the Senate and the House of Representatives. Its chief of state is the President of the United States and its head of government, the governor.

Since 1917, people born in Puerto Rico are U.S. citizens and as such, are entitled to vote at the federal level. When a Puerto Rican establishes residence within any of the 50 U.S. states, he or she can also vote for president. The currency of Puerto Rico is the dollar.

LISTA A Curso de Comunicación Intercultural	**LISTA B** Asociación de Estudiantes Hispanos
Proyecto nº 1: Entrevista 1. Argentina 2. Bolivia 3. Chile 4. Costa Rica 5. Ecuador 6. España 7. Guatemala 8. Honduras 9. República Dominicana 10. Perú 11. Puerto Rico 12. Uruguay	**Lista de alumnos hispanos:** Alba, José (República Dominicana) Castro, Lucía (Perú) Domínguez, César (Chile) Estévez, Nuria (Honduras) Fernández, Alberto (Uruguay) González, Luis (Puerto Rico) Jiménez, Alejandro (España) Montiel, Rafael (Guatemala) Palacios, Susana (Bolivia) Silvestrini, Juan (Argentina) Trojaola, Cecilia (Costa Rica) Balenciaga, Gladys (Ecuador)

¿SABES QUE...?

The number of international students enrolled in colleges and universities in the U.S. reached a record high of 723,277 in the 2010–11 academic year. The number of students from Mexico increased 2% from the previous year to 13,713, and the number from Colombia dropped 7% from 2009–10, but the enrollment of students from Venezuela increased 11%. The most popular fields of study are Business and Management.

During the 2009–10 academic year, 270,604 students participated in study abroad programs, a slight increase compared to 2008–09. Of all Americans studying abroad, Latin America hosted 15%, with Peru, Argentina, and Ecuador showing increases over the previous year. Spain is the third leading destination of U.S. study abroad students. Mexico, the 8th leading destination, was down 2% from the previous year.

[1]**Sabes...** Do you know that... ?

Describing yourself and others using cognates

PLUS For more practice, see **Grammar Handbook** found in *WileyPLUS*.

GRAMÁTICA

¡Manos a la obra!

Using cognates to describe yourself and others: Gender and number of adjectives

3

A number of words in Spanish and English are cognates—words that are identical or similar in both languages and that have the same meaning. Below is a list of adjectives commonly used with the verb **ser** to describe people. All these adjectives are cognates.

Soy modest**a** y un poco introvertid**a**, pero muy romántic**a**.

©John Wiley & Sons, Inc.

For additional practice on this grammar point, see PowerPoint slides on BCS and in *WileyPLUS*.

Most adjectives have a masculine form (ending in **-o**), used when describing a masculine noun, and a feminine form (ending in **-a**), used when describing a feminine noun.

- Adjectives that change **-o** to **-a** when describing a female:

ambicioso/a	atlético/a	cómico/a	creativo/a
dinámico/a	extrovertido/a	generoso/a	impulsivo/a
introvertido/a	modesto/a	organizado/a	práctico/a
religioso/a	romántico/a	serio/a	tranquilo/a

El señor Blanco es ambicios**o**.   La profesora Ruiz es ambicios**a**.
Pablo es extrovertid**o**.   Alejandra es extrovertid**a**.

- Adjectives that end in **-e, -ista,** or **most consonants** do not change in form when describing a female:

arrogante	eficiente	egoísta	flexible
independiente	inteligente	irresponsable	materialista
optimista	paciente	pesimista	puntual
rebelde	responsable	sentimental	tolerante

Luis es eficient**e**.   Mónica también (*also*) es eficient**e**.
Alberto es optimist**a**.   Sara también es optimist**a**.

To describe more than one person, adjectives are made plural by adding **-s** to those that end in a vowel and **-es** to those that end in a consonant:

optimista   →   optimista**s**   Luis y Mónica son optimista**s**.
puntual   →   puntual**es**   David y Diego son puntual**es**.

Sometimes students have difficulty recognizing cognates, particularly in the spoken vs. written form. Review the cognates listed and have students identify their English equivalents. Then have students volunteer a brief description of themselves, using two or three cognates from the lists.

¡En acción!

¡Oye! Before beginning, in order to make sure the class knows each person mentioned, ask: **¿Sabes quién es... ?/ ¿Sabes quiénes son... ?** *(Do you know who... is?/ Do you know who... are?)* Students then respond **Sí, lo sé** *(Yes, I know)* and provide the information, or **No, no lo sé.**

Guión para ¡Oye!
1. Eva Longoria es **dinámica.** *C*
2. Chris Rock es **tranquilo.** *F*
3. Donald Trump es **ambicioso.** *C*
4. J. K. Rowling es **creativa.** *C*
5. Hillary Clinton es **independiente.** *C*
6. Lady Gaga es **rebelde.** *C*
7. Will Farrell es **extrovertido.** *C*
8. Oprah Winfrey y Ellen DeGeneres son **introvertidas.** *F*
9. Bill y Melinda Gates son **generosos.** *C*
10. Serena Williams y Venus Williams son **atléticas.** *C*

¡Oye!   Los célebres y famosos

How much do you know about the following famous people? You will hear statements describing them. Say whether the description is true **(cierto)** or false **(falso).**

1-9 Los estudiantes hispanos

Paso 1. You have completed the interviews for your intercultural communications class (Act. 1-8), and you have gotten together with your partner to review the results. Look over your notes (see below) and summarize what the students said about themselves. Take turns.

MODELO

E1:   *¿Cómo es Rafael?* [1]

E2:   *Es optimista y responsable. No es cómico.*

Rafael	optimista	✓
	cómico	✗
	responsable	✓
Lucía	romántica	✓
	generosa	✓
	ambiciosa	✗
Susana	seria	✗
	práctica	✓
	responsable	✓
Nuria	eficiente	✗
	seria	✓
	creativa	✓
César	religioso	✓
	modesto	✓
	impulsivo	✗
Gladys	atlética	✓
	dinámica	✓
	modesta	✗
Alejandro	cómico	✓
	paciente	✗
	extrovertido	✓

Paso 2. You made some other observations about the students you interviewed that were not in your notes.

MODELO

Lucía / organizado →*Lucía es organizada.*

1. Susana y Nuria / independiente
   Susana y Nuria son independientes.
2. Alejandro / impulsivo
   Alejandro es impulsivo.
3. César y Gladys / práctico
   César y Gladys son prácticos.
4. Lucía / creativo
   Lucía es creativa.
5. Rafael / tolerante
   Rafael es tolerante.
6. Nuria y Gladys / muy religioso
   Nuria y Gladys son muy religiosas.

[1]**¿Cómo...** What is Rafael like?

PALABRAS FRECUENTES

un poco *a little*	también *also*	y *and*
muy *very*	tampoco *not either*	o *or*
pero *but*		

Y becomes **e** before words beginning with an **i** or **hi**:
  Luisa es generosa **e** inteligente.
  Madre **e** hijo son modestos.

O becomes **u** before words beginning with **o** or **ho**:
  ¿Eres pesimista **u** optimista?
  ¿Es deshonesto **u** honesto?

. . . y algo más   Answering questions affirmatively and negatively

- To answer a yes/no question affirmatively, **sí** (*yes*) is used before the statement: *Sí,* **soy práctico.**

- To answer a yes/no question negatively, **no** is used before the statement and also before the verb: *No, no* **soy práctico.**

- To make a statement negative, **no** is used before the verb: **Carlos** *no* **es muy religioso.**

1-10   ¿Cómo son? ¿Cómo somos?

Paso 1. What are some of the personality traits of the students in your Spanish class? To find out, walk around the classroom and ask at least *six* of your classmates yes/no questions.

MODELO

E1:	Pablo, ¿eres optimista?	**o:**	E1:	Susana, ¿eres puntual?
E2:	Sí, soy optimista. ¿Y tú?		E2:	No, no soy puntual. ¿Y tú?
E1:	Yo también soy optimista.		E1:	Yo tampoco.

Paso 2. Report one of your classmates' personality traits to the class. Also indicate *one* or *two* traits you and a classmate have in common.

MODELO
Pablo es optimista. Susana y yo no somos puntuales, pero sí somos muy responsables.

1-11   Mi personalidad

Paso 1. The tutor for your study group wants to get to know each of you and asks you to write a description of yourself. Write *four* sentences using cognates from the chart on page 11, and words like **y, un poco, muy, también,** and **tampoco** as applicable.

Paso 2. The tutor wants the study group to get along well and encourages members to get to know each other and discover what they have in common. In groups of *four*, read your descriptions to each other, noting similarities and/or differences.

MODELO
Yo soy romántico/a y Mónica también es romántica. Yo soy un poco serio/a, pero Pedro es muy cómico.

For more practice, see **Grammar Handbook** found in *WileyPLUS*.

For additional practice on this grammar point, see PowerPoint slides on BCS and in *WileyPLUS*.

1-10 Make sure that every student is asked questions about his/her personality. Step in and make inquiries yourself, if needed.

¿SABES QUE...?

A number of Spanish words are used in English. Examples include *rodeo, lasso, gusto, fiesta, salsa, taco, arena, burro, armadillo, llama, amigo, guerrilla, adios, loco,* and many more.

1-11 First, ask students to give you feedback on traits they have in common with their classmates, then ask them to report differences.

Paso IV

Counting to 59

Have students practice the numbers in the chart by counting in even numbers, in odd numbers, and by fives. Clip football game scores from your local newspaper, write them on the board, and have students read the numbers.

WILEY PLUS For more practice, see **Grammar Handbook** found in *WileyPLUS*.

For additional practice on numbers, see PowerPoint slides on BCS and in *WileyPLUS*.

LOS NÚMEROS DEL 0 AL 59

¡BINGO!					
0 cero	1 uno	2 dos	3 tres	4 cuatro	5 cinco
6 seis	7 siete	8 ocho	9 nueve	10 diez	11 once
12 doce	13 trece	14 catorce	15 quince	16 dieciséis	17 diecisiete
18 dieciocho	19 diecinueve	20 veinte	21 veintiuno	22 veintidós	23 veintitrés
24 veinticuatro	25 veinticinco	26 veintiséis	27 veintisiete	28 veintiocho	29 veintinueve
30 treinta	31 treinta y uno	40 cuarenta	41 cuarenta y uno	50 cincuenta	59 cincuenta y nueve

. . . y algo más   Writing numbers

- The numbers from 16 to 29 are usually written as one word. Those from 31 on are written as three words. What numbers carry accent marks?

- **Uno** shortens to **un** before a masculine noun and becomes **una** before a feminine noun: **un** amigo, **una** amiga.

- Likewise, **veintiuno** shortens to **veintiún** before a masculine noun and becomes **veintiuna** before a feminine noun: **veintiún** profesores, **veintiuna** profesoras. The same changes take place with **treinta y uno, cuarenta y uno,** and so on.

¡En acción!

 ¡Oye! ¡Bingo!

On a sheet of paper, make a Bingo board with five squares across and five down. Fill it *only* with the following 25 numbers: 0–20, 30, 40, 50, 59. Be sure to place the numbers in random order.

Listen as your instructor calls out numbers and circle those that appear on your board. Call out *Bingo!* if you complete a horizontal, vertical, or diagonal row. Then call out your marked row of numbers to the class for confirmation.

¡Oye! Call out numbers in random order, keeping track of those called. Continue the game until several students call out *¡Bingo!*

Guión para ¡Oye!
1, 5, 30,...

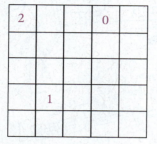

1-12   Las matemáticas

 Paso 1. You are tutoring a Spanish-speaking first grader who needs to review his/her addition and subtraction facts. When you call out the numbers to be added or subtracted, your pupil gives the answers. After five items, switch roles.

MODELO

Tú: 4 + 2 = → *Cuatro* **más** *dos* **son**...

Alumno/a: *seis*

1. 6 + 3 = 9
2. 7 + 8 = 15
3. 10 + 4 = 14
4. 18 + 6 = 24
5. (your choice)

6. 17 – 5 = 12
7. 13 – 12 = 1
8. 45 – 15 = 30
9. 59 – 49 = 10
10. (your choice)

Palabras útiles are for use in a particular activity.

> **Palabras útiles**
> más +
> menos –
> son/es =

 Paso 2. Now you want to make sure your pupil knows how to spell numbers. Say the following numbers, and he/she writes them out. After four items, switch roles. Then check each other's answers.

MODELO

Tú: *29*

Alumno/a: (writes) *veintinueve*

1. 16
2. 22
3. 15
4. 17

5. 23
6. 10
7. 33
8. 56

For additional practice on numbers, see PowerPoint slides on BCS and in *WileyPLUS*.

1-12 ANOTHER STEP: Write on the board **¿Cuál es tu número de teléfono?** and use your phone number as an example for an answer: **Es el 796...** Then encourage students to find out from a couple of classmates their phone numbers.

¹La clase

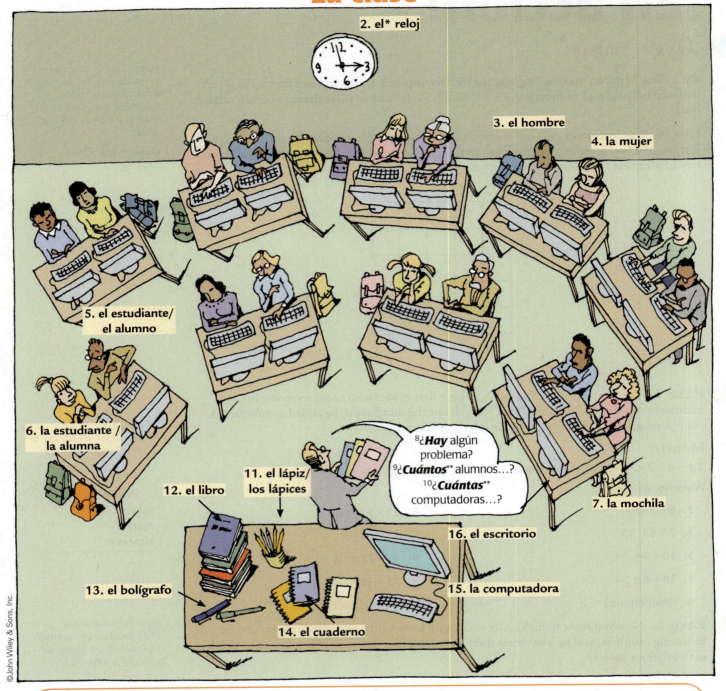

1. class 2. clock, watch 3. man 4. woman 5. student (*m.*) 6. student (*f.*) 7. backpack 8. Is there...? **Hay** There is/ There are; **¿Hay...?** Is there/Are there? 9. How many (*m.pl.*)? 10. How many (*f.pl.*)? 11. pencil/s 12. book 13. pen 14. notebook 15. computer 16. desk

An additional presentation of classroom vocabulary is provided in *Capítulo 2*.

For additional vocabulary practice, see PowerPoint slides on BCS and in *WileyPLUS*.

*The definite articles **el** and **la** (*the*) are included to indicate whether the noun is masculine or feminine.
¿Cuántos...? is used with masculine nouns (generally designated by the definite article **el or **los**). ¿Cuántas...? is used with feminine nouns (generally designated by **la** or **las**).

. . . **y algo más**   Pluralizing nouns

To make nouns plural:

- add **-s** if the word ends in **a, e, i, o, u:** estudiante → estudiantes
- add **-es** if it ends in any other letter: mujer → mujeres

 1-13 ¿Cuántos hay?

How observant are you? Study the classroom scene on page 16 and then take turns asking and answering the following questions.

MODELO

E1:   *¿Cuántos libros hay en el escritorio del profesor?*

E2:   *Hay cuatro.*

E1:   *¡Sí, hay cuatro!* (In cases where the answer is incorrect, say *No, no hay...*)

1. ¿Cuántos estudiantes hay en la clase? 18
2. ¿Cuántos hombres hay? ¿Y mujeres? 10 hombres (9 estudiantes y 1 profesor), 9 mujeres
3. ¿Cuántas computadoras hay? ¿Y cuántos relojes? 19 computadoras, 1 reloj
4. ¿Cuántos profesores hay en la clase? 1
5. ¿Cuántos lápices hay en el escritorio del profesor? ¿Y cuántos bolígrafos? 5 lápices, 2 bolígrafos
6. ¿Cuántos cuadernos hay en el escritorio? 3
7. ¿Cuántas mochilas hay en la clase? 11

You may use the PowerPoint slide to share the scene with the class.

1-13 Tell your students that numbers do not add any plural ending: **Hay cuatro libros**.

 1-14   Vamos a contar[1]

In groups of *four*, determine how many of the following items are visible in your class. If there are none, write **cero.** The first team to complete the chart is the winner. One member of the winning team reads the numbers in each category to the class, and the class determines whether they are correct.

estudiantes	
mujeres	
hombres	
computadoras	
televisores	
mapas	
mochilas	
relojes de clase	
iPods	
cuadernos	
diccionarios	
celulares	
lápices	
suéteres	

1-14 ANOTHER STEP: Have students find out who in their group has the highest number of the following items in his/her backpack: **libros, cuadernos, lápices, bolígrafos,...** Students jot down the numbers and report their conclusions to the class: **En la mochila de José hay ocho libros.**

[1]**Vamos...** Let's count

You may use the PowerPoint slide of the clocks to present telling time.

You might want to point out to students that in the Hispanic world the 24-hour clock is used in place of "am" and "pm".

You might present the option of telling time on digital clocks, for example: (clock with *) **Son las ocho cuarenta,** (clock with **) **Son las ocho cincuenta.**

Paso V

Telling time

¿Qué hora es?[1]

Es la una (en punto).
It's one o'clock sharp.

Son las cinco (en punto).
It is five o'clock sharp.

Son las ocho y diez.
It is ten after eight.

Son las ocho y cuarto.
Son las ocho y quince.
It is quarter after eight.

Son las ocho y media.
Son las ocho y treinta.
It is eight thirty.

* Son veinte para las nueve.
** Son diez para las nueve.

Son las nueve menos veinte.*
It is twenty to nine.

Son las nueve menos cuarto.
It is quarter to nine.

Son las nueve menos diez.**
It is ten to nine.

Es mediodía.
It is noon.

Es medianoche.
It is midnight.

For additional practice on telling time, see PowerPoint slides on BCS and in *WileyPLUS*.

Son las siete de la mañana.
It is seven in the morning.

Son las dos de la tarde.
It is two in the afternoon.

Son las once de la noche.
It is eleven at night.

De paso

In most Spanish-speaking countries, **de la tarde** is used as long as there is daylight.

[1]¿**Qué...** What time is it?

¡En acción!

¡Oye! ¿Qué hora es?

Draw six clock faces on a sheet of paper while a volunteer does the same on the board. When you hear a clock time, draw the time on your clock. Your instructor will indicate whether it is correct. Continue until all the clocks have hands indicating the stated times.

1-15 ¡Vamos a practicar la hora!

Your instructor will call out the time on each of the clocks below in random order, and you identify the corresponding clock by number. Repeat the activity with a partner. Take turns.

MODELO

Son las nueve menos diez de la mañana. ⟶ *El número 8.*

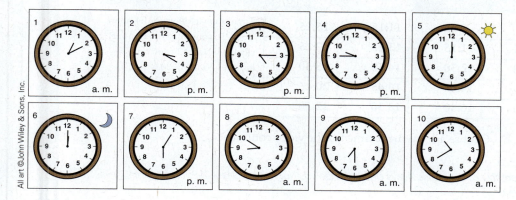

1-16 La rutina de Mónica

You know Mónica's schedule well, and can usually tell where she is at any given time. Your partner wants to know where she is during the times indicated on the chart, and you respond selecting the appropriate place according to the illustrations. After three items, switch roles.

MODELO

E1: *Son las ocho y media de la mañana. ¿Dónde está Mónica ahora?*

E2: *En el gimnasio (D)*

¡Oye! Ask **¿Qué hora es?** and then say a time, such as **Son las tres.** Continue by giving five more clock times. Repeat the activity with a new volunteer, asking a student or students to call out the times. Use the clocks on the board to confirm answers.

1-15 You may use the PowerPoint slide of the clocks to read the following times. Once students have identified the correct clock, point to it on the slide. *Times:* Son las cinco y cuarto (quince) de la tarde. [3]; Son las siete y media (treinta) de la mañana. [9]; Es la una y diez de la mañana. [1]; Es mediodía. [5]; Es medianoche. [6]; Son las diez menos cuarto (quince) de la noche. [4]; Son las seis y cinco de la tarde. [7]; Son las once menos veinte de la mañana. [10]; Son las tres y veinte de la tarde. [2]

1-16 ANSWERS:
1. Modelo, 2. E, 3. C, 4. B, 5. A, 6. F

Palabras útiles
¿Dónde? *Where?*

| 1. 8:30 a. m. |
| 2. 10:20 a. m. |
| 3. 12:00 ☀ |
| 4. 2:45 p. m. |
| 5. 6:15 p. m. |
| 6. 10:00 p. m. |

A
En el restaurante

B
En la clase de historia

C
En la cafetería

D
En el gimnasio

E
En la clase de inglés

F
En su carro

1-17 Husos horarios[1]

1-17 Explain that the 24-hour clock is often used on maps, for transportation schedules, for TV and movie times, and so on. *Option:* Before beginning *Actividad 1-17*, ask the class to convert all PM times on the chart from the 24-hour clock to the 12-hour clock. For example: 15:15 minus 12 equals 3:15 PM.

1-17 ANOTHER STEP: Your students may be able to find different time zones using their mobile devices. Ask them to look for cities such as Lima, Madrid, Santiago de Chile, etc.

For additional practice on telling time, see PowerPoint slides on BCS and in *WileyPLUS*.

Paso 1. The student organization at your school in New Orleans is setting up a video conference with similar organizations in other cities around the world. You and a friend have offered to find a time that will work for everyone. As you mention each city, your friend gives the time there, according to the time zone chart below. Take turns playing each role.

MODELO

E1: *Cuando[2] son las ocho y cuarto de la mañana aquí, ¿qué hora es en Nueva York?*

E2: *Son las nueve y cuarto de la mañana.*

E1: *¿Y en Buenos Aires?*

E2: *Son las once y cuarto de la mañana.*

E1: *¿Y en Barcelona?*

E2: *Son las tres y cuarto de la tarde.*

Nueva Orleans	Nueva York	Buenos Aires	Barcelona
8:15	9:15	11:15	15:15
10:15	11:15	13:15	17:15
11:30	12:30	14:30	18:30
13:45	14:45	16:45	20:45
15:30	16:30	18:30	22:30

Times shown follow the 24-hour clock. To convert to the 12-hour clock, subtract 12 from times beginning with 13:00.

Paso 2. Choose a convenient time for the video conference.

MODELO

La conferencia es a las[3]... de Nueva Orleans; a las... de Nueva York; a las... de Buenos Aires; y a las... de Barcelona.

Paso VI

Indicating days of the week and dates

Write the days of the week on the board with the letters scrambled: sulne = **lunes,** and so on. Have students unscramble each day, writing it correctly. This activity helps with spelling and placement of accents.

For more practice, see **Grammar Handbook** found in *WileyPLUS*.

LOS DÍAS DE LA SEMANA

lunes*	martes	miércoles	jueves	viernes	sábado	domingo
Monday	*Tuesday*	*Wednesday*	*Thursday*	*Friday*	*Saturday*	*Sunday*

*Note that the Spanish calendar starts with Monday and ends with Sunday, and that the days of the week are not capitalized.

. . . y algo más Indicating the days of the week

- The days of the week are masculine: **el lunes, el martes,** and so on.

- **El lunes** means *on Monday,* **el martes** means *on Tuesday,* and so on.

  La fiesta es **el sábado.** *The party is on Saturday.*

- **Los lunes** means *on Mondays, every Monday,* **los martes** means *on Tuesdays, every Tuesday,* and so on.

  Los viernes vamos al gimnasio. *On Fridays/Every Friday we go to the gym.*

[1]**Husos...** Time zones, [2]When, [3]**a...** at

¡En acción!

¡Oye! Los días de la semana

Your instructor is absent-minded and sometimes gets confused about what day it is, when events take place, and so on. Indicate whether the statements he/she makes are true or false by saying «¡Sí!» or «¡No!» If they are false, correct them.

1-18 Programación en televisión

Paso 1. You and your friend are checking out the TV programs of the week. Ask each other questions to find out what days of the week certain programs are featured.

MODELO

E1: *¿Qué días hay partidos?*

E2: *El martes hay partido de golf, el miércoles...*

1. partidos
2. noticias
3. películas
4. documentales
5. programas especiales

1-18 ANSWERS: 1. Martes, miércoles y domingo; 2. Lunes, martes, miércoles y jueves; 3. Lunes, miércoles, jueves, viernes, sábado y domingo; 4. Lunes, martes, viernes y domingo; 5. Jueves y sábado.

For additional practice on days of the week, see PowerPoint slides on BCS and in *WileyPLUS*.

Guión para ¡Oye!
1. Hoy es... (*give wrong day*).
2. La clase de español es el/los..., ... (*give correct day/s*).
3. En muchas universidades hay fiestas los sábados.
4. También hay fiestas los lunes por la noche.
5. El día favorito de los estudiantes es el lunes.
6. Un día muy, muy malo para los estudiantes es el viernes.

Palabras útiles
la película *movie*
el partido de béisbol *baseball game*
las noticias *news*

	lunes 4	martes 5	miércoles 6	jueves 7	viernes 8	sábado 9	domingo 10
CANAL 15 7:00	Noticias de Asia	Documental: *Turismo en Costa Rica*	Noticias de Europa	Noticias de Latino-américa	Documental: *La diabetes y la obesidad*	Especial: *Concierto de guitarra*	Partido de tenis
CANAL 37 8:30	Documental: *Animales en extinción*	Noticias internacio-nales	Partido de béisbol	Especial: *Casas de los famosos*	Película: *Los juegos del hambre*[2] J. Lawrence J. Hutcherson L Hemsworth	Película: *Frida* S. Hayek	Película: *Harry Potter y el príncipe mestizo*
CANAL 46 11:00	Película: *Piratas del Caribe* J. Depp	Partido de golf	Película: *Crepúsculo* K. Stewart R. Pattinson	Película: *Diarios de motocicleta* G. García Bernal	Documental: *Exploración del espacio*	Película: *Shrek III* M. Myers E. Murphy	Documental: *Historia del chocolate*

Paso 2. Individually, review all the programs, films, and other offerings and circle the ones you want to see. Then share the information with your classmate, indicating on which day each is featured.

MODELO

E1: *¿Qué quieres ver[1] en la televisión?*

E2: *El lunes, quiero ver el documental* **Animales en extinción***. El martes,... ¿Y tú?*

DESEOS

querer	*to want, wish, love*
¿Quieres...?	*Do you want...?*
Quiero...	*I want...*

1-18 Students preview two forms of the verb **querer** and the structure **querer + infinitive**: **¿quieres...? / quiero...**

[1]to see, [2]Hunger Games

LOS MESES DEL AÑO

enero	febrero	marzo	abril	mayo	junio
julio	agosto	septiembre	octubre	noviembre	diciembre

Write each month on a separate sheet of paper. Have twelve students, each holding up one of the months, stand in front of the class out of order. Then have the class close their books and rearrange the students chronologically. Next, remove (randomly) several of the students from the lineup and have the class provide the missing months.

¿SABES QUE...?

Thanksgiving is not celebrated in Hispanic countries, but Hispanics in the U.S. sometimes observe the holiday, calling it **el Día de Acción de Gracias.**

For additional practice on dates, see PowerPoint slides on BCS and in *WileyPLUS.*

De paso

¿Qué fecha es hoy?

el + (día) + **de** + (mes)   Hoy es **el 8 de** julio.

The first day of the month is **el primero.**   **El primero de mayo** = *May 1*

In Spanish, numerical dates are written with the day first, followed by the month. Example: 22/10 = the 22nd of October.

LA FECHA

¿Qué fecha es hoy?	*What is today's date?*
¿Cuándo es...?	*When is...?*
Hoy es...	*Today is...*
mi/tu cumpleaños	*my/your birthday*
la Navidad	*Christmas*
el Año Nuevo	*New Year's*

¡Oye! Review the celebrations/holidays with your students prior to beginning the activity.

Guión para ¡Oye!
1. El Año Nuevo. ¿Es en enero o en febrero?
2. La Navidad. ¿Es en noviembre o en diciembre?
3. El Día de San Valentín. ¿Es en enero o en febrero?
4. El Día de San Patricio. ¿Es en marzo o en mayo?
5. El Día de la Madre. ¿Es en marzo o en mayo?
6. El Día del Padre. ¿Es en abril o en junio?
7. El Día de la Independencia de EE. UU. ¿Es en julio o en agosto?
8. El Día de Halloween. ¿Es en septiembre o en octubre?
9. El Día de Acción de Gracias (*Thanksgiving*). ¿Es en noviembre o en diciembre?

¡Oye! Los meses del año

Your instructor will name some important annual celebrations. Name the month in which each takes place, selecting from the months you hear.

1-19 Meses en común

Walk around the classroom calling out the month of your birthday in Spanish, to find classmates with birthdays in the same month. You have *three* minutes. Form groups according to the month and then share your birth dates with each other.

MODELO

E1: *Mi cumpleaños es el 24 de septiembre.*

E2: *Mi cumpleaños es en septiembre también.*

1-20 Los cumpleaños de personas influyentes

Your instructor wants to know if you can identify the birthday dates of the following people. Remember that in Spanish, numerical dates are written with the day first, followed by the month. Repeat the activity with a partner. Take turns.

MODELO

¿Quién celebra su cumpleaños el 4 de septiembre?

E: *¿El 4 de septiembre? Beyoncé Knowles.*

1. Barack Obama 4/8
2. Tina Fey 18/5
3. Beyoncé Knowles 4/9
4. Ryan Gosling 12/11
5. Oprah Winfrey 29/1
6. Mark Zuckerberg 14/5

1-20 ANOTHER STEP: You may want to ask your students to write down the names of two friends or family members (**mi mamá, mi papá,...**) and their birthdays (day/month). They should include their name on the slip of paper, and turn it in to you. Students should keep a copy. Call out birthday dates at random (**Su cumpleaños es el 8 de enero. ¿Quién es?**) and the appropriate student identifies whose birthday it is (**Es mi amigo/a Joe/ Mary**) and confirms the date (**Su cumpleaños es el 8 de enero**).

ENERO

LUNES MONDAY	MARTES TUESDAY	MIÉRCOLES WEDNESDAY	JUEVES THURSDAY	VIERNES FRIDAY	SÁBADO SATURDAY	DOMINGO SUNDAY
○ LUNA LLENA *FULL MOON* 1st-31st - DÍA 1-31	C. MENGUANTE *LAST QUARTER* 9th - DÍA 9	LUNA NUEVA *NEW MOON* 17th - DÍA 17	C. CRECIENTE *FIRST QUARTER* 24th - DÍA 24	**1** AÑO NUEVO *NEW YEAR'S DAY*	**2** SAN BASILIO M.	**3** S. ANTERO PAPA
4 SAN PRISCO	**5** S. TELESFORO	**6** LOS REYES MAGOS (*EPIPHANY*)	**7** SAN RAIMUNDO	**8** SAN APOLINAR	**9** SAN MARCELINO	**10** SAN GONZALO
11 S. HIGINIO PAPA	**12** S. ARCADIO	**13** S. HILARIO	**14** SAN FÉLIX	**15** S. MAURO ABAD	**16** SAN MARCELO	**17** SAN ANTONIO ABAD
18 STA. PRISCA	**19** SAN MARIO	**20** SAN FABIÁN	**21** SAN FRUCTUOSO	**22** SAN VICENTE	**23** SAN ALBERTO	**24** SAN FRANCISCO DE S.
25 STA. ELVIRA	**26** S. TIMOTEO	**27** STA. ÁNGELA	**28** STO. TOMÁS DE A.	**29** SAN VALERIO	**30** STA. MARTINA	**31** S. JUAN BOSCO

©John Wiley & Sons, Inc.

¿Cuándo celebra Ángela el día de su santo? El 27 de enero, ¿verdad? ¿Y Elvira? ¿Alberto? ¿Martina? ¿Tomás?

¿SABES QUE...?

A Hispanic tradition is the celebration of one's **santo**, or saint's day. For example, March 19 is Saint Joseph's Day (**el día de San José**), so people named José celebrate on that date, as well as on their birthday.

 ## 1-21 ¿Cuál es tu signo del zodíaco?

Walk around the classroom asking as many students as possible the dates of their birthdays. Then identify their zodiac sign (see chart below) and jot down the information: name and sign. You have *five* minutes. The person who finds the most students with different zodiac signs wins! Report your findings to the class for confirmation.

MODELO

E1: *¿Cuándo es tu cumpleaños?*
E2: *El 24 de julio.*

E1: *¿Eres Leo?*
E2: *¡Sí!*

1-21 ANOTHER STEP: Have students line up in two teams. Each team rearranges itself according to birthdays (month and day, not year) by asking each other **¿Cuándo es tu cumpleaños?** and getting into the appropriate order. No English is allowed! The first team to complete the lineup wins. The winning team members call out their individual birthdays to confirm the lineup.

Aries	♈	20 de marzo – 19 de abril	Libra	♎	23 de septiembre – 22 de octubre
Tauro	♉	20 de abril – 20 de mayo	Escorpión	♏	23 de octubre – 22 de noviembre
Géminis	♊	21 de mayo – 20 de junio	Sagitario	♐	23 de noviembre – 20 de diciembre
Cáncer	♋	21 de junio – 22 de julio	Capricornio	♑	21 de diciembre – 19 de enero
Leo	♌	23 de julio – 22 de agosto	Acuario	♒	20 de enero – 18 de febrero
Virgo	♍	23 de agosto – 22 de septiembre	Piscis	♓	19 de febrero – 19 de marzo

©John Wiley & Sons, Inc.

1-22 Averigua[1] la fecha

You **(E1)** have a list of some important events for the month of May, but forgot to mark the dates on your calendar. Let's see if you can find out the exact date of each one from your brother/sister **(E2)**, who has marked them all (shown sideways). Play this game by asking first what *day* of the week the event takes place, and then the *date*. After four items, change roles.

MODELO

E1: *La inauguración del museo, ¿es el viernes?*

E2: *No, después.*

E1: *¿Es el domingo?*

E2: *Sí.*

E1: *¿Es el veintiséis?*

E2: *No, antes.*

E1: *¿Es el doce?*

E2: *¡Sí! La inauguración del museo es el 12 de mayo.*

Agenda para mayo (E2)

La inauguración del museo: 12
El fin del año académico: 16
La cita con el doctor Gómez: 20
El cumpleaños de la tía Rita: 1
El concierto de jazz: 17
El picnic con la familia: 25
La reunión con amigos: 14
La fiesta de Cristóbal: 31
La celebración del 5 de mayo: 5

Agenda para mayo (E1)

La inauguración del museo
El fin del año académico
La cita con el doctor Gómez
El cumpleaños de la tía Rita
El concierto de jazz
El picnic con la familia
La reunión con amigos
La fiesta de Cristóbal
La celebración del 5 de mayo

MAYO

LUNES	MARTES	MIÉRCOLES	JUEVES	VIERNES	SÁBADO	DOMINGO
			1	2	3	4	5
6	7	8	9	10	11	12 inauguración del museo
13	14	15	16	17	18	19
20	21	22	23	24	25	26
27	28	29	30	31		

For additional practice on dates, see PowerPoint slides on BCS and in *WileyPLUS*.

Skjold Photographs/The Image Works

A *Cinco de Mayo* parade in St. Paul, Minnesota. *Cinco de Mayo* celebrations are becoming more and more popular in the U.S. On that day, Mexican culture is celebrated with parades, floats, music, dancing, and typical Mexican food. This date commemorates the victory of the Mexicans over the French at Puebla.

[1]Find out

Tu mundo cultural

Breve historia del español

Año 218* a. C.[1]: el latín llega[2] a Hispania

WILEY PLUS Go to *WileyPLUS* to see the video related to this chapter.

Reading strategy: Tell your students that they do not need to know every word in order to understand the general meaning of a text. Encourage them to guess the meaning of unknown words by context.

Meets ACTFL Standards 1.2, interpretive reading, and 3.1, other disciplines.

For an additional activity related to this cultural theme, see the PowerPoint slides on BCS and in *WileyPLUS*.

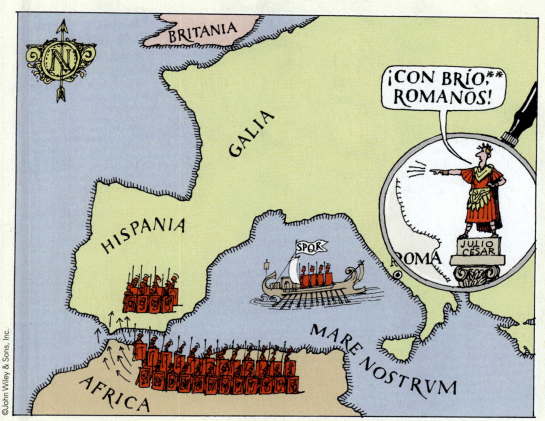

©John Wiley & Sons, Inc.

¿SABES QUE...?

Spanish, like French, Italian, Portuguese, and Romanian, comes from Latin. These are called Romance languages because of their Roman origin. The Latin word **Hispania** evolved into the Spanish word **España** (*Spain*).

Los romanos conquistan la Península Ibérica (218–204 a. C.) y la llaman **Hispania.** El latín, la lengua[3] de los soldados y comerciantes[4] romanos, se introduce en la península y se convierte en la lengua oficial del nuevo territorio romano. Con el paso de los siglos[5], el latín se transforma en lo que hoy llamamos castellano o español.

©John Wiley & Sons, Inc.

¿SABES QUE...?

The title of this text, *¡Con brío!*, comes from a Spanish expression that has an interesting origin. The word **brío** relates to the Celtic word *brig* which denotes strength. To do something with **brío** refers to the energy and determination with which one moves, works or does anything that requires effort. Other possible meanings include: with spirit, enthusiasm, gusto, grace, vigor, and courage.

[1]B.C., [2]arrives, [3]language, [4]merchants, [5]centuries

*218 **doscientos dieciocho**, **CON BRÍO** *With gusto, determination and courage*

Año 1492*: el idioma[1] español llega a América

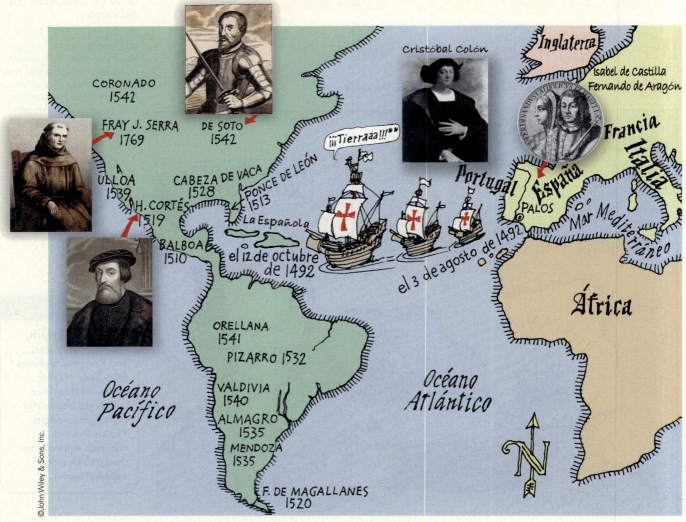

El 12 de octubre de 1492, Cristóbal Colón llega a América. Con la exploración, conquista y cristianización del continente americano, el español se convierte en la lengua oficial de gran parte del Nuevo Mundo[2].

Photos: BL: Bettmann/©Corbis; L: Lake County Museum/©Corbis; TC: Chris Keller/©Corbis; TR: Bettmann/©Corbis; R: ©Corbis

¿SABES QUE...?

The year 1492 was a turning point for both Spain and the Americas. Spain became unified politically and religiously under Ferdinand and Isabella. As a result, Jews (in 1492) and Muslims (in 1502) refusing to convert to Christianity were expelled from the country. Also, in 1492 Spain broadly expanded its territories by conquering the native civilizations of the Americas, with profound consequences for both. For the natives of the New World it marked the beginning of the destruction of their civilization.

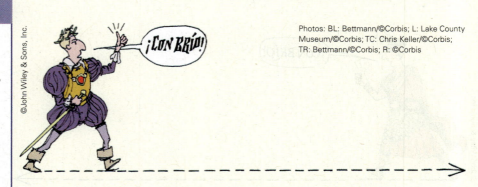

[1]language, [2]**Nuevo...** New World

*1492 **mil cuatrocientos noventa y dos,** **¡Tierra!** *Land!*

Año 1492–presente: el español continúa su expansión

©John Wiley & Sons, Inc.

En el siglo XIX, incluso[1] después de su independencia, la mayoría de los países[2] que anteriormente formaban parte de España conservan el español como lengua oficial. Actualmente el español es la lengua oficial de 21** países: España, 19 países en América y Guinea Ecuatorial, una antigua colonia española situada en África. El español es también la lengua de más de 40 millones de personas residentes en EE. UU.[3], adonde por razones políticas o económicas, continúan llegando inmigrantes procedentes de países hispanohablantes[4] (véanse las flechas[5] en el mapa).

¿Qué aprendiste?[6]

Mark the correct option for each question.

1. ¿De qué lengua se deriva el castellano o español?
   ☐ del italiano ☑ del latín ☐ del inglés
2. ¿En qué año llega el español a América?
   ☐ en el año 218 a. C. ☐ en 1776 ☑ en 1492
3. En este momento, ¿en cuántos países es el español la lengua oficial?
   ☑ en 20 ☐ en 19 ☐ en 10
4. En EE. UU., ¿aproximadamente cuántas personas son hispanohablantes?
   ☐ 5 millones ☐ 13 millones ☑ 41 millones

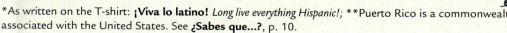

[1]even, [2]countries, [3]United States, [4]Spanish-speaking, [5]arrows, [6]**¿Qué...** What did you learn?

¿SABES QUE...?

The term **castellano** (*Castilian*) refers to the Spanish spoken in **Castilla** (*Castile*) in central Spain. Many Spanish-speakers use it as a synonym for **español.**

¿SABES QUE...?

The term Hispanic designates a cultural identity, not a race. Spanish-speaking countries, as you will learn in **Capítulo 9**, are racially diverse, including indigenous peoples of the Americas, Africans, Caucasians, and mixtures of the three.

¿SABES QUE...?

The Instituto Cervantes, founded in 1991 by the government of Spain, promotes the Spanish language and Hispanic culture through its centers all over the world, including five in the U.S.: New York, Boston, Chicago, Albuquerque, and Seattle. To celebrate the language and the worldwide Hispanic community it unifies, the Instituto Cervantes created **el día E**, the international day of Spanish, which takes place on the Saturday in June closest to the summer solstice.

©John Wiley & Sons, Inc.

*As written on the T-shirt: **¡Viva lo latino!** *Long live everything Hispanic!;* **Puerto Rico is a commonwealth associated with the United States. See **¿Sabes que...?**, p. 10.

Tu mundo en vivo

¡Video en acción!

¡Bienvenido al mundo hispano!

1. **Antes de ver el video**
   a. Do you know how many countries in the world are Spanish-speaking? 21
   b. Besides language, what else do Hispanic countries have in common? Culture, customs...
   c. What kind of greeting customs do we have in the U.S.? For example, how do you greet your friends? Professors? Work colleagues? Family members? Have you noticed any differences across the U.S. in this respect?

 Go to *WileyPLUS* to complete the **Mientras ves el video** activity.

2. **Después de ver el video**
   a. In small groups, discuss with your classmates the differences between greeting customs in your own culture and those in the Hispanic world. What might be the consequences if someone is unaware of the greeting customs in a particular region? Later, share your thoughts with the whole group.

¡Diálogos en acción!

1.1 Saludos y presentaciones informales

Olivia, a student from Spain, and her friend Marta, from Ecuador, run into Olivia's friend Claudio on campus. The three of them exchange greetings.

Paso 1. First, read the **Expresiones útiles** in p. A-1. Next, listen to the dialogue twice and answer the questions your instructor will ask.

Paso 2. Look at the transcript of this dialogue (p. A-15) and act it out with a partner. Switch roles. Now, go to p. A-1 to complete **Paso 3** and **4.**

1.2 Saludos y presentaciones formales

Marta Ledesma, a student from Ecuador, and her friend Olivia Torres, from Spain, run into Marta's professor González on their way to class. The three of them exchange greetings.

 Go to *WileyPLUS* to listen to and practice this dialogue.

Diálogo 1.1 models the functions of informal greetings, introductions, and leave-taking, as well as asking and explaining where one is from.
Diálogo 1.2 models formal greetings, introductions and leave-taking.

¡Lectura en acción!

Anuncios de actividades para niños[1]

The following advertisements from a Mexican newspaper publicize summer and weekend activities for children.

Paso 1. Without trying to understand these ads yet, simply look at the individual words and circle all the ones you know or are pretty certain of what they mean.

Paso 2. Now focusing primarily on the words you have circled, answer the following questions in Spanish, when possible, or in English, if necessary.

← **ANUNCIO 1**

1. When is this event?

2. How much does it cost to participate?

3. Who can participate?

4. Where is this event held?

ANUNCIO 2 →

1. When are these classes? What days? What times? What dates?

2. How much do they cost (in Mexican pesos)?

3. Who can participate?

4. Where are the classes?

Paso 3. Using all of the words you understand from each ad, as well as the images in each one, answer these questions, in English.

1. What do you think *ajedrez* is? How did you guess?

2. Can you figure out what *artes plásticas* are? What are some examples? What information helped you to make your guess?

[1]children

Gobierno del Distrito Federal, Delegación Coyoacán, Dirección General de Cultura Coyoacán: Cultura para Todos/México.

Reprinted by permission of la Escuela Nacional de Artes Plásticas/UNAM.

Reading Strategy

Skimming a Text for Cognates and Other Familiar Words or Information

When approaching your first readings in Spanish, it is important to focus on what you do know in order to not become overwhelmed by all the unfamiliar words. One way to overcome this is to highlight all the words that are familiar to you and use those words to decipher meaning from the context they help create.

Reading Strategy

Using Images to Understand Content

Frequently the images in a reading will offer clues to the text. What do the ones used here tell you?

¡A conversar!

¡A conversar! strategies will help you have more meaningful interpersonal communication in Spanish both in and out of class. You can record your **¡A conversar!** activities on *WileyPLUS* voice boards or with your own cell phones or tablet computers. Let's try it with this activity...

El primer día de clases

With a partner, talk about this term's first day of classes. Did anything funny or unusual happen? Listen carefully as your partner speaks, breaking in occasionally to summarize the information. Take turns telling your stories.

¡A escribir!

The strategies that accompany **¡A escribir!** activities are integrated into the steps of the writing process: prewriting, writing, revising, and peer correction. If you have access to a blog or a wiki, create a writing portfolio with your **¡A escribir!** assignments. You will see how your skills develop over time. Now, you'll practice the prewriting strategy of listing information with the following activity.

¡Preséntate!

How would you introduce yourself to your classmates in a blog? Jot down words and phrases in English related to your studies, work, family, and leisure activities. Once your list is complete, arrange the elements of your self-introduction in a logical order. You're ready to begin the first draft of your blog entry!

If you have access to a blog or wiki, you may wish to ask students to complete and post self-introductions outside of class based on the information they listed for this activity.

¡A investigar!

¡A investigar! strategies will assist you in finding and using appropriate sources, both online and in your own community, to answer questions about a variety of cultural topics. To share your **¡A investigar!** research results, you can create PowerPoint slides for class presentations, post reports to a wiki or blog, and even make podcasts and videos! You can also use the tools offered by your course management system. Let's try it with this activity...

Ruinas romanas en España

In **Tu mundo cultural** you learned Spanish comes from Latin, the language of the Romans. What architectural evidence of the Roman presence can still be seen in Spain and where are they? Work in groups of *three* and select one video or two images of one specific archaeological site, noting the location of the site and the URLs of your search results. Post your information online or bring it to class to share. As you and your classmates view the images, mark the locations of the sites on a map of Spain. Which would you like to visit?

If your access to technology is limited, have the students create posters to use as visual aids as they speak.

*You may assign the appropriate **Pasos** of **¡A investigar!** for pairs or small groups to complete outside of class.*

Trivia

Show off what you know about the Spanish-speaking world by answering *Trivia* questions. If you need some help, look at the map on the inside front cover of the book.

1. ¿Cómo se llama la capital de España? ¿Y la capital de México?

2. ¿Hay petróleo en España? ¿Y en México?

Very good! You might even win a trivia contest! *1. Madrid. Ciudad de México. 2. No. Sí.*

Vocabulario: Capítulo 1

Saludos *Greetings*
Hola. *Hello. Hi.*
Buenos días. *Good morning.*
Buenas tardes. *Good afternoon.*
Buenas noches. *Good evening. Good night.*

Despedidas *Good-byes*
Adiós. *Good-bye.*
Chao. *Bye.*
Hasta luego. *See you later.*
Hasta mañana. *See you tomorrow.*

Presentaciones *Introductions*
¿Cómo te llamas? *What is your name?*
      (informal)
¿Cómo se llama usted? *What is your name?*
      (formal)
Me llamo... *My name is...*
Le presento a... *Let me introduce you to...*
      (formal)
Te presento a... *Let me introduce you to...*
      (informal)
Encantado/a. *I'm delighted to meet you.*
Mucho gusto. *Nice/Pleased to meet you.*

Preguntas y respuestas
Questions and answers
¿Cómo estás? *How are you? (informal)*
¿Cómo está usted? *How are you? (formal)*
¿De dónde eres? *Where are you from?*
      (informal)
¿De dónde es usted? *Where are you from?*
      (formal)
¿Qué tal? *How are you (doing)? (informal)*
¿Y tú? ¿Y usted? *And you? (informal/*
      formal)
Bien./ Muy bien, gracias. *Fine.*
      Very well, thanks.
Regular. *Okay. So, so.*
Mal. *Not so well. Bad.*

Otras palabras y expresiones
Other words and expressions
Con permiso. *Excuse me (to ask permission to*
      pass by someone or to leave).
Perdón. *Pardon me/ Excuse me (to get some*
      one's attention or to seek forgiveness).
Gracias. *Thanks.*
De nada. *You're welcome.*
(el) señor (Sr.) *Mr., Sir*
(la) señora (Sra.) *Mrs., Ma'am*
(la) señorita (Srta.) *Miss*
el profesor/ la profesora *professor (m./f.)*
el amigo/ la amiga *friend (m./f.)*
el hombre *man*
la mujer *woman*
un poco *a little*
muy *very*

pero *but*
también *also*
tampoco *not either*
y *and*
o *or*

Los números del 0 al 59
Numbers 0 to 59
cero *zero*
uno *one*
dos *two*
tres *three*
cuatro *four*
cinco *five*
seis *six*
siete *seven*
ocho *eight*
nueve *nine*
diez *ten*
once *eleven*
doce *twelve*
trece *thirteen*
catorce *fourteen*
quince *fifteen*
dieciséis *sixteen*
diecisiete *seventeen*
dieciocho *eighteen*
diecinueve *nineteen*
veinte *twenty*
veintiuno *twenty-one*
veintidós *twenty-two*
veintitrés *twenty-three*
veinticuatro *twenty-four*
veinticinco *twenty-five*
veintiséis *twenty-six*
veintisiete *twenty-seven*
veintiocho *twenty-eight*
veintinueve *twenty-nine*
treinta *thirty*
treinta y uno *thirty-one*
cuarenta *forty*
cuarenta y uno *forty-one*
cincuenta *fifty*
cincuenta y nueve *fifty nine*
¿cuántos?/ ¿cuántas? *How many? (m./f. pl.)*

La clase *Class*
el bolígrafo *pen*
la computadora *computer*
el cuaderno *notebook*
el escritorio *desk*
el estudiante/el alumno *student (m.)*
la estudiante/la alumna *student (f.)*
el lápiz *pencil*
el libro *book*
la mochila *backpack*
el reloj *clock, watch*

Los días *Days*
el lunes *Monday*
el martes *Tuesday*
el miércoles *Wednesday*
el jueves *Thursday*
el viernes *Friday*
el sábado *Saturday*
el domingo *Sunday*

Los meses *Months*
enero *January*
febrero *February*
marzo *March*
abril *April*
mayo *May*
junio *June*
julio *July*
agosto *August*
septiembre *September*
octubre *October*
noviembre *November*
diciembre *December*

Las fechas *Dates*
¿Qué fecha es hoy? *What is today's date?*
¿Cuándo es...? *When is...?*
Hoy es... *Today is...*
mi/ tu cumpleaños *my/ your birthday*
la Navidad *Christmas*
el Año Nuevo *New Year's*

¿Qué hora es? *What time is it?*
y cuarto *fifteen past or quarter after*
y media *half past or thirty*
menos *less (literally), to*
menos cuarto *quarter to*
en punto *on the dot, sharp*
de la mañana *in the morning*
de la tarde *in the afternoon*
de la noche *in the evening*
Es mediodía. *It's noon.*
Es medianoche. *It's midnight.*

Verbos y expresiones verbales
Verbs and verbal expressions
hay *there is, there are*
ser *to be*
querer *to want, wish, love*
¿Quieres...? *Do you want...?*
Quiero... *I want...*

¡Próximamente!¹

Historietas² ¡Con brío!

Meet the main characters of the ¡Con brío! comic strips! They will accompany you throughout the text, beginning in Chapter 2 (see p. 41).

¡Hola! ¿Qué tal? Me llamo Jennifer. Soy de Puerto Rico. Estudio derecho³.

Jennifer

Me llamo Fabio. Soy policía y estudiante. Soy estadounidense de origen mexicano.

Fabio

¡Hola! Me llamo Ysenia. Soy de Ecuador. Soy estudiante de la universidad y amiga de Jennifer y de Mabel.

Ysenia

¿Qué tal? Me llamo Ernesto. Soy cubano. Me gusta⁴ el béisbol. Soy amigo de Fabio y de Mario. Estudio ingeniería.

Ernesto

¿Cómo están? Me llamo Mabel. Soy dominicana. Soy enfermera⁵ y también⁶ estudio en la universidad.

Mabel

¡Hola! ¿Qué tal? Soy Mario y soy de Chile. Me gustan las computadoras. Soy amigo de Fabio y de Ernesto.

Mario

Nosotros somos los padres de Jennifer. Somos puertorriqueños.

Los señores Rivera

Me llamo Yolanda. Mi mamá es Jennifer.

Yolanda

Yo soy Olivia y mi papá es Fabio.

Olivia

¹Coming up!, ²Comic strips, ³law, ⁴Me... I like, ⁵nurse, ⁶also

Capítulo 2

La universidad y el trabajo

WILEY PLUS

Additional activities and **Autopruebas** for each **Escena** available online.

Steve Hix/Fuse/Getty Images, Inc.

Escena 1
El campus universitario

GRAMÁTICA:
· Gender & number of nouns; definite & indefinite articles
· *Estar* (to be) + location

CULTURA:
Dos universidades hispanas

Escena 2
En clase

GRAMÁTICA:
· *Estar* + condition

CULTURA:
La influencia hispana en EE. UU.

Escena 3
Las profesiones y el trabajo

GRAMÁTICA:
· *Ir* (to go) + *a* + destination
· Interrogative words

CULTURA:
El español en el mundo laboral

TU MUNDO EN VIVO

¡**Videos en acción!** Una visita a la UNAM; Ser bilingüe
¡**Diálogos en acción!** Requesting Information; Greeting, Complaining, and Inviting
¡**Lectura en acción!** Utilizing Background Knowledge
¡**A conversar!** Requesting Repetitions
¡**A escribir!** Listing Information
¡**A investigar!** Finding Spanish-Language Sources

LEARNING OBJECTIVES

By the end of this chapter you will be able to:
· Give your class schedule.
· State where places are located on campus.
· Describe the classroom.
· Express to whom things belong.
· Ask and describe how someone is feeling or doing.
· Talk about professions.
· Tell where you are going on campus.
· Ask questions.
· Discuss the influence of Spanish and Hispanic culture in the USA.

El campus universitario

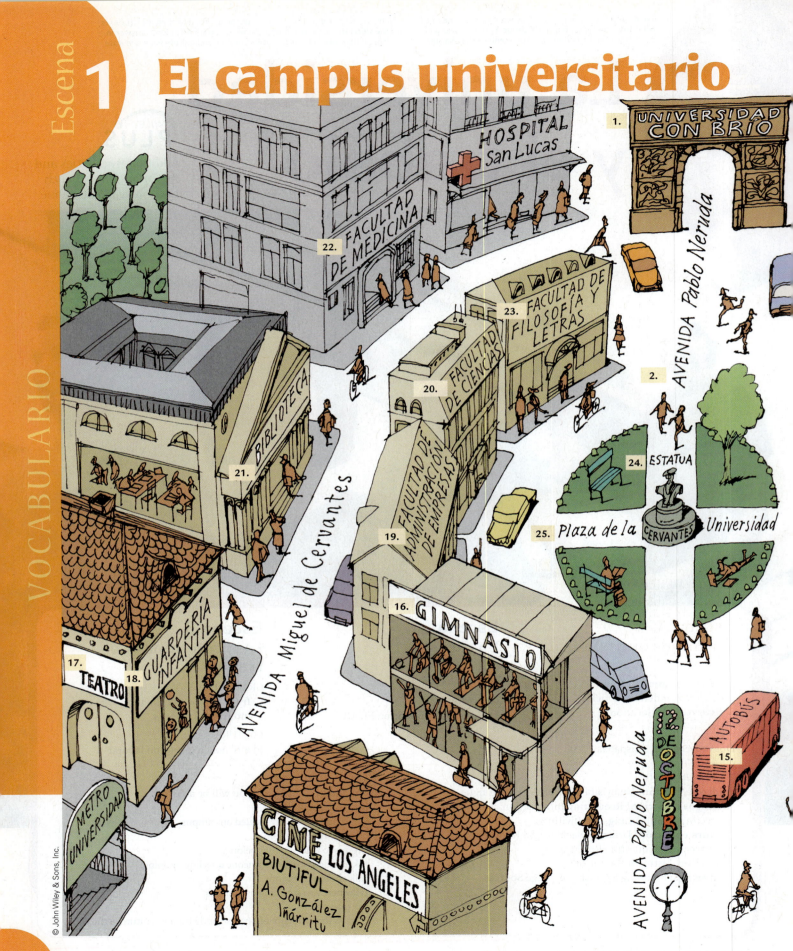

1. UNIVERSIDAD CON BRÍO
HOSPITAL San Lucas
22. FACULTAD DE MEDICINA
23. FACULTAD DE FILOSOFÍA Y LETRAS
20. FACULTAD DE CIENCIAS
2. AVENIDA Pablo Neruda
BIBLIOTECA
21.
24. ESTATUA
CERVANTES
25. Plaza de la Universidad
19. FACULTAD DE ADMINISTRACIÓN DE EMPRESAS
AVENIDA Miguel de Cervantes
16. GIMNASIO
17. TEATRO
18. GUARDERÍA INFANTIL
METRO UNIVERSIDAD
CINE LOS ÁNGELES
BIUTIFUL
A. González Iñárritu
AVENIDA Pablo Neruda
2 DE OCTUBRE
15. AUTOBÚS

© John Wiley & Sons, Inc.

Pronunciación: Practice pronunciation of the chapter's new vocabulary in *WileyPLUS*.

1. university
2. avenue
3. Law School*
4. building
5. street
6. stadium
7. Registrar's Office
8. student center
9. cafeteria
10. bookstore; stationery store
11. parking
12. bicycles
13. cars
14. dormitory, residence hall
15. bus
16. gym
17. theater
18. daycare center
19. Business School
20. School of Sciences
21. library
22. Medical School
23. School of Arts
24. statue
25. square, plaza

***La Facultad** is a school or a college within a university. The word for *faculty* is **el profesorado**.

You may use the PowerPoint slides of all scenes to present and practice the vocabulary.

Note: Be careful with the false cognate *librería*, which looks like *library* but actually means *bookstore*. *Biblioteca* is *library*.

¡La pronunciación!

Pay attention to the correct pronunciation of Spanish **vowels** and **diphthongs** (see P-1, P-2).

autobús estadio
bicicleta universidad

¡En acción!

2-1   En tu universidad

Indicate whether these statements apply to your campus by saying «**Cierto**» or «**Falso**».

MODELO

Profesor/a: *Hay un teatro.*

Tú: Cierto.   **o:**   Falso. No hay un teatro.

1. Hay una cafetería.
2. Hay una guardería infantil.
3. Hay una Facultad de Derecho.
4. Hay una biblioteca.
5. Hay una Facultad de Medicina.
6. Hay un centro estudiantil.
7. Hay un gimnasio.
8. Hay un estadio de deportes.
9. Hay una librería-papelería.
10. Hay residencias estudiantiles.
11. Hay una Facultad de Administración de Empresas.
12. Hay una estatua.

2-2   El campus universitario   RECYCLES numbers, telling time, dates.

A friend is visiting you at the *Universidad Con brío*. While touring the campus, he/she asks you about the school. One of you plays the role of the friend, and the other responds according to what he/she sees in the scene on pages 34–35. Take turns. Partial answers are provided for items 1 and 2.

1. ¿Qué facultades hay en la Universidad Con Brío? *La Facultad de...*
2. ¿En qué avenida hay un autobús? *En la avenida...* ¿Y una biblioteca? ¿Y un centro estudiantil?
3. ¿Cuántos carros hay en el estacionamiento? ¿Y cuántas bicicletas?
4. ¿Cómo se llama la cafetería? ¿Y la librería-papelería? ¿Y la residencia estudiantil?
5. ¿En qué calle hay un estadio de deportes? ¿Y en qué avenida hay una galería infantil?
6. ¿Cuántos estudiantes hay en la plaza de la universidad? ¿Cómo se llama la persona famosa representada en la estatua?
7. ¿Hay estudiantes en el gimnasio? ¿Cuántos hay?
8. En el campus, ¿hay un teatro? ¿y un cine? ¿y una parada de metro[1]?
9. ¿Qué hora es en el reloj de la avenida Pablo Neruda? ¿Qué fecha es?

¿SABES QUE...?

The streets in Spanish-speaking countries are often named after famous people (see opener scene). Calle Colón is named after **Cristóbal Colón** (Christopher Columbus) who was born in Genoa, Italy and died in Spain (1450 or 1451–1506). **Miguel de Cervantes** from Spain (1547–1616) is the author of the masterpiece *Don Quijote de la Mancha*. **Frida Kahlo** from Mexico (1907–1954) is a famous painter. She was married to the muralist Diego Rivera. **Pablo Neruda** from Chile (1904–1973) is a poet and winner of a Nobel prize in literature.

2-2 PERSONALIZED QUESTIONS: A prospective Spanish-speaking exchange student asks you, ¿Cómo se llama tu *college* o universidad? ¿Hay residencias estudiantiles? ¿Cuántas? ¿Qué otros edificios hay en el campus? Several students respond, each providing one building.

[1]**parada...** subway stop

Asignaturas y especialidades *Subjects and majors*

Asignaturas y especialidades vocabulary is passive.

Estudio...

alemán[1]
árabe
chino
español
francés
inglés
italiano
japonés
portugués
ruso

Yo estudio...

arte
ciencias políticas
filosofía
geografía
historia
literatura
música
oratoria[6]
religión
sociología

Y yo estudio...

álgebra
biología
cálculo
contabilidad[2]
economía
estadística[3]
física
geometría
informática[4]
matemáticas
(p)sicología
química
salud[5]

Y tú, ¿qué estudias?

¿SABES QUE...?

The word **álgebra**, along with more than 5,000 others, comes from Arabic. The Moors (Muslims of mixed Arab and Berber origin, from northern Africa) invaded Spain in the eighth century and occupied most of the peninsula for nearly 800 years (711–1492). Many of the Spanish words borrowed from Arabic begin with **al**.

Otras especialidades y carreras:

arquitectura
cine
derecho *law*
enfermería *nursing*
estudios medioambientales *enviromental studies*
hotelería *hotel management*

ingeniería *engineering*
medicina
negocios *business*
terapia del lenguaje *speech therapy*
terapia física
trabajo social *social work*

Most of the courses your students take should appear listed here. If they are taking a specialized course, such as child psychology, they can simply say that they are taking a course in **psicología**. Indicate to students that most of the subjects are cognates and, therefore, recognizable and easy to learn.

Articles have been omitted, since they are not necessary for expressing what one studies.

For additional practice on this grammar point, see PowerPoint slides on BCS and in *WileyPLUS*.

De paso

To talk about a certain class or book, use **de** + *noun:* **la clase de contabilidad** *accounting class;* **el diccionario de español** *Spanish dictionary.*

 ## 2-3 Y tú, ¿qué estudias?

Ask each other **¿Qué estudias?** to find out what the other person is studying. Respond saying **Estudio...**, adding subjects from those listed above. Take turns.

2-3 This activity previews the verb **estudiar**, to be presented formally on p. 80. Tell your students that when talking about actions performed by oneself the verb ends in **-o** as in estudi**o** versus the ending **-as** used when asking someone we address with **tú** as in estudi**as**. Follow up by asking students to name their major: **Mi especialidad es...**

[1]German, [2]accounting, [3]statistics, [4]computer science, [5]health, [6]speech

For more practice, see **Grammar Handbook** found in *WileyPLUS*.

For additional practice on this grammar point, see PowerPoint slides on BCS and in *WileyPLUS*.

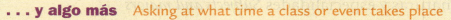

. . . y algo más — Asking at what time a class or event takes place

To ask *(At) what time* a class or event takes place, use **¿A qué hora...?** In your answer, use **a la una/a las dos...**

> **¿A qué hora** es la clase de biología? Es **a las 11:00** de la mañana.
> **¿A qué hora** es el examen? Es **a la 1:00** de la tarde.

2-4 Mi horario y tu horario RECYCLES days of the week and telling time.

Paso 1.   First, list your classes on a sheet of paper, without indicating the day/s or time/s, and give the list to your partner. Your partner does the same. Then ask your partner when each of his/her classes takes place (day/s and time/s) and in what building. Jot down the information. Take turns.

¿SABES QUE...?

In Spanish-speaking countries, there is no equivalent of the American two-year community college. Therefore, when referring to it, call it *college* or *universidad*.

MODELO

E1: *¿Qué días es tu clase de inglés?*

E2: *Los martes y jueves.*

E1: *¿A qué hora?*

E2: *A las 6:30 de la tarde.*

E1: *¿En qué edificio?*

E2: *En Washington Hall.*

> **Palabras útiles**
> la clase en línea *online class*
> la clase híbrida *hybrid class*

El horario de mi compañero/a de clase

	lunes	martes	miércoles	jueves	viernes
CLASE		inglés		inglés	
HORA		6:30 de la tarde		6:30 de la tarde	
EDIFICIO		Washington Hall		Washington Hall	

2-4 For *Paso 2*, focus on one day at a time. Ask students to volunteer information as to who takes classes (and what classes they take) on that particular day.

Paso 2.   Exchange schedules to confirm their accuracy and compare results. Who has more classes? Be prepared to share some of the information with the class.

🎧 ¡A escuchar![1] ¡Bienvenidos!

Paso 1.   You have just arrived at the *Universidad Con Brío*. Listen to the walking tour given to new students. Look at the university scene on pages 34–35 while you listen.

PLUS Go to *WileyPLUS* to complete **Paso 2** of this listening activity.

> **Palabras útiles**
> aquí *here*
> allí *there*

The scripts and recordings for the ¡A escuchar! sections are included on the Book Companion Site (BCS) for instructors and in *WileyPLUS*.

[1]¡A... Let's listen!

Jennifer habla con su hija Yolanda sobre[1] su primer día de universidad.

¡Mañana es tu primer día de universidad, mamá! ¿Cuál es tu primera clase y a qué hora es?

Es **la** clase de ciencias políticas, a **las** diez y media de **la** mañana.

¿Hay **una** parada[2] de autobús o de metro en **el** campus?

Sí, hay **un** autobús y **un** metro hasta[3] **el** campus.

¡Qué bien, mamá! ¿Estás nerviosa?

No, ¡estoy contenta porque es **una** universidad fantástica y **los** profesores son brillantes!

© John Wiley & Sons, Inc.

GRAMÁTICA

¡Manos a la obra![4]

Identifying gender and number: Nouns and definite and indefinite articles

1

The gender of nouns

Nouns are the names of people, animals, things, ideas, and concepts. All nouns in Spanish have *gender:* they are either masculine or feminine.

- Nouns *referring to males* and most nouns that *end in -o* are masculine:

    el hombre   el profesor   el lib**ro**   el teat**ro**

- Nouns *referring to females* and most nouns that *end in -a, -ión, or -dad/-tad* are feminine:

    la mujer   la profesor**a**   la plaz**a**   la lecc**ión**   la facul**tad**

- In other instances, learn the gender of the noun by memorizing the noun along with its corresponding masculine **(el)** or feminine **(la)** article.

    el cine   la calle   el hospital   el autobús

Forming the plural of nouns

Remember that you need to add **-s** to nouns ending in a vowel:

    carro → carro**s**
    calle → calle**s**

Remember that you need to add **-es** to nouns ending in a consonant:

    universida**d** → universidad**es**
    hospita**l** → hospital**es**

Definite and indefinite articles

- Both the **definite article** (*the*—specific) and the **indefinite article** (*a, some*—nonspecific) agree in gender and number with the noun they modify.

DEFINITE ARTICLES			INDEFINITE ARTICLES		
	singular	*plural*		*singular*	*plural*
masculine	**el** libro	**los** libros	masculine	**un** carro	**unos** carros
feminine	**la** mochila	**las** mochilas	feminine	**una** avenida	**unas** avenidas

- A mixed masculine/ feminine group calls for the masculine plural article:

    el profesor y **la** profesora → **los** profesores
    un alumno y **una** alumna → **unos** alumnos

- Some exceptions are **el mapa**, **el día**, **la mano** (*hand*). Cognates ending in **-ma** are masculine: **el problema**, **el programa**.

For additional practice on this grammar point, see PowerPoint slides on BCS and in *WileyPLUS*.

PLUS Go to *WileyPLUS* to review this grammar point with the help of the **Animated Grammar Tutorial**. For more practice, go to the **Grammar Handbook**.

To introduce students to nouns and articles used in context, have them take parts and read the **historieta** out loud. To check their comprehension and call their attention to the nouns and articles, ask the following questions:
1. **¿Cuál es la primera clase de Jennifer?**
2. **¿Son inteligentes los profesores de la universidad?**

Call out nouns and have students supply the appropriate definite article: **clase → la clase, estudiante, hombre, mujer, profesor, profesora, reloj, mochila, lápiz, libro, bolígrafo, cuaderno, edificio, calle, avenida, cine, estadio,** and so on. Repeat with the indefinite articles, then have students change nouns from singular to plural, using the plural definite article: **clase → las clases.**

[1]about, [2]stop, [3](that go) up to, [4]Let's get down to work!

¡En acción!

¡Oye! Las paradas[1] del autobús nº 5

You may use the PowerPoint slide of the opener scene to chart the route that the bus takes.

You have just arrived on campus and are taking a guided bus tour. Listen to the guide tell you about the various stops. Then answer the questions (**sí** or **no**) to see how well you have learned the bus route.

Guión para ¡Oye!

Hay paradas del autobús universitario n° 5...

... en **el** hospital San Lucas, donde hay **una** clínica para estudiantes;

... en **la** biblioteca, donde muchos estudian (*point to students seen studying in library*);

... en **la** guardería infantil, que es para **los** hijos (*point to children seen through windows*) de **los** estudiantes y de **los** profesores;

... en **el** Cine Los Ángeles, donde dan **la** película *Biutiful* (*point to film title*);

... en **la** residencia estudiantil San Carlos, donde viven muchos estudiantes;

... y en **el** estadio de deportes, donde hay partidos de fútbol.

2-5 ¡Exacto!

First, add the correct missing definite article (**el, la, los, las**) in front of the words in the second column. Then, your partner, who often forgets the names of places on campus, reads the information in the first column and you complete it with the corresponding word from the second column. If you are right, your partner says **¡Exacto!** Take turns.

1. Los estudiantes levantan pesas[2] y montan en bicicleta en...	c.	a. ... _la_ librería.		
2. Muchos estudiantes estudian en...	d.	b. ... _la_ cafetería.		
3. Dan películas[3] como *Biutiful* en...	e.	c. ... _el_ gimnasio.		
4. Se estudia medicina, ciencias, etc. en...	g.	d. ... _la_ biblioteca.		
5. Hay partidos[4] de fútbol en...	f.	e. ... _el_ cine.		
6. Sirven sándwiches deliciosos en...	b.	f. ... _el_ estadio.		
7. Hay carros y bicicletas en...	h.	g. ... _las_ facultades.		
8. Venden[5] libros en...	a.	h. ... _los_ estacionamientos.		

Comprensión para ¡Oye!
¿Sí o no?

¿Hay una parada en...

... el hospital? *sí*

... la Facultad de Medicina? *no*

... la biblioteca? *sí*

... la guardería infantil? *sí*

... la estación de metro? *no*

... el Cine Los Ángeles? *sí*

... la librería-papelería Cervantes? *no*

... la residencia estudiantil San Carlos? *sí*

... el estadio de deportes? *sí*

2-6 Remind students that after **Hay** the indefinite article is always used, not the definite article: **Hay + un/una/unos/unas**.

Contrast **hay** (which denotes *existence*) and **estar** (which indicates *location*): **Hay 30 estudiantes en el salón de clase./ Los estudiantes están en el salón de clase.**

2-6 En la Universidad Con Brío

What is on campus? Complete each statement with the appropriate indefinite articles (**un, una, unos, unas**). Then observe the scene on pages 34–35 to determine whether each statement is true (**cierto**) or false (**falso**). If it is false, provide the correct information. Take turns.

MODELO

C	F	
☐	☑	Hay **una** guardería infantil en la avenida Frida Kahlo.

Falso. Hay una guardería infantil en la avenida Miguel de Cervantes.

C	F	
☑	☐	**1.** Hay _una_ biblioteca en la avenida Miguel de Cervantes.
☑	☐	**2.** _Unos_ estudiantes entran a la residencia estudiantil.
☑	☐	**3.** Hay _un_ autobús en la Calle Colón.
☑	☐	**4.** En el estacionamiento hay _unas_ bicicletas.
☐	☑	**5.** Hay _una_ estatua y _un_ reloj en la avenida Frida Kahlo.
☐	☑	**6.** Hay _un_ carro en la avenida Miguel de Cervantes.
☐	☑	**7.** En el campus no hay _una_ plaza.
☑	☐	**8.** Hay _una_ facultad de Filosofía y Letras en la avenida Pablo Neruda.

Falso. La estatua está en la plaza de la Universidad y el reloj está en la Avenida Pablo Neruda.

Falso. Hay bicicletas en la Avenida Miguel de Cervantes.

Falso. Hay una plaza; la plaza de la Universidad.

[1]stops, [2]**levantan...** lift weights, [3]**Dan...** They show movies, [4]matches, [5]They sell

2-7 El inventario de la librería RECYCLES numbers and classroom vocabulary.

 You and a classmate have been hired to update the inventory of the Librería-Papelería Cervantes. One person reads the inventory from May 15 and the other states the current inventory. Take turns.

MODELO

E1: *Un lápiz.*

E2: *Ocho lápices.* (**E1** and **E2** both write *lápices*)

Inventario del 15 de mayo	
1	lápiz
1	calculadora
1	cuaderno
1	mochila
1	libro de español
1	mapa
1	reloj

Inventario actual	
8	lápices
25	veinticinco calculadoras
36	treinta y seis cuadernos
43	cuarenta y tres mochilas
57	cincuenta y siete libros de español
12	doce mapas
15	quince relojes

© John Wiley & Sons, Inc.

Es el primer día de universidad. Jennifer habla[1] con Fabio, otro estudiante.

Hola, perdón. ¿Dónde **está** la Facultad de Ciencias?

Está en la plaza.

También **está** en la plaza.

¿Y dónde **está** la secretaría?

¿Eres estudiante?

Sí, estudio derecho penal[2].

© John Wiley & Sons, Inc.

GRAMÁTICA

¡Manos a la obra!

2

Saying where you are: The verb **estar** (to be) + location

As you may have noticed, Spanish has two verbs that mean *to be*: **ser** and **estar.** Let's look at examples based on Jennifer and Fabio's encounter on campus.

—¿De dónde **es** Fabio? —**Es** de Estados Unidos. *(origin)*

—¿Qué **es**? —Es una mochila. *(identification)*

—¿Qué hora **es**, Jennifer? —**Es** la una. *(time)*

—¿Qué fecha **es**? —**Es** el 20 de agosto, el primer día de universidad. *(date)*

—¿Cómo eres? —**Soy** responsable y organizado. *(description)*

—¿Cómo **estás**, Fabio? —**Estoy** muy bien, gracias. *(how one is doing/feeling)*

Now you are going to use **estar** to talk about the location of people, places and things.

Jennifer y Fabio **están** en el campus de la universidad.
La secretaría **está** en la plaza.

estar + en + lugar *(place)*	
(yo)* **estoy**	*I am*
(tú) **estás**	*you are*
(usted/ Ud., él, ella) **está**	*you are, he, she, it is*
(nosotros/as) **estamos**	*we are*
(vosotros/as) **estáis**	*you are*
(ustedes/ Uds., ellos/as) **están**	*you are, they are*

*The subject pronouns, unless used to clarify or contrast, are usually omitted.

[1]speaks, [2]**derecho...** *Criminal law*

WILEY PLUS Go to *WileyPLUS* to review this grammar point with the help of the **Animated Grammar Tutorial** and **Verb Conjugator.** For more practice, go to the **Grammar Handbook.**

For additional practice on this grammar point, see PowerPoint slides on BCS and in *WileyPLUS*.

To introduce students to the forms of the verb **estar** used in context, have them take parts and read the **historieta** out loud. To check their comprehension and call their attention to the verb forms, ask the following questions: 1. ¿Está la **Facultad de Ciencias en la plaza?** 2. ¿Dónde está la secretaría?

¡En acción!

¡Oye! El horario de Mariana

Mariana leads a very structured life. Listen carefully as she tells you where she is on Tuesdays at certain times. Then answer the questions, selecting the correct option.

¡Oye!
Write on the board: **en casa** *at home,* **en el trabajo** *at work.*

Also write the following times and point to each one as you narrate Mariana's schedule: 8:00, 8:15, 10:30, 12:00, 1:00, 4:00, 5:30, 10:00.

Guión para ¡Oye!
Los martes...

1. A las ocho en punto de la mañana, estoy en el estacionamiento de la universidad.

2. A las ocho y cuarto estoy en mi clase de química, y a las diez y media, en el laboratorio de biología. Estudio para ser médica.

3. A las doce en punto estoy con mis amigas en la cafetería Oaxaca. Tomamos un café y un sándwich.

4. A la una de la tarde estoy en la biblioteca, y a las cuatro, voy al gimnasio y hago ejercicio (*mime doing exercises*).

5. A las cinco y media de la tarde, estoy en el trabajo (trabajo en el Hospital San Lucas).

6. A las diez de la noche estoy en casa, escribiendo en la computadora.

2-8 ¿Dónde están?

Take turns guessing where each of the following people or things are on the campus of *Universidad Con Brío*. Use **está** or **están** as appropriate. Use the scene on pages 34–35 as a guide.

MODELO

E1: *¿Dónde está Luis?*

E2: *Está en la residencia estudiantil.*

E1: *Falso. Está en el gimnasio.*

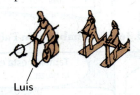

Luis

1.
Adela y Raúl
la biblioteca

2.
el reloj
la avenida P. Neruda

3.
el profesor
la cafetería

4.
las bicicletas
el estacionamiento

5.
la estatua
la plaza

6.
Sofía
la librería

All art © John Wiley & Sons, Inc.

2-9 Mi horario[1] RECYCLES telling time.

Paso 1. You and your classmate want to get together to study. First, fill in the **¿Dónde estoy?** column to indicate where you usually are on the days and at the times indicated. Then ask questions to find out where your classmate is on those days and at those times. Write the information in the fourth column. Take turns.

MODELO

E1: *Normalmente, ¿dónde **estás** los lunes a las nueve de la mañana?*

E2: ***Estoy** en el trabajo. ¿Y tú?*

> **Palabras útiles**
> en el trabajo *at work*
> en casa *at home*
> estar libre/s *to be free (available)*

Días	Horas	¿Dónde estoy?	¿Dónde está él/ella?
los lunes	9:00 a. m.	Estoy...	Está...
los martes	11:00 a. m.		
los miércoles	12:00 (mediodía)		
los jueves	1:00 p. m.		
los viernes	4:00 p. m.		
los sábados	11:00 p. m.		
los domingos	9:00 p. m.		

Paso 2. Now tell the class when you are both free to study together:

MODELO

*Los jueves a la una de la tarde… y yo **estamos** libres para estudiar.*

[1]schedule

Comprensión para ¡Oye!

1. Los martes, a las ocho en punto de la mañana, ¿está Mariana en casa o en el estacionamiento?

2. A las ocho y cuarto, ¿está en la clase de literatura o en la clase de química? Y a las diez y media, ¿está en el laboratorio de física o en el de biología?

ADVERBIOS Y PREPOSICIONES DE LUGAR[1]

Here are some common words and expressions to say where things are:

aquí	*here*	cerca de	*near*
allí	*there*	lejos de	*far from*
en	*in, at, on*	detrás de	*behind*
entre	*between*	delante de	*in front of*
al lado de	*beside*	enfrente de	*opposite, facing*

De paso

de + el → del   La Facultad de Medicina está al lado **del** hospital.

de + la (no change)   El estacionamiento está enfrente **de la** cafetería Oaxaca.

2-10   ¿Dónde está...?

Paso 1.   You are trying to locate certain places on campus. First, study the map on pages 34–35 to determine where certain places are. Select the appropriate response.

1. La Facultad de Medicina está ***entre/ enfrente de*** la biblioteca y el hospital.
2. El gimnasio está ***detrás del/ delante del*** Cine Los Ángeles.
3. El estadio está ***lejos del/ cerca del*** campus.
4. La librería-papelería Cervantes está ***al lado de/ detrás de*** la cafetería Oaxaca.
5. La estatua de Cervantes está ***enfrente de/ en*** la plaza.

Paso 2.   Now you are driving around campus and cannot find certain places. You stop the car, call a friend on your cell phone, and he/she helps you locate them, according to the map on pages 34–35. Take turns playing the two roles, using the sites below.

MODELO

la Facultad de Medicina

E1:   *¿Dónde está la Facultad de Medicina?*

E2:   *Está **detrás de** la Facultad de Filosofía y Letras y **al lado del** hospital.*

E1:   *Aquí está. Gracias.*

1. la Facultad de Ciencias
2. la biblioteca
3. el estacionamiento
4. la Calle Colón
5. el hospital San Lucas
6. el Cine Los Ángeles

2-11   Sesión de orientación   RECYCLES greetings, **hay**, and saying goodbye.

Imagine that you are a college mentor and that a new student needs information. Play the two roles, following the outline below.

- Greet each other and exchange names.
- The new student asks where certain places are located—the bookstore, the cafeteria, the library, and so on. The mentor replies, naming their location.
- The new student asks if certain places or services can be found on campus—a stadium, a movie theater, a day care, a subway, a bus, and so on. *¿Hay...?* The mentor replies.
- The new student thanks the mentor, and they say good-bye.

[1]location

(See p. 42 for beginning of **Guión para ¡Oye!**).

3. A las doce, ¿está en la cafetería o en el gimnasio?
4. A la una de la tarde, ¿está en la biblioteca o en el gimnasio?
5. A las cinco y media de la tarde, ¿está en casa o en la clínica San Miguel?
6. A las diez de la noche, ¿está en el trabajo o en casa?

Follow up with some personal questions, asking students where they are at the indicated times: **¿Dónde estás tú a las ocho de la mañana?**

For additional practice on this grammar point, see PowerPoint slides on BCS and in *WileyPLUS*.

2-10   Students may complete *Paso 1* individually or in pairs, with answers reviewed by the instructor. ANSWERS (*Paso 1*):
1. entre 2. detrás del
3. cerca del 4. al lado de
5. en

2-10   Point out that **ser** is used to identify something (**Es la Facultad de Medicina.**) and **estar,** to indicate location (**Está al lado del hospital.**).

2-11   Remind students that after **hay** (see the third item) the *indefinite* article is used: **¿Hay un estadio en la universidad?** When students have completed their conversation, ask a pair to perform in front of the class. Encourage applause!

Meets ACTFL Standards 1.2, interpretive reading; 2.1, cultural practices; 2.2, cultural products; and 4.2, cultural comparisons.

For an additional activity related to this cultural theme, see the PowerPoint slides on BCS and in *WileyPLUS*.

The *Tu mundo cultural* sections may be assigned as homework and reviewed in class, or they may be done entirely in class. Review the *¿Qué aprendiste?* section with students and allow them time to work in pairs to complete the *Actividad cultural* and the *Contraste cultural.*

Reading strategy: Encourage students to glean information about a text using context (**Mira las páginas web...**) and cognates. In the following text, ask students to identify and circle the cognates.

Tu mundo cultural

Dos universidades hispanas

¿Quieres estudiar español en una universidad hispana? Mira la información de dos universidades con larga tradición y muy frecuentadas por estudiantes de todo el mundo.

La Universidad Nacional Autónoma de México (UNAM), fundada en 1553, y la Universidad de Salamanca, fundada en 1218, ofrecen cursos de español para extranjeros[1] durante todo el año.

Ciudad de México, México   Salamanca, España

© John Wiley & Sons, Inc.

Visita la página web de la UNAM: www.unam.mx

La Universidad Nacional Autónoma de México (UNAM)

Cursos intensivos y superintensivos de español:
Nivel elemental, intermedio y avanzado (2, 3, 4 y 10 semanas)

Cursos de cultura:
Arte: salsa y danza tradicional, teatro mexicano, arte popular mexicano y prehispánico
Historia: Historia general de México e Historia de la independencia a la revolución
Literatura: Literatura mexicana, Narrativa de la revolución

Actividades culturales:
Conciertos, fiestas y especialidades típicas mexicanas, y visitas guiadas a sitios arqueológicos o históricos de la Ciudad de México

Residencia:
Habitaciones (dobles o individuales) en casas[2] de familias mexicanas o en departamentos[3]

Excursiones:
Puebla, Taxco, Cuernavaca y las pirámides del Sol y la Luna en San Juan de Teotihuacán

Página web:
www.unam.mx

¿SABES QUE...?

The Hispanic world has numerous prestigious universities, both public and private, with most located in capitals and other larger cities. Completing an undergraduate degree program or **carrera** may require from four to five years depending on the discipline and the country, but unlike programs in the US, students take no general education courses. Many Hispanic universities now offer hybrid and online classes just as colleges and universities in this country do.

[1]foreigners, [2]homes, [3]apartments

La Universidad de Salamanca

Cursos «a la carta»:
Clases individuales o para grupos

Cursos de lengua:
Pronunciación, conversación, gramática y español comercial

Cursos de cultura:
Cultura y civilización española, historia del arte español y teatro español contemporáneo, danza y gastronomía española, visitas guiadas de la ciudad de Salamanca para visitar su espléndida arquitectura, ciclos de cine[1] español, fiestas y café y tertulia[2] diaria en la famosa Plaza Mayor

Excursiones:
A Madrid, Toledo, Segovia, Ávila, Granada, Sevilla y Barcelona

Residencia:
En casas de familias españolas o en residencias estudiantiles

Página web:
www.usal.es

Visita la página web de la Universidad de Salamanca: www.usal.es

Comunicación Universidad de Salamanca. Used by permission.

 ¿Qué aprendiste?

1. ¿Dónde están situadas dos universidades hispanas de larga tradición? México y España.
2. ¿Son de fundación reciente? No.
3. ¿Qué ofrecen al estudiante extranjero? Cursos de lengua y cultura españolas, excursiones, actividades culturales,...

 Actividad cultural

Complete the form to indicate which of the two universities you would like to attend and your preferences as to month/s, courses, activities, and so on. Then compare the information with your classmate's.

Universidad:_____	Está en: _____	Fundada en: _____
Mes/es:		
Cursos:		
Actividades:		
Excursiones:		
Residencia en:		

 Contraste cultural

In English, compare your college or university with **la UNAM** and **la Universidad de Salamanca.** Talk about the courses, lodging, activities, and excursions offered to foreign students at your school.

[1]**ciclos...** film series, [2]gathering

2 En clase

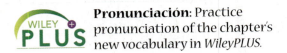

Pronunciación: Practice pronunciation of the chapter's new vocabulary in *WileyPLUS*.

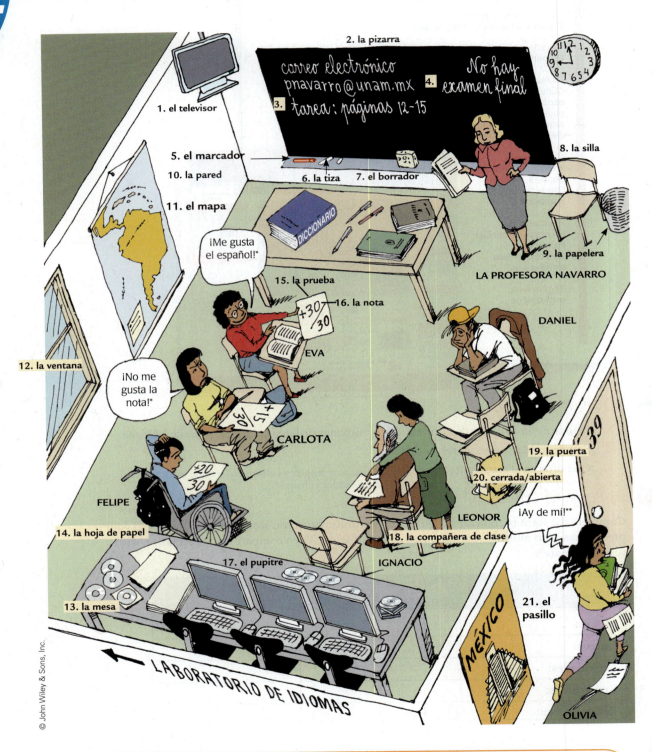

1. television set 2. chalkboard 3. homework 4. (final) exam 5. marker 6. chalk 7. eraser 8. chair 9. wastebasket 10. wall 11. map 12. window
13. table 14. sheet of paper 15. quiz, test 16. grade 17. desk (student's) 18. classmate (*f.*) **compañero** (*m.*) 19. door 20. closed/open 21. hallway

@ **arroba**, *¡**Me gusta**/ **No me gusta...**! *I like/I do not like . . . !* ** ¡**Ay de mí!** *Oh, my!*

¡En acción!

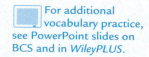
For additional vocabulary practice, see PowerPoint slides on BCS and in *WileyPLUS*.

2-12   ¿Qué hay en nuestro salón de clase[1]?   RECYCLES prepositions of location.

First, read each statement and indicate whether it applies to your classroom by marking **Sí** or **No**. Then take turns asking and answering questions according to the model.

MODELO

un televisor enfrente de la clase

E1:   *¿Hay un televisor enfrente de la clase?*

E2:   *Sí, hay un televisor.*   **o:**   *No, no hay un televisor.*

Sí	No	
☐	☐	**1.** una pizarra detrás del escritorio del/de la profesor/a
☐	☐	**2.** un mapa en la pared
☐	☐	**3.** una papelera cerca de la puerta
☐	☐	**4.** una mesa con computadoras
☐	☐	**5.** un reloj al lado de la pizarra
☐	☐	**6.** unos lápices en los pupitres
☐	☐	**7.** unas mochilas al lado de los estudiantes
☐	☐	**8.** unos libros y unas hojas de papel en el escritorio del/de la profesor/a

2-13   En la clase de español

Describe what the classroom on page 46 is like and what is happening there. Work with your partner to answer the questions.

1. En la puerta del salón de clase hay un número. ¿Qué número es? ¿La puerta está cerrada o abierta?

2. Según[2] la información que hay en la pizarra, ¿hay tarea? ¿Y examen final?

3. ¿Cuántas mochilas hay en el salón de clase? ¿Y cuántos pupitres?

4. ¿Qué otras cosas[3] hay en el salón de clase?

5. ¿Es buena o mala la nota de la prueba de Eva? ¿Qué dice[4] ella?

6. ¿Carlota está bien o mal? ¿Es buena o mala su nota? ¿Qué dice?

7. ¿Felipe está preocupado o contento? Y Daniel, ¿está contento?

8. ¿Cómo se llama la compañera de clase que está detrás de Ignacio?

9. ¿Dónde está Olivia? ¿Qué dice?

10. ¿Hay un laboratorio de idiomas[5] cerca del salón de clase?

2-13   This activity may be assigned for homework or done in class. You may want to show the PowerPoint slide of the scene to check the answers. Note that **estar** + *condition* is previewed.

2-13 PERSONALIZED QUESTIONS:
¿Qué hay en mi escritorio? Be sure to place several items on your desk. ¿Qué cosas hay en este salón de clase?

---

[1]**salón de clase** classroom (also **el aula, la clase**), [2]according to, [3]things, [4]**¿Qué...** What does she say?, [5]**laboratorio...** language lab

You may use the PowerPoint slide of the scene to practice colors, identifying the colors of the sweaters, backpacks, and other items.

To reinforce **me gusta,** informally introduced in the previous scene, ask personal questions: **¿Qué color te gusta más, el... o el...? Gustar** is introduced formally on p. 112.

PLUS For more practice, see **Grammar Handbook** found in *WileyPLUS*.

You may want to tell students that in Spanish, an adjective can function as a noun if it is preceded by an article, as in the model sentence, "Son los (libros) amarillos" (They are the yellow ones).

. . . y algo más Colors

© John Wiley & Sons, Inc.

Colors, like the cognates you encountered in Capítulo 1—**romántico, cómica, inteligente**—function as adjectives.

- Those ending in **-o** change **-o** to **-a** to modify feminine nouns.

  un libro negro   una silla roja

- Those ending in **-e** or a consonant do not change to reflect gender.

  la mochila verde   el suéter verde

- All have plural forms, except **beige** and (**color**) **café.**

  unos lápices amarillos   unos bolígrafos azules   unos cuadernos (**color**) **café**

2-14 Compañíalibros.com RECYCLES numbers.

You and your partner are packing orders at compañíalibros.com's warehouse. As one reads the items from the chart (p.49), the other indicates which they are according to the company's color-coded system.

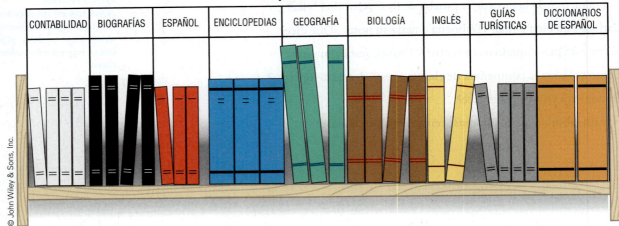

© John Wiley & Sons, Inc.

Compañíalibros.com

| CONTABILIDAD | BIOGRAFÍAS | ESPAÑOL | ENCICLOPEDIAS | GEOGRAFÍA | BIOLOGÍA | INGLÉS | GUÍAS TURÍSTICAS | DICCIONARIOS DE ESPAÑOL |

MODELO

11 libros de inglés

E1:   *Necesito 11 libros de inglés.*

E2:   *Son los (libros) amarillos.*

11 *libros de inglés* ....
43 *diccionarios de español* ....
30 *libros de contabilidad* ....
50 *enciclopedias* ....
15 *libros de biología* ....
19 *guías turísticas* ....
38 *libros de geografía* ....
10 *biografías* ....

De paso

Ser + de

You have already used **ser + de** to indicate origin: **Soy de California**. You can also use **ser + de** to indicate possession.

Es el libro **de** Ana.   **Son** los libros **de** Carlos.

To ask who owns something, use **¿De quién es...? ¿De quiénes son...?** *Whose is/are...?*

¿De quién es el cuaderno rojo?   **Es de** Mónica. (o) **Es del** profesor.
¿De quiénes son los libros?   **Son de** los estudiantes.

 2-15 ¿De quiénes son? RECYCLES classroom vocabulary.

Find the following items in the classroom scene on page 46 and identify the owners.

1. La mochila amarilla *es de Leonor*.

2. El diccionario morado *es de la profesora Navarro*.

3. El suéter rojo ____*es de Eva*____.

4. El lápiz y los bolígrafos que están en el escritorio *son de la profesora Navarro*.

5. La prueba con la nota + 15/30 ____*es de Carlota*____.

6. El suéter azul ____*es de Felipe*____.

7. La gorra de béisbol anaranjada y la chaqueta (color) café ____*son de Daniel*____.

8. Las mochilas que están en el salón de clase *son de los estudiantes*.

Paso 2. Now answer your instructor's questions (**¿De quién es/son...?** /**¿De quiénes es/son...?**) to indicate who owns what.

Dave and Les Jacobs/Blend Images/ Getty Images

¿Dónde están los estudiantes?

For additional practice on this grammar point, see PowerPoint slides on BCS and in *WileyPLUS*.

... y algo más
To introduce **ser + de**, gather various classroom and personal items belonging to students and put them on your desk. Students need not know how to identify the items in Spanish, as each is mentioned in the questions you ask. Pick up one item at a time and ask to whom it belongs, giving two options—the owner of the item and one other student: **¿De quién es este libro de español? ¿Es de... o es de...? ¿De quién son estos zapatos? ¿Son de... o son de...?**

Palabras útiles
15/30 = quince sobre treinta

2-15 You may want to show the PowerPoint slide of the scene to check answers.

ANOTHER STEP: You might want to teach your students how to claim ownership by saying: **Es mío/a. Son míos/as.**

¹Orders

2-16 En el laboratorio   RECYCLES classroom vocabulary.

Paso 1.   Some students have left their belongings behind in the computer lab. The lab director wants to know to whom these items belong, identifying each by its color. The director's assistant, who remembers where the students sat, responds. Play the two roles, with the director looking at drawing **A**, and the assistant, drawing **B**.

MODELO

Director: *¿De quién es el diccionario gris?*

Asistenta: *Es de la señora Gómez.*

Paso 2.   Five students stand in front of the class. One student describes an object belonging to someone in class stating its color. Others guess to whom it belongs. Students two through five then do the same.

MODELO

E1:   *Es un suéter blanco. ¿De quién es?*

E2:   *¿Es de Rafael?*

E1:   *Sí, es de Rafael. o: No, no es de Rafael.*

¡A escuchar!   ¡Ofertas!

Paso 1.   Listen to this radio ad for a sale at the university bookstore.

Palabras útiles
camiseta *T-shirt*

 Go to *WileyPLUS* to complete **Paso 2** of this listening activity.

Es el primer día de clase. Jennifer saluda a sus amigas Mabel e Ysenia.

Hola chicas, ¿cómo están?

Jenni, ¡qué sorpresa!¹

Yo **estoy muy cansada** porque son las 8 de la mañana.

¡Y yo, muy bien!

Pues yo **estoy estresada**... La familia, las clases y mi hija² Yolanda, ¡qué responsabilidad!

© John Wiley & Sons, Inc.

GRAMÁTICA

¡Manos a la obra!

3

Describing people's current conditions: Estar + condition

You have used **estar** to indicate location (**Están en el gimnasio.**) and you have also used it to ask or state how someone is feeling/doing (**¿Cómo estás? ¡Muy bien, gracias!**). Now you are going to expand on this use of **estar** with certain adjectives to express a broader range of feelings or conditions.

Let's consider examples based on the conversation that takes place when Jennifer meets her friends Mabel and Ysenia.

Ysenia está **cansada**. Su amiga Mabel está **contenta**.

• Remember, adjectives that end in **-o** change **-o** to **-a** to modify a feminine noun:

Mi amiga Jennifer está estresad**a**. Mi amigo Fabio está estresad**o**.

• All adjectives have plural forms:

Ysenia y Mabel están ocupada**s**. Fabio y Mario están aburrido**s**.

¿CÓMO ESTÁS?

The following adjectives are used with **estar** to express mental, emotional, or physical conditions—how a person is feeling /doing at a given time. Which words do you recognize?

 contento/a

 enojado/a

enfermo/a

 triste

estresado/a

ocupado/a

aburrido/a

 nervioso/a

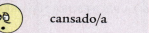 cansado/a

 preocupado/a

All art © John Wiley & Sons, Inc.

¹**¡qué...** what a surprise!, ²**mi...** my daughter

¡En acción!

¡Oye! ¿Cómo están Uds.?

Listen to the following university-related situations and imagine yourself in each circumstance. Then answer the follow-up questions to state how you feel.

2-17 ¿Cómo están los estudiantes? ¿Y tú?

Observe these people and describe how they are doing, selecting one or more items from the list. Then indicate if you are feeling the same as each of them or different. Follow the model.

MODELO

E1: *¿Cómo está Eva?*

E2: *Está contenta. ¿Y tú, estás contento/a?*

E1: *Estoy contento/a también.* **o:** *Estoy triste. ¿Y tú?*

E2: *Estoy…*

> aburrido/a   cansado/a   contento/a   enfermo/a   enojado/a
> estresado/a   nervioso/a   ocupado/a   preocupado/a   triste

1. EVA

2. CARLOTA

3. FELIPE

All art © John Wiley & Sons, Inc.

4. DANIEL

5. OLIVIA

6. LA PROFESORA NAVARRO

2-18 ¿Cómo están ellos?

Tell your partner how one of the people in the illustrations is feeling, but do not give the person's name. Your partner guesses who it is. Take turns.

2-18 You may review answers using the PowerPoint slide of the illustrations.

MODELO

E1: *Está muy contenta.*

E2: *Es doña Lolita.*

E1: *¡Sí! o: No, inténtalo otra vez¹.*

Doña Lolita

1. Paco

2. Linda

3. el señor Wang y el señor Smith

All art © John Wiley & Sons, Inc.

4. la señora Romero

5. Gonzalo

6. Carolina

2-19 Y tú, ¿cómo estás hoy?

Walk around the classroom to find classmates that are tired, happy, etc. (see list below). As you find each one, jot down his/her name under the corresponding condition. At the conclusion of the activity, share what you learned with the class.

2-19 At the conclusion of the activity, for each condition, ask students: **¿Quiénes están cansados?**, etc. They respond according to what they learned: **E1: Lisa está cansada. E2: José está cansado. E3:...**

cansado/a	contento/a	triste	estresado/a	enfermo/a	muy ocupado/a

MODELO

E1: *Lisa, ¿estás cansada?*

E2: *Sí, estoy cansada.* (Write down her name. If she says no, ask another student.)

¹**inténtalo...** try again

Tu mundo cultural

Meets ACTFL Standards
1.2, interpretive reading;
2.2, cultural products; and
4.2, cultural comparisons.

La influencia hispana en EE. UU.

For an additional activity related to this cultural theme, see the PowerPoint slides on BCS and in *WileyPLUS*.

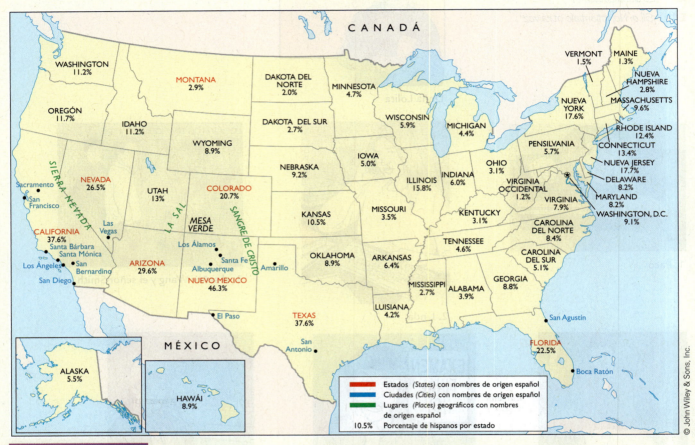

Estados *(States)* con nombres de origen español
Ciudades *(Cities)* con nombres de origen español
Lugares *(Places)* geográficos con nombres de origen español
10.5% Porcentaje de hispanos por estado

© John Wiley & Sons, Inc.

UNIVISIÓN canal 73
3:00 Entrevista con Salma Hayek

TELEMUNDO canal 19
5:00 Deportes: Copa mundial de fútbol

GALAVISIÓN canal 15
7:00 Ana Luisa, una historia romántica

CNN EN ESPAÑOL canal 27
7:30 Reportaje desde las Islas Galápagos

Con el rápido aumento de la población hispana (40% en la última década según el censo de 2010), los canales de televisión de EE. UU. tienen un enorme interés en el mercado hispano. Un ejemplo de esto es *CNN en español* que ha abierto estudios en Nueva York, Los Ángeles y recientemente, en Miami, "la capital de Latinoamérica" en EE. UU. Sin duda alguna[4], la oferta de canales de televisión en español va a continuar multiplicándose.

- En EE. UU., como resultado de la exploración española, y por ser gran parte del país antiguo[1] territorio mexicano, muchos lugares[2] tienen nombres de origen español. (Véase el mapa.)

- En el siglo XX mucha de la inmigración procede de México, Puerto Rico y Cuba. En años más recientes llegan[3] inmigrantes de América Central, República Dominicana, Colombia, Ecuador, Perú y Venezuela.

- Se calcula que hay más de 50 millones de hispanos en EE. UU. y se estima que para el año 2050 un tercio de la población va a ser hispana. En consecuencia, la influencia hispana continúa en aumento y es evidente en diversos aspectos de la cultura estadounidense.

¿SABES QUE...?

Based on figures from the 2010 US Census, the United States is now the second-largest "Spanish-speaking country" in the world, surpassed only by Mexico, which has a population of approximately 112 million people.

[1]former, [2]places, [3]arrive, [4]**Sin**... Without doubt

Hispanos famosos que forman parte de la vida estadounidense

1. Guillermo del Toro, director y productor mexicano, vive en Los Ángeles. Es reconocido por sus películas de terror y de fantasía, incluyendo *Mimic* (1997), *Hellboy* (2004), *El laberinto del fauno* (2006) y *El orfanato* (2007). La Academia de Hollywood nominó a *El laberinto del fauno* para el Oscar como mejor[1] película en lengua extranjera[2].

2. Julián Castro, alcalde[3] de San Antonio, Texas. Es uno de los alcaldes más jóvenes de EE. UU. Se graduó en Ciencias Políticas y Comunicaciones, en Stanford y en Derecho, en Harvard. Curiosamente, su hermano gemelo[4] también se graduó de esas dos universidades y es ahora representante del Congreso de Texas.

3. Sonia Sotomayor, hija de padres puertorriqueños, es la primera jueza hispana y la tercera mujer jueza del Tribunal Supremo de EE. UU. (2009). Estudió en la Universidad de Princeton, donde obtuvo su diploma "summa cum laude", y más tarde, se licenció como abogada en la Universidad de Yale.

4. Penélope Cruz, o *Pe* para los amigos, es una de las actrices españolas más reconocidas. En el año 2006 la Academia de Hollywood la nominó para el Oscar como mejor actriz por su película *Volver*. Finalmente, en el año 2009 ganó el Oscar por su papel secundario en *Vicky Cristina Barcelona*. Es una de las musas del famoso director Pedro Almodóvar.

5. Shakira, cantante[5] colombiana. Ha obtenido un premio *Grammy* y ocho *Grammys* latinos. Es la fundadora de *Pies Descalzos*, una fundación para ayudar a los niños necesitados.

6. Johan Santana, jugador de béisbol venezolano, ha obtenido en dos ocasiones el premio *Cy Young* por ser el mejor *pitcher* de las grandes ligas. La Fundación Johan Santana organiza programas para mejorar la calidad de vida[6] de familias en Venezuela y Minnesota.

¿Qué aprendiste?

1. ¿Qué estados, ciudades[7] y otros puntos geográficos hay en EE. UU. con nombres de origen español? ¿Por qué hay nombres de origen español? *Ver mapa.* Por la influencia española y mexicana.

2. ¿Cuáles son siete de los estados con mayor porcentaje (%) de hispanos? ¿Cuál es el porcentaje de hispanos en tu estado? NM, TX, CA, AZ, NV, FL, CO

3. ¿Cuántos hispanos hay en EE. UU. aproximadamente? Más de 50 millones.

Actividad cultural

In groups of *five*, list as many items as you can in each category. You have five minutes.

- Restaurantes hispanos de su ciudad y las especialidades que sirven
- Cantantes, actores y actrices, artistas, políticos y deportistas[8] hispanos
- Compañeros, profesores y empleados hispanos de su universidad. ¿De dónde son?

Contraste cultural

In groups of *five*, talk in English about: **(a)** your Hispanic acquaintances and/or family members and the countries they come from; **(b)** the Hispanic influence in your college or community.

[1]best, [2]foreign, [3]major, [4]twin, [5]singer, [6]life, [7]cities, [8]athletes

¿SABES QUE...?

In the Americas, the terms **latino** and **hispano** are used interchangeably in the media and by most Spanish-speakers when referring to people from the Caribbean, Mexico, and Central and South America.

Ask students what states and cities boast large Mexican, Puerto Rican, and Cuban populations. Also ask about other Hispanic minorities. They may want to research this information on the web.

Pronunciación: Practice pronunciation of the chapter's new vocabulary in *WileyPLUS*.

2. **el dependiente/** la dependienta

3. el cajero/**la cajera**
4. **el mesero**/la mesera

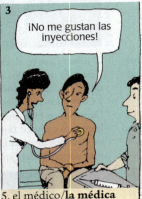

¡No me gustan las inyecciones!

5. el médico/**la médica**
6. **el enfermero/** la enfermera

7. **el policía**/la (mujer) policía

POLICÍA

TELEX

8. el hombre de negocios/ **la mujer de negocios**
9. el secretario/**la secretaria**
10. **el recepcionista/** la recepcionista

¡Hoy hay [11]**mucho** trabajo!

12. el programador/ **la programadora**
13. **el contador/** la contadora

Me gusta esta clase.

Tarea: págs. 10-30.

¡Hay mucha tarea!

14. **el maestro**/la maestra

Estoy [15]**en casa.**

16. **el ama** (*f.*) **de casa**

© John Wiley & Sons, Inc.

Hay muchos problemas.

17. **el abogado**/la abogada

SERVICIOS SOCIALES

¡Buenos días!

18. el trabajador social/**la trabajadora social**

Hoy hay muchas emergencias.

19. **el bombero/la bombera**

20. **el soldado/la soldado**

1. work, job 2. salesclerk 3. cashier 4. server 5. doctor 6. nurse 7. police officer 8. business executive 9. secretary 10. receptionist 11. much, a lot **(mucho/a);** many **(muchos/as)** 12. programmer 13. accountant 14. teacher 15. at home 16. homemaker 17. lawyer 18. social worker 19. firefighter 20. soldier

¡En acción!

2-20 ¿Dónde están?

Where would one usually find the following people when they are working? Draw a line from the profession to the appropriate location according to the scene on page 56. More than one answer may apply.

1.	el abogado _e_		a.	la escuela
2.	el policía _d_		b.	el hospital
3.	la programadora _h_		c.	la librería-papelería
4.	el mesero _g_		d.	la avenida
5.	la médica _b_		e.	el tribunal
6.	la bombera _i_		f.	la compañía
7.	el dependiente _c_		g.	la cafetería
8.	la mujer de negocios _f, h_		h.	la oficina
9.	el maestro _a_		i.	la estación de bomberos

De paso

When simply identifying someone's profession, the indefinite article is omitted:
Es abogado. Es maestra.

If the profession is modified, however, the indefinite article is included:
Es un abogado famoso. Es una maestra muy buena.

2-21 ¿Quién es?

Can you identify each profession or occupation? Observe the scenes on page 56 and work with your partner to answer the questions. Several have multiple answers.

1. ¿Quiénes trabajan en la oficina? ¿Qué dice el contador?
2. ¿Quiénes trabajan en el hospital? ¿Qué dice el paciente?
3. ¿Está contento el maestro con sus alumnos? ¿Hay mucha tarea?
4. ¿Quién defiende a los «inocentes»? ¿Qué dice el abogado?
5. ¿Quiénes defienden la nación?
6. ¿Quiénes trabajan en el restaurante?
7. ¿Qué personas trabajan en situaciones de emergencia? ¿Qué dice la bombera?
8. ¿Quién trabaja en servicios sociales?
9. ¿Qué persona trabaja predominantemente en casa?
10. ¿Quién trabaja en la librería?

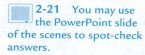

For additional vocabulary practice, see PowerPoint slides on BCS and in *WileyPLUS*.

2-20 Have students share responses in pairs or with the class.

2-20 ANOTHER STEP: Students or the instructor make incorrect and correct statements about where people usually are when they are working. If incorrect, the class gives the correct information: **El maestro está en el hospital. → ¡No! El maestro está en la escuela.**

2-21 You may use the PowerPoint slide of the scenes to spot-check answers.

2-21 PERSONALIZED QUESTIONS: ¿Hay meseros o meseras en la clase? ¿Dependientes o dependientas? ¿Abogados o abogadas? And so on.

Palabras útiles
trabaja *he/she works*
trabajan *they work*

2-21 This activity previews the verb **trabajar**, formally presented on p. 80.

Let your students know that a feminine word that begins with a stressed **a** or **ha**, such as **ama de casa**, uses the masculine article **el/un** in the singular. However, in the plural, it uses the feminine article: **el ama de casa → las amas de casa**.

2-22 With a student secretary at the board, have individuals call out one of their desired professions while others with the same preference raise their hands. The secretary records the results. The class then determines which professions are the most popular.

2-22 Me gustaría ser…

Take turns naming *three* professions you would like to have and *three* you would not. Then share your information with the class to determine which professions are the most popular.

MODELO

E1: *Quiero/Me gustaría ser bombero.*   **o:**   *No quiero/me gustaría ser bombero.*

E2: *Me gustaría ser…*

> **Palabras útiles**
> Me gustaría (ser)…
> *I would like (to be)…*

¡A escuchar!   ¡Ofertas de trabajo!

Paso 1.   Listen to the job opportunities offered in the radio ad by the Martínez employment agency.

WILEY PLUS Go to *WileyPLUS* to complete **Paso 2** of this listening activity.

To introduce students to the verb **ir** used in context, have them take parts and read the **historieta** out loud. To check their comprehension and call their attention to the verb forms, ask the following questions:
1. ¿Adónde va Ysenia esta tarde?
2. ¿Adónde va Jennifer?

Al mediodía, Mabel, Ysenia y Jennifer van a la cafetería.

WILEY PLUS Go to *WileyPLUS* to review this grammar point with the help of the **Animated Grammar Tutorial** and **Verb Conjugator**. For more practice, go to the **Grammar Handbook**.

For additional practice on this grammar point, see PowerPoint slides on BCS and in *WileyPLUS*.

Ask students to divide into small circles. One student starts by asking another: **¿Adónde vas hoy después de la clase de español?** The next student responds: **Voy a** + *the class or location* where he or she is going. Once all students have asked and answered the question, each student says where the student to his or her right is going: **Mary va a…**

GRAMÁTICA

¡Manos a la obra!

4

Talking about going places: **Ir (to go)** + **a** + destination

To ask where someone is going, say **¿Adónde vas (tú)?** (informal) or **¿Adónde va (Ud.)?** (formal). Let's see where Mabel, Jennifer, and Ysenia are going.

Voy a la clínica.	*I am going to the clinic.*
Jennifer **va** a la escuela de Yolanda.	*Jennifer is going to Yolanda's school.*
Vamos al estacionamiento.	*We are going to the parking lot.*

(yo)	**voy**	*I go/am going*
(tú)	**vas**	*you go/are going*
(Ud., él, ella)	**va**	*you go/are going; he, she, it goes/is going*
(nosotros/as)	**vamos**	*we go/are going*
(vosotros/as)	**vais**	*you go/are going*
(Uds., ellos, ellas)	**van**	*you go/are going; they go/are going*

• **a + el → al**   Voy **al** hospital.   **a + la** (no change)   Vamos **a la** cafetería.

[1]Who

¡En acción!

¡Oye! ¿Adónde?

It is 8:30 AM and everyone is going off to work. Listen to discover where they are going according to their professions. Then answer the questions by selecting the appropriate option.

2-23   ¿Adónde van…?   RECYCLES vocabulary from the chapter-opener scene.

Paso 1.   Where do students go on or off campus to do certain things? Select the correct verb form and then fill in the blank to indicate the appropriate destination. *Hint*: Review the campus vocabulary on pages 34–35.

MODELO

Para ver partidos de fútbol, Carlos *va/ vas* _____.

*Para ver partidos de fútbol, Carlos **va al estadio de deportes**.*

1. Para hacer ejercicio y levantar pesas nosotros *van/ vamos* _____.
2. Para conversar con amigos y otros estudiantes Matilde y Alicia *van/ vas* _____.
3. Para comer un sándwich la profesora Juárez *voy/ va* _____.
4. Para recibir atención médica mis amigos y yo *van/ vamos* _____.
5. Para estacionar el carro o la bicicleta Pablo *va/ vas* _____.
6. Para ver *Hamlet* los señores Benítez *van/ voy* _____.
7. Para estudiar y consultar libros mis amigos y yo *voy/ vamos* _____.
8. Para comprar libros, cuadernos, lápices y bolígrafos tú *va/ vas* _____.

Paso 2.   Tell each other what places on campus you frequently go to, and those where you almost never go. Then share the information with the class to determine the most frequented campus locations.

MODELO

E1:   *Con frecuencia **voy al** gimnasio y a la biblioteca. Casi nunca **voy al** centro estudiantil. ¿Y tú?*

EXPRESIONES DE TIEMPO[1]	
ahora	*now*
más tarde	*later*
después de clase	*after class*
hoy	*today*
mañana	*tomorrow*
esta mañana	*this morning*
esta tarde	*this afternoon*
esta noche	*tonight*
este fin de semana	*this weekend*
por la mañana/ tarde/ noche	*in the morning/ afternoon/ at night*

Remind your students that **de la mañana/tarde/noche** is used when a specific time is indicated. **Por** initiates the expression where no time is given: **Voy al trabajo a las cuatro de la tarde. Voy al trabajo por la tarde.**

[1]time

Guión para ¡Oye!
Son las 8:30 de la mañana.
1. José y Ana son maestros; van a la escuela.
2. La señorita García es médica; va al hospital.
3. … y yo somos profesores/profesoras; vamos a la universidad.
4. Elena es dependienta; va a la librería-papelería Cervantes.
5. Alberto es hombre de negocios; va a la oficina.

Comprensión para ¡Oye!
1. ¿Van los maestros a la escuela o a la oficina?
2. ¿Va la médica al hospital o a la clínica?
3. ¿Van los profesores/las profesoras a la universidad o a la escuela?
4. ¿Va la dependienta al restaurante o a la librería?
5. ¿Va el hombre de negocios al hospital o a la oficina?

> **Palabras útiles**
> con frecuencia *frequently*
> casi nunca *almost never*

2-23   Encourage students to guess meaning by context.
ANSWERS:
1. … vamos al gimnasio.
2. … van al centro estudiantil.
3. … va a la cafetería.
4. … vamos al hospital.
5. … va al estacionamiento.
6. … van al teatro.
7. … vamos a la biblioteca.
8. … vas a la librería–papelería.

2-24 Sondeo[1]

Paso 1. Where do you and your classmates go during the time periods mentioned? First, fill in the **Yo** column to indicate where *you* usually go. Then, ask *two* classmates each of the following questions. Jot down the person's name and where he/she is going.

¿Adónde vas...	Yo:	E1:	E2:
1. ... después de clase?	*Voy al trabajo.*	*Ana va al gimnasio.*	*Pablo va a casa.*
2. ... hoy por la tarde?			
3. ... esta noche?			
4. ... mañana por la mañana?			
5. ... el viernes por la noche?			
6. ... este fin de semana?			

Paso 2. Your instructor wants to know where your classmates go during the time periods in the chart. Answer his/her questions.

2-25 Mi semana

Paso 1. Think of your schedule of two or three days this week and share it with your partner. Include where you or you and your friends go during specific time periods.

MODELO

E1: *El martes por la mañana voy a clase de economía. Por la tarde... ¿Y tú?*

E2: *Yo, el martes...*

Paso 2. Now share some of the information you have about your partner with the class.

MODELO

E1: *El martes, mi compañero Nick...*

E2: *El martes, mi compañera Christine...*

Jennifer y Fabio se encuentran[2] y charlan[3] en el campus.

[1]Survey, [2]meet, [3]chat, [4]demanding

© John Wiley & Sons, Inc.

¡Manos a la obra!

GRAMÁTICA

5

Asking questions: Interrogative words

You have been using interrogative words (*Who? What? When?*) since *Capítulo 1*.

Let's look at a few examples based on Fabio and Jennifer's conversation about their class.

¿Cómo estás, Jennifer?   **¿Dónde** está la oficina del profesor Gutiérrez?
¿De dónde es él?   **¿Cuántos** exámenes hay en la clase?

¿Cómo?	*How?*	**¿Cómo** estás?
¿Cuál/ Cuáles?*	*Which (one/s)?*	**¿Cuáles** son tus maestros favoritos?
¿Cuándo?	*When?*	**¿Cuándo** vas a casa?
¿Cuánto/ Cuánta?	*How much?*	**¿Cuánto** trabajo hay?
¿Cuántos/ Cuántas?	*How many?*	**¿Cuántos** abogados hay en el tribunal?
¿Dónde?	*Where?*	**¿Dónde** está la escuela?
¿Adónde?	*(To) where?*	**¿Adónde** vamos?
¿De dónde?	*From where?*	**¿De dónde** es la mesera?
¿Qué?*	*What?*	**¿Qué** es?
¿Por qué?	*Why?*	**¿Por qué** no está en el trabajo?
¿Quién/ Quiénes?	*Who?*	**¿Quién** es ella?
¿De quién/ quiénes?	*Whose?*	**¿De quién** es?

*To ask for a choice in Spanish, the general rule is: **¿Cuál/ Cuáles** + *verb*? or **¿Qué** + *noun*?
¿Cuál es tu gimnasio favorito? *Which is your favorite gym?*
¿Qué días vas al gimnasio? *What/ Which days do you go to the gym?*

. . . y algo más   *Que, cuando, porque*

The following words are similar to the interrogatives but have a different function and at times a different meaning. Note that they do not carry an accent.

que *that, which, who* La mujer policía **que** está allí es muy eficiente.
cuando *when(ever)* **Cuando** no hay clase, estoy en casa.
porque *because* La secretaria no está hoy en la oficina **porque** está enferma.
¿Por qué estás triste? **Porque** es lunes y hay mucho trabajo.

To introduce students to interrogative words used in context, have them take parts and read the **historieta** out loud in page 60. To check their comprehension and call their attention to the interrogatives, ask the following questions: 1. ¿Adónde van Fabio y Jennifer? 2. ¿Cuántos exámenes hay en la clase? 3. ¿Quién es el profesor?

For additional practice on this grammar point, see PowerPoint slides on BCS and in *WileyPLUS*.

For more practice, see **Grammar Handbook** found in *WileyPLUS*.

¡En acción!

 ¡Oye! Unas vacaciones

Your instructor is planning to take a trip. Listen to the description of the trip. Then answer the questions by choosing the correct option.

2-26 ¿Quién lo pregunta?

Observe the scenes on page 56 to determine who might ask each question.

MODELO

¿**Qué** desean, café o té? → *el mesero*

1. ¿**Cómo** están Uds. hoy?
2. ¿**Cuántos** cuadernos necesita?
3. ¿**Adónde** vamos ahora?
4. ¿**Cuándo** vas al supermercado?
5. ¿**Quién** es el inocente?
6. ¿**Por qué** hay tanto tráfico hoy?
7. ¿**Cuál** es el total?
8. ¿**Quiénes** están en el salón de conferencias?

2-27 Mi profesor/a

Your professor will make some negative statements about him/herself. In order to get the correct information, ask questions using the interrogative words.

MODELO

Profesor/a: *No estoy triste ni preocupado/a hoy.*

E1: ¿***Cómo*** *está usted hoy?*

Profesor/a: *Estoy muy bien, gracias.*

1. No soy de Francia.
   ¿ De dónde es usted?
2. No tengo ocho hijos[1].
   ¿ Cuántos hijos tiene usted?
3. No voy al gimnasio después de clase.
   ¿ Adónde va usted después de clase?
4. No voy a mi oficina a las seis de la mañana.
   ¿ A qué hora va usted a su oficina?
5. Por la tarde, no estoy en casa.
   ¿ Cuándo está usted en casa?
6. Este fin de semana, no voy al cine con mis estudiantes.
   ¿Con quién va al cine este fin de semana?
7. Enero no es mi mes favorito.
   ¿ Cuál es su mes favorito?

[1] children, sons and daughters

Sidebar

¡Oye!
Write **playas**, **bosques**, and **flores** on the board and draw an image of each. If you like, personalize the information. Ask students to jot down answers.

Guión para ¡Oye!
El quince de junio, ¡voy a Costa Rica! Voy con dos amigos/as,... y... ¡Vamos a estar allí dos semanas! En Costa Rica hay playas magníficas, volcanes activos (*draw a volcano*), bosques tropicales y flores de muchos colores. ¡Es un lugar fascinante!

Comprensión para ¡Oye!
1. **¿Adónde** voy? ¿A Cancún o a Costa Rica?
2. **¿Cuándo** voy? ¿El quince de junio o el quince de julio?
3. **¿Con quién** voy? ¿Con dos o con tres amigos/as?
4. **¿Cuántas** semanas vamos a estar allí? ¿Dos o tres?
5. **¿Por qué** vamos? ¿Porque está lejos, o porque es fascinante?
6. **¿Qué** atracciones hay?
(*Students provide responses.*)

2-26 ANSWERS: 1. la trabajadora social (o) el maestro 2. el dependiente 3. el/la soldado (o) el bombero/la bombera 4. el ama de casa 5. el abogado 6. el policía 7. el contador 8. la mujer de negocios

2-28 Una entrevista[1]
RECYCLES greetings, origin, **estar**, **ser**, **ir**, months, dates, days of the week.

Paso 1. In order to get to know your partner better, interview him/her using the questions in the first column. He/She responds following the cues in the second column. In the third column, write down what your partner said. Then switch roles.

Preguntas	Respuestas	Información escrita[2]
1. ¿Cómo te llamas?	Me llamo…	Se llama…
2. ¿De dónde eres?	Soy de…	Es de…
3. ¿Dónde está tu familia?	Está en…	Está en…
4. ¿Cuándo es tu cumpleaños?	Es el…	Es el…
5. ¿Qué días vas al trabajo?	Voy los…	Va los…
6. ¿Cuál es tu profesor/a favorito/a?	Mi…	Su…
7. ¿Cuántos libros hay en tu mochila? ¿Y cuántos cuadernos?	Hay…	Hay…
8. ¿Cuál es tu e-mail? ¿Y tu número de teléfono?	Es…	Es…

Paso 2. Using the information in the third column, report what you learned about your partner to another classmate and/or to the class.

2-29 Mi clase favorita
RECYCLES days, time, **estar**, **ser**, and numbers.

Paso 1. You want to know about your partner's favorite class. Ask him/her which class it is, when it takes place, where it takes place, who the professor is, and how many students are in it. Take notes, following the chart below. Then switch roles.

Clase	Día/hora	Edificio	Profesor/a	Nº de estudiantes
¿Cuál es tu clase favorita?	¿Cuándo…?	¿Dónde…?	¿Quién…?	¿Cuántos…?

Paso 2. Read the information to your partner for accuracy. Then compare your results with two other pairs of classmates, to see if there is a consensus.

De paso

If you want to say that a class or an event *takes place* in a certain building or location, use **ser**.

La clase **es** en el edificio Colón. The class *takes place* in the Colón building.

2-28 This activity, following standard interview procedure, enables students to speak, listen, write, and report back to the class. For feedback (*Paso 2*), ask several students questions, such as **¿Cómo se llama tu amigo/a?** Keep other students attentive by asking them follow-up questions: **¿Cómo se llama el amigo de...?**

Since many activities in *¡Con brío!* are done in pairs, make sure that students change partners often. To reassign students, have them count off (in a class of 20) from 1 to 10, and then from 1 to 10 again. Student #1 joins with the other student #1, and so on.

2-29 After two or three students share what they learned with the class, get feedback from all students as to their partners' favorite class. A student records the information on the board. Finally, students determine which classes are the most popular.

For additional practice on this grammar point, see PowerPoint slides on BCS and in *WileyPLUS*.

[1]interview, [2]written

WILEY PLUS Go to *WileyPLUS* to see the video related to this reading.

For an additional activity related to this cultural theme, see the PowerPoint slides on BCS and in *WileyPLUS*.

Meets ACTFL Standards 1.2, interpretive reading; 2.1, cultural practices; and 4.2, cultural comparisons.

Tu mundo cultural

El español en el mundo laboral

El enorme crecimiento[1] de la población hispana en EE. UU. es evidente, con un aumento del 58%* entre los años 1990* y 2000* y un 43% entre los años 2000 y 2010. Una de cada seis personas en EE. UU. es hispana.

En EE. UU. hay más de dos millones y medio de compañías con propietarios[2] hispanos que emplean a un millón novecientas mil personas y generan ingresos de unos 345 mil millones[3] de dólares. Más de una tercera parte[4] de esas[5] compañías son administradas por mujeres.

Los expertos de mercado[6] y muchas compañías como American Airlines, Office Max, Kmart o Bank of America confirman que la forma de atraer al consumidor hispano es comunicarse en su lengua y estar familiarizado con su cultura. En consecuencia, el conocimiento del español y de las culturas hispanas es ya una necesidad económica en EE. UU.

Sabemos por qué vuelas® **American Airlines®** AA.com

Muchas compañías estadounidenses como American Airlines anuncian sus servicios y productos en español para atraer al consumidor hispanohablante.

Creatas/Age Fotostock America, Inc.

La demanda de médicos y enfermeras bilingües que hablan inglés y español es cada día mayor.

[1]growth, [2]owners, [3]mil... billion, [4]una... a third, [5]those, [6]marketing

*% **por ciento**; 1990 **mil novecientos noventa**; 2000 **dos mil**

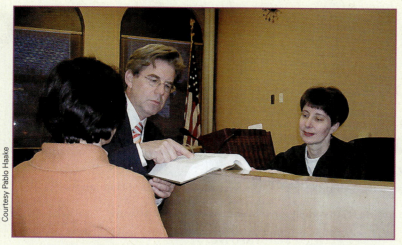

Courtesy Pablo Haake

En los tribunales de EE. UU., el uso del español es con frecuencia necesario.

SE NECESITA EXPERTO EN MARKETING
- Persona bilingüe con inglés y español
- Familiaridad con el mercado hispano
- Sueldo[1] muy atractivo

Llame al tel. 378-216843 o
envíe su currículo a P.O. Box 432
Compañía multinacional, Chicago, Illinois

¡URGENTE! RECEPCIONISTA Y SECRETARIA
- Trabajo en oficina de abogados
- Contacto con clientela hispana
- Experiencia con computadoras
- Buen sueldo y seguro médico

Enviar currículo a la
**Oficina principal en Nueva York
P.O. Box 467893**

COOPERATIVA FAMILIAR
- Necesitamos asistente social
- Imprescindible: español e inglés
- Horario flexible

Se requiere recomendación
Enviar currículo a Fax: 341-87-24
Alamosa, CO.

¿Qué aprendiste?

1. ¿Qué sector de la población de EE. UU. está experimentando un crecimiento considerable? Explica.
   Los hispanos. Debido, por ejemplo, a la necesidad del uso del español en el mundo laboral.
2. Según los expertos de mercado y muchas compañías de EE. UU., ¿cuál es la forma de atraer al cliente hispano?
   Conociendo su lengua y su cultura.

Actividad cultural

A. Imagine you and your partner are fluent in both English and Spanish. As students, you are considering career opportunities for the future. List in Spanish the professions in which you are most likely to use your bilingual skills. For inspiration, see the photo captions and ads above, and the list of professions on page 56.

B. Now you are actually looking for employment. Study the three job ads and select the one that appeals to you most, mentioning the reasons. For example: **sueldo muy atractivo**.

Contraste cultural

Imagine that your job requires frequent contact both with Hispanic employees and with clients who speak little English and who are unfamiliar with U.S. culture. In English, make a list of measures necessary to communicate effectively with this important sector of the population. Work in groups of *four*.

[1]salary

Go to *WileyPLUS* to see the videos and to find more activities for ¡Diálogos en acción!, ¡A conversar!, ¡A escribir! and ¡A investigar!

Meets ACTFL Standards 1.2, interpretive listening; 2.2, cultural products; and 4.2, cultural comparisons.

Tu mundo en vivo

¡Videos en acción!

2.1 Una visita a la UNAM

1. **Antes de ver el video**
   a. Why do you study Spanish?
   b. What do you think might be the best way to learn another language?

   Go to *WileyPLUS* to complete the **Mientras ves el video** activity.

2. **Después de ver el video** Marca **Sí** o **No.**
   a. El narrador habla[1] con estudiantes que son de:

_Sí_ Australia	_Sí_ Haití	_No_ Vietnam
_Sí_ Rusia	_Sí_ Corea	_No_ Venezuela
_No_ Senegal	_Sí_ Japón	

   b. A los estudiantes les gusta la UNAM porque:
   _____ Hay clases para aprender[2] la historia y cultura de México.
   __X__ Los maestros están motivados.
   __X__ Hay oportunidades para aprender y practicar español.

2.2 Ser bilingüe

Meets ACTFL Standards 1.1, interpersonal speaking, 1.2, interpretive listening, and 2.1, cultural practices.

1. **Antes de ver el video**
   a. Do you know a student that speaks Spanish very well?
   b. In what jobs or professions in the U.S.A. do you think knowing Spanish might be useful?

   Go to *WileyPLUS* to complete the **Mientras ves el video** activity.

You can also find the **transcripts** for the **Diálogos** in the PowerPoint slides on the BCS and in *WileyPLUS*.

2. **Después de ver el video**
   Do you agree that learning about the culture of a country is as important as learning its language? Defend your opinion.

¡Diálogos en acción!

2.1 ¿Dónde está?

Dialogue Tips: Play the dialogue once all the way through. Check comprehension by asking students to tell you everything they understood (English is OK). Then play it a second time, pausing after each sentence or phrase and asking students what was said.

Jorge is a Mexican student new to campus. He asks a passerby for information.

Paso 1.   First, read the **Expresiones útiles** in p. A-2. Next, listen to the dialogue twice and answer the questions your instructor will ask.

Paso 2.   Look at the transcript of this dialogue (p. A-15) and act it out with a partner. Switch roles. Now, go to p. A-2 to complete **Pasos 3** and **4.**

2.2 ¡Mis clases son difíciles!

Diálogo 2.1 models the linguistic functions of soliciting and providing information. It also practices **estar** and prepositions.
Diálogo 2.2 models the functions of greeting, complaining, and inviting. It also practices **ir** and **estar** + adjective.

Verónica and Alejandro, two Mexican students, run into each other on campus.

Go to *WileyPLUS* to listen to and practice this dialogue.

[1]speaks, [2]learn

¡Lectura en acción!

Orientación para la universidad

The following website describes for Latino students and their families the new student orientation activities available on the Ann Arbor campus.

Paso 1. Thinking about the title and introduction for this reading, and your own experiences attending new-student orientations in the past, check off each box in column 1 below that includes the types of information that you would expect to be included.

1 2

☐ ☐ information about the campus and its services

☐ ☐ a campus tour

1 2

☐ ☐ meet and talk to current students

☐ ☐ placement exams

1 2

☐ ☐ registration assistance

☐ ☐ general academic advising

Paso 2. Now, read the program description from the website. Don't worry about understanding every single word. Instead, focus on what you do understand. As you identify some of the activities and information from **Paso 1,** put a check in the box in column 2 above.

University of Michigan, Portal en Español. Used by permission.

M UNIVERSITY OF MICHIGAN

PORTAL EN ESPAÑOL

accesibilidad | inglés | texto
contacto   recursos para discapacitados

PORTAL EN ESPAÑOL   ADMISIONES Y ASUNTOS ACADÉMICOS   NOTICIAS EN ESPAÑOL   NOTICIAS UMHS

red ⦿   directorio ○   Buscar [buscar texto]   (IR)

Orientación

Como llegar a la U de Michigan

Oficina de Programas para Nuevos Estudiantes (ONSP)

Programa de Bienvenida (ALMA)

Orientación para Padres

- Hispanic Heritage Month en la Universidad de Michigan
- ¡Solicite su Admisión Ahora! Presente su solicitud por línea
- En nuestras propias palabras
- Calculador Financiero

Orientación

☐+ programas de orientación
☐+ información de viaje
☐+ preguntas más frecuentes

La Oficina de Programas para Nuevos Estudiantes, *ONSP*, tiene tres distintos programas de orientación para que estudiantes y padres se familiaricen con la Universidad de Michigan y la ciudad de Ann Arbor. Hay programas de orientación para nuevos estudiantes, para estudiantes de transferencia y para Padres.

Orientación para Nuevos Estudiantes: Es el primer paso en la transición hacia la universidad y un puente entre la Escuela Secundaria y la Educación Superior. El programa muestra en pocos días a los nuevos alumnos un resumen de la vida académica, social y práctica en la universidad y Ann Arbor en la que los estudiantes aprenden desde tomar el autobus del campus, llegar a la librería, buscar una clase de química y literatura, encontrar los comedores, utilizar los sistemas de accesos de información interna para estudiantes y en general, tener la experiencia típica de un alumno de la UM.

Orientación para estudiantes de transferencia: Ofrece información particular de acuerdo con la experiencia e historia de los estudiantes que se han transferido desde otras universidades. Ayuda a los alumnos a conocer a otros estudiantes de la UM, que están en una situación similar, que hace más fácil la transición a una universidad grande.

Durante ambos programas, los estudiantes finalizan los procedimientos para la matriculación en las clases, realizan los exámenes de suficiencia en ciertas materias y reciben consejos académicos.

Paso 3. Now, read the passage a second time and answer the questions below.

1. ¿Cuántos programas de orientación ofrece la Universidad de Michigan? ¿Para quiénes son?

2. Imagina que vas a estudiar en esta universidad. ¿A cuál de los programas de orientación vas a ir?

3. ¿Qué programa es para estudiantes recién graduados de la escuela secundaria[1]? ¿Cuál no es para estudiantes? ¿Es obligatorio[2] o no?

[1]high school, [2]required

Reading Strategy

Utilizing Your Background Knowledge

Before reading an unfamiliar text, it can be helpful to think about what you already know about the main topic, and to anticipate some of the information that will be included.

Prior to beginning **Paso 1,** ask students to recall words they already know that might be related to the topic at hand. Write them on a chalkboard or overhead projector so that students can see the list and thus add items their classmates suggest to their own lists.

Meets ACTFL Standards 1.2, interpretive reading, and 3.2, acquiring information.

Find out if your own institution (or others in your area) offers its webpage information in Spanish and point this out to your students. Ask them why it might be a good marketing step for a school to offer information related to its programs and admission process in Spanish. To whom is this information likely to be targeted: students or parents? Why?

Remind students of the previous **Reading Strategy,** presented in Capítulo 1 on p. 29: *Skimming a text for cognates and other familiar words or information.* Encourage them to utilize and practice previous reading strategies while adding new ones to their repertoire.

¡A conversar!

Speaking Strategy

Requesting Repetitions

Using speaking strategies will help you communicate more successfully. For example, certain phrases will make it easier to obtain assistance when it is hard to comprehend other speakers. If you do not understand, say "**Lo siento, pero no entiendo.**" If you need a person to speak more slowly, say "**Más despacio, por favor.**" To request a repetition of what was just said, use "**Repita, por favor.**" If you memorize these phrases, you will be ready to ask for help when you need it.

¿Adónde vas?

Role-play meeting a friend on campus. Greet each other and then ask:

- how you are
- where you're going after class
- at what time you're going home or to work
- then say goodbye

¡A escribir!

¿Quién soy yo?

You may wish to assign certain steps of the ¡A escribir! writing process for students to complete outside of class.

Write a brief description of yourself for a Spanish-speaking student you are going to mentor.

- Tell your name (*Me...*).
- Tell your occupation or profession, if you have one (*Soy...*).
- Indicate your nationality and where you are from (city, state, and so on).
- Say when your birthday is.
- Describe yourself using the cognates on page 11.
- Indicate your weekly schedule: on what days and at what times you go to class/work.
- Say what your favorite class is (*Mi clase favorita...*), who the instructor is, and how many students are in the class.
- Make sure to ask him or her some questions as well (see page 61).

Writing Strategy

Listing Information

Before you begin writing your description, quickly jot down words and phrases that apply to each of the items listed. Example: *Susana Gómez/ dependienta y estudiante...*

Steps:

1. *Prewriting:* List information.
2. *Writing:* Now turn your words and phrases into full sentences, and where applicable, give as much information as possible.
3. *Revising:* Read your composition carefully. Have you included all of the information requested and checked for correct spelling and punctuation? Have you (a) used **ser** and **estar** correctly, (b) omitted the article when indicating the profession, and (c) not capitalized nationality, days of the week, and months of the year?
4. *Peer correction:* Exchange papers with a classmate. Circle errors or areas where there are questions, and then talk about them. Make corrections on your own paper as appropriate.

¡A investigar!

Las universidades de los países hispanos

Where do students in Hispanic countries study? What are their universities like? You are already familiar with programs for international students at the Universidad de Salamanca and at UNAM, the Universidad Nacional Autónoma de México. Find out how other institutions are organized and what programs they offer to their domestic students by conducting a search limited to Spanish-language sites.

Paso 1. Your instructor will divide you into groups of *three* and assign each group a country. Using your search engine's language tools and key words such as *universidad* and your country name, find the official website of one of that country's universities. Working with your partners and relying on your background knowledge, cognates, and the website's images and graphics, examine the main page and the various sections of the site. Focus on headings and lists.

Paso 2. Based on your review, prepare a table that provides the following information about the university and post it to a wiki:

- The name of the university (*El nombre de la universidad*)
- Website URL (*La dirección en internet*)
- Where the university is located (*La ubicación de la universidad*)
- The names of three of the colleges or departments (*Tres facultades / departamentos*)
- The names of two academic programs from each of the colleges or departments (*Dos programas académicos*)
- Contact information (*El número de teléfono, el e-mail*)

Paso 3. After each group posts its table to the wiki and all groups have had an opportunity to review the information, compare, in English, the information available on these websites with what is presented on your own college or university site.

You may assign the appropriate **Pasos** of **¡A investigar!** for pairs or small groups to complete outside of class.

Meets ACTFL Standards 1.2, interpretive reading; 1.3, presentational writing; 2.2, cultural products; 3.2, acquiring information; and 4.2, cultural comparisons.

If your access to technology is limited, have students create poster charts or Word document tables.

Research Strategy

Finding Spanish-Language Sources

When studying a language and the culture of its speakers, it is useful to develop the skills needed to research aspects of the culture that interest you professionally, academically, or personally. Spanish-language websites created for a Hispanic audience will provide a perspective that English-language sites may not. The major Internet search engines allow you to select the language used to conduct searches, and you may even be able to limit results to a particular country. Look for advanced search instructions, language tools, and international sites on the homepage of your favorite search engine.

Trivia

Can you answer the following questions?

1. ¿Dónde hay más habitantes: en España o en México? ¿Es México el país hispano con más millones de habitantes?

2. Más o menos, ¿cuántos millones de habitantes hay en Cuba? ¿Y en Puerto Rico?

3. ¿Cuáles son las lenguas oficiales de España? ¿Y las lenguas oficiales de México, Cuba y Puerto Rico?

1. En México. Sí. 2. Cuba: 11 millones. Puerto Rico: 4 millones. 3. En España: el castellano, el catalán, el euskera y el gallego. En México: el español y algunas lenguas indígenas. En Cuba: el español. En Puerto Rico: el español y el inglés.

If you don't know the answers, take a look at the front inside cover of the textbook. Try to respond in complete sentences.

Vocabulario: Capítulo 2

Escena 1

En la calle   *In the street*
el autobús *bus*
la bicicleta *bicycle*
el carro *car*
el estacionamiento *parking*
la avenida *avenue*
la estatua *statue*
la plaza *square, plaza*

Los edificios   *Buildings*
la biblioteca *library*
la cafetería *cafeteria*
el centro estudiantil *student center*
el edificio *building*
el estadio de deportes *stadium*
la Facultad de Administración de
    Empresas *Business School*
la Facultad de Ciencias *School of Sciences*
la Facultad de Derecho *Law School*
la Facultad de Filosofía y Letras
    School of Arts
la Facultad de Medicina *Medical School*
la librería *bookstore*
la guardería infantil *daycare center*
el gimnasio *gym*
la residencia estudiantil *dormitory,*
    residence hall
la Secretaría *Registrar's Office*
el teatro *theater*
la universidad *university*

Preposiciones   *Prepositions*
al lado de *beside*
allí *there*
aquí *here*
cerca de *near*
delante de *in front of*
detrás de *behind*
en *in, at, on*
enfrente de *opposite, facing*
entre *between*
lejos de *far from*

Verbo   *Verb*
estar *to be*

Asignaturas y especialidades
    Subjects and majors
See page 37 for a listing of subjects and
majors (passive vocabulary).

Escena 2

En clase   *In class*
el borrador *eraser*
el compañero/ la compañera de
    clase *classmate*
el examen (final) *(final) exam*
la hoja de papel *sheet of paper*
el marcador *marker*
el mapa *map*
la mesa *table*
la nota *grade*
la papelera *wastebasket*
la pared *wall*
el pasillo *hallway*
la pizarra *chalkboard*
la prueba *quiz, test*
la puerta *door*
el pupitre *desk (student's)*
la silla *chair*
la tarea *homework*
el televisor *television*
la tiza *chalk*
la ventana *window*

Los colores   *Colors*
amarillo/a *yellow*
anaranjado/a *orange*
azul *blue*
blanco/a *white*
beige *beige*
(color) café *brown*
gris *gray*
morado/a *purple*
negro/a *black*
rojo/a *red*
rosado/a *pink*
verde *green*

Condiciones   *Conditions*
abierto/a *open*
aburrido/a *bored*
cansado/a *tired*
cerrado/a *closed*
contento/a *happy*
enfermo/a *sick*
enojado/a *angry*
estresado/a *stressed*
nervioso/a *nervous*
ocupado/a *busy*
preocupado/a *worried*
triste *sad*

Escena 3

El trabajo   *Work, job*
el abogado/ la abogada *lawyer*
el ama (f.) de casa *homemaker*
el bombero/ la bombera *firefighter*
el cajero/ la cajera *cashier*
el contador/ la contadora *accountant*
el dependiente/ la dependienta *salesclerk*
el enfermero/ la enfermera *nurse*
el hombre/ la mujer de negocios
    business executive
el maestro/ la maestra *teacher*
el médico/ la médica *doctor*
el mesero/ la mesera *server*
el policía/ la (mujer) policía *police officer*
el programador/ la programadora
    programmer
el/la recepcionista *receptionist*
el secretario/ la secretaria *secretary*
el soldado/ la soldado *soldier*
el trabajador social/ la trabajadora social
    social worker
en casa *at home*
en la escuela *at school*

¿Cuándo?   *When?*
ahora *now*
después de clase *after class*
esta mañana *this morning*
esta noche *tonight*
esta tarde *this afternoon*
este fin de semana *this weekend*
hoy *today*
mañana *tomorrow*
más tarde *later*
por la mañana/ tarde/ noche *in the*
    morning/ afternoon/ at night

Adjetivos   *Adjectives*
mucho/a/os/as *much, many, a lot*

Palabras interrogativas
    Interrogative words
¿Adónde? *(To) where?*
¿Cómo? *How?*
¿Cuál? ¿Cuáles? *Which (one/s)?*
¿Cuándo? *When?*
¿Cuánto/a? *How much?*
¿Cuántos/as? *How many?*
¿De dónde? *From where?*
¿De quién? ¿De quiénes? *Whose?*
¿Dónde? *Where?*
¿Por qué? *Why?*
¿Qué? *What?*
¿Quién? ¿Quiénes? *Who?*

Verbos   *Verbs*
ir *to go*
ir a *to go to*

Capítulo 3

La familia y los amigos

WILEY PLUS

Additional activities and **Autopruebas** for each **Escena** available online.

Ariel Skelley/Taxi/Getty Images, Inc.

Escena 1
La familia

GRAMÁTICA:
· Possessive adjectives
· The present indicative of regular *-ar* verbs

CULTURA:
La familia hispana

Escena 2
Los mejores amigos

GRAMÁTICA:
· *Ser* + descriptive adjectives

CULTURA:
Diferencias culturales

Escena 3
Las relaciones humanas

GRAMÁTICA:
· A summary of *ser* and *estar*

CULTURA:
Momentos importantes de la vida

TU MUNDO EN VIVO

¡Videos en acción! La familia hispana; Momentos importantes de la vida

¡Diálogos en acción! Describing Physical and Personality Traits; Inquiring About and Describing Family Plans

¡Lectura en acción! Guessing Meaning from Context

¡A conversar! Increasing Participation Through Questions

¡A escribir! Thinking About your Audience

¡A investigar! Applying Reading Strategies to Research

LEARNING OBJECTIVES

By the end of this chapter you will be able to:
· Talk about family and friends.
· Indicate possession and tell age.
· Talk about the present.
· Tell someone you address informally what to do.
· Describe people, places and things.
· Express marital status.
· Discuss family traditions, values and trends in the Hispanic world.

La familia

La nueva familia de María Luisa

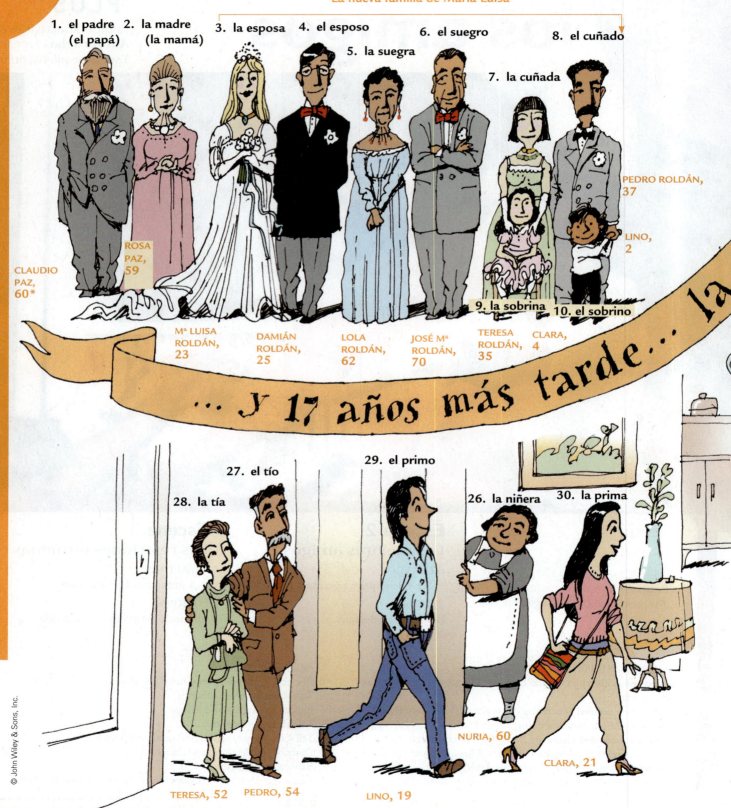

1. el padre (el papá)
2. la madre (la mamá)
3. la esposa
4. el esposo
5. la suegra
6. el suegro
7. la cuñada
8. el cuñado
9. la sobrina
10. el sobrino

CLAUDIO PAZ, 60*

ROSA PAZ, 59

Mª LUISA ROLDÁN, 23

DAMIÁN ROLDÁN, 25

LOLA ROLDÁN, 62

JOSÉ Mª ROLDÁN, 70

TERESA ROLDÁN, 35

CLARA, 4

PEDRO ROLDÁN, 37

LINO, 2

... y 17 años más tarde... la

27. el tío
28. la tía
29. el primo
26. la niñera
30. la prima

TERESA, 52

PEDRO, 54

LINO, 19

NURIA, 60

CLARA, 21

Pronunciación: Practice pronunciation of the chapter's new vocabulary in *WileyPLUS*.

familia Roldán...

11. los parientes

1. father
2. mother
3. wife
4. husband
5. mother-in-law
6. father-in-law
7. sister-in-law
8. brother-in-law
9. niece
10. nephew
11. relatives
12. grandson
13. grandfather
14. parents
15. baby (*f.*); **el bebé** baby (*m.*)
16. grandmother
17. granddaughter
18. dog
19. (older) brother
20. (younger) brother
21. son
22. daughter
23. (younger) sister
24. (older) sister
25. cat
26. nanny
27. uncle
28. aunt
29. cousin (*m.*)
30. cousin (*f.*)

*60 = 60 años *60 years old*
**¡Sonrían! *Smile!*

See *Palabras útiles* on p. 75 for additional vocabulary applicable to family relationships.

You may use the PowerPoint slides of all scenes to present and practice the vocabulary.

13. el abuelo
DON CLAUDIO, 77

16. la abuela
DOÑA ROSA, 76

14. los padres

12. el nieto

17. la nieta

¡Hola tíos, hola primos!

15. la bebé
ANITA, 3 meses

19. el hermano (mayor)

21. el hijo

20. el hermano (menor)

22. la hija

24. la hermana (mayor)

23. la hermana (menor)

ÁNGEL, 16

Mª LUISA, 40   DAMIÁN, 42

GUADALUPE, 14

ROBERTITO, 3

CARMEN, 9

25. el gato
CALISTO

iguau! iguau!

18. el perro
PACHÁ

¡Sonrían!**

¡La pronunciación!
Pay attention to the silent **h** and the correct pronunciation of Spanish **ñ** (see P-3, P-4).

hermano   **h**ija
cu**ñ**ado   ni**ñ**era

For additional vocabulary practice, see PowerPoint slides on BCS and in *WileyPLUS*.

¡En acción!

3-1 Mi familia y mis parientes

3-1 Students may complete the activity individually or in pairs, with answers reviewed by the instructor.

Can you identify the members of your family? Combine elements from each column to describe the ties.

MODELO

1f. Mi abuela es la madre de mi padre.

	es/son	
1. Mi abuela es f.		a. la hija de mis padres
2. Mi tío es d.		b. el esposo de mi hermana
3. Mis sobrinos son e.		c. los padres de mi esposo/a
4. Mi hermana es a.		d. el hermano de mi madre
5. Mi cuñado es b.		e. los hijos de mi hermano/a
6. Mis nietos son g.		f. la madre de mi padre
7. Mis primas son h.		g. los hijos de mis hijos
8. Mis suegros son c.		h. las hijas de mis tíos

¿SABES QUE...?

Because of their Catholic heritage, Hispanic women are often named **María**, in combination with another name: **María Luisa**, for example. Hispanic men may also be named **María**, in which case **María** follows the first name: **José María**, for example. The abbreviation of **María** is **Mª**.

De paso

The words **hijos, esposos, suegros, hermanos,** and so on, like the word **ellos,** represent both an all-male or a mixed-gender group.

For additional practice on this grammar point, see PowerPoint slides on BCS and in *WileyPLUS*.

3-2 La familia

Look at the wedding portrait and at the scene of the Roldán family seventeen years later (pages 72–73). Can you identify everyone? Take turns asking and answering the questions below.

¿SABES QUE...?

Doña (Dª) is a title of respect given to a married woman, or to a single woman that has reached an older age. **Don (D.)** is the masculine equivalent. Both titles are used in front of the first name: **Doña** Rosa, **Don** Carlos. **Doña** is often abbreviated to **Dª**.

La familia, el día del matrimonio

1. ¿Quién es la esposa de Damián? *Es...*

2. ¿Cómo se llaman los padres de Mª Luisa? ¿Y los de Damián?

3. ¿Quiénes son los suegros de Mª Luisa? ¿Y los de Damián? *Son...*

4. ¿Quiénes son los cuñados de Mª Luisa?

5. ¿Quiénes son los sobrinos de Mª Luisa y Damián?

La familia, diecisiete años más tarde

6. ¿Quién es la madre de los cinco hijos? ¿Y el padre?

7. ¿Cómo se llaman los hijos de Mª Luisa y Damián? ¿Quién es la bebé?

8. ¿Quién es el hermano menor de Ángel? ¿Y quiénes son las hermanas mayores de Anita?

9. ¿Cómo se llaman los abuelos? ¿Quiénes son sus nietos?

10. ¿Quiénes son Pedro y Teresa? ¿Y Clara y Lino?

11. ¿Cómo se llama el perro? ¿Y el gato?

12. ¿Quién es Nuria? ¿Y las personas que están en las fotos de la pared?

3-2 After students complete the activity, you may want to spot-check answers using the PowerPoint slide of the opener scene.

Go to *WileyPLUS* to review this grammar point with the help of the **Animated Grammar Tutorial** and **Verb Conjugator**. For more practice, go to the **Grammar Handbook**.

For additional practice on this grammar point, see PowerPoint slides on BCS and in *WileyPLUS*.

. . . y algo más   *Tener to express ownership*

tener *to have*

To talk about your family—how many brothers or sisters, how many children, etc. you have—use the verb **tener**.

—¿**Tienes** hermanos? —Sí, **tengo** tres hermanos y cuatro hermanas.
—¿Cuántos hijos **tiene** Pedro? —**Tiene** dos hijos.

(yo)	**tengo**	(nosotros/as)	**tenemos**
(tú)	**tienes**	(vosotros/as)	**tenéis**
(Ud., él, ella)	**tiene**	(Uds., ellos/as)	**tienen**

Tener is also used to express ownership: **Tenemos un gato y dos perros.**

3-2 PERSONALIZED QUESTIONS: Ask several students: **¿Cómo se llaman tus padres? ¿Quiénes tienen hermanos?** Ask each student who raised his/her hand: **¿Cuántos hermanos tienes?** If you have older students, ask: **¿Quiénes de Uds. son: madres o padres/abuelos o abuelas/tíos o tías?**

3-3   La familia de mi compañero/a

Paso 1.   Would you like to know about your classmate's family? Ask him/her questions according to the chart. Write the information in the second column. Take turns asking and responding.

MODELO

E1:   ¿**Tienes** hermanos?

E2:   Sí, **tengo** dos hermanos y una hermana. ¿Y tú?

3-2 and 3-3   Tell the class about your family using various forms of the verb **tener: Tengo...; Tenemos un perro...; Mis hijos tienen...**and so on, followed by true /false comprehension questions.

¿Tienes...?	La familia de... (*classmate's name*)
hermanos medio hermanos/ hermanastros	...*tiene* dos hermanos y una hermana.
esposo/a suegros cuñados y sobrinos	
hijos/ hijastros nietos	
abuelos tíos primos	
gatos y/o perros	

Palabras útiles
padrastro *stepfather*
madrastra *stepmother*
medio/a hermano/a *half-brother / half-sister*
hermanastro/a *stepbrother / stepsister*
hijastro/a *stepson / stepdaughter*
yerno *son-in-law*
nuera *daughter-in-law*

Paso 2.   Answer your instructor's question **¿Qué sabes de[1] tu compañero/a?** by sharing interesting information about your partner's family with the class. Also mention one or two things that you have in common: *... y yo **tenemos** dos gatos.*

3-3   In preparation for the introduction of the verb **saber** in ch. 4, the question **¿Qué sabes de...** will appear often so students become familiar with this use of **saber**. With that purpose also, point to the title of the box on top that reads **¿Sabes que...?** and mention to your students that **saber** in both cases refers to having that information.

[1]**Qué...** What do you know about

¿SABES QUE...?
Terms such as **madrastra** and **padrastro** carry negative connotations in some Spanish-speaking countries. Therefore some people prefer to say **el esposo de mi madre** (*stepfather*) and **la esposa de mi padre** (*stepmother*).

¿SABES QUE...?

Rubén Blades, the Panamanian salsa musician and actor, served as his country's minister of tourism from 2004 to 2009. In 2011 he received the Harry Chapin Humanitarian Award from the American Society of Composers, Authors and Publishers in recognition for his work with WhyHunger, a non-profit organization fighting hunger and poverty in the US and abroad.

3-4 Have students ask the ages of the individuals seated around them, then share the information with the class.

Review the numbers 0–59, then count by fives to 100.

To provide additional practice with numbers, have students in pairs play a game. E1 states a number under 100: **ochenta y tres** and E2 reverses the digits and says: **treinta y ocho.**

For further practice, have students walk around the classroom asking for (and jotting down) each other's phone numbers, with the digits given in pairs: 5-68-72-85.

Before the class determines who has the oldest or youngest family member, elicit feedback from many students.

¡A escuchar! Un cantante de salsa y su familia

Paso 1.   Listen to Alicia talk about her favorite salsa singer, Rubén Blades.

PLUS Go to *WileyPLUS* to complete this listening activity.

. . . y algo más   *Tener to express age*

tener... años *to be... years old*

The verb **tener** (*to have*), used previously to express possession or family relationships, is also used to express age. English, in contrast, uses the verb *to be*.

—¿Cuántos años **tienes**? *How old are you?*   —**Tengo** veintiún años. *I'm 21.*

Tengo treinta y nueve **años**. Y tú, ¿**cuántos años tienes**?

Tengo cuarenta y un **años**.

Courtesy of Laila Dawson

LOS NÚMEROS DEL 60 AL 100

To tell the age of those over 59, you will need to know the following numbers:

60 sesenta   70 setenta   80 ochenta   90 noventa   100 cien

Review the numbers 0–59 on page 14.

3-4   El mayor y el menor de la familia   RECYCLES numbers 0-59.

Paso 1.   In groups of *four*, ask each other **¿Quién es la persona mayor de tu familia? ¿Cuántos años tiene? ¿Y quién es la persona menor de tu familia? ¿Cuántos años tiene?** Jot down the name of each classmate who responds and the information given.

Nombre de compañero/a	El/La mayor de su familia	El/La menor de su familia
Juan	su[1] abuelo, 96 años	su[2] sobrina, dos meses

Paso 2.   Share information with the class to determine who has the oldest family member: *¡El abuelo de Juan tiene noventa y seis años!* Then do the same to discover who has the youngest family member: *¡La sobrina de Juan tiene dos meses!*

3-5   ¿Quién es?

Looking at the picture of the Roldán family seventeen years later (pages 72–73), **(a)** give the age of a particular member of the family without stating who the person is, and **(b)** name one family member closely related to him/her. **(c)** Can your partner identify the person? Take turns.

MODELO

E1:   *Tiene cuarenta años. Su esposo se llama Damián.*

E2:   *Es Mª Luisa, la madre.*

E1:   *¡Correcto!*   **o:**   *No, inténtalo otra vez.*

[1]his, [2]her

Jennifer y Fabio están en el centro estudiantil y hablan de sus familias.

Mira[1], Fabio, **mi** familia. Luis y Dolores, **mis** padres; son de Puerto Rico. ¡Ah! ¡Y mira, **sus** ocho nietos! **Nuestra** familia está muy unida[2].

Estoy divorciada y tengo una hija; se llama Yolanda. **Mi** hija tiene 5 años. ¿Cómo es **tu** familia, Fabio?

Soy hijo único. Yo también estoy divorciado. Tengo una hija de 8 años; se llama Olivia. **Su** madre es de Nicaragua, pero yo soy americano, de origen mexicano.

Go to *WileyPLUS* to review this grammar point with the help of the **Animated Grammar Tutorial**. For more practice, go to the **Grammar Handbook**.

For additional practice on this grammar point, see PowerPoint slides on BCS and in *WileyPLUS*.

GRAMÁTICA

¡Manos a la obra!

1

Indicating possession: Possessive adjectives

To express possession, you have used **de** and **tener**. Let's look at examples based on Jennifer's conversation with Fabio.

> Yolanda es la hija **de** Jennifer.
> Fabio también **tiene** una hija.

Now you will be introduced to the possessive adjectives (*my, your, his,* etc.) in Spanish:

mi, mis	*my*	**nuestro/a** **nuestros/as**	*our*
tu, tus	*your* (informal)	**vuestro/a** **vuestros/as**	*your* (informal, Spain)
su, sus	*his, her, its*	**su, sus**	*their, your (formal/informal)*

- Possessive adjectives agree in number with the noun that follows them:

  mi madre   **mis** padres

  tu amigo   **tus** amigos

- The **nosotros** and **vosotros** forms also agree in gender with the noun they modify:

  nuestro nieto   **nuestra** familia

  nuestros nietos   **nuestras** familias

- If the ownership referred to by **su** or **sus** is unclear from the context, you can clarify using **de** + *person's name* or **de** + *pronoun:*

  Es **su** hija ➔ Es la hija **de Jennifer.** (o) Es la hija **de ella.**

  Son **sus** padres. ➔ Son los padres **de Jennifer**. (o) Son los padres **de ella.**

* Keep in mind that **nuestro/a/os/as** (*our*) is different from **nosotros**/as (*we*)

To introduce students to possessive adjectives used in context, have them take parts and read the **historieta** out loud. To check their comprehension and call their attention to possessives, ask the following questions: 1.¿Cómo se llaman los padres de Jennifer? ¿Y su hija? 2. ¿Cómo se llama la hija de Fabio? ¿De dónde es su madre?

To illustrate the possessive adjectives, gather objects from students such as two books, two pencils, a backpack, a sweater, etc. Then ask, for example: ¿Son mis libros? The owner of the books says: No, no son sus* libros. Son mis libros. Then say: ¿Es verdad? ¿Son sus libros? The class responds: Sí, son sus libros.

*If you prefer that your students address you informally, change the sus to tus.

[1]Look, [2]close

Palabras útiles
los lápices de colores *colored pencils*
la pelota *ball*

¡En acción!

¡Oye!   ¿De quién es?

Your instructor will "borrow" items from you and your classmates and then claim to own them. Respond by saying «**¡No, no es su... !**» or «**¡No, no son sus... !**» Then set the record straight by declaring to whom each item belongs.

3-6   ¿Qué dicen?[1]

To find out what belongs to whom, first, complete the speech bubbles, putting yourself in the place of each character. Indicate to whom something belongs or to whom someone is related. The arrows point to the possessor/s. Your instructor will then ask you what each person is saying.

1. ¿Qué dice Robertito?

2. ¿Qué dice Nuria?

3. ¿Qué dicen don Claudio y doña Rosa?

4. ¿Qué dice Damián?

5. ¿Qué dice Guadalupe?

6. ¿Qué dice Ángel?

[1]¿**Qué...** What are they saying?

All art © John Wiley & Sons, Inc.

3-7 Mis favoritos

Paso 1. Indicate your favorites by filling in the **yo** column. Then tell your partner your preferences and ask for his/hers. Use **mi/mis** or **tu/tus**. In the third column, write down what your classmate says. Take turns asking and responding.

MODELO

E1: *Mi color favorito es el azul. ¿Y tu color favorito?*

E2: *Es el (color) rojo.*

E2: *Mis clases favoritas son la clase de… y la clase de… ¿Y tus clases favoritas?*

	yo	mi compañero/a
1. color	azul	rojo
2. clases		
3. amigo/a o persona		
4. restaurantes		
5. películas[1]		
6. programa (*m.*) de televisión		
7. carro		
8. aparatos electrónicos		

Paso 2. Join another pair of students and compare your answers for the following categories: **clases, restaurantes, películas, programas de televisión, aparatos electrónicos.**

MODELO

E1: (Asks the two students from the other pair) *¿Cuáles son sus clases favoritas?*

E2: (Answers on behalf of both) *Mis clases favoritas son… y sus clases favoritas son…*

o: *Nuestras clases favoritas son…*

3-8 Mi familia

First, fill in the family tree with members of your family. Then, describe some of them to your partner. Tell their relationship to you and include their names, ages, and places of origin. Take turns.

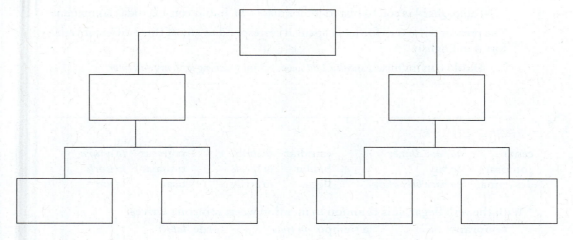

[1]films

3-7 For paired activities, walk around the classroom listening to students and providing assistance where necessary. At the conclusion of an activity, spot-check answers for accuracy. For item #6, remind students that **programa**, though ending in **-a,** is masculine.

3-7 **ANOTHER STEP:** Poll the class to determine their favorite restaurants, films, etc.

You may want to have your students ask you about your favorite restaurants, films, etc.

Jennifer y Fabio continúan su conversación en el centro estudiantil.

¿**Trabajas**?

Sí, soy policía y también estudiante, ¿y tú?

Estudio derecho, como[1] tú. Quiero ser abogada.

¡Qué interesante! Oye, ¿estás libre[2] esta noche?

Pues sí. Hoy Yolanda está con mi madre. **Regresan** a casa a las once.

¡Sí! ¡Es una idea estupenda!

¿**Cenamos** juntos[3]?

PLUS Go to *WileyPLUS* to review this grammar point with the help of the **Animated Grammar Tutorial** and **Verb Conjugator**. For more practice, go to the **Grammar Handbook**.

To introduce students to –ar verbs used in context, have them take parts and read the **historieta** out loud. To check their comprehension, ask the following questions: **1. ¿Qué estudia Jennifer? 2. ¿Quiénes cenan juntos? 3. ¿Cuándo regresan la hija de Jennifer y su madre?**

For additional practice on this grammar point, see PowerPoint slides on BCS and in *WileyPLUS*.

Note that English present tense expresses habitual present actions, not those occurring right now. Ex: I speak with her every day. I speak with her now. Spanish present tense expresses both habitual present and actions occurring right now: **Hablo con ella todos los días. Hablo con ella ahora.**

GRAMÁTICA

¡Manos a la obra!

Talking about the present: The present indicative of regular *-ar* verbs

2

- In English, the infinitive form of a verb is two words: *to speak*. In Spanish, it is just one word: **hablar.**
- There are three infinitive forms in Spanish, each with a different ending: **-ar, -er,** and **-ir:**

  estudi**ar** *to study*   aprend**er** *to learn*   viv**ir** *to live*

- There are regular verbs and irregular verbs. So far, you have learned four irregular verbs: **ser, estar, ir,** and **tener.**
- The different tenses (such as present and past) of regular verbs follow a set pattern: the infinitive ending is dropped and new endings are added, according to the tense and the subject of the verb.

hablar *to speak* (a regular verb) **hablar** habl- + *endings*			
(yo)	habl**o**	(nosotros/as)	habl**amos**
(tú)	habl**as**	(vosotros/as)	habl**áis**
(Ud., él, ella)	habl**a**	(Uds., ellos/as)	habl**an**

  —Fabio, **¿hablas** con tu hija todos los días? —Sí, **hablo** con ella todas las mañanas.

- The present tense verb forms in Spanish correspond to any of three different verb forms in English.

  —**Hablo** con mi hija. *I speak / I do speak / I am speaking with my daughter.*

VERBOS EN *-AR*

cenar	*to have dinner*	estudiar	*to study*	regresar	*to return*
comprar	*to buy*	hablar	*to speak*	trabajar	*to work*
desayunar	*to have breakfast*	llegar*	*to arrive*	usar	*to use*

* With the verb **llegar**, it is common to mention when someone arrives:

temprano *early*   **a tiempo** *on time*   **tarde** *late*

[1]like, [2]**estás...** are you free?, [3]together

© John Wiley & Sons, Inc.

¡En acción!

¡Oye! Ana y Andrés

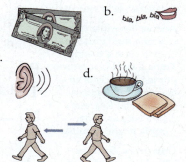

You will hear about the daily routines of two students who are very different from each other. Then you will hear each statement again, in random order. Say whether the description fits Ana or Andrés.

Guión para ¡Oye!
(see p. 82)

3-9 Acciones del momento

Take turns matching the verbs below with the symbol that represents them at the right. To do so, write the letter of the symbol in the space provided and share it with your partner.

1. __c__ Escuchas. 2. __b__ Hablamos. 3. __e__ Regresan. 4. __d__ Desayuno. 5. __a__ Compras.

All art © John Wiley & Sons, Inc.

3-10 Un día con los Roldán

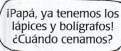

The kids arrive home from school, mom is at work and dad is "holding down the fort" until mom comes home from her shift at the hospital. In pairs, read what each person says and, judging from the remarks, report what they are doing. Select the correct verb from the list provided.

¡Hola, papá! ¡Ya estamos en casa! ¿Dónde está mamá?

Está en la sala de emergencias, ¡y todavía[1] tiene catorce pacientes!

Papá, vamos un momento a la papelería. Necesitamos lápices y bolígrafos.

Bueno. ¿Tienen dinero ($)?

compran	desayuna
estudian	habla
van	llegan
regresan	trabaja

1. Los hijos ____llegan____ a casa de la escuela. Su madre ____trabaja____ en el hospital.

2. Los hijos ____van____ a la papelería y allí ____compran____ lo que necesitan para la escuela.

¡Papá, ya tenemos los lápices y bolígrafos! ¿Cuándo cenamos?

Muy pronto.

Abuelo, esta noche no es posible. Ángel y yo tenemos mucha tarea.

Sí, sí, la tarea es muy importante. Vamos el sábado.

3. Los hijos ____regresan____ a casa y tienen hambre[2].

4. Guadalupe ____habla____ con su abuelo por teléfono. Esta noche ella y Ángel ____estudian____ porque tienen mucha tarea.

3-10 Have students in pairs read the dialogues to the class, with other individuals providing the follow-up responses.

All art © John Wiley & Sons, Inc.

Niños, ¿qué prefieren, cereal o croissants y fruta?

¿Y tú, mi amor[3]?

¡Croissants y fruta, mamá!

Yo también, y un cafecito, por favor.

3-10 Remind students that **la familia** is singular, and as such, requires a singular verb: **La familia desayuna...**

5. Al día siguiente, a las 8:00 de la mañana, la familia ____desayuna____ croissants y fruta.

[1]still, [2]**tienen...** are hungry, [3]love

Guión para ¡Oye!
(from p. 81)
Ana normalmente llega a clase tarde. No estudia mucho y no trabaja. Habla por el celular con sus amigas constantemente. Los sábados por la noche, va a la discoteca y regresa a casa ¡a las tres de la mañana!

Andrés desayuna en la cafetería por la mañana. Llega a clase a tiempo. Trabaja en el laboratorio por la tarde, y está en la computadora constantemente. Regresa a casa a las seis, cena, y por la noche, estudia.

Comprensión para ¡Oye! Repeat each of Ana and Andrés' actions in random order and have students call out the name of the person described.

3-11 If students prefer not to write in their textbooks, they can draw the numbered squares in their notebooks and write the names there.

Play ¡Bingo! once or twice more, as time allows. If time is at a premium, students in groups of four ask each other the questions and jot down names.

¿Con qué frecuencia? Tell your students that **nunca**, like the other adverbs in the purple box, can go in front of or after the verb. When it goes after the verb, **No** needs to be in front of the verb: **No desayuno nunca. / Nunca desayuno.**

3-11 ¡Bingo!

Paso 1. Walk around the classroom asking your classmates the questions on the Bingo board. In each square, jot down the name of the student who answers affirmatively. The first student to complete a horizontal, vertical, or diagonal line shouts **Bingo!** and informs the class of each answer: *1. Jason estudia en la biblioteca,...* Then play again!

MODELO

E1: *¿**Estudias** en la biblioteca?*

E2: *Sí, **estudio** en la biblioteca.* (**E1** jots down the name of **E2** in the box.)

o: *No, no **estudio** en la biblioteca.* (**E1** asks someone else.)

B I N G O

1. ¿**Estudias** en la biblioteca? _____	2. ¿**Trabajas** por la noche? _____	3. ¿**Desayunas** en la cafetería? _____
4. ¿**Compras** tus libros por Internet? _____	5. ¿**Llegas** a clase temprano? _____	6. ¿**Usas** las computadoras del laboratorio? _____
7. ¿**Cenas** en casa normalmente? _____	8. ¿**Regresas** a casa después de las nueve? _____	9. ¿**Hablas** con tus amigos por el celular? _____

Paso 2. Now share with the class two activities that you and a classmate have in common: *… y yo **desayunamos** en la cafetería,...*

¿CON QUÉ FRECUENCIA?

(casi) siempre *(almost) always*
(casi) nunca *(almost) never*
a veces *sometimes*
una vez/ dos veces por semana
  once/ twice per week
con frecuencia *frequently*

todo el día *all day*
todos los días *every day*
todas las mañanas/ tardes/ noches
  every morning/ afternoon/ evening, night
los fines de semana *on weekends*

3-12 ¿Con qué frecuencia?

Ask your partner questions to find out how often he/she participates in each of the following activities. Your partner will respond using the expressions in the box above. Jot down his/her responses. Take turns asking and responding.

MODELO

E1: *¿Con qué frecuencia estudias español?*

E2: ***Dos veces por semana.*** (**E1** writes the information on the chart.) *¿Y tú?*

E1: *Estudio español **¡todas las noches!*** (**E2** writes the information on the chart.)

Preguntas: ¿Con qué frecuencia...	Frecuencia
1. *estudiar* español?	
2. *desayunar* en casa?	
3. *llegar* a clase tarde?	
4. *cenar* en un restaurante?	
5. *comprar* comida rápida[1]?	

3-12 Instructor's questions for *Paso 2:* ¿Con qué frecuencia estudian español los estudiantes de la clase? **E1: Elena estudia español dos veces por semana. E2: Juan estudia español...** For each question, elicit responses from several students.

ANOTHER STEP: In preparation for the introduction of the verb **saber** in ch. 4, the question **¿Qué sabes de...** will appear often so students become familiar with this use of the **saber**.

PLUS Go to *WileyPLUS* to review this grammar point with the help of the **Animated Grammar Tutorial** and **Verb Conjugator.** For more practice, go to the **Grammar Handbook.**

You may want to use the PPT for activity 3–13 and ask students to read the text out loud for the class.

In this textbook tú affirmative commands are introduced at the same time as the present tense of the verbs is presented (chapters 3-6).

. . . y algo más   *Tú* affirmative commands for *-ar* verbs

Now that you have learned the present tense of regular **-ar** verbs, it would be very simple for you to use that as the basis for giving orders to people you address informally with **tú** such as a classmate, a friend, or a family member.

Just think of the **tú** form and drop the "s": —Mamá, com**pra** más chocolate: —Muy bien hija. Y tú, estu**dia** mucho.

3-13   Desean y ordenan

Paso 1.   Take turns reading the bubbles saying what the family members want from Angel and observe how to give orders in Spanish.

¡Ángel, **llega** a clase a tiempo!

¡Y **habla** con respeto a tus maestros!

¡Hijo, **desayuna** ahora con tus hermanos!

¡Hijo, **escucha** lo que dice tu hermanito!

¡Ángel, **regresa** pronto de la escuela!

© John Wiley & Sons, Inc

Paso 2.   Now give orders to each other using the verbs provided inside *Palabras útiles* box.

3-14   La rutina diaria   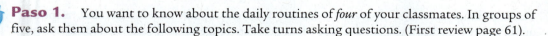 RECYCLES telling *at what time.*

Paso 1.   You want to know about the daily routines of *four* of your classmates. In groups of five, ask them about the following topics. Take turns asking questions. (First review page 61).

• where and when you have breakfast
• where you or members of your family work
• at what time you usually arrive at the university or at work and return home at night
• where, when, and with whom you usually have dinner

MODELO

E1: *¿Dónde y cuándo desayunan Uds.?*   **E2:** *Yo desayuno en la cafetería, a las 9 de la mañana.*

E3: *Desayuno en casa, a las 8 y media.* (**E4** asks next and then **E1** starts with next question)

Paso 2.   One member of each group tells the rest of the class about some of his/her classmates' routine activities.

---

[1]**comida...** fast food

Palabras útiles

Estudiar español
Usar WileyPLUS
Trabajar mucho para la clase de español
Comprar un diccionario de español
Desayunar siempre
Llegar a tiempo
Hablar español más
Cenar con tu familia o amigos

3-14 At the conclusion of the activity, one member shares with the class one interesting item from his/her group's conversation.

Tu mundo cultural

La familia hispana

¿Qué sabes de la familia hispana y de sus costumbres?

¿SABES QUE...?

Fernando Botero, born in Medellín, Colombia in 1932, is one of the most celebrated living artists in Latin America. Among his main influences are Dalí, Picasso, Mexican muralists, and painters from the Italian Renaissance. The Museo Botero of Bogota not only houses 123 pieces of his own drawings, paintings and sculptures, but his private collection of international works of art. Visit the Museo Botero online.

¿SABES QUE...?

Marcelo Ebrard, the mayor of Mexico's Distrito Federal elected in 2006 is an example of the new openness toward liberal social policies among politicians in many Hispanic countries. During his administration, same-sex marriage was approved by the legislature for couples in the Distrito Federal. Same-sex marriages performed in the Distrito Federal are recognized through the country.

Hijos por familia en México
· hace 30 años[5]: 7.3 hijos
· hace 10 años: 3.4 hijos
· actualmente: 2.2 hijos

© Fernando Botero, courtesy Marlborough Gallery, New York

Una familia (1989), óleo sobre lienzo, 241x195 cm, del pintor colombiano Fernando Botero. Museo Botero de Bogotá, Colombia.

La familia es una de las instituciones más sólidas de la sociedad hispana. En general, la vida[1] de los hispanos se centra en la familia.

Tradicionalmente, como se observa en el cuadro[2] de Botero, el padre tiene la autoridad, mientras que la madre se dedica a cuidar y a educar a los hijos. Pero esto está cambiando[3] debido al número ascendente de mujeres universitarias y profesionales que cada día son más independientes.

Además, ahora muchas mujeres hispanas son madres a los 30 años o más tarde. En muchos casos, no quieren tener muchos hijos porque los dos padres trabajan y no tienen tiempo para estar con ellos, y también porque mantener a los hijos cuesta mucho dinero.

Las familias hispanas tradicionalmente son numerosas (mira la foto de la página 85). Pero en años más recientes esto ha cambiado, tal como indican las estadísticas de México. En algunos casos más de una generación reside en la misma[4] casa, y por lo general, los hijos no se independizan hasta el día de su matrimonio.

Otro factor que es importante considerar cuando se habla de la familia hispana de hoy es la aceptación social en muchos países hispanos de un modelo de familia distinto al tradicional.

[1]life, [2]painting, [3]changing, [4]same, [5]hace... thirty years ago

Courtesy Gladys Navarro

Una familia de Quito, Ecuador. La familia incluye a los parientes más inmediatos (madre, padre, hijos, hermanos) y también a los abuelos, tíos, primos, etc.

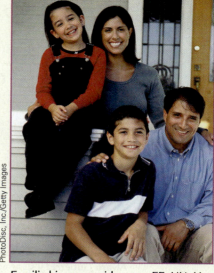

PhotoDisc, Inc./Getty Images

Familia hispana residente en EE. UU. Hoy día el núcleo familiar es, en general, más pequeño[1], con dos o tres hijos nada más.

¿Qué aprendiste?

1. ¿De dónde es Fernando Botero? ¿Cuántos miembros tiene la familia del cuadro? Según el cuadro, en la familia tradicional hispana, ¿quién tiene la autoridad?

2. En la primera fotografía, ¿cuántas personas hay en la familia? ¿De dónde son? ¿Dónde están? ¿Y en la tercera fotografía?

3. ¿Qué nuevo modelo de familia está apareciendo en la sociedad hispana?

Actividad cultural

Jaime, a student from Mexico, will be spending one month with your family. Write an e-mail to tell him the name, relation, and age of each person in your family. Indicate professions where appropriate.

Pablo Alfaro/RM//Getty Images, Inc.

Con los cambios en la sociedad hispana moderna están apareciendo nuevos modelos de familia, como es el caso de Ricky Martin y sus dos hijos gemelos[2] que vemos en esta fotografía. En el año 2010, el famoso cantante anunció **Soy quien soy, un hombre gay y lo digo bien alto**[3]. Su familia, que es muy católica, lo ha aceptado a él y a sus hijos, concebidos en un "vientre de alquiler"[4].

| To: | Jamie@novanet.com |
| Subject: | Mi familia |

Querido Jaime:
Te escribo para informarte acerca de mi familia. Mi...
...
Tu amigo/a,
...

Contraste cultural

In English, compare some characteristics of your family with those of the families described above, or with a Hispanic family you know. Talk about closeness of family members, how many generations live under the same roof, who makes what decisions, when children become independent, and to what degree family influences all aspects of life. Work in a group of *three*.

[1]**más...** smaller, [2]**twins**, [3]**lo digo...** I'm saying it loud and clear, [4]**vientre...** through a surrogate mother

¿SABES QUE...?

In some Hispanic countries, traditional family roles are changing. For example, in Spain it has been legal since 2005 for persons of the same gender to marry and to adopt children. As of this book's publication, the only Hispanic countries that have legalized gay marriage are Spain (2005) and Argentina (2010). However, Uruguay, Ecuador, and Colombia, and cities like Mexico City and the Mexican state of Coahuila, recognize some rights for same-sex unions.

Pronunciación: Practice pronunciation of the chapter's new vocabulary in *WileyPLUS*.

WILEY **PLUS**

¹Los mejores amigos

VOCABULARIO

A

COMPAÑÍA CON BRÍO S.A.*

2. rubio
3. fuerte
5. ayudar
4. desordenado

Álvaro Gutiérrez y su amigo Damián

B

6. morena
7. bonita/ guapa**
8. simpática
10. necesitar
9. llamar

Mi hija...

¡¡¡Mamááá!!!
ROBERTITO

Y mi hija...

Fátima Almanza y su amiga Mª Luisa

C

¡Ja, ja, ja!
16. amar
11. pelirroja
12. divertida
13. joven
14. delgada
15. visitar

PUERTO RICO

Dolores Toledo y su "amigo" Ángel

D

17. alta
18. baja
19. limpiar

Julia y Elena, las amigas de Guadalupe

E

20. cuidar
21. llorar
22. besar
23. abrazar
24. (muy) cariñosa

© John Wiley & Sons, Inc.

Nuria, la niñera, con Anita

F

¿Qué tal en la escuela, Carmen?...
¡Fenomenal!
25. calvo
26. viejo
27. charlar (con)
¡miau, miau!
29. pequeño
28. grande

Don Gonzalo, un amigo de los Roldán, con Carmen

1. best friends 2. blond 3. strong 4. disorganized, messy 5. to help 6. dark-haired/ dark-skinned 7. pretty/ good looking 8. nice, likeable 9. to call 10. to need 11. red-headed 12. funny, fun 13. young 14. thin, slender 15. to visit 16. to love 17. tall 18. short 19. to clean 20. to take care of 21. to cry 22. to kiss 23. to hug 24. (very) affectionate 25. bald 26. old 27. to chat (with) 28. large, big 29. small

*S.A. (Sociedad Anónima) *Inc*. **Guapo/a is only used to refer to people.

¡En acción!

 3-15 ¿Cómo son?[1]

Take a close look at the friends of the Roldán family (scenes, page 86). Then see if you can match their faces with the adjectives provided in the box. Take turns asking and responding.

MODELO

E1: ¿Cómo es Fátima?   **E2:** Es simpática.

Fátima

Calisto

Álvaro

Pachá

Dolores Toledo

Don Gonzalo

Nuria

Elena

> baja
> cariñosa
> delgada
> desordenado
> grande
> pequeño
> simpática
> viejo

 3-16 Los mejores amigos

Find out more about the Roldán family and their best friends. Look at the scenes on page 86 and work with your partner to answer the questions.

1. ¿Quién es el mejor amigo y compañero de trabajo de Damián Roldán? ¿Cómo es Álvaro? ¿Ayuda Damián a su amigo?

2. ¿Con quién habla Fátima Almanza? ¿De quiénes hablan? ¿Cómo es Fátima? ¿Quién llama a su mamá? ¿Necesita a su mamá?

3. ¿Quién visita a Ángel? ¿Cómo es ella? ¿Ama Ángel a Dolores?

4. ¿Quiénes son Julia y Elena? ¿Cómo son? ¿A qué hora llegan a la casa de Guadalupe para estudiar? ¿Quién limpia la casa cuando llegan?

5. ¿Quién llora? ¿Quién cuida a Anita? ¿Besa y abraza a la bebé? ¿Cómo es Nuria?

6. ¿Con quién charla Carmen? ¿Cómo es don Gonzalo? ¿Es Pachá, el perro, grande o pequeño? ¿Y Calisto, el gato?

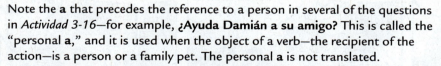

> **. . . y algo más**   The personal *a*
>
> Note the **a** that precedes the reference to a person in several of the questions in *Actividad 3-16*—for example, **¿Ayuda Damián a su amigo?** This is called the "personal **a**," and it is used when the object of a verb—the recipient of the action—is a person or a family pet. The personal **a** is not translated.
>
> The following verbs, presented on page 86, normally have a person as their object: **ayudar, llamar, necesitar, visitar, amar, cuidar, besar,** and **abrazar.**
>
> *Note:* The personal **a** is not used with the verb **tener. Tengo dos hermanos.**

 For additional practice on this grammar point, see PowerPoint slides on BCS and in *WileyPLUS*.

[1]What are they like?

Sidebar (right column):

For additional vocabulary practice, see PowerPoint slides on BCS and in *WileyPLUS*.

3-15 ANSWERS (may vary): Fátima / (provided); Calisto / pequeño; Álvaro / desordenado; Pachá / grande; Dolores Toledo / delgada; Don Gonzalo / viejo; Nuria / cariñosa; Elena / baja.

3-16 After students complete the activity, you may want to project the opener scene using the PowerPoint slide. Have students describe the various sets of friends.

3-16 PERSONALIZED QUESTIONS: Ask several students: **¿Cómo se llama tu mejor amigo/a? ¿Cómo es?** Assist them with adjective agreement.

> **¿SABES QUE...?**
>
> Many Mexican women are named Guadalupe (Lupe, Lupita), after the Virgen de Guadalupe, patron saint of Mexico.

PLUS For more practice, see **Grammar Handbook** found in *WileyPLUS*.

To visually present the personal **a**, write **Llamo, un taxi, María,** and a on four sheets of paper. Four students stand in front of the class, each holding up one of the sheets. Position students to form a sentence, placing or removing them according to the object (**un taxi** or **María**).

3-17 Mi vida personal

3-17 As students provide answers, be sure to ask whether they responded **sí** or **no** to the statement.

Get to know a classmate! First, add the personal **a** to each statement as needed. Then decide if for you, the statement is true or not. Mark **Sí** or **No.** Share the information with your partner.

Sí   No

☐   ☐   **1.** Tengo ____ novio/a o esposo/a.

☐   ☐   **2.** Tengo ____ hijo/a/os/as.

☐   ☐   **3.** Cuido _a_ mis sobrinos o _a_ mis hermanos menores con frecuencia.

☐   ☐   **4.** Necesito _a_ mis amigos. Son muy importantes en mi vida.

☐   ☐   **5.** Llamo _a_ mis abuelos dos veces por semana.

☐   ☐   **6.** Limpio ____ mi carro todas las semanas.

☐   ☐   **7.** No ayudo _a_ mis compañeros con la tarea.

☐   ☐   **8.** Visito ____ museos con frecuencia.

3-18 Personas importantes de nuestras vidas

3-18 Call out each action and students volunteer their responses. You may want to use the PowerPoint slide of the scenes to point out each action being described.

In groups of *three*, observe the scenes on page 86, looking for people doing things for/to others. Describe what is happening. Use each of the following verbs: **abrazar, amar, ayudar, besar, cuidar, llamar, necesitar, visitar.**

MODELO

*Nuria cuida **a** Anita. Carmen cuida **a** Pachá.*

3-19 Preguntas personales

3-19 For the feedback, provide a model: **Tina llama a su novio con frecuencia.**

To share additional aspects of your personal life, ask each other the following questions. Jot down the responses. Then change partners and share what you learned.

MODELO

E1: *¿A quién llamas por teléfono con frecuencia?* **E2:** *Llamo a... ¿Y tú?*

¿A quién...?
- visitas los fines de semana
- amas con todo tu corazón ❤
- ayudas a veces
- besas y abrazas

> **Palabras útiles**
> novio/a *boyfriend/ girlfriend*
> prometido/a *fiancé/ fiancée*
> a nadie *nobody*

¡A escuchar! El nuevo amigo de Manuela

Paso 1.   Listen to the dialogue between two friends.

PLUS Go to *WileyPLUS* to complete **Paso 2** of this listening activity.

Jennifer está en casa de sus padres. Ellos le preguntan acerca de la universidad.

¡Manos a la obra!

GRAMÁTICA

3

Describing people and things: *Ser* + descriptive adjectives

You have used adjectives with **estar** to express the mental, emotional, or physical condition of a person: Su hija **está contenta**. To describe the basic characteristics of someone or something, you use **ser** + *descriptive adjective*: Yolanda **es bonita**.

Let's look at descriptions of the people and activities in Jennifer's life.

- Adjectives that end in **-o** change **-o** to **-a** when describing a feminine noun.

  Su madre es moren**a**; es simpátic**a**. Su padre es moren**o**; es simpátic**o**.

- Adjectives ending in **-e**, **-ista**, or most consonants *do not change* in form when describing a feminine noun.

  Fabio es jove**n** y fuert**e**; es optim**ista**. Jennifer es jove**n** y fuert**e**; es optim**ista**.

- When describing more than one person or thing, the plural form of the adjective is used. Adjectives ending in a vowel add **-s**, and adjectives ending in a consonant add **-es**.

  Sus clases son buena**s**, pero difícil**es**. Los estudiantes son trabajador**es**.

- Most descriptive adjectives *follow* the nouns they modify—just the opposite of English:

  una universidad **fantástica**   *a fantastic university*

- Two types of adjectives precede the noun:

  Adjectives of quantity: **cuatro** clases   **muchos** amigos
  Possessive adjectives: **mis** padres   **nuestra** familia

Go to *WileyPLUS* to review this grammar point with the help of the **Animated Grammar Tutorial** and **Verb Conjugator**. For more practice, go to the **Grammar Handbook**.

To introduce students to descriptive adjectives used in context, have them take parts and read the **historieta** out loud. To check their comprehension and call their attention to the adjectives, ask the following questions: 1. **¿Cómo son los profesores de Jennifer?** 2. **¿Cómo es Fabio?**

For additional practice on this grammar point, see PowerPoint slides on BCS and in *WileyPLUS*.

Write **él, ella, ellos,** and **ellas** on the board accompanied by stick figures representing each. Use adjectives such as **romántico, inteligente, guapo,** and **sentimental** to describe the figures on the board, indicating the changes in the adjectives, where applicable.

ADJETIVOS Y SUS OPUESTOS

Here are some adjectives and their opposites, some of which you already know.

bonito/a	feo/a	*pretty*	*ugly*	joven	viejo/a***	*young*	*old*
bueno/a	malo/a	*good*	*bad*	listo/a	tonto/a	*smart*	*silly, dumb*
delgado/a*	gordo/a**	*thin*	*fat*	nuevo/a	viejo/a	*new*	*old*
divertido/a	aburrido/a	*fun*	*boring*	rico/a	pobre	*rich*	*poor*
fácil	difícil	*easy*	*difficult*	simpático/a	antipático/a	*nice*	*unpleasant*
grande	pequeño/a	*large*	*small*	trabajador/a	perezoso/a	*hard-working*	*lazy*

*Or **flaco/a** *thin, skinny*.   **To soften, use **gordito** or **gordita**.   *** To soften, use **persona mayor** *older/elderly* person

ESCENA 2

ochenta y nueve   **89**

¡En acción!

¡Oye! Be expressive and dramatic when you read the descriptions.

Guión para ¡Oye!

1. El señor Gómez no tiene casa y no tiene trabajo. ¿Es rico o pobre?
2. Héctor no trabaja, no estudia y con frecuencia mira la televisión. ¿Es perezoso o trabajador?
3. Víctor trabaja ocho horas al día, estudia y también es voluntario en el hospital. ¿Es perezoso o trabajador?
4. Penélope tiene sólo ocho años y ya resuelve problemas de álgebra. ¿Es lista o tonta?
5. Marta tiene doce años. ¿Es joven o vieja?
6. El gato de Marta tiene veintidós años. ¿Es joven o viejo?
7. Tina va a muchas fiestas, a discotecas y a restaurantes con sus amigos. ¿Es aburrida o divertida?
8. Los padres de Tina están en casa todas las noches y normalmente no hablan por teléfono con sus amigos. ¿Son aburridos o divertidos?

. . . y algo más You may want to present adjectives that change meaning according to their position: **un amigo viejo** (*old in years*); **un viejo amigo** (*old = long-standing*); **un carro nuevo** (*brand-new*); **un nuevo carro** (*new to owner, different*).

3-20 For item #4, **Mi familia...**, remind students that although the word **familia** refers to more than one person, the word itself is singular. Thus, the accompanying verb and adjectives must be singular as well: **Mi familia es divertida.**

3-20 Prior to moving on to *Paso 2*, elicit responses for each category from several students.

3-20 ANOTHER STEP: Students volunteer descriptions of their boy/girlfriends or significant others.

¡Oye! Los opuestos

You will hear statements describing various people or their pets. In the follow-up questions, select the adjective that best describes each one.

PLUS For more practice, see **Grammar Handbook** found in *WileyPLUS*.

. . . y algo más The adjectives *bueno/a, malo/a,* and *grande*

The adjectives **bueno/a** and **malo/a** may appear either before or after the noun. Before the noun, the masculine forms **bueno** and **malo** are shortened to *buen* and *mal*:

un libro **bueno** (o) un **buen** libro *a good book*
un estudiante **malo** (o) un **mal** estudiante *a bad student*

When it appears before a singular noun, the adjective **grande** changes to **gran**, and its meaning changes from *large* to **great**.

una mujer **grande** *a large woman*   una **gran** mujer *a great woman*
un libro **grande** *a large book*   un **gran** libro *a great book*

For additional practice on this grammar point, see PowerPoint slides on BCS and in *WileyPLUS*.

3-20 Profesores, amigos y familia

Paso 1. Check the characteristics that best describe each of the following.

1. Mis profesores, por lo general, son:
   - ☐ fáciles ☐ difíciles ☐ interesantes ☐ aburridos
   - ☐ buenos ☐ malos ☐ jóvenes ☐ viejos

2. Mis amigos, por lo general, son:
   - ☐ perezosos ☐ trabajadores ☐ simpáticos ☐ antipáticos
   - ☐ divertidos ☐ aburridos ☐ listos ☐ tontos

3. Mi mejor amigo/a es:
   - ☐ simpático/a ☐ antipático/a ☐ ordenado/a ☐ desordenado/a
   - ☐ trabajador/a ☐ perezoso/a ☐ guapo/a ☐ feo/a

4. Mi familia es:
   - ☐ grande ☐ pequeña ☐ aburrida ☐ divertida
   - ☐ ordenada ☐ desordenada ☐ extrovertida ☐ introvertida

Paso 2. Compare your results with those of a classmate, noting similarities and differences. Then report at least one observation to the class: *Mis amigos son perezosos, pero los amigos de… son trabajadores. (o) Mis amigos y los amigos de… son perezosos.*

3-21 ¿Cómo son? ¡Descríbelos!

You and your friend sometimes gossip about others. Describe the people, pets, and objects in the illustrations using the following adjectives. Remember to make the adjectives agree with the nouns!

alto	calvo	desordenado	gordo	moreno	aburrido
antipático	cariñoso	divertido	grande	pequeño	simpático
atlético	bueno	feo	inteligente	perezoso	trabajador
bajo	delgado	fuerte	joven	rubio	viejo

3-21 You may want to project the corresponding PowerPoint slide of the illustrations. Have students describe the various characters, preferably with their books closed.

MODELO

Juan y Anita son jóvenes y fuertes.

Juan   Anita

1.   Pedro   Pablo   Pepe

2.   Raimundo

3.   el carro rojo   el carro azul

4.   Ana   Sergio   Samuel

5.   el Sr. Gómez

6.   el Sr. Gutiérrez

7.   Tomás   Juanita

8.   Noé   Nicolás
los dos perros

 3-22 Mi mejor amigo/a

Paso 1. In groups of *four*, take turns describing your best friend. Take notes as others speak. Include the following:

- nombre de tu amigo/a
- origen: de dónde es
- edad: cuántos años tiene
- trabajo, profesión u ocupación
- descripción física
- descripción de su personalidad

Paso 2. Determine who in your group has the most interesting best friend. The student to the right of that person tells the class why the selection was made.

¿SABES QUE...?

Human imitations of animal sounds vary from language to language. In Spanish, dogs say **¡guau guau!**, cats say **¡miau miau!**, birds say **¡pío pío!**, and roosters say **¡Quiquiriquí!**

Tu mundo cultural

Diferencias culturales

¿Es fácil adaptarse a una cultura y a una lengua diferentes? Antes de responder, lee[1] la correspondencia entre dos amigas mexicanas: Marta y Josefina. Marta reside en EE. UU. con su esposo y tres hijos, y Josefina, en Monterrey, México.

To:	josefinam@tecnonet.com
Subject:	¡Llega mi mamá de México!

Querida Josefina:
¿Cómo estás? Yo estoy bien, pero un poco preocupada. Mi mamá llega esta semana y va a pasar dos meses con nosotros. No conoce[2] esta cultura y posiblemente va a tener problemas con mis hijas adolescentes: no quieren hablar español y tampoco quieren estar con la familia, solamente con sus amigos. Ya sabes, en México, normalmente los hijos pasan mucho tiempo con la familia, especialmente los fines de semana y durante las vacaciones. Escríbeme pronto.

Un fuerte abrazo,

Marta

P.D. En el anexo hay una foto de los chicos.

¿SABES QUE...?

P.D. is the abbreviation of **posdata,** which is equivalent to the English P.S. (postscript).

Anexo

Courtesy Conchita Lucas

Elena, 13 años; Pablo, 4 años; Alexandra, 14 años

[1]read, [2]**No...** She does not know

Para:	martag@mensajes.com
Asunto:	Re: ¡Llega mi mamá de México!

Querida Marta:

¡Qué alegría[1] recibir tu mensaje y la foto! Nosotros estamos todos muy bien aquí en Monterrey. ¡Qué padre! Finalmente tu mamá va a visitar EE. UU. Comprendo tu preocupación. Es cierto que aquí los jóvenes pasan más tiempo en familia, pero tu mamá va a comprender que tus hijas están en otra cultura, y a aceptar las diferencias. Va a ser una experiencia positiva. Tu mamá va a cuidar a tu hijo y a preparar comida casera[2] todos los días mientras tú estás en el trabajo. Tus hijas van a hablar español con ella porque tu mamá no habla inglés y posiblemente, van a pasar más tiempo en casa para que la abuela esté contenta.[3] ¡Buena suerte![4]

Con cariño,

Tu amiga Josefina

© John Wiley & Sons, Inc.

 ## ¿Qué aprendiste?

1. ¿De dónde son las dos amigas? ¿Dónde están ahora?
   De México. Una en México y la otra en EE. UU.
2. ¿Quién va a visitar a Marta pronto? ¿Por qué está preocupada?
   Su mamá. Porque los jóvenes no se comportan igual en EE. UU. que en México.
3. Según[5] Marta, ¿qué es diferente en México?
   En México, los jóvenes pasan más tiempo en familia.
4. ¿Qué aspectos positivos menciona Josefina en relación con la visita de la madre de Marta a EE. UU.? Respuestas posibles: Su mamá va a cuidar a su hijo y a preparar comidas caseras.

 ## Actividad cultural

Look at the photo in the attachment that Marta sent to Josefina. Describe Marta's three children: physical characteristics, personality, and age. Also indicate how they appear to be (estar). Take turns.

 ## Contraste cultural

Think of people that you know in your family or in your community who have immigrated from other countries. In English, talk about the aspects of U.S. life that a foreigner might find hard to adjust to, as well as which aspects that person might enjoy most.

[1]Qué... What a joy it was, [2]comida... homemade food, [3]Para que... so that grandma will be happy, [4]Buena... Good luck!, [5]According to

Las relaciones humanas

Pronunciación: Practice pronunciation of the chapter's new vocabulary in *WileyPLUS*.

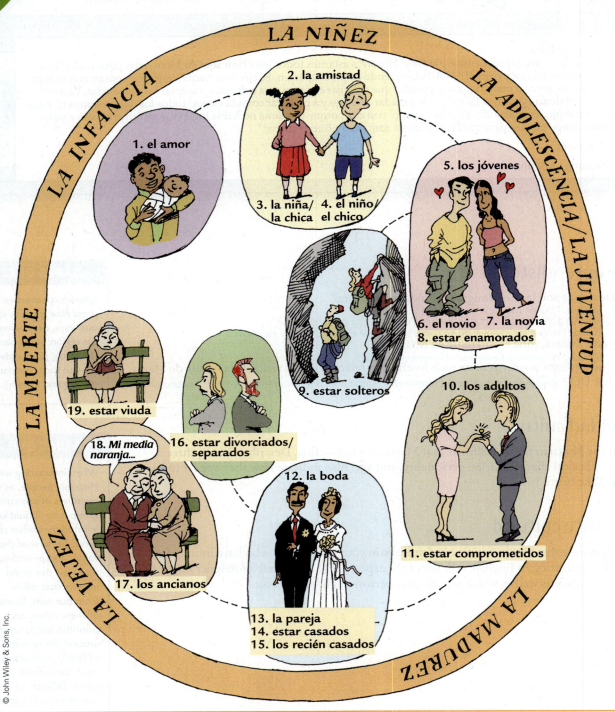

LA NIÑEZ

LA INFANCIA

LA ADOLESCENCIA/LA JUVENTUD

LA MUERTE

LA VEJEZ

LA MADUREZ

1. el amor

2. la amistad

3. la niña/ la chica   4. el niño/ el chico

5. los jóvenes

6. el novio   7. la novia
8. estar enamorados

9. estar solteros

10. los adultos

11. estar comprometidos

12. la boda

13. la pareja
14. estar casados
15. los recién casados

16. estar divorciados/ separados

18. *Mi media naranja...*

19. estar viuda

17. los ancianos

© John Wiley & Sons, Inc.

1. love 2. friendship 3. child (*f.*), girl 4. child (*m.*), boy 5. young people 6. boyfriend 7. girlfriend 8. to be in love 9. to be single 10. adults
11. to be engaged 12. wedding 13. couple; **mi pareja** my significant other 14. to be married 15. newlyweds 16. to be divorced/ separated
17. elderly (*noun*) 18. my soul mate 19. to be a widow; **viudo** widower

¡En acción!

 3-23 Estados civiles y emocionales

You are riding on the subway and overhear snatches of conversations about people's relationships with others. On the basis of what you hear, can you determine the marital or emotional status of each person? Use the adjectives provided. Sometimes more than one assumption is possible. Take turns reading the statements and responding.

casado/a	comprometido/a	divorciado/a	enamorado/a
separado/a	soltero/a	viudo/a	

1. Rosa dice: "Mi esposo es profesor de química". Ella está _casada_.
2. La señora García dice: "Mi ex es gordo". Ella está _separada/divorciada_.
3. Catalina dice: "Mi novio es perfecto". Ella está _enamorada_.
4. Jorge dice: "Mi boda va a ser el 22 de junio". Él está _comprometido_.
5. Héctor dice: "Mi esposa es enfermera". Él está _casado_.
6. Alonso dice: "Mi esposa murió[1]". Él está _viudo_.
7. Ramona dice: "No tengo novio". Ella está _soltera_.
8. Inés y Luz dicen: "Nuestros ex esposos están casados". Ellas están _divorciadas_.

De paso

In general, **estar** is used with adjectives that denote marital status because the characteristic attributed to the subject (**estar casado, estar divorciado**, etc.) is considered the result of an action, a change, or is subject to change. When **ser** is used, particularly with **soltero/a** or **viudo/a**, it emphasizes that the condition of being single or a widow/er is seen as of a more inherent nature.

Mis hermanas **están casadas**,   Mi abuela **es viuda**.
   pero yo **soy soltero**.
My sisters are married, but I am single.   *My grandmother is a widow.*

3-24 Las relaciones humanas

Comment on the various stages of life that you see in the scenes on page 94. Work with your partner to answer the questions.

1. En la escena que representa el amor, ¿quién ama al bebé?
2. En la escena que representa la amistad, ¿quiénes son los mejores amigos? ¿Cómo son?
3. ¿Quiénes están enamorados? ¿Cuántos años tienen los jóvenes, aproximadamente?
4. ¿Cómo están los dos adultos que están comprometidos?
5. ¿Qué celebran los recién casados? ¿Cómo son el esposo y la esposa?
6. El hombre y la mujer que escalan las montañas, ¿están casados o están solteros?
7. Hay una pareja que no está muy contenta. ¿Están casados o divorciados?
8. ¿Están enamorados los ancianos que están en el parque? ¿Qué dice él?
9. ¿Por qué está triste la anciana?
10. ¿Qué palabras (p. 94) asocias con los términos "infancia", "niñez", "juventud" y "vejez"?

For additional vocabulary practice, see PowerPoint slides on BCS and in *WileyPLUS*.

3-23 *Option:* Students may complete the activity in pairs. Then, to confirm answers, ask eight students to read the statements and another eight to provide the subsequent responses.

For additional practice on this grammar point, see PowerPoint slides on BCS and in *WileyPLUS*.

3-24 Before students begin *Actividad 3-24*, you may want to project the PowerPoint slide of the opener scene. Review the stages of life presented in the outer circle, and see if students can guess the meaning of each by context. **La infancia =** *Infancy,* and so on.

3-24 PERSONALIZED QUESTIONS: Ask several students each question. **¿Cuántos estudiantes están solteros?** Students respond with a show of hands. The class counts them and then states how many students are single. **¿Cuántos están enamorados? ¿Cuántos tienen pareja? ¿Cuántos están casados?**

3-25 La familia y los amigos

In groups of *three*, talk about the status of each other's friends and/or relatives. Also mention how they are doing.

> casado/a   comprometido/a   divorciado/a   separado/a   enamorado/a   soltero/a   viudo/a

MODELO

casado/a

E1: *¿Cuáles de tus parientes o amigos están casados?*

E2: *Mi hermano Gonzalo está casado·y está muy enamorado de su esposa.*

E3: *Mi amiga Marisela está casada, pero su matrimonio no va bien.*

¡A escuchar! Dos ancianos en el parque

Paso 1. Listen to the dialogue between don Tomás and doña Remedios. They are sitting on a bench in the park observing the young people passing by.

PLUS Go to *WileyPLUS* to complete **Paso 2** of this listening activity.

3-26 Una pareja encantadora[1]

Let's test your memory! First, take a quick look at the information provided below about this couple. Then one of you will talk about Antonio and the other about María. Use the list of items to be covered that follows. Let's see who remembers more.

Make sure to cover the following information about each person:

1. origin or nationality   **2.** occupation   **3.** marital status

4. emotional condition   **5.** personality traits   **6.** location in the photo

Wiley Archive

Antonio **es** un joven español que estudia en Estados Unidos. Es un chico muy responsable y está siempre contento. **Está** comprometido con María, su novia. En este momento está en el parque y habla con ella por el celular.

Courtesy of Conchita Lucas

María **es** una joven universitaria ecuatoriana. **Está** muy enamorada de Antonio y pronto van a casarse. La boda **es** en el mes de abril, y ahora está en casa y planea los últimos detalles. Es una chica encantadora.

[1]charming

You may want to use the PPT to show the two photos to your students so they can talk as much as they can about this couple.

Fabio llega al centro estudiantil. Allí, su amigo Mario le presenta a Ernesto.

Hola, ¿cómo **estás**?

Estoy un poco cansado. Trabajo por la noche y estudio por la mañana.

Te presento a Ernesto.

Hola, Ernesto. **Soy** de Nueva York. Y tú, ¿de dónde **eres**?

Soy cubano. Estudio ingeniería, ¿y tú?

Yo estudio derecho penal.

© John Wiley & Sons, Inc.

¡Manos a la obra!

GRAMÁTICA

4

Describing people, places, and things: A summary of *ser* and *estar*

You have used both **ser** and **estar** (*to be*) in a number of different situations. Here is a synopsis of their uses thus far, with examples based on Fabio's friends and family.

Ser is used to express:	Examples:	Estar is used to express:	Examples:
1. **Where** the subject* is **from** (*ser + de*)	Fabio **es de** Nueva York.	1. **Where** the subject is **located**	Hoy Mario **está** en el centro estudiantil. Sus hermanos **están** en Chile.
2. **What** the subject is **like** (physical characteristics and basic personality traits)	Mi amigo Mario **es** alto, delgado y muy inteligente. Su motocicleta **es** nueva; **es** roja y negra.	2. **How** the subject is **feeling** or what **condition** the subject is in at a given time (physical, emotional, and mental states that may change)	Fabio **está** cansado porque **está** muy ocupado. Su carro **está** viejo, pero su computadora **está** nueva.
3. **Who** or **what** the subject is (including nationality, political and religious affiliations, occupation)	Mabel **es** dominicana, conservadora y católica. **Es** enfermera y trabaja en una clínica.	3. The third use of **estar** (present progressive) will be presented in Ch. 5.	
4. **Day, date,** and **time**	Hoy **es** martes, 20 de septiembre. **Es** el cumpleaños de Ernesto. **Son** las tres y media de la tarde.		
5. **Possession**	El suéter **es de** Ysenia. **Es** su mochila.		

Subject refers to the person, animal, place, or thing that is described or performs the action.

To introduce students to the uses of **ser** and **estar** in context, have them take parts and read the **historieta** out loud. To check their comprehension and call their attention to the two verbs, ask the following questions: 1. ¿Cómo está Fabio? ¿Por qué? 2. ¿De dónde es Fabio? ¿Y Ernesto?

For additional practice on this grammar point, see PowerPoint slides on BCS and in *WileyPLUS*.

Have students identify each of the ser/estar concepts illustrated in the ¡Oye! activity that follows this grammar presentation.

Let students know that many adjectives can be used with both **ser** and **estar,** conveying different meanings. For example: **Él es aburrido** (*is boring*)./ **Él está aburrido** (*is bored*). **Ella es bonita** (*is pretty*)./ **Ella está bonita** (*looks good*) **hoy.** **Ella es lista** (*is smart*)./ **Ella está lista** (*is ready*). **Él es muy rico** (*is very rich*)./ **El pastel está rico** (*is delicious*). **El libro es nuevo** (*is new*). / **El libro está nuevo** (*in good shape*). **El libro es viejo** (*is old*). / **El libro está viejo** (*in bad shape*).

Ask students to determine the difference in meaning between **Camila es/está delgada** and **Paco es/está nervioso.**

¡En acción!

¡Oye! Víctor, un estudiante universitario

Listen to the description of Víctor. Then answer the questions, selecting the correct response.

3-27 Answers on page 99.

3-27 Mensajes de amigos y familiares

Paso 1. Read the voice messages that several people have left on Lucía's cell phone. Then organize the information according to the categories indicated in the chart below.

Guión para ¡Oye!
Víctor es enfermero y estudia en la universidad. Es joven, guapo y muy trabajador. Es de República Dominicana, pero ahora su familia está en Nueva York. Hoy Víctor está muy preocupado y no está contento porque tiene problemas en el trabajo, y mañana tiene un examen muy difícil en la clase de biología.

1. Soy Amelia, tu prima extrovertida y un poco loca de Miami. Hoy estoy en casa porque estoy enferma. Llámame.

2. Somos Paco y Pepe, ¿recuerdas? Los meseros morenos y guapos de tu café favorito de Boston. Ahora estamos muy contentos y de vacaciones en Nueva York. Llámanos.

3. ¿Quién soy? Adán, tu novio, el hombre más inteligente y divertido de California. Estoy aquí, muy ocupado, en la biblioteca de San Diego. Tengo dos exámenes finales. Llámame.

4. Hola, soy tu tía Julia, de Guadalajara. Estoy un poco nerviosa. Estoy en mi carro en el centro y hay mucho tráfico. Ya sabes que soy impaciente. ¿Estás bien? Llámame. Estoy preocupada por ti.

Comprensión para ¡Oye!
1. ¿Es Víctor profesor o enfermero?
2. ¿Es joven o viejo?, ¿guapo o feo?, ¿trabajador o perezoso?
3. ¿Es de República Dominicana o de Nueva York?
4. ¿Está su familia en República Dominicana o en Nueva York?
5. ¿Está preocupado o contento?
6. ¿Tiene problemas en el trabajo o con la familia?
7. ¿Tiene uno o dos exámenes mañana?

Personas que llaman	¿Quién es/ Quiénes son?	¿De dónde es/son?	¿Dónde está(n)?	¿Cómo es/son?	¿Cómo está(n)?
1. Amelia	Es su prima.	Es de…			
2. Paco y Pepe	Son…	Son de…			
3. Adán					
4. Julia					

Paso 2. **¿Qué sabes ahora de Lucía?** According to the information you have gathered, tell your classmates what you found out about Lucía's friends and relatives.

3-28 Un día con una mujer extraordinaria   RECYCLES interrogative words

Your friend has arranged for you to attend a party organized by an extraordinary woman. To learn about the person, and to ultimately find out whose party you are attending, ask questions with **ser** and **estar**. One of you (**E1**) asks questions following the model to cover categories 1-7. The other (**E2**) uses chart **A** to provide the information in complete sentences. Then switch roles, and do the same with chart **B**. Review the interrogative words on page 61.

A.
1. España
2. morena, bonita y delgada
3. casada
4. ocupada y contenta
5. en Madrid y en EE. UU.
6. actriz
7. Mira su foto en la pág. 55.

MODELO

E1: ¿De dónde es?

E2: Es de…

1. Origen
2. Descripción
3. Estado civil[1]
4. Cómo está probablemente
5. Dónde está frecuentemente
6. Su profesión u ocupación
7. Identificación de la persona (¿Es…? ¿Quién es?)

B.
1. Colombia
2. rubia, guapa y delgada
3. soltera
4. muy ocupada y contenta
5. en Bogotá y Barcelona
6. cantante, bailarina y compositora
7. Mira su foto en la pág. 55.

[1]**Estado…** marital status

3-29 ¿Cómo es normalmente? ¿Cómo está hoy?

Paso 1.   Today, at your workplace, some of your coworkers are not their usual selves, but rather the opposite. *Three* of you talk about the situation:

Employee 1 describes what the coworker is *usually* like (first column). **Employee 2** indicates a *change* in the person's disposition (choosing from the adjectives in the second column). **Employee 3** asks *why*. **Employee 1 or 2** provides an answer (third column). Be creative!

MODELO

E1:   *Normalmente, Marta **es** muy enérgica, ¿verdad?*

E2:   *Sí, pero hoy **está** un poco cansada.*

E3:   *¿Por qué?*

E1 o E2:   *Porque tiene mucho trabajo, tres clases y un hijo enfermo.*

3-27   (from page 98) To check answers, first, ask who the caller is: **¿Quién es Amelia?** Then ask the subsequent questions in the chart: **¿De dónde es Amelia?...** *Paso 2* may also be completed by students in pairs.

3-27 ANSWERS: (from p. 98)
Amelia es su prima. Es de Miami. Está en casa. Es extrovertida y un poco loca. Está enferma. **Paco y Pepe** son meseros. Son de Boston. Están en Nueva York. Son morenos y guapos. Están contentos. **Adán** es su novio. Es de California. Está en la biblioteca de San Diego. Es inteligente y divertido. Está muy ocupado. **Julia** es su tía. Es de Guadalajara. Está en su carro en el centro. Es impaciente. Está nerviosa y preocupada.

Normalmente...	hoy...	porque...
1. Marta *es* muy enérgica.	aburrido/a	
2. Enrique *es* muy tranquilo.	cansado/a	
3. Elena *es* optimista y no tiene preocupaciones.	contento/a nervioso/a	
4. Ricardo *es* muy animado y curioso.		
5. Pepa *es* una persona muy alegre (*cheerful*).	preocupado/a	
6. Raimundo *es* una persona triste.	triste	

Paso 2.   Following the same pattern, tell each other something about yourselves: *Normalmente, **soy**..., pero hoy **estoy**... porque...*

 3-30 Tu pariente/a favorito/a

Paso 1.   Interview your partner to find out who his/her favorite relative is and what the relative is like. Ask the following questions and take notes. Then switch roles.

3-30 *Option:* Each student brings to class a photo of his/her family or favorite relative/s.

1. ¿Cómo se llama?
2. ¿Qué relación tienes con él/ella?
3. ¿De dónde es? (o) ¿Cuál es su nacionalidad*?
4. ¿Dónde está ahora?
5. ¿Está soltero/a o casado/a?
6. ¿Qué profesión u ocupación tiene?
7. ¿Cómo es?
8. ¿Cómo está probablemente?

 Paso 2.   *Four* students volunteer to report on their classmate's favorite relative: *El/La pariente/a favorito/a de... se llama....* The class then votes on the four, to determine who in the class has the most interesting family member.

---

* For a listing of the nationalities of the world, see the inside back cover of your textbook.

Tu mundo cultural

Meets ACTFL Standards
1.2, interpretive reading;
2.1, cultural practices;
2.2, cultural products; and
4.2, cultural comparisons.

Momentos importantes de la vida

El matrimonio

📺 For an additional activity related to this cultural theme, see the PowerPoint slides on BCS and in *WileyPLUS*.

Los novios[1] o recién casados bailan al ritmo de la música de los mariachis para celebrar el día de su matrimonio.

Tell students that in some Latin American countries **el matrimonio** (in addition to **la boda**) is used for *wedding*. **Matrimonio** can also mean *marriage, matrimony,* and *young married couple.*

Rodrigo Marín Vivar
Mª Nieves Alba González

Pedro Enrique Altuna Gómez
Dolores Simón Camino

Participan el próximo enlace matrimonial de sus hijos

Olivia y Alejandro

y tienen el gusto de invitarle(s) a la ceremonia religiosa que se celebrará el sábado 15 de julio, a las 7 de la tarde, en la iglesia de Santa Lucía, y al banquete que se servirá a continuación en La Hacienda del Valle.

Calle Las Palomas n° 17
Sotogrande
Bogotá
Tel. 534 20 96

Se ruega confirmación.

Una invitación de matrimonio. ¿Qué diferencias hay entre esta invitación y las invitaciones de matrimonio en EE. UU.?

El nacimiento[2] y el bautizo[3]

El bautizo de un niño en una iglesia católica. La madrina[4] tiene al niño mientras el padrino y los padres observan atentamente.

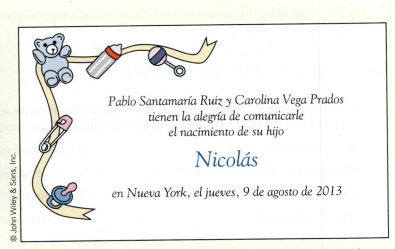

Pablo Santamaría Ruiz y Carolina Vega Prados
tienen la alegría de comunicarle
el nacimiento de su hijo

Nicolás

en Nueva York, el jueves, 9 de agosto de 2013

Una participación de nacimiento[5], costumbre que los hispanos residentes en EE. UU. están adoptando para comunicar a sus familiares y amigos el feliz evento.

[1]bride and groom, [2]birth, [3]christening, [4]godmother, [5]**participación...** birth announcement

La fiesta de quinceañera

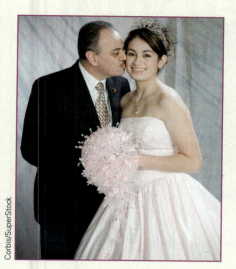

Corbis/SuperStock

Un padre y su hija en México, el día de la fiesta. Se llama quinceañera a la fiesta de los quince años, un ritual que celebran las jóvenes hispano-americanas para decir adiós a la niñez. Se celebra con una misa[1], una recepción y un baile[2]. En EE. UU. se venden vestidos[3] de quinceañera porque las jóvenes hispanas residentes aquí también la celebran. Algunas chicas prefieren hacer un viaje[4] en lugar de celebrar la fiesta.

DE NIÑA A MUJER.
UN AÑO MUY IMPORTANTE
EN TU VIDA

FELICES

15

¡ ES TU QUINCEAÑERA !

©John Wiley & Sons, Inc.

Una tarjeta[5] de quinceañera

¿Qué aprendiste?

1. ¿Cómo se llaman los novios de la invitación? ¿Dónde y en qué fecha se celebra la boda? ¿Qué hay después de la ceremonia? Olivia y Alejandro. 15 de julio a las 7 de la tarde en Bogotá. Un banquete.

2. En los países hispanos, ¿quiénes participan en la ceremonia del bautizo? Los padrinos y los padres, principalmente.

3. ¿Cómo se celebra la quinceañera? ¿Se celebra sólo en Latinoamérica? Con una misa, una recepción y un baile. Se celebra también en algunos lugares de EE. UU.

Actividad cultural

You have just received an invitation (see page 100) to attend the wedding of your friend Alejandro, a former Colombian exchange student. Write an e-mail to your significant other to give him/her details of the wedding so that he/she can attend with you.

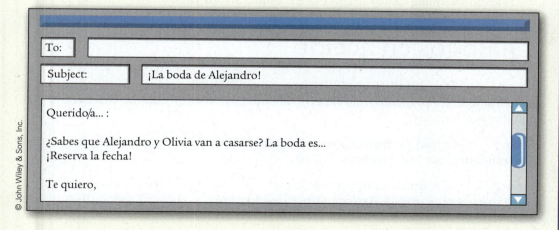

© John Wiley & Sons, Inc.

To:

Subject: ¡La boda de Alejandro!

Querido/a... :

¿Sabes que Alejandro y Olivia van a casarse? La boda es...
¡Reserva la fecha!

Te quiero,

Contraste cultural

In English, talk to your partner about which of the celebrations you have just read about are similar to ones in your family or culture and which are new to you. Have you attended a **quinceañera** in the United States, or a Hispanic wedding or christening?

[1]mass, [2]dance, [3]dresses, [4]trip, [5]card

Go to **WileyPLUS** to see these **videos** and to find more activities for **¡Diálogos en acción!**, **¡A conversar!**, **¡A escribir!** and **¡A investigar!**

Meets ACTFL Standards 1.2, interpretive listening; 2.1, cultural practices; and 4.2, cultural comparisons.

Tu mundo en vivo

¡Videos en acción!

3.1 La familia hispana

1. Antes de ver el video

   In the Carvajal family, what do you think the main responsibilities of the grandmother might be?

   Go to *WileyPLUS* to complete the **Mientras ves el video** activity.

2. Después de ver el video

   Are there differences between the Carvajal family and your family? Explain.

3.2 Momentos importantes de la vida

1. Antes de ver el video

   a. What special celebrations take place in your home? Who attends?

   b. Mark the special occasions you think the family of Rocío and Rogelio might celebrate. Confirm your predictions after seeing the video.

_____ Bautizos	_____ Día de Acción de Gracias
_____ Bodas	_____ Navidad
_____ Primeras comuniones	_____ Año Nuevo

   Go to *WileyPLUS* to complete the **Mientras ves el video** activity.

2. Después de ver el video

   Is Rocío's wedding similar to those in the United States? Explain.

Meets ACTFL Standards 1.1, interpersonal speaking, 1.2, interpretive listening and 2.1, cultural practices.

You can find the **transcripts** for the **Diálogos** in the Power-Point slides on the BCS and in *WileyPLUS*.

Dialogue tips: Play the dialogue once all the way through. Check comprehension by asking students to tell you everything they understood (English is OK). Then play it a second time, pausing after each sentence or phrase and asking students what was said.

¡Diálogos en acción!

3.1 El novio de Graciela

Graciela and Juan, two friends from Mexico, run into each other on campus. Graciela tells Juan about her new boyfriend.

Paso 1.   First, read the **Expresiones útiles** in p. A–3. Next, listen to the dialogue twice and answer the questions your instructor will ask.

Paso 2.   Look at the transcript of this dialogue (p. A–16) and act it out with a partner. Switch roles. Now, go to p. A–3 to complete **Pasos 3** and **4**.

3.2 La familia

Leticia and Juan are two classmates from Mexico chatting over coffee.

Go to *WileyPLUS* to listen to and practice this dialogue.

Diálogo 3.1 models the linguistic functions of greeting, describing physical and personality traits, making social plans, and leave-taking. It also practices **ser** + *descriptive adjective*.
Diálogo 3.2 models the functions of inquiring about and describing plans and family, and leave-taking. It also practices family vocabulary, possessive adjectives, **tener**, **estar** + *adjective*, and recycles **llamarse**.

¡Lectura en acción!

Uno de cada tres niños nace fuera del matrimonio[1] en España; el doble que hace 10 años

Meets ACTFL Standards 1.2, interpretive reading, and 3.2, acquiring information.

The following article from the newspaper *El País* reports on a dramatic recent change in family structure in Spain.

Paso 1. Read the article one time to get a general sense of the information it contains. Note the italicized words that are likely to be unfamiliar to you. Resist the urge to look them up! Just read through it to get the overall idea of the article.

> ### La proporción de bebés de madre no casada se duplica en una década
> - El *auge*[2] de las uniones de hecho[3] y la *inmigración impulsan la transformación*
>
> **En 10 años serán *mayoría* los hijos extramatrimoniales, declara una experta**
>
> En el año 1981, el Código Civil *eliminó* las diferencias que existían entre los niños nacidos dentro y fuera del matrimonio y se convirtieron en iguales ante la ley. En 1981 el porcentaje de bebés nacidos fuera del matrimonio era el 4,4%. Según el Instituto Nacional de Estadística, en el año 2009 alcanzaron el 34,5% (170.604 bebés).
>
> ¿A qué obedece ese cambio tan rápido? "Se han modernizado las parejas[4], y las madres españolas en poco tiempo han pasado a ser casi como las suecas[5] o las británicas en este aspecto", explica Tobío. "Este cambio es resultado de la secularización de la sociedad, de la tolerancia, de la autonomía de las madres –que ya no necesitan la seguridad matrimonial para procrear –, de la inmigración y de la igualdad jurídica de los hijos sin tener en cuenta[6] el estado civil de los padres", afirma la socióloga. Ser madre soltera ya no se considera un estigma.
>
> Según esta experta, el aumento de la procreación fuera del matrimonio es un "fenómeno generacional", "una moda" que protagonizan los que tienen menos de 35 años cuyos[7] padres aceptan con normalidad que sus hijos convivan sin casarse", explica Daniel Devolder, investigador del Centro de Estudios Demográficos de la Universidad Autónoma de Barcelona. "Hay una evolución del sistema de pareja, ya no se piensa en una para toda la vida".
>
> © Charo Nogueira / El País S.L. 2011

Reading Strategy

Guessing Meaning from Context

When you come across an unfamiliar word or phrase that is key to a passage, analyze the context closely to see if you can guess its meaning.

Remind students of the previous Reading Strategies, already presented on pages 29 and 67: *Skimming a Text for Cognates and Other Familar Words or Information* and *Utilizing your Background Knowledge*. Encourage them to utilize and practice previous reading strategies while adding new ones to their repertoire. To help with this, you may wish to ask a few questions after reading the article title to find out what your students know about this topic as it applies to the US. Also help students focus on all the familiar words and cognates that should help them interpret the text.

Remind your students that in Spanish we mark the thousand with a period, not a comma, while English uses periods to mark decimals.

Paso 2. Next, looking at the italicized words, which ones can you figure out from the context? Even if you can't determine a word's exact meaning, by answering the following questions, you can probably get close enough to understand the general idea.

- Can you figure out what part of speech the word is? (noun, verb, adjective, etc.)
- Does the word appear to be a cognate?
- What clues do the surrounding words provide about the word's meaning?

Paso 3. Now, read the passage one more time and check your comprehension with the questions below.

1. ¿Cuál es la transformación familiar más reciente que se menciona en el artículo? ¿Ha sido una transformación rápida o gradual?
2. Nombra dos causas importantes de este cambio social, según el artículo.
3. ¿Hay un estigma hacia la madre soltera en España hoy en día?

[1]**nace...** is born outside of marriage, [2]rise, [3]civil unions, [4]couples, [5]Swedish women, [6]**sin...** without taking it into account, [7]whose

¡A conversar!

¡Estoy enamorado/a!

One student plays the role of a teenager madly in love. *Two* students are the parents, who want to know who the son or daughter is in love with, and what that person is like. The teenager provides the information and the parents ask questions, including questions about the person's family. Their questions could include:

- The person's name
- Where he or she studies
- If he or she works
- What he or she is like
- If he or she is responsible (nice, hard-working...)
- What his or her family is like

You may wish to assign certain steps of the ¡A escribir! writing process for students to complete outside of class.

¡A escribir!

Busco[1] compañero/a de apartamento

You need someone to share living expenses with you. Using the format shown below, write a personal ad to find a roommate. First, state the qualities you seek in the other person. Use adjectives from the **Palabras útiles** list or others. Then, describe yourself with the following information:

- Where you are from
- Physical characteristics, personality, age
- Profession or vocation
- Work/study schedule
- Friends and family

BUSCO COMPAÑERO/A DE APARTAMENTO

Busco un/a compañero/a...
Soy de...
Soy...
Estudio...
Trabajo...
Tengo...
...

Palabras útiles	
ordenado/a	responsable
independiente	honesto/a
realista	paciente
flexible	sincero/a
inteligente	

Writing Strategy

Thinking About Your Audience

Think first about who might be reading your ad. In order to make a positive impression on your reader, consider how to state diplomatically the qualities of the person you seek, and how to best present yourself.

Steps:

1. *Prewriting:* Quickly jot down your initial ideas (**¡en español!**), keeping in mind the accompanying strategy.

2. *Writing:* Turn your thoughts and ideas into sentences, and for smooth transitions, be sure to use transitioning words like **y, o, pero, también, tampoco**.

3. *Revising:* Read your composition carefully. Have you included all of the information requested and checked for correct spelling and punctuation? **¡Ojo!** Have you (a) made your adjectives agree in gender and number with the nouns they describe, (b) made your subjects agree with your verbs, and (c) omitted the article when indicating the profession?

4. *Peer correction:* Exchange papers with a classmate. On each other's compositions, circle errors or areas where there are questions, and then talk about them. Make corrections on your own paper as appropriate.

[1] I am looking for

¡A investigar!
La familia en el arte

How are families portrayed in works of art created by artists from the Hispanic world? You learned about Colombian painter Fernando Botero earlier in this chapter, and you discussed his work *Una familia* (1989). Has Botero painted other works that represent the family? What other Hispanic artists have used the family as an artistic theme?

Paso 1. Your instructor will divide the class into groups of *three* and assign an artist to each group. The artists may include but not be limited to the following: Diego Velázquez, Francisco de Goya, Pablo Picasso and Fernando Botero. Working together, use the research strategies you learned in *Capítulo 2* to find a Spanish-language website that presents information about your artist and images of his or her paintings. Skim the text for information about the artist and identify a painting that portrays a family.

Paso 2. Collaborate to write and edit a brief description of the painting, and post it to your class wiki or blog to share it with the other groups. Include:

- The name of the artist (*El/ la artista es...*)
- Where the artist is from (*Es de...*)
- The title of the painting (*El cuadro se llama...*)
- The century the painting is from (*Es del siglo...*)
- The relationship of the family members portrayed (*El hombre es el padre de...*)
- A description of the physical characteristics of the family members and their emotional state (*La madre es... La madre está...*)
- The URL of the painting's website (*La dirección en internet de la Web del cuadro es...*)

Paso 3. After each group posts its description and the class has viewed them, share whether or not you like each painting and why. In English, compare the representation of the family in older and newer works of art from the Hispanic world.

You may assign the appropriate **Pasos** of **¡A investigar!** for pairs or small groups to complete outside of class.

Meets ACTFL Standards 1.2, interpretive reading; 1.3, presentational writing; 2.2, cultural products; 3.1, other disciplines; 3.2, acquiring information; and 4.2, cultural comparisions.

Palabras útiles

el artista *male artist*
la artista *female artist*
el cuadro *painting*

If your access to technology is limited, have the students create Word documents to submit the description of their paintings.

Research Strategy

Applying Reading Strategies to Research

When you find a Spanish-language source about a topic, you must be able to comprehend it well enough to find the information you want. You have already learned several reading strategies that will help. First, use your background knowledge. What do you already know about the topic? Second, look at the images and graphics. Do they provide clues about the content? Next, skim the headings, links and text, looking for cognates and familiar words. Finally, use the context to guess the meaning of unknown words. These strategies will enable you to locate what you need.

Trivia

Can you answer the following questions?

1. ¿Sabes qué productos exporta Colombia? ¿Y Panamá? Menciona dos, como mínimo.
2. ¿Dónde hay más indígenas, en Colombia o en Panamá?
3. ¿Qué país es más grande, Honduras o Panamá?

1. (Answers will vary among: a) alimentos, petróleo, ropa y calzado, oro, esmeraldas, café, flores y textiles b) cemento y materiales de construcción, refinado de azúcar) 2. En Panamá. 3. Honduras.

If you don't know the answers, take a look at the front inside cover of the textbook. Try to respond in complete sentences.

Vocabulario: Capítulo 3

Escena 1

La familia y sus mascotas
The family and their pets

la abuela/ el abuelo *grandmother/ grandfather*
la bebé/ el bebé *baby (f./m.)*
la cuñada/ el cuñado *sister-in-law/ brother-in-law*
la esposa/ el esposo *wife/ husband*
el gato *cat*
la hermana/ el hermano *sister/ brother*
la hija/ el hijo *daughter/ son*
la madre/ el padre *mother/ father*
la mamá/ el papá *mother/ father*
la nieta/ el nieto *granddaughter/ grandson*
la niñera *nanny*
los padres *parents*
los parientes *relatives*
el perro *dog*
la prima/ el primo *cousin (f./m.)*
la sobrina/ el sobrino *niece/ nephew*
la suegra/ el suegro *mother-in-law/ father-in-law*
la tía/ el tío *aunt/ uncle*
mayor/ menor *older/ younger*

Los números del 60 al 100
Numbers 60 to 100

sesenta *sixty*
setenta *seventy*
ochenta *eighty*
noventa *ninety*
cien *one hundred*

Adverbios *Adverbs*

a tiempo *on time*
tarde *late*
temprano *early*

Verbos *Verbs*

cenar *to have dinner*
comprar *to buy*
desayunar *to have breakfast*
estudiar *to study*
hablar *to speak*
llegar *to arrive*
regresar *to return*
tener *to have*
trabajar *to work*
usar *to use*

¿Con qué frecuencia? *How often?*

a veces *sometimes*
una vez/ dos veces por semana *once/ twice per week*
(casi) nunca *(almost) never*
(casi) siempre *(almost) always*
con frecuencia *frequently*
los fines de semana *on weekends*
todas las mañanas *every morning*
todas las noches *every night*
todas las tardes *every afternoon*
todo el día *all day*
todos los días *every day*

Escena 2

Descripciones *Descriptions*

aburrido/a *boring*
alto/a *tall*
antipático/a *disagreeable, unpleasant*
bajo/a *short*
bonito/a *pretty*
bueno/a *good*
calvo/a *bald*
cariñoso/a (muy) *affectionate (very)*
delgado/a *thin, slender*
desordenado/a *disorganized, messy*
difícil *difficult*
divertido/a *funny, fun*
fácil *easy*
feo/a (un poco) *ugly (a little bit)*
fuerte *strong*
gordo/a (un poco) *fat (a little bit)*
grande *large, big*
guapo/a *good looking*
joven *young*
listo/a *smart*
malo/a *bad*
moreno/a *dark-haired/ dark-skinned*
nuevo/a *new*
pelirrojo/a *red-headed*
pequeño/a *small*
perezoso/a *lazy*
persona mayor *older/elderly person*
pobre *poor*
rico/a *rich*
rubio/a *blond*
simpático/a *nice, likeable*
tonto/a *silly, dumb*
trabajador/a *hard-working*
viejo/a *old*
el mejor amigo/ la mejor amiga *best friend (m./f.)*

Verbos *Verbs*

abrazar *to hug*
amar *to love*
ayudar *to help*
besar *to kiss*
charlar (con) *to chat (with)*
cuidar *to take care of*
limpiar *to clean*
llamar *to call*
llorar *to cry*
necesitar *to need*
visitar *to visit*

Escena 3

Las personas *People*

los adultos *adults*
los ancianos *elderly (noun)*
los jóvenes *young people*
la niña/ la chica *child (f.), girl*
el niño/ el chico *child (m.), boy*

Los estados civiles y emocionales
Marital status and emotional ties

estar casado/a/os/as *to be married*
estar comprometido/a/os/as *to be engaged*
estar divorciado/a/os/as *to be divorced*
estar enamorado/a/os/as *to be in love*
estar separado/a/os/as *to be separated*
estar soltero/a/os/as *to be single*
estar viudo/a/os/as *to be a widow/ widower*

mi media naranja *my soul mate*
la novia/ el novio *girlfriend/ boyfriend*
la pareja *couple*
mi pareja *my significant other*
los recién casados *newlyweds*

la amistad *friendship*
el amor *love*
la boda *wedding*

To introduce the theme, you may want to play one of the videos from this chapter, with or without the audio, and then ask students what they think the chapter is about. You may also want to use the video to motivate cultural discussion, even if students answer in English for the first chapters. At the end of the chapter, ask students if their predictions about its content and culture were accurate.

El tiempo libre

Additional activities and **Autopruebas** for each **Escena** available online.

Oliver Furrer/Brand X Pictures/Getty Images

Escena 1
Actividades al aire libre

GRAMÁTICA:
· *Gustar*
· Present of regular *-er* and *-ir* verbs

CULTURA:
Dos deportes nacionales

Escena 2
Diversiones con la familia y amigos

GRAMÁTICA:
· Present of verbs with an irregular *yo* form

CULTURA:
Un sábado entre hispanos

Escena 3
El clima y las estaciones

GRAMÁTICA:
· *Saber* and *conocer*
· The future with *ir + a +* infinitive

CULTURA:
Lugares fascinantes para conocer

TU MUNDO EN VIVO
¡Videos en acción! El fútbol: pasión hispana; Fines de semana entre hispanos
¡Diálogos en acción! Issuing and Accepting Invitations; Providing Information and Discussing Plans
¡Lectura en acción! Scanning for Specific Information
¡A conversar! Handling Unknown Words
¡A escribir! Gathering Information
¡A investigar! Using Geography and Climate Resources Online

LEARNING OBJECTIVES
By the end of the chapter you will be able to:
· Talk about likes, dislikes, pastimes and other activities in the present.
· Tell someone you address informally what to do.
· Express opinions, doubts and obligations.
· Talk about the weather and the seasons.
· Talk about who and what you know.
· Express future activities.
· Discuss typical leisure activities in the Hispanic world.

Actividades al aire libre*

1. las montañas
2. esquiar
3. ganar
COMPETENCIA INTERNACIONAL
4. el lago
5. patinar
6. acampar
7. el bosque
8. caminar
9. el valle
10. la granja
11. el campo
12. montar a caballo
13. montar en bicicleta
14. manejar
15. el río
16. pescar
17. el pez

© John Wiley & Sons, Inc.

1. mountains
2. to ski
3. to win
4. lake
5. to skate
6. to camp
7. forest
8. to walk
9. valley
10. farm
11. field, countryside
12. to ride horseback/go horseback riding
13. to ride a bicycle
14. to drive
15. river
16. to fish
17. fish (living); **los peces** *(pl.)*
18. beach
19. island
20. to rest
21. to go by boat/ship
22. sea
23. to swim
24. to snorkel
25. to sunbathe
26. to eat
27. to drink
28. sand
29. to run
30. to play volleyball
31. to play, go out for sports
32. ball
33. to lift weights
34. to read
35. much, a lot
36. little, not much
37. to write
38. to draw
39. to paint (a painting)

18. la playa
20. descansar
19. la isla
¡Me encanta el mar!**
21. ir en barco
22. el mar
23. nadar
24. bucear
32. la pelota
31. practicar deportes
30. jugar al vólibol
29. correr
28. la arena
27. beber
26. comer
25. tomar el sol
No, leo ³⁶**poco**.
Y tú, ¿lees ³⁵**mucho**?
33. levantar pesas
PARQUE BUENAVISTA
39. pintar (un cuadro)
38. dibujar
34. leer
37. escribir

*Actividades al aire libre *Outdoor activities*
**¡Me encanta el mar! *I love the sea!*

You may use the PowerPoint slides of all scenes to present and practice the vocabulary.

¡La pronunciación!

Pay attention to the correct pronunciation of the Spanish que and qui combinations (see P-4).

bosque   esquiar

¡En acción!

For additional vocabulary practice, see PowerPoint slides on BCS and in *WileyPLUS*.

4-1 Students may complete the activity individually or in pairs, with answers reviewed by the instructor. As students provide responses, you may use the PowerPoint slide of the opener scene to point out each activity mentioned.

4-1 ¿Se puede o no?

Indicate whether the following activities can or cannot take place in each of the locations mentioned. If the response is negative, say what activities can be done there. Use the scene on pages 108–109 as a guide.

MODELO

Sí	No	
☐	☑	En las montañas se puede bucear.

No, no se puede bucear. Se puede esquiar y acampar.

Sí	No	
☑	☐	**1.** En el bosque, se puede caminar.
☐	☑	**2.** En el río, se puede montar en bicicleta.
☐	☑	**3.** En el mar, se puede jugar al tenis.
☐	☑	**4.** En la playa, se puede patinar.
☐	☑	**5.** En la isla, se puede manejar.
☐	☑	**6.** En el Parque Buenavista, se puede pescar.

Palabras útiles

Se puede... *You can/ One can...*

No se puede... *You cannot/ One cannot...*

For additional practice on this grammar point, see PowerPoint slides on BCS and in *WileyPLUS*.

De paso

The **preposition por,** when expressing spatial relationships, means *across, through, along, around*.

El río pasa **por** el bosque. *The river passes **through** the forest.*
Todos los días caminamos **por** la playa. *Every day we walk **along** the beach.*
Patinan **por** el lago. *They skate **around/ across** the lake.*

¿SABES QUE...?

Spain currently has several outstanding sports figures including **Fernando Alonso**, two-time world champion in Formula One; **Alberto Contador**, winner of several Tour de France, Giro d'Italia and Vuelta a España bicycle races and considered the best climber and stage racer in the world; the basketball player **Pau Gasol** has won two NBA championships with the Lakers, in 2009 and 2010; tennis player **Rafael Nadal** (see p. 133) and last but not least; mountain climber **Edurne Pasabán** (see p. 141).

4-2 After students complete *Actividad 4-2*, you may want to project the PowerPoint slides of the opener scene and ask the class to describe it, one section at a time.

4-2 PERSONALIZED QUESTIONS: ¿Qué haces cuando vas a las montañas? ¿Y cuando estás en la playa?

4-2 Actividades al aire libre

What is happening in the scene on pages 108–109? To find out, work with your partner to answer the questions.

En las montañas

1. ¿Quién gana la competencia, la esquiadora[1] número 9 o el esquiador número 3?

2. ¿Qué se puede hacer[2] en el lago?

3. ¿Dónde acampan unas personas?

4. ¿Cuántas personas caminan por el bosque?

[1]skier (*f*), [2]to do

5. ¿Quién monta a caballo, un hombre o una mujer?

6. ¿Pasa el río por el bosque o por la granja? ¿Quién pesca en el río? ¿Hay muchos peces?

7. ¿Cuántas chicas montan en bicicleta?

8. ¿Maneja bien el joven? ¿De qué color es su carro?

En la playa

9. ¿Cuántas islas hay en el mar? ¿Quién descansa en la hamaca?

10. Según la escena, ¿qué se puede hacer en el mar? ¿Qué dice la persona del barco?

11. ¿Qué deporte practican los jóvenes en la playa? ¿Qué usan para jugar?

12. ¿Qué más se puede hacer en la playa? ¿Y qué se puede hacer en el Parque Buenavista?

De paso

Note how **the verb jugar** changes **u** to **ue** in all persons except **nosotros/as** and **vosotros/as**.

j**ue**go, j**ue**gas, j**ue**ga, jugamos, jugáis, j**ue**gan

¿**Juegan** Uds. al tenis? No, **jugamos** al béisbol.

Use **jugar** with these common sports: **jugar al...** básquetbol, béisbol, fútbol *(soccer)*, fútbol americano, golf, tenis, ping pong.

In some Latin American countries, **jugar** is used without the **a: Juego fútbol**.

 ## 4-3 ¿Mucho, poco o nunca?

Paso 1. How often do you take part in the activities presented in the scene on pages 108–109? Write down a minimum of *three* in each category. Then share the information with your partner using the present tense. Follow the model. All regular verbs (-*ar*, -*er* and -*ir*) use the ending **-o** for the present tense of *yo*.

Mucho	Poco	Nunca
manejar	*leer*	*escribir*

MODELO

manejar

E1: **Manejo** *mucho, pero* **leo** *poco y no* **escribo** *nunca.*

E2: *Pues, yo....*

 Paso 2. Which activities are the most popular? Share yours with the class and a student secretary will keep a tally on the board.

 ## ¡A escuchar! Las vacaciones de tres compañeros de trabajo

Paso 1. Listen to three teachers talking about their vacations.

PLUS Go to *WileyPLUS* to complete **Paso 2** of this listening activity.

Introduce **jugar** by asking students if they play a particular sport: **¿Juegas al tenis?**

At this time you may want to mention to your students that **jugar** is one of many stem-changing verbs, and as such, changes the **u** to **ue** in its stem (**jug-**) in the persons indicated. **Jugar** and other stem-changing verbs are formally introduced on p. 164.

For additional practice on this grammar point, see PowerPoint slides on BCS and in *WileyPLUS*.

4-3 Students are introduced here to the present tense *yo* form of -**er** and -**ir** verbs. It will be activated in the next scene.

4-3 As students volunteer their activities from the **Mucho** column, a student secretary jots them on the board, keeping track of those that are repeated. The class then determines the most popular activities. If time allows, do the same with the **Nunca** column to discover the least popular activities.

4-3 Remind students that when **Nunca** is placed after the verb, one needs to put *No* in front of the verb as in *No manejo nunca*. But *Nunca manejo*.

The scripts and recordings for the **¡A escuchar!** sections are included in the Book Companion Site (BCS) for instructors and in *WileyPLUS*.

Fabio, Ernesto y Mario están en el parque jugando al básquetbol.

For additional practice on this grammar point, see PowerPoint slides on BCS and in *WileyPLUS*.

Go to *WileyPLUS* to review this grammar point with the help of the **Animated Grammar Tutorial** and **Verb Conjugator**. For more practice, go to the **Grammar Handbook**.

To introduce students to the verb **gustar** used in context, have them take parts and read the **historieta** out loud. To check their comprehension and call their attention to the verb forms, ask the following questions:
1. **¿Qué deporte le gusta a Ernesto? ¿Y a Mario?**
2. **¿Qué otra actividad le gusta a Mario?**

To introduce **gustar**, write **Me gusta...** on the board. Tell students one activity that you like to do, for example **Me gusta jugar al tenis.** (Act it out.) Follow up by asking several students if they like to do the same: **¿Te gusta jugar al tenis?** Then test your students' memory by asking them to write on the board what persons in the class (and the instructor) like to do: **A Rosa le gusta jugar al tenis; a Luis le...**, etc.

Remind your students that with **gustar** the person to whom something is pleasing or displeasing is the recipient (the indirect object).

GRAMÁTICA

¡Manos a la obra!

1

• Expressing likes and dislikes: The verb *gustar*

The verb **gustar** does not function like other **-ar** verbs, and it also functions differently from the English *to like*. **Gustar** means *to be pleasing (to someone)*. The thing that is pleasing or displeasing (liked or disliked), which follows **gustar**, is the subject of the sentence, and so the verb agrees with it.

Let's look at examples based on Fabio, Ernesto, and Mario's conversation about sports.

> **Me gusta** el béisbol. *I like baseball. (Literally, Baseball is pleasing to me.)*
> ¿**Te gusta** el fútbol? *Do you like soccer? (Is soccer pleasing to you?)*

If the subject (the thing that is pleasing or displeasing) is plural—for instance, **los deportes**—the plural form of **gustar (gustan)** is used.

> **Me gustan** los deportes. *I like sports. (Sports are pleasing to me.)*

Person to whom something is pleasing		*gusta* or *gustan*	thing/s liked
me	*to me*		
te	*to you (fam.)*	+ **gusta**	+ **el** o **la** + *singular noun*
le	*to you (form.) him, her*	+ **gustan**	+ **los** o **las** + *plural noun*
nos	*to us*		
os	*to you (fam.)*		
les	*to you (form.), them*		

• To say one likes or does not like *to do something*, the singular form of **gustar (gusta)** + *one or more infinitives* is used:

> Nos **gusta correr** y **practicar** deportes.   *We like to run and play sports.*
> No les **gusta jugar** al vólibol.   *They do not like to play volleyball.*

(Note that **no** is used before **me, te, le,** etc.)

• As **le** and **les** have several meanings, the preposition **a** + *person* is often used to clarify:

> **A él** le gusta comer en el café.   *He likes to eat in the café.*
> **A Mario** le gusta correr.   *Mario likes to run.*

• Note how Spanish speakers express varying degrees of liking something:

> **Me gusta.**   **¡Me gusta mucho!**   **¡No me gusta nada!**
> *I like it.*   *I like it a lot!*   *I do not like it at all!*

...y algo más   The verb *encantar*

Similar to **gustar mucho,** the verb **encantar** means *to love* or *like a lot.*

A Ernesto **le encanta** jugar al béisbol.   *Ernesto loves to play baseball.*
Nos encantan las actividades al aire libre.   *We love outdoor activities.*
Me encantan mis* amigos.   *I love (like a lot) my friends.*

*After **gustar** and **encantar,** el/la/los/las may be replaced by a possessive adjective.

...y algo más   Emphasizing who likes something: *a mí, a ti, a él,* etc.

To emphasize the person who likes or does not like to do something, the following is used in front of the verb forms of **gustar** or **encantar.**

a mí	**a nosotros/as**
a ti	**a vosotros/as**
a él, a ella, a Ud.	**a ellos, a ellas, a Uds.**

A mí no me gusta levantar pesas.   *I do not like to lift weights.*
A ella sí le gusta.   *She does (like to lift weights).*

¡En acción!

¡Oye!   Los lugares¹ que me gustan o me encantan

Listen as your instructor tells you about some of the geographical places he/she likes and what he/she likes to do there. Then respond **sí** or **no** to the options that follow.

4-4   ¿A quiénes les gusta?

In order to know who likes what, first, complete each bubble with **me, te, le, nos,** or **les** as appropriate. Then match each bubble to the person/s saying it or thinking it (illustrations a-d).

1. A mi esposa <u>le</u> encanta el mar.

2. ¡A mí <u>me</u> encanta montar en bicicleta! ¿Y a ti <u>te</u> gusta?

3. A nosostros siempre <u>nos</u> gusta acampar aquí, ¿verdad?

4. A los jóvenes <u>les</u> gusta charlar.

© John Wiley & Sons, Inc

3. **a.**

4. **b.**

2. **c.**

1. **d.**

¹places

For additional practice on these grammar points, see PowerPoint slides on BCS and in *WileyPLUS*.

For more practice, see Grammar Handbook found in *WileyPLUS*.

Guión para ¡Oye!
1. Soy una persona muy aventurera. Me encantan las playas de Hawái porque me gusta nadar, bucear, hacer surf y tomar el sol.
2. **Me gustan** los bosques y lagos de Minnesota porque me encanta acampar, pescar e ir en canoa.
3. También **me gustan** las montañas de Utah y Colorado porque me encanta esquiar y hacer *snowboard.*

Write on the board:
aventurero/a *adventurous;* **canoa** (*draw a canoe on a lake*). Feel free to change some of the locations. Act out as many of the activities as possible!

Comprensión para ¡Oye!
¿Sí o no?
1. **En las playas de Hawái...**
me gusta nadar y bucear. ¿Sí o no? ¡*Sí*!
me gusta esquiar y hacer *snowboard.* ¡*No*!
me gusta hacer surf y tomar el sol. ¡*Sí*!
2. **En los bosques y lagos de Minnesota...**
me encanta bucear y tomar el sol. ¡*No*!
me encanta acampar y pescar. ¡*Sí*!
me encanta ir en canoa. ¡*Sí*!
3. **En las montañas de Utah y Colorado...**
me gusta hacer surf. ¡*No*!
me gusta esquiar y hacer *snowboard.* ¡*Sí*!
me gusta tomar el sol. ¡*No*!

¡Oye! Add a brief follow-up by asking who in the class likes to do several of the activities mentioned:
¿A quién le gusta acampar? Students indicate their preference with a show of hands and a verbal reply: **¡A mí! ¡A mí, no!** Tally the totals and write them on the board: A X estudiantes **les gusta/ no les gusta acampar,** etc.

4-5 Remind your students that the verb stays singular even if the subject consists of multiple infinitive verbs. **Me gusta pintar, leer y escribir.**

4-5 ¿Te gusta o no?

Paso 1. What are your partner's preferences? Look at the drawing on pages 108–109 and tell him/her at least *six* things you like or love to do and *two* that you do not like to do. Take turns asking and responding.

MODELO

E1: *Me gusta esquiar. ¿Y a ti?*

E2: *A mí me gusta esquiar también. Y además, me encanta patinar.*

o: *No me gusta esquiar, pero me gusta patinar.*

> **Palabras útiles**
> además *in addition*

Paso 2. Now share with the class at least one thing you both like to do and one that you do not: *A... y a mí nos gusta correr. / No nos gusta...*

4-6 Las vacaciones de los ricos y famosos

Paso 1. The host of the talk show **Miércoles Magnífico** is interviewing movie stars, comedians, and musicians about their vacation preferences. You and your partner will play the roles of the host and one celebrity of your choice. If you cannot think of one, you can pick one of the options below. The talk show host asks the questions in the first column, the celebrity responds following the cues in the second column, and the host writes down the information in the third column. Take turns playing host and celebrity.

(Before beginning, identify which celebrity you are.)

MODELO

Soy Javier Bardem.

4-6 If you wish to personalize the activity, have students working in pairs ask each other the questions in the chart.

> **Palabras útiles**
> hacer *to do*
> durante *during*

Preguntas	Respuestas	Información
1. Javier, ¿adónde **te gusta** ir de vacaciones para escaparte de los paparazzi?	*Me gusta ir a...*	*A Javier Bardem le gusta ir de vacaciones a...*
2. ¿Con quién **te gusta** ir?	*Me gusta ir con...*	*Le gusta ir con...*
3. ¿Qué **les gusta** hacer a Uds. durante las vacaciones?	*Nos gusta...*	*A él y a su/s... les gusta...*

Paso 2. Each talk-show host shares **(a)** the identity of the famous person interviewed and **(b)** his/her likes and dislikes. The audience (the class) then determines what the most popular vacation spots and activities of the rich and famous might be.

> **Javier Bardem**, actor español
>
> **Zoe Saldana**, actriz de padre dominicano y madre puertorriqueña
>
> **Juanes**, cantante colombiano
>
> **Salma Hayek**, actriz mexicana
>
> **Penélope Cruz**, actriz española
>
> **Marc Anthony**, cantante de padres puertorriqueños
>
> **Sofía Vergara**, actriz colombiana
>
> **George López**, cómico mexicano-americano

Después de jugar al básquetbol, Ernesto, Mario y Fabio van a un café.

A ver,[1] ¿qué **bebemos**?
Una Coca-Cola para mí.
Y para mí.

Tres Cocas, por favor. Invito yo.
Gracias, Mario.
¡Gracias!
De nada.

¡Es estupendo, Ernesto! **¡Vives**[2] al lado de un campo de béisbol!
Sí, **vivo** enfrente del Parque Buenavista.

¡Ah sí! A Jennifer le encanta ese parque. Allí su hija **aprende**[3] a jugar al vólibol y Jennifer **lee** novelas y **escribe** su tarea.
A veces mi amigo y yo **corremos** por allí. Es muy grande.

© John Wiley & Sons, Inc

GRAMÁTICA

¡Manos a la obra!

2

Talking about the present: Regular -er and -ir verbs

All verbs in Spanish fall into three categories: verbs with infinitives ending in **-ar,** verbs ending in **-er,** and those ending in **-ir.** You have already learned the present tense of **-ar** ending verbs. Those ending in **-er** and **-ir** follow the same pattern, i.e., they drop the infinitive ending and add the endings shown below.

leer *to read*	**escribir** *to write*
leer → le + *endings*	**escribir → escrib** + *endings*
(yo) le**o**	escrib**o**
(tú) le**es**	escrib**es**
(Ud., él, ella) le**e**	escrib**e**
(nosotros/as) le**emos**	escrib**imos**
(vosotros/as) le**éis**	escrib**ís**
(Uds., ellos/as) le**en**	escrib**en**

Let's look at examples based on Jennifer's activities in the **park.**

—Jennifer, **¿lees y escribes** mucho en el parque? Sí, **leo** novelas y **escribo.**

Note that the endings are the same for both **-er** and **-ir** verbs, except for the **nosotros** and the **vosotros** forms.

. . . y algo más   *Tú* affirmative commands of -er and -ir verbs

As with **-ar** verbs, the **tú** affirmative commands of **-er** and **-ir** verbs are formed by dropping the "s" in the **tú** form of the present tense.

Tú lees y escribes poco → lees y escribes. → Por favor, **¡lee** y **escribe** más!

---

[1]**A...** Let's see, [2](you) live, [3]learns

To introduce students to -*er* and -*ir* verbs used in context, have them take parts and read the **historieta** out loud. To check their comprehension and call their attention to the verb forms, ask the following questions:
1. ¿Qué aprende la hija de Jennifer en el parque?
2. ¿Qué hacen Mario y su amigo allí?

PLUS Go to *WileyPLUS* to review these grammar points with the help of the **Animated Grammar Tutorial** and **Verb Conjugator.** For more practice, go to the **Grammar Handbook.**

For additional practice on these grammar points, see PowerPoint slides on BCS and in *WileyPLUS*.

Present -er and -ir verbs by writing model verbs on the board with endings highlighted.

Have the class stand in a circle. State a model sentence (Leo novelas románticas.), then call out a subject pronoun (ellos,...) and tap a student on the shoulder. He/She restates the sentence (Leen novelas románticas.), provides a different subject pronoun (tú,...), and taps another student on the shoulder. After five or six rounds, provide another model sentence. Encourage students to keep a fast pace!

Remind your students that chapter 6 will include a summary of all affirmative commands.

MÁS VERBOS EN -ER, -IR

You learned five **-er** and **-ir** verbs in the first scene. Here are some others:

aprender	to learn	deber (+ infinitive)	should/ must/ ought to (do something)
aprender (+ a + *infinitive*)	to learn how to do something	compartir	to share (something)
creer	to believe (something)	vivir	to live
creer (+ que + clause)	to believe/ think (that)		

WILEY PLUS For more practice, see **Grammar Handbook** found in *WileyPLUS*.

For additional practice on this grammar point, see PowerPoint slides on BCS and in *WileyPLUS*.

¡Oye! Write on the board: dibujen *draw*; tiburón *shark* (*or draw a shark*). Read each statement slowly, followed by a pause to allow time for drawing.

Guión para ¡Oye!
1. Dibujen el mar y mucha arena.
2. Una señora corre por la arena.
3. Otra señora toma el sol y su esposo lee una novela.
4. Un niño come una banana.
5. Dos niñas comparten un sándwich.
6. Un joven bebe una limonada.
7. Dos niños juegan al vólibol.
8. Dos personas nadan en el mar.
9. Un grupo de amigos va en barco.
10. ¡Qué horror! ¡Creo que hay un tiburón en el mar! Dibujen un tiburón grande. **Finalmente, escriban su nombre en el cuadro.**

At the conclusion of the *¡Oye!* activity, divide the class into groups of four and have students take turns describing activities in their drawings.

4-7 First, review with the class the **nosotros** form of each verb, contrasting the endings of **-ar**, **-er**, and **-ir** verbs. Student then complete the activity individually, prior to sharing information with a partner or the class.

. . . y algo más   Uses of *creer, deber, aprender*

The verbs **creer**, **deber**, and **aprender** are useful to . . .

- express an opinion: **creer que...**

  Reportero: ¿**Crees que** el fútbol es un deporte divertido?
  Aficionado: Yo **creo que** sí, pero mis amigos **creen que** no.

- express duty and obligation: **deber +** *infinitive*

  Madre: Hijo, **debes** estudiar más. Tu maestro dice que eres perezoso.
  Hijo: Sí, es verdad, mamá. **Debo** estudiar todos los días.

- indicate that one learns to do something: **aprender a +** *infinitive*

  Profesor: ¿Qué **aprendes** en la clase de la profesora Navarro?
  Estudiante: **Aprendo a hablar** y **a escribir** español.

¡En acción!

¡Oye! Un día en la playa

How artistic are you? On a sheet of paper, draw the beach scene that your instructor describes.

4-7 En la playa RECYCLES -ar verbs.

When you go to the beach or to a picnic with your family or friends, do you do the following? If you do, check **Sí** and jot down with whom you do it. If not, check **No**. Then tell the class what you do there and what you don't do. Use the **nosotros** form of the verb.

MODELO

Persona/s	Sí	No	
Mi primo y yo...	☑	☐	bucear en el mar.

Sí, mi primo y yo **buceamos** *en el mar.*

Persona/s	Sí	No	
1. _____ y yo...	☐	☐	*nadar* en el mar
2. _____ y yo...	☐	☐	*leer* novelas
3. _____ y yo...	☐	☐	*comer* sándwiches y *beber* Coca-Cola
4. _____ y yo...	☐	☐	*jugar* al fútbol y *correr* por la playa
5. _____ y yo...	☐	☐	*tomar* el sol y *compartir* el protector solar
6. _____ y yo...	☐	☐	*escribir* poemas
7. _____ y yo...	☐	☐	*aprender* a hacer surf

4-8 Actividades del fin de semana

Paso 1. In groups of *four*, find out how popular the following activities are among your classmates. When everyone has answered all the questions, a secretary, with the help of the group, records the names of the persons and what they answered. Follow the model.

MODELO

E1:   *Los fines de semana, ¿**corres** por el parque?*

E2:   *Sí, (No, no) **corro** por el parque. ¿Y tú?* (**E2** asks **E3,** and so on).

The secretary, records: *John **corre**…; Liz, no **corre**…; …*

Los fines de semana, …	
1. ¿**corres** por el parque?	4. ¿**lees** libros?
2. ¿**escribes** mensajes en Facebook?	5. ¿**vas** al cine o al centro comercial?
3. ¿**comes** en un restaurante?	6. ¿**aprendes** a bailar salsa?

Paso 2. Now answer your instructor's question **¿Qué saben de sus compañeros?** and provide your feedback regarding students' weekend activities. Each group takes turns answering his/her questions. Follow the model.

MODELO

¿Qué saben de sus compañeros?

Profesor/a: *¿**Corren** los estudiantes por el parque los fines de semana?*

Grupo 1:   *Creemos que sí porque en nuestro grupo tres estudiantes **corren** por el parque.*

o: *Creemos que no porque en nuestro grupo nadie/ casi nadie corre por el parque.*

4-9 Anuncios para estudiantes   RECYCLES **ser** and **-ar** verbs.

Paso 1. Native speakers of Spanish at *Con Brío University* often introduce themselves by posting ads on the bulletin board. Complete the following personal ads as if you were the person/s in the ads. Use the verbs given.

1. Federico y Ricardo

Somos salvadoreños. _Somos_ muy responsables y estudiosos. _Leemos_ muchos libros y no _practicamos_ deportes. A Federico le _gustan_ sus catorce perros y a mí, mis veinte gatos. Nosotros dos _compartimos_ el amor por los animales.

compartir, gustar, leer, practicar, ser

Gary Conner/PhotoEdit

2. Miranda

Soy dominicana. _Tengo_ veintitrés años. Mi familia _vive_ en el Caribe. Cuando yo _estoy_ allí, _practico_ toda clase de deportes. _Corro_ cinco kilómetros por la playa todos los días y _nado_ en el mar. Me _gusta_ ir a la playa y tomar el sol. Yo _creo_ que soy muy afortunada.

correr, creer, estar, gustar, nadar, practicar, ser, tener, vivir

Purestock/Getty Images

3. Ángela

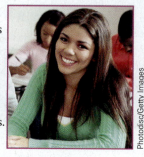

Soy venezolana. _Hablo_ inglés muy bien y _soy_ un poco introvertida. _Leo_ muchas novelas, especialmente las románticas. También _pinto_ cuadros. _Paso_ mucho tiempo con mi familia y con mis amigos. Y me _encantan_ los animales.

encantar, hablar, leer, pasar, pintar, ser (use it twice)

Photodisc/Getty Images

Paso 2. Now Federico, Ricardo, Miranda and Angela want you to participate in their favorite activities. Fill in the bubbles with the most likely suggestions they would give you, based on what they like. Use the affirmative **tú** commands of the following verbs:

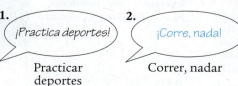

1. ¡Practica deportes!
Practicar deportes

2. ¡Corre, nada!
Correr, nadar

3. ¡Pinta, pasa tiempo con la familia!
Pintar, pasar tiempo con la familia

Palabras útiles
nadie *no one, nobody*
la mayoría *the majority*

4-8 In preparation for the introduction of the verb **saber** in ch. 4, the question **¿Qué sabes de…**will appear often so students become familiar with this use of the verb **saber**.

4-9 Students may complete the ads individually or in pairs, with answers reviewed by the instructor. To review responses, ask three students to read the ads for the class.

4-9 When students have finished, ask the class to determine whether Ángela or Miranda would be the more compatible friend to Federico and Ricardo. Students defend their opinions: **A Miranda/ Ángela (no) le gusta…**

WILEY PLUS Go to *WileyPLUS* to see the video related to this reading.

For an additional activity related to this cultural theme, see the PowerPoint slides on BCS and in *WileyPLUS*.

Meets ACTFL Standards 1.2, interpretive reading; 2.1, cultural practices; 2.2, cultural products; and 4.2, cultural comparisons.

¿SABES QUE...?

The Spanish World Cup victory has helped place the name of Spain on the map. Their victory has also been one of the best forms of publicity concerning tourism and business opportunities. Since winning the World Cup, Spain has received a record number of tourists. There is also increased demand to learn Spanish, the language of the 2010 World Cup Champions!

Tu mundo cultural

Dos deportes nacionales: el fútbol y...

En tu país, ¿cuál es el deporte más popular? Sin duda alguna, el fútbol es el deporte más popular en todo el mundo hispano, excepto en el área del Caribe, donde hay más afición al béisbol. Los dos se pueden practicar durante todo el año y en casi todos los climas de los países hispanos.

Photo by Simon Bruty/Sports Illustrated/Getty Images

El equipo[1] de la selección española celebrando su triunfo de campeón del mundo de fútbol en Sudáfrica, después de ganar a Holanda, en julio de 2010.

Cada[2] cuatro años, se celebra la Copa Mundial de Fútbol, donde los equipos de gran número de países hispanos son los favoritos. El día de la victoria española en Sudáfrica, la cantante colombiana Shakira cantó la canción oficial llamada "Waka Waka"(Esto es África). El próximo campeonato va a ser en Brasil, en el año 2014.

Cuando hay partidos importantes, la vida en los países hispanos se paraliza y en la calle, en casa y en los bares, se escuchan gritos[3] de ¡¡¡gol!!! Después del partido, los hinchas[4] o aficionados salen[5] a la calle para celebrar con entusiasmo la victoria de su equipo.

AP/Wide World Photos

Lionel Messi (Rosario, Argentina, 1987) es el mejor jugador del mundo de la generación actual. Juega para el Fútbol Club Barcelona, familiarmente conocido como "El Barça".

Los equipos de fútbol (1–6) de Argentina, Chile, Honduras, México, Paraguay y Uruguay.

Photos: (tl) ©AP/Wide World Photos; (tlc) © KIMIMASA MAYAMA/epa/Corbis; (trc) Andy Mead/YCJ/Icon SMI/© Corbis; (tr) © Kelley L. Cox/ISiphotos.com/Corbis; (bl) © Catherine Ivil/AMA/Corbis; (br) © Sampics/Corbis

[1]team, [2]Each, [3]shouts, [4]fans, [5]go out

... el béisbol.

Paul A. Souders/© Corbis

Niños panameños aficionados al béisbol. En los países hispanos del Caribe, el béisbol es más popular que el fútbol. Allí, el sueño[1] de muchos niños es ser jugadores de un equipo estadounidense.

© Greg Nelson/Sports Illustrated/ Getty Images

Albert Pujols, de República Dominicana (Saint Louis Cardinals)

Getty Images

Aramis Ramírez, de República Dominicana (Chicago Cubs)

Tom DiPace/Sports Illustrated/ Getty Images

Carlos Beltrán, de Puerto Rico (New York Mets)

Rob Tringali/Getty Images

Edgar Rentería, de Colombia (Cincinnati Reds)

MLB Photos via Getty Images

Francisco Rodríguez, de Venezuela (Los Angeles Angels)

Photo by Robbie Rogers/ MLB Photos via Getty Images

Mariano Rivera, de Panamá (New York Yankees)

Estas fotos son de unos pocos de los muchos jugadores de béisbol hispanos que juegan en los equipos de las Grandes Ligas de EE. UU.

¿Qué aprendiste?

1. ¿Cuáles son los deportes más populares entre los hispanos?
   el fútbol y el béisbol
2. ¿Qué evento futbolístico importante ocurre cada cuatro años?
   la Copa Mundial de fútbol
3. ¿Cuál es el sueño de muchos niños hispanos que juegan al béisbol?
   ser jugadores de un equipo estadounidense

Actividad cultural

In groups of *three*, browse through the ¿Sabes que...? notes on the pages of this chapter and summarize the information you have gathered about other successful Hispanic stars in the world of sports.

Contraste cultural

If you were to introduce a Hispanic to the sports culture of the US, which sports would you focus on, and to which sports events would you take him/her? In groups of *three*, discuss this topic in English.

[1]dream

2 Diversiones con la familia y amigos

WILEY PLUS

Pronunciación: Practice pronunciation of the chapter's new vocabulary in *WileyPLUS*.

A

1. salir de paseo/ dar un paseo
2. escuchar (música)

Guadalupe, Carmen y Pachá

B

¡Con brío, Ángel!
4. dar fiestas   3. bailar

Dolores Toledo, Ángel y sus amigos

C

5. cantar
La La La
6. tocar (la guitarra)
7. hacer ejercicio

Ángel y Guadalupe

D

9. pasar el tiempo (con la familia)
8. ver la televisión

Don Claudio y doña Rosa con los nietos

E

11. el partido de fútbol
10. el equipo   12. mirar

Lino, su equipo de fútbol y su familia

F

CENTRO COMERCIAL
13. ir de compras

Fátima y Mª Luisa

G

CONCIERTO Y EXPOSICIÓN DE ARTE
14. asistir a
© John Wiley & Sons, Inc

Álvaro y su novia

H

15. mandar y recibir mensajes electrónicos/e-mails
16. navegar por la Red

Carmen Roldán

I

18. hacer un viaje (al campo/a la ciudad)
17. viajar
OAXACA
19. disfrutar de (las vacaciones)

Los Roldán

---

1. to take a walk/ stroll 2. to listen to (music) 3. to dance 4. to give/ throw parties 5. to sing 6. to play (the guitar) 7. to exercise 8. to watch TV 9. to spend time (with the family) 10. the team 11. the soccer game 12. to look at, watch 13. to go shopping 14. to attend 15. to send and receive e-mail messages 16. to surf the Web 17. to travel 18. to take a trip (to the country/ to the city) 19. to enjoy (the vacation)

¡En acción!

 For additional vocabulary practice, see PowerPoint slides on BCS and in *WileyPLUS*.

 4-10 Distintas aficiones

People enjoy their free time in different ways. Observe the scenes on page 120. Then read the situation in the first column to your partner, who will choose the statement in the second that corresponds to it. Take turns.

4-10 *Option:* Students complete the activity individually, then check their answers in pairs.

Students may be interested in knowing that the term *e-mail* is now used in most Spanish-speaking countries, and that it already appears in many dictionaries. It's also known as *correo electrónico* or *mensaje electrónico*.

1. Guadalupe, Carmen y Pachá salen de paseo. h.

2. Dolores Toledo, Ángel y sus amigos dan una fiesta. e.

3. Guadalupe hace ejercicio. a.

4. Ángel canta y toca la guitarra. c.

5. Don Claudio y doña Rosa pasan el tiempo con sus nietos. b.

6. Lino y su familia miran un partido de fútbol. d.

7. Carmen Roldán navega por la Red y manda y recibe *e-mails*. g.

8. Los Roldán hacen un viaje en carro. f.

a. Le gusta estar delgada y en buena forma.

b. Les encanta estar con la familia.

c. Tiene afición a la música.

d. Observan a dos grupos de jugadores que corren detrás de una pelota.

e. Escuchan música y bailan.

f. Disfrutan de las vacaciones.

g. Está informándose y comunicándose gracias a la computadora.

h. Les gusta caminar por el parque.

 4-11 Diversiones con la familia y amigos

How do the Roldán family and their friends spend their free time? Find out by observing the scenes on page 120. Work with your partner to answer the questions.

1. ¿Quiénes salen de paseo? ¿Qué escuchan Guadalupe y Carmen?

2. ¿A quién le gusta dar fiestas? ¿Quiénes bailan?

3. ¿Cuál es la diversión favorita de Ángel? ¿Y de Guadalupe?

4. ¿A quiénes les gusta pasar el tiempo con los nietos y ver la televisión?

5. ¿Quiénes juegan al fútbol? ¿Hay muchos aficionados que miran el partido?

6. ¿Adónde van de compras Fátima y Mª Luisa en su tiempo libre?

7. ¿Con quién está Álvaro? ¿A qué asisten?

8. ¿Cuáles son las diversiones favoritas de Carmen cuando está en casa?

9. ¿A quiénes les gusta viajar? ¿Hacen un viaje al campo o a la ciudad?

4-11 After students complete the activity, you may want to project the PowerPoint slides of the scenes and have students describe each one.

4-11 PERSONALIZED QUESTIONS: ¿Qué te gusta más, escuchar música o bailar? ¿Hacer ejercicio o ir de compras? ¿Ver la televisión o navegar por la Red? ¿Viajar o estar en casa? Ask several students each question and add other combinations.

4-11 ANOTHER STEP: Have students take turns describing each scene and what the people are doing in it. E1 gives the information (**dónde están; cuántos hay; cómo son; qué hacen**), and then E2 guesses who is being described (**Es/ Son...**).

4-12 Mis pasatiempos favoritos   RECYCLES gustar.

Paso 1. How do you spend your free time? Jot down your *five* favorite pastimes, in order of importance. Use the vocabulary from the scenes on page 120 and the *Palabras útiles* as needed.

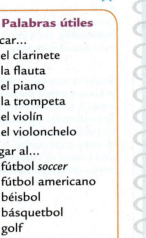

1. *Me gusta escuchar música.*

2.

3.

4.

5.

Paso 2. Walk around the classroom interviewing at least *five* classmates to find out if any of them share your interests: *¿Te gusta...?* Then report common interests to the class: *A... y a mí nos gusta escuchar música.*

¡A escuchar! Las diversiones: una encuesta

Paso 1. Listen to Pelayo's survey for his Sociology class. His assignment is to uncover the favorite pastimes of three different age groups.

PLUS Go to *WileyPLUS* to complete **Paso 2** of this listening activity.

Fabio llama a Ernesto para preguntarle si quiere ir al cine con Mario y con él.

[1]**asientos...** free seats

¡Manos a la obra!

3

Talking about activities in the present: Verbs with an irregular *yo* form

You have learned the present tense of *regular* verbs—those that follow a consistent pattern. The following nine verbs are *irregular* in the first-person **(yo)** form.

hacer *to do, make*		**poner** *to put, place*		**salir** *to leave, go out*	
hago	hacemos	**pongo**	ponemos	**salgo**	salimos
haces	hacéis	pones	ponéis	sales	salís
hace	hacen	pone	ponen	sale	salen

traer *to bring*		**oír** *to hear*		**decir** *to say, tell*	
traigo	traemos	**oigo**	oímos	**digo**	decimos
traes	traéis	oyes	oís	dices	decís
trae	traen	oye	oyen	dice	dicen

venir *to come*		**dar** *to give*		**ver** *to see*	
vengo	venimos	**doy**	damos	**veo**	vemos
v**ie**nes	venís	das	dais *(no accent)*	ves	veis *(no accent)*
v**ie**ne	v**ie**nen	da	dan	ve	ven

- There are seven verbs with **yo** forms that end in **–go** (often called "yo-go" verbs).
- Observe the uses of **salir** with examples based on the plans Fabio, Mario, and Ernesto make for the evening.

    salir de... *to exit/ leave a certain place*   **salir con...** *to go out with*

    Ernesto **sale de** casa y va al cine.   Fabio va a **salir con** Ernesto y Mario.

- Note that **oír** changes **i** to **y** in three persons;
- Note that **decir** changes **e** to **i** in four persons.
- **Dar** (**doy, das, ...**) is similar to **ir** (**voy, vas, ...**).
- **Venir** (**vengo, vienes**, ...) is similar to **tener** (**tengo, tienes**, ...).

. . . y algo más   *Tú affirmative commands for decir, hacer, poner, salir and venir*

Affirmative **tú** commands for **decir, hacer, poner, salir** and **venir** are irregular, but easy to remember because they consist of just one syllable: **di, haz, pon, sal** and **ven.**

   ¡**Di** la verdad[1]! ¡**Haz** ejercicio! ¡**Pon** tu chaqueta aquí! ¡**Sal** de paseo! ¡**Ven** al cine!

[1]truth

For additional practice on these grammar points, see PowerPoint slides on BCS and in *WileyPLUS.*

WILEY PLUS Go to *WileyPLUS* to review these grammar points with the help of the **Animated Grammar Tutorial** and **Verb Conjugator.** For more practice, go to the **Grammar Handbook.**

To introduce students to the forms of these irregular *yo* form verbs used in context, have them take parts and read the **historieta** out loud. To check their comprehension and call their attention to the verb forms, ask the following questions:
1. ¿Qué hace Ernesto cuando llama Fabio?
2. ¿Con quiénes sale Ernesto esta noche?
3. ¿Dónde pone Fabio su chaqueta?

Using the irregular **yo** verbs, tell a student one activity you usually do, and ask if he/she does it as well: *Salgo* **con mi familia los fines de semana. ¿Y tú?** If the student answers affirmatively, tell the class **...y yo** salimos **con nuestras familias los fines de semana.** You may ask a second student the same question, and if both respond in the same way, say **...y...** salen **con sus familias los fines de semana.** *More examples:* **Hago ejercicio todos los días. Siempre traigo mis libros a clase. Doy fiestas con frecuencia. Veo la televisión todos los fines de semana.**

Remind your students that ch. 6 will include a summary of all affirmative commands.

¡En acción!

¡Oye! ¿Es introvertido/a o extrovertido/a?

You are looking for a roommate whose personality matches yours. Listen to what the following people say about themselves, and then determine, in your opinion, whether each one is an *introvert* or an *extrovert*. Later you will have the opportunity to choose your roommate.

4-13 Para ti, ¿es la amistad una prioridad?   RECYCLES possessive adjectives.

Paso 1.   Read the following statements and check **Sí** or **No** according to what you do.

Sí	No	
☐	☐	1. **Salgo** con mis amigos/as con mucha frecuencia.
☐	☐	2. Cuando los **oigo**[1] hablar de sus problemas, escucho con interés.
☐	☐	3. Cuando hablo con ellos/ ellas, siempre **digo** la verdad[2].
☐	☐	4. Muchas veces, **veo** las películas que a ellos les gustan.
☐	☐	5. **Pongo** sus fotos en Facebook.
☐	☐	6. A veces, no **vengo** a clase para estar con ellos.
☐	☐	7. **Traigo** mi celular a la universidad o *college* para mandarles mensajes.
☐	☐	8. Cuando están enfermos/as, **hago** cosas por ellos/ ellas.

Paso 2.   Your partner asks you if you do each activity, and after hearing all of your answers, determines if friendship is a priority for you. Then change roles.

MODELO

E1: ¿*Sales* con tus amigos/as con frecuencia?

E2: *Sí, (No, no)* **salgo** con mis amigos/as con frecuencia.

Conclusión: *Creo que para ti la amistad…* ☐ es una prioridad ☐ no es una prioridad.

4-14 Por la mañana

Paso 1.   Your instructor plays the role of Paco and describes what he does before going to work. Identify the number of the illustration that corresponds to the activity.

1

Las noticias de hoy…

2

3

© John Wiley & Sons, Inc

Paso 2.   Now take turns describing Paco's routine in sequential order, using the following verbs: **ver, hacer, poner**[3] **música, dar, desayunar, salir**. After you describe each scene, tell each other if you do or don't do those activities in the morning.

MODELO

E1: *Por la mañana, Paco ve las noticias en la tele. Yo también/no veo las noticias.*

[1]**los…** I hear them, [2]*truth*,
[3]**poner**, in addition to meaning to *put, place*, means *to turn on* (music, iPods, computers, lights, etc.)

4-15 ¿Por qué lo haces?

Paso 1. Look at the list of activities in the box in the margin and share with your partner which ones you do or don't do. Also indicate how often you do them (see vocabulary box on p. 82) and explain why. Follow the model.

MODELO

Hacer ejercicio

E1: **Hago** ejercicio con frecuencia porque creo que es importante.

E2: Pues, yo (no) **hago**…

For actions that your partner doesn't do and you consider worth doing, tell her/him to do it and give a reason. Use **tú** affirmative commands: **¡Haz** ejercicio! ¡Es importante!

Paso 2. Now share with the rest of the class one activity that both of you do or don't do and explain why.

Nosotros/as dos (no) hacemos ejercicio porque creemos que…

Palabras útiles
Creo que es …
necesario *necessary*/
bueno/ malo/
divertido

---

hacer ejercicio
oír el/la radio
poner música
venir tarde a clase
decir tonterías[1] con
frecuencia
traer el celular a clase
dar las gracias

Remind your students that ch. 6 will include a summary of all affirmative **tú** commands.

4-15 Suggested instructor-led questions for *Paso 2*: **¿Quién hace yoga todas las semanas?** Various students provide answers. If no one engages in a particular activity, introduce **Nadie…**

4-16 Lo que hacemos todas las semanas

RECYCLES regular verbs in the present tense.

Paso 1. What do your classmates do on a weekly basis? Find out by walking around the classroom and asking them questions. In each category, jot down the names of students who answer affirmatively. Work efficiently. You have *six* minutes.

MODELO

hacer yoga

E1: ¿**Haces** yoga todas las semanas?

E2: Sí, **hago** yoga todas las semanas.   **o:** No, no **hago** yoga todas las semanas.

Actividad	Nombre	Actividad	Nombre
1. *hacer* yoga		6. *dar* fiestas	
2. *ir* de compras		7. *tocar* un instrumento (piano, guitarra,…)	
3. *salir* con tus amigos/as		8. *practicar* un deporte ¿cuál?	
4. *asistir* a un concierto		9. *limpiar* tu casa o apartamento	
5. *ver* un DVD en casa o una película[2] en el cine		10. *oír* las noticias en la radio o *ver* las noticias en la televisión	

Paso 2. Now, answer your instructor's question **¿Qué sabes de las actividades semanales de tus compañeros?** according to the information you have gathered.

4-16 In preparation for the introduction of the verb **saber** in ch. 4, the question **¿Qué sabes de…**will appear often so students become familiar with this use of the verb **saber**.

4-17 ¿Qué haces los sábados?

Write down all of the activities that you typically do on Saturdays. Your instructor will set a time limit. Then read your responses to a classmate, and count your activities. The student with the most activities wins and reads his/her list to the class.

MODELO

Profesor/a: ¿Qué haces los sábados?

Estudiante: Por la mañana, trabajo,…

4-17 Remind students that, as in English, when **hacer** is used in a question, it is only rarely used in the answer as well: ¿Qué **haces** los lunes por la noche? → **Hago** ejercicio y **hago** la tarea. In most cases, as in English, a different verb is used: ¿Qué **haces** los sábados? → **Trabajo, voy de compras,…**

[1]silly things, [2]movie

Meets ACTFL Standards 1.1, interpersonal speaking; 1.2, interpretive reading; 2.1, cultural practices; 2.2, cultural products; and 4.2, cultural comparisons

Tu mundo cultural

For an additional activity related to this cultural theme, see the PowerPoint slides on BCS and in *WileyPLUS*.

Un sábado entre[1] hispanos

Donde tú vives, ¿cuáles son las diversiones favoritas de la gente los fines de semana? ¿Sabes cuáles son las de muchos hispanos?

En general, los hispanos son gente[2] muy sociable y sus diversiones favoritas con frecuencia incluyen a la familia y a los amigos. La mayoría vive en países con climas no demasiado extremos. Por eso, muchas de sus actividades tienen lugar[3] en la calle.

Es la hora de salir de paseo

Paseo de Pereda, Santander, España. El paseo es una de las actividades preferidas de los españoles. A diversas horas del día, y en especial, los fines de semana, en las calles principales de los pueblos y ciudades de España se observa a niños, jóvenes y mayores que salen de paseo. En muchas partes de Latinoamérica a la gente también le gusta salir a la calle y pasear, incluso por la noche.

Courtesy Conchita Lucas

Es la hora de tomar un café

© Yadid Levy/Getty Images

Tomar un café es siempre una buena excusa para charlar con familiares y amigos a cualquier hora del día. Los cafés al aire libre tienen una larga tradición en los países hispanos. El café de los países hispanos es fuerte, por eso normalmente uno es suficiente y no se repite. También, al contrario de lo que ocurre en EE. UU., no es frecuente ver a la gente bebiendo café por los pasillos, por la calle o en el carro.

© FogStock Collection/Age Fotostock America, Inc.

En algunos países hispanos, los jóvenes frecuentan los cibercafés o cafés Internet para conectarse a la Red y tomarse un café o un refresco[4]. Allí pasan horas «chateando» con amigos y familiares.

[1]among, [2]people, [3]tienen... take place, [4]soft drink

Es la hora de ir al baile

Courtesy Bettina Bolger

El baile tiene una larga tradición en el mundo hispano. Los fines de semana, por la noche, las discotecas y salas de baile se llenan de jóvenes y mayores. Los ritmos del Caribe, como la salsa, la cumbia o el merengue, son los favoritos. Los bailes latinos son cada vez más populares entre los estadounidenses.

 ## ¿Qué aprendiste?

1. ¿Con quiénes prefieren pasar los hispanos su tiempo libre?
   con la familia y los amigos
2. ¿Cuáles son algunas de las costumbres y diversiones favoritas de los hispanos? Descríbelas.
   salir de paseo, tomar un café, bailar…
3. ¿Qué bailes latinos son populares en EE. UU.?
   salsa, cumbia, merengue

¿SABES QUE…?

Have you seen Víctor Cruz, wide receiver for the New York Giants, dance a few salsa steps whenever he scores a touchdown? Of Puerto Rican and African-American descent, the New Jersey-raised athlete was even asked to perform his signature move while presenting an award at the 2012 Grammy ceremony. Cruz willingly obliged.

 ## Actividad cultural

Look at the map of the Hispanic world on the inside front cover of your book, and choose one city that both of you would like to visit. Imagine that you have just arrived there on a business trip, you have a Saturday free, and you would like to meet and chat with some Spanish-speaking people. Use the chart below to jot down at least *two* activities that you might like to do during each of the time periods listed.

Destino: _____

Por la mañana	*Nos gustaría… y también…*
Por la tarde	
Por la noche	

Share the information with two other classmates and/or with the class.

 ## Contraste cultural

In groups of *three*, discuss in English ways in which the leisure activities you have just read about are similar to or different from those of your culture.

Pronunciación: Practice pronunciation of the chapter's new vocabulary in *WileyPLUS*.

²¿Qué tal el clima? o ¿Qué tiempo hace?

3. la nieve

4. Nieva.

¿Te gusta hacer *snowboard*?

5. Hace (mucho) frío.

6. el invierno

7. Está (muy) nublado.

9. la lluvia

10. Llueve.

8. la nube

12. el pájaro

11. las flores

13. Hace (muy) buen/(muy) mal tiempo.

14. la primavera

20. la luna

21. las estrellas

15. Hace (mucho) sol.

16. el cielo

Hacer surf aquí es fantástico.

17. la ola

18. Hace (mucho) calor.

19. el verano

22. Hace (mucho) viento.

23. las hojas

24. el árbol

25. Hace fresco.

26. el otoño

© John Wiley & Sons, Inc

---

1. seasons 2. What is the weather like? 3. snow 4. It is snowing./ It snows. **nevar (ie)** to snow 5. It is (very) cold. 6. winter 7. It is (very) cloudy.
8. cloud 9. the rain 10. It is raining./ It rains. **llover (ue)** to rain 11. flowers 12. bird 13. The weather is (very) nice/ bad. 14. spring 15. It is (very) sunny; **sol** sun 16. sky 17. wave 18. It is (very) hot; **calor** heat. 19. summer 20. moon 21. stars 22. It is (very) windy; **viento** wind 23. leaves
24. tree 25. It is cool. 26. fall, autumn

¡En acción!

4-18 Las estaciones

 Paso 1. Identify the season that corresponds to each description.

> el invierno   la primavera   el verano   el otoño

1. Se puede esquiar y hacer *snowboard*.
2. Se juega al fútbol americano.
3. Se juega al béisbol.
4. Hace sol y se puede nadar en el mar.
5. Hace mucho frío y hay nieve.
6. Hace calor y los pájaros cantan.
7. Hace fresco y viento, y las hojas cambian[1] de color.
8. Llueve y hay muchas flores.

 Paso 2. Ask your partner which season is his/her favorite (*¿Cuál es tu estación favorita?*) and why. Then participate in a class poll to determine your classmates' preferences.

4-19 El clima y las estaciones

What is the weather like? To find out, observe the scenes on page 128 and work with your partner to answer the questions.

El invierno

1. ¿Qué tal el clima? ¿Te gusta la nieve?
2. ¿Cuáles son algunas diversiones o actividades típicas del invierno?

La primavera

3. ¿Qué tal el clima? ¿Hay nubes en el cielo? ¿Te gusta la lluvia?
4. ¿De qué color son las flores? ¿Cuántos pájaros hay? ¿De qué color son?
5. En EE. UU., ¿qué se asocia con la primavera, el béisbol o el fútbol americano?

El verano

6. ¿Es un buen día para ir a la playa? ¿Por qué?
7. ¿Cuáles son algunas diversiones o actividades típicas del verano?
8. Cuando no está nublado, ¿qué observamos por la noche en el cielo?

El otoño

9. ¿Qué tiempo hace?
10. Donde tú vives, ¿se caen[2] las hojas de los árboles en otoño?
11. ¿Qué hacen las dos chicas? Y tú, ¿escuchas música cuando corres o haces *jogging*?
12. En EE.UU., ¿qué se asocia con el otoño, el béisbol o el fútbol americano?

[1]change, [2]se... fall

For additional vocabulary practice, see PowerPoint slides on BCS and in *WileyPLUS*.

4-18 Students may complete the activity individually or in pairs, with answers reviewed by the instructor. ANSWERS: **1. el invierno 2. el otoño 3. la primavera (o) el verano 4. el verano 5. el invierno 6. el verano 7. el otoño 8. la primavera.**

Point out that weather expressions use either **muy** or **mucho** as an intensifier: **muy** for adjectives (e.g. **Hace muy buen tiempo**) and **mucho** for nouns (e.g. **Hace mucho sol**). Exception: The intensifier is not normally used with **Hace fresco**.

4-19 After students complete the activity, you may want to project the PowerPoint slide of the scenes. Have students describe the weather conditions and the activities, preferably with books closed.

4-19 PERSONALIZED QUESTIONS: A prospective Spanish-speaking exchange student asks you, **¿Qué tal el clima en verano (invierno, primavera, otoño) donde Uds. viven?** Have several students respond, each adding something, season by season.

4-20 El clima el 15 de julio

 Paso 1. You and a classmate are about to go on separate trips to multiple destinations in Latin America. You are both looking at the same website (see map below), helping each other find out how the weather is in each location. Follow the model and take turns initiating each inquiry.

MODELO

Cliente: *Voy a La Habana, en Cuba. ¿Qué tal el clima?*

Servicio: *Hace sol. La temperatura máxima es de 32 grados centígrados (Celsius) y la mínima es de 24.*

4-20 Encourage students to examine the thermometer in the art that includes the conversion from Fahrenheit to Celsius degrees.

4-20 At the end of *Paso 1*, you may want to project the PowerPoint slide of the map and have pairs of students role-play for the class. For *Paso 2*, pairs going to the same location add up their lists. The pairs with the highest number of activities in each of the three categories are the winners. They each read their list of activities to the class.

EL CLIMA: jueves, 15 de julio

© John Wiley & Sons, Inc

 Paso 2. You and a friend are planning a vacation to one of the destinations given below. (Your instructor will assign you one of the three.) Jot down outdoor and indoor activities appropriate to your location, taking into consideration the weather on July 15. How many activities can you think of in *two* minutes?

Playa del Carmen (México)	Portillo (Chile)	Buenos Aires (Argentina)

¡A escuchar! Hemisferios opuestos

The scripts and recordings for the ¡A escuchar! sections are included in the Book Companion Site (BCS) for instructors and in WileyPLUS.

Paso 1. Listen to the dialogue between Tere, in the United States, and her mother in Uruguay.

PLUS Go to *WileyPLUS* to complete **Paso 2** of this listening activity.

Ernesto, Mario y Fabio salen del cine y hablan de adónde ir a cenar.

© John Wiley & Sons, Inc

Ask students to read the **historieta** out loud. Ask the following questions:
1. ¿Conocen Mario y Fabio el restaurante?
2. ¿Qué saben preparar en "La Habana"?

For additional practice on this grammar point, see PowerPoint slides on BCS and in *WileyPLUS*.

PLUS Go to *WileyPLUS* to review this grammar point with the help of the **Animated Grammar Tutorial** and **Verb Conjugator**. For more practice, go to the **Grammar Handbook**.

GRAMÁTICA

¡Manos a la obra!

4

Knowing facts, skills, people, and places: *Saber* and *conocer*

Just as Spanish has two verbs (**ser** and **estar**) that express *to be,* it also has two verbs that express *to know.* These verbs are **saber** and **conocer.**

Let's look at examples based on what Ernesto, Mario, and Fabio know about the restaurant **La Habana.**

- **Saber** means *to know facts or information.*

  —¿**Sabes** cómo es el restaurante "La Habana"?
  —No, pero **sé** que es muy bueno.

- **Saber** + *infinitive* means *to know how to do something.*

  Saben preparar especialidades cubanas, pero no **saben** hacer especialidades mexicanas.

- **Conocer** means *to know or to be acquainted with a person, place, or thing.* It also means *to meet a person for the first time.*

  Ellos no **conocen** "La Habana".   *They do not know "La Habana".*
  ¿**Conoces** al* mesero?   *Do you know the waiter?*
  Conozco a* Marta, la cajera del restaurante.   *I know Marta, the restaurant's cashier.*

- Both verbs are irregular in the **yo** form only:

saber		conocer	
sé	sabemos	**conozco**	conocemos
sabes	sabéis	conoces	conocéis
sabe	saben	conoce	conocen

*Remember to include the personal **a** after **conocer** when the object of the verb is a person.

¹I'm so hungry!

¿SABES QUE...?

By now you have read many ¿Sabes que...? notes. Do you know why *saber* and not *conocer* is used in this question? To confirm your answer, read the upside down explanation.

Because it asks if you know certain facts or information.

To introduce the uses of **saber** and **conocer,** ask questions to illustrate each concept: ¿Sabes cuáles son los mejores equipos de básquetbol de EE. UU.? ¿Sabes jugar al vólibol, al tenis o al golf? ¿Conoces las montañas de Colorado? ¿Sabes esquiar o hacer *snowboard*? ¿Conoces a un/a jugador/a de básquetbol, de fútbol americano o de tenis famoso/a? ¿Quién es?

¡Oye! Write on the board: **mundo** *world.* If you would like to use this *¡Oye!* to introduce the uses of **saber** and **conocer**, write the following on the board for reference while making the corresponding statements: **Saber**—*knowledge, information* (items 1, 2); **Saber**—*skills, how to...* (items 3–5); **Conocer**—*people* (items 6, 7); and **Conocer**—*places* (8–10) Personalize the suggested statements, mixing true and false ones.

Guión para ¡Oye!
¿Es verdad o mentira?
1. Sé los nombres de todos los estudiantes de la clase.
2. Sé la fecha del cumpleaños de casi todos los estudiantes.
3. Sé hablar español, francés, ruso, chino, italiano...
4. Sé tocar el violín.
5. Sé jugar al...
6. Conozco a todos los estudiantes de la clase.
7. Conozco personalmente a Shakira, la cantante colombiana.
8. Conozco bien la ciudad de Tokio.
9. Conozco el parque nacional Yosemite.
10. Conozco... (*name a local place*).

4-21 After students complete *Paso 2,* open the floor for questions: **¿Saben de dónde soy?** Students respond: **Sí, lo sé/ sabemos. Ud. es de...** (or) **No, no lo sé/ sabemos. ¿De dónde es Ud.?**

4-22 ANOTHER STEP: Divide the class into two teams. Then call out the names of Spanish-speaking countries, one at a time. The teams alternate in identifying the capital. If one team does not know the answer, the other team replies. The team with the most correct answers wins.

¡En acción!

¡Oye! ¿Es verdad o mentira?[1]

Your instructor will make personal statements using **saber** and **conocer.** You cannot, however, believe everything he/she says! Using your best judgment, say «**¡Es verdad!**» or «**¡Es mentira!**» after each declaration.

4-21 ¿Conoces bien a tu profesor/a?

Paso 1. Do you know the following about your instructor? Mark the appropriate column.

¿Sabes...	Sí, lo sé.	No, no lo sé.
1. ...de dónde es?	☐	☐
2. ...dónde vive?	☐	☐
3. ...cuántos hijos tiene?	☐	☐
4. ...adónde va en verano?	☐	☐
5. ...qué música le gusta?	☐	☐
6. ...si toca un instrumento de música?	☐	☐
7. ...si juega a algún deporte?	☐	☐

Paso 2. With a partner, take turns asking each other the questions and compare answers. After completing the activity, where you both responded **No, no lo sé**, ask your instructor for the information.

MODELO

E1: *¿Sabes de dónde es el/la profesor/a? No lo sé.*

E2: *Yo tampoco.*

(Al final.)

E1: *Profesor/a, ¿de dónde es Ud.?*

4-22 Capitales

Paso 1. Do you know the capitals of the Spanish-speaking countries? Look at the map of the Spanish-speaking world on the inside front cover of your textbook and ask your partner if he/she knows what the capital of a particular country is. Your partner answers without looking at the map. After *six* questions, switch roles. Keep score to determine the winner.

MODELO

E1: *¿Sabes cuál es la capital de Uruguay?*

E2: *Sí lo sé. Es Montevideo.* (scores one point)

o: *No lo sé. Un momento, por favor.* (looks for answer on map) *Ah, es Montevideo.*

Paso 2. What capital cities are you familiar with? List those in the United States and/ or abroad that you have visited. The person with the longest list reads it to the class: *Conozco Sacramento, ...* Others add cities not mentioned: Y yo *conozco...*

[1]Is it true or a lie?

4-23 ¿Sabes quién es? ¿Quieres conocerlo/la?

Can you identify the famous Hispanic people below? Ask your partner if he/she knows who each one is, and if he/she would like to meet that person. Take turns.

MODELO

Eva Longoria

E1: ¿Sabes quién es?

E2: Sí, sé quién es.

o: No, no sé quién es.

(If you answer no, see answers below.)

E1: ¿Quieres conocerla?

E2: Sí, quiero conocerla.

o: No, no quiero conocerla.

1. Penélope Cruz
2. Sandra Cisneros
3. Laura Chinchilla

4. Alex Rodríguez
5. Antonio Villaraigosa
6. Rafael Nadal

7. ... (escoge tú)
8. ... (escoge tú)
9. ... (escoge tú)

Modelo Eva Longoria, actriz, de padres mexicanos (Texas)
1. Penélope Cruz, actriz (España)
2. Sandra Cisneros, escritora, de padres mexicanos (Chicago)
3. Laura Chinchilla, presidenta de Costa Rica
4. Alex Rodríguez, jugador de béisbol, de padres dominicanos (Nueva York)
5. Antonio Villaraigosa, alcalde (*mayor*) de Los Ángeles, de padres mexicanos
6. Rafael Nadal, jugador de tenis (España)

© John Wiley & Sons, Inc

4-24 ¿Lo sabes hacer? RECYCLES vocabulary and **aprender a**.

Paso 1. List *two* sports/ outdoor activities that you know how to do, *two* that you do not know how to do, and *two* that you want to learn how to do.

Sé...	No sé...	Quiero aprender a...
1.		
2.		

Paso 2. You and your partner take turns asking and answering questions about your lists. Take notes on what he or she says in order to share information with the class and your instructor.

MODELO

E1: Ana, ¿qué **sabes** hacer?

E2: **Sé** esquiar y nadar.

E1: ¿Qué no **sabes** hacer?

E2: No **sé** patinar y no **sé** montar a caballo.

E1: ¿Qué quieres **aprender a** hacer?

E2: Quiero **aprender a** hacer snowboard y a pilotar un helicóptero.

Palabras útiles

¿Quieres conocerlo/la? *Do you want to meet him/her?*
Quiero conocerlo/la. *I want to meet him/her.*

¿SABES QUE...?

Rafael Nadal (1986 –), commonly known as *Rafa*, has come off the tennis courts of his native Mallorca, Spain, to take the tennis world by storm. His string of successes, including winning the gold medal in men's singles at the Beijing Olympics (2008) and his win over Roger Federer for the championship of the 2009 Australian Open, has positioned him among the top male tennis players in the world. He completed the career Grand Slam by winning the 2010 US Open.

Palabras útiles

balsismo *(rafting)*
saltar en paracaídas *(to sky dive)*
puentismo *(bungee jumping)*
pilotar un helicóptero/avión *(airplane)*

4-24 Ask students first to share information about the special talents of people in their group, then have them mention things that people want to learn to do. On the basis of the information provided for the latter, the class decides the following: If they could have a group instructor for only one activity, what would it be?

4-25 En clase de español: ¿qué sabes y a quién conoces?

Paso 1.   Since starting your Spanish class, you have learned a number of things and become acquainted with new people and places. In groups of *four*, talk about what you now know using the chart below.

Cosas que sé ahora	Cosas que sé hacer ahora	Personas y lugares que conozco ahora
Sé el vocabulario de…	**Sé** hablar…	**Conozco** a…
Sé el verbo…		**Conozco**…
Sé que la capital de Perú es Lima.		

Paso 2.   The winning group in each category reports the information to the class: *Sabemos…*

Después del cine, Mario, Fabio y Ernesto van a cenar al restaurante cubano "La Habana".

© John Wiley & Sons, Inc

For additional practice on this grammar point, see PowerPoint slides on BCS and in *WileyPLUS*.

GRAMÁTICA

¡Manos a la obra!

5

Talking about the future: ***Ir + a + infinitive***

To talk about actions that are going to happen, English uses *going to + infinitive* and Spanish uses **ir + a + infinitive.**

Let's look at examples based on Mario, Fabio, and Ernesto's conversation in the Cuban restaurant.

—¿Qué **vas a hacer** ahora, Ernesto?   *What are you going to do now, Ernesto?*
—**Voy a ir** a casa.   *I am going to go home.*
—¿Qué **van a hacer** Uds. mañana?   *What are you going to do tomorrow?*
—**Vamos a jugar** al básquetbol.   *We are going to play basketball.*
For review, here are the present-tense forms of the verb **ir** *to go*.

(yo)	**voy**	(nosotros/as)	**vamos**
(tú)	**vas**	(vosotros/as)	**váis**
(Ud., él, ella)	**va**	(Uds., ellos/as)	**van**

*A way of making "Let's" commands in Spanish is using the structure **vamos** + **a** + infinitive.
Fabio, Mario, **vamos a ver** el documental juntos. *Fabio, Mario, let's watch the documentary together.*

¡En acción!

¡Oye! Federico habla de sus planes

Federico has some plans that are feasible, and others that are crazy. As you hear each one, react by saying «**¡Es un buen plan!**» or «**¡Está loco!**»

4-26 El clima   RECYCLES weather expressions

Paso 1. Imagine that you and your classmates live in Chicago, near Lake Michigan, and have the next five days off. Before planning your activities, you decide to check the weather on ¡Con brío! Divide into groups of *three*. First, one student describes the weather forecast for a particular day. Second, the other students each suggest at least *one* activity to do that day. Follow the model and switch roles.

MODELO

Hoy, martes

E1: *Hoy* **la temperatura máxima** *va a ser* **de** 24 **grados** *y la mínima,* **de** 13 **grados.** **Hace muy buen tiempo y hay poca humedad**.

E2: **Vamos a nadar** *en el lago.*

E3: *Y después,* **vamos a tomar** *el sol en la playa.*

E1: *¡Qué buena idea! Y luego,* **vamos a comer** *la famosa pizza de Chicago.*

El tiempo ¡Con brío! → Chicago → Illinois → Estados Unidos, 16 de junio					
		Temperatura (°C) Máxima	Temperatura (°C) Mínima	Humedad	
HOY, MARTES		24°C	13°C	40%	Sol y cielo despejado
MIÉRCOLES		19°C	10°C	49%	Parcialmente nublado
JUEVES		23°C	10°C	51%	Lloviznas ocasionales
VIERNES		17°C	10°C	67%	Nubes por la mañana soleado por la tarde
SÁBADO		21°C	13°C	78%	Tormentas

© John Wiley & Sons, Inc

Paso 2. One spokesperson from each group now shares the forecast and plans for the day with the class.

¿SABES QUE...?

As you know, Hispanic countries express the temperature in Celsius instead of Farenheit. When travelling to those countries or talking to Spanish-speakers, you should be aware of the following formulas to convert Celsius into Farenheit. **Hint:** 0 Celsius = 32 Farenheit

$°C \times 9/5 + 32 = °F$

Can you tell what's the temperature in Farenheit in two days of the chart above?

You are already familiar with many of these expressions. Which ones are new to you?

momentos precisos	
esta noche	*tonight*
mañana	*tomorrow*
pasado mañana	*day after tomorrow*
mañana por la mañana/ tarde/ noche	*tomorrow morning/ afternoon/ night*
la semana que viene	*next week*
la próxima semana	*next week*
el mes/ año/ verano que viene	*next month/ year/ summer*
el próximo mes/ año/ verano	*next month/ year/ summer*
momentos imprecisos	
algún día	*someday, some time*
un día	*one day*

4-27 ¿Qué van a hacer?

Paso 1. What are your classmates going to do in each of the time periods below? In groups of *four,* ask each other questions to find out. Take notes, jotting down the names and the information.

MODELO

E1: ¿Qué **van a hacer** Uds. esta noche?

E2: Yo **voy a estudiar.** Tengo un examen.

E3: Yo también.

E4: Y yo **voy a salir** con mis amigos. (**E4** asks **E1**) Julio, ¿qué **vas a hacer** tú?

¿Qué van a hacer?	1. *Silvia*	2. _____	3. _____
esta noche	va a estudiar.		
mañana por la mañana			
el próximo sábado			
el verano que viene			
el año que viene			
algún día			

Paso 2. Your instructor will ask for feedback, one time period at a time. Share what you learned, being sure to report unusual plans to the class: *El verano que viene José* **va a trabajar** *en Nueva York.*

4-28 La adivina[1]   RECYCLES tener, ser, estar, and regular verbs in the present.

Paso 1.   A fortune-teller (your classmate in disguise) asks you questions about your current life. You respond, and then he/she predicts your future, indicating the time frame. Write the information in the third column. Then switch roles.

MODELO

E1: *¿Dónde vives ahora?*

E2: *Vivo en un apartamento en la ciudad.*

E1: *En dos años, vas a vivir en una casa roja en el campo, en Uruguay.*

E2: (Reacts using the expressions provided)
         ¡Qué bien!

© John Wiley & Sons, Inc

Palabras útiles
¡Qué bien!
¡Qué horror!
¡Qué extraño!
   How strange!
¡Qué suerte!
   What luck!

Preguntas de la adivina	Yo, ahora	Yo, en el futuro, según la adivina
1. ¿Dónde vives?	*Vivo en…*	*En dos años, voy a vivir en…*
2. ¿Dónde trabajas?		
3. ¿Qué estudias?		
4. ¿Tienes pareja?		
5. ¿Cuáles son tus diversiones favoritas?		
6. ¿Eres ambicioso/a?		
7. ¿Cómo estás en este momento?		

Paso 2.   Join another pair of students, and take turns reading some of the predictions to each other. Then share unusual information with the class.

[1]The fortune-teller

Tu mundo cultural

Lugares fascinantes para conocer

Aquí tienes varios ejemplos de lugares fascinantes que puedes visitar si viajas a América Latina.

© John Wiley & Sons, Inc

1.

Buddy Mays/© Corbis

Corbis Images

Portillo es una de las primeras estaciones[1] de esquí chilenas. Está situada en Los Andes, en la base del Aconcagua, el pico más alto del hemisferio occidental (a 7.266 metros/ 22.835 pies sobre el nivel del mar[2]). Tiene vistas sobre la bella Laguna del Inca. Los mejores meses del año para esquiar y hacer *snowboard* allí son agosto y septiembre.

3.

PhotoDisc, Inc./Getty Images

Courtesy Conchita Lucas

Courtesy Conchita Lucas

2.

Jaques Jangoux/Photo Researchers, Inc.

Macduff Everton/© Corbis

El Salto[3] Ángel, situado en el parque nacional Canaima de Venezuela, es el salto de agua más alto del mundo (3.281 pies/ 979 metros). Es cuatro veces más alto que las cataratas del Niágara. Se puede ver desde el aire, en helicóptero, o haciendo una excursión que consiste en navegar primero en canoa por dos ríos, y después caminar por la selva[4].

La playa del Carmen, situada en la península de Yucatán en el mar Caribe mexicano, está a 60 kilómetros de Cancún. Cerca de la playa están la isla de Cozumel y los templos mayas de Chichén Itzá y Tulúm. En los parques naturales de Xelhá y Xcaret se puede bucear y nadar con los delfines.

[1]resorts, [2]**sobre...** above sea level, [3]fall, [4]jungle

4.

Ralph Lee Hopkins/NGS/Getty Images

Las islas Galápagos, situadas en el océano Pacífico a 970 km/ 600 millas de la costa ecuatoriana, son un tesoro[1] ecológico. El 90%* de su territorio es un parque nacional. En 1835 Charles Darwin se inspira allí para su Teoría de la evolución de las especies. Entre su fauna observamos una increíble variedad de pájaros y aves, como los piqueros azules[2], los pelícanos y los pingüinos. Allí, también se pueden ver tortugas[3] gigantes, iguanas marinas y, en muchas de las playas, lobos marinos[4] tomando el sol.

Wolfgang Kaehler/© Corbis

Courtesy Laila Dawson

¿Qué aprendiste?

1. ¿Dónde están Portillo y el Salto Ángel? ¿Qué son y qué se puede hacer allí?
   La estación de esquí Portillo está en Chile y la catarata el Salto Ángel, en Venezuela. Las respuestas variarán.
2. ¿Dónde podemos visitar ruinas mayas? ¿Qué otras actividades se pueden hacer allí?
   En Chichen Itzá y en Tulúm. En los parques naturales de Xelhá y Xcaret se puede bucear y nadar con los delfines.
3. ¿Dónde están las islas Galápagos? ¿Qué animales hay en las islas? ¿Con qué científico famoso se relacionan?
   Están en Ecuador y hay diferentes especies de pájaros y aves, tortugas, iguanas marinas, y lobos marinos.

Actividad cultural

 Paso 1. Select one of the four vacation spots on pages 138–139, and complete the following chart.

Nombre del lugar	Situación geográfica	Actividades o deportes para hacer o practicar allí	¿Otras atracciones?

 Paso 2. Compare your information with that of two other classmates. Were your choices the same or different?

Contraste cultural

Your Chilean pen pal is planning a trip to your country. He/She asks you to send him/her information about *three* or *four* very different places that it would be worthwhile to visit. In English, discuss what places you would choose and why.

[1]treasure, [2]**piqueros...** blue-footed boobies, [3]turtles, [4]**lobos...** sea lions.

*% **por ciento**

Go to *WileyPLUS* to see these **videos** and to find more activities for **¡Diálogos en acción!**, **¡A conversar!**, **¡A escribir!** and **¡A investigar!**

Meets ACTFL Standards 1.2, interpretive listening; 2.1, cultural practices; 2.2, cultural products; 3.2, acquiring information; and 4.2, cultural comparisons.

Meets ACTFL Standards 1.1, interpersonal speaking, 1.2, interpretive listening and 2.1, cultural practices.

Dialogue Tips: Play the dialogue once all the way through. Check comprehension by asking students to tell you everything they understood (English is OK). Then play it a second time, pausing after each sentence or phrase and asking students what was said.

You can also find the **transcripts** for the **Diálogos** in the PowerPoint slides on the BCS and in *WileyPLUS*.

Tu mundo en vivo

¡Videos en acción!

4.1 El fútbol: pasión hispana

1. Antes de ver el video
   a. Do you play any sport or participate in an organized activity?
   b. What do you like about your sport or activity?

Go to *WileyPLUS* to complete the **Mientras ves el video** activity.

2. Después de ver el video
   a. Why is soccer so popular among Hispanics?
   b. In your opinion, what is the most popular sport in the U.S.?

4.2 Fines de semana entre hispanos

1. Antes de ver el video Name 5 activities you do on the weekends.

Go to *WileyPLUS* to complete the **Mientras ves el video** activity.

2. Después de ver el video Are there differences between what you do on weekends and what the persons interviewed do? Explain.

¡Diálogos en acción!

4.1 La fiesta cubana

Magali and William are two co-workers from Cuba living in New York City. Magali runs into William and invites him to a party she is having.

Paso 1. First, read the **Expresiones útiles** on p. A-4. Next, listen to the dialogue twice and answer the questions your instructor will ask.

Paso 2. Look at the transcript of this dialogue (p. A-17) and act it out with a partner. Switch roles. Now, go to pp. A-4, A-5 to complete **Pasos 3** and **4.**

4.2 Planes para Navidades

Magali and William are co-workers from Cuba living in New York City. They run into each other shortly before the Christmas holiday and inquire about each other's plans.

Go to *WileyPLUS* to listen to and practice this dialogue.

Diálogo 4.1 models the linguistic functions of issuing, accepting, and rejecting invitations. It also practices the verbs **dar, ver, traer, venir, creer, decir, saber,** and **ir** + **a** + *infinitive*.
Diálogo 4.2 models the functions of discussing plans in the near future, describing weather, and well-wishing. It also practices **ir** + **a** + *infinitive*, in addition to weather and activities vocabulary.

¡Lectura en acción!

Una alpinista[1] de excepción

The following news story, from the Spanish newspaper *El diario montañés* from Santander, tells about the incredible feats of Edurne Pasabán, a female mountain climber from the Basque region of Spain.

Paso 1.   Skim the following passage, looking specifically for the following information:

a. her main accomplishment

b. the height of the summits and how many there are

c. the time it took her to achieve her main accomplishment

d. her other accomplishments and current occupations

As students search for the information requested in *Paso 1*, remind them that they do not need to understand the unfamiliar words included in the passage to find the requested information.

Reading Strategy

Scanning for Specific Information

Often when reading, we only seek specific information and are able to skim or scan the passage while skipping those details that don't pertain to our search.

Edurne Pasabán, la primera mujer que conquista las montañas más altas del planeta

La alpinista Edurne Pasabán Lirrizábar (Tolosa, Gipuzkoa, 1973) va a ofrecer una conferencia el próximo día 17, en el Palacio de Festivales de Santander, para hablar de sus experiencias en la gesta histórica de la coronación de catorce montañas con 8.000 metros de altitud.

Es la primera mujer en la historia del planeta en ascender a los catorce "ochomiles" (montañas de más de 8.000 metros). Para hacerlo, necesitó 9 años. En el año 2001 comenzó con el Everest, para continuar después con el Makalu, Cho-Oyu, Lhostse, Gasherbrum II, Gasherbrum I, K2, Nanga Parbat, Broad Peak, Dhaulagiri, Manaslu, Kangchenjunga, Annapurna, Shisha Pangma y Tajahierro.

Edurne tiene una carrera singular. Se interesó por el deporte desde niña y además, es ingeniera técnica industrial. También, tiene un restaurante y alojamiento[2] rural que se llama "El Abeletxe", situado en Zizurkil, Guipuzkoa (www.abeletxe.com). Curiosamente, una de las especialidades del menú es "el pulpo[3] a feira" con sal rosa del Himalaya. Además, la alpinista se dedica a dar conferencias por todo el país, con contrataciones a través de su página web oficial: http://www.edurnepasaban.com/conferencias/.

Diego Ruiz: "Edurne Pasabán y su '14 × 8.000', en Santander 06.11.10," *El Diario Montañés*, sábado, 6 de noviembre de 2010. Used by permission.

Pierre-Philippe Marcou/AFP/Getty Images

8.000 metros = *26,246 feet*

Meets ACTFL Standards 1.2, interpretive reading, and 3.2, acquiring information.

Paso 2.   Based on your responses in **Paso 1**, determine if the following statements are true or false. Mark **Cierto** or **Falso**.

If your students' interest is high, you may wish to encourage them to search online for more information about Edurne Pasabán and to bring back their findings to class.

Cierto	Falso	
☐	☐	Es una alpinista que escala las montañas más altas del mundo.
☐	☐	Edurne Pasabán Lirrizábar ha conquistado los catorce "ochomiles".
☐	☐	Es la primera mujer en la historia que lo hace.

[1]mountain climber, [2]lodging, [3]octopus

¡A conversar! Meets ACTFL Standard 1.1, interpersonal speaking.

Planes para todas las estaciones del año

Imagine that *three* of you are going to take a trip together each season in the coming year. Make your plans. Think of:

- Estación del año, destino: *El próximo verano vamos a...*

- Fecha de salida: *Salimos el...*

- El clima típico en esa estación: *Allí, en verano, normalmente hace... y...*

- Actividades: *Vamos a..., ..., ... Vamos a ver...*

- Fecha de regreso a casa: *Vamos a regresar el...*

¡A escribir!

Un fin de semana con mis amigos

A long weekend holiday is approaching, and you and three friends are going away. They have asked you to plan the trip. Write an itinerary for the group for Friday-Monday, using the following list as a guide. Include:

Información general:

- Adónde van

- Cómo es el clima allí (*Normalmente hace...*)

Itinerario del viernes al lunes

- Cuándo y dónde van a desayunar

- A qué hora van a salir del hotel por la mañana

- Qué van a aprender a hacer (*¿parasailing?, etc.*)

- A qué hora y dónde van a cenar

- Qué van a hacer por la noche

- A qué hora van a regresar al hotel

Writing Strategy

Gathering Information

Before you begin writing your itinerary, gather information about the potential place for the weekend get-away. Check out likely places on the Internet (be adventurous!) or draw from your own experiences.

Steps:

1. *Prewriting*: After gathering your information (see strategy), jot down your initial ideas in words and phrases, **¡en español!**

2. *Writing*: Complete the itinerary using complete sentences, but in bulleted format. So that your readers can quickly identify each item, underline a key word or phrase in each sentence: **desayunar**, etc.

3. *Revising*: Read your composition carefully. Have you included the requested information and checked for correct spelling and punctuation? **¡Ojo!** Have you used **a la/s...** to express *at what time*, and correctly used the **ir** + **a** + *infinitive* construction?

4. *Peer correction*: Exchange papers, circle errors or areas where there are questions, talk about them, and then make corrections on your own paper.

¡A investigar!

Un congreso internacional

Meets ACTFL Standards 1.3, presentational writing and speaking; 2.1, cultural practices; 3.1, other disciplines; and 3.2, acquiring information.

Your company has been hired to plan a conference for an international organization. The conference will take place next June. Your client's headquarters is in Spain, and they have limited knowledge of Latin America, but because many of their organization's members live in the Americas, they are interested in the following cities as possible conference sites: Santiago, Chile; Santo Domingo, República Dominicana; and Quito, Ecuador. The conference must include free time for participants to explore the area, and many of them are interested in sports and outdoor activities. Your challenge is to recommend to your client the best site based on the desires of the organization's members and when the conference will take place.

Paso 1.　Work in teams of *three* to prepare your proposal. Research the locations and for each one write and edit a short description that includes:

- The typical weather in June in the city (*En...normalmente hace...*)
- The geography of the area (*Hay..., Está cerca de...*)
- The activities available for visitors (*Se puede...*)

You may assign the appropriate **Pasos** of **¡A investigar!** for pairs or small groups to complete outside of class.

Paso 2.　When the descriptions are ready, combine them in a PowerPoint presentation that includes links to Spanish-language websites and videos about the cities and the activities you've mentioned.

Paso 3.　Collaborate with your group members to select the city to recommend to your client and be ready to defend your choice (*Creemos que Uds. deben organizar su congreso en...porque...*).

If your access to technology is limited, have the students create Word documents for their proposals and posters to use as visual aids as they speak.

Paso 4.　Make your presentation to your client (your classmates) and state your recommendation.

The class can decide which teams made the right choice for their client. If time is short, students could produce PowerPoints with recorded narrations and post them to a wiki or blog for others to review outside of class.

Research Strategy

Using Geography and Climate Resources Online

To find out about the geography, climate, and current weather conditions in Hispanic countries, consider websites such as the CIA World Factbook, the World Meteorological Organization, and the World Weather Information Service, in addition to sites such as Yahoo! En español. Mapping applications such as Google Maps and Google Earth can also help you learn about a country's geographical features.

Trivia

Can you answer the following questions?

1. ¿Sabes qué estación del año es ahora en Chile? ¿Y en la República Dominicana?

2. ¿Sabes qué dos países hispanos no tienen acceso al mar?

3. ¿Cómo se llaman las islas que están en el océano Pacífico y son territorio de Ecuador?

　　　1. (Answers will vary.) 2. Bolivia y Paraguay 3. Islas Galápagos

If you don't know the answers, take a look at the front inside cover of the textbook. Try to respond in complete sentences.

Vocabulario: Capítulo 4

Escena 1

Los lugares al aire libre
Outdoor places

la arena *sand*
el bosque *forest*
el campo *field, countryside*
la granja *farm*
la isla *island*
el lago *lake*
el mar *sea*
la montaña *mountain*
la playa *beach*
el río *river*
el valle *valley*

Las actividades al aire libre
Outdoor activities

acampar *to camp*
bucear *to snorkel*
caminar *to walk*
correr *to run*
esquiar *to ski*
ir en barco *to go by boat/ ship*
jugar (ue) al vólibol *to play volleyball*
manejar *to drive*
montar a caballo *to ride horseback/
    go horseback riding*
montar en bicicleta *to ride a bicycle*
nadar *to swim*
patinar *to skate*
pescar *to fish*
practicar deportes *to play, go out for sports*
tomar el sol *to sunbathe*
la pelota *ball*
el pez/ los peces *fish (living) (s./pl.)*

Otros verbos y expresiones
verbales *Other verbs and verbal*
expressions

aprender (a) *to learn (to)*
beber *to drink*
comer *to eat*
compartir *to share*
creer (que) *to believe/ think (that)*
deber (+ *infinitive*) *should/ must/ ought to (do
    something)*
descansar *to rest*
dibujar *to draw*
encantar *to love, like a lot*

escribir *to write*
ganar *to win*
gustar *to like*
levantar pesas *to lift weights*
leer *to read*
pintar (un cuadro) *to paint (a painting)*
vivir *to live*

Adverbios *Adverbs*
mucho/ poco *much, a lot/ little, not much*

Escena 2

Los deportes *Sports*
el equipo *the team*
el partido de fútbol *the soccer game*

Las actividades *Activities*
asistir a... *to attend . . .*
bailar *to dance*
cantar *to sing*
dar fiestas *to give/ throw parties*
escuchar (música) *to listen to (music)*
hacer ejercicio *to exercise*
hacer un viaje (al campo/ a la ciudad)
    to take a trip (to the country/ to the city)
ir de compras *to go shopping*
mandar y recibir mensajes electrónicos
    to send and receive e-mail messages/ e-mails
mirar *to look at, watch*
navegar por la Red *to surf the Web*
pasar el tiempo (con la familia) *to spend
    time (with the family)*
salir de paseo/dar un paseo *to take
    a walk/ stroll*
tocar (la guitarra) *to play (the guitar)*
ver la televisión *to watch TV*
viajar *to travel*

Más verbos *More verbs*
dar *to give*
decir *to say, tell*
disfrutar de... *to enjoy . . .*
hacer *to make, do*
oír *to hear*
poner *to put*
salir *to leave, go out*
traer *to bring*
venir *to come*
ver *to see*

Escena 3

La naturaleza *Nature*
el árbol *tree*
el cielo *sky*
la estrella *star*
la flor *flower*
la hoja *leaf*
la lluvia *rain*
la luna *moon*
la nieve *snow*
la nube *cloud*
la ola *wave*
el pájaro *bird*
el sol *sun*
el viento *wind*

Las estaciones *Seasons*
el invierno *winter*
el otoño *fall, autumn*
la primavera *spring*
el verano *summer*

El clima *Weather*
Está (muy) nublado. *It is (very) cloudy.*
Hace (muy) buen/ mal tiempo. *The weather
    is (very) nice/ bad.*
Hace (mucho) calor. *It is (very) hot.*
Hace fresco. *It is cool.*
Hace (mucho) frío. *It is (very) cold.*
Hace (mucho) sol. *It is (very) sunny.*
Hace (mucho) viento. *It is (very) windy.*
llover (ue) *to rain*
Llueve. *It is raining/ It rains.*
nevar (ie) *to snow*
Nieva. *It is snowing/ It snows.*

¿Qué tal el clima?/ ¿Qué tiempo hace?
    What is the weather like?

El futuro *The future*
algún día *someday, some time*
mañana por la mañana/ tarde/
    noche *tomorrow morning/ afternoon/ night*
pasado mañana *day after tomorrow*
la semana que viene *next week*
el mes/ año/ verano que viene *next month/
    year/ summer*
la próxima semana *next week*
el próximo mes/ año/ verano *next month/
    year/ summer*

Más verbos *More verbs*
conocer *to know, be acquainted with*
saber *to know (facts, information), to know
    how (skills)*

To introduce the theme, you may want to play one of the videos from this chapter, with or without the audio, and then ask students what they think the chapter is about. You may also want to use the video to motivate cultural discussion, in Spanish from this chapter on. At the end of the chapter, ask students if their predictions about its content and culture were accurate.

La comida

WILEY PLUS

Additional activities and **Autopruebas** for each **Escena** available online.

Martin Jacobs/StockFood Creative/Getty Images, Inc.

Escena 1
En el mercado

GRAMÁTICA:
· Direct object pronouns

CULTURA:
Los productos hispanos y su historia

Escena 2
En el restaurante

GRAMÁTICA:
· Stem-changing verbs

CULTURA:
Platos típicos de algunos países hispanos

Escena 3
Preparativos para una fiesta

GRAMÁTICA:
· The present progressive

CULTURA:
Dos recetas típicamente hispanas

TU MUNDO EN VIVO

¡Videos en acción! En el supermercado; En el restaurante

¡Diálogos en acción! Interacting with a Server in a Restaurant; Issuing and Accepting an Invitation, and Negotiating a Complication

¡Lectura en acción! Summarizing

¡A conversar! Using Descriptions to Avoid Lapses

¡A escribir! Let the First Draft Flow

¡A investigar! Using Bilingual Dictionaries

LEARNING OBJECTIVES

By the end of this chapter you will be able to:

· Buy, order and talk about food in a market, restaurant, etc.
· Express large quantities, prices and dates.
· Refer to people, places and things.
· Talk about actions, desires and preferences in the present.
· Tell someone you address informally what to do.
· Describe an action in progress.
· Tell the origin of produce and describe typical meals from the Hispanic world.

En el mercado

1. MERCADO CENTRAL

2. las frutas

FRUTERÍA

36. las carnes

CARNICERÍA

37. las salchichas

39. el bistec

40. la carne de res

195 pesos el kilo.

3. la sandía

38. el jamón

41. las chuletas de cerdo

42. el pollo

43. el pavo

4. las naranjas

7. las manzanas

5. los limones

¿Cuánto 6cuestan las naranjas?

PANADERÍA

9. las cerezas

8. las peras

NURIA

11. los duraznos

13. las piñas

33Busco las flores.

¡Allí están!

10. las uvas

12. las fresas

¡Me encanta el maíz!

32. el pan

¡Qué rico!*

19. desear

14. las bananas

18. el maíz

CARMEN

ROBERTITO

23. el brócoli

25. los tomates

27. los frijoles

21. las zanahorias

17. las papas

16. el ajo

20. las arvejas, los chícharos

22. los pimientos

15.

LEGUMBRES - VERDURAS

24. la lechuga

28. ARROZ

26. las cebollas

© John Wiley & Sons, Inc.

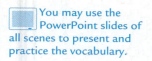

 WILEY PLUS

Pronunciación: Practice pronunciation of the chapter's new vocabulary in *WileyPLUS*.

PESCADERÍA - MARISQUERÍA

44. el pescado

45. los mariscos

47. la langosta

46. los camarones

Los vendedores aquí son muy [31]amables.

34. SE VENDE
35. QUESO

29. el dinero

30. contar (ue)

1. market
2. fruit
3. watermelon
4. oranges
5. lemons; **el limón** (s.)
6. cost; **costar (ue)** to cost
7. apples
8. pears
9. cherries
10. grapes
11. peaches
12. strawberries
13. pineapples
14. bananas
15. vegetables
16. garlic
17. potatoes
18. corn
19. to want, to wish, to desire
20. peas
21. carrots
22. green/red peppers
23. broccoli
24. lettuce
25. tomatoes
26. onions
27. beans
28. rice
29. money
30. to count
31. kind, pleasant
32. bread
33. I'm looking for ...; **buscar** to look for
34. for sale; **vender** to sell
35. cheese
36. meats
37. sausages
38. ham
39. steak
40. beef
41. pork chops
42. chicken
43. turkey
44. fish
45. seafood, shellfish
46. shrimp; **el camarón** (s.)
47. lobster

*¡Qué rico! *How delicious / tasty!*

 ¡La pronunciación!
Pay attention to the correct pronunciation of the Spanish **r** and **rr** (see P-4).

pe**r**a   a**r**veja
a**rr**oz   **r**ico

¡En acción!

5-1 Los ingredientes para la cena

Paso 1. Esta noche tienes invitados. Vas a preparar una ensalada mixta, un plato principal y una ensalada de frutas. En cada columna, escribe por lo menos *cinco* ingredientes que vas a comprar para la cena.

Para la ensalada mixta voy a comprar...	Para el plato principal voy a comprar...	Para la ensalada de frutas voy a comprar...

Paso 2. Háganse preguntas[1] para saber lo que[2] van a comprar.

MODELO

E1: ¿Qué vas a comprar para la ensalada mixta?

E2: Voy a comprar lechuga,... ,... ,... y...

5-2 En el mercado

¿Qué se vende en el Mercado Central? Observen la escena de las páginas 146–147 y contesten las preguntas.

1. ¿Qué frutas se venden en la frutería?
2. ¿Cuánto cuestan las naranjas?
3. ¿Qué legumbre desea la niña que está con su madre? ¿Qué otras verduras se venden allí?
4. ¿Se venden arroz y frijoles en el mercado? ¿A ti te gustan los frijoles?
5. ¿Quiénes están en la panadería? ¿Le gusta el pan a Robertito? ¿Qué dice?
6. ¿Qué se vende al lado de la panadería?
7. ¿Qué busca Nuria? ¿Qué hace la vendedora de flores?
8. ¿Qué clase de carne se vende en la carnicería?
9. ¿Qué se vende en la pescadería-marisquería? ¿Qué mira la señora?
10. ¿Cuántas personas salen del mercado? Según las señoras que charlan, ¿cómo son los vendedores del mercado?

De paso

mirar *to look at, watch*   **buscar** *to look for, search for*

Whereas English includes corresponding prepositions in the expressions *to look at* and *to look (search) for,* Spanish does not use a preposition after **mirar** and **buscar**.

Miran las frutas.   *They are **looking at** the fruits.*
Buscan las uvas.   *They are **looking for** the grapes.*

The personal **a** (see page 87) *is* used when the object of **mirar** and **buscar** is a person.

Busco **a** mi hija.   *I am looking for my daughter.*
Miro **a** los vendedores.   *I am looking at the salespeople.*

Can you find where **buscar** and **mirar** are used in *Actividad 5-2*?

[1]**Háganse...** Ask each other questions, [2]**lo...** what

WILEY PLUS For more practice, see **Grammar Handbook** found in *WileyPLUS*.

. . . y algo más The impersonal *se*

To explain what one does or is done without reference to the person performing the action, Spanish uses **se** + *verb* (*third person*).

> **Se vende** queso. *Cheese for sale. (or) Cheese is sold here.*
> En México **se come** bien. *One eats well in Mexico.*

If the noun that follows the verb is plural, the plural form of the verb is commonly used.

> **Se venden** flores en el mercado. *Flowers are sold at the market.*

Can you find where **se** + **vende/n** is used in the *Actividad 5-2* questions?

For additional practice on this grammar point, see PowerPoint slides on BCS and in *WileyPLUS*.

The Bridgeman Art Library, International

La inscripción **Viva la vida**[1] en la sandía es muy significativa porque Frida Kahlo pintó este cuadro solamente ocho días antes de su muerte.

¿SABES QUE...?

Hispanic countries boast many specialty food shops. In general, the names of these shops are easy to decipher: **la panadería** → *bread shop*; **la carnicería** → *butcher's shop*. The words are feminine, and the ending is always **-ería**.

¿SABES QUE...?

The names of fruits, vegetables, and other foods can vary from one Spanish-speaking country to another. The terms used in one country or region, however, are usually understood in others. Some examples:

peas
arvejas (Colombia, Ecuador, Chile, Argentina, Uruguay)
chícharos (Mexico, Honduras, Cuba)
guisantes (Venezuela, Spain)
pitipuas (Dominican Republic, Puerto Rico, Cuba)

bananas
guineos (Central America, Dominican Republic, Puerto Rico, Colombia, Ecuador, Peru)
bananas (most Spanish-American countries)
plátanos (Spain and other Spanish-speaking countries)
cambures (Venezuela)

corn
elote (Mexico and Central America)
jojoto (Venezuela)
choclo (Ecuador, Argentina)
maíz (Spain, Colombia, and other Spanish-speaking countries)

green beans
judías verdes (Spain)
ejotes (Mexico)
habichuelas (Colombia, Cuba)
chauchas (Chile, Argentina)
vainitas (Ecuador)

potatoes
papas (Spanish-speaking countries except most parts of Spain)
patatas (Spain)

¿SABES QUE...?

In some Latin American countries, such as Venezuela, Peru, and Mexico, *limes* are called **limones** and *lemons* are called **limones amarillos**.

[1]**Viva...** Long live life!

Practice the numbers by dividing students into groups of six and having them count from 0 to 1000 by 50s. To make it into a game (chaotic, but fun), have them tap rhythmically on their desk tops as they say the numbers, and then clap once between the numbers.

Have students write historic dates on the board, at random—1776, 1492, 1929, 2000—and have them practice reading the dates according to the third item in the chart below.

LOS NÚMEROS DEL 100 AL...

100	cien	800	ochocientos/as
101	ciento uno/a	900	novecientos/as
200	doscientos/as	1.000	mil
300	trescientos/as	2.000	dos mil
400	cuatrocientos/as	100.000	cien mil
500	quinientos/as	200.000	doscientos mil
600	seiscientos/as	1.000.000	un millón (de + noun)
700	setecientos/as	2.000.000	dos millones (de + noun)

WILEY PLUS For more practice, see **Grammar Handbook** found in *WileyPLUS*.

. . . y algo más   Numbers from 200 to 999

- Numbers between 200–999 agree with the nouns that follow them:

  tresci**entos** alumn**os**   ochoci**entas** person**as**

- Although *and* can be used in English between hundreds and smaller numbers, **y** is not used in Spanish.

  450/ *four hundred (and) fifty* = **cuatrocientos cincuenta**

- The years above 1000 are not broken into two-digit groups as they are in English.

  1998/ *nineteen ninety-eight* = **mil novecientos noventa y ocho**

- In writing numbers, Spanish commonly uses a comma where English uses a period, and vice versa.

  English: 9.75 meters; 150,000 inhabitants   Spanish: **9,75** metros; **150.000** habitantes

- When **millón/ millones** is immediately followed by a noun, the preposition **de** is used.

  un millón *de* **pesos**   **dos millones** *de* **euros**

- A billion dollars = **mil millones** de dólares.

- A trillion dollars = **un billón** de dólares.

For additional practice on this grammar point, see PowerPoint slides on BCS and in *WileyPLUS*.

5-3   ¿En qué año?   RECYCLES: Numbers up to 100.

Primero, escucha los años de fundación de los restaurantes que lee tu profesor/a y escríbelos en la tercera columna. Luego, pon los restaurantes con sus años en orden cronológico y léeselos a la clase.

5-3   Read the name and the location of each restaurant, and the year it opened: a. [...] 1836, b. [...] 1905, c. [...] 1515, d. [...] 1860, e. [...] 1858, f. [...] 1725, g. [...] 1930. Then ask students to read the years in chronological order. For visual confirmation, write the years on the board. At the end of the activity, ask students to identify the oldest restaurant in their city or town.

Nombre del restaurante	Lugar[1]	Año
3 a. Delmonico's	Nueva York, EE. UU.	1836
6 b. El Cordano	Lima, Perú	1905
7 c. Restaurante La Diligencia	Tarragona, España	1515
5 d. Hostería Santo Domingo	Ciudad de México, México	1860
4 e. Café Tortoni	Buenos Aires, Argentina	1858
2 f. Casa Botín	Madrid, España	1725
7 g. Restaurante El Quijote	Nueva York, EE. UU.	1930

[1]place

5-4 En un supermercado de Santiago de Chile

Paso 1. Tu amigo está enfermo y tú vas al supermercado por él. En su casa, él mira las ofertas especiales que se anuncian en la Red y te dice por teléfono *cinco* cosas que necesita, y la cantidad[1]. Tú escribes la información.

MODELO

Amigo: *Quiero un kilo de manzanas, dos kilos de zanahorias, tres pimientos rojos, dos pizzas con mozzarella y un pollo entero.*

Tú: *Bueno.* (Apuntas la información.)

5-4 Before the class does *Actividad 5-4*, practice the numbers by having students read the price of each item aloud.

> *Note:*
> 1 U.S. dollar = approx. 486 Chilean pesos. (03-12)
> Kg = kilo(gram) (1 kilo = 2.2 lbs.)

manzanas, 1kg 299 pesos

peras, 1 kg 549 pesos

bananas, 1 kg 329 pesos

zanahorias, 1 kg 180 pesos

pimientos rojos, 1 unidad 199 pesos

cebollas, 1 kg 468 pesos

lechuga, 1 unidad 352 pesos

pizza con *mozzarella*, 980 pesos

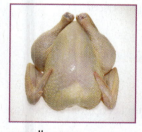

un pollo entero, aprox. 2 kg 2.750 pesos

carne molida, 7%, 1 kg 1.599 pesos

bistec, 1kg 3.052 pesos

panecitos frescos para hamburguesas, una docena 839 pesos

Paso 2. Después, llevas[2] las compras a la casa de tu amigo. Él te da las gracias y te pregunta cuánto es. Le dices los precios de cada cosa[3] y el total.

MODELO

Amigo: *¡Muchas gracias! ¿Cuánto es?* (Escribe la información que obtienes de tu amigo para confirmar que el total es correcto.)

Tú: *A ver, un kilo de manzanas, 299 pesos,... Y el precio total es...*

[1]quantity, [2]take, [3]**cada...** each item

5-4 If time allows, have students switch roles. As a follow-up to *Paso 2*, have some students call out their totals while others write them on the board, with the class making any necessary corrections.

5-5 Preparativos para una boda

 Paso 1. Linda va a casarse en seis meses en Miami. Hoy va a ver el menú del chef Adolfo para escoger la comida para el banquete. Léelo para familiarizarte con lo que hay.

EL MENÚ DEL CHEF ADOLFO

sopa de mariscos
$8.25

sopa de pollo
$7.50

aperitivos variados
$5 por persona

ensalada
de la casa
$7.00

ensalada
de frutas
tropicales
$7.00

pollo al vino con
arroz y zanahorias
$20.00

salmón con puré
de papas y espárragos
$25.75

bistec con papas fritas y brócoli
$27.00

plato vegetariano: arroz,
frijoles y verduras variadas
$15.00

pasta con camarones
al limón
$18.50

pastel de bodas
(de fresa, limón o vainilla) $700

pan (blanco o integral[1])
$1.50 por persona

© John Wiley & Sons, Inc.

 Paso 2. Ahora, Linda y su madre hablan con el chef Adolfo y escogen la comida. Hagan los tres papeles[2] según el modelo.

- El chef saluda[3] a Linda y a su madre.
- El chef les pregunta el número total de invitados y lo apunta.
- La madre y la hija leen el menú del chef y hacen la selección para cada categoría.
- El chef lo apunta y les da el precio total de cada categoría; madre o hija reaccionan al oír[4] los precios.
- Al final, la madre y la hija preguntan cuál es la suma total y el chef responde.
- La madre y la hija deciden si aceptan o no. Todos se despiden[5].

[1]whole wheat, [2]**Hagan...** Play the three roles, [3]greets, [4]**al...** upon hearing, [5]**se...** say goodbye

MODELO

Chef: *Buenas tardes, ¿en qué puedo servirles?*

Madre: *Buenas tardes. Mi hija va a casarse y venimos a escoger¹ la comida para la recepción.*

Chef: *A ver²... ¿Cuántos invitados van a tener?*

Hija: *Cincuenta.*

Chef: *(Apunta el número.) Bien. ¿Desean aperitivos?*

Hija: *Sí, aperitivos variados.*

Chef: *Los aperitivos son 5.00 dólares por persona. El total es 250 dólares.*

Madre: *¡Caramba! ¡Qué caro! (o) Muy bien.*

NÚMERO DE INVITADOS: <u>50</u>

Comida	Descripción	Precio por persona	Total
aperitivos	aperitivos variados	$5.00	$250
sopa			
ensalada			
tres platos principales			
pan			
pastel de bodas			
			SUMA TOTAL: _____

5-5 Point out to students that when pronouncing the following two words the stress goes on the "o" in d**ó**lares and on the "a" in tot**a**l. By doing so they would avoid confusing **dólares** with **dolores** (pains).

5-5 You may project the PowerPoint slide of chef Adolfo's menu and ask students in groups of three to role-play their parts for the class. One group makes selections for soup and salad, another for the main dish, and so on, as time permits.

The scripts and recordings for the **¡A escuchar!** sections are included on the Book Companion Site (BCS) for instructors and in *WileyPLUS*.

¡A escuchar! La lista de compras³

Paso 1. Gabriel le dice a su esposa que va a ir al supermercado y que necesita su ayuda para completar la lista de compras. Escucha la conversación.

WILEY PLUS Go to *WileyPLUS* to complete **Paso 2** of this listening activity.

Jennifer e Ysenia están en el supermercado. Van a hacer las compras para la cena en la casa de Jennifer.

© John Wiley & Sons, Inc.

To introduce students to direct object pronouns used in context, have them take parts and read the **historieta** out loud. To check their comprehension and call their attention to the pronouns, ask the following questions: **1.** ¿Cómo cocina Ysenia la carne? ¿Y el pescado? **2.** ¿Va a invitar Jennifer a Fabio y a sus amigos?

¹choose, ²A... Let's see..., ³**lista...** grocery list

Go to *WileyPLUS* to review this grammar point with the help of the **Animated Grammar Tutorial.** For more practice, go to the **Grammar Handbook.**

For additional practice on this grammar point, see PowerPoint slides on BCS and in *WileyPLUS.*

Remind students that these direct object pronouns are different from those previously seen with **gustar,** which are *indirect* object pronouns (Ch. 7).

Write the direct object pronouns on the board or on a transparency. Present a few sample questions and answers (use student names): **¿Conoces a Marta? Sí, la conozco. ¿Conoces a Pedro? No, no lo conozco. ¿Conoces a Ana y a Linda? Sí, las conozco. ¿Conoces a Martín y a Tomás? No, no los conozco.**

To demonstrate placement of direct object pronouns, write: **no, te, llamo, quiero,** and **llamar** on separate sheets of paper and give them to five students. Have the three students holding **llamo, te** and **no** (out of sequence) step forward, and have the class help place the words in the correct order. Replace the student holding **llamo** with the two students holding **quiero** and **llamar.** Again have the class help arrange the students (and words) in the correct order: **No te quiero llamar,** (or) **No quiero llamarte.**

GRAMÁTICA

¡Manos a la obra!

Referring to people, places, and things: Direct object pronouns

Direct object nouns or pronouns answer the questions *what?* or *who?/whom?* in relation to the verb. Let's look at examples based on the conversation of Jennifer and Ysenia as they shop.

—¿Compra Jennifer **la carne** para la cena?　—Sí, **la** compra.
—¿Invita a **los amigos** de Fabio?　—Sí, **los** invita.

You use direct object pronouns to refer to persons, places and things without mentioning their names. Direct object pronouns agree in gender and number with the nouns they replace or refer to.

—¿Tienes **el dinero**, Jennifer?　*Do you have the money, Jennifer?*
—Sí, **lo** tengo.　*Yes, I have it.*
—¿Y tienes **la lista de compras**?　*Do you have the shopping list?*
— Sí, **la** tengo.　*Yes, I have it.*

The direct object pronouns are:

me	*me*	**nos**	*us*
te	*you (fam.)*	**os**	*you (fam.)*
lo	*you (m., form.), him, it (m.)*	**los**	*you (m., form.), them (m.)*
la	*you (f., form.), her, it (f.)*	**las**	*you (f., form.), them (f.)*

Placement:

- Direct object pronouns are placed immediately *before* a conjugated verb.

  Ysenia prepara **las verduras**.　　**Las** prepara.

- If a conjugated verb is followed by an infinitive, the direct object pronoun is placed either *before the conjugated* verb or *attached to the infinitive.*

  Jennifer va a invitar a **Fabio**.　→　**Lo** va a invitar. (o) Va a invitar**lo**.

- When the direct object pronoun is placed before the conjugated verb, **no** precedes the pronoun to make a question or statement negative.

  —¿**No lo** compras?　*Aren't you buying it?*
  —**No, no lo** compro.　*No, I'm not buying it.*

- Direct object pronouns are attached to affirmative **tú** commands. A written accent is added to the stressed syllable of regular command forms. No accent is added to irregular **tú** commands with an attached pronoun.

  Jennifer, prepara **la carne**.　　Prepár**ala**.
  Ysenia, corta **las papas**.　　Córt**alas**.
  Haz **el pescado**.　　Haz**lo**.

¡En acción!

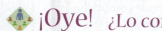

¡Oye! ¿Lo compran o no?

Escucha la información acerca de Luis, Ana y Jaime, y di qué compra o no compra cada uno. Responde con: «**Sí, lo/ la/ los/ las compra.**» (o) «**No, no lo/ la/ los/ las compra.**»

5-6 Un compañero muy distraído[1]   RECYCLES prepositions of location.

Pepe está preparando tacos. Como es muy distraído, no encuentra[2] los ingredientes y le pregunta a su compañero Ricardo dónde están. Hagan los dos papeles, completando la conversación con la información apropiada. Primero repasen el vocabulario de la página 43 y luego presten atención a los pronombres (**me, te, lo,...**).

huevos

tortillas

carne

cebollas

Pepe: Ricardo, **te** estoy hablando, ¿no **me** oyes?

Ricardo: Sí, **te** oigo.

Pepe: ¿Dónde están los tomates? No **los** encuentro.

Ricardo: En el refrigerador, al lado de __la lechuga__. ¿No **los** ves?

Pepe: Ah, sí, ahora **los** veo. ¿Y la carne?

Ricardo: Está debajo de[3] __la lechuga__ y al lado de __las zanahorias__.

Pepe: Ahora **la** veo. ¿Y el queso?

Ricardo: Pepe, ¡qué distraído eres! No buscas bien. ¿No **lo** ves?

Pepe: ¡Ah sí! Aquí está, __al lado__ de __los huevos__. ¿Y la salsa? Ah, también **la** veo. Está __al lado__ de __la leche__.

Ricardo: Bueno, ya no **me** necesitas más, ¿verdad?

Pepe: Pues, sólo una pregunta más. ¿Dónde están las tortillas y las cebollas? No **las** veo en el refrigerador.

Ricardo: ¡Están en __la mesa__! ¿Para qué **las** quieres?

Pepe: Es obvio, ¿no? ¡Para preparar los __tacos__!

Ricardo: Ah, ¡estupendo! ¡Qué hambre tengo![4]

Pepe: David y Tomás **nos** van a llamar a las siete. ¿Quieres invitar**los** a __cenar__?

Ricardo: __[...] (Last answer will vary.)__.

[1]absentminded, [2]find, [3]**debajo...** under, [4]**Qué...** How hungry I am!

¡Oye! Encourage students to jot down their yes/no answers rather than call them out. After most have done so, elicit responses in full sentences. This encourages participation by all students rather than by only a few.

Guión para ¡Oye!
1. Luis es un **vegetariano** muy estricto. Para el almuerzo, ¿compra o no lo siguiente?
· camarones
· uvas
· brócoli
· chuletas de cerdo
· ajo y cebollas
· frijoles
· huevos
2. El plato favorito de Ana es la **sopa de pollo con verduras.** Para prepararla, ¿compra o no lo siguiente?
· pollo
· zanahorias
· arvejas
· pescado
· manzanas
· cebolla
· mariscos
3. A Jaime le gusta **la ensalada mixta.** Para prepararla, ¿compra o no lo siguiente?
· pimientos rojos y verdes
· papas
· lechuga
· tomates
· arroz
· cerezas
· carne

5-6 You may use the PowerPoint slide of the illustration to confirm answers. Then have two students read the dialogue in front of the class. Encourage them to be expressive!

5-6 ANOTHER STEP: Ask the following questions: **Según la conversación, ¿oye Pepe a Ricardo?** *Sí, lo oye.* **¿Encuentra Pepe los tomates?** *Sí, los encuentra.* **¿Busca Pepe la leche?** *No, no la busca.* **¿Y las zanahorias?** *No, no las busca.* **¿Y la carne?** *Sí, la busca.* **¿Encuentra Pepe todos los ingredientes que busca?** *Sí, los encuentra.* **¿Va Pepe a preparar tacos?** *Sí, va a prepararlos.* (o) *Sí, los va a preparar.*

© John Wiley & Sons, Inc.

5-7 This activity may be completed by students working in pairs, or as an instructor-led activity, with the instructor asking the questions.

5-7 ANOTHER STEP: Ask students to name and give some information about shops in their city or town that specialize in a particular food: **Donde yo vivo hay una quesería que vende quesos muy buenos.**

5-8 Have two students perform for the class. You can also set up a "market" in the classroom, with food items either drawn by students (provide markers and paper) or cut from magazines. Students move from stand to stand purchasing items.

5-9 Answers will vary. Make sure students use the informal command with the appropriate pronoun.

5-7 ¿En qué clase de tienda?

Este mes trabajas de voluntario/a en un pueblo hispano. Allí, hay muchas tiendas que se especializan en un solo producto. Pregúntale a una persona del pueblo dónde compra los productos de la lista. Él/Ella contesta usando **lo, la, los** o **las**. Hagan los dos papeles.

> Panadería Luz   Floristería Rosa   Tortillería López   Quesería Sol   Frutería Pérez
> Pescadería Cruz   Marisquería Marina   Taquería Lupe   Carnicería Tomás

MODELO

E1: ¿Dónde compras el pescado?   E2: *Lo* compro en la Pescadería Cruz.

1. el pescado   3. el pan   5. la carne   7. el queso   9. las piñas y fresas
2. los camarones   4. los tacos   6. las tortillas   8. las flores

5-8 Compras para la cena   RECYCLES gustar.

Paso 1. Uds. dos van al Mercado Central (págs. 146–147) para comprar los ingredientes para la cena. Pasen por las secciones en el orden que se indica abajo, y escojan lo que necesitan. Compren sólo los ingredientes que les gustan a los dos. Usen **lo, la, los, las** según el modelo. Después de cada sección cambien de papel[1]. Tienen *cinco* minutos.

> LEGUMBRES-VERDURAS → FRUTERÍA → CARNICERÍA → PESCADERÍA- MARISQUERÍA → PANADERÍA

MODELO

E1: (LEGUMBRES-VERDURAS) A mí me gusta el brócoli, ¿y a ti?

E2: Sí, me gusta.   **o:**   No, no me gusta.

E1: Bueno, **lo** compramos.   **o:**   Bueno, no **lo** compramos.

Paso 2. Díganle a otra pareja o a la clase los ingredientes que compraron y compartan su menú.

5-9 ¡Expresa tus deseos!

Hoy ustedes han decidido expresar muy claramente sus deseos. Tú miras la lista (1–6) y comunicas tus deseos con los mandatos de **tú**. En sus respuestas, tu compañero/a usa los pronombres apropiados (**me, te lo, la, los, las**) en lugar de las palabras subrayadas[2]. Túrnense.

MODELO
Invitar*me* a comer

E1: Invíta*me* a comer.

E2: Muy bien, **te** invito.   **o:**   No **te** invito.

1. *Escuchar*me   3. *Escribir* la lista de compras   5. *Pagar* las bebidas también
2. *Buscar* un lápiz   4. *Comprar* los ingredientes   6. *Hacer* los sándwiches
                                    con tu dinero

> ### . . . y algo más   The suffix *-ísimo*
>
> The suffix **-ísimo** can be added to many adjectives to intensify their meaning. In *Actividad 5-9*, note the following:
>
> **mucho** *a lot* → **muchísimo** *very much*   **rico** *delicious* → **riquísimo** *very delicious*
> (Note spelling change.)
>
> Can you intensify the adjectives **alto** and **divertido**?

For additional practice on this grammar point, see PowerPoint slides on BCS and in *WileyPLUS*.

PLUS For more practice, see **Grammar Handbook** found in *WileyPLUS*.

[1]**cambien...** change roles [2]underlined

5-10 Celebraciones a la luz de la luna

Paso 1. En la terraza de un restaurante del Caribe, *cuatro* parejas celebran el Día de los Enamorados (San Valentín). Primero, completen los espacios en blanco con el verbo indicado y los pronombres **me** o **te** correspondientes. Luego, lean las conversaciones con expresión. Finalmente, escriban en las líneas en blanco del margen, el número que corresponde con la información de cada pareja (1, 2, 3 o 4).

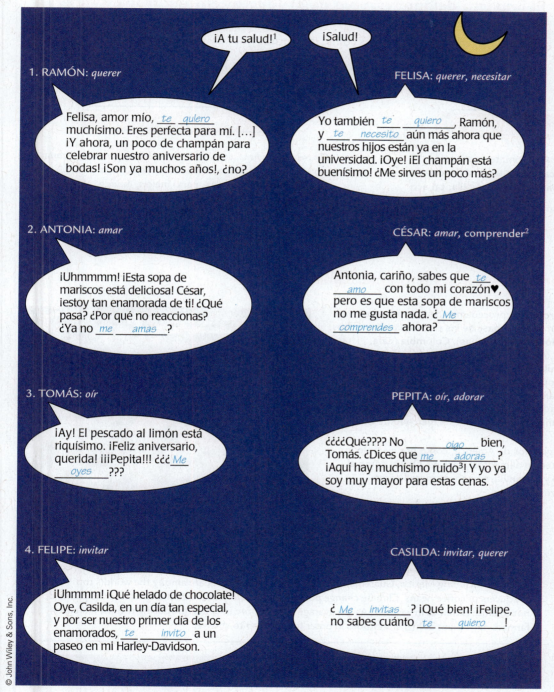

1. RAMÓN: *querer*

¡A tu salud!¹

Felisa, amor mío, _te quiero_ muchísimo. Eres perfecta para mí. [...] ¡Y ahora, un poco de champán para celebrar nuestro aniversario de bodas! ¡Son ya muchos años!, ¿no?

FELISA: *querer, necesitar*

¡Salud!

Yo también _te quiero_, Ramón, y _te necesito_ aún más ahora que nuestros hijos están ya en la universidad. ¡Oye! ¡El champán está buenísimo! ¿Me sirves un poco más?

2. ANTONIA: *amar*

¡Uhmmmm! ¡Esta sopa de mariscos está deliciosa! César, ¡estoy tan enamorada de ti! ¿Qué pasa? ¿Por qué no reaccionas? ¿Ya no _me amas_?

CÉSAR: *amar, comprender²*

Antonia, cariño, sabes que _te amo_ con todo mi corazón♥, pero es que esta sopa de mariscos no me gusta nada. ¿_Me comprendes_ ahora?

3. TOMÁS: *oír*

¡Ay! El pescado al limón está riquísimo. ¡Feliz aniversario, querida! ¡¡¡Pepita!!! ¿¿¿_Me oyes_???

PEPITA: *oír, adorar*

¿¿¿¿Qué???? No ___ _oigo_ bien, Tomás. ¿Dices que _me adoras_? ¡Aquí hay muchísimo ruido³! Y yo ya soy muy mayor para estas cenas.

4. FELIPE: *invitar*

¡Uhmmm! ¡Qué helado de chocolate! Oye, Casilda, en un día tan especial, y por ser nuestro primer día de los enamorados, _te invito_ a un paseo en mi Harley-Davidson.

CASILDA: *invitar, querer*

¿_Me invitas_? ¡Qué bien! ¡Felipe, no sabes cuánto _te quiero_!

Paso 2. El Día de los Enamorados decides dejar⁴ un mensaje especial para el amor de tu vida (real o imaginario) en el contestador de su teléfono. En *cuatro* oraciones, expresa tus sentimientos por esa persona. Usa los verbos del *Paso 1. Mi amor,…*

¹Cheers!, ²to understand, ³noise, ⁴leave

© John Wiley & Sons, Inc.

---

4 Es un matrimonio mayor que celebra sus bodas de oro (50 años de casados).

3 Es una pareja joven que celebra su primer día de San Valentín.

2 Es una pareja de recién casados.

1 Es un matrimonio que celebra sus bodas de plata (25 años de casados).

5-10 Review the answers for *Paso 1* before two pairs perform their dialogues in front of the class. Encourage them to read with great theatrical expression! (Applause is always in order!)

5-10 ANOTHER STEP: After students complete *Paso 2*, have them tell their Valentine's Day special messages to each other in groups of five. Students then nominate individuals with unique or clever messages, who in turn read their messages to the class.

5-10 Students will further practice direct object pronouns in the third scene of this chapter, along with the present progressive.

For an additional activity related to this cultural theme, see the PowerPoint slides on BCS and in *WileyPLUS*.

WILEY PLUS Go to *WileyPLUS* to see the video related to this reading.

Meets ACTFL Standards 1.1, interpersonal speaking; 1.2, interpretive reading; 2.2, cultural products; and 4.2, cultural comparisons.

Some students may find it interesting to know that many products brought from Europe to America originally came to Spain from Asia and Africa and that a number of them had been introduced in Spain as a result of the Moorish invasion.

Tu mundo cultural

Los productos hispanos y su historia

El impacto del intercambio de productos entre Europa y América

¿Sabes el origen de muchas de tus comidas favoritas y de sus ingredientes?

A raíz del[1] encuentro entre[2] el Viejo y el Nuevo Mundo (1492), comienza el intercambio de productos entre Europa y América. Su impacto es enorme en los dos continentes.

América → Europa

Flora: papa, batata *sweet potato*, tomate, pimiento, aguacate *avocado*, cacao, yuca, maní *peanut*, chile, calabaza *pumpkin*, frijol, maíz, piña, papaya, fresa, vainilla, tabaco

Fauna: pavo, bacalao *cod*, alpaca, llama

Europa → América

Flora: trigo *wheat*, café, caña de azúcar *sugar cane*, lechuga, ajo, cebolla, zanahoria, espinaca, arveja, banana, uva, naranja, limón, manzana, pera, melón, mango, almendra, aceituna/oliva, pimienta *pepper*, canela *cinnamon*, mostaza *mustard*

Fauna: vaca *cow*, cerdo, gallina *hen*, caballo *horse*

El impacto del intercambio en la dieta americana y europea

En América, algunos de los productos procedentes de Europa se cultivan con tal éxito[3], que constituyen ahora la base de las economías de muchos de sus países. Por ejemplo: **Honduras** (bananas), **Colombia** (café, segundo productor mundial), **Argentina** (trigo, uno de los primeros productores del mundo) y **Chile** (uvas, vino). Lo mismo[4] ocurre con los animales procedentes de Europa. Entre los primeros países del mundo en producción ganadera[5] están Argentina, Uruguay y Paraguay. Los tres exportan carne de gran calidad. ¿De qué continente son originarias las uvas, las manzanas y las naranjas que se ven en este mercado de Chile?

En Europa, los productos originarios de América, como por ejemplo la papa y el bacalao, se convierten en alimentos[6] básicos. Otros, como el tomate, el cacao, el pimiento y la vainilla, son ahora ingredientes indispensables en la dieta europea.

PictureGarden/The Image Bank/Getty Images, Inc.

¿SABES QUE...?

Guatemala is the world's leading producer of chewing gum (**chicle**). The revenue from gum exports totals more than $2 million a year. Until 1973, Guatemala exported gum solely to the United States.

¿SABES QUE...?

Europeans brought coffee to the Americas in the 18th century, and a number of Spanish-American countries including Mexico, Guatemala, Costa Rica, and Colombia are among the world's top producers of coffee beans. Climate change poses a threat to coffee production because the plants do not tolerate extremes in weather. As the average temperature in coffee-producing regions increases, farmers must plant at higher altitudes in order for the crop to survive.

¿SABES QUE...?

Vanilla, the aromatic substance added to baked goods and cosmetics, has its origins in Mexico, and like cacao, it was cultivated by Pre-Columbian peoples. The Spanish word **vainilla** is the diminutive form of **vaina** or *seed pod*. Vanilla beans grow in pods produced by a type of orchid.

[1]**A...** As a result of, [2]between, [3]**tal...** such success, [4]**Lo...** The same thing, [5]cattle, [6]foods

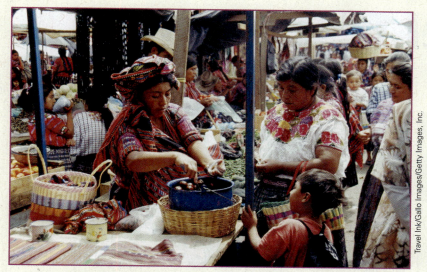

En un mercado de Guatemala.

Travel Ink/Gallo Images/Getty Images, Inc.

Beginning with this chapter, *Contraste cultural* sections are in Spanish, giving students the opportunity to talk in the target language. You may prefer to allow English for a few minutes, however, for a more in-depth discussion.

To more fully respond to the first item in the *Contraste cultural*, remind students that they can find the Spanish names of the countries in the inside back cover of their textbooks.

chiles de México
espárragos blancos de Perú
papayas y **mangos** de México
uvas de Chile
bananas de Honduras
pescado de Chile
camarones de Ecuador
aceitunas y **aceite de oliva** de España
café de Colombia, Costa Rica, Guatemala y Puerto Rico
vino de Chile y de España

Los supermercados en EE. UU. y su selección de productos hispanos

La influencia hispana es evidente en numerosos aspectos de la vida estadounidense y los supermercados no son una excepción. Observa las etiquetas[1] de los productos en tu supermercado. Te va a sorprender la cantidad de productos originarios de países hispanos que se importan en EE. UU., como los de la lista azul del margen.

¿Qué aprendiste?

1. ¿A partir de qué año se inicia el intercambio de productos entre Europa y América?
   1492.
2. ¿Cuáles son algunos de los productos procedentes de Europa que constituyen ahora la base de la economía de algunos países de América?
   Bananas, café, trigo, uvas, vino.
3. ¿Qué productos originarios de América son parte indispensable de la dieta o de la cocina europea?
   El tomate, el cacao, el pimiento y la vainilla.

Actividad cultural

Escribe una lista de: **(a)** *tres* productos originarios de América que te gustan; **(b)** *tres* productos procedentes de Europa que te gustan; **(c)** *tres* productos hispanos importados que compras en tu supermercado. Luego, compártela con un compañero/a de clase.

Contraste cultural

En grupos de *cuatro*, hablen de:

- las comidas o productos de otros países o continentes que Uds. comen o compran (China, Japón, Tailandia, Vietnam, la India, Oriente Medio[2], África,...)

- las comidas o productos de su país o región que son populares en otros países

¿SABES QUE...?

The olive tree dates back to 4000 B.C. Spain is the world's leading supplier of olive oil, producing two million tons a year with a value of US$1.7 billion.

¿SABES QUE...?

Chocolate is made by crushing the beans of the cacao fruit into cocoa powder and mixing it with other ingredients such as sugar milk, vanilla and cinnamon. The word **cacao** is Mayan, and the Aztecs used cacao beans as currency. An officer of Hernán Cortés, the Spanish conquistador, observed Moctezuma, the Aztec leader, drinking 50 flagons (more than a gallon) of chocolate a day.

Masterfile

[1]labels, [2]**Oriente...** Middle East

2 En el restaurante

Pronunciación: Practice pronunciation of the chapter's new vocabulary in *WileyPLUS*.

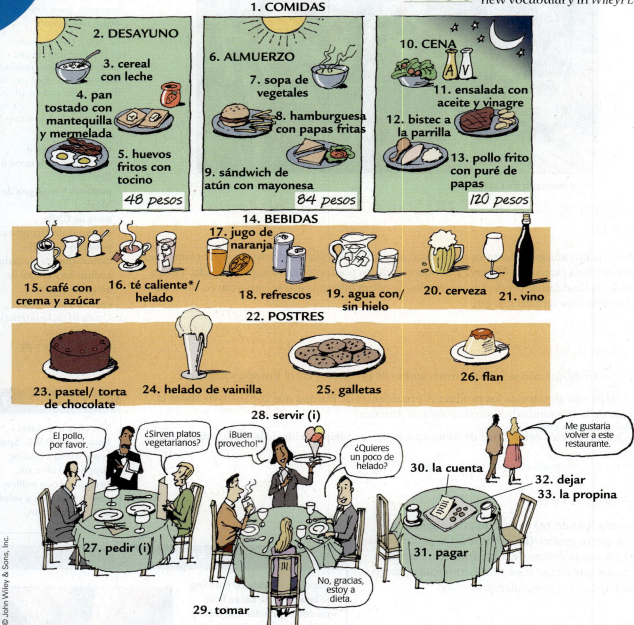

1. meals, food 2. breakfast (*m.*) 3. cereal (*m.*) with milk 4. toast with butter and jam 5. fried eggs with bacon 6. lunch (*m.*) 7. vegetable soup 8. hamburger with French fries 9. tuna salad sandwich (*m.*) 10. dinner (*f.*) 11. salad with oil and vinegar 12. grilled steak 13. fried chicken with mashed potatoes 14. drinks, beverages 15. coffee (*m.*) with cream and sugar 16. hot tea (*m.*)/ iced tea 17. orange juice 18. soft drinks, sodas 19. water with/ without ice 20. beer 21. wine 22. desserts 23. chocolate cake; **pastel** (*m.*) 24. vanilla ice cream 25. cookies 26. caramel custard (*m.*) 27. to order, ask for 28. to serve 29. to drink, take 30. the bill 31. to pay (for) 32. to leave (behind) 33. tip

*caliente *hot (temperature)*; picante *hot (spicy)* ** ¡Buen provecho! *Enjoy your meal!*

¡En acción!

5-11 El menú

Paso 1. De los menús de la página 160, ¿qué va a pedir tu compañero/a? Hazle las preguntas de la primera columna. Él/Ella responde según el modelo de la segunda columna, y tú escribes la información en la tercera. Luego, cambien de papel.

5-11 Answers will vary.

Preguntas	Respuestas	Información escrita
1. ¿Qué vas a pedir en el desayuno? ¿Y para beber?	*Voy a pedir cereal con leche...*	*Samuel va a pedir cereal con leche...*
2. ¿Qué vas a pedir en el almuerzo? ¿Y para beber? ¿Y de postre?		
3. ¿Qué vas a pedir en la cena? ¿Y para beber? ¿Y de postre?		

Paso 2. Ahora, comparte la información de la tercera columna con la clase, para saber cuáles son las comidas más populares del desayuno, del almuerzo y de la cena.

. . . y algo más   Describing food

- You have noticed how Spanish speakers say *orange juice* (**jugo de naranja**), *chocolate cake* (**torta de chocolate**), and *vanilla ice cream* (**helado de vainilla**). How many types of juice, cakes/ pies, and ice cream can you identify?

   dish + **de** + *flavor*

- You have also learned how to talk about sandwiches (and other foods) with multiple ingredients: **sándwich *de* atún *con* mayonesa.** What other combinations of sandwiches can you think of?

   sandwich + **de** + *main ingredient* + **con** + *other ingredients*

For more practice, see **Grammar Handbook** found in *WileyPLUS*.

5-12 Tema de conversación: las comidas

Observen la escena de la página 160 y háganse las siguientes preguntas para saber las preferencias de cada uno/a.

1. De las tres comidas del día, ¿cuál es tu favorita?

2. ¿A qué hora desayunas, almuerzas y cenas?

3. ¿Qué desayunas[1] ? ¿Y qué jugo o bebida caliente tomas?

4. ¿Cuál es tu sopa favorita? ¿Y tu sándwich favorito?

5. ¿Qué bebida te gusta más con el almuerzo? ¿Y con la cena?

(continúa)

[1]**Qué...** What do you have for breakfast?

5-12 You may review responses using the PowerPoint slide of the menu/ restaurant scene.

You may want to point out to your students that **desayunar, almorzar** and **cenar** mean to have breakfast, lunch and dinner, respectively. Each of those infinitives already contain the idea of "to have" and therefore is not necessary to add anything else.

5-12 PERSONALIZED QUESTIONS: Una persona de un país hispano les pregunta lo siguiente: En su país, ¿qué se come normalmente en el desayuno? ¿En el almuerzo? ¿Y en la cena? ¿A qué hora se come cada comida?

6. Cuando cenas en un restaurante, normalmente, ¿pides sopa? ¿ensalada? ¿postre?

7. ¿Qué postres se sirven en el restaurante de la página 160? ¿Cuál es tu postre favorito?

8. En el restaurante, ¿qué pide el señor? ¿Es vegetariana la señora?

9. ¿Qué sirve la mesera? ¿Qué dice? ¿Quién no desea tomar helado? ¿Por qué?

10. ¿Qué pagamos en un restaurante después de comer o cenar? ¿Dejas una buena propina en los restaurantes?

11. ¿Qué dice la señora que sale del restaurante con su esposo?

5-13 Los restaurantes favoritos

¿SABES QUE...?

People in most Hispanic countries, when possible, eat the main meal of the day with their families, usually between 1:00 and 2:00 p.m. Breakfast is normally quite light, and dinner is generally later than in the United States, typically between 8:00 and 9:00 p.m. Spain is known for its late lunches and dinners, particularly on weekends.

DreamPictures/Taxi/Getty Images, Inc.

En EE. UU. la comida mexicana es muy popular y los restaurantes mexicanos forman ya parte de las opciones culinarias preferidas por los estadounidenses.

 Paso 1.   ¿Cuál es el restaurante favorito de tu compañero/a de clase? ¿Qué se sirve allí? Pregúntale lo siguiente y apunta la información. Luego, cambien de papel.

Incluyan:

5-13   At the conclusion of *Paso 1*, poll the class to determine their favorite restaurants.

- nombre y ubicación[1] del restaurante (¿Cómo se llama? ¿Dónde está?)

- clase de comidas que se sirven allí (¿Mexicana? ¿Italiana? ¿Tailandesa?...)

- platos y bebidas que le gustan de allí (ensalada, plato principal, verduras, postre)

- precio de los platos principales (cuestan... dólares)

- frecuencia con la que come allí (todas las semanas, una vez al mes,...)

 Paso 2.   Ahora, con la información obtenida, comparte con la clase la información acerca del restaurante favorito de tu compañero/a. Da todos los detalles posibles.

[1]location

¡A escuchar! Una cena especial

Paso 1. Los señores Alvar están en su restaurante favorito para celebrar el 23° aniversario de su matrimonio. Escucha la conversación entre ellos y el mesero.

WILEY PLUS Go to *WileyPLUS* to complete **Paso 2** of this listening activity.

Ejemplos de comidas de los restaurantes del mundo hispano

Desayuno de México: quesadillas, frijoles y papaya con jugo de naranja y café con leche.

Almuerzo de Costa Rica: pescado a la parrilla con limón y ensalada de tomate, pepino y cebolla.

Cena típica de Venezuela: carne de res, arroz, frijoles negros y plátanos fritos, con pan y jugo de frutas naturales.

Merienda[1] de España: chocolate con churros.

Almuerzo típico de Uruguay: parrillada con diferentes carnes

Postre típico de Argentina: dulce de leche.

[1]Afternoon snack

Fabio y sus amigos compran las bebidas para la cena con los padres de Jennifer.

¿Qué **piensan** de este supermercado?

Pienso que es estupendo. Aquí **podemos** comprar todas las bebidas.

¿**Quieren** refrescos o jugo?

Yo **prefiero** jugo de piña, ¿y ustedes?

Podemos llevar varios jugos y también, una botella de vino.

¡Qué buena idea!

Y ahora,... **volvemos** al carro... ¡y a cenar!

© John Wiley & Sons, Inc.

Go to *WileyPLUS* to review this grammar point with the help of the **Animated Grammar Tutorial** and **Verb Conjugator**. For more practice, go to the **Grammar Handbook**.

For additional practice on this grammar point, see PowerPoint slides on BCS and in *WileyPLUS*.

To introduce students to stem-changing verbs used in context, have them take parts and read the **historieta** out loud. To check their comprehension and call their attention to the verbs, ask the following questions: **1. ¿Qué bebidas pueden llevar? 2. Después de comprar las bebidas, ¿adónde vuelven?**

Show students the "shoe" patterns of stem changes, visible with the three singular forms on the left, the three plural on the right, and a line enclosing all verb forms with a stem change.

Name one activity you usually do, and ask several students if they do it too: *Almuerzo* **en la cafetería. ¿Y tú?** Try to find a student who does, so you can say [...] y yo *almorzamos* **en la cafetería.** If two students respond in the same way, say [...] y [...] *almuerzan* **en la cafetería, ¿verdad?** *More examples:* **Prefiero cenar en casa. Pido camarones a veces. Juego al... Duermo ocho horas.**

GRAMÁTICA

¡Manos a la obra!

2

Talking about actions, desires, and preferences in the present: Stem-changing verbs

You know how to form the present tense of regular verbs: you drop the infinitive ending (**-ar, -er** or **-ir**) and add the present tense endings, according to the person.

Some verbs also change the *stem*—the portion left after you drop the infinitive ending. The last vowel before the ending changes in all persons except **nosotros** and **vosotros.**

e → ie		o → ue		e → i	
querer (ie) *to want, love*		**dormir (ue)** *to sleep*		**pedir (i)** *to ask for, order*	
quiero	queremos	duermo	dormimos	pido	pedimos
quieres	queréis	duermes	dormís	pides	pedís
quiere	quieren	duerme	duermen	pide	piden

Let's look at examples based on the three friends' conversation in the supermarket.

e → ie

entender (ie) *to understand* — ¿Entiendes la lista de ingredientes?
pensar (ie) *to think* — ¿Piensan Uds. que aquí venden jugo de piña?
preferir (ie) *to prefer* — Prefiero comprar todas las bebidas.

o → ue

almorzar (ue) *to eat lunch* — ¿A qué hora almuerzas, Mario?
contar (ue) *to count* — Cuento los refrescos para ver si hay suficientes.
costar (ue) *to cost* — ¿Cuánto cuesta la botella de vino?
poder (ue) *to be able* — Fabio, ¿pueden Uds. cenar a las siete?
volver (ue) *to return* — Los tres amigos vuelven al carro.
jugar* (ue) *to play sports/games* — Mario, ¿juegas al básquetbol antes del almuerzo?

e → i

repetir (i) *to repeat* — La madre de Jennifer repite el menú.
servir (i) to serve — ¿Qué sirven sus padres?

The affirmative **tú** commands of these verbs also have the stem change.

Fabio, **vuelve** al supermercado.   *Fabio, return to the supermarket.*
Pide otro jugo.   *Ask for another juice.*

*The verb **jugar** changes the **u** to **ue**. See page 111.

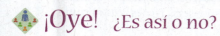

¡En acción!

 ¡Oye! ¿Es así o no?

Escucha lo que dice tu profesor/a y di si piensas que es cierto o no lo siguiente.

5-14 ¿Es así en nuestra universidad?

Paso 1. En grupos de *cuatro*, un/a estudiante lee la siguiente[1] información en voz alta y cada persona del grupo marca **Sí** o **No** según su opinión.

Sí	No	
☐	☐	**1.** Los estudiantes **pueden** estacionar *(park)* sin dificultad en la universidad.
☐	☐	**2.** La cafetería **sirve** comida muy nutritiva.
☐	☐	**3.** Los estudiantes **piensan** que casi todas las clases son buenas.
☐	☐	**4.** Los profesores **entienden** los problemas de los estudiantes.
☐	☐	**5.** Los estudiantes **prefieren** estudiar en la biblioteca.
☐	☐	**6.** Muchos estudiantes **vuelven** tarde a casa porque trabajan.

Paso 2. Comparen sus respuestas. En los casos en que todos coincidan en su respuesta, díganselo a su profesor/a, que quiere saber sus opiniones: En nuestra **opinión**, los estudiantes (no) **pueden** estacionar sin dificultad.

> **. . . y algo más** Uses of *pensar*
>
> Note four uses of **pensar**.
> - **pensar de:** to ask for an opinion. ¿Qué **piensas de...**? *What do you think about...?*
> - **Pensar en:** to think about something or someone ¿**En** qué **piensas**? *What are you thinking about* **Pienso en** mis notas. *I'm thinking about my grades*
> - **pensar que:** to state an opinion. **Pienso que...** *I think (that)...*
> - **pensar +** *infinitive:* to plan/ intend to do something. **Pienso ir.** *I plan/ intend to go.*

 5-15 Una conversación por Skype™

Juan, un estudiante de Quito, capital de Ecuador, va a estudiar en tu college o universidad el próximo semestre. En este momento, habla contigo por Skype y tiene muchas preguntas para ti. Hagan los dos papeles. Luego, túrnense.

MODELO Juan quiere saber si[2] las clases son difíciles y **entiendes** bien a tus profesores.

Juan: *¿Son difíciles las clases? ¿**Entiendes** bien a tus profesores?*

Tú: *Algunas son difíciles, pero en general, **entiendo** si voy a clase y hago la tarea.*

JUAN QUIERE SABER:

1. si las clases son difíciles y si **entiendes** bien a tus profesores
2. qué clases **prefieres** y cuánto **cuesta** cada clase
3. dónde **almuerzan** los estudiantes y qué tipo de comida **se sirve** allí
4. a qué deportes **juegan** los estudiantes
5. qué **piensas de** tus profesores y **de** los otros estudiantes

[1]following, [2]if

¡Oye! After students guess whether each of your statements is true, set the record straight by providing the correct information.

Guión para ¡Oye!
1. **Quiero** estudiar chino. ¿Sí o no?
2. **Entiendo** francés.
3. **Juego** muy bien al ping-pong.
4. **Prefiero** vivir en el campo.
5. Durante la semana, **vuelvo** a casa a las diez de la noche.
6. **Duermo** cinco horas todas las noches.
7. **Almuerzo** en mi oficina.
8. En los restaurantes, **pido** cerveza.
9. **Pienso** en mis estudiantes día y noche.

For additional practice on this grammar point, see PowerPoint slides on BCS and in *WileyPLUS*.

For more practice, see **Grammar Handbook** found in *WileyPLUS*.

Art: © John Wiley & Sons, Inc., Photo: Hola Images/Getty Images, Inc.

5-16 If time is at a premium, ask students to get feedback from *two* rather than *three* classmates for each question. *Option:* Students may complete the activity in groups of four.

5-16   ANOTHER STEP: Ask each student to share one item that they had in common with a classmate they interviewed (thus practicing the **nosotros** form): [...] y yo pedimos mariscos cuando vamos a un buen restaurante a cenar.

5-16 ¡Hablemos de comida!

Paso 1.   ¿Quieres conocer los hábitos de comer de tus compañeros? Camina por la clase y hazles cada pregunta a *tres* estudiantes diferentes. Apunta las respuestas. Tienes *ocho* minutos.

SONDEO

1. ¿Dónde **almuerzas** durante la semana? ¿A qué hora?

   dónde   a. _____   b. _____   c. _____

   a qué hora   a. _____   b. _____   c. _____

2. ¿Qué **prefieres** comer y beber en el desayuno?

   comer   a. _____   b. _____   c. _____

   beber   a. _____   b. _____   c. _____

3. Cuando vas a un buen restaurante a cenar, ¿qué **pides**?

                  a. _____   b. _____   c. _____

4. En general, ¿qué **piensas** de la «comida rápida»?

   Pienso que...   a. _____   b. _____   c. _____

5. ¿Qué comida **puedes** preparar tú solo/a?

                  a. _____   b. _____   c. _____

6. ¿Qué platos **quieres** aprender a preparar?

                  a. _____   b. _____   c. _____

7. Los fines de semana, ¿**duermes** la siesta después del almuerzo?

                  a. _____   b. _____   c. _____

Paso 2.   En grupos de *seis*, comparen las respuestas a cada pregunta y apunten las que tienen en común varios estudiantes. Luego, una persona de cada grupo informa al resto de la clase: *En nuestro grupo, la mayoría de los estudiantes **almuerza** en la cafetería al mediodía.*

5-17 En el Café Ibérico de Chicago

Paso 1.   Estás con dos amigos en el **Café Ibérico,** un restaurante de Chicago que sirve comida española y se especializa en tapas. Antes de llamar[1] al mesero, Uds. leen el menú y hablan de los platos que prefieren o piensan pedir. Usen los verbos siguientes.

You might want to tell your students to keep an open mind with regard to food and to be adventurous by trying new dishes. After all, the food we like is an acquired taste.

> querer   preferir   pedir   pensar

MODELO

E1:   *¿Qué **quieren** pedir Uds.?*

E2:   *Yo **pienso** pedir dos o tres tapas; unas calientes y otras frías.*

E3:   *Pues, yo aquí siempre **pido** ensalada, pero hoy **prefiero** la sopa.*

[1]**Antes...** Before calling

Café Ibérico — TAPAS BAR

ENSALADAS

Ensalada de la casa	$ 4.50

House salad with sherry vinaigrette and olive oil.

Ensalada mixta	$ 5.50

Spanish style mixed salad with asparagus, beets, hearts of palm, endive, dressed with our vinaigrette and wine dressing.

Ensalada de legumbres	$ 4.50

A combination of seasonal grilled vegetables marinated with sherry vinaigrette.

TAPAS FRÍAS

Aceitunas aliñadas	$ 5.50

Marinated Spanish olives.

Canelón de atún	$ 5.95

Tuna cannelloni served with a creamy whitewine sauce.

Pimientos asados	$ 4.50

Fire roasted three color peppers with olive oil.

Patatas ali-oli	$ 5.50

Red potatoes with garlic mayonnaise sauce.

Jamón ibérico	$ 7.95

Spanish style cured ham with manchego cheese and tomato bread.

Tortilla española	$ 5.50

Spanish omelet.

SOPAS

Caldo gallego	$ 3.95

Galician style soup with white beans and rappini.

Sopa de fideos	$ 3.95

Chicken noodle soup.

TAPAS CALIENTES

Patatas bravas	$ 5.50

Spicy potatoes with special tomato sauce.

Pincho de pollo	$ 5.50

Chicken brochette with caramelized onions and rice.

Pincho de solomillo	$ 7.50

Beef tenderloin skewer with fries and caramelized onions.

Calamares a la plancha	$ 6.50

Grilled squid with olive oil, garlic and lemon juice.

Pulpo a la plancha	$ 8.50

Grilled octopus with potatoes and olive oil.

Chorizo y morcilla	$ 4.50

A combination platter of grilled Spanish style sausages.

Queso de cabra	$ 7.50

Baked goat cheese with fresh tomato basil sauce.

POSTRES

Flan de caramelo	$ 3.95

Caramel custard.

Arroz con leche	$ 3.95

Baked rice pudding with milk and cinnamon.

CAFÉS

Café solo	$ 2.00

Espresso.

Café cortado	$ 2.00

Espresso with a touch of milk.

Café con leche	$ 2.00

Espresso with lots of steamed milk.

Used by permission of CAFÉ IBÉRICO Company.

Courtesy Conchita Lucas

El bar llamado **Tapas Barcelona** en Evanston, Illinois. **Las tapas** son pequeñas porciones de diferentes especialidades de comida española. En España se sirven en todos los bares. Ahora son también populares en EE. UU.

Joff Lee/Photolibrary/Getty Images, Inc.

Paso 2. Ahora, Uds. ya están listos[1] para pedir su comida. Hagan los papeles de mesero/a y de tres clientes. Incluyan lo siguiente en sus diálogos:

- saludos
- preguntas acerca de las ensaladas, sopas y tapas que sirven
- lo que piden para comer
- lo que piden de postre y la clase de café que prefieren
- pedir la cuenta y pagar (con tarjeta de crédito)
- las despedidas

5-18 Cómo entrenar a un/a mesero/a

Eres el dueño[2] de un restaurante y hoy entrenas a un/a nuevo/a mesero/a. En la columna de la izquierda está lo que le has explicado esta mañana. Ahora es tarde y estás cansado/a y sin paciencia, por eso le das mandatos directos para cada cosa. Sigue el modelo. Túrnense.

ESTA MAÑANA

1. Primero, *cuentas* las personas.
2. Luego, *explicas* el menú.
3. A continuación, *sirves* las bebidas.
4. Después, *repites* el menú, si es necesario.
5. Más tarde, *vuelves* para ver si necesitan algo más.

AHORA

→ **Cuenta** las personas que hay.

→

→

→

→

[1]ready, [2]owner

Palabras útiles

¡Buen provecho!
Enjoy your meal!
Quisiera... *I would like... (polite)*

5-17 ANOTHER STEP: In groups of three, students play chefs writing their menu for the "dinner special" of their restaurant, to include soup, salad, a main course, and dessert, listing ingredients where appropriate. Menus are then shared with the class, with votes taken to determine the best one/s.

5-18 ANOTHER STEP: You can ask students to give the orders using the corresponding pronouns instead of the direct objects.

Go to *WileyPLUS* to see the video related to this reading.

For an additional activity related to this cultural theme, see the PowerPoint slides on BCS and in *WileyPLUS*.

Meets ACTFL Standards
1.1, interpersonal speaking
1.2, interpretive reading;
2.2, cultural products; and
4.2, cultural comparisons.

Tu mundo cultural

Platos típicos de algunos países hispanos

Dónde tú vives, ¿hay restaurantes que se especializan en comidas de países hispanos? ¿Cuáles has comido?

La gastronomía del mundo hispano es un reflejo de su diversidad. Los países hispanohablantes, que están en continentes y hemisferios distintos, tienen climas y geografía muy variados, un rico pasado y una gran diversidad cultural. En consecuencia, sus platos típicos incluyen todos los productos, colores, sabores[1] y métodos culinarios imaginables.

Lo interesante es que la mayoría de esos platos se pueden encontrar ahora en los restaurantes de todas las grandes ciudades de EE. UU. Esto es el resultado de la presencia cada vez mayor en este país de inmigrantes procedentes de diversos países hispanos. ¿Cuáles de estos platos te gustaría comer?

Bob Daemmrich/The Image Works

Los tamales (del azteca *tamal-i*) son típicos de Guatemala, Puerto Rico, México y otros países hispanoamericanos. En su masa[2] de maíz se pone carne (de res, puerco, pavo o pollo), cebolla, ajo, tomate, especias, y a veces, papas, garbanzos, pasas[3] o aceitunas[4]. Los tamales se cuecen al vapor[5], en hojas de maíz o plátano. Se sirven en Navidad y en ocasiones especiales.

Monica Stevenson/FPX/Getty Images, Inc.

Ingram/Alamy

El ajiaco o sancocho criollo es uno de los platos preferidos de países del Caribe como República Dominicana, Puerto Rico y Cuba. Esta sopa tropical tiene maíz, plátanos verdes, jugo de limón, yuca, batata, ñame (variedad de batata) y calabaza[6].

El mole poblano, original de la ciudad de Puebla, en México, es una salsa de chocolate, chiles y especias que se sirve con pavo o pollo. Se come en días especiales.

[1]flavors, [2]dough, [3]raisins, [4]olives, [5]**se...** are steamed, [6]squash

Lew Robertson/FPX/Getty Images, Inc.

Ropa vieja es una especialidad de países del Caribe, como Cuba. Sus ingredientes son carne de res preparada con cebolla, ají (chile) rojo y verde, ajo, orégano, pimentón, tomate frito, aceite de oliva y un poco de vino blanco. Se sirve con arroz, frijoles y plátanos fritos.

© Corbis

El cebiche (o ceviche) es típico de Perú y del sur de Ecuador, y es popular en otros países hispanos de la costa. Se prepara con pescado o marisco crudo[1], marinado en jugo de limón o de naranja; lleva también cebolla, tomates, aceite de oliva, ají, sal, pimienta y cilantro. Se sirve de aperitivo o como plato ligero[2].

PinoDita/Flickr/Getty Images, Inc.

Tom Grill/The Image Bank/Getty Images, Inc.

La paella es un plato típico español de la región mediterránea de Valencia, aunque se prepara en toda España. Sus ingredientes varían de una región a otra. Tradicionalmente, se prepara al aire libre con arroz, carne o mariscos, pimientos rojos y verdes, tomates, aceitunas, ajo, cebolla, limón, azafrán[3], sal y aceite de oliva.

Las empanadas son una especialidad de Argentina; también se preparan en España, Chile, Bolivia, Colombia, Paraguay, Cuba y otros países. Consisten en una masa de harina rellena de carne, papas, cebolla, arvejas, aceitunas, pasas, huevos y especias.

¿Qué aprendiste?

1. ¿Por qué es tan variada la gastronomía hispana?
   Por la gran diversidad cultural, climática y geográfica de sus países.
2. ¿Por qué se sirven muchos platos hispanos en restaurantes estadounidenses?
   Por la inmigración hispana.
3. ¿Cuáles son algunas especialidades de México, el Caribe, Perú, Ecuador, Argentina y España?
   México: mole poblano, tamales. Caribe: ropa vieja, ajiaco. Perú y Ecuador: cebiche.
   Argentina: empanadas. España: paella.

Actividad cultural

Uds. quieren preparar dos platos típicamente hispanos. Decidan cuáles van a hacer y por qué. Luego, escriban una lista de lo que van a comprar en el supermercado, según los ingredientes de cada plato.

Contraste cultural

Habla con tu compañero/a de dos o tres platos representativos de la región donde vives. Dile los ingredientes que tienen, las ocasiones cuando se preparan, cuál es tu favorito y por qué. Túrnense.

[1]raw, [2]light, [3]saffron

Preparativos para una fiesta

Pronunciación: Practice pronunciation of the chapter's new vocabulary in *WileyPLUS*.

1. la cocina
3. ¿**Otro*** regalo?
¡Qué rica!
Necesita 6**más** 7**sal** y 8**pimienta**.
Me encanta 9**cocinar**.
GUADALUPE
2. los regalos
4. probar (ue)
D* ROSA
5. preparar
CALISTO
10. cortar
AZÚCAR
HARINA
11.
DAMIÁN
ÁNGEL
NURIA

¡Feliz cumpleaños, Robertito!

24. las copas
23. los vasos
22. las tazas
M* LUISA
21. los platos
12¡**Tengo hambre!**
19. los cuchillos
20. las cucharas
17. los tenedores
18. las servilletas
RAFAEL
16. la merienda
PACHÁ
15. las aceitunas
13¡**Tengo sed!** Quiero limonada.
14. el mantel
ROBERTITO
CARMEN
DON CLAUDIO

© John Wiley & Sons, Inc.

1. kitchen 2. gifts 3. another 4. to taste, to try 5. to prepare 6. more; **menos** *less* 7. salt (*f.*) 8. pepper 9. to cook 10. to cut 11. flour
12. I'm hungry! **tener hambre** to be hungry 13. I'm thirsty! **tener sed** to be thirsty 14. tablecloth 15. olives 16. afternoon snack 17. forks (*m.*)
18. napkins 19. knives 20. spoons 21. plates, dishes 22. cups 23. glasses 24. wine glasses, goblets

***Otro regalo/ otra galleta** *Another gift/ another cookie.* Note that **otro/a** does *not* include **un/una** before it.

¡En acción!

5-19 ¿Cierto o falso?

Lee las oraciones e indica si son ciertas o falsas. Si son falsas, corrígelas.

MODELO

C	F	
☐	☑	Para tomar sopa se usa un cuchillo.

Falso. Se usa una cuchara.

C	F	
☐	☐	**1.** La comida se sirve en platos.
☐	☐	**2.** El vino se sirve en una taza.
☐	☐	**3.** Para beber té helado, se usan copas.
☐	☐	**4.** Para comer un huevo frito, se necesita una cuchara.
☐	☐	**5.** Para cortar el bistec, se usa un tenedor.
☐	☐	**6.** Cuando se comen espaguetis, se necesita una servilleta.
☐	☐	**7.** Cuando se tiene mucha hambre, se come una ensalada de lechuga.
☐	☐	**8.** Cuando se tiene mucha sed y hace calor, se bebe agua o un refresco.

ANSWERS: *Cierto:* 1, 6, 8; *Falso:* 2. Se sirve en una copa 3. Se usan vasos 4. Se necesita un tenedor 5. Se usa un cuchillo 7. [...] (Answers will vary.)

5-20 Preparativos para una fiesta

Los Roldán están muy ocupados en la cocina. ¿Qué pasa? Observen la escena de la página 170 y contesten las preguntas.

1. ¿Qué fiesta celebran? ¿Cuántos años cumple Robertito?
2. ¿Qué hace Guadalupe? ¿Qué dice?
3. ¿Qué ingredientes necesita Ángel para preparar la ensalada?
4. ¿Qué ingredientes usa Nuria para preparar los pasteles? ¿Qué hace? ¿Le gusta cocinar a ella?
5. ¿Dónde está Calisto, el gato? ¿Qué hace? ¿Y Pachá, el perro?
6. ¿Para quién son los regalos que están en la mesa? ¿Qué dice la abuela?
7. ¿Qué va a poner Mª Luisa en la mesa? ¿De qué color es el mantel?
8. ¿Qué comidas van a servir en la merienda? ¿Qué prueba Carmen?
9. ¿Quién tiene hambre? ¿Qué quiere probar? ¿Quién tiene sed? ¿Qué quiere beber?
10. En la otra mesa hay utensilios y otras cosas. ¿Cuáles se usan para beber? ¿Y para comer?

Courtesy Conchita Lucas

5-20 PERSONALIZED QUESTIONS: Ask several students each question. ¿Te gusta cocinar? ¿Qué platos te gusta preparar? Cuando tienes mucha hambre, ¿qué comes? Y cuando tienes mucha sed, ¿qué bebes?

Cocina mexicana con paredes de cerámica o azulejos, decoración tradicional de muchas cocinas hispanas. En ella se ve a una cocinera preparando tortillas de maíz.

For additional vocabulary practice, see PowerPoint slides on BCS and in *WileyPLUS*.

5-19   *Option:* Students may do *Actividad 5-19* in pairs. Remind them of the "impersonal se," using the model as an example: [...] **se usa una cuchara** *one uses a spoon/ a spoon is used*. Pause after each sentence to allow students to decide whether it is true or false.

¿SABES QUE...?

Maricel Presilla, the owner and chef of Cucharamama and co-owner of Zafra, two restaurants located in Hoboken, New Jersey, was named Best Chef in the Mid-Atlantic region in 2012 by the James Beard Foundation. Of Cuban descent, Presilla has a PhD in medieval Spanish history. She has taught at Rutgers University, and she is the author of *Gran Cocina Latina: The Food of Latin America*, among other books. She travels throughout Latin America gathering recipes, cooking techniques, and ingredients in order to introduce them to the American market.

5-20   After students complete the activity, you may project the PowerPoint slide of the scene. The class then describes the scene, or, ask several students to go to the front and take turns describing it.

¿SABES QUE...?

The term **salario** (*salary*) derives from the word **sal.** Before refrigerators, salt was used to preserve meats and other foods. A valuable commodity, salt served as a currency of trade.

In many Hispanic countries, **la merienda**—a snack between lunch and dinner, similar to tea in England—is a part of daily life. It can be a cold snack such as a sandwich, or a cup of hot chocolate, coffee, or tea with pastries or cake. Birthday parties and other special occasions are celebrated with a **merienda**.

5-21 ¡La abuela cumple 100 años!

Paso 1. ¿Qué se va a servir en la celebración del cumpleaños de tu abuela? Escribe una lista que incluya dos platos, dos postres y tres bebidas.

Paso 2. Una amiga te ayuda a poner[1] la mesa. Tú le dices lo que se va a servir y ella te indica lo que se necesita para la mesa. Hagan los dos papeles y al final cambien de papel. (Antes de empezar anota en el cuadernito lo que se va a servir.)

MODELO

Tú: Para beber, vamos a servir agua y vino.

Tu amigo/a: Necesitamos vasos de agua y copas de vino.

Palabras útiles

las palomitas de maíz *popcorn*
el plato sopero *soup bowl*

5-21 Ask if anyone in the class has a birthday today, this week, or this month. Have the class sing **¡Cumpleaños feliz!** to that person, replacing "abuela" in the lyrics at right with the birthday boy/girl's name.

Para beber:	agua y vino
Para comer:	
Para postre:	

¡Cumpleaños feliz!

¡Cum-ple - a - ños fel - iz, cum-ple - a - ños fel - iz, Te de - sea - mos a - bue - la, cum-ple - a - ños fel - iz!

© John Wiley & Sons, Inc.

¡A escuchar! Preparativos para un picnic

Paso 1. La familia Martínez está haciendo los preparativos para un picnic en el campo. Escucha la conversación.

PLUS Go to *WileyPLUS* to complete **Paso 2** of this listening activity.

[1]set

La madre de Jennifer está preparando la cena. Jennifer entra a la cocina para ayudarla.

© John Wiley & Sons, Inc.

GRAMÁTICA

¡Manos a la obra!

3

Saying that an action is in progress: The present progressive

When you want to stress that something is happening right at the moment, you use the present progressive, as you saw in Jennifer's conversation with her mother:

En este momento, su madre **está cocinando** ropa vieja.

Her mother is cooking ropa vieja *right now.*

The present progressive consists of:

the present tense of **estar** + ***the present participle*** (the *-ing* form) of a verb.

The *regular* present participle is formed by dropping the infinitive ending and adding:

-ando (**-ar** verbs) or **-iendo** (**-er** and **-ir** verbs):

	habl**ar**	com**er**	escrib**ir**
estoy estás está estamos estáis están	habl**ando**	com**iendo**	escrib**iendo**

- Unlike English speakers, Spanish speakers use the present tense **(hablo, como, escribo)** to describe an ongoing action in the present—*I am speaking, I am eating, I am writing*—rather than the present progressive. They use the present progressive only to emphasize that something is happening *right now.*

- Direct object pronouns are placed *before* **estar** or *attached to the present participle.*

  Tiene muchas verduras. **Las** está cortando. (o) Está cortándo**las**.*

- Spanish also has *irregular* present participles. Here are five verbs you know whose present participles are irregular. The first four have stem changes.

dec**ir** (i)	d**i**ciendo	dorm**ir** (u)	d**u**rmiendo
ped**ir** (i)	p**i**diendo	leer	leyendo
serv**ir** (i)	s**i**rviendo		

*When a pronoun is attached to the present participle, a written accent is placed above the stressed vowel of the participle, which is always the vowel that precedes the *n*:
Está ayudándome, Está sirviéndolo.

For additional practice on this grammar point, see PowerPoint slides on BCS and in *WileyPLUS*.

To introduce students to the present progressive used in context, have them take parts and read the **historieta** out loud. To check their comprehension and call their attention to this verb tense, ask the following questions: **1. ¿Qué está haciendo la madre de Jennifer? 2. ¿Qué está haciendo su hija?**

WILEY PLUS Go to *WileyPLUS* to review this grammar point with the help of the **Animated Grammar** Tutorial and **Verb Conjugator**. For more practice, go to the **Grammar Handbook**.

To present the present progressive, mime several actions while telling the class what you are doing: **Estoy cantando/ hablando/ bailando/ comiendo/ escribiendo...** Contrast the present and the present progressive: **Ceno en casa./ Estoy cenando ahora.**

<!-- margin notes -->

¡Oye! Mime each of the actions as you read them.

Guión para ¡Oye!

1. Un niño **está comiendo** toda la comida y otro **está bebiendo** todas las bebidas que hay en el refrigerador.
2. Dos niñas **están preparando** galletas de chocolate. Una **está leyendo** la receta y la otra **está buscando** los ingredientes. Hay ingredientes por todas partes: harina, azúcar, huevos, chocolate...
3. Un niño **está cortando** una manzana con un cuchillo muy grande.
4. Otro **está poniendo** mermelada en el pan... y la **está probando**.
5. El gato **está bebiendo** la leche del bol que está en la mesa.
6. Y el perro, muy tranquilo, **está durmiendo**. (cont.)

Palabras útiles

empezar (ie) *to begin*
sacar *to remove*
la sartén *frying pan*
la estufa *stove*

Comprensión para ¡Oye!
In the follow-up, assign parts to eight students according to items 1–6 above. Read the actions again, allowing students to act out their parts after each statement. Then have each student mime his/her action without your prompts while the class identifies what is happening.

5-22 Before students begin the activity, you may want to project the PowerPoint slide of the photos. Then read items 2–7 in random order and have students identify the corresponding photo. For example: **Y finalmente, estoy sirviendo la sopa. [7]**

When the class has completed the activity, point out the appropriate photo as students read each step aloud.

¡En acción!

¡Oye! ¡Qué desastre en la cocina!

Los señores Gutiérrez no están en casa y sus hijos están con unos amigos en la cocina. Escuchen lo que está pasando. Luego, ocho estudiantes representan lo que ocurre haciendo los papeles de los seis niños, el gato y el perro.

5-22 encasadekristina.com

En casa de Kristina es un programa de televisión. Hoy Kristina está preparando sopa de calabaza para una ocasión festiva. Primero, escuchen los pasos de preparación que lee su profesor/a e identifiquen la foto que le corresponde a cada uno. Luego, completen los pasos con la ayuda de las fotos. Usen la forma **yo** del presente progresivo. Túrnense.

1. ¡Muy buenos días! En estos momentos (*empezar*) ___estoy___ ___empezando___ a preparar una sopa muy rica: crema de calabaza.

2. Primero, como Uds. ven, (*lavar*) ___estoy___ ___lavando___ muy bien la calabaza.

3. Ahora, con un bol y un lápiz (*hacer*) ___estoy___ ___haciendo___ un círculo en la parte superior de la calabaza.

4. En este momento, (*cortar*) ___estoy___ ___cortando___ la calabaza con un cuchillo, siguiendo la marca del círculo.

5. A continuación, ven Uds. que (*sacar*) ___estoy___ ___sacando___ la pulpa de la calabaza.

6. Ahora, (*poner*) ___estoy___ ___poniendo___ en la estufa la sartén con la pulpa, un poquito de aceite, ajo y sal.

7. Y finalmente, (*servir*) ___estoy___ ___sirviendo___ la sopa. Y como ven, uso la calabaza como recipiente.

2

3

4

5

6

7

All photos on this page are courtesy Conchita Lucas

5-23 **¿Dónde están?** RECYCLES estar + *location*.

 Un/a estudiante les dice a las otras tres personas de su grupo lo que está ocurriendo en uno de los siguientes lugares[1], pero sin dar el nombre del lugar. Las tres personas tienen que adivinarlo[2]. Túrnense.

MODELO

E1:   *Una persona **está usando** la computadora, otra **está hablando** por teléfono,...*

Los otros: *¡Están en la oficina!*

E1:   *¡Correcto!*

1. en la clase
2. en la oficina
3. en la cocina
4. en la biblioteca
5. en la playa
6. en las montañas

 5-24 **La fiesta de Robertito**

Un/a estudiante pregunta quién está haciendo cierta cosa y el/la otro/a dice quién es según la escena de la página 170. Túrnense. Usen los verbos de la lista en sus preguntas y los pronombres **lo, la, los, las** en sus respuestas.

> comer   cortar   dormir   observar   poner   preparar   probar   decir

MODELO

E1:   *¿Quién **está observando** a los niños?*

E2:   *Don Claudio **los** está observando.*   **o:**   *Don Claudio está observándo**los**.*

E1:   *¡Exacto!*   **o:**   *No, inténtalo otra vez.*

5-25 **¿Por qué lo están haciendo?**

Digan lo que están haciendo las siguientes personas y expliquen por qué.

MODELO

E1:   *Las dos chicas **están decorando** un pastel de cumpleaños. ¿Por qué?*

E2:   ***Lo están decorando** porque es el cumpleaños de su amiga Ana. (o)*

     *Están decorándo**lo** porque es el cumpleaños de su amiga Ana.*

decorar

preparar

beber

comer

comprar

leer

decir

[1]places, [2]**tienen...** have to guess it

For an additional activity related to this cultural theme, see the PowerPoint slides on BCS and in *WileyPLUS*.

Meets ACTFL Standards
1.1, interpersonal speaking;
1.2, interpretive reading;
2.2, cultural products; and
4.2, cultural comparisons.

Palabras útiles
¼ un cuarto
  one quarter
½ medio/a *half*

Tu mundo cultural

Dos recetas típicamente hispanas

¿Te gusta cocinar? ¿Quieres aprender a hacer algo rico y fácil? A continuación vas a ver dos recetas de dos especialidades hispanas que puedes probar en numerosos restaurantes de EE. UU.

ARROZ CON POLLO
(receta para seis personas)

Tiempo de preparación: 20 minutos
Tiempo de cocción: 50 minutos
Grado de dificultad: fácil
Costo: razonable

Courtesy Laila Dawson

El arroz con pollo, el plato del Caribe más popular.

Glosario:

Corbis Images

una olla

Courtesy Conchita Lucas

machacar

Courtesy Conchita Lucas

picar

DK Limited/Dave Murray/© Corbis

Achiote u onoto[7]: especia de color rojo extraída de una flor de la América tropical

Ingredientes:

4 pechugas[1] de pollo sin hueso[2], cortadas
¼ taza de aceite de oliva
2 dientes de ajo machacados
media cebolla picada
½ pimiento verde picado
1 tomate picado
2 tazas de caldo[3] de pollo
¼ de una cucharadita de achiote disuelto en caldo

½ cucharadita de sal (o más, al gusto)
pimienta al gusto
1½ tazas de arroz blanco
½ lata[4] de garbanzos
½ taza de chícharos
½ lata de cerveza
unos cinco espárragos cocidos al vapor y un huevo duro para decorar

Preparación:

En una olla se fríe el pollo con aceite de oliva y se le añade un poco de sal.
Se saca[5] el pollo de la olla.
En la olla se fríen el ajo, la cebolla, el pimiento verde y el tomate.
Se añade[6] el caldo de pollo caliente, el achiote, la sal y la pimienta.
Se añade el arroz.
Se añaden el pollo, los garbanzos, los chícharos y los pimientos.
Se añade la cerveza.
Se cocina a fuego moderado durante unos 30 minutos hasta que el arroz absorba el líquido.
Luego se deja reposar unos minutos antes de servirlo y decorarlo.

Se sirve adornado con los espárragos y el huevo.

[1]breasts, [2]bone, [3]broth, [4]can, [5]Se... Take out, [6]Se... Add, [7]annatto

FLAN

(receta española para seis personas)

Tiempo de preparación: 10-15 minutos
Tiempo de cocción: 45 minutos
Grado de dificultad: fácil
Costo: muy económico

El flan, postre típico de los países hispanos. Dependiendo del país, varían los ingredientes. Por ejemplo, en el Caribe a veces se añade coco o piña.

Ingredientes:

Para el caramelo:
dos cucharadas grandes de agua y tres de azúcar

Para el flan:
4 ó 5 huevos
1 lata de leche condensada (con azúcar) de
    396 gr./ 14 oz.
1½ tazas de leche
½ cucharadita de extracto de vainilla

Recipientes necesarios:

flanera

fuente para el baño María

Preparación:

1. *El caramelo:*
Se pone el agua y el azúcar en el molde a fuego lento[1].
Cuando el agua y el azúcar adquieren un color dorado[2], se extiende bien por el molde.
Se aparta el molde durante unos cinco minutos hasta que se enfríe.

2. *El flan:*
Se baten[3] los huevos.
Se añade la leche condensada y la leche, y se mezclan[4].
Se añade la vainilla y se mezcla todo.
Se pone en el molde caramelizado.
Se pone en el horno[5] *al baño María* durante 45 minutos a una temperatura de 375° (Fahrenheit).
Se saca del horno y se deja enfriar. Si no se va a comer durante unos días, se puede dejar en el refrigerador.
Antes de servir el flan se vuelca[6] el molde en un plato.

El caramelo es un almíbar que se forma cuando se calienta el agua con el azúcar.

El baño María[7] consiste en poner el molde con el flan dentro de otro recipiente que contiene agua.

 ## ¿Qué aprendiste?

1. ¿De dónde es típico el arroz con pollo? ¿Qué verduras tiene?
Del Caribe. Ajo, cebolla, pimientos, garbanzos, chícharos y tomate.
2. ¿De dónde es típico el flan? ¿Qué ingredientes le ponen a veces en el Caribe?
De varios países hispanos, como España.
3. ¿Qué se prepara primero, el caramelo o el flan? ¿Se sirve frío o caliente?
El caramelo. Frío.

 ## Actividad cultural

Sigan las recetas y preparen los dos platos.

Contraste cultural

¿Cuáles son las recetas favoritas de su familia? ¿Son típicas de la región donde Uds. viven? ¿Son típicas de EE. UU.?

Cuando el flan está frío, se separa sin dificultad de los bordes del molde con un cuchillo y se vuelca en el plato de servir.

All photos on this page are courtesy Conchita Lucas.

Palabras útiles
(gr.) gramo *gram*

---

[1]**fuego...** low heat, [2]**golden**, [3]**Se...** Beat, [4]**se...** mix them, [5]**oven**, [6]**se...** turn it out onto, [7]**double-boiler**

Tu mundo en vivo

¡Videos en acción!

5.1 En el supermercado

1. Antes de ver el video

   a. ¿Conoces un supermercado hispano? ¿Cuál?

   b. ¿Qué platos y comidas típicas de países hispanos te gusta comer?

   Go to *WileyPLUS* to complete the Mientras ves el video activity.

2. Después de ver el video

   Completa los espacios en blanco.

   a. ¿Por qué se ofrece cada vez más variedad de productos hispanos en los supermercados de EE. UU.? porque los hispanos son la población que gasta más dinero en comida

   b. Nombra 5 productos que se muestran en el video.
   plátanos maduros, limones, cervezas, queso, jugos de fruta, café, carne...

5.2 En el restaurante

1. Antes de ver el video

   a. ¿Conoces un restaurante hispano que no sea mexicano?

   b. ¿Qué platos pides cuando vas?

   Go to *WileyPLUS* to complete the Mientras ves el video activity.

2. Después de ver el video

   ¿Te gusta este restaurante? ¿Qué plato te gustaría probar?

¡Diálogos en acción!

5.1 En el Café Ibérico

Un señor cubano va a almorzar a El Café Ibérico donde trabaja una mesera que también es cubana.

Paso 1. Primero, mira las **Expresiones útiles** de la página A-5. Luego, escucha el diálogo dos veces y contesta las preguntas de tu profesor/a.

Paso 2. Mira la transcripción del diálogo (pág. A-17) y represéntalo con tu compañero/a. Túrnense. Ahora, vete a la página A-5 para completar los **Pasos 3** y **4**.

5. 2 Chiles rellenos

Alejandro y Verónica son dos estudiantes mexicanos. Cuando se encuentran en el campus, Verónica invita a Alejandro a cenar en su casa.

Go to *WileyPLUS* to listen to and practice this dialogue.

Diálogo 5.1 models the linguistic function of interacting with a server in a restaurant. It also practices food and drink vocabulary as well as the verbs **querer, almorzar, pedir, creer, preferir,** and **volver.**

Diálogo 5.2 models the linguistic functions of issuing and accepting an invitation, negotiating a complication, thanking, greeting and leave-taking. It also practices the verbs **querer** and **pensar.**

¡Lectura en acción!

Gastón Acurio y su *La Mar* neoyorquino

La siguiente reseña[1] es de **Pie derecho**, una revista en español publicada en Nueva York.

Paso 1. Primero, lee el texto concentrándote en los detalles que te parezcan importantes.

Lino Estrada/NewsCom

Used by permission of the author, Denisse Oller.

El embajador del sabor[2] peruano

Llega a conquistar a los neoyorquinos por el estómago. El célebre chef limeño[3] inaugura en estos días su primer restaurante en el corazón de Manhattan.

Es un hombre de temperamento tranquilo, tiene todo bajo control, y con su mirada recorre hasta el menor rincón[4] de su nuevo restaurante *La Mar* en la calle Madison, para que todo resulte perfecto. Es jovial, sencillo[5], con sentido del humor y siempre dispuesto a charlar con cualquier interlocutor que tenga enfrente, incluso en Nueva York, donde el ritmo de vida es siempre vertiginoso, y cuando habla de su trabajo, lo hace con pasión.

Se inició como chef después de abandonar sus estudios de ciencias políticas en París para introducirse en el mundo de la cocina de los bistros franceses. El resto es historia. "Me importa mucho la gastronomía peruana", dice Acurio, "es ya mi vida, y quiero que se conozca en todo el mundo, por eso abro este restaurante ahora en Nueva York".

El chef, de origen limeño, describe a la cocina de su país como "maravillosa", y le da tal calificativo porque tiene la riqueza de la cultura negra, blanca, india mestiza, española, china, y japonesa, el mosaico racial que amalgama en su geografía. "Y todo esto quiero que se convierta en una industria", dice, "que cree trabajo para miles de familias peruanas, que permita el reconocimiento de nuestro sabor en los paladares[6] de todo el mundo, que impulse nuestros ingredientes, que cree empleos dentro y fuera del Perú".

Además de su restaurante original en Lima, *Astrid y Gastón*, que inició junto con su esposa, el chef ha abierto ya más de diez en diversas partes del mundo, en sociedad con corporaciones e inversionistas, pero en todos, se nota su toque personal, los platillos peruanos que sólo él puede recrear, y en todos impone su estilo gerencial[7].

En el menú de *La Mar* neoyorquino no faltan los platos típicos de la gastronomía del país, pero también se aventura a agregar al típico ceviche una salsa de tamarindo, o al clásico tiradito[8], preparado con pescado en salsa lechosa, añadirle un aderezo de ajonjolí[9]. Sus fusiones y recreaciones no tienen límite.

Paso 2. Ahora, marca lo que corresponde para ver si entendiste la información más importante de la reseña.

1. Gastón Acurio se inició como chef en...
- ☑ París
- ☐ Lima
- ☐ Nueva York

2. La comida peruana tiene influencias de la cultura negra, blanca, india mestiza, ...
- ☑ china
- ☑ española
- ☐ colombiana
- ☑ japonesa
- ☐ mexicana

3. El chef limeño quiere convertir la cocina peruana en una industria para...
- ☐ viajar por el mundo
- ☑ dar trabajo a los peruanos
- ☐ hacerla universal

Paso 3. Finalmente, con tus propias palabras, resume la reseña, concentrándote en la información más importante.

---

[1]review, [2]taste, [3]from Lima, [4]corner, [5]humble, [6]palates, [7]**estilo...** CEO style, [8]Peruvian dish of raw fish, [9]sesame

Sidebar

Encourage students to focus on what they do understand in the text and to think about how they would summarize the passage. Remind them that they do not need to understand every word to complete this task.

Reading Strategy

Summarizing

Summarizing the main points of a text can help you focus on the important details and help you determine what you did and did not understand.

Meets ACTFL Standards 1.2, interpretive reading, 2.2, cultural products; and 3.2, acquiring information.

¿SABES QUE...?

Ceviche is the Peruvian flag-dish, a fusion of three distinct culinary traditions: Inca hot peppers, Spanish limes and onions, and Japanese raw fish marinated in citrus juices. **Tiradito**, another Peruvian specialty, also has its origins in the way Japanese immigrants in Peru prepare fish. However, while **ceviche** is cut in bite-size cubes and is prepared with onions, tiradito is sliced in long, fine pieces with no onions.

Using Descriptions to Avoid Lapses

To avoid a lapse in communication when you lack the word to name something, you can simply point at the object if it's nearby. But what if your surroundings don't include that object? One strategy is to describe its appearance or use. For example, if *cherry* is the word you need, you could say **Es una fruta roja y pequeña**. Or, if *cup* is the word, you could say **Se usa para tomar café o té**. Upon recognizing what you're describing, the person you are speaking to will often provide the word for you.

¡A conversar!

Una fiesta en familia

En grupos de *tres*, hablen de la fiesta que más se celebra en su familia. En la conversación, hablen y pregunten acerca de lo siguiente:

- Estación y fecha del año cuando se celebra
- Ocasión y momento del día cuando ocurre
- Personas que asisten
- Comidas y bebidas que se preparan y se sirven, y sus ingredientes principales
- Tradiciones familiares de la celebración
- Otras cosas curiosas que ocurren o se hacen en esa ocasión

¡A escribir!

Las costumbres de la comida

Escribe un mensaje electrónico a un/a amigo/a de Argentina que quiere saber acerca de las costumbres estadounidenses relacionadas con las comidas. Incluye:

- A qué hora se desayuna, se almuerza y se cena
- Cuáles son los platos típicos del desayuno, del almuerzo, de la cena
- Si[1] se cocina mucho en casa (explica qué platos) o si se va a restaurantes de "comida rápida" con frecuencia (explica)
- En qué ocasiones se reúne toda la familia para compartir el almuerzo o la cena
- Si muchas personas están a dieta y explica en qué consiste

Meets ACTFL Standard 1.3, presentational writing.

You may wish to assign certain steps of the **¡A escribir!** writing process for students to complete outside of class.

Palabras útiles

(no) tener tiempo *to (not) have time*

Let the First Draft Flow

Write your first draft *quickly*, without stopping to check spelling or grammar. Let your ideas flow!

Steps:

1. *Prewriting*: Jot down your initial ideas in words and phrases.
2. *Writing*: See strategy.
3. *Revising*: Read your composition carefully. Do you want to add to, delete, or re-group some of your information? Have you included all of the information requested and checked for correct spelling and punctuation? **¡Ojo!** Have you (a) used **a la/s…** to express *at what time*, (b) used the impersonal **se** + *verb* in several of your sentences, and (c) checked for agreement between articles and nouns?
4. *Peer correction*: Exchange papers, circle errors or areas where there are questions, talk about them, and then make corrections on your own paper.

[1]if

¡A investigar!

El maíz y la dieta mexicana y centroamericana

Los pueblos indígenas de las Américas cultivan maíz desde hace más de cuatro mil años. Es uno de los ingredientes principales de muchas comidas y bebidas que se preparan en México y en América Central.

Paso 1. Primero, cada estudiante va a buscar el nombre de un plato preparado con maíz. ¿De qué país es el plato? No se limiten a los platos que ya conozcan.

Paso 2. Con la ayuda de su profesor/a y sus compañeros de clase, preparen una lista de todos los platos y sus países de origen. Van a trabajar en grupos de *tres* para investigar una comida o bebida.

Paso 3. Usen las estrategias de investigación del *Capítulo 2* y busquen una receta para el plato de su grupo. Léanla juntos y usen un diccionario bilingüe para entenderla si es necesario. Hagan una lista escrita de los ingredientes que se necesitan para preparar la receta y publiquen la lista con el nombre del plato en un blog o wiki para compartirla con los otros estudiantes.

Paso 4. Después de leer las listas, decidan qué platos quieren probar. ¿Se sirven los platos en los restaurantes de su pueblo o ciudad? ¿Se pueden comprar los ingredientes en los supermercados?

Meets ACTFL Standards 1.2, interpretive reading; 1.3, presentational writing; 2.2, cultural products; 3.2, acquiring information; and 4.2, cultural comparisons.

You may assign the appropriate **Pasos** of **¡A investigar!** for pairs or small groups to complete outside of class.

If your access to technology is limited, have the students create Word documents with their ingredient lists.

Research Strategy

Using Bilingual Dictionaries

Using reading strategies can help you comprehend many of the main points of a text, but sometimes you simply must use a dictionary to determine the meaning of key words of a Spanish-language source. Bilingual dictionaries list the singular forms of nouns, the masculine, singular forms of adjectives, and the infinitives of verbs. Once you've found the word, you should read the entire entry and any examples provided, as many words have multiple meanings, and you must select the meaning that fits the context.

Trivia

A ver cuánto sabes.

1. ¿Sabes qué cuatro países hispanohablantes de Centroamérica y uno de África exportan café? ¿Y cacao? a. Costa Rica, Guatemala, Honduras, República Dominicana, Guinea Ecuatorial   b. República Dominicana, Guinea Ecuatorial, Ecuador
2. ¿Puedes decir el nombre de un país hispano de Sudamérica que exporta carne? ¿Y pescado? a. Answers will vary: Argentina, Uruguay y Paraguay b. Chile, Perú
3. ¿Puedes decir el nombre de un país hispano de Sudamérica que exporta flores? ¿Y dos de Sudamérica que exportan tabaco?
   a. Colombia b. Colombia y Bolivia

If you don't know the answers, take a look at the front inside cover of the textbook. Try to respond in complete sentences.

Vocabulario: Capítulo 5

Escena 1

Las carnes y los mariscos
Meats and seafood/ shellfish

el bistec *steak*
el camarón *shrimp*
la carne de res *beef*
la chuleta de cerdo *pork chop*
el jamón *ham*
la langosta *lobster*
el pavo *turkey*
el pescado *fish*
el pollo *chicken*
la salchicha *sausage*

Las frutas *Fruits*

la banana *banana*
la cereza *cherry*
el durazno *peach*
la fresa *strawberry*
el limón *lemon*
la manzana *apple*
la naranja *orange*
la pera *pear*
la piña *pineapple*
la sandía *watermelon*
la uva *grape*

Las legumbres/ las verduras
Vegetables

la arveja, el chícharo *pea*
el brócoli *broccoli*
la cebolla *onion*
el frijol *bean*
la lechuga *lettuce*
el maíz *corn*
la papa *potato*
el pimiento verde/ rojo *green/red pepper*
el tomate *tomato*
la zanahoria *carrot*

Más comidas y otras palabras
More foods and other words

el ajo *garlic*
el arroz *rice*
el pan *bread*
el queso *cheese*

el dinero *money*
el mercado *market*

Los números del 100 al...
Numbers from 100 to...

cien *one hundred*
ciento uno/a *one hundred and one*
doscientos/as *two hundred*
trescientos/as *three hundred*
cuatrocientos/as *four hundred*
quinientos/as *five hundred*
seiscientos/as *six hundred*
setecientos/as *seven hundred*
ochocientos/as *eight hundred*

novecientos/as *nine hundred*
mil *one thousand*
dos mil *two thousand*
cien mil *one hundred thousand*
doscientos mil *two hundred thousand*
un millón *one million*
dos millones *two million*

Adjetivo *Adjective*

amable *kind, pleasant*

Verbos *Verbs*

buscar *to look for*
contar (ue) *to count*
costar (ue) *to cost*
desear *to want, wish, desire*
vender *to sell*
se vende *for sale*

Escena 2

Las comidas del día *Meals of the day*

el desayuno *breakfast*
el almuerzo *lunch*
la cena *dinner*

Las comidas *Foods*

el atún *tuna*
el cereal *cereal*
la ensalada *salad*
la hamburguesa *hamburger*
el huevo (frito) *(fried) egg*
el pan tostado *toast*
las papas fritas *French fries*
el puré de papas *mashed potatoes*
el sándwich *sandwich*
la sopa *soup*
el tocino *bacon*

Las bebidas *Drinks*

el agua *water*
el café *coffee*
la cerveza *beer*
el jugo (de naranja) *(orange) juice*
la leche *milk*
el refresco *soft drink, soda*
el té (caliente/ helado) *(hot/ iced) tea*
el vino *wine*

Los postres *Desserts*

el flan *caramel custard*
la galleta *cookie*
el helado (de vainilla) *(vanilla) ice cream*
el pastel/ la torta (de chocolate) *(chocolate) cake*

Más comidas y otras palabras
More foods and other words

el aceite *oil*
el azúcar *sugar*
la crema *cream*
el hielo *ice*
la mantequilla *butter*

la mayonesa *mayonnaise*
la mermelada *jam*
el vinagre *vinegar*
frito/a *fried*
a la parrilla *grilled*

la cuenta *bill*
la propina *tip*

Preposiciones *Prepositions*

con/ sin *with/ without*

Verbos *Verbs*

almorzar (ue) *to have lunch*
dejar *to leave (behind)*
dormir (ue) *to sleep*
entender (ie) *to understand*
pagar *to pay (for)*
pedir (i) *to ask for, order*
pensar (ie) (+ infinitivo) *to think, plan/ intend (to do something)*
poder (ue) *to be able*
preferir (ie) *to prefer*
querer (ie) *to want, love*
repetir (i) *to repeat*
servir (i) *to serve*
tomar *to drink, take*
volver (ue) *to return*

Escena 3

Para poner la mesa *To set the table*

la copa *wine glass, goblet*
la cuchara *spoon*
el cuchillo *knife*
el mantel *tablecloth*
el plato *plate, dish*
la servilleta *napkin*
la taza *cup*
el tenedor *fork*
el vaso *glass*

Más comidas y otras palabras
More foods and other words

la aceituna *olive*
la cocina *kitchen*
la harina *flour*
la merienda *afternoon snack*
la pimienta *pepper*
el regalo *gift*
la sal *salt*

más/ menos *more/ less*
otro/a *another*
otros/as *other*

Verbos y expresiones verbales
Verbs and verbal expressions

cocinar *to cook*
cortar *to cut*
preparar *to prepare*
probar (ue) *to taste, try*
tener hambre/ sed *to be hungry/ thirsty*

To introduce the theme, you may want to play one of the videos from this chapter, with or without the audio, and then ask students what they think the chapter is about. You may also want to use the video to motivate cultural discussion in Spanish. At the end of the chapter, ask students if their predictions about its content and culture were accurate.

En casa

WILEY PLUS

Additional activities and **Autopruebas** for each **Escena** available online.

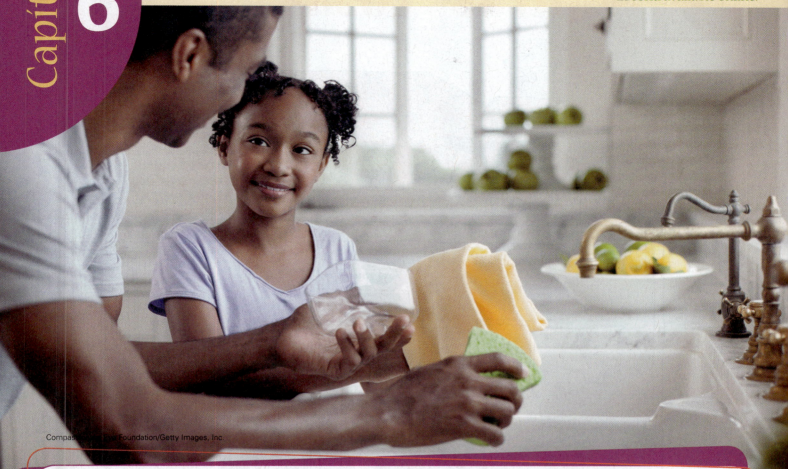

Compassionate Eye Foundation/Getty Images, Inc.

Escena 1
Cuartos, muebles y otras cosas

GRAMÁTICA:
· Prepositions
· Demonstrative adjectives

CULTURA:
Las casas de estilo tradicional español

Escena 2
La vida diaria

GRAMÁTICA:
· Reflexive verbs

CULTURA:
La vida diaria: costumbres y horarios

Escena 3
Los quehaceres domésticos

GRAMÁTICA:
· Informal commands: *tú* affirmative (recap) and negative

CULTURA:
Los quehaceres y el servicio doméstico

TU MUNDO EN VIVO

¡Videos en acción! Mi vida aburrida; Los quehaceres
¡Diálogos en acción! Answering and Inquiring about an Ad; Showing Someone Around and Negotiating Task-sharing
¡Lectura en acción! Making Lists as you Read
¡A conversar! Using Nonverbal Cues
¡A escribir! Developing a Good Topic Sentence
¡A investigar! Including Photo and Video Sources

LEARNING OBJECTIVES

By the end of the chapter you will be able to:
· Describe a house or an apartment and its contents.
· Indicate where people, places and things are in relation to oneself.
· Talk about daily routines and household chores.
· Use commands in informal situations.
· Identify features typical of Hispanic architecture.
· Become familiar with the habits and schedule of daily life in the Spanish-speaking countries.

¹Cuartos, ²muebles y otras ³cosas

4. el techo

7. el ropero

5. la cómoda

6. la cama

8. el dormitorio/el cuarto

DAMIÁN

10. subir

CALISTO

9. el segundo piso

ROBERTITO

el dormitorio de Robertito

22. la lámpara
DON CLAUDIO

17. el estante

18. la chimenea

Hogar, dulce hogar

Dª ROSA

19. la alfombra

20. el suelo, el piso

21. el sofá

23. el sillón

24. la sala

25. la escalera

26. bajar

PACHÁ

27. el primer piso

28. las cortinas

GUADALUPE

29. el comedor

© John Wiley & Sons, Inc.

Pronunciación: Practice pronunciation of the chapter's new vocabulary in *WileyPLUS*.

1. rooms
2. furniture (*m.*)
3. things
4. roof, ceiling
5. dresser
6. bed
7. closet
8. bedroom, room
9. second floor
10. to go up
11. bathtub
12. shower
13. mirror
14. sink (bathroom)
15. toilet
16. bathroom
17. bookcase, shelf
18. fireplace, chimney
19. rug, carpet
20. floor
21. sofa
22. lamp
23. easy chair
24. living room
25. stairs
26. to go down
27. first floor
28. curtains
29. dining room
30. refrigerator
31. microwave
32. stove
33. kitchen sink
34. dishwasher
35. to ring (phone), go off (alarm clock)
36. to answer
37. kitchen
38. basement
39. light, electricity
40. for rent; **alquilar** to rent
41. garage
42. garbage can
43. garden

*Hogar, dulce hogar →
Home, sweet home

You may use the PowerPoint slides of all scenes to present and practice the vocabulary.

12. la ducha
13. el espejo
39. la luz
40. SE ALQUILA CUARTO PARA ESTUDIANTE
11. la bañera
14. el lavabo
CARMEN
15. el inodoro
16. el (cuarto de) baño
41. el garaje
30. el refrigerador
31. el microondas
¡Rin! ¡Rin!
NURIA
35. sonar (ue)
32. la estufa
36. contestar
33. el fregadero
43. el jardín
Mª LUISA
34. el lavaplatos
42. el cubo de la basura
37. la cocina
38. el sótano

¡La pronunciación!
Pay attention to the correct pronunciation of the Spanish **je** and **ge** combinations (see P-3).
gara**je**   refri**ge**rador

¡En acción!

6-1 ¿Qué es?

Con la ayuda de la escena de las páginas 184–185, indica a qué corresponde cada descripción.

1. _la... cama_ Está en el dormitorio; es para dormir.

2. _la alfombra_ Se pone sobre el piso; algunas son muy caras.

3. _el estante_ Sirve para poner los libros.

4. _el refrigerador_ Dentro se conserva la comida; está en la cocina.

5. _la escalera_ Conecta el primer piso con el segundo.

6. _la chimenea_ Está en la sala; se usa para calentar[1] la casa.

7. _la bañera_ Está en el baño; allí, en el agua caliente, nos relajamos.

8. _la estufa_ Es esencial para cocinar; está en la cocina.

6-2 La casa de los Roldán

¿Cómo es la casa de los Roldán y cómo es la vida en ella? Observen la escena de las páginas 184–185 y contesten las preguntas.

1. ¿De qué color es el techo de la casa de los Roldán? ¿Tiene ático y sótano?

2. ¿Qué hay en el dormitorio principal? ¿Quién está allí? ¿Qué está haciendo?

3. ¿Qué hace Robertito en su dormitorio? ¿Qué muebles hay en su cuarto?

4. ¿Quién está en el cuarto de baño? ¿Qué cosas hay allí?

5. ¿Quién está subiendo por las escaleras al segundo piso? ¿Y quién está bajando al primer piso?

6. ¿Qué hay en la sala? ¿Qué están haciendo don Claudio y doña Rosa?

7. ¿Qué muebles y otras cosas hay en el comedor? ¿Qué hace Guadalupe?

8. ¿Qué pasa en la cocina? ¿Qué electrodomésticos[2] hay allí?

9. ¿Qué hay en el garaje? ¿Y en el jardín?

10. ¿Qué se alquila?

WILEY PLUS For more practice, see **Grammar Handbook** found in *WileyPLUS*.

> ### . . . y algo más Affirmative and negative words: *alguien, nadie, algo, nada*
>
> You have already used some affirmative and negative words in Spanish:
> **siempre/a veces** *always/ sometimes* → **nunca** *never;* **también** *also* → **tampoco** *neither, not either.*
>
> Here are four more:
>
> | | | |
> |---|---|---|
> | **alguien** | *someone* | —¿Hay **alguien** en la cocina? |
> | **nadie** | *no one, not anyone, nobody* | —No, **no** hay **nadie.** |
> | **algo** | *something* | —¿Hay **algo** en la mesa? |
> | **nada** | *nothing* | —No, **no** hay **nada.** |
>
> Negative words such as **nadie, nada, nunca,** and **tampoco** may be placed either before the verb (**Nadie** contesta.) or after the verb, with **no** preceding it, in a "double negative" construction (**No** contesta **nadie.**).

[1]warm up, [2]appliances

For additional vocabulary practice, see PowerPoint slides on BCS and in *WileyPLUS*.

6-1 Present alternatives to vocabulary items at your discretion: **el dormitorio/ el cuarto/ la recámara/ la alcoba; el ropero/ el clóset/ el armario** (the latter may also mean *armoire*). Have students note that **la cómoda** (a noun) means *dresser* and that **cómodo/a** (an adjective) means *comfortable*.

6-2 You may want to project the PowerPoint slide of the opener scene, and have the class describe both each room in the house and the corresponding activities.

6-2 PERSONALIZED QUESTIONS: En tu casa, o en la casa de tu familia, ¿cuál es tu cuarto favorito? ¿Por qué? Ask several students the questions, then poll the class to find out which rooms are their favorites.

6-2 ANOTHER STEP: Write on the board: **el dormitorio, el baño, la cocina, el comedor, la sala.** Project the PowerPoint slide of the opener scene. Call out the names of pieces of furniture, appliances, and so on, and have students identify the room in which they each belong: **la cama → el dormitorio.** As they do so, point to the particular room.

For additional practice on this grammar point, see PowerPoint slides on BCS and in *WileyPLUS*.

You may want to explain to students that if **a nadie** and **nada** are direct objects they sound unnatural at the beginning of the sentence. Ex: **No veo nada.** or **No veo a nadie.** vs. **Nada veo.** or **A nadie veo.** When **nadie** or **nada** is a subject, its position is flexible: **No contesta nadie.** Or **Nadie contesta. No existe nada.** Or **Nada existe.**

6-3 ¿Hay alguien o algo allí?

¿Tienen buena memoria visual? Observen la escena de las páginas 184–185. Luego, lean las preguntas y respondan según el modelo. Usen **algo/ nada/ alguien/ nadie** en sus respuestas. Túrnense.

MODELO

E1: *¿Está durmiendo **alguien** en el dormitorio principal?*

E2: *No, **nadie** está durmiendo allí, pero **alguien** está haciendo ejercicio.*

E1: *Cierto. (Si la respuesta es incorrecta, **E1** la corrige.)*

E2: *¿Hay **algo** en la pared del dormitorio principal?*

E1: *Sí, hay **algo**. Hay dos cuadros.*

1. ¿Hay **algo** en la cómoda del dormitorio principal?
2. ¿Hay **alguien** en la computadora del dormitorio de los niños?
3. ¿Hay **alguien** en el baño?
4. ¿Hay **algo** en el piso del baño?
5. ¿Hay **algo** en el piso de la sala?
6. ¿Está durmiendo **alguien** en el sofá de la sala?
7. ¿Está cocinando **alguien** en la cocina?
8. ¿Hay **algo** en el fregadero?

¡A escuchar! Buscando casa

Paso 1.   Un matrimonio tiene una cita con la agente de una agencia de bienes raíces[1] para ver una casa. Escucha la conversación.

PLUS Go to *WileyPLUS* to complete **Paso 2** of this listening activity.

En la casa del futuro, ¿qué te interesa más?

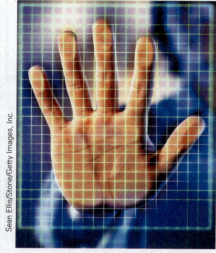

En la casa del futuro, **la llave** es algo obsoleto; un escáner reconoce la palma de la mano para abrir la puerta.

El espejo del futuro sabe qué hay en el ropero y lo que va bien con la ropa que llevas[2].

[1]**agencia...** real estate agency, [2]you are wearing

Explain that whereas in English "double negatives" are ungrammatical, in Spanish they are commonly used: **No** hay **nadie** aquí.

Remind students that when **Hay** is followed by an article it is always an indefinite article (un, una, unos, unas) and never a definite article.

Also remind them the difference between *Hay* (*There is /are*) to express existence, as in **Hay un espejo en el baño,** and *Estar* (*to be located*) to indicate location, as in **El espejo está encima del lavabo.**

6-3   You may want to review answers using the PowerPoint slide of the opener scene.

ANSWERS: 1. Sí, hay algo. Hay una lámpara y un reloj. 2. No, no hay nadie en la computadora, pero hay alguien en la cama. 3. Sí, hay alguien en el baño. Carmen está allí. 4. No, no hay nada en el piso del baño, pero hay algo en la bañera. 5. Sí, hay algo. Hay dos alfombras. 6. No, nadie está durmiendo en el sofá, pero alguien está leyendo. 7. Sí, alguien está cocinando. Es Nuria. 8. No, no hay nada en el fregadero, pero hay algo en la estufa.

The scripts and recordings for the ¡A escuchar! sections are included on the Book Companion Site (BCS) for instructors and in *WileyPLUS*.

Remind students that the verb **interesar** works just like the verb **gustar**.

6-4 For *Paso 1*, have several students indicate which house or apartment they plan to rent and why. For *Paso 2*, ask two students to role-play their telephone conversation for the class.

You may want to do this activity with the class using the PowerPoint slide.

6-4 ¿Buscan casa o apartamento para alquilar?

Paso 1. Lean los anuncios de dos casas y de un apartamento de Miami. Comenten qué les gusta de cada uno. Luego, digan cuál quieren alquilar y por qué.

MODELO

E1: *Me gusta esta casa porque tiene...*

E2: *Y a mí me gusta esta casa porque...*

E1: *Quiero alquilar esta casa/ este apartamento porque...*

> **Palabras útiles**
>
> esta casa *this house*
> este apartamento *this apartment*

> **¿SABES QUE...?**
>
> When answering the phone, one says ¿Aló? (in most Spanish-speaking countries), ¿Bueno? (in Mexico), ¿Diga? (in Spain), and ¿Hola? (in Argentina). To ask who is calling, one says ¿Quién llama/es? or ¿De parte de quién?

Dormitorios: 3
Baños: 2
Pisos: 1
Garaje: 2 carros
Aire acondicionado central
Casa ideal para pareja joven; con gimnasio y sauna. Está cerca de escuelas buenas, del centro comercial y del hospital.

Dormitorios: 5
Baños: 3
Pisos: 2
Garaje: 3 carros
sótano en muy buenas condiciones
Aire acondicionado central
Bonita casa con piscina[1] y jardín. Zona muy tranquila y elegante. Situada muy cerca de la autopista.

Dormitorios: 2
Baños: 1
Pisos: 1
Garaje: 1 carro
Aire acondicionado central
Apartamento elegante con patio para barbacoa y jardín; piscina comunitaria, cancha de tenis y gimnasio; muy próximo a la universidad.

Paso 2. Un agente de bienes raíces[2] habla por teléfono con una clienta que busca casa o apartamento. Hagan los dos papeles.

MODELO

Agente: *¿Aló?*   **Clienta:** *Buenas tardes, señor/ señora/ señorita... Busco... Me gustaría ver...*

Al volver del supermercado, Mario y Fabio tienen una propuesta interesante para Ernesto.

[1]swimming pool, [2]**agente... real state agent**

¡Manos a la obra!

GRAMÁTICA

1

Expressing relationships in space and time: More about prepositions

Prepositions are connectors; they describe relationships between people, places, or things. You have learned already many of these:

Prepositions of place

cerca de/ lejos de	*close, near (to)/ far from*
debajo de/ encima de	*beneath, below, under/ on top of, above*
dentro de/ fuera de	*within, inside (of)/ outside (of)*
detrás de/ delante de	*behind/ in front of*
en	*on, in*
enfrente de	*opposite, facing, in front of*
al lado de	*beside, next to*
entre	*between*
sobre	*above*
por	*by, through, around, alongside*

Other prepositions

sobre, acerca de	*about (a topic)*
antes de/ después de	*before/ after*
durante	*during*
en vez de	*in place of, instead of*
para	*for*
para + *infinitivo*	*in order to (do something)*
al + *infinitivo*	*upon (doing something)*

Let's look at examples based on the three friends' conversation about the apartment:

- In Spanish, a verb following a preposition is always in the infinitive (**-ar, -er, -ir**) form. English typically uses the *-ing* form.

  En vez de **vivir** en la residencia, Ernesto quiere vivir con Fabio y Mario.
  *Instead of **living** in the dormitory, Ernesto wants to live with Fabio and Mario.*

- Prepositions often used with infinitives: **antes de, después de, en vez de, al, sin.**

  Al volver, hablan del apartamento.   ***Upon returning**, they talk about the apartment.*

  Pasan por allí **antes de cenar**.   *They go by there **before having dinner**.*

- Use **para** + *infinitive* to express *in order to* (purpose, goal).

  Su compañero de apartamento va a Argentina **para estudiar.**
  *Their roommate is going to Argentina **to (in order to) study**.*

Object-of-preposition pronouns

- In Spanish, the pronouns that serve as objects of most prepositions are identical in form to the subject pronouns, except for **mí** and **ti**.

> **mí, ti, Ud., él, ella, nosotros/as, vosotros/as, Uds., ellos, ellas**

  —¿Viven Uds. lejos de **mí**? —¿Lejos de **ti**? No, vivimos en la calle 51.
- The preposition **entre** is followed by subject pronouns.

  Entre tú y **yo** tenemos suficientes muebles para el apartamento.
- **Con + mí = conmigo** (*with me*) and **con + ti = contigo** (*with you*).

  —¿Quién vive **contigo**, Fabio? —¿**Conmigo**? Mario.

WILEY PLUS Go to *WileyPLUS* to review this grammar point with the help of the **Animated Grammar Tutorial**. For more practice, go to the **Grammar Handbook**.

For additional practice on this grammar point, see PowerPoint slides on BCS and in *WileyPLUS*.

To introduce students to these prepositions used in context, have them take parts and read the **historieta** out loud. To check their comprehension and call their attention to the prepositions, ask the following questions: 1. **¿Por qué buscan Fabio y Mario compañero de apartamento? 2. ¿Dónde está el apartamento?**

Additional uses of **por** and **para** are presented in *Capítulo 8* and *Capítulo 11*. Use the *¡Oye!* listening activity to review the prepositions of location.

To familiarize students with the prepositions, send them to the board to write original sentences using the prepositions of place to describe locations on campus. Assign two prepositions per pair of students. Other students could write example sentences using prepositions from the "Other prepositions" list, related to what takes place in Spanish class.

¡En acción!

¡Oye! ¿Dónde está la araña?

Tu profesor/a tiene una araña muy activa. Escucha las preguntas y contesta para indicar dónde está en cada momento.

6-5 La invasión de los gatos

En grupos de *tres*, identifiquen dónde están los gatos, usando las preposiciones de la página 189. Apunten la información. ¿Qué grupo puede decir dónde está el mayor número de gatos? Tienen *cinco* minutos.

MODELO

Un gato está **encima del** *sofá. Otro está…*

© John Wiley & Sons, Inc.

Ofelia   Sofía   Maya

6-6 Hogar, dulce hogar: en casa de los Roldán

Observa el dibujo de las páginas 184–185 y di lo que hacen los Roldán en casa. Completa las oraciones con la preposición apropiada. En algunos casos se puede usar más de una.

| al | antes de | después de | durante | en vez de | para | acerca de |

1. Probablemente, Damián va a ducharse ___después de___ hacer ejercicio.

2. Robertito, ___en vez de___ estar con el resto de la familia, está durmiendo la siesta.

3. ___Al / Después de___ entrar al baño, Carmen siempre se mira al espejo.

4. En la sala, la abuela Rosa está leyendo un libro ___acerca de___ los incas.

5. Don Claudio lee el periódico ___para___ saber lo que pasa en el mundo.

6. ___Antes de___ cenar, Guadalupe sirve agua en los vasos.

7. ___Durante___ la cena, no antes ni después, todos van a hablar de las vacaciones.

¡Oye! Bring a shoe box or similar container to class, with a rubber or paper spider in it (or something similar).

Guión para ¡Oye!
1. ¿Dónde está la araña? (*Shake the box.*) Ah…, aquí está, ¡dentro de la caja!
2. ¿Y dónde está ahora? Fuera de la caja.
3. ¿Y ahora? Encima de la caja, y… debajo de la caja, y… al lado de la caja.
4. ¿Y ahora? Está delante de la caja, y… detrás de la caja.
5. (*Toss it into the wastebasket.*) Ahora está dentro de la papelera, pero no le gusta estar allí. Ahora está fuera de la papelera.
6. Le gusta la clase de español. Ahora está enfrente de la clase.
7. La araña quiere conocer a (*name student*). Está cerca de… (*same student*).
8. (*Toss spider out the door.*) Ya no está cerca de los estudiantes. Está lejos de ellos.

Comprensión para ¡Oye! Place the spider again in the various locations (1–8 above) and have students say where it is. For each location, give them two options to choose from: **¿Está la araña dentro o fuera de la caja?**

6-5 After students complete their work, you may want to have the winning group present their description of the location of each cat, using the PowerPoint slide of the illustration.

6-6 Students may complete the activity individually or in pairs, with answers reviewed by the instructor. Using the PowerPoint slide of the opener scene, point to each area as students provide answers.

6-6 PERSONALIZED QUESTIONS: Ask students to complete the following sentences to reflect aspects of their personal lives: **Por la mañana, después de salir de casa,…; Al regresar a casa,…; Antes de preparar la cena,…; Por la noche, en vez de…**

RECYCLES prepositions of location

6-7 Un juego: ¡Busca la llave!

Paso 1. Tu compañero/a esconde[1] la llave de tu carro en un lugar de la casa (págs. 184–185) y tú quieres saber en qué cuarto está y dónde exactamente. Usen las preposiciones de lugar. Túrnense. Tienen *cinco* minutos para esconder y encontrar la llave varias veces.

MODELO

Tú: ¿Está en el dormitorio? → **Tu compañero/a:** *Sí, está allí. (o) No, no está allí.*

Tú: ¿Está **debajo de** la cama? → **Tu compañero/a:** *Sí, está allí. (o) No, no está allí.*

Tú: (Si la encuentras, di con entusiasmo:) *¡¡¡La encontré[2] !!! ¡Te toca[3]!*

Paso 2. Al terminar, díganle a la clase en qué lugares encontraron la llave.

Ernesto va al apartamento de Fabio y Mario para ver el cuarto que alquilan.

GRAMÁTICA

¡Manos a la obra!

Pointing out things and people: Demonstrative adjectives

2

Demonstrative adjectives

Demonstrative adjectives are used to point out specific objects or people. Like other adjectives, demonstrative adjectives agree in gender and number with the word they describe. The demonstrative adjective you use depends upon how close you are to the item you are pointing out.

aquí *here* (close to speaker)		**ahí** *there* (at a short distance from speaker)		**allí** or **allá** *over there* (far from speaker)	
this	(m.) **este** sillón	*that*	**ese** sillón	*that*	**aquel** sillón
	(f.) **esta** silla		**esa** silla		**aquella** silla
these	(m.) **estos** cuadros	*those*	**esos** cuadros	*those*	**aquellos** cuadros
	(f.) **estas** cortinas		**esas** cortinas		**aquellas** cortinas

Memory tip: "This" and "these" have "t's"!

Let's consider comments Ernesto might make about the apartment:

Me gusta **esta** cama y **esa** cómoda.   *I like **this** bed and **that** dresser.*

¿De quién son **esos** libros y **aquel** estante?   *Whose are **those** books and **that** bookshelf?*

[1]hides, [2]**La...** I found it, [3]Your turn!

For additional practice on this grammar point, see PowerPoint slides on BCS and in *WileyPLUS.*

6-7 Have students jot down the hiding place so they can show it to their partner later. Advise students doing the guessing to first find out the floor or room where the key is located, then to proceed to find out its exact location.

WILEY PLUS Go to *WileyPLUS* to review this grammar point with the help of the **Animated Grammar Tutorial.** For more practice, go to the **Grammar Handbook.**

To introduce students to demonstrative adjectives used in context, have them take parts and read the **historieta** out loud. To check their comprehension and call their attention to the demonstratives, ask the following questions: 1. ¿Dónde está el cuarto de baño del apartamento? 2. ¿Dónde se puede estacionar?

To practice neuter demonstratives, write on the board: ¡Esto es un desastre! ¡Esto/ Eso es el colmo! (*This/That is the limit/ the last straw!*) ¡Eso es genial! ¿Qué es esto? Students use the expressions to respond to each of the following: 1. Entras en el cuarto de tu hermano y está todo desordenado. 2. Llegas a tu apartamento después de un día horrible en el trabajo y descubres que no hay agua ni en la cocina, ni en el baño. 3. Una amiga te dice que va a comprar un apartamento con vistas maravillosas al mar Caribe. 4. Ves algo en el cubo de la basura y no sabes lo que es.

Go to *WileyPLUS* to review this grammar point with the help of the **Animated Grammar Tutorial**. For more practice, go to the **Grammar Handbook**.

Place three books in three different locations—near you, farther away, and very far away. Do the same with three backpacks, three baseball caps, and three pairs of tennis shoes. Illustrate the demonstratives by describing each: **Este libro es azul. Ese de ahí es…, y aquel (que está allí, lejos) es…**

Project PowerPoint slides for this **¡Oye!** or draw on the board: (1) Three houses, the first in the foreground—new, large, and two stories; the second farther away—smaller and two stories, with a two-car garage; the third farthest away—one story with large trees and lots of flowers around it. (2) Three cars, the first in the foreground (write the year 2000 next to it); the second farther away (year 2006); the third farthest away (year 2010).

Guión para ¡Oye!, primera parte
Write down prices throughout, as you say them.
1. **Esta** casa (*point to largest house*) es nueva y es de dos pisos. Tiene cuatro habitaciones y cuatro baños. Cuesta 250.000 dólares.
2. **Esa** casa (*point to it*) también es de dos pisos y es muy bonita. Tiene tres habitaciones, tres baños y un garaje para dos carros. Cuesta 175.000 dólares.
3. **Aquella** casa (*point to it*) es de un piso; tiene dos habitaciones, dos baños y un jardín muy bonito, con árboles grandes y muchas flores. Cuesta 140.000 dólares. ¿Cuál prefieres, **esta, esa** o **aquella**? ¿Por qué?

6-8 ANSWERS *Luis:*
1. (modelo) 2. … esa… pequeña 3. … esos…feos
4. … esas… viejas
5. … ese…desordenado
6. … esos… viejos
7. … esas…bajas
8. … esos…pequeños.

For additional practice on this grammar point, see PowerPoint slides on BCS and in *WileyPLUS.*

The spelling changes announced by the Real Academia Española in 2010 included the decision to drop accent marks from demonstrative pronouns.

¡En acción!

¡Oye! Buscando casa y carro

Escucha con atención la descripción de tres casas y decide cuál prefieres. Luego, haz lo mismo después de escuchar la descripción de los tres carros.

6-8 Dos casas completamente opuestas

RECYCLES adjectives of opposite meaning.

Ana y Luis buscan casa. Con los planos en la mano, Ana comenta acerca de la casa que les gusta, y Luis, acerca de la otra, que es todo lo opuesto. Hagan de pareja. Ana usa **este/ esta/ estos/ estas** según la información del 1 al 8, y Luis responde con **ese/ esa/ esos/ esas,** y lo opuesto de la palabra en cursiva. Sigan el modelo de las burbujas[1].

Esta casa está *cerca* del trabajo.

En cambio[2], **esa** casa está *lejos* del trabajo.

© John Wiley & Sons, Inc.

Ana habla de la casa que les gusta…

1. *Esta* . casa está *cerca* del trabajo.
2. *Esta* . cocina es *grande*.
3. *Estos*. dormitorios son *bonitos*.
4. *Estas* . alfombras son *nuevas*.
5. *Este* . garaje está *ordenado*.
6. *Estos*. baños son *nuevos*.
7. *Estas*. paredes son *altas*.
8. *Estos*. roperos son *grandes*.

[1]bubble, [2]**En…** On the other hand

6-9 La mudanza[1]

Un/a estudiante ayuda a otro con la mudanza y le pregunta dónde debe poner los muebles y cosas de la casa. Su compañero/a contesta, indicando el lugar apropiado. Usen los demostrativos. Después de completar del 1 al 6, cambien de papel.

MODELO

el sofá

E1: *¿Dónde pongo **este** sofá?*

E2: ***Ese**, en la sala.*

1. las sillas
2. los platos
3. la cómoda
4. el estante
5. el espejo
6. la lámpara
7. el televisor
8. la alfombra

6-10 En la tienda[2] de muebles

Uno/a de Uds. necesita muebles para la sala y el comedor de su apartamento. Hagan de cliente/a (**A** en el dibujo) y de dependiente/a (**B** en el dibujo). Combinen muebles clásicos y modernos, si lo desean.

Necesitas: sofá, sillón, cuadros, mesita, alfombra, lámparas, mesa y sillas de comedor

MODELO

Cliente/a:	*Busco un sofá para mi apartamento.*
Dependiente/a:	*Tenemos **este** de flores o **este** rojo.*
Cliente/a:	*Prefiero **ese**. Me gustan las flores y el estilo. ¿Cuánto cuesta?*
Dependiente/a:	*2.500 dólares.*
Cliente/a:	*¡Qué caro! ¿Y cuánto cuesta **ese**?*
Dependiente/a:	*¿**Este**? 1.500 dólares.*
Cliente/a:	*Pues, **ese**.*

Palabras útiles

¡Qué barato!	*How inexpensive*
¡Qué caro/a!	*How expensive!*
¡Qué bonito/a!	*How pretty!*
¡Es mucho dinero!	*It is a lot of money!*

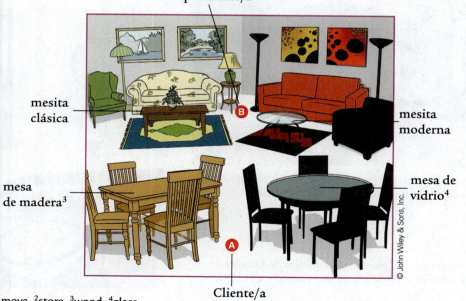

Dependiente/a

mesita clásica

mesita moderna

mesa de madera[3]

mesa de vidrio[4]

© John Wiley & Sons, Inc.

B

A

Cliente/a

[1]The move, [2]store, [3]wood, [4]glass

Tu mundo cultural

Las casas de estilo tradicional español

For an additional activity related to this cultural theme, see the PowerPoint slides on BCS and in *WileyPLUS*.

Meets ACTFL Standards
1.1, interpersonal speaking;
1.2, interpretive reading;
2.2, cultural products; and
4.2, cultural comparisons.

¿Sabes cómo son las casas de estilo tradicional español? ¿Hay alguna en tu pueblo o ciudad?

Hay casas de estilo tradicional español que, aunque estén situadas en países, continentes, hemisferios y climas diferentes, tienen rasgos[1] comunes en su arquitectura y decoración. Estos rasgos, resultado de la influencia romana y árabe en España, se introducen en el Nuevo Mundo con la llegada de los españoles.

> *Elementos característicos*: cuartos alrededor de[2] un patio interior; jardín o patio exterior; techos de teja[3]; pisos de madera[4] o cerámica; cocinas y baños decorados con mosaicos; balcones y ventanas exteriores con rejas[5]. En muchos casos, una valla[6] de rejas rodea la casa y el jardín.

Arquitectura de estilo tradicional español en Estados Unidos

La influencia hispana también se observa en el diseño de las casas de EE. UU., no sólo en el sudoeste, cerca de la frontera mexicana, sino en muchas otras partes del país.

Casa de estilo tradicional español en Fort Myers, Florida. En muchas partes de EE. UU. se encuentran casas de este estilo, muestra de la presencia hispana en la historia de este país.

Jeff Greenberg/The Image Works

Santiago Fdez Fuentes/Age Fotostock America, Inc.

El típico patio central de las casas de estilo tradicional español se encuentra también en muchas casas de EE. UU.

Courtesy Conchita Lucas

Baño de una casa de Colorado. La cerámica de Talavera se produce también en México y de allí se exporta a EE. UU.

[1]features, [2]**alrededor...** surrounding, [3]tile, [4]wood, [5]metal railings, [6]fence

Los apartamentos de las ciudades hispanas modernas

Con la expansión urbana, tanto[1] en España como en Latinoamérica, la mayoría de la gente[2] que vive en las ciudades y pueblos grandes reside en edificios de apartamentos (departamentos). Estos apartamentos conservan algunos elementos de las casas tradicionales como los techos de teja, los balcones, el patio interior o la decoración de baños, cocina y pisos con cerámica.

Lin Alder/Danita Delimont

 ## ¿Qué aprendiste?

1. ¿Cuáles son las características del interior y exterior de las casas de estilo tradicional español?
   Patio interior, jardín, techos de teja, pisos de madera o cerámica, mosaicos, balcones o rejas.
2. ¿Dónde se encuentran casas de estilo tradicional español en EE. UU.?
   En zonas de presencia hispana como Florida y en muchas otras partes del país.
3. En las ciudades o pueblos grandes del mundo hispano, ¿dónde reside la mayoría de la gente? ¿Qué características conservan esos edificios de las casas tradicionales?
   En apartamentos. Techos de teja, balcones, cerámica o patio interior.

Actividad cultural

 Paso 1. Eres arquitecto/a y alguien que desea construir una casa de estilo tradicional español te consulta sobre los rasgos más característicos de esa clase de casas. Escribe la información para tu cliente/a en el espacio provisto:

Edificio de apartamentos de Buenos Aires, en Argentina. Como se puede observar, el balcón es un elemento que tienen en común las casas y edificios de todos los países hispanos.

Techo:
Ubicación[3] de los cuartos:
Piso y decoración de la cocina y los baños:
Elementos en el exterior del edificio:
Otros rasgos típicos:

 Paso 2. Ahora llama por teléfono a tu cliente/a para darle tus ideas. Luego, cambien de papel.

Carmen Nasarre/Age Fotostock America, Inc.

Contraste cultural

Descríbele a tu compañero/a algunas características de tu casa o apartamento con la ayuda de la siguiente lista. Menciona también las diferencias que observas con las casas o apartamentos hispanos. Luego, cambien de papel.

En los países hispanos es común colgar la ropa[7] en la ventana o en el balcón.

CARACTERÍSTICAS:

· techo de (teja, metal, tablilla[4])	· piso de (madera, cerámica o alfombra)
· número de pisos, dormitorios y baños	· patio interior o exterior o terraza[5]
· exterior de (madera, cemento, estuco, ladrillo[6])	· ventanas con o sin rejas, garaje, jardín, valla, vistas...

[1]as much, [2]people, [3]location, [4]shingle, [5]deck, [6]brick, [7] **colgar...** hang clothes

Inform your students that the verbs in this scene are *reflexive verbs*, formed with the reflexive pronoun **se**.

La vida diaria

Pronunciación: Practice pronunciation of the chapter's new vocabulary in *WileyPLUS*.

¹La vida diaria de Lola, una enfermera

- 5:00
- 2. despertarse (ie)
- 3. el despertador
- 5:15
- 4. levantarse
- 5:20
- 5. cepillarse (los dientes)
- 6. el cepillo de dientes
- 7. la pasta de dientes
- 8. el jabón
- 5:25
- 9. ducharse
- 10. lavarse (el pelo)
- 11. el champú
- 5:35
- 12. afeitarse

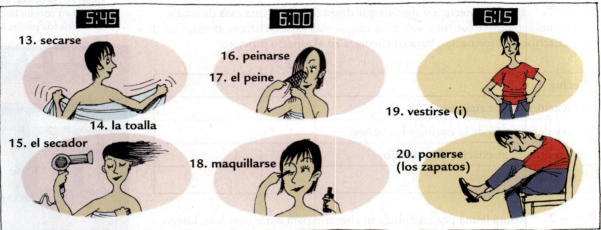

- 5:45
- 13. secarse
- 14. la toalla
- 15. el secador
- 6:00
- 16. peinarse
- 17. el peine
- 18. maquillarse
- 6:15
- 19. vestirse (i)
- 20. ponerse (los zapatos)

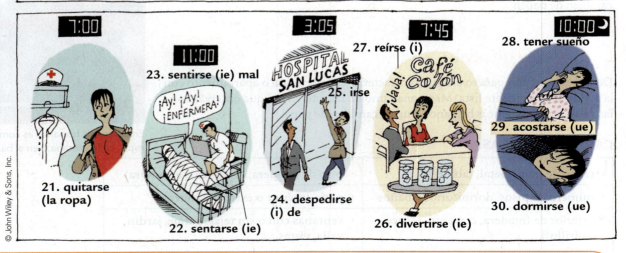

- 7:00
- 21. quitarse (la ropa)
- 11:00
- 22. sentarse (ie)
- 23. sentirse (ie) mal
- ¡Ay! ¡Ay! ¡ENFERMERA!
- HOSPITAL SAN LUCAS
- 3:05
- 24. despedirse (i) de
- 25. irse
- 27. reírse (i)
- 7:45
- Café Colón
- ¡Jajá!
- 26. divertirse (ie)
- 10:00
- 28. tener sueño
- 29. acostarse (ue)
- 30. dormirse (ue)

© John Wiley & Sons, Inc.

1. daily life 2. to wake up 3. alarm clock 4. to get up 5. to brush (one's teeth) 6. toothbrush 7. toothpaste 8. soap 9. to take a shower; **bañarse** to take a bath 10. to wash (one's hair) 11. shampoo 12. to shave 13. to dry oneself 14. towel 15. hairdryer 16. to comb one's hair 17. comb 18. to put on makeup 19. to get dressed 20. to put on (one's shoes, etc.) 21. to take off (one's clothes, etc.) 22. to sit down 23. to feel bad/ sick; **sentirse bien** to feel well 24. to say good-bye (to) 25. to go away 26. to have fun/ a good time 27. to laugh 28. to be sleepy 29. to go to bed 30. to fall asleep

¡En acción!

6-11 Mi lista de compras

Paso 1. Es el primer día en tu nueva casa y ves que no tienes lo que necesitas para tu rutina diaria. Escribe en un papel lo que tienes que comprar.

Mi rutina:

1. para despertar**me** a tiempo
2. para bañar**me** o ducharme
3. para lavar**me** el pelo
4. para secar**me** el pelo
5. para cepillar**me** los dientes
6. para secar**me** las manos[1]
7. para peinar**me**

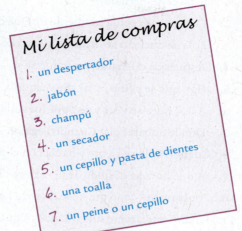

Mi lista de compras

1. un despertador
2. jabón
3. champú
4. un secador
5. un cepillo y pasta de dientes
6. una toalla
7. un peine o un cepillo

Paso 2. Ahora, compara tu lista de compras con la de un/a compañero/a.

6-12 Lola y su rutina   RECYCLES estar + *location*.

Según las situaciones de la página 196, pongan las actividades de Lola en orden cronológico. Luego, indiquen dónde está en cada momento.

__5__ Habla con los pacientes que **se** sienten mal. _Está en el hospital/ en el trabajo._

__1__ **Se** levanta a las cinco y cuarto de la mañana. _Está en el dormitorio/ cuarto._

__8__ **Se** quita la ropa y **se** acuesta. _Está en el dormitorio/ cuarto._

__7__ Sale con sus amigos a cenar y **se** divierte. _Está en el Café Colón._

__2__ **Se** ducha y **se** lava el pelo. _Está en el (cuarto de) baño._

__6__ **Se** despide de sus compañeros. _Está fuera del hospital._

__4__ **Se** viste y **se** pone los zapatos. _Está en el dormitorio/ cuarto._

__3__ **Se** seca el pelo y **se** peina. _Está en el (cuarto de) baño._

Inform your students that *Actividad 6-12* will serve as an introduction to *reflexive* verbs. The verbs in it are *reflexive verbs*, formed with the reflexive pronoun **se**. Point out that the pronoun **se** goes in front of the verb and refers to an action performed by **él, ella, Ud.**, or their plural counterparts. If your students are ready, introduce the rest of the reflexive pronouns: **me, te, nos**, and **os**, so they start becoming familiar with them.

6-12 Students may complete the activity individually or in pairs, with answers reviewed by the instructor.

¿SABES QUE...?

In Spanish, as in English, names are frequently shortened. For example:
Conchita (Concepción); **Lola** (Dolores); **Paco** (Francisco); **Pepe** (José); **Lupe** (Guadalupe); **Toño** (Antonio); **Quique** (Enrique); **Charo** (Rosario).

---

[1]hands

6-13 La vida diaria de Lola

Observen las escenas de la página 196 y contesten las preguntas.

1. ¿A qué hora **se** despierta Lola? *Se despierta a las...* ¿**Se** levanta inmediatamente cuando suena el despertador?

2. ¿Con qué **se** cepilla los dientes? ¿Qué otra cosa hay en el lavabo?

3. ¿Lola **se** ducha o **se** baña? ¿Qué usa para lavar**se** el pelo? ¿**Se** afeita las piernas[1]?

4. Después de duchar**se**, ¿con qué **se** seca? ¿Qué usa para secar**se** el pelo?

5. ¿Con qué **se** peina Lola? ¿**Se** maquilla Lola?

6. ¿A qué hora **se** viste y **se** pone los zapatos?

7. ¿Dónde trabaja Lola? Cuando llega allí, ¿qué hace antes de poner**se** el uniforme de enfermera?

8. Cuando Lola **se** sienta y habla con el paciente, ¿qué dice él? ¿Y cómo **se** siente?

9. ¿A qué hora **se** despide de un colega y **se** va Lola del hospital?

10. Por la noche, ¿con quién **se** divierte Lola? ¿Quién **se** ríe?

11. Finalmente, ¿tiene sueño Lola? ¿A qué hora **se** acuesta? ¿**Se** duerme rápidamente?

> **. . . y algo más**   Adverbs in *-mente*
>
> In Spanish, many adverbs are formed by adding **-mente** (equivalent to the English *-ly*) to an adjective. Can you identify the adverbs in *Actividad 6-13*?
>
> - Add **-mente** to adjectives ending in **-e** or a consonant.
>   posible → posible**mente**   personal → personal**mente**
> - Add **-mente** to the feminine singular form of adjectives ending in **-o**.
>   inmediato → inmediata**mente**   rápido → rápida**mente**

¡A escuchar! ¡Esto sí que es vida!

Paso 1. Dos amigos están pasando juntos unos días de vacaciones y comentan la experiencia. Escucha la conversación.

Go to *WileyPLUS* to complete **Paso 2** of this listening activity.

 En el carro, camino a casa de Jennifer, Fabio y sus amigos hablan de su rutina diaria.

[1]legs

¡Manos a la obra!

3

Talking about daily routines: Reflexive verbs

Uses of reflexive verbs

Some verbs use the reflexive pronouns (**me, te, se, nos, os, se**) to show that the person is doing the action to himself/herself. This *pronoun + verb* construction often describes daily routines or personal care. In these examples based on the routines of Fabio's friends, note the change in meaning when the reflexive pronoun is used.

Jennifer **se baña**.	*Jennifer is bathing (herself).*
Jennifer **baña** a su hija.	*Jennifer is bathing her daugher.*
Debo **levantarme**.	*I should get up (get myself up).*
Debo **levantar** a Mario.	*I should get Mario up.*

Although many reflexive verbs do describe actions a person does to himself/ herself, others, such as **sentirse** *to feel*, and **dormirse** *to fall asleep*, are idioms in which there is no logical explanation for the pronoun. The non-reflexive counterparts of these verbs usually have a somewhat different meaning (e.g. **dormir** *to sleep* vs. **dormirse** *to fall asleep*).

The formation of reflexive verbs

Note that the reflexive pronoun and the subject of the verb refer to the same person.

(yo)	**me** visto	(nosotros/as)	**nos** vestimos
(tú)	**te** vistes	(vosotros/as)	**os** vestís
(Ud., él, ella)	**se** viste	(Uds., ellos, ellas)	**se** visten

- As with direct and indirect object pronouns, reflexive pronouns are either placed immediately before the conjugated verb or attached to the infinitive and the present participle.

  Me tengo que duchar. (o) Tengo que duchar**me**.
  Mario no se está afeitando. (o) Mario no está afeitándo**se**.

- The reflexive pronoun **te** is attached to the end of **tú** affirmative commands. A written accent is added to the stressed syllable of regular command forms.

Ernesto, levánta**te**. Ya son las 7:30.	*Ernesto, get up. It's already 7:30.*
Víste**te** rápidamente.	*Get dressed quickly.*

- In the reflexive construction, use the definite article, not the possessive (**mi, tu, su,...**) to refer to parts of the person's body or to articles of clothing.

—Mamá, ¿vas a lavarte **el** pelo?	*Mama, are you going to wash **your** hair?*
—No, voy a cepillarme **los** dientes.	*No, I'm going to brush **my** teeth.*

- The pronouns **nos, os,** and **se** are also used to express reciprocal* or mutual actions.

Ysenia y Mabel **se** conocen bien.	*Ysenia and Mabel know **each other** well.*
Mis padres y yo **nos** queremos mucho.	*My parents and I love **each other** very much.*

  * The reciprocal construction is used passively in *¡Con brío!*

For additional practice on this grammar point, see PowerPoint slides on BCS and in *WileyPLUS*.

To familiarize students with the reflexive verbs, have the class stand in a circle. State an example sentence: **Me ducho por la mañana.**

Then call out a subject pronoun (**ellos,...**) and tap a student on the shoulder. He/She restates the sentence (**Se duchan por la mañana**), provides a different subject pronoun (**tú,...**), and taps another student on the shoulder.

WILEY PLUS Go to *WileyPLUS* to review this grammar point with the help of the **Animated Grammar Tutorial** and **Verb Conjugator**. For more practice, go to the **Grammar Handbook**.

(First, see the example: **Me ducho por la mañana.**) To illustrate the position of reflexive pronouns, write **debo, bañar, me, estoy, bañando,** and **baño** on separate sheets of paper. Give the papers with **baño** and **me** to a pair of students and ask them to place themselves in the correct order. Then use sets of three students for the infinitive and **-ando** constructions, giving them both options for the placement of pronouns: **Debo bañarme/ Me debo bañar** and **Estoy bañándome/ Me estoy bañando.** (Write in the accent mark on **bañándome**.)

¡En acción!

You may want to project the PowerPoint slide of the *Escena 2* scenes. Point to the appropriate scene as you describe it.

Guión para ¡Oye!
Por la mañana...
1. Lola se despierta a las seis de la mañana. *No. ... a las cinco...*
2. Se cepilla los dientes después de ducharse. *No. ... antes de...*
3. Se lava el pelo en la ducha. *Sí.*
4. Se afeita las piernas (*act out*) en la ducha. *Sí.*
5. Lola se seca el pelo con una toalla. *No. ... con secador.*
6. Lola se maquilla antes de peinarse. *No. ... después de...*
7. Lola se viste antes de ponerse los zapatos. *Sí.*

En el hospital...
8. El paciente se siente bien. *No. Se siente mal.*
9. A las dos y cinco de la tarde, Lola se despide de un compañero y se va. *No. ... a las tres y cinco...*

Por la noche...
10. Lola se ríe y se divierte con sus amigos. *Sí.*
11. Se acuesta a medianoche porque no tiene sueño. *No. ... a las 10:00 porque...*

6-14 To practice the **nosotros** form, ask students to report to the class answers they both had in common: *... y yo no nos despertamos temprano.*

6-15 To assist students, write on the board: E1: **acción;** E2: **cuándo;** E3: **dónde;** E4: **con qué.** At the end of each series, ask students from several groups to repeat their extended sentence for the class.

6-15 ANOTHER STEP: Six volunteers each act out one of the actions provided, and the other students describe what each is doing: **Joe está duchándose.** (o) **Joe se está duchando.**

¡Oye! La rutina de Lola

Observa las escenas de la página 196. Escucha la rutina de Lola y responde «¡Sí!» o «¡No!» para indicar si lo que oyes es cierto o falso. Si es falso, corrígelo.

6-14 ¿Es así tu rutina diaria?

Paso 1. Primero, completa los espacios en blanco con la forma **yo** de cada verbo. Luego, marca **Sí** o **No** para indicar si es así o no, según tu rutina.

Sí	No	Normalmente...
☐	☐	1. (*despertarse*) __Me__ __despierto__ muy temprano.
☐	☐	2. (*ducharse*) __Me__ __ducho__ por la mañana.
☐	☐	3. (*lavarse*) __Me__ __lavo__ el pelo todos los días.
☐	☐	4. (*afeitarse*) __Me__ __afeito__ todas las mañanas.
☐	☐	5. (*cepillarse*) __Me__ __cepillo__ los dientes tres veces al día.
☐	☐	6. (*peinarse*) __Me__ __peino__ varias veces al día.
☐	☐	7. (*ponerse*) __Me__ __pongo__ ropa limpia una vez por semana.
☐	☐	8. (*divertirse*) __Me__ __divierto__ con mi familia los fines de semana.
☐	☐	9. (*acostarse*) __Me__ __acuesto__ entre las diez y las once de la noche.

Paso 2. Ahora, compara las respuestas con las de tu compañero/a. En los casos donde contestaron **no,** den la información correcta.

MODELO

E1: *Yo **no me despierto** muy temprano. **Me despierto** a las diez. ¿Y tú?*

E2: *Yo sí **me despierto** muy temprano. **Me despierto** a las siete de la mañana.*

6-15 Un juego

La clase se divide en grupos de *cuatro*. Su profesor/a dice un número del 1 al 6. **E1** observa el objeto que hay junto al número y dice lo que hacen todos, según el modelo. **E2** lo repite y añade[1] **cuándo** lo hacen; **E3** lo repite todo y añade **dónde;** y **E4** lo repite todo y añade **con qué.** Luego, otro/a estudiante del grupo es **E1** y el juego continúa, empezando con otro número.

MODELO

Profesor/a: número 2

E1: *Nos duchamos.*

E2: *Nos duchamos **por la mañana.***

E3: *Nos duchamos por la mañana **en la ducha.***

E4: *Nos duchamos por la mañana en la ducha **con jabón.***

1. 2. 3. 4. 5. 6.

¹adds

All art © John Wiley & Sons, Inc.

6-16   La rutina de mis compañeros de clase

Paso 1.   Camina por la clase y pregúntales a tus compañeros si hacen lo siguiente. Apunta el nombre de cada estudiante que responde *afirmativamente*. A ver cuántas respuestas afirmativas puedes obtener en *cinco* minutos.

MODELO

E1:   ¿*Te despiertas* sin despertador?

E2:   Sí, *me despierto* sin despertador. (Apuntas el nombre.)

o: *No, no me despierto* sin despertador. (Buscas a otro/a estudiante.)

1. ¿**Te levantas** inmediatamente al sonar el despertador?	1. *Mario*
2. ¿**Te secas** el pelo con secador?	2.
3. ¿**Te afeitas** todos los días?	3.
4. ¿**Te bañas** o duchas por la noche?	4.
5. ¿**Te lavas** el pelo con jabón?	5.
6. ¿**Te cepillas** los dientes antes del desayuno?	6.
7. ¿**Te acuestas** después de medianoche?	7.
8. Después de **acostarte**, ¿**te duermes** rápidamente?	8.

Paso 2.   Ahora, el/la profesor/a quiere saber algo de la rutina de los estudiantes. Contesten sus preguntas según la información que tienen.

MODELO

Profesor/a: ¿Quién *se levanta* inmediatamente al sonar el despertador?

E1:   *Mario se levanta* inmediatamente.

6-17   Mi rutina diaria

Paso 1.   Describan su rutina diaria en orden cronológico, en *seis* oraciones. Incluyan expresiones de la lista. Túrnense.

> Por la mañana, **me despierto** a…

Paso 2.   Ahora comparte con la clase alguna información sobre la rutina diaria de tu compañero/a.

6-18   ¿Qué está haciendo Lola?

Paso 1.   Observen las escenas de la página 196. Un/a estudiante dice lo que hace Lola en un momento determinado del día (no en orden cronológico). Su compañero/a encuentra la escena que corresponde y dice *la hora* y *el lugar*. Después de *seis* acciones, cambien de papel.

MODELO

E1:   Lola *se divierte*.

E2:   ¡Ah! La veo. Son las 7:45 de la noche y *se divierte* en un café con sus amigos.

Paso 2.   Ahora, den *cuatro* ejemplos de cómo se diferencia su rutina de la rutina de Lola:
*A las cinco y cuarto de la mañana yo estoy en la cama. No **me levanto** hasta las nueve.*

After students learn the reflexive verbs, they may have the tendency to make all verbs reflexive (**Me desayuno…**). Warn students not to catch the disease called "reflexivitis"!

6-16   Instructor's questions (for *Paso 2* follow up): ¿**Quién se levanta inmediatamente al sonar el despertador?** Several students respond. After the feedback for each question, ask the class to summarize the degree of participation for each activity: **Muchas personas/ Pocas personas/ Nadie…**

Palabras útiles
Por la mañana
Primero
Luego
Normalmente
Después
Más tarde
Finalmente

6-18   You may want to project the PowerPoint slide of the scenes, and elicit feedback on *Paso 2*. ¿**En qué se diferencia su rutina diaria de la rutina de Lola?**

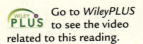
Go to *WileyPLUS* to see the video related to this reading.

For an additional activity related to this cultural theme, see the PowerPoint slides on BCS and in *WileyPLUS*.

Tu mundo cultural

Meets ACTFL Standards
1.1, interpersonal speaking;
1.2, interpretive reading;
2.1, cultural practices; and
4.2, cultural comparisons.

La vida diaria: costumbres y horarios[1]

¿Almuerzas o cenas diariamente en casa con tu familia, tu pareja o amigos? En tu familia, ¿son el desayuno, el almuerzo o la cena ocasiones para reunirse y charlar?

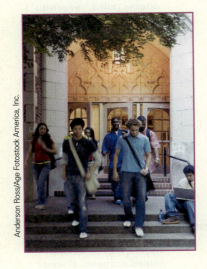

Anderson Ross/Age Fotostock America, Inc.

En el mundo hispano, los niños y los universitarios salen de clase para ir a casa a almorzar. Regresan a clase después del almuerzo.

Ariel Skelley/Blend/Getty Images, Inc.

Familia de San Miguel de Allende, México. A la hora del almuerzo, tres generaciones de una familia mexicana hacen una pausa en la jornada escolar y laboral[2] para comer juntos[3].

La hora del almuerzo marca la jornada laboral

A muchos hispanos les gusta comer en familia; por esa razón, los horarios se organizan de acuerdo con las comidas. El almuerzo es la comida principal, cuando los miembros de la familia se reúnen para estar juntos y comentar los eventos del día. Para el almuerzo se pone la mesa y se sirve comida casera[4] que requiere tiempo para su preparación. La hora exacta varía de país a país, pero en general, el almuerzo es entre la una y las dos de la tarde.

Courtesy Conchita Lucas

QUO viajes **HORARIOS** QUO viajes

Mañanas: 9,30 - 13,30
Tardes: 16,30 - 20,00
Sábados: 10,00 - 13,00

¿SABES QUE...?

In the Hispanic world, after lunch it is common to have a **sobremesa,** a time in which family members converse about the events of the day while sipping a cup of coffee.

Courtesy Conchita Lucas

Heidelberg
Restaurante

HORARIO AL PUBLICO
De 13,30 a 16,00
y 20 ,00 a 23,30
DESCANSO SEMANAL
DOMINGO

Durante el almuerzo se cierran las tiendas[5] y casi todos los trabajos, y los hispanos van a casa. Los domingos y días festivos son también para la familia; no se trabaja y no se abren las tiendas. En algunas capitales y grandes ciudades se están empezando a abrir tiendas los domingos, pero es todavía más la excepción que la regla.

Los restaurantes son los pocos lugares abiertos a la hora del almuerzo. Durante la semana son frecuentes en ellos los almuerzos de negocios. Cuando los clientes terminan de almorzar, los restaurantes se cierran y no se abren hasta la hora de la cena, tal como se observa en el horario de la fotografía.

[1]schedules, [2]**jornada...** school and work day, [3]together, [4]homemade, [5]stores

Consejo para los que no son hispanos

Cuando se trata con hispanos, es fundamental conocer sus horarios y cómo influye en ellos la familia. Saber esto es esencial para evitar[1] graves problemas de comunicación. Los hombres y mujeres estadounidenses que hacen negocios con países hispanos tienen que conocer estos dos aspectos tan característicos de la cultura hispana; desconocerlos puede tener repercusiones en el éxito[2] de sus negocios.

 ## ¿Qué aprendiste?

1. ¿Dónde almuerzan la mayoría de las familias hispanas diariamente? ¿Qué hacen y qué comen durante el almuerzo? ¿Qué es costumbre hacer después del almuerzo?
En casa. Comentan los eventos del día. La sobremesa.
2. Por lo general, ¿se abren las tiendas los domingos y días festivos en los países hispanos? ¿Por qué?
No. Es el momento de estar en familia.
3. ¿Cuáles son algunos aspectos de la cultura hispana que deben conocer los hombres y las mujeres de negocios estadounidenses? ¿Por qué?
Los horarios y la importancia de estar en familia.

Actividad cultural

 Paso 1. Completa los espacios en el recuadro para comparar los horarios típicos de una ciudad hispana y los de tu pueblo o ciudad.

	Ciudad hispana	Tu pueblo o ciudad
1. Horario del almuerzo en las casas, a diario		
2. Horario de las tiendas, a diario		
3. Horario de los restaurantes, a diario		
4. Horario de las tiendas, los domingos y días festivos		

 Paso 2. Comparen y comenten los resultados.

 ## Contraste cultural

En grupos de *tres*, hablen acerca de las ventajas[3] y desventajas de la costumbre hispana de no abrir las tiendas durante el almuerzo, ni los domingos ni días festivos. Mencionen los beneficios que tiene en las relaciones con la familia y amigos, y cómo afecta a la salud y al bienestar[4].

¿SABES QUE...?

The **siesta**, the tradition of resting in the early afternoon after eating the main meal of the day, has its origins in the Roman custom of taking a break from work and from the heat at the **hora sexta** or sixth hour of the day counting from dawn. In some places the modern-day legacy of the Romans's **hora sexta** in Hispanic countries is the closing of schools and businesses so that families can enjoy a meal together and rest before returning to their obligations later in the afternoon.

¹Los quehaceres domésticos
²¿Qué tienen que hacer?

WILEY PLUS

Pronunciación: Practice pronunciation of the chapter's new vocabulary in *WileyPLUS*.

3. hacer la cama
DAMIÁN

4. guardar (la ropa)
Mª LUISA

5. limpiar el polvo
6. ordenar (el cuarto)
7. pasar la aspiradora

GUADALUPE CARMEN ÁNGEL

8. poner la mesa
9. quitar la mesa

DOÑA ROSA   DON CLAUDIO

10. lavar (los platos)
11. secar (los platos)

DAMIÁN CARMEN   NURIA

14. doblar la ropa
12. la lavadora 13. la secadora 15. planchar
NURIA   Mª LUISA

17. hacer las compras

16. barrer
NURIA   Mª LUISA

18. sacar la basura 19. reciclar
CARMEN   GUADALUPE

20. cortar el césped
21. regar (ie) (las plantas)

ÁNGEL   DOÑA ROSA

---

1. household chores 2. What do they have to do? **tener que** + *infinitivo* = to have to do something 3. to make the bed 4. to put away (clothes)
5. to dust 6. to straighten up (the room) 7. to vacuum 8. to set the table 9. to clear the table 10. to wash (the dishes) 11. to dry (the dishes)
12. washing machine 13. dryer 14. to fold the clothes 15. to iron 16. to sweep 17. to buy groceries, run errands 18. to take out the trash
19. to recycle 20. to mow the lawn 21. to water (the plants)

© John Wiley & Sons, Inc.

¡En acción!

6-19 ¿Qué haces antes y después?
RECYCLES the preposition + *infinitive* construction.

Completa cada acción con la que le corresponde.

1. Después de levantarme,... e.	a. ... quito la mesa.
2. Después de quitarme el suéter,... d.	b. ... paso la aspiradora y limpio el polvo.
3. Antes de llegar los invitados,... b. (o) g.	c. ... los seco.
4. Antes de preparar la cena,... f.	d. ... lo guardo en el ropero.
5. Antes de comer,... g.	e. ... hago la cama.
6. Después de comer,... a.	f. ... compro los ingredientes.
7. Después de lavar los platos,... c.	g. ... pongo la mesa.
8. Después de lavar la ropa,... h.	h. ... la doblo y, a veces, la plancho.

6-20 Los quehaceres domésticos

¿Quién los hace en casa de los Roldán? Observen los dibujos de la página 204 y contesten las preguntas.

1. ¿Dónde están Damián y Mª Luisa? ¿Qué están haciendo?

2. ¿Qué hacen Guadalupe y Carmen en la sala? ¿Y Ángel?

3. ¿Quiénes están poniendo y quitando la mesa en el comedor?

4. ¿Qué están haciendo Damián y Carmen en la cocina? ¿Quién prepara la comida?

5. ¿Qué hacen Nuria y Mª Luisa? ¿Qué electrodomésticos usan para lavar y secar la ropa?

6. ¿Quién barre la entrada de la casa? ¿Y quién hace las compras?

7. ¿Qué hace Carmen en el garaje? ¿Y qué hace Guadalupe con los periódicos?

8. ¿Qué están haciendo Ángel y doña Rosa en el jardín?

6-21 ¿Quién tiene que hacerlo?

Paso 1. Digan quién tiene que hacer en su casa los quehaceres representados en los dibujos de la página 204.

MODELO

E1: *En mi casa, yo tengo que poner la mesa y mi pareja tiene que quitarla.*

E2: *En mi casa, mis hijos tienen que poner la mesa, y...*

Paso 2. Ahora comenten acerca de la división de quehaceres en su casa. ¿Participan los hombres igual que las mujeres? ¿Y los jóvenes igual que los mayores?

6-22 ¡Qué obediente! RECYCLES tú affirmative commands.

Tu profesor/a le ordena cinco cosas a un/a estudiante de la clase. Este/a las representa por medio de mímica[1]. Si él/ ella sigue bien las órdenes, la clase dice: "**¡Así es!**". En caso contrario, dice "**¡Así no es!**" y le indica cómo se hace. Luego, tu profesor/a le da otras cinco órdenes a un/a estudiante diferente.

[1]mime

For additional vocabulary practice, see PowerPoint slides on BCS and in *WileyPLUS*.

6-19 Students may complete the activity in pairs, with answers reviewed by the instructor.

6-19 Remind your students that in Spanish a verb that follows a preposition remains in the infinitive, as it is the case in numbers 1-8. Add that the reflexive pronoun must refer to the appropriate subject **después de levantarme, yo...**, not ~~después de levantarse, yo...~~

6-19 ANOTHER STEP: Write on the board: **el dormitorio, la sala, el comedor, la cocina, el lavadero** (*laundry room*)**, el garaje, el jardín.** Students in pairs have five minutes to list as many chores as possible appropriate to each location: **el dormitorio →
hacer la cama, guardar la ropa,...**

6-20 After students answer the questions, you may want to project the PowerPoint slide of the scenes. Have various students describe the scenes to the class.

6-20 PERSONALIZED QUESTIONS: ¿Qué quehaceres les gusta hacer a Uds.? ¿Y cuáles no les gustan o detestan?

Guión para actividad 6-22
1. Pasa la aspiradora.
2. Limpia el polvo.
3. Haz la cama.
4. Pon la mesa.
5. Lava los platos.
6. Corta el césped.
7. Riega las plantas.
8. Plancha la ropa.
9. Come la pizza y bebe el refresco.
10. Sal de casa. (*The student leaves the class for a second—open the door for him/her—then invite the student back by saying* **Entra, por favor.**)

WILEY PLUS Go to *WileyPLUS* to review the grammar point below with the help of the **Animated Grammar Tutorial** and **Verb Conjugator**. For more practice, go to the **Grammar Handbook**.

¡A escuchar! Los quehaceres de la casa nunca se terminan

Paso 1. Dos amas de casa hablan de sus quehaceres domésticos. Escucha la conversación.

WILEY PLUS Go to *WileyPLUS* to complete **Paso 2** of this listening activity.

Jennifer y su madre están preparando la casa para la cena. Las dos les dicen a todos lo que tienen que hacer.

Yolanda, haz la cama y ordena tu cuarto. **No juegues** ahora, por favor.

¡Ay papi, por favor, **no mires** ahora la televisión! ¡Ve a la cocina con mamá!

Jennifer, pon la mesa, por favor, pero **no sirvas** el agua **ni cortes** el pan todavía.

Levántate, vamos a ayudar a Jennifer.

© John Wiley & Sons, Inc.

For additional practice on this grammar point, see PowerPoint slides on BCS and in *WileyPLUS*.

To introduce students to informal commands used in context, have them read the **historieta** out loud. Ask the following questions: 1. ¿Qué **tiene que hacer Yolanda?** 2. ¿Y Jennifer?

After presenting the **tú** affirmative commands, ask students to open their books to the opener scene (page 204). Call out a household chore such as **hacer la cama**. Have students identify the place where the command would be given: **En el dormitorio**. Then have them turn the expression into a command—¡**Haz la cama!**—followed by the more emphatic ¡**Hazla!**

GRAMÁTICA

¡Manos a la obra!

Giving orders and advice: Informal commands (tú affirmative and negative)

Tú affirmative commands

You already know the affirmative informal commands used to give orders or advice to people you address as **tú** (see pages 83 and 115).

- The regular **tú** affirmative command is formed by dropping the "**s**" in the **tú** form of the present tense.

Yolanda, **ordena** tu cuarto.	*Yolanda, straighten up your room.*
Jennifer, **trae** los platos de la cocina.	*Jennifer, bring the plates from the kitchen.*

- Some **tú** affirmative commands are irregular. You learned the forms for **decir, hacer, poner, salir** and **venir** (**di, haz, pon, sal,** and **ven**) (see page 123).

The **tú** affirmative commands for **ir, ser,** and **tener** are also irregular.

Ve a la cocina.	*Go to the kitchen.*
Sé buena, Yolanda.	*Be good, Yolanda.*
Ten paciencia.	*Have patience (Be patient).*

Tú negative commands

- **Tú** affirmative and negative commands differ from one another. The **tú** negative commands are formed by dropping the **-o** from the **yo** form of the present tense and adding **-es** (to **-ar** verbs) or **-as** (to **-er** and **-ir** verbs).

hablar	→	habl**o**	→	habl**es**	¡No habl**es**!
volver	→	vuelv**o**	→	vuelv**as**	¡No vuelv**as**!
salir	→	salg**o**	→	salg**as**	¡No salg**as**!

- In some verbs, the **tú** negative command form is irregular. Here are two:

    ¡No **vayas**!   *Don't go!*   ¡No **seas** desordenada!   *Don't be messy!*

- As you learned previously, object and reflexive pronouns (pages 154 and 199) are *attached to the end of* **tú** affirmative commands. In negative commands, pronouns are placed immediately *before the verb*.

    Negative: ¡No **la** mires!   ¡No **lo** cortes!   ¡No **te** levantes!
    Affirmative: ¡Mira**la**!   ¡Córta**lo**!   ¡Levánta**te**!

- Some verbs undergo a spelling change in the **tú** negative command form:

c → qu: **g → gu:**   **z → c:**

buscar No lo busques.	**llegar** No llegues tarde.	**abrazar** No me abraces.
sacar No saques la basura.	**pagar** No lo pagues.	**almorzar** No almuerces allí.
tocar No toques la guitarra.	**regar** No riegues.	

In the case of **c → qu** and **g → gu**, the spelling change preserves the sound of the consonant in the infinitive.

¡En acción!

¡Oye! ¿Quién lo dice?

Escucha los mandatos y di quién los dice: **1.** una madre a su hijo, **2.** un profesor a un estudiante o **3.** un novio celoso[1] a su novia.

6-23 Quehaceres y más quehaceres

Paso 1.   Un sábado, los padres tienen que ir a trabajar y le dejan a su hija mayor la lista de las cosas que tiene que hacer. Como ella no quiere hacerlas, le dice a su hermano menor que las haga él (mandatos de **tú**). Túrnense entre los estudiantes haciendo de hermana mayor que da órdenes y de hermano menor que las representa mediante mímica para toda la clase.

MODELO

Hermana mayor: *Saca la basura, por favor.*
Hermano menor: (Lo hace mediante mímica.)

1. **sacar** la basura	4. **regar** las plantas	7. **escribir** la lista de compras
2. **pasar** la aspiradora	5. **poner** la mesa	8. **barrer** la cocina
3. **hacer** las camas	6. **doblar** la ropa limpia	9. **lavar** y **secar** los platos

Paso 2.   Ahora, hagan lo mismo, pero en parejas. El hermano menor está ya cansado y no quiere hacer nada. En sus respuestas usa **lo, la, los, las**:

Hermana mayor: *Saca la basura, por favor.*
Hermano menor: *No quiero. Sácala tú.*

[1]jealous

To demonstrate the placement of object pronouns in commands, write **lo, no, hagas**, and **haz** on separate sheets of paper and give them to four students. First, the two students holding **haz** and **lo** position themselves and the class confirms **¡Sí!** or **¡No!**, according to their placement. The student holding **no** enters and the other students reposition or replace each other (**hagas** for **haz**). Repeat the same procedure with a reflexive verb: **te, no, acuestes, acuesta**. Be sure to add the accent to **acuéstate**.

¡Oye! Ask for a volunteer to come to the front. In the first round, as you call out the commands, the student acts them out.

Guión para ¡Oye!
1. Después de clase, **no hables** con tu ex-novio. *3*
2. **No comas** galletas antes de la cena. *1*
3. **No salgas** con otros chicos; eres mi novia. *3*
4. **No vengas** a clase sin la tarea terminada. *2*
5. **No dejes** tu ropa en el suelo. *1*
6. **No vayas** al cine con tus amigas; ven conmigo. *3*
7. **No traigas** comida a clase. *2*
8. **No llegues** tarde a clase. *2*

6-23 In *Paso 1*, seated students take turns giving the commands, and then either one or several students can play the role of the younger brother who acts out the commands in front of the class. ANSWERS for both *Paso 1* and *Paso 2*: 1. (provided) 2. Pasa… / Pásala tú. 3. Haz… / Hazlas tú. 4. Riega… / Riégalas tú. 5. Pon… / Ponla tú. 6. Dobla… / Dóblala tú. 7. Escribe… / Escríbela tú. 8. Barre… / Bárrela tú. 9. Lava y seca… / Lávalos y sécalos tú.

6-24 ¡Que llegan los tíos!

Paso 1. ¡Los tíos llaman para decir que en una hora llegan para cenar y pasar la noche! Paco y Nacho rápidamente se ponen en acción para ordenar la casa, hacer la cena y prepararse. Paco le da órdenes a Nacho y viceversa. Hagan los dos papeles. Usen los mandatos de **tú**.

6-24 Have pairs call out answers. **ANSWERS:** *Paco* 1. (provided) 2. No prepares... 3. Ve... y pon... 4. Corta... y no sirvas... 5. Sé... 6. Dúchate y aféitate *Nacho:* 2. Ve... 3. Ven... 4. Haz... y ordena... 5. No limpies 6. Vístete y péinate.

> ¡**Dime** qué ingredientes necesitamos! ¡Los tíos llegan en una hora!

> ¡**Ten** la lista y **sal** ya de la casa! No tenemos mucho tiempo.

Paco le dice a Nacho	Nacho le dice a Paco
1. *decirme* qué ingredientes necesitamos	1. *tener* la lista, y *salir* ya de la casa
2. No *preparar* la comida; la preparo yo.	2. *ir* a la panadería
3. *ir* al comedor y *poner* la mesa	3. *venir* a casa con todo lo necesario
4. *cortar* el pan y no *servir* el agua todavía[1]	4. *hacer* las camas y *ordenar* la sala
5. *ser* eficiente	5. No *limpiar* el baño; lo limpio yo.
6. *ducharse* y *afeitarse*	6. *vestirse* y *peinarse*

Paso 2. ¿Cómo está hoy tu casa o apartamento? Imagina que tus padres llegan esta noche. Tu compañero/a se ofrece para ayudarte. Dile *cinco* cosas que tiene que hacer: *Por favor, …* Luego cambien de papel.

6-25 Los consejos de Carmela Casas

6-25 Have seven students each present one of Carmela's recommendations. Then have the class indicate which ones they consider important.

Lee los consejos de Carmela, una experta ama de casa. Primero, marca **sí** o **no** para indicar si tú haces cada cosa. Luego, completa los espacios en blanco con el mandato negativo (**tú**).

Sí   No

☐ ☑ **1.** (*barrer*) No   barras   el garaje cuando hace viento.

☐ ☐ **2.** (*ver*) No   veas   la televisión cuando hay tormenta.

☐ ☐ **3.** (*limpiar*) No   limpies   los muebles de madera[2] con agua.

☐ ☐ **4.** (*regar*) No   riegues   las plantas por la noche.

☐ ☐ **5.** (*hacer*) No   hagas   las compras cuando tienes hambre.

☐ ☐ **6.** (*poner*) No   pongas   la pasta en agua fría cuando la cocinas.

☐ ☐ **7.** (*servir*) No   sirvas   el vino tinto[3] con hielo.

6-26 No te preocupes

6-26 ANSWERS:
Problemas en la universidad:
1. (Modelo) 2. ¡No te sientes...! 3. ¡No te duermas...! 4. ¡No saques...!
Problemas en el trabajo:
1. ¡No llegues...! 2. ¡No los llames...! 3. ¡No salgas...! 4. ¡No te vayas...!

Manuel no es ni un estudiante, ni un empleado modelo. Hoy su novia le da el ultimátum, diciéndole lo que no debe hacer (**tú** negativo). Hagan los dos papeles. Cambien después del n° 4.

MODELO

Novia: *Manuel, ¡no comas enchiladas en clase!*

Manuel: *No te preocupes, no voy a comer enchiladas en clase nunca más.*

Problemas en la universidad:

1. Come enchiladas en clase.
2. Se sienta en el escritorio del profesor.
3. Se duerme en las clases.
4. Saca malas notas.

Problemas en el trabajo:

1. Llega tarde.
2. Llama a sus amigos en vez de trabajar.
3. Sale de la oficina para tomar café.
4. Se va del trabajo antes de la hora.

[1]yet, [2]wood, [3]red

6-27 Nuestro amigo Humberto y su cuarto: dos perspectivas diferentes

Paso 1. Uds, que son súperordenados, son dos amigos de Humberto que van a verlo y al entrar a su cuarto observan con horror el desastre que hay allí. Díganle con tono enérgico todo lo que tiene que hacer para que él y su cuarto estén decentes. Usen los mandatos afirmativos (tú).

MODELO

E1: ¡Humberto, por favor, **riega** la planta!

E2: ¡Sí, **riégala** ya[1]. Necesita agua!

Paso 2. Un poco más tarde, Uds, que son dos amigos diferentes de Humberto muy desordenados, entran a su cuarto y lo encuentran preocupado por todo lo que tiene que hacer para poner orden y asearse[2]. Como Uds. son muy comprensivos, díganle con un tono compasivo, todo lo que **no** tiene que hacer. Usen los mandatos negativos (tú).

MODELO

E1: ¡**No riegues** la planta!

E2: ¡**No la riegues**! **Hazlo** mañana.

6-27 You may want to project the PowerPoint slide of Humberto's messy room and have students volunteer commands.

6-27 Before starting the activity, you may want to encourage the class to observe the room and Humberto with careful attention. Then ask them to tell you all the things that need to be done in order to straighten up the room and make Humberto presentable.

© John Wiley & Sons, Inc.

[1]right now, [2]to freshen up

Go to *WileyPLUS* to see the video related to this reading.

Tu mundo cultural

Los quehaceres y el servicio doméstico

Meets ACTFL Standards
1.1, interpersonal speaking;
1.2, interpretive reading;
2.1, cultural practices; and
4.2, cultural comparisons.

For an additional activity related to this cultural theme, see the PowerPoint slides on BCS and in *WileyPLUS*.

En las relaciones de pareja de tu sociedad, ¿están muy definidos los papeles? ¿O están cambiando[1]?

Courtesy Conchita Lucas

Como se observa en la fotografía, el hombre hispano moderno ayuda cada vez más en las tareas domésticas.

Getty Images, Inc.

Cada vez son más las mujeres hispanas que se incorporan a la vida profesional.

Hasta[2] la presente generación, en la sociedad hispana los papeles de los esposos estaban muy definidos. El hombre tenía las responsabilidades de su trabajo o profesión y la mujer, las de madre y ama de casa. Con la reciente incorporación de un alto porcentaje de mujeres hispanas al trabajo, la familia hispana contemporánea ha experimentado grandes cambios[3]. Ahora, cada vez más parejas se dividen las tareas domésticas, y en la generación más joven, los hombres ayudan con los hijos, cocinan, hacen las camas y limpian. También comienza a verse a más mujeres hispanas en viajes de negocios y en otras actividades profesionales. Los datos que siguen sirven para ilustrarlo:

- Actualmente, las mujeres hispanas representan el 4.9% de toda la fuerza laboral[4] de Estados Unidos y muchas trabajan ya en puestos de gerencia[5].

- En 1990, el 37.9% de las mujeres latinoamericanas trabajaba de forma remunerada y en 2012, el 53%. Esta tendencia sigue en aumento.

¿SABES QUE...?

Nicaragua, Panamá, and Chile have had female presidents. Violeta Chamorro was president of Nicaragua (1990–1997), Mireya Moscoso was president of Panamá (1999–2004), and Michelle Bachelet was president of Chile (2006–2010). In Argentina, Cristina Fernández de Kirchner was elected president in 2011, and in Costa Rica, Laura Chinchilla was elected president in 2010. In Spain, María Teresa Fernández de la Vega Sanz was vice-president (2004–2010) and also Elena Salgado Méndez (2009–2011) who also served as the minister of economy and finance.

[1]changing, [2]Until, [3]changes, [4]**la fuerza...** the work force, [5]**puestos...** managerial positions

Es cierto que en el mundo hispano se están experimentando grandes cambios hacia la igualdad, pero queda[1] mucho por hacer. A muchas mujeres hispanas todavía[2] no se les permite trabajar fuera del hogar y el cambio de papeles crea tensiones.

En la clase media y alta de los países hispanos es común el servicio doméstico y como allí no es muy costoso, cuentan con[3] mucha ayuda en casa. Las empleadas domésticas cuidan a los niños, preparan las comidas caseras, lavan la ropa y limpian la casa.

En EE. UU., algunas familias, sean hispanas o no, tienen también servicio doméstico. En algunos casos, las personas que hacen las labores de sirvientas, cocineras, niñeras o jardineros son hispanas.

Empleada doméstica limpiando el polvo.

¿SABES QUE...?

According to the International Labor Organization, between 14 and 18 million women in Latin America work as domestic employees. That represents between 7% and 9% of the work force. About 500,000 of those women migrate to look for work in neighboring countries that have a higher demand for domestic work. In some cases they have to travel from Peru to Chile; in others, from Nicaragua to Costa Rica, or from Paraguay to Argentina.

¿Qué aprendiste?

1. ¿Cuáles son los papeles tradicionales del hombre y de la mujer hispanos? ¿Qué factor está contribuyendo a su cambio? El hombre dedicado al trabajo y la mujer al hogar. La incorporación de la mujer al trabajo.

2. ¿Qué nuevas responsabilidades domésticas tienen ahora muchos hombres hispanos? Ayudan con los hijos, cocinan o limpian.

3. ¿Dónde y en qué familias es común el servicio doméstico? En las de clase media y alta de los países hispanos. En EE. UU. muchos hispanos hacen labores domésticas.

Actividad cultural

Completen la tabla para indicar las obligaciones que tienen, en general, los hombres y las mujeres en la familia tradicional y en la contemporánea.

Familia tradicional: hispana o estadounidense		Familia contemporánea: hispana o estadounidense	
Quehaceres	Persona/s responsable/s	Quehaceres	Persona/s responsable/s

Contraste cultural

En grupos de *tres*, hablen de los siguientes aspectos de sus familias. Después, establezcan dos o tres contrastes entre sus familias y una familia hispana típica.

- Mujeres de sus familias que son profesionales o empleadas. Incluyan más de una generación.

- Quehaceres domésticos que hacen los hombres de sus familias.

- Responsabilidades con respecto a los hijos en sus familias.

[1]remains, [2]still, [3]**cuentan...** count on

Tu mundo en vivo

¡Videos en acción!

6.1 Mi vida aburrida

1. **Antes de ver el video**
   ¿Es tu vida aburrida? ¿Por qué?

WILEY PLUS Go to *WileyPLUS* to complete the **Mientras ves el video** activity.

2. **Después de ver el video**
   ¿Qué se observa en la foto?

© John Wiley & Sons, Inc.

6.2 Los quehaceres

1. **Antes de ver el video**
   ¿Qué quehaceres haces en tu casa?

WILEY PLUS Go to *WileyPLUS* to complete the **Mientras ves el video** activity.

2. **Después de ver el video**
   En tu opinión, ¿hacen Aaron y Alexa suficientes quehaceres? Explica.

¡Diálogos en acción!

6.1 En busca de compañera de piso[1]

María busca piso en Madrid y llama para informarse sobre uno que se anuncia en Craigslist.

Paso 1. Primero, mira las **Expresiones útiles** de la página A-6. Luego, escucha el diálogo dos veces y contesta las preguntas de tu profesor/a.

Paso 2. Mira la transcripción del diálogo (pág. A-18) y represéntalo con tu compañero/a. Túrnense. Ahora vete a la página A-6 para completar los **Pasos 3** y **4.**

6.2 El piso de Paula

María llega al piso de Paula para ver el cuarto que se alquila y decidir si lo quiere.

WILEY PLUS Go to *WileyPLUS* to listen to and practice this dialogue.

[1]apartment

¡Lectura en acción!

La casa de vacaciones de tus sueños

En este anuncio de un periódico chileno se hace publicidad de casas de vacaciones construidas en una zona muy atractiva de la costa, a sólo dos horas de Santiago de Chile.

Paso 1. Antes de leer el texto, escribe una lista de los aspectos que piensas que se van a mencionar en el anuncio.

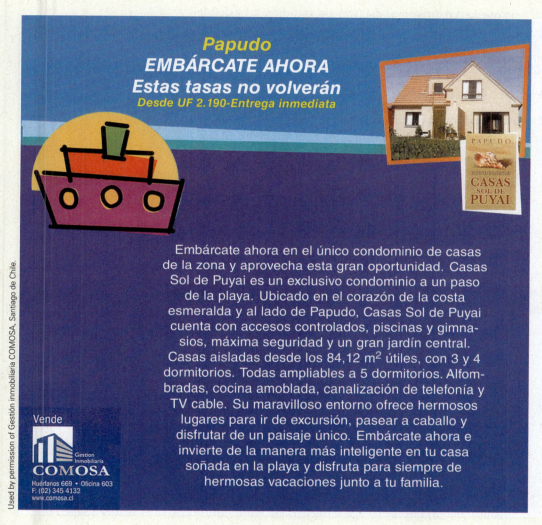

Used by permission of Gestión inmobiliaria COMOSA, Santiago de Chile.

Paso 2. Ahora, lee el anuncio y escribe una lista de las características que se mencionan, incluyendo información sobre las casas y la comunidad donde están situadas.

Paso 3. Responde a las siguientes preguntas para ver si entendiste la información más importante del anuncio.

1. Compara tus dos listas. ¿Hay algo que te sorprende[1] ver en la publicidad de estas casas?

2. ¿Cuántos dormitorios tienen las casas?

3. ¿A quiénes se dirige[2] este anuncio, a personas solteras, jubiladas, o a familias?

4. ¿Te gustaría comprar una casa en *Casas Sol de Puyai*? ¿Por qué?

[1]surprises, [2]se... is targeted, directed

Meets ACTFL Standard 1.3, presentational writing.

You may want to assign a minimum number of words or sentences as appropriate for the **¡A escribir!** task. Students can use the word count tool available in their word processing application to check the length of their work before and after the revising step of the writing process.

¡A conversar!

Mi vida diaria

En *parejas*, hablen del lugar donde viven y de su rutina diaria. Túrnense. Incluyan lo siguiente:

- el lugar donde Uds. viven: dónde está y cómo es
- las personas con quiénes viven
- su rutina en casa desde que se despiertan
- lo que hacen durante el día (trabajo, estudios, ...) y dónde

¡A escribir!

Una familia muy querida

Describe a tu familia o a una familia que conoces bien. Incluye:

- el número de personas que hay
- cómo son las personas
- su edad[1]
- su profesión u ocupación
- dónde viven
- una descripción detallada de su casa o apartamento
- lo que hacen normalmente—su rutina y pasatiempos favoritos

Writing Strategy

Developing a Good Topic Sentence

After deciding what family you are going to write about and brainstorming on the content, write a topic sentence that will serve as an introduction to the family. Make it of interest to your readers, perhaps highlighting something that sets the family apart.

Steps:

1. *Prewriting:* Jot down your initial ideas in words and phrases.
2. *Writing:* After your topic sentence (see strategy), write about the information listed with as much detail as possible.
3. *Revising:* Read your composition carefully. Have you included all of the information requested and checked for correct spelling and punctuation? **¡Ojo!** Have you (a) expressed age correctly, (b) used **ser** and **estar** correctly, (c) used reflexive verbs properly when talking about the family's routine, and (d) checked for agreement between articles and nouns, and nouns and adjectives?
4. *Peer correction:* Exchange papers, circle errors or areas where there are questions, talk about them, and then make corrections on your own paper.

[1]age

¡A investigar!

Las casas del mundo hispano

Ya saben que muchas casas del mundo hispano y de partes de EE. UU. son de estilo tradicional español. Tienen rasgos comunes, como un jardín interior, techos de teja, y balcones y ventanas exteriores con rejas (miren la página 194). Estos rasgos son el resultado de la influencia de los romanos y árabes en España. ¿Tienen esas características todas las casas del mundo hispano? ¿Hay otros estilos?

Paso 1.   Trabajen en grupos de *tres*. Su profesor/a les va a asignar uno de estos países: España, México, Puerto Rico, Colombia, Bolivia o Chile. Usando uno de los sitios de Internet donde se comparten fotos, busquen tres fotos de casas o apartamentos de su país. Apunten los URL de las fotos y cualquier otra información que les pida su profesor/a.

Paso 2.   Cada miembro del grupo va a preparar una descripción de una de las casas. Incluyan:

- Dónde están las casas o apartamentos (país, ciudad o pueblo)
- Cómo son las casas
- Si tienen los elementos del estilo tradicional español y cuáles son
- Si tienen otros elementos y cuáles son

Después, todos los estudiantes del grupo van a colaborar para mejorar las descripciones y crear un PowerPoint con las fotos. Túrnense para hablar. Otra opción es crear una presentación que tenga un comentario grabado[1]. Pueden poner las presentaciones grabadas en el blog o wiki de la clase.

Paso 3.   Después de ver las presentaciones de todos los grupos, comparen las casas o apartamentos de un país con los de otros países hispanos y con los de EE. UU.

Research Strategy

Including Photo and Video Sources

For those interested in learning about Hispanic culture, the Internet offers much more than text-based sources of information. Photos and videos, either amateur or professional, can provide a fascinating perspective on the people and places of the Spanish-speaking world. Online photo and video sharing sites such as Flickr and YouTube are excellent resources for language students, and some photographers allow the use of their photos in class presentations and other projects under certain conditions.

Trivia

A ver cuánto sabes.

1. ¿Sabes qué dos países hispanohablantes no están en América?

2. ¿Sabes qué cinco países hispanos no tienen costa en el océano Atlántico?

3. ¿Puedes decir el nombre un país hispano que ocupa la mitad de una isla?

1. España y Guinea Ecuatorial   2. Guatemala, El Salvador, Ecuador, Perú, Chile
3. República Dominicana

Meets ACTFL Standards 1.3, presentational speaking; 2.2, cultural products; and 4.2, cultural comparisons.

If your access to technology is limited, have the students create posters or transparencies to use as visual aids as they speak.

You may assign the appropriate **Pasos** of **¡A investigar!** for pairs or small groups to complete outside of class.

If you don't know the answers, take a look at the front inside cover of the textbook. Try to respond in complete sentences.

[1]recorded

Vocabulario: Capítulo 6

Escena 1

La casa y sus cuartos
The house and its rooms

el (cuarto de) baño *bathroom*
la cocina *kitchen*
el comedor *dining room*
el dormitorio *bedroom*
la sala *living room*
la chimenea *fireplace, chimney*
la escalera *stairs*
el garaje *garage*
el jardín *garden*
el primer piso *first floor*
el segundo piso *second floor*
el sótano *basement*
el suelo, el piso *floor*
el techo *roof, ceiling*

Los muebles y otras cosas
Furniture and other things

la alfombra *rug, carpet*
la bañera *bathtub*
la cama *bed*
la cómoda *dresser*
las cortinas *curtains*
el cubo de la basura *garbage can*
la ducha *shower*
el espejo *mirror*
el estante *bookcase, shelf*
la estufa *stove*
el fregadero *kitchen sink*
el inodoro *toilet*
la lámpara *lamp*
el lavabo *sink (bathroom)*
el lavaplatos *dishwasher*
la luz *light, electricity*
el microondas *microwave*
el refrigerador *refrigerator*
el ropero *closet*
el sillón *easy chair*
el sofá *sofa*

Palabras afirmativas y negativas
Affirmative and negative words

algo *something*
alguien *someone*
nada *nothing*
nadie *no one, not anyone, nobody*

Preposiciones   *Prepositions*

acerca de *about (a topic)*
al + *infinitivo* *upon (doing something)*
antes de *before*
debajo de *beneath, below, under*
dentro de *within, inside (of)*
después de *after*
durante *during*
encima de *on top of, above*
en vez de *in place of, instead of*
fuera de *outside (of)*
para *for*
para + *infinitivo* *in order to (do something)*
por *by, through, around, alongside*
sobre *on, above; about (a topic)*

Verbos y expresiones verbales
Verbs and verbal expressions

alquilar *to rent*
bajar *to go down*
contestar *to answer*
sonar (ue) *to ring (phone), go off (alarm clock)*
subir *to go up*
se alquila *for rent*

Escena 2

Los artículos de uso personal
Personal items

el cepillo de dientes *toothbrush*
el champú *shampoo*
el despertador *alarm clock*
el jabón *soap*
la pasta de dientes *toothpaste*
el peine *comb*
el secador *hairdryer*
la toalla *towel*

La vida diaria   *Daily life*

acostarse (ue) *to go to bed*
afeitarse *to shave*
bañarse *to take a bath*
cepillarse (los dientes) *to brush (one's teeth)*
despedirse (i) (de) *to say good-bye (to)*
despertarse (ie) *to wake up*
divertirse (ie) *to have fun/ a good time*
dormirse (ue) *to fall asleep*
ducharse *to take a shower*
irse *to go away*
lavarse (el pelo) *to wash (one's hair)*

levantarse *to get up*
maquillarse *to put on makeup*
peinarse *to comb one's hair*
ponerse (los zapatos, etc.) *to put on (one's shoes, etc.)*
quitarse (la ropa, etc.) *to take off (one's clothes, etc.)*
reírse (i) *to laugh*
secarse *to dry oneself*
sentarse (ie) *to sit down*
sentirse (ie) mal/ bien *to feel bad, sick/ well*
tener sueño *to be sleepy*
vestirse (i) *to get dressed*

Escena 3

Los quehaceres domésticos
Household chores

barrer *to sweep*
cortar el césped *to mow the lawn*
doblar la ropa *to fold the clothes*
guardar (la ropa) *to put away (clothes)*
hacer la cama *to make the bed*
hacer las compras *to buy groceries*
lavar (los platos) *to wash (the dishes)*
limpiar el polvo *to dust*
ordenar (el cuarto) *to straighten up (the room)*
pasar la aspiradora *to vacuum*
planchar *to iron*
poner la mesa *to set the table*
quitar la mesa *to clear the table*
reciclar *to recycle*
regar (ie) (las plantas) *to water (the plants)*
sacar la basura *to take out the trash*
secar (los platos) *to dry (the dishes)*
tener que + *infinitivo* *to have to do something*

Los electrodomésticos   *Appliances*

la lavadora *washer*
la secadora *dryer*

Capítulo 7

La ciudad

WILEY **PLUS**

Additional activities and **Autopruebas** for each **Escena** available online.

Robert Fried/Alamy

Escena 1
En la ciudad

GRAMÁTICA:
- Formal commands (*Ud.* and *Uds.*)
- The preterit tense of regular *–ar* verbs

CULTURA:
La plaza: el corazón de la ciudad

Escena 2
La vida urbana

GRAMÁTICA:
- The preterit tense of regular *-er* and *-ir* verbs
- The preterit tense of four irregular verbs: *dar*, *ser*, *ir*, and *hacer*

CULTURA:
Un viaje a Machu Picchu

Escena 3
En la carretera

GRAMÁTICA:
- To whom? For whom? Indirect object pronouns

CULTURA:
El transporte público

TU MUNDO EN VIVO

¡Videos en acción! La plaza: el centro de la ciudad hispana; El transporte público: el metro

¡Diálogos en acción! Formally Soliciting and Providing Advice and Directions; Inquiring About and Narrating Past Activities

¡Lectura en acción! Identifying the Target Audience

¡A conversar! Using Strategic Pauses

¡A escribir! Using Sequencing Words

¡A investigar! Exploring Cities Online

LEARNING OBJECTIVES

By the end of the chapter you will be able to:
- Use commands in formal situations.
- Talk about places and things in the city.
- Talk about actions in the past.
- Carry out transactions at the post office and the bank.
- Talk about to whom or for whom something is done.
- Describe Machu Picchu, a world heritage site.
- Indicate how to use the subway in Mexico City.

En la ciudad

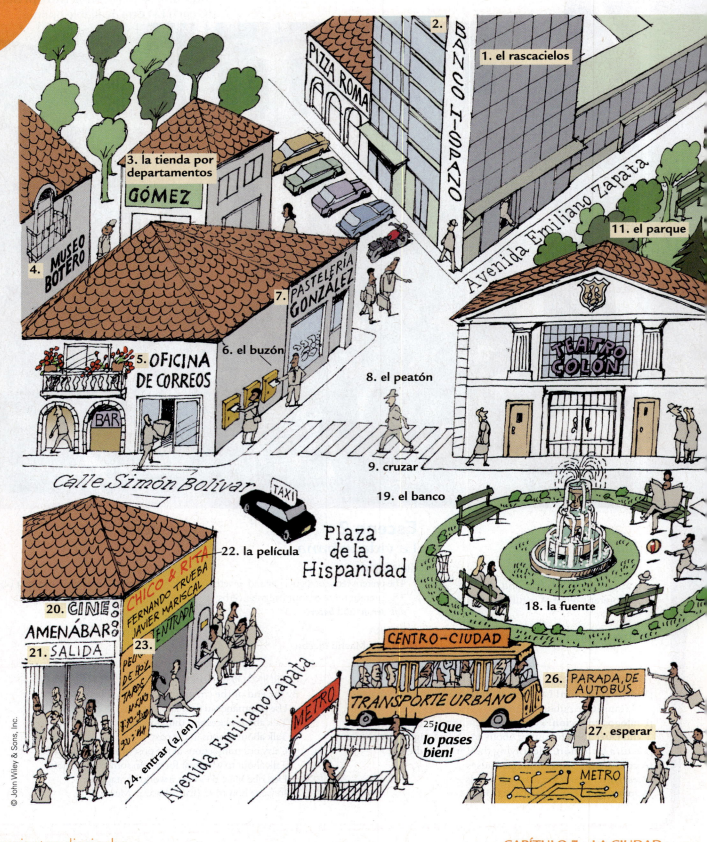

1. el rascacielos
2. (Banco Hispano)
3. la tienda por departamentos — GÓMEZ
4. MUSEO BOTERO
5. OFICINA DE CORREOS
6. el buzón
7. PASTELERÍA GONZÁLEZ
8. el peatón
9. cruzar
11. el parque
18. la fuente
19. el banco
20. CINE AMENÁBAR
21. SALIDA
22. la película
23.
24. entrar (a/en)
25. ¡Que lo pases bien!
26. PARADA DE AUTOBÚS
27. esperar

PIZZA ROMA

Avenida Emiliano Zapata

TEATRO COLÓN

Calle Simón Bolívar

TAXI

Plaza de la Hispanidad

CHICO & RITA — FERNANDO TRUEBA — JAVIER MARISCAL — ENTRADA

CENTRO-CIUDAD — TRANSPORTE URBANO

METRO

BAR

© John Wiley & Sons, Inc.

1. skyscraper
2. bank
3. department store
4. museum
5. post office
6. mailbox
7. pastry shop
8. pedestrian
9. to cross
10. church
11. park
12. train station
13. downtown
14. bridge
15. motorcycle
16. traffic light
17. (no) parking
18. fountain
19. bench
20. movie theater
21. exit
22. film
23. entrance
24. to enter
25. Have a good time!
    pasarlo bien to have a good time
26. bus stop
27. to wait (for)
28. newsstand
29. magazine
30. newspaper
31. news
32. a block away
33. corner
34. hair salon
35. jewelry store
36. shoe store
37. stores

*La Mina de Oro *The Gold Mine*

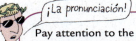 You may use the PowerPoint slides of all scenes to present and practice the vocabulary.

Calle del Río

AEROPUERTO
ESTACIÓN DE TREN
CIUDAD ANTIGUA
12.
13. CENTRO

14. el puente

15. la motocicleta

16. el semáforo

10.
IGLESIA DE SANTA ANA

Calle del Puente

17. (no) estacionar

CAFÉ COLON

34.
PELUQUERÍA ELENA

35.
JOYERÍA LA MINA DE ORO*

36.
ZAPATERÍA TERESA

DISCOTECA ¡CON BRÍO!

33. la esquina

28. el quiosco

Calle José Martí

37. las tiendas

FARMACIA A UNA CUADRA

32.

29. la revista
30. el periódico
31. las noticias

¡La pronunciación!

Pay attention to the correct pronunciation of Spanish **words with a written accent** (see P-5).

estación   joyería
película   semáforo

For additional vocabulary practice, see PowerPoint slides on BCS and in *WileyPLUS*.

7-1 Present alternatives to vocabulary items at your discretion: **autobús/camión** (Mexico)/**guagua** (Puerto Rico, Cuba)/**bus** (Colombia).

Remember that verbs preceded by prepositions must be in the infinitive form. **Voy al banco para depositar el dinero.**

7-2 You may want to project the PowerPoint slide of the opener scene and have the class describe it.

7-2 PERSONALIZED QUESTIONS: ¿Qué ciudades les gusta visitar a Uds.? ¿Qué medios de transporte usan cuando están en ciudades grandes? ¿Y qué les gusta hacer allí?

Point out to your students the expression for # 4: **¡Que lo pases bien!** Expressions like these will be learned in Ch. 10.

7-2 ANOTHER STEP: Students walk around the classroom inviting classmates to accompany them to various places in the city (recycles **conmigo, contigo,** and **tener que**). E1: **Voy al parque esta tarde. ¿Quieres ir conmigo?**
E2: **Sí, ¡gracias! Voy contigo.** (o) **Lo siento, pero no puedo ir contigo. Tengo que limpiar mi casa.**

¡En acción!

7-1 ¿Adónde van?

Uds. tienen un profesor nuevo que no conoce bien la ciudad donde está su *college* o universidad. Por eso, él quiere saber adónde van Uds. para hacer lo siguiente.

MODELO
depositar dinero
Profesor: *¿Adónde van Uds. para depositar dinero?*
E1: *Yo voy al Banco Central.*
E2: *Y yo, al Banco...*

1. cortarse el pelo
2. ver películas
3. ver obras de teatro
4. comprar ropa o zapatos
5. comprar revistas y periódicos
6. comprar pasteles
7. comer bien
8. pasarlo bien o descansar

¿SABES QUE...?

As is the custom in Spanish-speaking countries, the streets in the opener city scene are named after famous historical and literary figures. **Simón Bolívar** (1783–1830) was a Venezuelan revolutionary leader who fought for the independence of Hispanic America from Spain. **José Martí** (1853–1895) was a Cuban poet, writer, and lawyer who fought and died for Cuba's independence from Spain. **Emiliano Zapata** (around 1879–1919) was a Mexican revolutionary who fought for the rights of the farmers.

7-2 En la ciudad

¿Qué hay en el centro y qué pasa allí? Observen la escena de las páginas 218–219 y contesten las preguntas.

1. ¿Cómo se llaman los edificios muy altos de la Avenida Emiliano Zapata? ¿Y el banco que está en uno de ellos?
2. ¿Quién cruza la avenida en dirección a la oficina de correos? ¿Cuántos buzones hay allí?
3. ¿Qué película se puede ver en el Cine Amenábar? ¿Llega tarde o temprano la pareja que se ve a la entrada? ¿Por dónde salen las personas del cine?
4. ¿Dónde espera la mujer el autobús? ¿Qué le dice a su amigo el señor que está cerca de la entrada del metro?
5. ¿Qué se vende en el quiosco?
6. ¿Qué conecta el centro de la ciudad con la estación de tren? ¿Qué se ve y qué pasa por allí?
7. ¿Se puede estacionar en la esquina de la calle del Río y la calle del Puente?
8. ¿Qué tiendas hay en la calle José Martí? ¿A qué distancia está la farmacia?
9. ¿Qué centros culturales y religiosos hay en la ciudad?

7-3 ¿Con qué frecuencia lo haces?

RECYCLES expressions of frequency with the present tense.

Paso 1. Marca con qué frecuencia haces lo siguiente.

¿Con qué frecuencia lo haces?	Con (mucha) frecuencia	A veces	Nunca o casi nunca
1. *ir* de compras a tiendas por departamentos			
2. *ir* a museos de arte o de ciencias			
3. *ir* al cine			
4. *ir* a la oficina de correos			
5. *esperar* en la parada del autobús			
5. *comprar* revistas			
6. *leer* el periódico			
7. *ir* a un servicio religioso (a la iglesia, a la mezquita, al templo o a la sinagoga)			

Paso 2. Ahora, compara tus respuestas con las de tu compañero/a.

MODELO

E1: *Yo voy de compras a tiendas por departamentos con mucha frecuencia. ¿Y tú?*

E2: *Yo nunca voy. (o) No voy nunca. Prefiero las tiendas pequeñas.*

¡A escuchar! Una mañana en el centro

Paso 1. María y su amiga Elvira pasan juntas una mañana en el centro. Escucha la conversación observando la escena de la ciudad (págs. 218–219).

PLUS Go to *WileyPLUS* to complete **Paso 2** of this listening activity.

7-3 Remind students that when **nunca** follows the verb, **no** is still needed in front of the verb in order to make the sentence negative: **Nunca voy** but **No voy nunca.**

The scripts and recordings for the **¡A escuchar!** sections are included on the Book Companion Site (BCS) for instructors and in *WileyPLUS*.

Fabio y sus amigos llegan a casa de Jennifer. En la mesa, el padre de Jennifer les da instrucciones.

To introduce students to formal commands used in context, have them take parts and read the **historieta** out loud. To check their comprehension and call their attention to the commands, ask the following questions: **1. Según las instrucciones del chiste del padre de Jennifer, ¿qué no deben hacer? 2. En realidad, ¿qué pueden hacer?**

[1]joke

© John Wiley & Sons, Inc.

WILEY PLUS

Go to *WileyPLUS* to review this grammar point with the help of the **Animated Grammar Tutorial** and **Verb Conjugator**. For more practice, go to the **Grammar Handbook**.

For additional practice on this grammar point, see PowerPoint slides on BCS and in *WileyPLUS*.

Point out that formal commands, like **Ud./Uds.** as a form of address, are used with persons one is less familiar with (e.g., on a last-name basis) and to show respect and courtesy.

To illustrate the placement of object pronouns in commands, write the following words on sheets of paper, one word per sheet: **haga, lo, no, acueste, se.** Have two students come to the front and give them **lo** and **haga.** Then have them place themselves in the correct order for the affirmative **Ud.** command (you can add the accent). Give the **no** to a third student and have the students reposition themselves for the negative **Ud.** command, minus accent. Follow the same procedure for **se** and **acueste.**

GRAMÁTICA

¡Manos a la obra!

Giving orders and instructions: Formal commands (*Ud.* and *Uds.*)

You have already reviewed how to give *informal,* or **tú,** commands (**¡Saca la basura!**). *Formal* commands are the ones you give to people with whom you have a more formal relationship—people you would address as **usted.** Plural commands in the Uds. form are used to address multiple people both formally and informally in Latin America. In Spain, "Uds" is used only as a formal plural pronoun, since "vosotros" is informal plural. (Go to **Instrucciones para la clase** commands on page i at the beginning of the book.).

The **Ud./Uds.** commands are formed by dropping the **-o** from the **yo** form of the present tense and adding:

-e (Ud.) or -en (Uds.) to -ar verbs and
-a (Ud.) or -an (Uds.) to -er and -ir verbs.

infinitive	yo form	Ud.	Uds.
habl**ar**	habl**ø**	habl**e**	habl**en**
jug**ar**	jueg**ø**	juegu**e**	juegu**en**
com**er**	com**ø**	com**a**	com**an**
volv**er**	vuelv**ø**	vuelv**a**	vuelv**an**
escrib**ir**	escrib**ø**	escrib**a**	escrib**an**
ped**ir**	pid**ø**	pid**a**	pid**an**

Unlike **tú** commands, the formal commands are the same in both the affirmative and negative forms.

Let's look at examples based on the dinner conversation at Jennifer's parents house.
Por favor, **prueben** este plato típico de Puerto Rico, pero no lo **coman** si no les gusta.

- Some **Ud.** and **Uds.** commands undergo the same spelling changes as the negative **tú** commands (see page 208).
  Busque las tazas.   No **lleguen** tarde.   No **almuercen** allí.

- Some verbs have irregular **Ud./Uds.** command forms. Here are three of them.

ir → **vaya/n**	**¡Vaya** con Dios! *God be with you!*
ser → **sea/n**	No **sean** tímidos. *Don't be shy.*
estar → **esté/n**	**Estén** listos a las cinco. *Be ready at 5:00.*

Formal commands + *pronouns*

The placement of object and reflexive pronouns is the same as for the **tú** commands.

- In affirmative commands, object and reflexive pronouns are *attached* to the command form.

  ¡Láven**se** las manos!*   *Wash your hands!*
  Prepáre**lo**.   *Prepare it.*

- In negative commands, the pronoun is placed immediately *before* the verb.

  No **se** levanten sin permiso.   *Don't get up without permission.*
  No **los** sirva.   *Don't serve them.*

Nosotros commands

Similar to **Ud.** and **Uds.** commands, **nosotros/as** commands are made by changing the –**amos** ending of –**ar** verbs to –**emos**, and the –**emos** ending of –**er** and –**ir** verbs to –**amos**.

  Comamos en el patio.   *Let's eat on the deck.*

*There is a written accent when the stress falls on the third-to-last syllable.

¡En acción!

 ¡Oye! La rutina de una mañana

Escucha las instrucciones de tu profesor/a y representa cada acción con mímica.

7-4 Son órdenes del alcalde[1]

Paso 1. El alcalde de Villabonita tiene órdenes para sus ciudadanos. Léanlas en voz alta e indiquen con la inicial correspondiente el propósito de cada orden: **L** Limpieza; **T** Tráfico; **E** Embellecimiento[2] de la ciudad.

<u>L</u> **1.** No **boten**[3] latas de aluminio, botellas y papeles en las calles o en las aceras. **Deposítenlos** en los cubos de basura o de reciclaje.

<u>T</u> **2.** Los semáforos también son para los peatones. **Miren** antes de cruzar la calle.

<u>E</u> **3.** **Planten** flores delante de su edificio. **Riéguenlas**, pero **háganlo** antes de las 8:00 de la mañana.

<u>T</u> **4.** **Estén** atentos a las señales de tráfico y **respétenlas** cuando manejen.

<u>L</u> **5.** Si sus perros hacen sus necesidades en la calle, por favor, **pónganlas** inmediatamente en una bolsita de plástico.

<u>E</u> **6.** Si tienen césped enfrente de su casa, **córtenlo** todas las semanas.

Paso 2. Ahora, Uds. son el alcalde y su asistente. Anoten *seis* órdenes para sus ciudadanos, *dos* en cada categoría. Usen los verbos de la lista u otros. Luego, túrnense con las otras parejas para dar órdenes a sus ciudadanos (la clase).

Limpieza	Tráfico	Embellecimiento
barrer, (no) poner, ...	manejar, (no) estacionar, ...	pintar, decorar, ...
Barran ...		

Es importante usar el cinturón de seguridad, como dice este anuncio en un peaje[4] en Perú. Y tú, ¿usas siempre el cinturón de seguridad?

Courtesy Elena Herrero

[1]mayor, [2]beautification, [3]to throw, [4]toll

¡Oye! Write on the board: **a pie** *by foot.*
Before beginning, rehearse commands that include **a pie** through a demonstration, having students walk in their places when they hear **Vayan a la oficina a pie; Regresen a casa a pie.**

Guión para ¡Oye!
1. Levántense.
2. Lávense la cara.
(continue)

Palabras útiles
la acera *sidewalk*
con cuidado *with care*
los escaparates *storefront windows*
los letreros *signs*

3. Vístanse.
4. Desayunen.
5. Péinense.
6. Cepíllense los dientes.
7. Pónganse la chaqueta.
8. Vayan a la oficina a pie.
9. Saluden a sus compañeros/as de trabajo.
10. Siéntense y usen la computadora.
11. Hagan llamadas telefónicas.
12. Salgan de la oficina.
13. Regresen a casa a pie.
14. Siéntense a la mesa.
15. Almuercen.
16. Es la hora de la siesta. Duérmanse.

7-4 Students may complete the activity individually or in pairs. To review answers, ask six readers to each present one of the mayor's recommendations and the class identifies the category (**L, T,** or **E**). After students complete *Paso 2,* write the three categories on the board: **Limpieza / Tráfico / Embellecimiento de la ciudad.** Students call out the commands related to each.

7-5 La tradición de *"Trick or treat"*

7-5 *Option:* Students write the commands. Write the two categories on the board and as students provide answers for each, jot them down.

7-5 *Paso 2* ANSWERS:
Adultos: 1. (provided) Tengan... 3. Acompañen...
5. Dejen...
6. Compren...
8. Inspeccionen...
Niños: 2. No vayan...
4. Caminen... crucen...
7. No se pongan...

7-6 Have six students read each of the ads aloud. The other students volunteer the recommendations that apply to each.

Paso 1. Pronto es *Halloween*. Eres el jefe de policía y decides mandar información en español para los adultos y niños de tu distrito que no entienden inglés. Para organizarte, primero indica a cuál de los dos grupos se dirige cada consejo: **A** adultos, **N** niños.

Recomendaciones para el día de *Halloween*

_A_ **1.** Deben **tener** suficientes dulces[1] en casa para todos los niños.

_N_ **2.** *No* deben **ir** a casas que no conocen.

_A_ **3.** Deben **acompañar** a sus hijos menores.

_N_ **4.** Deben **caminar** en grupos y **cruzar** las calles por los semáforos.

_A_ **5.** Deben **dejar** sus perros y gatos dentro de casa.

_A_ **6.** Deben **comprar** disfraces[2] reflectantes para sus hijos.

_N_ **7.** *No* deben **ponerse** máscaras; es mejor maquillarse.

_A_ **8.** Deben **inspeccionar** los dulces que reciben sus hijos.

Paso 2. Ahora, dales consejos a los adultos y a los niños de tu ciudad. Usa los mandatos de **Uds.**: (para los adultos) *Tengan suficientes dulces...*

7-6 Los consejos de la famosa periodista Celia Ciudad

Paso 1. Cada semana, Celia escribe una columna con consejos para quienes visitan su ciudad, pero hoy está enferma, y tienen que hacerlo Uds. Lean **(a)** lo que ella comenzó a escribir antes de enfermarse, y **(b)** los anuncios de periódico que tiene para preparar su columna semanal. Luego, según la información que tienen, escriban *seis* consejos con varios mandatos de **Ud.** en cada uno.

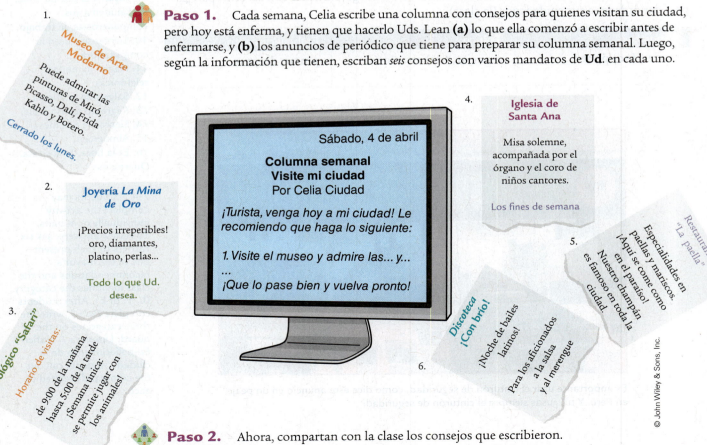

1. **Museo de Arte Moderno**
Puede admirar las pinturas de Miró, Picasso, Dalí, Frida Kahlo y Botero.
Cerrado los lunes.

2. **Joyería *La Mina de Oro***
¡Precios irrepetibles! oro, diamantes, platino, perlas...
Todo lo que Ud. desea.

3. **Zoológico «Safari»**
Horario de visitas: de 9:00 de la mañana hasta 5:00 de la tarde.
¡Semana única: se permite jugar con los animales!

Sábado, 4 de abril
Columna semanal
Visite mi ciudad
Por Celia Ciudad

¡Turista, venga hoy a mi ciudad! Le recomiendo que haga lo siguiente:

1. Visite el museo y admire las... y...
...
¡Que lo pase bien y vuelva pronto!

4. **Iglesia de Santa Ana**
Misa solemne, acompañada por el órgano y el coro de niños cantores.
Los fines de semana

5. **Restaurante *"La paella"***
Especialidades en paellas y mariscos. ¡Aquí se come como en el paraíso! Nuestro champán es famoso en toda la ciudad.

6. **Discoteca ¡Con brío!**
¡Noche de bailes latinos!
Para los aficionados a la salsa y al merengue

Paso 2. Ahora, compartan con la clase los consejos que escribieron.

[1]candy, [2]costumes

PARA DAR INSTRUCCIONES

doblar	*to turn*
...a la derecha	*to the right, on the right*
...a la izquierda	*to the left, on the left*
seguir (i)	*to continue, follow*
... recto/ derecho	*straight ahead*
... una cuadra/ media cuadra	*one block/ half a block*
pasar por	*to pass, go by*
hasta llegar a...	*until you arrive at...*

7-6 ANOTHER STEP: Students write *three* suggestions (**Ud.** commands) directed to a person visiting their university town or city, then share them with the class. A volunteer writes the information on the board.

7-7 ¿Cómo se va?

7-7 For *Paso 1,* allow students a minute or two to complete the directions individually, prior to beginning their work in pairs. You may want to project the PowerPoint slide of the city scene, and as students call out the directions, trace the route to the final destination: **la pastelería González.**

To check answers for *Paso 2,* have students in pairs call out the directions from one place to another. Use the PowerPoint slide of the city scene to trace the route.

Paso 1.   Un turista está a la entrada de la zapatería Teresa (págs. 218–219) y te pregunta cómo se va a cierto lugar de la ciudad. Primero, completa las instrucciones que le das con los mandatos de **Ud.** Luego, léele las instrucciones a tu compañero/a y él/ella sigue la ruta por la Escena 1.

(*Caminar*) __Camine__ **media cuadra** por la calle José Martí **hasta llegar a** la esquina. (*Doblar*) __Doble__ **a la derecha** y (*seguir*) __siga__ **derecho hasta llegar a** la calle del Puente. (*Cruzar*) __Cruce__ la calle y (*doblar*) __doble__ **a la izquierda**. (*Pasar*) __Pase__ por la iglesia y el teatro. (*Cruzar*) __Cruce__ la Avenida Emiliano Zapata. Al ver los buzones, (*doblar*) __doble__ **a la derecha**. Allí está, al lado de la oficina de correos y cerca del Banco Hispano.

¿Sabes adónde llega el turista?

Paso 2.   Ahora una turista quiere saber cómo se llega a ciertos lugares de la ciudad (págs. 218–219) y un peatón muy amable le da instrucciones (mandatos de **Ud.**). Hagan los papeles de turista y peatón y túrnense.

El peatón y la turista están en...	→	La turista quiere ir a...
1. la oficina de correos	→	el Café Colón
2. la Joyería La Mina de Oro	→	el puente
3. el Cine Amenábar	→	el parque
4. la estación de tren	→	la Plaza de la Hispanidad

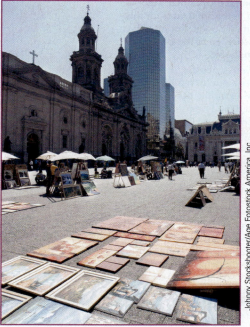

Johnny Stockshooter/Age Fotostock America, Inc.

Vista parcial de la Plaza de Armas, en el centro histórico de Santiago de Chile. La Catedral Metropolitana del siglo dieciocho y los otros edificios antiguos de la plaza contrastan con los modernos rascacielos que se ven a lo lejos.

Durante la cena, los tres amigos conversan con los padres y la hija de Jennifer.

¿Cómo **llegaron** hasta aquí?

Cruzamos por la plaza y **doblamos** a la izquierda en la calle del Puente. Fabio **manejó**.

… pero primero, **buscamos** la dirección en Google.

… y la **encontramos** sin ningún problema.

Mamá, ¿saben tus amigos dónde **pasamos** el fin de semana pasado?

Dinos, Yolanda, ¿dónde lo **pasaron**?

El sábado, mamá y yo **visitamos** el Museo de Bellas Artes. ¡Y **me gustó** mucho Botero!

¡Y el domingo, **manejamos** hasta el zoo!

© John Wiley & Sons, Inc.

¡Manos a la obra!

GRAMÁTICA

Talking about what happened: The preterit tense of regular -ar verbs

To talk about actions completed in the past, Spanish uses the *preterit* (simple past) tense, as shown in these examples based on Yolanda's weekend activities:

¿Dónde **pasaste** el fin de semana?	Where **did you spend** the weekend?
Visité el Museo de Bellas Artes.	I **visited** the Fine Arts Museum.
Mi madre **manejó** al zoo.	My mother **drove** to the zoo.

The preterit tense of regular **-ar** verbs is formed by dropping the infinitive ending and adding the endings below.

caminar *to walk*		
(yo)	**-é**	camin**é**
(tú)	**-aste**	camin**aste**
(Ud., él, ella)	**-ó**	camin**ó**
(nosotros/as)	**-amos**	camin**amos**
(vosotros/as)	**-asteis**	camin**asteis**
(Uds., ellos, ellas)	**-aron**	camin**aron**

—¿**Caminaste** por el museo el sábado?   —Sí, y el domingo **caminé** por el zoo.

- The **nosotros** forms in the present and in the preterit are the same. The context usually clarifies the meaning.

Visitamos el museo todos los días.	We **visit** the museum every day.
Visitamos el museo el sábado.	We **visited** the museum on Saturday.

- In the preterit, some verbs change spelling in the **yo** form, just like the ones you learned with the **Ud./Uds.** and negative **tú** commands. These include verbs that end in **-car, -gar,** and **-zar.**

-car   **c → qu:** buscar bus**qué**; pescar pes**qué**; sacar sa**qué**; tocar to**qué**

-gar   **g → gu:** jugar ju**gué**; llegar lle**gué**; navegar nave**gué**; pagar pa**gué**

-zar   **z → c:** abrazar abra**cé**; almorzar almor**cé**; cruzar cru**cé**

¡En acción!

¡Oye! ¿Leonardo no trabajó el lunes?

Escucha mientras[1] tu profesor/a te dice cómo pasó su día Leonardo. Luego responde «**¡Cierto!**» o «**¡Falso!**» a las afirmaciones. Si son falsas, corrígelas.

7-8 ¿Qué hiciste[2] ayer?

Completa las oraciones para decirle a tu compañero/a lo que hiciste ayer. Luego, pregúntale que hizo[3] él/ella. Túrnense.

MODELO

E1: *Ayer **desayuné** en casa. Y tú, ¿**desayunaste** en casa?*

E2: *Sí, (No, no) **desayuné** en casa,…*

1. **Desayuné…**
2. **Llegué** a la universidad a la/s…
3. **Hablé** con…
4. **Trabajé** en…
5. **Almorcé…**

6. **Jugué** al…
7. **Regresé** a casa a la/s…
8. **Cené…**
9. **Estudié…**
10. **Me acosté** a la/s…

7-9 Personalidades como el día y la noche

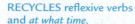 RECYCLES reflexive verbs and *at what time*.

Paso 1. **M**ateo es *muy activo y ordenado* y su amigo **T**omás es *tranquilo y desordenado*. Para indicar quién hizo cada cosa de la lista que sigue, escriban en los espacios en blanco la inicial que corresponde (**M** o **T**).

1. *levantarse* a las 6:45 de la mañana   <u>M</u>   *Mateo se levantó a las 6:45 de la mañana.*
2. *levantarse* a las 10:30 de la mañana   <u>T</u>   *se levantó…*
3. *lavar* la ropa, las sábanas[4] y las cortinas   <u>M</u>   *lavó…*
4. no *ordenar* la casa y pasar horas descansando en el sofá   <u>T</u>   *no ordenó…*
5. *levantar* pesas antes de salir de casa   <u>M</u>   *levantó…*
6. *mirar* la televisión unas horas   <u>T</u>   *miró…*
7. *bañarse* tranquilamente, escuchando la radio   <u>M</u>   *se bañó…*
8. *ducharse* rápidamente   <u>T</u>   *se duchó…*
9. *comprar* comida para toda la semana   <u>M</u>   *compró…*
10. *dejar* la cama sin hacer   <u>T</u>   *dejó…*

Paso 2. Ahora, uno/a de Uds. cuenta lo que hizo Mateo y su compañero/a cuenta lo que hizo Tomás. Luego, decidan con cuál tienen Uds. más en común. Explíquenlo.

[1]While, [2]did (you), [3]did (he/she), [4]sheets

¡Oye! Write on the board: **boleto** *ticket;* **jefe** *boss.* Trace Leonardo's route using the PowerPoint slide of the opener scene.

Guión para ¡Oye!

1. El lunes pasado, Leonardo no **trabajó** con la excusa de estar enfermo.
2. **Desayunó** en casa y luego **tomó** el metro al centro de la ciudad.
3. **Caminó** por la avenida Emiliano Zapata hasta llegar al parque.
4. Allí, **se sentó** en un banco para leer el periódico y tomar el sol.
5. Más tarde, **almorzó** en el café Colón.
6. Luego, **cruzó** el puente y **llegó** a la estación de tren.
7. Allí **compró** un boleto porque el próximo lunes va a visitar a su novia.
8. Después de comprar el boleto, **escuchó**… ¡la voz de su jefe!
9. El jefe le dijo: «Leonardo, ¿qué está haciendo Ud. aquí? ¿No está Ud. enfermo?» (*read dramatically*)
10. ¿**Inventó** Leonardo otra excusa? ¡Probablemente!.

Comprensión para ¡Oye!

1. El lunes pasado, Leonardo no trabajó con la excusa de estar enfermo. *Cierto.*
2. Tomó el autobús al centro. *Falso. Tomó el metro.*
3. Caminó hasta llegar al parque. *Cierto.*
4. Allí, se sentó en un banco para leer el periódico. *Cierto.*
5. Almorzó en el café Colón. *Cierto.*
6. Cruzó la calle para llegar a la estación de tren. *Falso. Cruzó…*
7. Compró un boleto para visitar a su novia. *Cierto.*
8. Después de comprar el boleto, escuchó la voz de su esposa. *Falso. Escuchó…*
9. Leonardo probablemente inventó otra excusa. *Cierto.*

7-9 At the conclusion of the activity, have two students read their list to the class. Poll students to find out who falls into the "active" or "laid back" category.

7-10 You may want to project the PowerPoint slide of the opener scene to review answers with the class.

7-10 ¿Dónde? RECYCLES vocabulary from chapter-opener scene and prepositions of location.

Marco y Sara, dos de tus amigos, visitaron el centro de la ciudad (págs. 218–219) recientemente. Tú no conoces bien el centro y por eso quieres saber dónde hicieron[1] cada cosa y dónde está cada lugar que mencionan. Ellos contestan. Hagan los *tres* papeles.

MODELO
comprar la pizza

Tú: *¿Dónde **compraron** la pizza?*

Marco: *La **compramos** en el Restaurante Pizza Roma.*

Tú: *¿Dónde está el Restaurante Pizza Roma?*

Sara: *Al lado del Banco Hispano.*

1. depositar dinero
2. tomar un café
3. comprar pasteles y zapatos
4. cortarse el pelo
5. descansar
6. tomar una cerveza
7. comprar el periódico
8. mirar *jeans* y suéteres

EN EL PASADO

Here are some common words and expressions for talking about the past:

anoche	*last night*
ayer	*yesterday*
anteayer	*the day before yesterday*
la semana pasada	*last week*
el fin de semana pasado	*last weekend*
el viernes/ sábado... pasado	*last Friday/ Saturday...*
el mes/ año pasado	*last month/ year*
ya	*already*

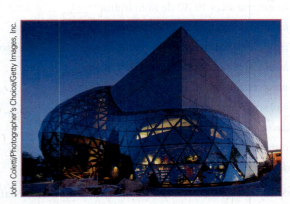

Benedicte Desrus/Alamy

El Museo Soumaya fue inaugurado en el año 2011, en la Ciudad de México. Es un edificio espectacular, de forma circular, con una extensión de 17.000 metros cuadrados distribuidos en seis pisos. El museo lleva el nombre de la difunta esposa del multimillonario mexicano Carlos Slim Helu, que construyó el museo que alberga su colección privada. Entre otras, allí se pueden admirar obras de Tintoretto, El Greco, Tiziano, Leonardo da Vinci, Renoir, Monet, Sorolla, Zurbarán, Van Gogh, Degas, Murillo y Toulousse Lautrec. Lo más destacado del museo es la colección de esculturas de Rodin, la mejor colección fuera de Francia.

John Coletti/Photographer's Choice/Getty Images, Inc.

El Museo Dalí fue inaugurado en el año 2011 en St. Petersburg, (Florida). El edificio es espectacular, con vistas a la Bahía de Tampa, y está hecho a prueba de huracanes. Contiene la colección más completa del pintor español Salvador Dalí fuera de España. Las obras de arte del museo son una donación de la familia de Albert Reynolds Morse, un ingeniero multimillonario de Ohio que fue amigo de Dalí y acumuló esta colección durante décadas. Lo más destacado es una escalera de caracol[2] que parece interminable y que representa el interés de Dalí por la estructura del ADN.[3]

[1]did, [2]**escalera...** spiral staircase, [3]DNA

7-11 ¿Qué pasó anoche, ayer,...?

Paso 1. Háganse las preguntas de la primera columna y respondan con una oración completa. Para cada pregunta, marquen su respuesta en la segunda columna y la de su compañero/a en la tercera. Sigan el modelo.

7-11 At the conclusion of the activity, get feedback from several students. Keep other students attentive by asking them to confirm what is being said: **¿Quiénes estudiaron anoche?**

MODELO

E1: ¿Anoche **estudiaste?** → **E2:** *Sí estudié.*

E1: ¿Para qué clase? → **E2:** *Para la clase de historia. ¿Y tú?*

E1: *Yo también estudié para la clase de historia.*

	Yo	Mi compañero/a
Anoche,...		
1. ¿... **estudiaste?** ¿Para qué clase?	☑ sí ☐ no ... *estudié...*	☑ sí ☐ no ... <u>estudió</u> ...
2. ¿... **navegaste** por la Red?	☐ sí ☐ no	☐ sí ☐ no ... _____ ...
Ayer o anteayer,...		
3. ¿... **jugaste** a... (*deporte*)?	☐ sí ☐ no	☐ sí ☐ no ... _____ ...
4. ¿... **charlaste** con alguien de tu familia? ¿Con quién?	☐ sí ☐ no	☐ sí ☐ no ... _____ ...
La semana pasada,...		
5. ¿... **compraste** algo? ¿Qué?	☐ sí ☐ no	☐ sí ☐ no ... _____ ...
6. ¿... **cenaste** en un restaurante? ¿Cuál? ¿Con quién?	☐ sí ☐ no	☐ sí ☐ no ... _____ ...
El verano pasado,...		
7. ¿... **viajaste** a alguna ciudad de Latinoamérica? ¿A cuál?	☐ sí ☐ no	☐ sí ☐ no ... _____ ...
8. ¿... **trabajaste?** ¿Dónde?	☐ sí ☐ no	☐ sí ☐ no ... _____ ...

Paso 2. Ahora, díganle a otra pareja o a la clase lo que Uds. tienen en común: *Anoche... y yo estudiamos para la clase de historia.*

Cartagena de Indias (1533), situada en la costa colombiana del Caribe, es una ciudad ideal para pasear por sus calles llenas de casas con balcones y admirar sus palacios, monasterios, plazas y casas antiguas. Su puerto es famoso por su enorme fortificación, construida para proteger allí los tesoros[1] de América antes de llevarlos a España. ¿Te gustaría conocer esta ciudad?

[1]treasures

Quito, la capital de Ecuador, tiene una zona antigua de gran belleza, con la catedral y otros edificios de arquitectura colonial. ¿Hay una zona antigua en tu ciudad?

Tu mundo cultural

La plaza: el corazón[1] de la ciudad

© John Wiley & Sons, Inc.

¿Conoces alguna plaza en EE. UU.? ¿Y alguna del mundo hispano?

La plaza es el centro de las actividades más importantes de la vida de toda ciudad y todo pueblo hispano. Allí se va a la hora del café, los días de mercado, y para celebrar la fiesta del santo patrón o de la santa patrona del pueblo o de la ciudad. Los edificios más representativos de la vida civil y religiosa están allí: la iglesia o catedral, y la casa presidencial o la alcaldía[2]. Generalmente, en la plaza hay también un teatro o cine, restaurantes, cafés y bares. Una característica típica de muchas plazas hispanas son sus portales, que sirven para protegerse del sol y de la lluvia. En el centro de la plaza normalmente hay una estatua o una fuente.

Wesley Bocxe/The Image Works

La Plaza Mayor de Lima, Perú (1535), con la fuente de bronce en el centro. La fuente es uno de los pocos elementos de la plaza original que no fue destruido por los terremotos[3] de Lima. En la plaza también están la catedral, el Palacio Presidencial, el Palacio del Arzobispo y otros edificios importantes. En el pasado, la plaza se usaba para corridas de toros[4].

La plaza de San José (1525), en San Juan de Puerto Rico, una de las favoritas de la juventud. Allí está la iglesia colonial de San José y en el centro, una estatua de bronce de Juan Ponce de León, el fundador de la ciudad. La plaza está situada en una zona muy popular, con vistas panorámicas, y bares y restaurantes donde se sirven hamburguesas deliciosas y comida criolla. Durante las fiestas, la plaza es el escenario de conciertos de rock, bailes de salsa, y competiciones de boxeo y gimnasia.

Dave G. Houser/© Corbis

[1]heart, [2]Mayor's office, [3]earthquakes, **corridas...** bullfights

Richard Elliott/Stone/Getty Images

La Plaza Real de Santa Fe (1607) en Nuevo México. Santa Fe es la segunda* ciudad más antigua de EE. UU. y ejemplo del legado[1] hispano. El Palacio del Gobernador está en la plaza, y a su alrededor hay museos, galerías de arte y gran variedad de tiendas.

 ¿Qué aprendiste?

1. ¿Qué importancia tiene la plaza en las ciudades hispanas? ¿Qué actividades se hacen allí?

   Es el corazón de la ciudad. Se toma café, se celebran fiestas o se va al mercado.

2. Por lo general, ¿qué edificios se encuentran en la plaza? ¿Y qué lugares hay para divertirse? ¿Qué hay a veces en el centro de la plaza? ¿Para qué sirven los portales de la plaza?

   Iglesia, alcaldía, bares, teatros,… A veces hay una fuente o estatua. Los portales sirven para resguardarse de la lluvia o el sol.

3. ¿Cuál de las tres plazas ha sido[2] destruida por terremotos? ¿Cuál tiene en el centro la estatua del fundador de la ciudad? ¿Y cuál representa el legado hispano en EE. UU.? ¿De qué año es?

   La Plaza Mayor de Lima. La Plaza de San José. La Plaza Real de Santa Fe, de 1607.

 ## Actividad cultural

Decidan a cuál de las tres plazas van a ir, y hagan una lista de lo que van a encontrar y van a hacer cuando estén allí.

 ## Contraste cultural

Háganse las siguientes preguntas: En tu pueblo o ciudad, ¿hay una plaza o un parque en el centro? Si no, ¿hay otros lugares comparables a la plaza? ¿Son puntos de encuentro para niños, jóvenes y mayores? ¿Qué se puede hacer en ellos? ¿Vas allí con frecuencia? ¿Con quién?

[1]legacy, [2]ha… has been

_____

*The oldest city in the United States is St. Augustine, Florida (1565), also of Hispanic heritage.

La vida urbana

Pronunciación: Practice pronunciation of the chapter's new vocabulary in *WileyPLUS*.

VOCABULARIO

A la entrada del Cine Amenábar

CHICO & RITA
FERNANDO TRUEBA ★ JAVIER MARISCAL TONO ERRANDO

PELÍCULA DE HOY FRIDA
TARDE/NOCHE
7:30 – 9:00
9:30 – 11:00

ENTRADA

3. la gente

1. empezar (ie)
2. terminar
4. el boleto
5. hacer fila

En el Banco Hispano

8. el cajero automático

HORARIO 9:00–14:00*

6. abrir
7. cerrar (ie)

9. sacar

Deseo abrir 10*una cuenta.*

Quiero depositar este 11*cheque* y 12*cobrar* el otro.

13*Fírmelos,* por favor.

En la oficina de correos

15. PAÍSES EXTRANJEROS
NACIONAL LOCAL

14. el paquete
16. la estampilla
17. la (tarjeta) postal
18. mandar una carta

En la Peluquería Elena

MANICURA
MASAJE

¿Va a 20*teñirse*?

De color rojo.

¿De qué color quiere 19*pintarse las uñas*?

21. cortarse el pelo

En el parque

La tienes que buscar.
¿Y la pelota?
¡Aquí está!

23. perder (ie)
24. encontrar (ue)

¡Hola, Ana!
¡Hola, Marta!

25. llevar

22. encontrarse (ue) con

© John Wiley & Sons, Inc.

En la calle del Río

Y también debe 27*abrocharse el cinturón.*

26. la licencia de manejar

29. la multa

28. mostrar (ue)

calle del Río

---

1. to begin, start 2. to finish 3. people 4. ticket (movie/ theater/ bus/ plane/ train) 5. to wait in line 6. to open 7. to close 8. ATM 9. to take out 10. an account 11. check (*m.*) 12. to cash, charge 13. Sign them; **firmar** *to sign* 14. package 15. foreign countries 16. stamp 17. postcard 18. to mail/ send a letter 19. to have one's nails painted, paint one's nails 20. **teñirse (i)** to have one's hair colored, color one's hair 21. to get a haircut, cut one's hair 22. to meet up (with) 23. to lose 24. to find 25. to take, carry 26. driver's license 27. to fasten one's seatbelt 28. to show 29. fine, ticket

*14:00 = *2:00 PM on the 24-hour clock.*

¡En acción!

7-12 Por la ciudad

Observen las escenas de la página 232. Luego, digan como mínimo *tres* actividades que se pueden hacer en los siguientes lugares.

el cine	el banco	la oficina de correos	la peluquería	el parque	la calle
comprar boletos ...					

7-13 La vida de la ciudad

¿Qué pasa en las distintas partes de la ciudad? Para saberlo, observen las escenas de la página 232 y contesten las preguntas.

1. ¿A qué hora empieza la primera película? ¿A qué hora termina?
2. ¿Qué hace la gente en la ventanilla? ¿Qué van a comprar?
3. ¿A qué hora se abre y se cierra el Banco Hispano? ¿Qué hace la gente que está allí?
4. ¿Qué lleva el señor que entra a la oficina de correos? ¿Qué hacen las personas que están cerca de los buzones?
5. En la peluquería, ¿qué hacen las clientas? ¿Qué otro servicio ofrece la peluquería?
6. ¿Quiénes se encuentran en el parque? ¿Qué más ocurre allí?
7. ¿Quién lleva a dos niños al parque? ¿Qué lleva el hombre al parque?
8. ¿Qué pasa en la calle del Río?

7-14 Conversaciones: En la ciudad

Hagan los siguientes papeles y conversen. Tienen 30 segundos para cada conversación. Túrnense.

1. **tú y el cajero del cine:**
   quieres saber las horas de las películas, cuánto cuestan los boletos,...

2. **tú y la empleada del banco:**
   quieres cobrar un cheque y abrir una cuenta

3. **tú y el empleado de la oficina de correos:**
   quieres mandar un paquete y comprar estampillas

4. **tú y la peluquera:**
   quieres cortarte y/o teñirte el pelo, quieres un masaje,...

5. **tú y un amigo/a con quien te encuentras en el parque:**
   lo/la saludas y hablan de sus planes para el fin de semana

> **Palabras útiles**
> ¿En qué puedo servirle?
> / ¿Qué desea?
> *How can I help you?*
> Me gustaría…
> *I would like…*

¡A escuchar! Una cita¹ en la ciudad

Paso 1.   Sonia y Candela van a la peluquería mientras sus amigos Miguel y Toño se ocupan de los detalles para la cita que tienen los cuatro esta noche.

WILEY PLUS Go to *WileyPLUS* to complete **Paso 2** of this listening activity.

¿SABES QUE...?

The streets and downtown areas of many Hispanic cities, founded centuries ago, were designed for pedestrians and not for cars, trucks, and buses. Streets are narrow, and therefore parking is a problem. In most Hispanic countries, citizens rely on public transportation.

Note: Tell your students that the verbs **cortarse** and **teñirse** are used in the reflexive form even when someone else cuts or dyes one's hair.

7-12   For each category, write items on the board as students volunteer them.

7-13   You may want to project the PowerPoint slide and have students in pairs describe each of the six vignettes. The class adds input as appropriate.

7-13 PERSONALIZED QUESTIONS: Una persona de un país hispano va a pasar un año en su pueblo o ciudad y tiene preguntas para Uds. ¿Dónde se cortan Uds. el pelo? ¿Dónde se puede comprar estampillas y mandar paquetes? ¿Qué lugares de recreo hay en su pueblo o ciudad? ¿Van Uds. al cine con frecuencia o alquilan películas?

7-13   Present alternatives to vocabulary items at your discretion: **boleto / billete** (Spain); **estampilla / sello** (Spain); **hacer fila / hacer cola** (Spain and other Spanish-speaking countries); **estacionar / aparcar** (Spain) / **parquear** (U.S.A., Colombia).

7-14   When students have completed the activity, have five pairs each present one of the conversations.

Jennifer, su madre y su hija Yolanda hablan del osito panda que visitaron en el zoo.

Mi esposo **oyó** en el radio que hay un osito panda en el zoo. Luego, lo **vimos** en la televisión y **leímos** en el periódico que se puede visitar.

¡¡Es lindísimo!! Cuando **abrieron** las puertas del zoo, **corrí** a verlo.

Y tomaste muchas fotos, ¿verdad?

¿Saben? A Yolanda **le gustó** tanto el panda que cuando **volvimos** a casa **escribió** una composición para su clase.

¡Y **recibió** una nota muy buena!

Luego, **comimos** en la cafetería del zoo y ¿saben qué **bebimos**? ¡Jugo de panda! Es una bebida preparada con coca cola y helado de vainilla.

Y Yolanda **decidió**... que va a ser veterinaria, ¿verdad?

Yolanda, tienes que conocer a mi hija Olivia. ¡Ella también quiere ser veterinaria!

© John Wiley & Sons, Inc.

To introduce students to the preterit of regular –er and –ir verbs used in context, have them take parts and read the **historieta** out loud. To check their comprehension and call their attention to the preterit, ask the following questions: 1. ¿Qué escribió Yolanda? 2. ¿Qué bebieron en la cafetería?

PLUS Go to *WileyPLUS* to review this grammar point with the help of the **Animated Grammar Tutorial** and **Verb Conjugator**. For more practice, go to the **Grammar Handbook**.

For additional practice on this grammar point, see PowerPoint slides on BCS and in *WileyPLUS*.

To introduce -er/-ir verbs, write a question/answer pair on board, e.g. **¿Leíste el periódico ayer? Sí, leí el periódico/No, no leí el periódico.** Ask a student the question, then have him/her pose the same question to a classmate. Repeat this procedure with different students, then ask them about their classmates, e.g. **¿Leyó [John] el periódico? [John] y [Mary], ¿leyeron Uds. el periódico?** etc. *Other examples:* ¿Viste las noticias? ¿Recibiste unos e-mails hoy? ¿Asististe a un concierto? ¿Corriste por el parque?

3

¡Manos a la obra!

GRAMÁTICA

Talking about what happened:The preterit tense of regular -er and -ir verbs

You have used **-ar** verbs to talk about actions completed in the past. Now you will learn to do the same with **–er** and **–ir** verbs, as in these examples based on Yolanda's experience at the zoo.

—¿Cuándo **volvieron** a casa ayer? — *When **did** you **return** home yesterday?*
—**Volvimos** por la tarde. — *We **returned** in the afternoon.*
—¿Qué nota **recibiste**? — *What grade **did** you **receive**?*
—**Recibí** una nota buena. — *I **received** a good grade.*

The preterit tense of regular **-er** and **-ir** verbs is formed by dropping the infinitive endings and adding the endings below. The endings for **-er** and **-ir** verbs are identical.

	-ar endings	*-er/ -ir endings*	**volver** *to return*	**abrir** *to open*
(yo)	-é	**-í**	volv**í**	abr**í**
(tú)	-aste	**-iste**	volv**iste**	abr**iste**
(Ud., él, ella)	-ó	**-ió**	volv**ió**	abr**ió**
(nosotros/as)	-amos	**-imos**	volv**imos**	abr**imos**
(vosotros/as)	-asteis	**-isteis**	volv**isteis**	abr**isteis**
(Uds., ellos, ellas)	-aron	**-ieron**	volv**ieron**	abr**ieron**

—¿**Comieron** en la cafetería? ¿Qué **bebieron**?
—Sí, **comimos** en la cafetería del zoo y **bebimos** jugo de panda.

- As with **-ar** verbs, the **nosotros** form of **-ir** verbs in the *present* and in the *preterit* is the same. The context usually clarifies the meaning.

  Salimos a las 9:00 todos los días. *We **leave** at 9:00 every day.*
  Salimos a las 9:00 ayer. *We **left** at 9:00 yesterday.*

- The **yo** and **Ud./ él/ ella** forms of **ver** have no accents, since they are only one syllable: **vi**, viste, **vio**, vimos, visteis, vieron

- In the preterit, the verbs **leer** and **oír** change the **i** of the third-person singular and plural endings to **y**. They also add accents to the **tú, nosotros,** and **vosotros** forms.

  leer: leí, leíste, le**y**ó, leímos, leísteis, le**y**eron
  oír: oí, oíste, o**y**ó, oímos, oísteis, o**y**eron

¡En acción!

¡Oye! Al volver a casa

Escucha y observa lo que tu profesor/a hizo una tarde. Luego, contesta las preguntas.

7-15   La semana de Carlota   RECYCLES days of the week and scene vocabulary.

Paso 1.   Lee el diario de Carlota y a continuación, completa las columnas con la información que corresponde.

(1) *El lunes* pasado **estacioné** en un lugar prohibido de la calle del Río y claro, **recibí** una multa. (2) *El martes*, para no tener una multa, no **manejé**; **salí** tarde de casa y ya en la estación, **oí** el tren, **corrí**, pero no **llegué** a tiempo. (3) *El miércoles*, para no gastar todo mi dinero, **abrí** una cuenta en el Banco Hispano. (4) *El jueves*, en mi casa, **leí** la sección de películas del periódico y le **escribí** un e-mail a mi novio para invitarlo a ir al cine. (5) Anteayer, *viernes*, **me lavé** y **me corté** el pelo en la peluquería. (6) Ayer *sábado*, **vi** una película con mi novio en el Cine Amenábar y **volví** a casa tarde. (7) Hoy *domingo*, por la mañana, **desayuné** con mis amigos en el Café Colón, mi favorito.

¿Cuándo?	¿Qué hizo o qué le pasó?	¿Dónde?
el lunes	1. ***Estacionó*** y ***recibió*** una multa.	*en un lugar prohibido*
el martes	2. *No manejó; salió…; oyó…; corrió…; pero no llegó…*	*en la estación*
el miércoles	3. *Abrió…*	*en el Banco Hispano*
el jueves	4. *Leyó…; escribió…*	*en su casa*
el viernes	5. *Se lavó y se cortó…*	*en la peluquería*
el sábado	6. *Vio…volvió…*	*en el Cine Amenábar*
el domingo	7. *Desayunó…*	*en el Café Colón*

Paso 2.   Ahora, pregúntale a tu compañero/a qué hizo Carlota cada día y dónde. Túrnense.

MODELO

E1:   *¿Qué hizo el lunes?*

E2:   ***Estacionó*** *en un lugar prohibido y* ***recibió*** *una multa. ¿Y el martes?*

¿SABES QUE…?

Chico & Rita, the film on the marquee in this chapter's opening scene, is a Spanish animated film directed by Fernando Trueba and Javier Mariscal. The story is set against backdrops of Havana, New York, Las Vegas, Hollywood, and Paris in the late 1940's and early 1950's. The film was nominated for Best Animated Feature Film for the 2012 Academy Awards and won the 2012 Goya Award in Spain for best-animated film.

¡Oye! Write on the board: **fui** *I went;* **prendí** *I turned on (the TV, etc.).* Consider bringing a few props to class to reinforce the content of this activity. To reinforce meaning, mime each action immediately after verbalizing it (where you see … in the script).

Guión para ¡Oye!
Volví a casa a las cuatro de la tarde, e inmediatamente **fui** a la cocina. … **Abrí** el refrigerador… y **saqué** una manzana. … La **comí.** … **Saqué** unas uvas,… y las **comí.** … Finalmente, **saqué** un refresco,… y lo **bebí.** … Me **senté** en el sofá. … Primero **leí** una revista. … Más tarde, **leí** el periódico. … **Prendí** el televisor. … Primero, **vi** las noticias y luego, un programa sobre las playas del Pacífico. … Un amigo me **llamó** y **hablé** con él. … A las 7:00 **salí** de casa… para cenar con él en un restaurante. …

Comprensión para ¡Oye!
Students do not need to produce the verbs in their responses.
1. ¿A qué hora volví a casa? *a las cuatro de la tarde*
2. ¿Qué comí? *una manzana, unas uvas*
3. ¿Qué bebí? *un refresco*
4. ¿Qué leí? *una revista y un periódico*
5. ¿Qué vi en la televisión? *las noticias y un programa sobre…*
6. ¿A qué hora salí de casa? *a las 7:00* ¿Para qué? *para cenar con un amigo*

7-16 Instructor's question for *Paso 2*: **¿Quién recibió un paquete el mes pasado?** Elicit responses from several students, asking follow-up questions such as **¿De quién?** To keep students attentive, ask for confirmation: **¿De quién recibió Tomás un paquete?** and so on.

7-16 El mes pasado

Paso 1. ¿Quieres saber lo que hizo tu compañero/a el mes pasado? Hazle las preguntas de la primera columna. Él/Ella responde según el modelo de la segunda y tú escribes la información en la tercera. Túrnense.

Preguntas	Respuestas	Información escrita
1. **¿Recibiste** un paquete? ¿De quién?	*Sí,* **recibí** *un paquete de mi tía.* ¿Y tú?	... **recibió**...
2. **¿Viste** una película interesante? ¿Cuál?		
3. **¿Leíste** una revista divertida? ¿Cuál?		
4. **¿Comiste** en un restaurante? ¿Dónde?		
5. **¿Escribiste** e-mails? ¿A quién?		
6. **¿Saliste** con tus amigos? ¿Adónde?		
7. **¿Te encontraste** con tus amigos en un café? ¿Cuándo?		
8. **¿Te cortaste** el pelo? ¿Dónde?		

Paso 2. Ahora, su profesor/a quiere saber lo que hicieron Uds. el mes pasado. Contesten sus preguntas.

7-17 To review answers, have the class call out Nacho's activities one day at a time. Be sure to get feedback on *Paso 2*.

7-17 Hijo adolescente y padres preocupados

Paso 1. Últimamente[1], su hijo Nacho no pasa mucho tiempo con la familia y el fin de semana pasado, nadie lo vio en casa. Un día, al vaciar[2] los bolsillos[3] para lavar su chaqueta, Uds., los padres, encuentran la "evidencia". Comenten lo que hizo Nacho *el viernes, el sábado* y *el domingo*. Usen todos los verbos que siguen (pág. 237).

[1]Lately, [2]empty, [3]pockets, [4]gold ring, [5]yours

© John Wiley & Sons, Inc.

asistir a	bailar	beber	comer	comprar	escribir	pagar	sacar	ver

For additional practice on this grammar point, see PowerPoint slides on BCS and in *WileyPLUS*.

MODELO

Madre: Bueno..., veo que el viernes **sacó** 500 pesos del Banco Hispano.

Padre: ... y veo que...

Palabras útiles

gastar demasiado
to spend too much

Go to *WileyPLUS* to review the grammar point below with the help of the **Animated Grammar Tutorial** and **Verb Conjugator**. For more practice, go to the **Grammar Handbook**.

Paso 2. Ahora, comenten lo que piensan que pasa con Nacho. ¿Creen Uds. que los padres de Nacho deben continuar preocupándose por su hijo? ¿Por qué?

Jennifer, su familia y sus amigos hablan mientras toman un café después de la cena.

¿Cuándo **decidieron** venir a vivir a Estados Unidos?

Lo **decidimos** hace treinta años.[1]

Fue muy difícil. Más tarde, **nacieron**[2] nuestros dos hijos, Enrique y Jennifer. Mira, ésta es Jennifer de bebé.

Hicimos muchos sacrificios para comprar esta casa y les **dimos** la mejor educación posible a nuestros hijos.

Fueron muy valientes[3]. Y tienen unos hijos muy guapos y listos.

© John Wiley & Sons, Inc.

GRAMÁTICA

¡Manos a la obra!

4

The preterit of four irregular verbs: *dar, ser, ir,* and *hacer*

The four verbs below, which have irregular forms in the present tense, also have irregular forms in the preterit.

dar *to give*		**ir** *to go* and **ser** *to be*		**hacer** *to do, make*	
di	dimos	fui	fuimos	hice	hicimos
diste	disteis	fuiste	fuisteis	hiciste	hicisteis
dio	dieron	fue	fueron	hizo	hicieron

• Let's imagine a conversation between Jennifer's parents that takes place that same evening.
—¿**Fuiste** al parque con Yolanda? ¿**Dieron** un paseo? ¿Qué más **hicieron**?
—Sí, **fuimos** y solamente **dimos** un paseo. No **hicimos** nada más.

• In the preterit, **dar** (an **-ar** verb) has **-ir** endings, but without accents.

• The preterit forms of **ser** and **ir** are identical; the context clarifies which verb is used:

Fueron a otro país.   They **went** to another country.
Fue muy difícil.   It **was** very difficult.

—Ask student B to do some exercises in front of the class. Ask the class: **¿Qué hizo...?**
—Ask student C to give two items to two different students. Then ask the class: **¿Qué le dio... a...? ¿Y qué le dio... a...?** This previews indirect objects, to be presented in Escena 3 of this chapter.

To introduce students to the preterit of these four irregular verbs used in context, have them take parts and read the **historieta** out loud. Ask 1. **¿Qué hicieron los padres para comprar su casa? 2. ¿Qué les dieron a sus hijos?**

Write the verbs **dar, ir,** and **hacer** on the board. Circle the appropriate verb after students complete each of the following instructions, and write the preterit form used in the demonstration under each. *Demonstration:* —Ask student A to go to the board, then to a window, and then to the classroom door. Ask the class: **¿Adónde fue...** (name of student) **primero? ¿Y después? ¿Y al final?**

[1]**hace...** twenty years ago, [2]were born, [3]brave

¡En acción!

¡Oye! ¿Es verdad o no?

Escucha lo que hizo tu profesor/a recientemente. Según lo que sabes de él/ella, responde diciendo: «**probablemente sí**» o «**probablemente no**».

7-18 ¿Qué hicieron tus compañeros?

Paso 1. Camina por la clase haciéndoles cada pregunta a *tres* estudiantes diferentes. Apunta sus nombres y las respuestas. Tienes *cinco* minutos.

Preguntas	E1: _____	E2: _____	E3: _____
1. ¿Adónde **fuiste** el fin de semana pasado?	... *fue a*...		
2. ¿**Hiciste** un viaje el verano pasado? ¿Adónde?			
3. ¿**Diste** una fiesta recientemente? ¿Cuál **fue** la ocasión?			

Paso 2. Al terminar, cuéntale a la clase una cosa que hicieron dos de tus compañeros/as: ... y... **fueron** al centro el fin de semana pasado. ¿Quién hizo la cosa más interesante?

7-19 Mi fin de semana en la Ciudad de México

RECYCLES regular verbs in the preterit along with **dar, hacer,** and **ir.**

Paso 1. Miren las fotos con los comentarios que colgó[1] Lola en su *blog*. Como lo hizo muy rápido, faltan algunos verbos. Escojan el verbo más apropiado de la lista para completarlos. Usen el pretérito. Tienen *ocho* minutos.

LA CIUDAD DE MÉXICO

VIERNES
Por la noche, __lleguê__ a la Ciudad de México; __me__ __registré__ en el hotel e inmediatamente __me__ __acosté__. [**acostarse, llegar, registrarse**]

SÁBADO

Topham/The Image Works

Por la mañana, __fui__ al Museo Nacional de Antropología y allí __admiré__ el famoso calendario azteca. [**admirar, ir**]

© PIXTAL/Age Fotostock America, Inc.

Por la tarde, __visité__ Chapultepec, un parque enorme con lagos y bosques, y __di__ un paseo por el jardín botánico. Por la noche, __cené__ en un restaurante buenísimo y __volví__ al hotel muy contenta. [**cenar, dar, visitar, volver**]

[1]posted

DOMINGO

Por la mañana, __me__ __desperté__ temprano; __desayuné__ huevos rancheros y café, y __tomé__ un taxi para ir al museo del Templo Mayor. Allí __vi__ pirámides construidas por los aztecas para sus dioses. [**desayunar, despertarse, tomar, ver**]

Al lado del Museo, en el Zócalo*, está el Palacio Nacional donde se pueden admirar los murales de Diego Rivera. El guía nos __explicó__ muy bien todo acerca de ellos. Al mediodía, __almorcé__ en una terraza; __comí__ pollo con mole y __bebí__ un licuado de frutas tropicales. [**almorzar, comer, beber, explicar**]

Por la tarde, no __hice__ mucho por estar cansada, pero por la noche, __fui__ al Palacio de Bellas Artes donde __vi__ el Ballet Folclórico. ¡Me __gustó__ muchísimo! ¡La Ciudad de México es fascinante! [**gustar, hacer, ir, ver**]

7-19 Regarding the last answer, remind students that **gustó/gustaron** are the forms of **gustar** used in the preterit.

 Paso 2. Imagínense que Uds. tienen solamente un día para visitar la Ciudad de México. Decidan *tres* cosas que van a hacer y compártanlas con la clase.

 7-20 **¿Dices siempre la verdad?** RECYCLES reflexive verbs and regular verbs in the preterit.

 Paso 1. Di *cinco* cosas que hiciste ayer. De ellas, *dos* no son verdad. Tus compañeros tienen que adivinar[1] cuáles no son ciertas. Túrnense.

MODELO

E1: *Ayer, **me levanté** a las siete y **me duché**. Luego, **estudié** unas horas. Después, **hablé** con el presidente de EE. UU. y **bailé** con Salma Hayek.*

E2: *¡Es mentira[2]! No **hablaste** con el presidente de EE. UU. y tampoco **bailaste** con Salma Hayek.*

E3: *Pues, yo ayer…*

Paso 2. Ahora, compartan con la clase las mentiras más divertidas.

[1]guess, [2]Es... lie   *Plaza principal de la Ciudad de México

¿SABES QUE...?

Air quality in Mexico City, one of the largest metropolitan areas in the world, was once so bad that children drew the sky using brown crayons and birds would drop dead while flying over the city. New, tough, environmental standards have changed all of this. Lead levels have dropped 95%, sulfur dioxide, 86%, and carbon monoxide, 74%.

Tu mundo cultural

Un viaje a Machu Picchu

For an additional activity related to this cultural theme, see the PowerPoint slides on BCS and in *WileyPLUS*.

Meets ACTFL Standards 1.1, interpersonal speaking; 1.2, interpretive reading; 2.2, cultural products; 3.1, other disciplines; and 4.2, cultural comparisons.

¿Te gustaría visitar una ciudad muy antigua del hemisferio sur? ¿Eres una persona aventurera? ¿Cómo prefieres viajar, en avión, en tren, en autobús o a pie[1]?

Machu Picchu, ciudad sagrada de los incas, fue descubierta en 1911 por Hiram Bingham, arqueólogo e historiador de la Universidad de Yale. Bingham buscaba *La Ciudad Perdida de los Incas* que, según la leyenda, fue el lugar donde se escondieron[2] de los españoles. Un indígena de nueve años le condujo hasta las ruinas y allí Bingham pudo admirar, por primera vez, templos y casas reales[3] cubiertos por la densa vegetación de la selva[4]. Fue una experiencia, sin duda, inolvidable. Desde entonces, miles de viajeros y aventureros de todo el mundo visitan este lugar, situado en medio de un paisaje[5] espectacular.

Para llegar a Machu Picchu, por su situación tan remota, son necesarios varios medios de transporte.

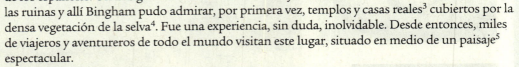

PERÚ
Lima
Machu Picchu
Cuzco

© John Wiley & Sons, Inc.

Información práctica:

- Líneas aéreas: LAN Perú; TANS; Nuevo Continente
- Temporada alta de turismo: junio–septiembre
- Para problemas de altura: infusión de hojas de coca, pastillas de coramina, glucosa o diamox

SGM/Age Fotostock America, Inc.

De Lima se va en avión a Cuzco donde se toma el tren que llega a la estación de Aguas Calientes, a media hora de Machu Picchu. El viaje dura cerca de cuatro horas, dependiendo del tren que se tome (hay tres trenes, de categoría y precios diversos: véase *www.perurail.com*). Hay vistas de paisajes majestuosos.

Jeremy Horner/©Corbis

Reuters/©Corbis

En Aguas Calientes se toma un autobús para llegar a las ruinas de Machu Picchu. Este trayecto de media hora se hace por una carretera estrecha[6] y zigzagueante. Para subir a pie se necesita aproximadamente una hora, si se está en buena forma.

Otra forma de ir de Cuzco a Machu Picchu es a pie, por el Camino del Inca. Es una opción para quienes estén en buena forma física, sean aventureros o les guste la naturaleza. Para ello, se toma el tren a Machu Picchu o un autobús hasta el kilómetro 82 u 88 de la vía a Machu Picchu. Desde allí, se camina entre 35 y 40 km. por lugares de gran belleza. Acompañados de guías, se tarda generalmente cuatro días, y se atraviesan diferentes ecosistemas que varían en altitud de los 8.000 a los 13.776 pies. Una ruta más corta sólo requiere dos días.

[1]a... on foot, [2]se... hid, [3]royal, [4]jungle, [5]landscape, [6]**carretera**... narrow highway

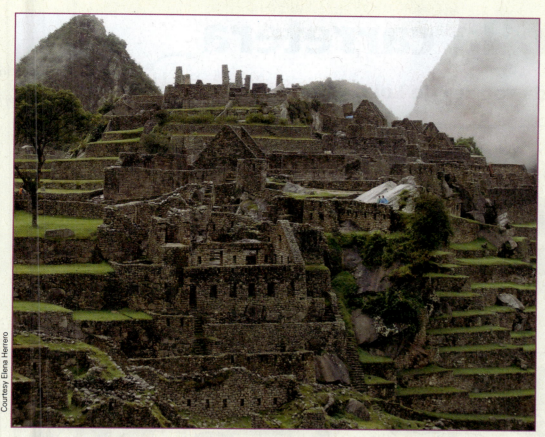

Courtesy Elena Herrero

Finalmente, se llega a la ciudad sagrada, situada a unos ocho mil pies sobre el nivel del mar. En este lugar majestuoso, con un paisaje espectacular, hay cerca de 200 casas y templos, acueductos, fuentes, tumbas y terrazas construidos todos de granito. Algo muy curioso es que no emplearon argamasa[1] para la construcción, pero las piedras[2] están tan unidas que no se puede poner ni un cuchillo entre ellas. Se estima que allí vivían cerca de 1.200 personas, la mayoría mujeres, niños y sacerdotes[3]. Y se cree que los conquistadores nunca la descubrieron.

¿Qué aprendiste?

1. ¿Quién descubrió Machu Picchu? ¿En qué año? ¿Qué buscaba?

   Hiram Bingham, en 1911. Buscaba *La Ciudad Perdida de los Incas.*

2. ¿Cómo se puede llegar a Machu Picchu? ¿Para qué clase de turistas es el Camino del Inca?

   En tren, en autobús y a pie. Para los más aventureros.

3. ¿Cómo es la ciudad sagrada? ¿A qué altura está?

   Cuenta con 200 casas y templos de granito. A 8.000 pies.

Actividad cultural

Planeen un viaje a Machu Picchu. Apunten **(a)** cuándo van a ir, **(b)** qué medios de transporte van a usar y por qué, **(c)** y qué piensan ver y hacer allí.

Contraste cultural

EE. UU. cuenta también en su historia con civilizaciones antiguas. Hablen de una de ellas y de los lugares donde se pueden visitar sus ruinas[4]. O si lo prefieren, hablen de la historia de su región y mencionen los edificios y monumentos más representativos.

[1]mortar, [2]stones, [3]priests, [4]remains

¿SABES QUE...?

With the permission of the Peruvian government, Bingham removed more than 45,000 artifacts from Machu Picchu for study in the United States. The pieces were stored at Yale University's Peabody Museum in New Haven, Connecticut. Almost 100 years after Hiram Bingham brought them to the US, the artifacts were returned to Peru in 2012, where they have been already exhibited to the public in the **Palacio de Gobierno** de Lima. Plans are underway to build a museum in Cuzco.

¿SABES QUE...?

A significant feature of **Machu Picchu** is the **intihuatana**, a column of stone rising out of a larger, altar-shaped block of stone. **Inti** was the Sun God of the Incas; **intihuatana** means *to catch or tie the sun.* In 2000, an advertising film crew, working on a beer commercial, chipped a chunk off the top of the stone when their crane fell on it.

En ¹la carretera

La vida caótica de Lola, la enfermera

WILEY **PLUS**

Pronunciación: Practice pronunciation of the chapter's new vocabulary in *WileyPLUS*.

VOCABULARIO

Ya llego, ²*estoy en camino.*

3. GASOLINERA A 200 METROS

90

76

4. la velocidad máxima

5. BAÑOS

AIRE

Por favor, ¿dónde están los baños?

Allí, a la izquierda.

GASOLINA

6. llenar el tanque

7. revisar (el aceite)

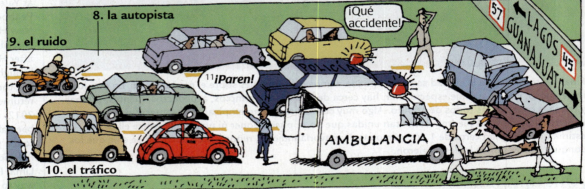

8. la autopista

9. el ruido

¡Qué accidente!

57 LAGOS GUANAJUATO 45

¹¹¡Paren!

POLICIA

AMBULANCIA

10. el tráfico

RESTAURANTE 2 KILÓMETROS↑ TALLER MECÁNICO 1 km →

12.

Sí, siga recto un kilómetro y está a la derecha.

¹³*Mi carro se descompuso.* ¿Hay un taller mecánico cerca?

POLICIA

14. ALTO

15. la señal de tráfico

© John Wiley & Sons, Inc.

TALLER MECÁNICO – REPARACIONES

¹⁶*Hay que* revisar ¹⁷*los frenos.*

18. reparar

²¹*¡Qué mala suerte!* ¡Una llanta pinchada y el motor ²²*no funciona!*

¡Ay! ¡Y también tiene ²⁰*una llanta pinchada!*

19. cambiar

23. las llaves

1. road 2. I'm on my way. 3. gas station 4. maximum speed 5. restrooms 6. to fill the tank 7. to check (the oil) 8. highway, freeway 9. noise
10. traffic 11. Stop! **parar** to stop 12. auto repair shop 13. My car broke down. 14. stop (road sign) 15. road sign 16. One must/ should
17. brakes 18. to repair, fix 19. to change, exchange 20. flat tire 21. What bad luck! 22. does not work; **funcionar** to work (machinery) 23. keys

¡En acción!

7-21 Una vida loca

Observa las escenas de la página 242 y completa la descripción de un día en la vida de Lola, la enfermera.

Lola maneja mientras habla por el celular con su novio. Le dice que está en camino, pero que tiene que ir a una gasolinera para __llenar__ el tanque. No __revisa__ el aceite, pero pregunta por los __baños__ y un señor muy amable le dice que están a la __izquierda__. De nuevo en la __autopista__, hay mucho __ruido__ y mucho __tráfico__. Un policía le dice a Lola y a otros conductores «¡__Paren__!» porque hay un accidente. Al final, Lola tiene muchos problemas. El motor de su carro no __funciona__ y tiene una __llanta__ pinchada. ¡Qué mala __suerte__!

7-22 Las aventuras de Lola en la carretera

¿Es caótica la vida de Lola? Para saberlo, observen las escenas de la página 242 y contesten las preguntas.

1. ¿En qué dirección dobla el carro rojo? ¿Qué dice Lola por su celular?
2. ¿Adónde va Lola, probablemente? ¿A qué distancia está la gasolinera?
3. ¿Cuál es la velocidad máxima (kilómetros por hora) en la carretera número 76?
4. ¿Qué pasa en la gasolinera?
5. ¿Hay mucho tráfico y ruido en la autopista? ¿Qué dice el policía? ¿Por qué?
6. Según el letrero[1] de la autopista, ¿en qué dirección se dobla para ir a Lagos? ¿Y para ir a Guanajuato?
7. Lola está cerca de la señal de tráfico que dice ALTO. ¿Qué pasa allí?
8. Finalmente, ¿adónde llega Lola? ¿Por qué dice «¡Qué mala suerte!»?
9. ¿Qué pasa dentro y fuera del taller?

Christof Sonderegger/Age Fotostock America, Inc.

La avenida 9 de Julio y el obelisco, que conmemora la fundación de Buenos Aires, son símbolos famosos de esta bella ciudad. A lo lejos se ve el Río de La Plata, que separa Argentina y Uruguay. ¿Te gustaría viajar a Buenos Aires?

[1]sign

Comic Strip: To introduce students to indirect object pronouns used in context, have them take parts and read the **historieta** out loud. To check their comprehension and call their attention to the pronouns, ask the following questions:
1. ¿Qué le presta Fabio a Mario? ¿Por qué?
2. ¿Qué tiene que hacer Mario?

7-23 Conversaciones: En camino

Hagan los siguientes papeles y conversen. Tienen 30 segundos para cada conversación. Túrnense.

1. **tú y un policía:**
   el policía te para por exceso de velocidad y va a ponerte una multa

2. **tú y el/la operador/a:**
   estás en tu carro, ves un accidente y llamas al 911

3. **tú y el/la empleado/a de una gasolinera:**
   buscas los baños, necesitas gasolina,...

4. **tú y el mecánico de un taller:**
   hablan de los problemas de tu carro

Danny Lehman/©Corbis

A veces lo milenario se encuentra con lo moderno, y el resultado tiene mucho encanto, tal como se observa en esta fotografía tomada en Guatemala.

¡A escuchar! ¡Un día de esos!

Paso 1. Dos enfermeras, Macarena y Pilar, se encuentran al entrar en el estacionamiento y charlan de los eventos del día.

WILEY PLUS Go to *WileyPLUS* to complete **Paso 2** of this listening activity.

Fabio, Mario y Ernesto vuelven a casa después de cenar con Jennifer y su familia.

¡Qué familia tan simpática! ¡Y qué cena tan deliciosa!

Sí. **Le** pedí la receta a la madre de Jennifer. Si quieren, un día **les** preparo "ropa vieja". ¡**Me** encanta cocinar!

Bueno, pero me devuelves el carro antes de las cinco, ¿verdad?

¡Estupendo! Oye, Fabio, ¿**me** prestas tu carro mañana? Mi carro está todavía en el taller.

Le prometí a Jennifer llevarla al cine.

Bueno, bueno. **Les** hablo de eso en otro momento.

Tranquilo, Fabio. **Te** lo devuelvo antes de las cinco.

Oye, ¿**nos** cuentas algo? ¡Esa relación va en serio!

© John Wiley & Sons, Inc.

¡Manos a la obra!

5

To whom? For whom?: Indirect object pronouns

You have learned that *direct* object pronouns answer the questions *Who?* and *What?* in relation to the verb. Let's look at examples based on Fabio's conversation with his friends after dinner.

Who? —¿Invitaste a Jennifer?   —Sí, **la** invité.
What? —¿Compraste los boletos?   —Sí, **los** compré.

Indirect object pronouns answer the questions ***To whom?*** and ***For whom?*** in relation to the verb. Thus, the person receives the action of the verb indirectly.

To whom? Mario **le** devolvió el carro.   *Mario returned the car to him.*
For whom? **Me** revisó los frenos.   *He checked the brakes for me.*

Indirect object pronouns are identical to direct object pronouns, except in the third-person singular and plural forms. You have been using them with the verb **gustar** since *Capítulo 4.*

direct object pronouns		indirect object pronouns	
me	*me*	me	*(to, for) me*
te	*you (fam.)*	te	*(to, for) you (fam.)*
lo	*you (m., form.), him, it (m.)*	**le**	*(to, for) you (form.), him, her*
la	*you (f., form.), her, it (f.)*		
nos	*us*	nos	*(to, for) us*
os	*you (fam.)*	os	*(to, for) you (fam.)*
los	*you (m., form.), them (m.)*	**les**	*(to, for) you (form.), them*
las	*you (f., form.), them (f.)*		

Indirect object pronouns follow the same rules for placement as direct object pronouns.

- They go immediately *before* a conjugated verb.

  Le presté el carro a él.   *I lent him the car./ I lent the car to him.*
  Le voy a prestar el carro.   *I am going to lend him the car./*
                              I am going to lend the car to him.

  Le estoy prestando el carro.   *I am lending him the car./*
                              I am lending the car to him.

- They go immediately *before* the verb in a negative command.

  Mario, no **me** llenes el tanque.   *Mario, don't fill up the tank for me.*
  No **le** digas que el motor no funciona.   *Don't tell him that the motor doesn't work.*

- They are always *attached to* an affirmative command.

  Pregúnta**le*** si quiere ir al cine.   *Ask her if she wants to go to the movies.*
  Cuénta**nos** qué pasa con Jennifer.   *Tells us what's happening with Jennifer.*

- They may be *attached to* an infinitive or present participle.

  Fabio va a dar**me** las llaves.   *Fabio is going to give me the keys./*
                              Fabio is going to give the keys to me.
  Está dándo**me*** las llaves.   *He is giving me the keys./*
                              He is giving the keys to me.

*There is a written accent when the stress falls on the third-to-last syllable.

WILEY PLUS Go to *WileyPLUS* to review this grammar point with the help of the **Animated Grammar Tutorial.** For more practice, go to the **Grammar Handbook.**

For additional practice on this grammar point, see PowerPoint slides on BCS and in *WileyPLUS.*

Review direct object pronouns. Highlight the differences between the third-person direct and the third-person indirect object forms. Illustrate the differences in concept—the action being received directly versus indirectly—through sample sentences: **Vi a Marta. Cuando la vi, le di el libro. Le regalé un carro a mi hijo. Lo compré por Internet.**

Illustrate indirect object pronouns as follows: Bring to class a little gift box (or draw one on a sheet of paper) and put it on a student's desk. Ask him/her to give it to you. Tell the class: **¡Juanita me dio un regalo!** (write the sentence on the board). Then ask several students: **¿Te dio Juanita un regalo?** They respond: **No, no me dio un regalo.** Summarize responses: **Juanita no le dio un regalo a..., ¡pero me dio un regalo a mí!** As a follow-up, have students give each other various "gifts," and then tell the class who gave them the item and what it was: **... me dio...** Students need to recall who gave what to whom: **... le dio** (*objeto*) **a...**

 Go to *WileyPLUS* to review this grammar point with the help of the **Animated Grammar Tutorial.** For more practice, go to the **Grammar Handbook.**

For additional practice on this grammar point, see PowerPoint slides on BCS and in *WileyPLUS.*

. . . y algo más   For whom or to whom happens: *Le* and *les*

- **Le** and **les** are commonly used even when the person *to* or *for whom* something happens is mentioned.

  El policía **le** pone una multa **a Elena.**   *The policeman gave a ticket to Elena.*
  Ella **les** contó **a sus hermanos** lo que pasó.   *She told her brothers what happened.*

- For emphasis or clarification, the following phrases may be used along with the indirect object pronouns: **a mí, a ti, a Ud., a él, a ella, a nosotros/as, a vosotros/as, a Uds., a ellos/as.**

  A mí me dieron un boleto para el teatro. ¿**Y a ti**?
  *They gave **me** a theater ticket. What about **you**?*

  A ellos les mandaron cuatro boletos y **a nosotros,** seis.
  *They sent **them** four tickets and (sent) **us,** six.*

You may find it helpful to present, along with the verb **prestar** *to lend,* the expression **pedir/ tomar prestado** *to borrow.*

Let your students know that these verbs take direct objects in addition to indirect objects, and can both occur within the same sentence, e.g. *Te explico el problema. Les presté mi nuevo carro.*

VERBOS PARA COMUNICARSE Y RELACIONARSE

Indirect objects are frequently used with certain verbs, as one generally gives, sends, shows, lends,... things *to someone.*

Verbs you already know:		Other verbs you need to learn:	
contestar*	*to answer*	contar (ue)	*to tell, narrate (a story or incident)*
dar	*to give*	devolver (ue)	*to return (something)*
decir (i)	*to say, tell*	explicar	*to explain*
escribir	*to write*	preguntar	*to ask*
mandar	*to send*	prestar	*to lend*
pedir (i)	*to ask for, request*	regalar	*to give (as a gift)*

¿SABES QUE...?

Cuba has the oldest arsenal of American cars made before 1960, the year of the US embargo to Cuba. Most of them were manufactured between 1920–1940. They are called **almendrones** because of their almond shape. About 10.000 circulate daily in Cuba. Almendrones are used as private cars, taxis or in car pools. They are also rented to nostalgic tourists. Considering that they are almost a century old, the fact that there are so many of them in working order is a testament to Cuban ingenuity.

Bachmann /Getty Images, Inc.

*In the case of *contestar*, if the object is human, it is considered indirect: **Le contesto a la profesora**; if it is inanimate, it is considered direct: **Contesto la pregunta → La contesto.**

¡En acción!

 ¡Oye! El carro de mi profesor/a

Escucha con atención mientras tu profesor/a te cuenta lo que le pasó con su carro. Luego, di si las afirmaciones son ciertas o falsas.

🖥 You may project the PPT slide of **un mal día en la autopista** and ask the students in groups of four (Álvaro, his brother, the policeman and a narrator) to play their parts for the class.

7-24 Un mal día en la autopista

Paso 1. Ayer Álvaro manejó al centro con su hermano Adrián por la autopista, pero... por encima del límite de velocidad. Un policía los paró. Para contar lo que pasó, llenen los espacios en blanco con **le** o **les.** Luego, sigan el modelo. Túrnense.

MODELO

*"¿Quieren explicarme adónde van Uds. tan rápido?" **les** preguntó el policía a Álvaro y a su hermano.*

1. ... _les_ preguntó el policía a **Álvaro y a su hermano.**

2. ... _le_ contestó Álvaro al policía.

3. _le_ dijo el policía y Álvaro _le_ mostró su licencia al policía.

4. ... _le_ explicó el policía a **Álvaro**, y _le_ devolvió la licencia.

5. ... _le_ dijo[1] Álvaro a **Adrián.**

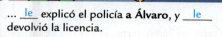

Ni Álvaro ni Adrián _les_ *contaron **a sus padres** lo que pasó.*

[1]said

(continúa en la pág. 248)

Guión para ¡Oye!
1. Voy al taller y **le cuento** al mecánico lo que le pasa a mi carro.
2. **Le explico** que el motor y los frenos no funcionan.
3. **Le muestro** las dos llantas pinchadas y **me dice:** «¡Qué mala suerte!»
4. **Le pregunto:** «¿Puede repararlo pronto? Lo necesito para mañana.»
5. **Me contesta:** «Sí, ¡por supuesto!»
6. Hace lo que promete y **me devuelve** el carro al día siguiente, a las dos de la tarde.
7. **Le digo:** «¡Mil gracias!» «¡Ud. es un mecánico fenomenal!».
8. **Le pregunto:** «¿Cuánto le tengo que pagar?»
9. **Me contesta:** «Para Ud., 250 dólares». (*Repeat.*)

Comprensión para ¡Oye!
Begin by having students write the numbers 1–9 on a sheet of paper. Then read the statements, pausing after each to give students time to jot down their responses before they call them out to the class. This procedure avoids having a few extroverts provide most of the responses.
1. Le cuento al mecánico lo que le pasa a mi carro. ¿Cierto o falso? *Cierto*
2. Le explico que la batería no funciona. *Falso*
3. Le muestro las tres llantas pinchadas. *Falso*
4. Le pregunto si puede reparar el carro pronto. *Cierto*
5. Me contesta: «¡Imposible!» *Falso*
6. Me devuelve el carro a tiempo. *Cierto*
7. Le digo: «¡Mil gracias!» *Cierto*
8. Le pregunto: «¿Cuánto le tengo que pagar?» *Cierto*
9. Me dice: «500 dólares». *Falso*

Paso 2. Ahora, háganse las siguientes preguntas para saber si les pasó algo similar.

1. ¿Alguna vez manejaste por encima del límite de velocidad?

2. ¿Te paró la policía? ¿Le mostraste la licencia de manejar? ¿Te puso una multa?

3. ¿Le contaste a tu familia lo que pasó?

7-25 Regalos para los Roldán

 Paso 1. Miren la lista de regalos de los Roldán de la Navidad pasada. Contesten las preguntas escogiendo el que probablemente recibió cada persona o pareja, y el perro. Sigan el modelo y usen **le** o **les** en las preguntas y respuestas. Usen la foto de la familia, páginas 72–73. Túrnense.

7-25 Review answers for *Paso 1.* Expect disagreement as to which gift is most appropriate for a person or people (or pet). After each response, ask the class **¿Es un buen regalo para... o no?**

Lista de regalos recibidos

a. una pelota

b. el último libro de *Crepúsculo*[1]

c. un suéter rosado con la inicial C

d. un DVD y un CD de Adele

e. unas vacaciones en la nieve para toda la familia

f. un hueso[2]

g. dos boletos para la ópera

h. una cena romántica para dos en su restaurante favorito

✓ i. boletos para el circo

j. un teléfono celular y una blusa bonita de flores

© John Wiley & Sons, Inc.

MODELO

Los abuelos → sus nietos

E1: *¿Qué **les** regalaron los abuelos a sus nietos?*

E2: *(i) **Les** regalaron boletos para el circo.*

1. Nuria → Robertito *¿Qué **le** regaló...?*

2. Los padres → sus hijos

3. Ángel → Guadalupe

4. Guadalupe → Carmen

5. Carmen → Ángel

6. Robertito→ Pachá, el perro

7. Los nietos → sus abuelos

8. Los hijos → sus padres

9. Todos → Nuria

Ahora, confirmen si escogieron bien los regalos.

Suggested answers: 1.a 2.e 3.b 4.c 5.d 6.f 7.g 8.h 9.j

 Paso 2. Ahora cada uno/a de Uds. piensa en un regalo que recibió, cuándo lo recibió y de quién. Compartan la información con la clase: *Mi tío **me** regaló una motocicleta el año pasado.* Luego, la clase decide quién recibió el mejor regalo.

[1]Twilight, [2]bone

7-26 ¿Recibiste algo de alguien? RECYCLES verbs in the preterit.

 Paso 1. Háganse preguntas para saber qué recibieron de otras personas recientemente. Si tu compañero/a responde **sí** a una pregunta, apunta en la segunda columna quién lo hizo.

MODELO

E1: ¿Alguien **te** mandó un paquete recientemente?

E2: Sí, mi tía **me** mandó un paquete. (**E1** escribe en la segunda columna la tía de Lisa.)

o: No, nadie **me** mandó un paquete. ¿Y a ti?

¿Alguien…?	¿Quién lo hizo?
1. *mandar* / un paquete	la tía de Lisa / nadie
2. *dejar* / un mensaje en Facebook	
3. *escribir* / un mensaje de texto	
4. *regalar* / algo especial	
5. *pagar* / el almuerzo o la cena	
6. *prestar* / su carro	
7. *explicar* / la tarea de español	
8. *dar* / un abrazo	
9. *contar* / un chiste	

 Paso 2. Ahora, dile a la clase qué información tienes de tu compañero/a: *La tía de Lisa le mandó un paquete recientemente.* **o:** *Nadie le mandó un paquete recientemente.*

7-27 En la ciudad y en la carretera RECYCLES verbs in the preterit, city vocabulary, and professions.

 Paso 1. Con frecuencia, en la ciudad y en la carretera se reciben servicios de otras personas. Mira la lista que sigue y marca con una X la/s persona/s de quién/es recibiste un servicio.

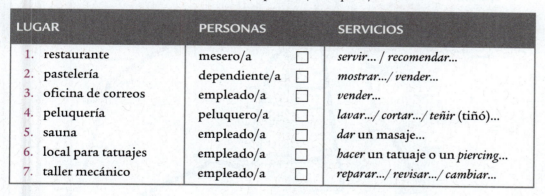

LUGAR	PERSONAS		SERVICIOS
1. restaurante	mesero/a	☐	*servir… / recomendar…*
2. pastelería	dependiente/a	☐	*mostrar…/ vender…*
3. oficina de correos	empleado/a	☐	*vender…*
4. peluquería	peluquero/a	☐	*lavar…/ cortar…/ teñir* (tiñó)…
5. sauna	empleado/a	☐	*dar* un masaje…
6. local para tatuajes	empleado/a	☐	*hacer* un tatuaje o un *piercing…*
7. taller mecánico	empleado/a	☐	*reparar…/ revisar…/ cambiar…*

Paso 2. Ahora, comuníquense los servicios que recibió cada uno/a de Uds. y mencionen dónde. Sigan el modelo y túrnense.

MODELO

E1: *El mesero* **me** *sirvió una copa de vino.*

E2: *¿Dónde?*

E1: *En el Restaurante ¡Con brío! ¿Y a ti?*

E2: *A mí, una mesera…*

Finalmente, díganle a la clase un servicio que Uds. dos recibieron: *Un peluquero* **nos** *cortó…*

7-27 ANOTHER STEP: For further writing practice, ask students to make a list of the services their classmate received, indicating who did them and where.

Tu mundo cultural

El transporte público

Para moverte por tu ciudad, ¿caminas, usas un medio de transporte o manejas tu carro?

La mayoría de las ciudades hispanas cuenta con medios de transporte urbano que permiten a los ciudadanos vivir sin necesidad de un carro. Un buen ejemplo es la capital de México, la segunda ciudad más poblada del mundo (22 millones de habitantes), por cuyo metro circulan diariamente unos cuatro millones de personas. Este metro cubre una extensión de 201.7 km (125.3 millas). Es uno de los metros más económicos del mundo (alrededor de 3 pesos = $0,22).

For an additional activity related to this cultural theme, see the PowerPoint slides on BCS and in *WileyPLUS*.

Meets ACTFL Standards 1.1, interpersonal speaking; 1.2, interpretive reading; 2.1, cultural practices; 2.2, cultural products; 3.2, acquiring information; and 4.2, cultural comparisons.

SISTEMA DE TRANSPORTE COLECTIVO
Red del Metro

Ciudad de México
Capital en Movimiento

SISTEMA DE TRANSPORTE COLECTIVO

Used by permission of Sistema de Transporte Colectivo, Red Metro Subway.

Roberto Velazquez/©AP/Wide World Photos

El metro es una solución ideal para una ciudad con problemas de tráfico y contaminación como ésta, pero su construcción no fue fácil. Durante las excavaciones se encontraron ruinas arqueológicas, que ahora se pueden ver en estaciones como la de *Pino Suárez*, y los restos de un mamut (10.000 a. C.), que se pueden observar en la estación *Talisman*. Allí también se encuentran murales interesantes como el de esta foto.

Este metro ofrece servicios para usuarios discapacitados: señalización en Braille y accesos para las personas en sillas de ruedas.

 ## ¿Qué aprendiste?

1. ¿Cuántas personas circulan por el metro de la ciudad de México diariamente?
   unos 4 millones de personas.
2. ¿Qué ventajas[1] ofrece este metro? Da ejemplos específicos.
   Es uno de los más económicos del mundo. Señalización en Braille y accesos para personas en sillas de ruedas.

 ## Actividad cultural

Imagínense que Uds. van a visitar la capital de México próximamente. Para familiarizarse con la ciudad, expliquen cómo se va a los siguientes destinos. Mencionen las líneas y los cambios necesarios. Antes de empezar, localicen en el mapa sus puntos de partida y sus destinos.

MODELO

Propósito:	visitar el Castillo de Chapultepec y pasear por el parque
Estación de salida:	Talismán (línea 4)
Estación de llegada:	Chapultepec (línea 1)

- Primero, **se toma** la línea 4 en Talismán **con dirección a** Santa Anita.
- **Se pasan** cuatro estaciones y luego **se llega** a Candelaria.
- **Se cambia**[2] a la línea 1 **con dirección a** Observatorio.
- **Se pasan** ocho estaciones y finalmente, **se llega a** Chapultepec.

Propósito	Estación de salida	Estación de llegada
a. visitar la Casa Azul, el Museo de Frida Kahlo, en *Coyoacán*	*Universidad* (línea 3)	*Coyoacán* (línea 3)
b. reunirse con unos amigos para tomar un café en la plaza principal de la capital	*Polanco* (línea 7)	*Zócalo* (línea 2)
c. tomar un autobús para visitar las Pirámides de Teotihuacán, situadas fuera de la capital	*Pino Suárez* (conexión entre la línea 1 y la línea 2)	*Autobuses del Norte* (línea 5)

 ## Contraste cultural

Comparen la vida en una cultura como la estadounidense, que depende del carro, con la cultura hispana en donde se depende más del transporte urbano. Comenten las consecuencias que esto tiene en las relaciones humanas, la economía, la salud[3], el ruido y la contaminación.

[1]advantages, [2]**Se...** One transfers, [3]health

Tu mundo en vivo

¡Videos en acción!

7.1 La plaza: el centro de la ciudad hispana

1. **Antes de ver el video** Mira los primeros 45 segundos del video 7.1 sin el sonido.

   ¿Qué imágenes ves? ¿Qué impresión tienes de esta plaza mexicana?

   Go to *WileyPLUS* to complete the **Mientras ves el video** activity.

2. **Después de ver el video** Relaciona las fotos con lo que dice cada persona.

A   B   C   D

©John Wiley & Sons, Inc.

   __C__ «El domingo... vinimos a la iglesia... vinimos a comer...»

   __D__ «Vine a la plaza para estar un poquito más tranquilo.»

   __A__ «El fin de semana pasado... visité las tiendas que están alrededor.»

   __B__ «Me gusta venir a la plaza... para ir al cine...»

7.2 El transporte público: el metro

1. **Antes de ver el video** ¿Qué idea tienes del metro de la Ciudad de México? ¿Crees que cuesta mucho? ¿Lo usan muchas personas?

   Go to *WileyPLUS* to complete the **Mientras ves el video** activity.

2. **Después de ver el video** ¿Tienes ahora una idea diferente de este metro que antes de ver el video? Explica tu respuesta.

¡Diálogos en acción!

7.1 ¿Cómo se llega al Museo Botero?

Verónica, una mexicana que está de visita en una ciudad que no conoce, le hace unas preguntas a un vendedor de periódicos.

Paso 1. Primero, mira las **Expresiones útiles** de la página A-7. Luego, escucha el diálogo dos veces y contesta las preguntas de tu profesor/a.

Paso 2. Mira la transcripción del diálogo (pág. A-18) y represéntalo con tu compañero/a. Túrnense. Ahora, vete a la página A-7 para completar los **Pasos 3** y **4**.

7.2 ¿Qué hiciste?

William y Magali son dos colegas cubanos que viven en Nueva York. Al regresar al trabajo el lunes, se preguntan sobre el fin de semana.

Go to *WileyPLUS* to listen to and practice this dialogue.

Diálogo 7.2 models the functions of narrating past events, informal greeting, and leave-taking. It practices regular preterit verbs, the irregular preterit of **ir** and **hacer**, and city vocabulary.

¡Lectura en acción!

Aviso público

Este aviso de la Secretaría de Turismo de la capital de México apareció en folletos[1] turísticos y periódicos de la ciudad.

Paso 1. Con sólo echarle un vistazo[2] a este aviso, contesta las siguientes preguntas.

1. ¿A quién se dirige? ¿Cómo lo sabes?

2. ¿Quién lo emitió[3]?

Paso 2. Piensa en la posible información que se puede transmitir en un aviso como este. Marca las respuestas más probables.

Información relacionada con...

☐ la seguridad del turista   ☐ interrupciones de tráfico
☐ atracciones turísticas   ☐ actividades culturales

> Used by permission of the Gobierno de Distrito Federal, Secretaría de Turismo.

ESTIMADO VISITANTE

La circulación vehicular en la avenida Paseo de la Reforma y en el Centro Histórico de la Ciudad de México ha sido bloqueada por un movimiento pacífico de resistencia civil derivado de nuestro reciente proceso electoral.

Por ello es importante informarle que:

- Estas zonas pueden ser recorridas a pie y de manera segura.

- Los hoteles, atractivos y servicios turísticos ubicados en estas zonas funcionan de manera normal.

- Para trasladarse, puede utilizar el Metro, el Metrobús, los autobuses del Sistema de Transporte Colectivo y taxis autorizados.

- Para mayor información:

  Información turística: 01 800 008 0909

  Teléfono de emergencia: 066

  www.mexicocity.gob.mx

¡Que su estancia en la Ciudad de México sea placentera!

GOBIERNO DEL DISTRITO FEDERAL
Secretaría de Turismo

Paso 3. Ahora, lee el aviso y responde a las siguientes preguntas para ver si entendiste la información más importante.

1. ¿Qué problema se comunica a quienes visiten la avenida Paseo de la Reforma y el Centro Histórico?

2. ¿Qué medios de transporte se recomiendan a los visitantes de esa zona? Marca las respuestas correctas.

   ☐ caminar   ☐ carros privados   ☐ autobuses   ☐ el metro   ☐ el metrobús
   ☐ taxis

3. Si alguien desea más información, ¿qué debe hacer?

4. ¿Por qué crees que la Secretaría de Turismo emitió este aviso?

[1]flyers, [2]glancing, [3]issued

Reading Strategy

Identifying the Target Audience and Point of View

Identifying the target audience of a passage and its point of view can assist you in understanding a reading, sometimes after only glancing at it.

Encourage students to think critically about the types of messages the *Secretaría de Turismo* is likely to promote in an announcement such as this one, as well as those that office would likely not advertise.

Meets ACTFL Standards 1.2, interpretive reading, and 3.2, acquiring information.

Remind students to focus on what they do understand from the text and to keep the context of the reading, the target audience, and the point of view of the *Secretaría de Turismo* in mind as they read the passage and answer the questions. Even without understanding a number of the individual words in the passage, they will likely be able to understand a great deal of the passage's message.

Meets ACTFL Standard 1.3, presentational writing.

You may want to assign a minimum number of words or sentences as appropriate for the ¡A escribir! task. Students can use the word count tool available in their word processing application to check the length of their work before and after the revising step of the writing process.

¡A conversar!

Meets ACTFL Standard 1.1, interpersonal speaking.

¿Un viaje estupendo o terrible?

En grupos de *tres*, un/a estudiante habla de un viaje estupendo o terrible que hizo. Los otros le hacen preguntas. Túrnense.

Preguntas:

- ¿Adónde fuiste?
- ¿Cómo fuiste (en carro, tren, etc.) y con quién/es?
- ¿Qué viste?
- ¿Qué comiste?
- ¿Qué hiciste?
- ¿Cuánto tiempo pasaste allí?
- ¿Te gustó?

¡A escribir!

Un día en la ciudad

Describe un día que pasaste en una ciudad. Incluye:

- el nombre de la ciudad y dónde está
- una descripción de lo que hay allí: tiendas, iglesias, museos, parques, etc.
- qué hiciste y quién fue contigo
- tus recomendaciones (mandatos de Ud.) *Visite...*

Writing Strategy

Using Sequencing Words to Connect your Sentences

When narrating a series of events or actions (see third bullet above), use words such as **primero**, **después**, **luego**, **más tarde**, **esa noche**, **finalmente**, etc., to convey the order of events and to smoothly transition from one activity to another.

Steps:

1. *Prewriting:* You already know about organizing your thoughts and jotting down lists and key words.

2. *Writing:* Begin with your topic sentence and then provide the descriptive content in a first draft, written without stopping to check spelling, punctuation, and grammar. Let the ideas flow. Where applicable, be sure to use sequencing words (see strategy).

3. *Revising:* As you read your composition, focus on its organization and appropriate division into paragraphs. Check your spelling and punctuation. **¡Ojo!** Have you (a) used the correct endings for the preterit tense, (b) used **ser** and **estar** correctly, and (c) checked for agreement between articles and nouns, and nouns and adjectives?

4. *Peer correction:* Exchange papers, circle errors or areas where there are questions, talk about them, and then make corrections on your own paper.

¡A investigar!

La exploración urbana

¿Quieren conocer las ciudades del mundo hispano? En comparación con el lugar donde viven, ¿cómo son las ciudades hispanas?

Paso 1. Trabajen en grupos de *tres*. Cada grupo va a escoger e investigar sobre ciudades diferentes.

Paso 2. Divídanse las tareas entre los miembros de su grupo. Usen las estrategias de investigación y recursos que ya conocen para preparar una breve presentación oral para su clase. Incluyan:

- Un plano[1] de las calles de la ciudad con los lugares de su presentación señalados en él
- Tres lugares públicos de la ciudad, como mínimo (plazas, parques, museos, etc.)
- Una descripción de los medios de transporte público disponibles
- Varias recomendaciones (usen los mandatos de Uds.) para quien quiera visitar la ciudad (*Visiten... porque... Tomen el autobús porque...*)

Trabajen juntos para organizar la información y hacer las correcciones necesarias. Creen un PowerPoint que tenga fotos y enlaces a videos y a páginas Web sobre los lugares. Añadan los URL de las fotos y cualquier otra información que requiera su profesor/a. Durante la presentación, túrnense para hablar.

Si no hay tiempo para las presentaciones en clase, creen presentaciones que tengan un comentario grabado y pónganlas en el blog o wiki de la clase.

Paso 3. Después de ver las presentaciones, comparen los lugares públicos de las ciudades que exploraron con los de las ciudades que conocen los otros estudiantes de la clase.

Meets ACTFL Standards 1.2, interpretive reading; 1.3, presentational speaking; 2.1, cultural practices; 2.2, cultural products; 3.2, acquiring information; and 4.2, cultural comparisons.

If your access to technology is limited, have the students create posters or transparencies to use as visual aids as they speak.

You may assign the appropriate Pasos of **¡A investigar!** for pairs or small groups to complete outside of class.

Research Strategy

Exploring Cities Online

Even when you can't travel abroad, you can still explore the cities of the Hispanic world via the Internet. Using the tools and strategies learned in previous chapters, you can find maps, photos and videos to experience cities visually. Try out Google Maps' "street view" feature: you can walk the streets as if you were there! By pairing search terms such as **museo, plaza, parque,** and **transporte público** with the names of cities, you can investigate cultural and leisure activities and find out how to go from one place to another within a city. With online resources, you will travel the neighborhoods without actually being there!

 Trivia

A ver cuánto sabes.

1. ¿Puedes nombrar cuatro países de América del Sur donde hay minerales?
   Bolivia, Chile, Ecuador, Perú
2. ¿En qué se basa la economía de Uruguay?
   carne, metales, textiles y productos agrícolas
3. ¿Y en qué se basa la economía de Paraguay?
   azúcar, carne, textiles, cemento, madera y minerales

If you don't know the answers, take a look at the front inside cover of the textbook. Try to respond in complete sentences.

[1]city map

Vocabulario: Capítulo 7

Escena 1

En el centro   *Downtown*
el banco *bank, bench*
el buzón *mailbox*
el cine *movie theater*
la entrada *entrance*
la esquina *corner*
la estación de tren *train station*
la fuente *fountain*
la iglesia *church*
la joyería *jewelry store*
la motocicleta *motorcycle*
el museo *museum*
la oficina de correos *post office*
la parada de autobús *bus stop*
el parque *park*
la pastelería *pastry shop*
el peatón *pedestrian*
la película *film*
la peluquería *hair salon*
el puente *bridge*
el quiosco *newsstand*
el rascacielos *skyscraper*
la salida *exit*
el semáforo *traffic light*
la tienda *store*
la tienda por departamentos *department store*
la zapatería *shoe store*

las noticias *news*
el periódico *newspaper*
la revista *magazine*

Instrucciones   *Directions*
a la derecha *to the right, on the right*
a la izquierda *to the left, on the left*
a una cuadra *a block away*
una cuadra/media cuadra *one block/ half a block*
recto/ derecho *straight ahead*
hasta llegar a… *until you arrive at…*

En el pasado   *In the past*
anoche *last night*
anteayer *day before yesterday*
ayer *yesterday*
el fin de semana pasado *last weekend*
el mes/ año pasado *last month/ year*
el viernes/ sábado… pasado *last Friday/ Saturday . . .*
la semana pasada *last week*
ya *already*

Escena 2

Por la ciudad   *In and around the city*
el boleto *ticket (movie/ theater/ bus/ plane/ train)*
el cajero automático *ATM*
el cheque *check*
la cuenta *account*
la estampilla *stamp*
la gente *people*
la licencia de manejar *driver's licence*
la multa *fine, ticket*
el paquete *package*
la tarjeta postal *postcard*

el país extranjero *foreign country*

Verbos y expresiones verbales   *Verbs and verbal expressions*
abrir *to open*
abrocharse el cinturón *to fasten one's seatbelt*
cerrar (ie) *to close*
cobrar *to cash, charge*
cortarse el pelo *to get a haircut, cut one's hair*
empezar (ie) *to begin, start*
encontrar (ue) *to find*
encontrarse (ue) (con) *to meet up (with)*
firmar *to sign*
hacer fila *to wait in line*
llevar *to take, carry*
mandar una carta *to mail/ send a letter*
mostrar (ue) *to show*
perder (ie) *to loose*
pintarse las uñas *to have one's nails painted, paint one's nails*

Verbos y expresiones verbales   *Verbs and verbal expressions*
cruzar *to cross*
doblar *to turn*
entrar (a/en) *to enter*
esperar *to wait for*
estacionar *to park*
pasarlo bien *to have a good time*
pasar por *to pass, go by*
seguir (i) *to continue, follow*

¡Que lo pases bien! *Have a good time!*

sacar *to take out*
teñirse (i) el pelo *to have one's hair colored, color one's hair*
terminar *to finish*

Escena 3

En la carretera   *On the road*
la autopista *highway, freeway*
el baño *restroom*
los frenos *brakes*
la gasolinera *gas station*
la llanta pinchada *flat tire*
la llave *key*
el ruido *noise*
la señal de tráfico *road sign*
el taller mecánico *auto repair shop*
el tráfico *traffic*
la velocidad máxima *maximum speed*

alto *stop (road sign)*
¡Qué mala suerte! *What bad luck!*

Verbos y expresiones verbales   *Verbs and verbal expressions*
cambiar *to change, exchange, transfer*
contar (ue) *to tell, narrate (a story or incident)*
devolver (ue) *to return (something)*
explicar *to explain*
funcionar *to work (machinery)*
llenar el tanque *to fill the tank*
parar *to stop*
preguntar *to ask*
prestar *to lend*
regalar *to give (as a gift)*
reparar *to repair, fix*
revisar (el aceite) *to check (the oil)*

Estoy en camino. *I'm on my way.*
Hay que… *One must/ should…*
Mi carro se descompuso. *My car broke down.*
¡Paren! *Stop!*

Capítulo 8

De compras

WILEY PLUS

Additional activities and **Autopruebas** for each **Escena** available online.

Gamma-Rapho/Getty Images, Inc.

Escena 1
En el centro comercial

GRAMÁTICA:
· More irregular verbs in the preterit

CULTURA:
El estilo de los hispanos

Escena 2
La ropa

GRAMÁTICA:
· Making equal comparisons
· Making unequal comparisons

CULTURA:
Diseñadores hispanos de fama internacional

Escena 3
Los aparatos electrónicos

GRAMÁTICA:
· Direct and indirect object pronouns
· Emphatic possessive adjectives and pronouns

CULTURA:
Los internautas hispanos

TU MUNDO EN VIVO

¡Videos en acción! De compras; La tecnología une a las familias

¡Diálogos en acción! Interacting with a Salesperson, Completing a Sales Transaction; Interacting with a Computer Repair Technician

¡Lectura en acción! Reading for the Main Idea

¡A conversar! Active Listening

¡A escribir! Providing Supporting Information

¡A investigar! Participating in Language Communities

LEARNING OBJECTIVES

By the end of this chapter you will be able to:
· Talk about purchasing clothes, shoes, accessories and gadgets.
· Carry out sales transactions.
· Talk about past events.
· Make comparisons.
· Talk about for whom something is done and to whom something is given.
· Indicate and emphasize possession.
· Describe styles and clothing preferences among Hispanics.
· Identify how Hispanics use the internet and social networks.

1 En el centro comercial

© John Wiley & Sons, Inc.

Las Mercedes

1. mall
2. clothes
3. jeans
4. t-shirt
5. shorts
6. sweatshirt
7. (baseball) cap
8. long pants
9. size
10. They don't fit me; **quedar bien/mal** to fit/ not fit
11. too (*adv.*)
12. I'm going to try them on; **probarse (ue)** to try on
13. credit / debit card
14. I would like (*polite variation of* **quiero**)
15. cheap, inexpensive
16. sales
17. to wear, carry
18. fashion
19. bag
20. gold and silver jewelry
21. necklace
22. chain
23. bracelet
24. earrings
25. price
26. (diamond) ring
27. expensive
28. to spend
29. cash
30. sneakers
31. sandals
32. boots
33. comfortable
34. (leather) jacket
35. purse, handbag
36. wallet
37. gloves
38. belt

You may use the PowerPoint slides of all scenes to present and practice the vocabulary.

¡La pronunciación!
Pay attention to the correct pronunciation of the Spanish **ll** (see P-4).

ani**ll**o co**ll**ar ta**ll**a bi**ll**etera

¡En acción!

For additional vocabulary practice, see PowerPoint slides on BCS and in *WileyPLUS*.

Present alternatives to vocabulary items at your discretion: **aretes/ pendientes/ zarcillos; camiseta/ franela/ remera.**

8-1 Write the five categories on the board. As each "winner" supplies answers, jot them down. Other students add their input as well.

8-1 Asociaciones

Paso 1. ¿Cuántas encuentran? Miren las páginas 258–259 y escriban como mínimo *tres* cosas o acciones que asocien con las siguientes palabras. Tienen *tres* minutos.

los *jeans*	el cuero	el oro	la zapatería	el precio
la camiseta				

Paso 2. Al terminar, la pareja con la lista más larga en cada categoría se la lee a la clase.

8-2 En el centro comercial Las Mercedes

¿Qué tiendas hay allí? ¿Qué se vende? Para saberlo, observen la escena de las páginas 258–259 y contesten las preguntas.

1. ¿Qué se vende en la tienda de ropa para jóvenes?
2. ¿Qué dicen los letreros[1] para indicar que la ropa está muy barata?
3. En los probadores, ¿cuántas chicas están probándose *jeans*? ¿Cómo reacciona cada una de ellas? ¿Les quedan bien los *jeans* a todas las chicas?
4. ¿Qué hacen o dicen los otros clientes y empleados que están en la tienda?
5. ¿Qué ropa lleva la chica que camina por el centro comercial con dos bolsas? Según una de las bolsas, ¿a qué tienda fue de compras?
6. ¿Qué clase de joyas se venden en la Joyería Ruiz? ¿Qué precio tiene el anillo de diamante? ¿Es caro o barato?
7. ¿Cómo paga el señor que habla con la cajera? ¿Qué dice?
8. ¿Qué clase de calzado[2] se vende en la Zapatería Fernández?
9. ¿Qué número de zapato necesita la señora? ¿Cómo son los zapatos que se está probando?
10. ¿De qué material son los artículos que se venden en la tienda Lara? ¿Qué accesorios tienen?

8-2 You may want to project the PowerPoint slide of the opener scene. Have the class describe the scene, or have small groups of students describe segments of it. Ask students to note when the **Perfumería Herrera** is open and closed, and to compare those days and times with the schedules of malls where they live.

8-2 PERSONALIZED QUESTIONS: ¿Adónde van Uds. de compras? ¿Qué clase de ropa o accesorios les gusta comprar?

¿SABES QUE...?

In some Hispanic countries, such as Ecuador and El Salvador, the U.S. dollar is the currency.

For additional practice on this grammar point, see PowerPoint slides on BCS and in *WileyPLUS*.

De paso

In *Capítulo 7* you learned that **llevar** means *to take* or *carry*:

Llevo a mi hijo al parque.   **Llevamos** los regalos a la fiesta.

Llevar also means *to wear* (clothing, shoes, jewelry, a hat, perfume,...) or *to carry a personal item* (a purse, wallet, umbrella,...).

to wear	Hoy Juan **lleva** unos *jeans* nuevos y botas de cuero.
	Doña Ana **lleva** unos aretes de oro y un cinturón rojo.
	¿Qué perfume **llevas** tú?
to carry	Luisa **lleva** una cartera azul y un paraguas porque va a llover.

[1]signs, [2]footwear

8-3 Las compras de tu compañero/a RECYCLES verbs in the preterit.

Paso 1. Entrevista a un/a compañero/a con las preguntas de la primera columna. Él/Ella responde siguiendo el modelo de la segunda columna, y tú escribes la información en la tercera columna. Después, cambien de papel.

Preguntas	Respuestas	Información escrita
1. ¿A qué tiendas **fuiste** recientemente?	*Fui a...*	*... fue a...*
2. ¿Con quién **fuiste**?		
3. ¿**Gastaste** mucho dinero?		
4. ¿**Te probaste** algo?		
5. ¿Te **quedó/quedaron** bien?		
6. ¿Qué **compraste**?		
7. ¿Cuánto **costó/costaron**?		
8. ¿Cómo **pagaste**?		
9. ¿Lo/La/Los/Las **devolviste**?		
10. ¿**Te** lo/la/los/las **pusiste** ya?		

Paso 2. Cambien de pareja y comuníquenle la información obtenida a otro/a compañero/a: *... fue a...* Luego, comparte con la clase una cosa que compró tu compañero/a, cuánto le costó, cómo lo pagó y si lo devolvió.

¡A escuchar! En el centro comercial Las Mercedes

Paso 1. Una madre y sus dos hijas van de compras al centro comercial. Escucha la conversación.

PLUS Go to *WileyPLUS* to complete **Paso 2** of this listening activity.

RubberBall/Alamy

Esta corbata[1] ecológica diseñada por *Agresearch* de Nueva Zelanda, es la primera corbata de hierba[2]. Se tiene que regar y fertilizar con nutrientes de calidad. Se recomienda no usarla cerca de animales rumiantes por peligro[3] a que se la coman. ¿Le queda bien la corbata? ¿Llevarías tú una corbata o una camisa de hierba? ¿Por qué?

[1]tie, [2]grass, [3]danger

8-3 For all paired activities, be sure students work with different partners each time. Either change seating periodically or divide the class in half and assign a number (1–10 and 1–10) to each student, with matching numbers forming pairs.

Palabras útiles
quedar *to fit*
   (it works like gustar)
Me queda/n bien.
   It fits me. / They fit me.
Me queda/n mal.
   It doesn't fit me. / They don't fit me.

The scripts and recordings for the ¡A escuchar! sections are included on the Book Companion Site (BCS) for instructors and in *WileyPLUS.*

Ask students to mention the advantages of a grass garment: easy to wash, do not need to iron it, etc.

Hoy Fabio pasa el día con su hija Olivia. Ahora están en la cocina hablando de lo que hicieron ayer.

—¿Qué **hiciste** ayer, papá?
—**Tuve** que estudiar para mis clases y luego fui al centro comercial.

—¿Compraste algo?
—No, no **pude**. **Estuve** allí poco tiempo.

—¿Pero... no viste ninguna sudadera bonita para mí?
—¡Ay, hija! No miré.

—Entonces, ¿no me **trajiste** nada del centro comercial?
—No, hijita. ¿No me **dijiste** la semana pasada que en tu ropero ya no cabe[1] toda tu ropa?

Go to *WileyPLUS* to review these grammar points with the help of the **Animated Grammar Tutorial** and **Verb Conjugator**. For more practice, go to the **Grammar Handbook**.

For additional practice on this grammar point, see PowerPoint slides on BCS and in *WileyPLUS*.

To introduce students to these irregular preterits used in context, have them take parts and read the **historieta** out loud. To check their comprehension and call their attention to the preterit forms, ask the following questions: 1. ¿Qué tuvo que hacer Fabio ayer? 2. ¿Por qué no pudo comprar nada en el centro comercial?

Help students become familiar with the preterit forms by calling out sample sentences and having individuals identify the infinitives: *Ayer hice ejercicio en el gimnasio. Quise hacer ejercicio dos horas, pero no pude. Estuve allí una hora y media, y luego tuve que irme.*

GRAMÁTICA

¡Manos a la obra!

Talking about what happened: More irregular verbs in the preterit

You have already learned the preterit of the irregular verbs **dar, ser, ir,** and **hacer** (see page 237). The following verbs follow a pattern similar to **hacer** (also shown below).

stem + irregular endings: -e, -iste, -o, -imos, -isteis, -ieron		
estar	**estuv-**	estuve, estuviste, estuvo, estuvimos, estuvisteis, estuvieron
poder	**pud-**	pude, pudiste, pudo, pudimos, pudisteis, pudieron
poner	**pus-**	puse, pusiste, puso, pusimos, pusisteis, pusieron
saber	**sup-**	supe, supiste, supo, supimos, supisteis, supieron
tener	**tuv-**	tuve, tuviste, tuvo, tuvimos, tuvisteis, tuvieron
hacer	**hic-**	hice, hiciste, hizo, hicimos, hicisteis, hicieron
querer	**quis-**	quise, quisiste, quiso, quisimos, quisisteis, quisieron
venir	**vin-**	vine, viniste, vino, vinimos, vinisteis, vinieron
decir	**dij-**	dije, dijiste, dijo, dijimos, dijisteis, dijeron*
traer	**traj-**	traje, trajiste, trajo, trajimos, trajisteis, trajeron

Let's look at the continuation of Fabio's conversation with his daughter:

—¿Dónde **estuviste** anoche, papá?   *Where **were** you last night, daddy?*
—Ernesto y Mario **vinieron** a verme.   *Ernesto and Mario **came** to see me.*
  Trajeron pizzas y refrescos.   *They **brought** pizzas and soft drinks.*

*Verbs whose stem ends in **j** add **-eron** instead of **-ieron.**

. . . y algo más   Different meaning in the preterit

The verbs **saber** *to know,* **querer** *to want,* and **poder** *to be able* convey a different meaning in the preterit than in the present.

saber	No lo **supe** hasta hoy.	*I didn't **find out** until today.*
querer	José **quiso** llamarla.	*José **tried** (and failed) to call her.*
	Ella **no quiso** hablar con él.	*She **refused** to speak with him.*
poder	**Pudimos** encontrar el carro.	*We **succeeded in** finding the car.*
	No pudimos encontrarlo.	*We **failed** (after trying) to find it.*

[1]fits

¡En acción!

¡Oye! ¿Qué pasó?

Escucha lo que le pasó a tu profesor/a anoche. Luego, di si las afirmaciones son ciertas o falsas.

8-4 ¿Qué hizo Ramón anoche? (See annotation for Actividad 8-4 & 8-5 on p. 264)

Paso 1. Anoche, Ramón y sus amigos, unos jóvenes de dieciséis años, organizaron una fiesta en casa de Ramón, aprovechando la ausencia de sus padres. Al volver los padres, la hermana de Ramón, alias "la espía", les contó lo que pasó. Lean lo que les dijo.

> Los amigos de Ramón **vinieron** a casa a las nueve de la noche ¡y **estuvieron** aquí hasta las dos de la mañana! **Trajeron** comida, bebidas y sus CD favoritos. **Pusieron** la música a todo volumen, bailaron e **hicieron** muchísimo ruido[1]. Por eso, los vecinos[2] no **pudieron** dormir, y unos policías que **supieron** de la fiesta por los vecinos **vinieron** a casa y nos **hicieron** muchas preguntas. Al llegar, uno de ellos **dijo**: "Jóvenes, es obvio que Uds. no **quisieron** perder un minuto durante la ausencia de sus padres." Ramón y sus amigos **tuvieron** que darles sus nombres a los policías y luego todos **se fueron** a sus casas.

Paso 2. Como es natural, Ramón tuvo que someterse a un largo interrogatorio de su padre. Hagan los dos papeles.

Padre	Ramón
1. ¿Quiénes **vinieron** a la fiesta?	1. *Bueno,… eh… mis amigos…*
2. ¿Cuánto tiempo **estuvieron** aquí?	2. …
3. ¿Qué **trajeron**?	3. …
4. ¿**Pusieron** Uds. la música muy alto?	4. …
5. ¿Qué más **hicieron** Uds.?	5. …
6. ¿Cómo **supieron** los policías de la fiesta?	6. …
7. ¿Qué **hicieron** los policías? ¿Qué les **dijeron**?	7. …
8. ¿Qué **tuvieron** que hacer Uds.?	8. …

8-5 Isidora, la famosa actriz, va de compras

Paso 1. Isidora va con frecuencia de compras con su novio a la tienda de ropa *¡Con brío!* Primero, *tres* estudiantes leen para la clase lo que dicen **Isidora, la dependienta** y **el novio**.

1. ISIDORA — ¡Me encanta la ropa de esta tienda! Me gustaría probarme estos *jeans*.
DEPENDIENTA — ¡Cuánto lo siento, señorita, pero no tenemos tallas tan pequeñas!

2. ISIDORA — ¡Qué lástima, porque esos *jeans* son divinos!
DEPENDIENTA — Señorita, pruébese estas camisetas y esos pantalones cortos; son la última moda.

3. ISIDORA — Me los compro. ¡Ay! ¡No veo la tarjeta de crédito en mi cartera!
Gracias, mi amor.
NOVIO — No te preocupes, Isidora, mi amor; yo lo pago todo con mi tarjeta.

4. ISIDORA — ¡Hasta pronto! ¡Su tienda es fantástica!
NOVIO

[1]noise, [2]neighbors

¡Oye! Write on the board: **llamar a la puerta** *to knock on the door;* **hubo…** *there was….*

Guión para ¡Oye!
Ayer, a las nueve de la noche, alguien llamó a la puerta de mi casa (*make knocking sound*). Abrí la puerta y vi a un policía que me **dijo** con un tono muy serio:
—Esta tarde hubo un crimen en esta calle y quiero hacerle a Ud. unas preguntas.
—Bueno —le **dije**.
—¿Dónde **estuvo** Ud. a las tres de la tarde? —me preguntó.
—**Estuve** en mi oficina —le contesté.
—¿A qué hora salió Ud. de la oficina? —me preguntó.
—**Quise** salir a las cuatro, pero no **pude**. Salí a las cinco —le **dije**.
—¿**Vino** directamente a casa? —me preguntó.
—No. **Tuve** que hacer unas compras y no llegué a casa hasta las seis de la tarde —le contesté.
—Bueno, gracias —me **dijo**, y se fue.
Nunca **supe** lo que pasó en mi calle, ni por qué **vino** el policía.

Comprensión para ¡Oye!
1. El policía vino a mi casa para hacerme unas preguntas. ¿Cierto o falso? *Cierto*
2. Le dije que estuve en casa a las tres de la tarde. *Falso*
3. Le dije que estuve en la oficina a las tres de la tarde. *Cierto*
4. Le dije que quise salir de la oficina a las tres, pero que no pude. *Falso*
5. Le dije que vine directamente a mi casa. *Falso*
6. Le dije que tuve que hacer unas compras. *Cierto*
7. El policía me contó lo que pasó esa tarde. *Falso*
8. Nunca supe lo que pasó en mi calle. *Cierto*

(continúa)

8-4 Have three students play the roles of parents and child and perform for the class. Encourage the parents to "grill" their son, being very stern in their inquiries.

8-4 ANOTHER STEP: Students make their own confessions. In groups of three, they talk about what they once did when their parents were not at home.

8-5 For *Paso 1,* ask three students to read the dialogue with expression. Students may complete *Paso 2* individually or in pairs, with answers reviewed by the instructor.

Paso 2. Ahora, completen el *e-mail* que la dependienta, gran admiradora de la actriz, envió a su mejor amiga. Usen los verbos que siguen:

| decir | encontrar | estar | irse | poder | probarse | querer | tener | venir |

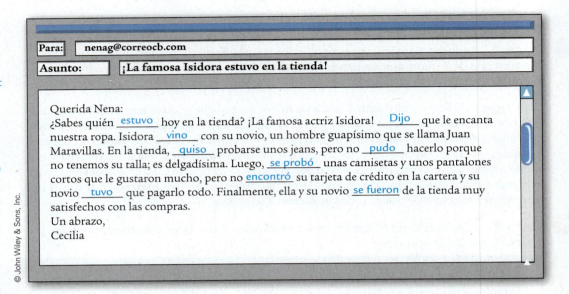

Para: nenag@correocb.com

Asunto: ¡La famosa Isidora estuvo en la tienda!

Querida Nena:

¿Sabes quién __estuvo__ hoy en la tienda? ¡La famosa actriz Isidora! __Dijo__ que le encanta nuestra ropa. Isidora __vino__ con su novio, un hombre guapísimo que se llama Juan Maravillas. En la tienda, __quiso__ probarse unos jeans, pero no __pudo__ hacerlo porque no tenemos su talla; es delgadísima. Luego, __se probó__ unas camisetas y unos pantalones cortos que le gustaron mucho, pero no __encontró__ su tarjeta de crédito en la cartera y su novio __tuvo__ que pagarlo todo. Finalmente, ella y su novio __se fueron__ de la tienda muy satisfechos con las compras.

Un abrazo,

Cecilia

© John Wiley & Sons, Inc.

8-6 Un sondeo de la clase

Paso 1. Camina por la clase y hazle cada pregunta a un/a estudiante diferente. Apunta el nombre de la persona que responde y la información obtenida. Tienes *seis* minutos.

Option: Students complete the activity in groups of 4-6 students.

8-6 For *Paso 2,* ask follow-up questions such as ¿Quién tuvo que trabajar la semana pasada? ¿Quién pudo descansar el fin de semana pasado? Elicit responses from several students.

Preguntas	Nombre	Información obtenida
1. **¿Tuviste** que trabajar la semana pasada? ¿Dónde **trabajaste?** ¿Cuántas horas?	*Luis*	*Sí, (No, no)* **tuvo** *que...*
2. **¿Pudiste** descansar el fin de semana pasado? ¿Qué **hiciste?**		
3. **¿Hiciste** ejercicio en el gimnasio la semana pasada? ¿Cuánto tiempo **pasaste** allí?		
4. **¿Quisiste** dormir más esta mañana?		
5. **¿Viniste** a la universidad en carro o en autobús?		
6. **¿Le dijiste** algo a tu profesor/a al entrar a clase?		
7. **¿Trajiste** hoy la tarea terminada?		
8. **¿Dónde pusiste** tus cosas después de entrar?		

Paso 2. Con la información obtenida, contesten las preguntas de su profesor/a.

8-7 Un robo en la Joyería Ruiz

¡AVISO! Ayer, viernes, alguien robó un anillo con un diamante de tres quilates[1] en la Joyería Ruiz. Hoy, sábado, el/la detective Rascacielos interroga a los tres sospechosos[2]: **Candelario Vega, Gertrudis Salazar** y **Humberto Ramos.** ¿Quién será el/la culpable?

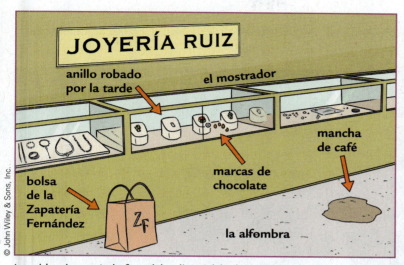

JOYERÍA RUIZ

anillo robado por la tarde

el mostrador

mancha de café

marcas de chocolate

bolsa de la Zapatería Fernández

ZF

la alfombra

© John Wiley & Sons, Inc.

La evidencia, según la foto del policía (el/la detective la estudia con cuidado)

8-7 Allow the detectives in each group one minute to study the "evidence" while the other three students determine which "suspect" they are each going to be. *The suspects close their books.* For *Paso 2*, have each of the detectives say who in their group is the likely robber and why. Note that there is no predetermined selection—the detective will make his/her decision based on the information provided by the suspects.

You may want to project the PowerPoint slide of this scene when detectives present their findings.

Paso 1. En grupos de *cuatro,* hagan los papeles de el/la detective y de los tres sospechosos. Ahora comienza el interrogatorio; los sospechosos contestan y la detective apunta la información.

Preguntas de el/la detective	Respuestas de Candelario Vega	Respuestas de Gertrudis Salazar	Respuestas de Humberto Ramos
1. Sabemos que Ud. **estuvo** en la Joyería Ruiz ayer. ¿En qué otras tiendas **estuvo** por la tarde?	*Yo* **estuve**...	*Yo...*	*Y yo...*
2. ¿Qué le gusta beber? ¿Y qué **bebió** ayer por la tarde?			
3. ¿Qué **comió** ayer por la tarde? ¿Le gusta el chocolate?			
4. Antes de ir a la joyería, ¿qué **compró** Ud.? ¿Perfume? ¿Zapatos? ¿Ropa?			
5. ¿Cuándo **supo** del robo?			

Paso 2. El/la detective decide quién es el posible autor del robo y se lo dice a la clase explicando sus razones. Finalmente, la clase vota por el/la detective que dio las razones más convincentes.

[1]carats, [2]suspects

Go to *WileyPLUS* to see the video related to this reading.

Tu mundo cultural

El estilo de los hispanos

La forma de vestir y el arreglo personal[1] varían de una cultura a otra. ¿Conoces algunas de las idiosincrasias hispanas?

Hay hispanos que prefieren llevar las camisetas y los *jeans* muy planchados.

Para muchos hispanos, particularmente los mayores, vestirse bien es importante, incluso para actividades tan corrientes como ir al mercado.

En los países hispanos la mayoría de las niñas llevan aretes desde que son bebés, tal como se ve en la fotografía. Y probablemente esta bebé lleva también colonia, otra costumbre muy extendida en esa cultura.

Prendas y accesorios hispanos fáciles de encontrar en EE. UU.

Muchos hispanos, aunque residan en EE. UU., no abandonan algunos de los aspectos típicos de su cultura en lo que se refiere al arreglo personal o al vestir, como se observa en la foto.

Las joyas de oro de estilo muy elaborado se llevan mucho entre los hispanos de Estados Unidos. Tanto las chicas como los chicos llevan pulseras, cadenas de oro y medallas religiosas. En los centros comerciales de EE. UU. hay joyerías especializadas en esta clase de trabajo en oro.

[1]**arreglo...** personal appearance

McLatchy-Tribune/Getty Images, Inc.

Courtesy Conchita Lucas

George Doyle/StockByte Platinum/Getty Images, Inc.

La guayabera es la prenda masculina del Caribe por excelencia. Es también popular en las regiones tropicales de EE. UU. La usan hombres tanto jóvenes como mayores para ocasiones informales o fiestas elegantes. Generalmente, es de lino o de algodón y lleva bordados, pliegues[1] y bolsillos[2].

El poncho, prenda de abrigo usada en toda América Latina y esencial para el gaucho[3] argentino, sirve de inspiración para una nueva moda en EE. UU., tal como se observa en la foto de estas jóvenes estadounidenses.

Algo que le llama la atención al extranjero que visita una ciudad hispana es la abundancia de zapaterías y tiendas de artículos de cuero que hay en sus calles y centros comerciales. EE. UU. importa grandes cantidades de zapatos y artículos de cuero de países como España, Argentina o Costa Rica.

¿Qué aprendiste?

1. ¿Qué aspectos del arreglo personal son comunes en muchos hispanos? Den ejemplos.
   Respuestas posibles: Las niñas llevan aretes; se usa colonia; la abundancia de zapaterías.
2. ¿Qué prendas o joyas hispanas se encuentran fácilmente en EE. UU.? ¿Dónde?
   Joyas de oro elaboradas, ponchos y guayaberas. En zonas tropicales.
3. ¿Qué artículos hispanos de cuero se importan a EE. UU.? ¿De qué países se importan?
   Zapatos. De España, Argentina o Costa Rica.

Actividad cultural

Paso 1. Hagan dos listas con lo siguiente:

- la ropa, accesorios, zapatos y costumbres hispanas relativas al vestir y al arreglo personal

- la ropa y los accesorios típicos de los jóvenes en tu universidad; o la ropa y los accesorios típicos de tus colegas en el trabajo (escojan una de las dos)

Paso 2. Luego, compárenlas con la otra pareja para ver si son similares.

Contraste cultural

Imaginen que van a pasar un año en un país hispano. Comenten a qué aspectos del arreglo personal y forma de vestirse se van a adaptar Uds. más fácilmente. Luego, digan a cuáles les va a costar más trabajo hacerlo y por qué.

[1]pleats, [2]pockets, [3]cowboy

La ropa

¿Qué llevan?

WILEY PLUS

Pronunciación: Practice pronunciation of the chapter's new vocabulary in *WileyPLUS*.

VOCABULARIO

En casa

Mamá, mi camiseta está ⁵*sucia* y no tengo otra ⁶*limpia*.

2. la ropa interior
1. los calcetines
3. las pantimedias
4. el/la pijama

En la calle

9. el gorro (de lana)
¡Qué frío!
13. el paraguas
8. la bufanda
7. el abrigo
10. el suéter
11. tener frío
12. el impermeable

En la universidad

14. la blusa (de algodón)
16. la camisa (de manga larga)
15. la falda (corta)
Ser o no ser, esa es la cuestión. W. Shakespeare

En la oficina

17. los lentes
19. la corbata
18. el traje
20. el vestido

En la playa

21. tener calor
23. las gafas de sol
24. el sombrero
25. el bikini
22. el traje de baño
¡Qué buena idea!
Me voy al agua. ¿Vienes conmigo?

© John Wiley & Sons, Inc.

1. socks 2. underwear 3. panty hose 4. pajamas 5. dirty 6. clean 7. coat 8. scarf 9. (wool) cap 10. sweater 11. to be cold 12. raincoat 13. umbrella 14. (cotton) blouse 15. (short) skirt 16. (long-sleeve) shirt 17. glasses; **lentes de contacto** contact lenses 18. suit 19. tie 20. dress 21. to be hot 22. swimsuit 23. sunglasses 24. hat 25. bikini

¡En acción!

For additional vocabulary practice, see PowerPoint slides on BCS and in *WileyPLUS*.

8-8 Ropa diferente para cada ocasión

¿Qué van a ponerse? Apunten la ropa y los accesorios apropiados para cada ocasión. Al terminar, compartan la información con la clase.

1. una cena de gala en el hotel Ritz
2. un picnic en el campo
3. una reunión de negocios
4. un día de esquí en Portillo, Chile

8-8 Write the four occasions on the board. As students provide responses, a secretary writes the information on the board.

8-9 You may want to project the PowerPoint slide of the scenes and have the class describe each vignette.

8-9 ¿Qué llevan?

Para saberlo, observen las escenas de la página 268 y contesten las preguntas.

1. ¿Qué ropa llevan las personas que están en casa? ¿Qué problema tiene la niña?
2. ¿Qué ropa y accesorios llevan las personas que están en la calle? ¿Qué tal está el clima? ¿Quién tiene frío?
3. En la universidad, ¿qué ropa llevan los estudiantes que están sentados? ¿Y los que están de pie[1]?
4. ¿Qué ropa llevan la señora y la joven que trabajan en la oficina? ¿Y el señor?
5. ¿Qué llevan las dos personas que están en la playa? ¿Quién tiene calor? ¿Qué van a hacer?

8-9 PERSONALIZED QUESTIONS: ¿Qué ropa les gusta a Uds. llevar cuando están en casa? ¿Y en la universidad? ¿Y en el trabajo?

8-10 ANOTHER STEP: Remind students that when it is winter in the northern hemisphere, it is summer in the southern.

8-10 ¿Qué van a empacar? RECYCLES the verb *ir* and weather expressions.

Paso 1. Uds. han decidido pasar el mes de julio en un país hispano para practicar español, pero cada uno/a en un país y hemisferio diferente. Antes de empacar, cada uno/a consulte el mapa que está detrás de la cubierta del libro para decidir a qué país va a ir. Luego, pongan (escriban) en la maleta[2] lo que van a llevar.

Paso 2. Ahora, tu compañero/a y tú háganse preguntas para informarse sobre **a)** el país adónde va a viajar su compañero/a, **b)** el clima que hace allí en julio **c)** y las cosas que va a empacar. Túrnense. Después, informen a la clase sobre los planes de su compañero/a.

8-10 You may want to project the slide for this activity in class.

LA MALETA

© John Wiley & Sons, Inc.

8-11 ¿Quién es?

Escribe *una* oración para describir la ropa y accesorios que lleva un/a estudiante de la clase, pero no digas quién es. Usa el vocabulario de las páginas 258–259 y 268. Dale la descripción a tu profesor/a. Luego, él/ella lee las descripciones y la clase adivina[3] quién es.

MODELO

Profesor/a: *Lleva unos jeans, una camiseta blanca y una gorra azul.*

Estudiante: *¡Es David!*

¡A escuchar! ¿Qué ropa llevar?

Paso 1. Adrián se va de viaje de negocios a Santiago de Chile. Su esposa Laura le ayuda a escoger la ropa que se va a poner durante su estancia en ese país. Escucha la conversación.

WILEY PLUS Go to *WileyPLUS* to complete **Paso 2** of this listening activity.

[1]de... standing, [2]suitcase, [3]guesses

Fabio y Olivia miran en el ropero de Olivia.

© John Wiley & Sons, Inc.

For additional practice on this grammar point, see PowerPoint slides on BCS and in *WileyPLUS*.

To introduce students to equal comparisons used in context, have them take parts and read the **historieta** out loud. To check their comprehension and call their attention to the comparisons, ask the following questions: 1. **¿Cuánta ropa tiene Olivia?** 2. **¿Cómo bailan y cantan Olivia y su amiga Susana?**

To introduce comparisons of equality, give an example like this: **Barack Obama tiene dos hijas. George Bush tiene dos hijas también. Entonces, Obama tiene tantas hijas como Bush.** Write **tantas... como** as you speak, and an = sign to make your meaning obvious. If you can find two students in class with the same number of pens/pencils or other items, use them as additional examples, e.g. **John tiene tantos lápices como Mary. John es tan alto como Jim.** Elicit opinions from students by saying things like, **En mi opinión, Beyoncé canta tan bien como Christina Aguilera. George Clooney es tan guapo como Brad Pitt. ¿Sí o no?**

PLUS Go to *WileyPLUS* to review this grammar point with the help of the **Animated Grammar Tutorial**. For more practice, go to the **Grammar Handbook**.

GRAMÁTICA

¡Manos a la obra!

Making equal comparisons

2

- When we compare things, as Olivia does when talking about her friend Susana, we look for similarities or differences between them. To compare things that are roughly equal, Spanish uses **tan** or **tanto/a/os/as** with **como**.

> **tan** + *adjective* or *adverb* + **como** = *as... as*

Olivia es **tan** bonita **como** Susana.   Su ropero es **tan** grande **como** el de Susana.
Es **tan** alta **como** su amiga.   Susana no canta **tan** bien **como** Olivia.

> **tanto/a** + *noun* + **como** = *as much... as*
> **tantos/as** + *noun* + **como** = *as many... as*

Olivia tiene **tantos** zapatos **como** Susana.   Quiere tener **tanta** ropa **como** ella.

Lleva **tantas** sudaderas **como** su amiga.   Susana se prueba **tantos** vestidos **como** Olivia.

- To compare *actions*, **tanto como** is used.

> *verb* + **tanto como** = *as much as*

Olivia baila **tanto como** Susana, pero no canta **tanto como** ella.
Olivia no va de compras **tanto como** su amiga.

De paso

Tan can also mean *so:*

    ¡Esa corbata es **tan** barata!   *That tie is **so** cheap!*

Tanto can also mean *so much,* and **tantos/as** can mean *so many:*

    ¡Él habla **tanto**!   *He talks **so much**!*
    ¡Tienes **tantas** camisetas!   *You have **so many** T-shirts!*

For additional practice on this grammar point, see PowerPoint slides on BCS and in *WileyPLUS*.

¹outfit, ²**¡Que...** Not at all!

¡En acción!

¡Oye! ¿Es verdad o no?

Escucha las comparaciones que hace tu profesor/a. Luego responde diciendo si son verdad o no.

8-12 ¡Comparaciones!

Compárate con una persona con quien tengas algo de lo siguiente en común. Luego, comparte tus observaciones con tu compañero/a.

1. características personales: **Soy tan... como...**
2. cosas que tienen: **Tengo tanto/a/os/as... como...**
3. actividades que hacen: **Yo** (verbo)**... tanto como...**

8-13 Irma e Imelda   RECYCLES descriptive adjectives.

Paso 1.   Irma e Imelda son gemelas[1]. Según la fotografía, hagan *cinco* comparaciones. Usen **tan... como** y *cinco* adjetivos que sean apropiados.

Jose Luis Pelaez/© Corbis

antipática   fea
divertida   rubia
bonita
inteligente   simpática
seria
vieja   morena   joven

MODELO
inteligente
Irma es tan inteligente como Imelda.

Paso 2.   Ahora, miren los roperos tan ordenados de Irma e Imelda: **E1** observa el de Irma y **E2,** el de Imelda. Digan lo que hay en cada uno y hagan comparaciones usando **tantos/as... como**. Túrnense.

MODELO

E1:   *Hay dos paraguas en el ropero de Irma.*

E2:   *También hay dos paraguas en el ropero de Imelda.*

E1:   *Imelda tiene **tantos** paraguas **como** Irma.*

Irma   Imelda

© John Wiley & Sons, Inc.

[1]twins

¡Oye! Fill in with names of students. After each statement, ask: **¿Es verdad o no?**

Guión para ¡Oye!
1. Soy tan fuerte como... (*show your muscles*) ¿Es verdad o no?
2. Soy tan alto/a como...
3. Soy tan simpático/a como...
4. Soy tan joven como...
5. Soy tan guapo/a como...
6. Soy tan trabajador/a como...
7. Soy tan organizado/a como...
8. Soy tan divertido/a como...

8-12   Get feedback from the class one category at a time, eliciting responses from as many students as possible.

8-13   For *Paso 1,* allow students a minute or two to think of comparisons, then elicit responses from the class. To review answers for *Paso 2,* you may want to project the PowerPoint slide of Irma's and Imelda's closets and have the entire class now make the comparisons, with input from as many students as possible.

Jennifer va de compras con Fabio. Buscan un regalo para la prima de Jennifer.

Estoy buscando un regalo para mi prima. ¿Te gusta esta mochila?

No mucho. No es **tan** bonita **como** esa, pero esa es mucho **más** cara **que** esta.

Sí, es verdad, y no quiero gastar **más de** 20 dólares.

¿Te gusta esta camiseta? Es **más** barata **que** la mochila y es muy bonita.

¡Ay, sí! ¡Me encanta! La voy a comprar para mi prima.

¡A Jennifer también le va a quedar muy bien!

© John Wiley & Sons, Inc.

Go to *WileyPLUS* to review this grammar point with the help of the **Animated Grammar Tutorial**. For more practice, go to the **Grammar Handbook**.

For additional practice on this grammar point, see PowerPoint slides on BCS and in *WileyPLUS*.

To introduce students to unequal comparisons used in context, have them take parts and read the **historieta** out loud. To check their comprehension and call their attention to the comparisons, ask the following questions: 1. ¿Cómo son las dos mochilas? 2. ¿Cómo es la camiseta?

Use students to illustrate unequal comparisons: **Mónica es más alta que la profesora. Jared es menos sentimental que Juan.** If you deem it appropriate and to bring the concept to life, have two volunteers arm wrestle. The class then declares: **... es más fuerte que...**

To reinforce the use of **de** before numbers, ask different students how much money they have on them (¿**Marta, tienes más/menos de diez dólares? ¿más/menos de doce?...**) until the amount is determined.

Inform your students that **mayor** and **menor** are also used to refer to sizes: **una talla mayor/menor** *a larger/smaller size*.

GRAMÁTICA

¡Manos a la obra!

Making unequal comparisons

3

- To compare *things* that are not equal, highlighting their differences, as Jennifer and Fabio do while shopping, Spanish uses

> **más/ menos** + *adjective/ adverb/ noun* + **que**
> *more / less (fewer)... than*

Esa mochila es **más** cara **que** esta.   *That backpack is **more** expensive **than** this one.*

Encontré un regalo **más** rápidamente **que** tú.   *I found a gift **more** quickly **than** you.*
En esta tienda hay **menos** camisetas **que** en esa.   *In this store there are **fewer** t-shirts **than** in that one.*

- To compare unequal *actions*, Spanish uses

> verb + **más/ menos que***
> *... more/ less than*

Jennifer gasta **más que** Fabio.   *Jennifer spends **more than** Fabio.*

*Before a number, **de** replaces **que**: Jennifer no pagó más **de** 20 dólares por la camiseta.

- Some adjectives and adverbs have irregular comparative forms. These forms do not use **más** or **menos.**

> bueno/a, bien → **mejor**   malo/a, mal → **peor**
> *good, well*   *better*   *bad, badly*   *worse*

Esta billetera es **buena**, pero esa es **mejor**.   *This wallet is **good**, but that one is **better**.*
Aquel centro comercial es **peor** que este.   *That mall is **worse** than this one.*
¿Se viste **mejor** o **peor** que su prima?   *Does she dress **better** or **worse** than her cousin?*

- To compare age, **mayor que** *older than* and **menor que** *younger than* are used.

Jennifer es **menor que** su prima.   *Jennifer is younger than her cousin.*
Fabio es **mayor que** Jennifer.   *Fabio is older than Jennifer.*

¡En acción!

¡Oye! Las mujeres son más inteligentes, ¿no?

Escucha las siguientes generalizaciones y para cada una di si, en tu opinión, son verdad o no.

8-14 ¡A comparar!

Paso 1. ¿Sabes cómo es tu compañero/a comparado con su mejor amigo/a? Hazle las preguntas de la primera columna. Luego, él/ella responde según el modelo de la segunda y tú apuntas la información en la tercera columna. Después, cambien de papel.

(Si el resultado de la comparación es que son iguales, usen **Tan... como.**)

Preguntas	Respuestas	Información escrita
1. ¿Eres **más** alto/a o **menos** alto/a **que** tu mejor amigo/a?	*Soy **más/ menos...***	*... es **más/ menos...***
2. ¿Eres **más** inteligente o **menos** inteligente **que** él/ella?		
3. ¿Eres **más** perezoso/a o **menos** perezoso/a **que** él/ella?		
4. ¿Hablas español **mejor** o **peor que** él/ella?		
5. ¿Eres **mayor** o **menor que** él/ella?		
6. ¿Te vistes **más** a la moda o **menos** a la moda **que** él/ella?		

Paso 2. Comuníquenle toda la información obtenida a otro/a compañero/a.

8-15 Un desfile de modas en YouTube   RECYCLES equal comparisons.

Paso 1. Uds. están mirando un desfile de modas en YouTube. Describan con todo detalle lo que lleva cada modelo.

Soraya lleva un vestido blanco, unos guantes negros,…

Paso 2. Ahora, hagan como mínimo ocho comparaciones entre la ropa, los accesorios y los cinco modelos. Usen comparativos de *igualdad* y *desigualdad* y los adjetivos de la lista, más otros de su elección.

MODELO

E1: *El vestido de Soraya es **más** largo **que** el vestido de Olivia.*

E2: *Las joyas de Penélope son **tan... como.**…*

caro/ barato	feo/ bonito
cómodo/ incómodo	formal/ informal
corto/ largo	moderno/ clásico

© John Wiley & Sons, Inc.

¡Oye! After each statement, ask: **¿Es verdad o no?**

Guión para ¡Oye!

1. La clase de español es más difícil que la clase de matemáticas. ¿Es verdad o no?
2. Las mujeres de esta clase son más inteligentes que los hombres.
3. Los hombres de esta clase son más trabajadores que las mujeres.
4. Las mujeres, en general, gastan menos dinero que los hombres.
5. Los hombres hispanos bailan mejor que los hombres estadounidenses.
6. Los carros americanos son mejores que los japoneses.
7. El dinero es más importante que el amor.
8. Vestirse bien (estar a la moda) es más importante que sacar buenas notas.

8-15 You may want to use the PowerPoint slide to review answers. *Option:* Turn the activity into a competition, to see which pair can come up with the longest list.

Go to *WileyPLUS* to review this grammar point with the help of the **Animated Grammar Tutorial**. For more practice, go to the **Grammar Handbook**.

For additional practice on this grammar point, see PowerPoint slides on BCS and in *WileyPLUS*.

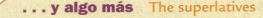

. . . y algo más   The superlatives

In Spanish, superlatives (*the most..., the least..., the tallest..., the best..., the worst...*) are expressed as follows:

> **el/ la/ los/ las** (*noun*) + **más/ menos** + *adjective or adverb* + **de** (*in*)...

Ella compró **el** vestido **más** caro **de** la tienda.
She bought the most expensive dress in the store.

> **el/ la/ los/ las** + **mejor(es)/ peor(es)** (*noun*) + **de**...

Esta es **la mejor** tienda **del** centro comercial. Aquella es **la peor** tienda **de** todas.
This is the best store in the mall. That one is the worst store of all.

el vestido:
 largo/corto
las joyas:
 caras/baratas
los zapatos:
 altos/bajos
la ropa:
 formal/informal
el/ la modelo:
 guapo/a /feo/a
el hombre/ la mujer:
 elegante

8-16   ¿Quién es el más/ menos… de todos?

En grupos de *tres*, vuelvan a ver el desfile de YouTube de la página 273 y comenten cuál es *el más o menos... de todos*, según las categorías de la lista del margen. Usen los superlativos. Túrnense.

MODELO

E1:   *El vestido de Soraya es **el más** largo **de** todos.*

E2:   *Pues, la ropa de …*

8-17   ¡El mejor o la mejor!

Paso 1.   En grupos de *tres*, escriban los nombres de *tres* personas o cosas que se distingan por ser las mejores o las peores en las siguientes categorías. Luego, compárenlas según el modelo. Un/a secretario/a apunta la información, según lo que decida el grupo.

MODELO

equipos de fútbol americano: bueno/ mejor/ el mejor → *Indianápolis, Chicago, Pittsburgh*

E1:   *El equipo de Chicago es **bueno**.*

E2:   *Creo que el equipo de Indianápolis es **mejor**.*

E3:   *En mi opinión, el equipo de Pittsburgh es **el mejor de** los tres.*

E1:   *No estoy de acuerdo. Creo que el equipo de... es **el mejor de** todos.*

1. equipos de béisbol: bueno/ mejor/ el mejor

2. centros comerciales: grande/ más grande/ el más grande

3. películas: divertida/ más divertida/ la más divertida

4. restaurantes: malo/ peor/ el peor

Paso 2.   Los secretarios comparten con la clase los resultados y algunos voluntarios los escriben en la pizarra. Luego, voten para decidir cuál es el/la mejor en cada categoría.

8-18   ¡Compra en línea!

Paso 1.   El próximo mes tienes una cena de negocios en Puerto Rico con un cliente importante. Por eso, decides comprar en línea algunas de las cosas que te vas a poner allí. Primero, mira la lista de lo que necesitas. Luego, escoge en el catálogo de la tienda *¡Con brío!* lo que más te guste de cada cosa.

To present the superlatives, write the formulas on the board and ask students to respond to the following: **¿Quién es el/la estudiante más rubio/a de la clase? ¿Quién es el/la más joven? ¿Quién es el/la más divertido/a? ¿Cuál es la tienda de ropa más cara de la ciudad? ¿Y la más barata? ¿Cuál es el libro más intrigante del año? ¿Cuál es la peor película del año? ¿Cuál es el peor carro de todos?**

8-17 Write the six categories on the board and have volunteers write the information as the secretaries provide it, one category at a time. Then the class votes, and the results are announced: **... es el mejor equipo de todos.**

	Lo que necesito en San Juan	
Para la cena de negocios:		*Para la playa o el barco:*
un traje / un vestido	unas gafas de sol	un traje de baño/ bikini
unos zapatos/ unas sandalias		unos zapatos/ unas sandalias

Tienda en línea ¡Con brío!

1.

Trajes de baño de dama   Trajes de baño de caballero

  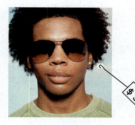

$ 60 $ 42 $ 39 $ 45

Photos: L: Westend61/
Getty Images, Inc.;
LC: Masterfile;
RC: Randi Sidman-
Moore/Masterfile;
R: Masterfile

2.

Gafas de sol de dama   Gafas de sol de caballero

$ 55 $ 90 $ 75 $ 94

Photos: L: David Lees/
Stone/Getty Images,
Inc.; LC: Altrendo/Getty
Images, Inc; RC: Ryan
McVay/Stone/Getty
Images, Inc.; R: Leland
Bobbe/The Image Bank/
Getty Images, Inc.

3.

Vestidos de dama   Trajes de caballero

$ 105 $ 129 $ 300 $ 240

Photos: L: iRepublic/
Masterfile; LC:
Gabrielle Revere/The
Image Bank/Getty
Images, Inc.; RC: Janet
Kimber/The Image
Bank/Getty Images,
Inc.; R: Bruce Laurance/
Taxi/Getty Images, Inc.

4.

Zapatos de dama   Zapatos de caballero

$ 62 $ 29 $ 35 $ 68

Photos: L: iStockphoto;
LC: Dorling Kindersley/
Getty Images, Inc.;
RC: iStockphoto;
R: iStockphoto

$ 80 $ 45 $ 145 $ 170

Photos: L: iStockphoto;
LC: iStockphoto;
RC: iStockphoto;
R: iStockphoto

 Paso 2.   Ahora, pregúntense qué cosas escogieron. Al responder, usen el superlativo, teniendo en cuenta lo siguiente: (**precio**) más caro/ más barato; (**estilo**) apropiado/ bonito/ práctico/ elegante/ cómodo… Añadan también otras razones para justificar su selección.

MODELO

E1: *¿Qué traje de baño pediste?*

E2: *Pedí el… porque es **el más barato de** los dos; es más bonito que el otro y me gusta el color.*

de tacón alto
  high heeled
de tacón bajo
  low heeled
zapato plano *flat shoe*

doscientos setenta y cinco   **275**

Tu mundo cultural

Meets ACTFL Standards
1.1, interpersonal speaking;
1.2, interpretive reading;
2.2, cultural products; and
4.2, cultural comparisons.

For an additional activity related to this cultural theme, see the PowerPoint slides on BCS and in *WileyPLUS*.

Diseñadores hispanos de fama internacional

¿Piensas que la moda que se lleva en los países hispanos es muy diferente de la moda que se lleva en EE. UU.?

El arte de la moda no siempre tiene el reconocimiento[1] que se da a otras artes, pero es indudable que para ser diseñador de ropa se requieren talento y cualidades artísticas que no todos poseen. Los cinco diseñadores hispanos que se mencionan a continuación ejercen gran influencia en múltiples esferas de la vida en EE. UU.

Carolina Herrera

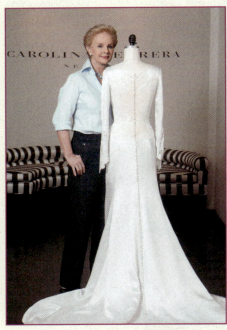

Summit Entertainment/

Vestido de novia diseñado por Carolina Herrera para Bella Swan en Amanecer[2], la última película de la saga de *Crepúsculo*[3] interpretada por la actriz Kristen Stewart. Carolina Herrera ha diseñado también trajes para Jacqueline Onassis, Caroline Kennedy, Renée Zellweger, Salma Hayek y varias esposas de presidentes de EE. UU. En el año 2004 recibió en Nueva York el premio[4] de la *Council of Fashion Designers of America* (CFDA) al mejor diseñador o diseñadora del año. El famoso artista Andy Warhol pintó tres retratos de Carolina Herrera. Esta famosa diseñadora nació en Venezuela.

Isabel Toledo

Chip Somodevilla/Getty Images

Modelo diseñado por Isabel Toledo. Michelle Obama lo llevó el 20 de enero de 2009, a la inauguración de su esposo como presidente de Estados Unidos. Isabel Toledo es una diseñadora cubana que estudió en *Parson's School of Design,* en Nueva York, ciudad donde reside.

Narciso Rodríguez

WireImage/Getty Images, Inc.

Modelo del diseñador Narciso Rodríguez. Este estadounidense de padres cubanos nació en Nueva Jersey y es diplomado de *Parson's School of Design* en Nueva York. Fue director de Cerruti en París y ha recibido dos años consecutivos el premio de la CFDA al mejor diseñador o diseñadora del año en la categoría de ropa de mujer. Diseñó el traje de novia de Carolyn Bessette, la esposa de John Kennedy Jr. Otras de sus clientas son Claire Danes, Julianna Margulies y Salma Hayek (en la foto). Narciso Rodríguez diseñó también el vestido negro y rojo que Michelle Obama llevó el 4 de noviembre de 2008, cuando su esposo fue elegido a la presidencia de Estados Unidos.

[1]recognition, [2]Breaking Dawn, [3]Twilight, [4]prize

Custodio y David Dalmau

WireImage/Getty Images, Inc.

WireImage/Getty Images, Inc.

Los hermanos españoles Custodio y David Dalmau, creadores de la marca **Custo Barcelona**, diseñan ropa para hombre y mujer. Con diseños de estilo innovador y original estos hermanos han obtenido fama internacional. Residen en Barcelona, pero sus tiendas se encuentran en varios continentes. Sus camisetas han aparecido en series televisivas como *Friends* y *Suddenly Susan*, y en MTV. Actrices de cine como Julia Roberts, Penélope Cruz, Sandra Bullock y Natalie Portman, y los músicos Dixie Chicks, Sarah McLachlan y LeAnn Rimes son algunos de sus clientes.

 ## ¿Qué aprendiste?

1. ¿De dónde son y dónde residen ahora los cinco diseñadores mencionados?
   Carolina Herrera, Venezuela. Isabel Toledo, Cuba. Narciso Rodríguez, EE. UU. Custo y David Dalmau, España.
2. ¿Cuáles son algunos de los clientes famosos de estos diseñadores?
   Respuestas posibles: Michelle Obama, Julia Roberts, Salma Hayek...
3. ¿Qué diseñadores hispanos han creado ropa para Michelle Obama? ¿Para qué acontecimientos importantes la diseñaron?
   Isabel Toledo, para la inauguración de su esposo como presidente de EE. UU. Narciso Rodríguez, para la elección de su marido a la presidencia de EE. UU.

 ## Actividad cultural

Uds. son expertos en moda y tienen que hacer un comentario sobre la noche de los *Óscar* o la de los premios MTV, donde se vieron los cinco modelos de las fotografías. Compárenlos en cuanto a colorido, elegancia y estilo. Digan cuál prefieren y por qué.

Contraste cultural

Piensen en los vestidos, chaquetas o pantalones de su ropero. Compárenlas con la ropa de Custo Barcelona y digan qué elementos tienen o no en común.

¿SABES QUE...?

Inditex, the Spanish group that owns the trademark **Zara**, among others, is the world leader in textile fashion and its founder is the 10th richest man in the world. It has 5,544 stores in 77 countries on four continents. Its recent international expansion has been such that it has captured the attention of professionals in the business world. Their success is studied at Harvard Business School, London Business School, the Indian School of Business, and others.

¿SABES QUE...?

Dominican designer **Oscar de la Renta** is the 2011 recipient of the Couture Council Artistry of Fashion Award, the highest award of the American Fashion industry.

Pronunciación:
Practice pronunciation
of the chapter's new
vocabulary in *WileyPLUS*.

VOCABULARIO

1. ad 2. electronic devices/ equipment 3. DVD/VCR player 4. speakers 5. flat-screen (TV) 6. to plug in 7. to turn on 8. remote control 9. to turn off
10. brand 11. support; **apoyar** to support 12. laptop 13. keyboard 14. (wireless USB) mouse 15. cell phone 16. cordless phone 17. answering machine
18. digital camera 19. to take photos 20. I would like/love to... 21. headphones

Note:* **el DVD/ el CD is said **el devedé/ el cedé**; **los DVD/ los CD** is said **los devedés/ los cedés.**

¡En acción!

8-19 Aparatos electrónicos

Paso 1. Observa los aparatos electrónicos y digitales de la página 278 y escribe en cada columna la información que corresponda, de acuerdo a tu situación, necesidades o preferencias.

Ya tengo:	Me gustaría tener:	No me interesa tener:
Una computadora		

Paso 2. Ahora, compara tu lista con la de un/a compañero/a.

8-20 En la tienda Tecnología Siglo XXI

¿Les gustan las tiendas de alta tecnología? Para saber lo que hay en esta, observen la escena de la página 278 y contesten las preguntas.

1. ¿Qué aparatos electrónicos y digitales se ven en el estante que está al fondo de la tienda? ¿Y en las dos mesas?

2. Según los anuncios que se ven por la tienda, ¿qué servicios ofrece?

3. ¿Qué hay en el estante que está a la derecha de la entrada a la tienda?

4. ¿Qué está haciendo cada persona que está en la tienda? ¿Y el joven que entra a la tienda?

5. Según el póster a la izquierda de la entrada, ¿qué se debe hacer para conectarse a la alta tecnología? Según el anuncio que está cerca de la entrada, ¿qué está en oferta?

For additional vocabulary practice, see PowerPoint slides on BCS and in *WileyPLUS*.

You might want to remind your students that the verb **interesar** works like **gustar**.

8-20 You may want to use the PowerPoint slide of the scene and have the class describe it, one area at a time.

8-20 PERSONALIZED QUESTIONS: De los aparatos electrónicos que se venden en la tienda Siglo XXI, ¿cuáles tienen ya? ¿Cuáles les gustaría tener? ¿Cuáles son los más útiles? ¿Por qué?

Smartphones are also called **teléfonos inteligentes.**

Matthew Lloyd/Getty Images, Inc.

Las tabletas como este iPad son aparatos multiusos que permiten leer los e-mails, participar en las redes sociales, escuchar música y usar aplicaciones para divertirse y aprender. ¿Crees que una tableta es un instrumento útil para aprender idiomas? ¿Por qué?

AFP/Getty Images, Inc.

¿Te gustaría tener un iPhone como este, o ya lo tienes?

¡Este globo es **para** ti!

¿**Para** mí? ¡Gracias!

De paso

Para and **por** are commonly used in the context of shopping.

PARA = *for, destined for, to give to...*
Compré un iPod **para** mi tía.
La cámara digital es **para** mí.

POR = *for, in exchange for...*
Pagué 99 dólares **por** el iPod.
La compré **por** 200 dólares.

 For additional practice on this grammar point, see PowerPoint slides on BCS and in *WileyPLUS*.

8-21 ¡Me encantan los aparatos electrónicos!

Paso 1. Uno/a de Uds. entra a la tienda Tecnología Siglo XXI (p. 278) para comprar *tres* regalos y habla con la dependienta. Hagan los papeles de cliente y dependienta y completen la conversación.

Dependienta: ¿En qué puedo servirle?

Cliente: Quisiera comprar _____ para _____.

Dependienta: Este(a)/ Estos(as) _____ de aquí es/son muy _____.

Cliente: ¿Cuánto cuesta/n?

Dependienta: ¿Para usted? ¡Sólo _____ dólares!

Cliente: A ver, ... también me gustaría comprar...

Palabras útiles
¡Qué bien! *Great!*
¡Genial! *Nice!*
¿Qué más? *What else?*

Paso 2. Cambien de pareja y háganse preguntas acerca de lo que compraron. Digan también cuánto pagaron por cada artículo.

MODELO

E1: *¿Qué compraste?*

E2: *Compré una computadora portátil **por** seiscientos dólares.*

E1: *¡Genial! ¿**Para** quién la compraste?*

E2: ***Para** mi hermano. ¿Y tú, qué compraste?*

8-21 Have two students role-play *Paso 1* for the class, followed by another pair buying a different gift. For *Paso 2*, get feedback from the entire class.

¡A escuchar! Siglo XXI, tu tienda

Paso 1. Un hijo encuentra en el periódico un anuncio de la nueva tienda de alta tecnología y se lo lee a su padre. Escucha la conversación.

PLUS Go to *WileyPLUS* to complete **Paso 2** of this listening activity.

Ysenia, Mabel y Jennifer, de compras, en el centro comercial.

Jennifer, ¡me encanta tu camiseta! ¿Cuándo **te la** compraste?

Me la compró Fabio ayer.

¿Oíste? **Se la** compró Fabio.

Sí, nos llevamos muy bien. **Te la** presto cuando quieras, Ysenia.

¿De verdad **me la** dejas? Tengo una cita este sábado con un chico que me gusta y no tengo nada que ponerme.

¡Entiendo, Ysenia! **Te la** doy mañana. Y devuélvemela cuando quieras.

Te lo agradezco, Jennifer. ¡Qué buena amiga eres!

Go to *WileyPLUS* to review this grammar point with the help of the **Animated Grammar Tutorial**. For more practice, go to the **Grammar Handbook**.

GRAMÁTICA

¡Manos a la obra!

Direct and indirect object pronouns together

4

You have studied direct objects (p. 154) and indirect objects (p. 245) separately.

- To combine them, as in Jennifer's conversation with her friends, place the indirect object pronoun first: **indirect + direct** (ID).

  Fabio **me la** compró.   *Fabio bought it for me.*

- In a negative statement, **no** precedes both object pronouns.

  Mi madre **no me la** compró.   *My mother did not buy it for me.*

- The indirect object pronouns **le** and **les** change to **se** when they precede the direct object pronouns **lo, la, los, las.**

  > **le** (*or*) **les + lo, la, los las → se + lo, la, los, las**

  —¿**Le** prestaste la camiseta a Ysenia?   *Did you lend the t-shirt to Ysenia?*
  —Sí, **se** la presté.   *Yes, I lent it to her.*

  —¿Quién **les** mostró a ellas el iPod?   *Who showed them the iPod?*
  —La dependienta **se** lo mostró.   *The clerk showed it to them.*

- Double object pronouns (like single ones) are placed *before* a conjugated verb, or may be *attached* to an infinitive or present participle.

  Se la doy.   Voy a dár**sela**.   Estoy dándo**sela**.

- They are always placed *before* negative commands, and *after* affirmative commands.

  No **me la** devuelvas inmediatamente.   Devuélve**mela** cuando quieras.

For additional practice on this grammar point, see PowerPoint slides on BCS and in *WileyPLUS*.

To introduce students to direct and indirect object pronouns used in context, have them take parts and read the **historieta** out loud. Ask the following questions: 1. ¿Quién le compró la camiseta a Jennifer? 2. ¿Cuándo le va a dar Jennifer la camiseta a Ysenia?

To demonstrate the position of two object pronouns, write the words **mandé, lo,** and **te** on separate sheets of paper. Also write the words **quiero** and **mandar** (to substitute for **mandé**) on two other sheets. Give the first three sheets to three students who, with the help of classmates, position themselves correctly. Then replace the student holding **mandé** with two others holding **quiero** and **mandar.** The students determine the correct order. *Note:* Provide a red marker to write in the accent as needed. Highlight the two options for placing the pronouns in the latter sentence. To demonstrate **le → se**, replace **te** in the sentences above with **le** (written on a separate sheet of paper, with **se** written on the back). Repeat the pronoun positioning process, showing how **se** replaces **le.**

¡En acción!

¡Oye! ¿Me lo prestas?

Primero, su profesor/a les pide que le den ciertas cosas. Luego, contesten las preguntas.

For **¡Oye!** instructions and **Guión** see p. 282.

8-22 "El empleado del mes"   RECYCLES direct objects and **pedir** in the preterit.

Paso 1.   Hoy, los clientes de la tienda Tecnología Siglo XXI comentan maravillas sobre "el empleado del mes". Completa lo que dijeron los clientes.

1. **Le** pedí un iPhone 4S, iy *me lo* vendió con descuento!
   Tania

2. **Le** llevé mi computadora portátil porque no funcionaba, iy *me la* reparó inmediatamente!
   Juan

3. **Le** pedimos unos DVD, iy *nos los* buscó rápidamente!
   Linda y Tomás

4. **Le** pedimos dos cámaras digitales, iy *nos las* dio más baratas!
   Sergio y Lucía

5. **Le** pedí _____, iy *me* ___ _____!
   Yo

Paso 2.   Ahora, cuéntale a tu compañero/a quién pidió cada cosa y qué hizo el empleado:
*Tania **le** pidió al empleado un iPhone 4S iy el empleado **se lo** vendió con un descuento!* Luego, tu compañero/a reacciona: *¡Qué empleado tan eficiente!* Túrnense.

8-22   After reviewing answers for *Paso 1,* you may want to provide cues for *Paso 2:* 2. Juan le llevó su... 3. Linda y Tomás le pidieron... 4. Sergio y Lucía le pidieron... 5. Yo le pedí...

(See p. 281) **¡Oye!**
Walk around the
classroom spotting
items that you would like
to borrow. If it is a ring or
another accessory that the
student is wearing, and he/
she agrees to lend it to you,
have the student take it off
and give it to you.

Guión para ¡Oye!
1. Me encanta esa
chaqueta. ¿Me la prestas?
2. Me encanta ese collar.
¿Me lo prestas?
3. … ese anillo, … esa
pulsera, … esa gorra
de béisbol, … esa bolsa,
… ese suéter, … esa
mochila, … ese celular, etc.

**Comprensión para
¡Oye!**
Hold up each item and ask
to whom it belongs. Then
ask if you should return it
to the owner. If the class
says yes, return the item
and thank the student.
If the class says no,
pretend to keep the
item, saying **¿Es para
mí? ¡Gracias!**
1. ¿De quién es esta
chaqueta? *Es de…* ¿Se la
devuelvo? ¿Sí o no?
2. ¿De quién es este collar?
etc.

8-23 Ask several pairs
of students to present
the question/answer
sequences. **ANSWERS:**
1. (modelo). 2. Se lo
presto a… (o) No se lo
presto a nadie. 3. Se las
regalo a… (o) No se las
regalo a nadie. 4. Se los
mando a… (o) No se
los mando a nadie. 5. Se
la doy a… (o) No se la doy
a nadie. 6. Se la preparo
a… (o) No se la preparo
a nadie. 7. Se la explico a…
(o) No se la explico a nadie.
8. Se la presto a… (o) No
se la presto a nadie.

8-24 Bring a bag to
class to put the slips of
paper in. Make sure students
do not write their names
on the papers. For *Paso 2*,
to keep students attentive,
ask follow-up questions:
**¿Quién le regaló a Sandra
el collar?,** etc.

8-23 ¿Para quién lo haces?

¿Son Uds. personas generosas o no? Háganse preguntas para saberlo. Túrnense.

MODELO

E1: *¿A quién **le** prestas dinero?*   E2: ***Se lo** presto a mi hermano.*   **o:** *No **se lo** presto a nadie.*

1. ¿A quién **le** prestas **dinero**?
2. ¿A quién **le** prestas tu carro?
3. ¿A quién **le** regalas flores?
4. ¿A quién **le** mandas mensajes?

5. ¿A quién **le** das propina?
6. ¿A quién **le** preparas comida?
7. ¿A quién **le** explicas la tarea?
8. ¿A quién **le** prestas tu ropa?

8-24 Regalos secretos

Paso 1.   Hoy cada estudiante le va a dar un regalo a una persona de la clase. Apunta en un papelito la descripción detallada de un regalo y ponlo en la bolsa que va pasando tu profesor/a. Luego, toma un papelito (tu regalo) de la bolsa y camina por la clase preguntando hasta saber quién te lo regaló.

MODELO   Each time that you give a piece of paper to a student say: **¡Es un regalo para** ti! and ask each student to react enthusiastically saying **¿Para mí?**

E1: *¿**Me** regalaste tú este celular de la marca…?*

E2: *Sí, yo **te lo** regalé.* (Dale las gracias y dile que te encanta.)

o: *No, yo no **te lo** regalé.* (Sigue preguntando a otra persona de la clase.)

Paso 2.   Tu profesor/a quiere saber qué regalos recibieron algunos de los estudiantes. Contesta según el modelo.

MODELO

Profesor/a: *Sandra, ¿qué recibiste?*

Sandra: *Un collar de oro.*

Profesor/a: *¿Quién **te lo** regaló?*

Sandra: ***Me lo** regaló Tina.* (Sandra le dice a Tina) *Gracias, por el collar de oro, Tina.*

8-25 En todas partes hay gente generosa

Paso 1.   Anoche robaron en su apartamento y Felipe perdió todas sus cosas. Hoy, llega a clase sin nada y Uds. le prestan algunas cosas. Un/a estudiante hace el papel de Felipe.

MODELO

Profesor/a: *¿Quién puede prestar**le** algo?*

E1: *Yo puedo prestar**le** mi iPod.* (El/La profesor/a escribe la palabra iPod en la pizarra.)

Profesor/a: *Excelente. ¿Quién puede prestar**le** otra cosa?*

Paso 2.   Un día después, Felipe, que ya ha recuperado[1] sus cosas, quiere devolverles a sus compañeros las que le prestaron. El problema es que no recuerda quién se las prestó[2].

MODELO

Felipe: *(Ve en la lista de la pizarra "iPod" y pregunta:) ¿Quién **me** prestó este iPod?*

E2: *Carlos **te lo** prestó.*

o:

E1: *Yo **te lo** presté.*

[1]ha… has recovered, [2]se… lent them to him

WILEY PLUS

Go to *WileyPLUS* to review this grammar point with the help of the **Animated Grammar Tutorial**. For more practice, go to the **Grammar Handbook**.

Ysenia tiene que comprar un celular para su madre.

El celular de mamá no funciona; y ahora quiere uno como **el mío**.

Pero **el tuyo** es muy antiguo, ¿no?

¿Antiguo? ¡¡Nooo!! Me lo compré hace 4 años[1].

¡Ja, ja, ja! Ysenia, me haces reír. ¿Sabes que ya no[2] venden modelos como **el tuyo**?

Mabel tiene razón. ¿Por qué no buscas uno como **los nuestros**? ¡Son chéveres[3]!

¡Porque **los suyos** son más caros! Mi madre, ¡seguro que lo pierde! Ella y yo somos muy despistadas.[4]

Perdón, señorita, ¿es **suyo** este celular?

¿¿Ven?? ¡Se lo dije!

© John Wiley & Sons, Inc.

GRAMÁTICA

¡Manos a la obra!

5

Expressing possession: Emphatic possessive adjectives and pronouns

You have learned how to express ownership or possession by using **de +** *person* and by using the possessive adjectives **mi, tu, su,...** (see pages 49 and 76) as in these examples based on the three friends' conversation at the mall.

Es el teléfono **de Jennifer.**   Es **mi** celular.

To stress the idea of ownership (*who* owns something), the emphatic possessives are used.

mío/a, míos/as	*mine*	Este celular no es **mío.**
tuyo/a, tuyos/as	*yours*	¿Es **tuyo**?
suyo/a, suyos/as	*his/ hers/ yours*	Las camisetas son **suyas.**
nuestro/a, nuestros/as	*ours*	Estos teléfonos no son **nuestros.**
vuestro/a, vuestros/as	*yours*	¿Son **vuestros**?
suyo/a, suyos/as	*theirs/ yours*	Dicen que la cámara digital es **suya.**

- Emphatic possessives agree in gender and number with the object possessed, and not with the possessor or owner:

  Los videos son **suyos.**   *The videos are **hers**.*
  Las camisetas son **mías.**   *The t-shirts are **mine**.*
  ¿Es **tuyo** ese celular, Ysenia?   *Is that cell phone **yours**, Ysenia?*
  Esa computadora es **nuestra.**   *That computer is **ours**.*

- The emphatic possessive adjectives follow the noun to indicate *of mine, of yours*, etc.

  Fui de compras con dos amigas **mías.**   *I went shopping with two friends **of mine**.*

- Emphatic possessive pronouns take the place of nouns and are generally used with definite articles. The article is often omitted when the pronoun follows the verb **ser.**

  –¿No quieres un celular como **los nuestros**? –No, **los suyos** son caros.

  –¿Es **tuya** esa computadora? –No, no es **mía.** Es de Mabel.

- To clarify who owns something in the third person, **de +** *pronoun* may be used.

  El celular es **suyo.** El celular es **de ella (de él, de Ud., de ellas, de ellos, de Uds.).**

[1]**hace...** four years ago, [2]no longer, [3]awesome, [4]absent-minded

For additional practice on this grammar point, see PowerPoint slides on BCS and in *WileyPLUS*.

To introduce students to emphatic possessives used in context, have them take parts and read the **historieta** out loud. Ask the following questions:
1. ¿Qué quiere la madre de Ysenia?
2. ¿Cómo es el celular de Ysenia? ¿Y los de sus amigas?

To illustrate gender and number changes in emphatic possessives, place four items (masculine singular and plural, feminine singular and plural) on your desk: **el libro, la mochila, los cuadernos, las gafas de sol.** Point to each and say that it is yours: **Este libro es mío, ¿verdad? Y esta mochila es mía..., estos cuadernos...** Then place the items on the desks of several students and say **Ahora vamos a ver de quiénes son estas cosas. Ese libro es suyo, ¿verdad? Y esa mochila es...** (allow the class to complete the sentences), **esos cuadernos son... y esas gafas de sol son....**

¡En acción!

¡Oye! ¡Son míos!

Observa lo que pasa y luego, contesta las preguntas de tu profesor/a para decidir de quién es cada cosa.

8-26 Los regalos de Navidad

Paso 1. Es la mañana del 25 de diciembre y hay muchos regalos en la casa de los Roldán. Decide qué regalo es el más apropiado para cada persona. Luego, escribe lo que dice cada uno/a.

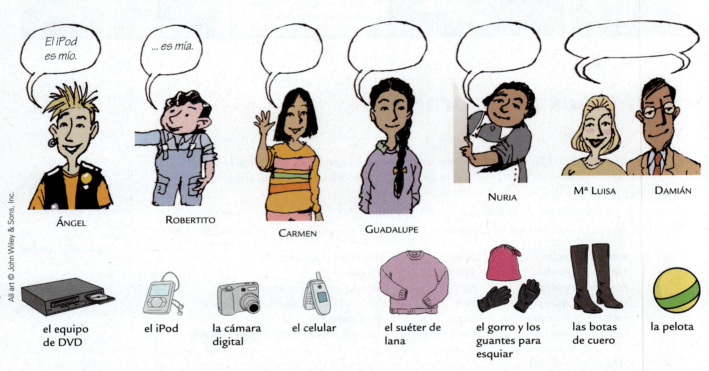

¡Oye! Bring to class four items in a bag—for example, **bufanda, guantes, gorro de lana, gafas de sol.** Choose an extroverted student as your partner. It is best to practice the dialogue once before the actual "performance."

For the *Actividad 8-26* annotation, see p. 285.

(For **Guión para ¡Oye!**, see below.)

Guión para ¡Oye!
1. *Profesor/a*: Esta bufanda es mía. (*You hold it up.*)
Estudiante: No es suya, ¡es mía! (*He/She grabs it from you.*)
Profesor/a: ¡Le digo que es mía! (*You grab it back.*)
Estudiante: Bueno, es suya. (*Sometimes the student yields, and sometimes not.*)
2. *Profesor/a*: Estos guantes son míos. (*You hold them up.*)
Estudiante: No son suyos, ¡son míos!
Profesor/a: ¡Son míos!
Estudiante: ¡No! ¡Son míos!
Follow the same procedure with the remaining items.
(continues on p. 285)

Paso 2. Según lo que se lee en las burbujas[1] que completaron Uds., digan qué regalo le corresponde a cada persona de la familia. En algunos casos, es posible que haya diferencias de opinión entre Uds. Túrnense.

MODELO

E1: *¿Qué dice Ángel?*

E2: *Dice que el iPod es* **suyo.**

8-27 ¡Rebajas increíbles en la tienda Siglo XXI!

Hoy, "viernes negro", hay precios únicos y los clientes, muy impacientes, compiten por llevarse las mejores gangas[2]. Primero, completen los diálogos (pág. 285) con el singular o plural de **mío/a, tuyo/a, nuestro/a,** según corresponda. Luego, hagan los siguientes papeles:

[1]bubbles, [2]bargains

284 doscientos ochenta y cuatro

CAPÍTULO 8   DE COMPRAS

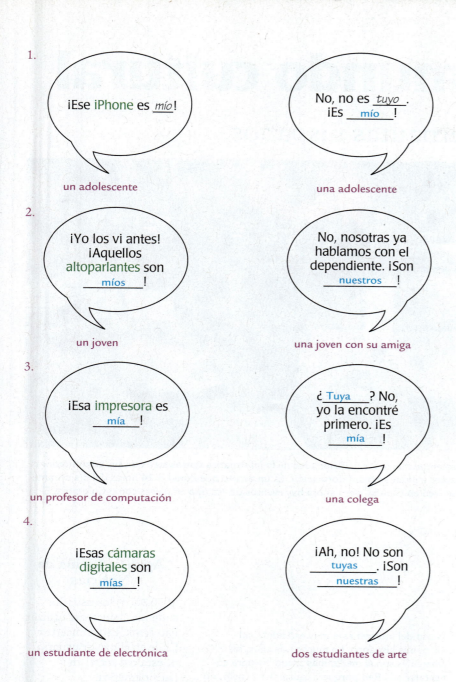

1.

¡Ese iPhone es _mío_!

un adolescente

No, no es _tuyo_. ¡Es _mío_!

una adolescente

2.

¡Yo los vi antes! ¡Aquellos altoparlantes son _míos_!

un joven

No, nosotras ya hablamos con el dependiente. ¡Son _nuestros_!

una joven con su amiga

3.

¡Esa impresora es _mía_!

un profesor de computación

¿_Tuya_? No, yo la encontré primero. ¡Es _mía_!

una colega

4.

¡Esas cámaras digitales son _mías_!

un estudiante de electrónica

¡Ah, no! No son _tuyas_. ¡Son _nuestras_!

dos estudiantes de arte

(from p. 284)

Comprensión para ¡Oye!
1. ¿De quién es esta bufanda? ¿Es mía o es suya (*pointing to student*)? *Es suya* (students respond pointing to you).
2. ¿De quién son estos guantes? ¿Son míos o son suyos?
3. ¿De quién es este gorro de lana? ¿Es mío o es suyo?
4. ¿De quién son estas gafas de sol? ¿Son mías o son suyas?

8-26 You may want to review answers for *Paso 1* using the PowerPoint slide of the illustrations. Expect answers to vary.

8-27 To confirm answers, ask pairs to take turns reading each set of statements. Encourage students to be expressive!

8-28 Objetos perdidos

(Para poder hacer esta actividad, cada estudiante tiene que poner una cosa en el escritorio de su profesor/a: zapatos, suéter, chaqueta, cuaderno, mochila,...)

Pronto termina el semestre y en la oficina de tu profesor/a se han acumulado muchas cosas perdidas. Ayúdale a localizar a los dueños[1] contestando sus preguntas.

MODELO

Profesor/a:	*Álex, ¿es **tuyo** este anillo?*
Estudiante:	*No, no es **mío**.*
Profesor/a (a toda la clase):	*¿Saben Uds. de quién es?*
Otro/a estudiante (apuntando a la persona dueña del objeto):	*Es **suyo**. (o) Es de...*

[1]owners

8-28 In some instances, say that a particular item is yours and, if possible, put it on. If someone in the class says **¡No es suyo! ¡Es mío!** return it to that person.

Go to *WileyPLUS* to see the video related to this reading.

For an additional activity related to this cultural theme, see the PowerPoint slides on BCS and in *WileyPLUS*.

Meets ACTFL Standards 1.1, interpersonal speaking; 1.2, interpretive reading; 2.1, cultural practices; and 4.2, cultural comparisons.

Tu mundo cultural

Los internautas hispanos

AP/Wide World Photos

Campus Party COLOMBIA es un evento anual que reúne a aficionados de la informática que asisten con sus computadoras para jugar, compartir, establecer contactos e intercambiar información. Es un evento que dura las 24 horas del día durante una semana. El primer Campus Party se creó en España, pero ahora hay eventos de ese tipo en países como Colombia, El Salvador, México, Ecuador, y Chile.

La Red en los países hispanos

Courtesy Conchita Lucas

El uso del Internet está muy extendido en los países hispanos. En muchos de ellos, los cibercafés son el medio más asequible para conectarse a la Red porque a causa de su costo, no todos pueden hacerlo en casa.
Observen este Cibercafé situado en un centro comercial de Quito, la capital de Ecuador.

Agencia Latina de Noticias

El 90,9% de los usuarios chilenos de internet utilizan Facebook. Eso convierte a Chile en el mayor usuario de esta red social en Latinoamérica.

Los hispanos en EE. UU. y su acceso a la Red

Gracias a su costo asequible, muchos hispanos residentes en EE. UU. pueden acceder a la Red para conectarse con sus familias, leer las noticias en los periódicos de sus países de origen, hacer compras y, en general, informarse. El 70% de los hispanos de EE. UU. ya navega por la Red y es la minoría que más rápido está conectándose.

IT Stock/Age Fotostock America, Inc.

Usuarios hispanos: resultados de encuesta[1] realizada en EE. UU.

- Argentina, Chile y España son los países hispanohablantes con mayor porcentaje de conexión a la Red. En el caso de los dos primeros lo hace más del 50%* de su población y en el caso de España, el 70%.
- México cuenta con 27,4% de usuarios (27 millones de personas)
- Colombia, Costa Rica y República Dominicana tienen un 30%
- El español es la tercera lengua más usada en la Red (136 millones de usuarios) por detrás del inglés y del chino.

La Red y los hispanos de EE. UU

- El 70% se conecta a la Red.
- El 50% tiene acceso a banda ancha.
- El 48% lo usa para mandar mensajes.
- El 32% lo usa para acceder a las redes sociales.
- El 22% lo hace para chatear.

Portales y sitios en la Red con información de toda clase en español

http://www.terra.com/

http://espanol.yahoo.com/

http://latino.msn.com/

http://www.us.starmedia.com/

Nota: También puedes escribir "portales en español" en tu buscador favorito.

¿Qué aprendiste?

1. Según la encuesta, ¿qué porcentaje de usuarios hispanos se conecta a la Red en EE. UU.? ¿Para qué se conectan?
   70%. Para leer la prensa, hacer compras o informarse.
2. ¿Por qué son tan populares los cibercafés en los países hispanos?
   Por su costo asequible.
3. ¿Cómo se puede aprender más del mundo hispano haciendo uso de la Red?
   Visitando portales en español.

Actividad cultural

Paso 1. Camina por la clase y pregunta a *tres* personas lo siguiente. Apunta la información.

1. ¿Dónde te conectas a la Red?

   ☐ en casa   ☐ en la universidad   ☐ en otro lugar

2. ¿Para qué te conectas?

   ☐ para escribir   ☐ para hacer   ☐ para entrar en   ☐ para otras cosas
      e-mails   compras   Facebook

3. ¿Cuánto tiempo pasas conectado/a cada día?

   ☐ menos de una hora ☐ más de una hora   ☐ más de dos horas ☐ más de tres horas

Paso 2. En grupos de *seis*, compartan sus resultados. Un/a secretario/a apunta la información y se la presenta a la clase.

Contraste cultural

Lean de nuevo los datos sobre los usuarios hispanos de la Red. Luego, hablen sobre cuáles serían los resultados más probables de una encuesta similar realizada entre los estudiantes de su *college* o universidad. Finalmente, compártanla con un/a compañero/a.

[1]poll

* % por ciento

Tu mundo en vivo

¡Videos en acción!

8.1 De compras

1. **Antes de ver el video**
   ¿Te gusta ir de compras solo/a o con otra persona?

   WILEY PLUS Go to *WileyPLUS* to complete the **Mientras ves el video** activity.

2. **Después de ver el video**
   Relaciona las fotos con lo que dice cada persona.

   _B_ «Esa no me gusta. Está muy corta.»

   _C_ «Ay, no, este es tan largo como este, pero este me gusta más.»

   _B_ «Este color te queda muy bien con el color de tus ojos.»

   _A_ «¿Trajiste suficiente dinero?»

8.2 La tecnología une a las familias

1. **Antes de ver el video**
   ¿Tienes familia que vive lejos de ti? ¿Cómo mantienes el contacto con ellos? ¿Usas Skype?

   WILEY PLUS Go to *WileyPLUS* to complete the **Mientras ves el video** activity.

2. **Después de ver el video**
   ¿Por qué dice la pareja del video que la computadora ayuda a la familia a estar más unida?

¡Diálogos en acción!

8.1 En la zapatería

Marta, una ecuatoriana, entra a una zapatería de Quito, capital de Ecuador.

Paso 1. Primero, mira las **Expresiones útiles** de la página A-8. Luego, escucha el diálogo dos veces y contesta las preguntas de tu profesor/a.

Paso 2. Mira la transcripción del diálogo (pág. A-19) y represéntalo con tu compañero/a. Túrnense. Ahora vete a la página A-8 para completar los **Pasos 3** y **4.**

8.2 ¡Mi computadora no funciona!

La computadora portátil de Claudia no funciona y la lleva a una tienda de reparaciones.

WILEY PLUS Go to *WileyPLUS* to listen to and practice this dialogue.

Diálogo 8.1 models the functions of interacting with a shoes salesperson (requesting help, asking for a size, completing a sales transaction, etc.) and making comparisons. It also practices shopping vocabulary and comparisons of inequality and equality.

Diálogo 8.2 models the function of interacting with a computer repair person (requesting help, soliciting and providing information, completing a business transaction). It also practices electronic vocabulary.

¡Lectura en acción!

El artículo que sigue a continuación trata del éxito obtenido por una joven diseñadora, hija de inmigrantes salvadoreños.

Paso 1. Basándote en otros casos que conozcas como este, ¿qué temas crees que se van a mencionar en el artículo? Coméntalo con un/a compañero/a.

Paso 2. Ahora lee el artículo. Después de cada párrafo, resume brevemente la idea principal en inglés.

APWide World Photos

La diseñadora Johana Hernández dio sus primeros pasos en fábricas[1] y hoy viste[2] a celebridades

La diseñadora Johana Hernández ha sacado su propia línea de ropa después de haber diseñado para conocidos artistas. "Este mes estoy lanzando la colección *Glaudi by Johanna Hernández* y me da mucho gusto presentarle esto al mundo, porque es una colección súper única y también porque ayudamos a los necesitados con las ventas de los vestidos", dijo Hernández, cuyo[3] interés por la moda se despertó en su infancia cuando acompañaba a sus padres al trabajo en unas fábrica de costura[4] de Los Ángeles. Allí, de niña, jugaba con trozos de tela[5] mientras sus padres trabajaban. La diseñadora señaló que su colección representa "al latino que es trabajador, al latino que somos la nueva generación y que estamos muy orgullosos[6] de nuestras raíces[7] y de dónde venimos".

Nacida el 21 de junio de 1986 en Los Ángeles, Johana Hernández es hija de inmigrantes salvadoreños. "Toda esta historia siento que regresa a lo que mi familia es: ellos fueron humildes, trabajaron en fábricas, y ahora yo soy la que estoy manejando las fábricas y soy la líder de los diseños de muchas compañías grandes", explicó Hernández. Y agregó, "he diseñado colecciones de ropa para Hannah Montana, Jonas Brothers, Bon Jovi y el grupo mexicano RBD que se han vendido en almacenes como Wal-Mart, Macy's y Kohl's".

Actualmente, Hernández es directora de diseños en la compañía Seven Jeans y dedica tiempo para impartir seminarios en el Instituto de Diseño de Modas y Mercadeo (FIDM), donde estudió. El año pasado, Hernández creó la fundación *Latinos con Corazón* para organizar cada año una noche de presentaciones de sus amigos artistas. El dinero recaudado para asistir al evento se dona a las personas necesitadas. Este año, la diseñadora va a donar el 50% de las ganancias de su colección *Estilo con Causa* al hogar[8] de niños con discapacidades *Padre Vito Guarato*, de El Salvador.

Por su parte, Gladys Hernández, de 52 años y madre de la diseñadora, dijo a Efe que se siente satisfecha de que los sueños que ella siempre tuvo los haya realizado Johana. "Mi hija es un orgullo hispano para demostrarle a los jóvenes que 'sí se puede' y que estudiando, luchando y con esfuerzo personal, los sueños en este país sí se pueden realizar."

Paso 3. Ahora, contesta las preguntas que siguen para ver si has entendido las ideas principales de este artículo.

1. ¿En qué lugar se despertó el interés de Johana Hernández por la moda?
2. ¿De dónde es Johana Hernández y de dónde son sus padres?
3. ¿Para quiénes ha diseñado ropa anteriormente?
4. ¿Para qué creó la fundación *Latinos con Corazón*? ¿Qué va a hacer con el 50% de las ganancias que obtenga?
5. Según la madre de Johana Hernández, ¿qué demuestra el éxito de su hija?

Paso 4. ¿Conoces a otras personas latinas exitosas que sean de origen humilde? Coméntalo con un/a compañero/a.

[1]factories, [2]*vestir* to dress, [3]whose, [4]sewing, [5]*trozos...* pieces of cloth, [6]proud, [7]roots, [8]home

Meets ACTFL Standard 1.1, interpersonal speaking.

¡A conversar!

¿Cómo hacer las compras?

En grupos de *tres*, hablen de cómo prefieren hacer sus compras, y de las ventajas y desventajas de hacerlo de una forma u otra.

- Por la Red (¿Qué sitios visitan con más frecuencia? ¿Qué compran?)
- Por catálogo (¿Qué catálogos reciben?)
- En los centros comerciales (¿Cuáles? ¿Qué tiendas prefieren?)
- En las tiendas de descuento (¿Cuáles prefieren?)

Speaking Strategy

Active Listening

To improve your comprehension, become an active listener! As you've learned in previous chapters, don't hesitate to request a repetition of what's been said. Observe the other person's body language, facial expressions, and gestures. Finally, as you listen, try to make predictions about what will be said based on the topic and the circumstances of the conversation.

¡A escribir!

Lo que necesitas para tu año en esta universidad

Un/a estudiante de Chile va a pasar un año en tu *college* o universidad y quiere saber qué ropa debe empacar. Escríbele un e-mail con las cosas que va a necesitar y explica por qué. Además de ropa y zapatos, incluye también aparatos electrónicos y otras cosas.

Ejemplos:

- *Debes traer una chaqueta, una gorra, una bufanda y unos guantes porque aquí en invierno hace frío. Y también, porque vamos a ir a esquiar.*
- *Trae tus CD y DVD; me los puedes prestar.*

Meets ACTFL Standard 1.3, presentational writing.

You may want to assign a minimum number of words or sentences as appropriate for the ¡A escribir! task. Students can use the word count tool available in their word processing application to check the length of their work before and after the revising step of the writing process.

Writing Strategy

Providing Supporting Information

In order to make your writing more meaningful, provide supporting information around the facts that you convey. For example, if you say to a friend, "Bring a bathing suit," you have conveyed simple information. You have painted a picture if you add "Where I live, it's very hot and sunny in the summer and we often go to the beach. Bring your bathing suit!"

Steps:

1. *Prewriting*: Make an outline of the information you want to convey.
2. *Writing*: Be sure to include a topic sentence. For each item or group of items you suggest, provide supporting information (see strategy).
3. *Revising*: Check your content. Have you included appropriate clothing and shoes for a variety of weather conditions and activities? And essential electronic devices? Is your information helpful? Have you checked for correct spelling and punctuation? ¡Ojo! Have you (a) used correct weather expressions, (b) used commands to give advice, and (c) checked for agreement of articles and nouns?
4. *Peer correction*: Exchange papers, circle errors or areas where there are questions, talk about them, and then make corrections on your own paper.

¡A investigar!

Las tiendas de nuestra ciudad

¿Hay una comunidad hispanohablante en tu ciudad? ¿Dónde hacen las compras? ¿Se ven anuncios y letreros[1] en español en los periódicos, las calles, las tiendas y los centros comerciales?

Paso 1. Trabajen en grupos de *tres* y con la ayuda de su profesor/a, identifiquen las tiendas y las publicaciones que sirven a los hispanohablantes de la ciudad. Cada persona del grupo debe visitar un lugar o recoger ejemplos de las publicaciones.

Paso 2. Después, colaboren para organizar un informe escrito de lo que encontraron. Incluyan:

- El nombre y la ubicación de las tiendas
- Los productos que se venden
- La información que está disponible en español en las tiendas
- Los anuncios y otras formas de publicidad en español

Trabajen juntos para escribir y revisar el informe y publíquenlo en un blog o wiki para compartirlo con sus compañeros de clase. Si es posible, incluyan fotos de los lugares que visitaron.

Paso 3. Después de leer los informes, hablen de las ventajas[2] de publicar información en español, para las tiendas y para los miembros de la comunidad, y comparen los productos que se venden en ellas con los de otras tiendas.

Research Strategy

Participating in Language Communities

Participate in the Spanish-speaking community in your area by noticing your surroundings and interacting with other students and local residents in the language. Look for ads, signs, and product information in Spanish in stores. By being observant, asking questions, and keeping a journal, you can improve your language skills and cultural awareness. Consider participating in the online community of Spanish speakers. Does your favorite online store have a Spanish-language version of their website or stores in other countries? Utilize the Web portals listed in **Los internautas hispanos** in *Escena 3*. On social networks, follow Hispanic individuals, businesses, and organizations. Use Spanish in both the physical and the virtual worlds!

 **Trivia**

A ver cuánto sabes.

1. ¿Qué cuatro países centroamericanos exportan textiles? ¿Y qué país de Sudamérica exporta esmeraldas? **a. Costa Rica, El Salvador, Guatemala, Honduras b. Colombia**
2. ¿Sabes qué dos países hispanos usan el dólar como moneda? **Ecuador y El Salvador**
3. ¿Cuál es la moneda de Paraguay? ¿Y la moneda de Costa Rica? **a. el guaraní b. el colón**

---

[1]signs, [2]advantages

Vocabulario: Capítulo 8

Escena 1

La ropa *Clothing*
la camiseta *t-shirt*
la chaqueta *jacket*
los jeans *jeans*
los pantalones cortos *shorts*
los pantalones largos *long pants*
la sudadera *sweatshirt*

El calzado *Footwear*
las botas *boots*
las sandalias *sandals*
los zapatos de tenis *sneakers*

Los artículos de cuero *Leather goods*
la billetera *wallet*
la cartera/ la bolsa *purse, handbag*
el cinturón *belt*
los guantes *gloves*

Las joyas *Jewelry*
el anillo (de diamante) *(diamond) ring*
los aretes *earrings*
la cadena *chain*
el collar *necklace*
la pulsera *bracelet*
de oro/ plata *gold/ silver*

Otras palabras y expresiones *Other words and expressions*
la bolsa *bag*
el centro comercial *mall*
la gorra (de béisbol) *(baseball) cap*
la moda *fashion*
el precio *price*
las rebajas *sales*
la talla *size*
la tarjeta de crédito/débito *credit/debit card*
en efectivo *cash*

Adjetivos *Adjectives*
barato/a *cheap, inexpensive*
caro/a *expensive*
cómodo/a *comfortable*
corto/a *short*
largo/a *long*

Adverbio *Adverb*
demasiado *too*

Verbos y expresiones verbales *Verbs and verbal expressions*
gastar *to spend*
llevar *to wear, carry*
probarse (ue) *to try on*
quedar bien/ mal *to fit/ not fit*
quisiera *I would like*

Escena 2

¿Qué llevan? *What are they wearing?*
el abrigo *coat*
el bikini *bikini*
la blusa *blouse*
la bufanda *scarf*
los calcetines *socks*
la camisa *shirt*
la corbata *tie*
la falda *skirt*
el gorro *cap*
el impermeable *raincoat*
las pantimedias *panty hose*
el/la pijama *pajamas*
la ropa interior *underwear*
el sombrero *hat*
el suéter *sweater*
el traje *suit*
el traje de baño *bathing suit*
el vestido *dress*
las gafas de sol *sunglasses*
los lentes *glasses*
los lentes de contacto *contact lenses*
el paraguas *umbrella*

Adjetivos y otras expresiones *Adjectives and other expressions*
limpio/a *clean*
sucio/a *dirty*

de algodón *cotton*
de lana *wool*
de manga larga/ corta *long-/ short-sleeved*

Comparaciones *Comparisons*
mejor/ peor *better/ worse*

Expresiones verbales *Verbal expressions*
tener calor *to be hot*
tener frío *to be cold*

Escena 3

Los aparatos electrónicos *Electronic devices/ equipment*
los altoparlantes *speakers*
los audífonos *headphones*
la cámara digital *digital camera*
el celular *cell phone*
la computadora portátil *laptop*
el contestador automático *answering machine*
el control remoto *remote control*
el equipo de DVD y video *DVD/VCR player*
el ratón (óptico USB) *(wireless USB) mouse*
el teclado *keyboard*
el teléfono inalámbrico *cordless phone*
(el televisor) de pantalla plana *flat screen (TV)*
el anuncio *ad*
el apoyo *support*
la marca *brand*

Verbos y expresiones verbales *Verbs and verbal expressions*
apagar *to turn off*
apoyar *to support*
enchufar *to plug in*
prender *to turn on*
tomar fotos *to take photos*
me gustaría... *I would like/love to...*

Capítulo 9

To introduce the theme, you may want to play one of the videos from this chapter, with or without the audio, and then ask students what they think the chapter is about. You may also want to use the video to motivate cultural discussion in Spanish. At the end of the chapter, ask students if their predictions about its content and culture were accurate.

La salud y las emergencias

Additional activities and **Autopruebas** for each **Escena** available online.

Chris Ryan/OJO Images/Getty Images, Inc.

Escena 1
En el consultorio médico

GRAMÁTICA
· The preterit of stem-changing verbs

CULTURA
La medicina natural en el mundo hispano

Escena 2
El cuerpo humano

GRAMÁTICA
· The imperfect

CULTURA
El lenguaje corporal

Escena 3
Situaciones de emergencia

GRAMÁTICA
· The preterit and the imperfect

CULTURA
La diversidad racial de los hispanos

TU MUNDO EN VIVO

¡Videos en acción! La medicina moderna y tradicional; ¿Qué significa ser hispano?

¡Diálogos en acción! Narrating a Past Accident; Describing Habitual Past Activities

¡Lectura en acción! Read, Look up, and Describe

¡A conversar! Borrowing New Words

¡A escribir! Drafting a Newspaper Article

¡A investigar! Identifying Healthcare Sources

LEARNING OBJECTIVES

By the end of this chapter you will be able to:
· Talk about actions in the past.
· Narrate actions and describe persons and things in the past.
· Identify parts of the body.
· Talk about health, illness and injuries.
· Describe some natural remedies.
· Determine what to say in emergency situations.
· Talk about the racial diversity in the Hispanic world.

Escena 1

En [1]el consultorio médico

VOCABULARIO

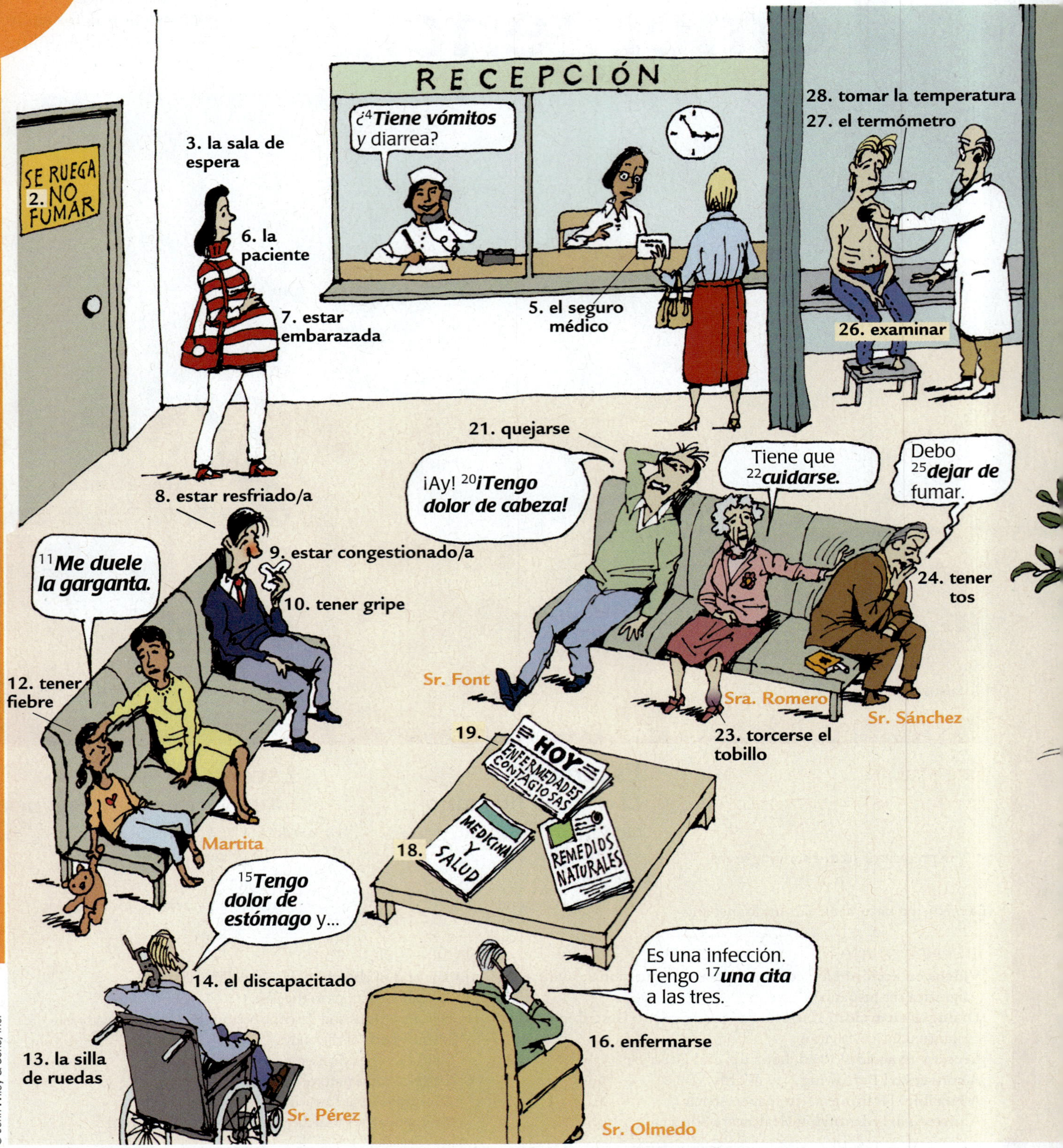

You may use the PowerPoint slides of all scenes to present and practice the vocabulary.

Pronunciación: Practice pronunciation of the chapter's new vocabulary in *WileyPLUS*.

1. the doctor's office
2. no smoking; **fumar** to smoke
3. waiting room
4. Are you vomiting. . . ? **tener vómitos** to be vomiting
5. medical insurance
6. patient (*f.*); **el paciente** (*m.*)
7. to be pregnant
8. to have a cold
9. to be congested
10. to have the flu
11. my throat hurts **doler (ue)** to hurt
12. to have a fever
13. wheelchair
14. disabled (*m.*); **la discapacitada** (*f.*)
15. I have a stomachache; **tener dolor de estómago** to have a stomachache
16. to get sick
17. an appointment, a date
18. health
19. illnesses, diseases (*f.*)
20. I have a headache; **tener dolor de cabeza** to have a headache
21. to complain
22. to take care of yourself/ oneself
23. to twist/ sprain one's ankle
24. to have a cough
25. to stop. . . **dejar de + *inf.*** to stop doing something
26. to examine
27. thermometer
28. to take one's temperature
29. X-ray
30. to take one's blood pressure
31. to give a shot
32. Do not be afraid. **tener miedo** to be afraid
33. to take blood
34. to stay, remain
35. skin (*f.*)
36. AIDS
37. cure
38. pills
39. prescription

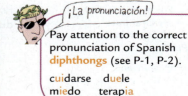
¡La pronunciación!
Pay attention to the correct pronunciation of Spanish **diphthongs** (see P-1, P-2).

cu**i**darse   d**ue**le
m**ie**do   terap**ia**

¡En acción!

9-1 Enfermedades, dolores y malestares

A ver cuánto sabes de remedios y curas. Empareja las palabras de la primera columna con las de la segunda para obtener oraciones lógicas.

1. Si tienes dolor de cabeza...	d.	a. ... debe comer pocas grasas y hacer ejercicio.
2. Cuando tengo gripe y fiebre,...	e.	b. ... haz gárgaras¹ con agua y sal.
3. Algunas personas que tienen alergias...	f.	c. ... deja de fumar.
4. Para el dolor de garganta,...	b.	d. ... toma una aspirina.
5. Alguien con el colesterol alto...	a.	e. ... bebo muchos líquidos y descanso.
6. Si tienes tos y adicción al tabaco...	c.	f. ... tienen que ponerse inyecciones.

> **. . . y algo más** Some expressions with *tener*
>
> **Tener** expressions learned to date:
>
> **tener hambre/ sed/ frío/ calor/ sueño/ miedo**
> **tener dolor de cabeza/ garganta/ estómago; tener fiebre/ gripe**

9-2 En el consultorio médico

¿Qué pasa allí? ¿Cuáles son los síntomas de los pacientes? Para saberlo, observen la escena de las páginas 294–295 y contesten las preguntas.

1. ¿Quién entra al consultorio médico? ¿Qué dice el letrero que se ve en la puerta?

2. ¿Qué pasa en la recepción? ¿Y en cada uno de los cuatro cuartos?

3. En la sala de espera, ¿qué síntomas tiene la niña? ¿Y el señor que está al lado de la mamá?

4. En el otro sofá, ¿qué problema tiene cada uno de los pacientes?

5. ¿Qué consejo le da la señora al señor que está a su lado? ¿Cómo responde él?

6. ¿Qué debe hacer el paciente que está con la enfermera?

7. ¿Qué síntomas tiene el señor que está en la silla de ruedas?

8. ¿Y qué le pasa al señor que está en el sillón? ¿A qué hora es su cita?

9. ¿Qué clase de revistas hay en la mesa? ¿Cuál te interesa más? *Me interesa...*

10. ¿Qué dicen los letreros que hay a la salida? ¿Qué pasa allí?

> **. . . y algo más** The verb *doler*
>
> The verb **doler (ue)** works like **gustar:**
>
> Present tense: **me** duele/n, **te** duele/n, **le** duele/n, **nos** duele/n, **os** duele/n, **les** duele/n.
>
> **Me duele** la garganta.   **Nos duelen** los pies.
> *My throat hurts.*   *Our feet hurt.*

¹**haz...** gargle

9-3 Síntomas con diagnóstico evidente

9-3 You may want to project the PowerPoint slide of the opener scene so students can better play their roles as doctors and nurses describing the six patients.

Primero, lean las burbujas con información sobre *seis* pacientes (vean sus nombres en la pág. 294) y anoten encima el nombre del paciente al que se refiere cada burbuja. Luego, escriban el diagnóstico en el espacio en blanco debajo de la burbuja con la forma del verbo que corresponde (**le duele**/**le duelen**) y la parte del cuerpo que les duele (vean la lista de Palabras útiles). Después, tu compañero/a hace de enfermero/a (lee lo que dice la burbuja) y tú haces de doctor/a que da el diagnóstico de lo que le duele. Finalmente, el/la enfermero/a lo confirma. Sigan el modelo. Túrnense.

1. *La señora Romero*

Se cayó por las escaleras y ahora tiene el pie izquierdo muy inflamado. Se lo torció y…

le duele el tobillo.

MODELO

El/La enfermero/a dice: *Se cayó por las escaleras y ahora tiene el pie izquierdo muy inflamado. Se lo torció y…*

El/La doctor/a: *Le duele el tobillo*

El/La enfermero/a: *Así es, doctor. A la señora Romero **le duele** el tobillo.*

Palabras útiles

el estómago
la garganta
los oídos *ears*
la cabeza
los pulmones *lungs*
el tobillo

2. El señor Font

Se queja mucho y se pone la mano en la frente. Dice que…

le duele la cabeza.

3. El señor Olmedo

No oye bien porque tiene **una infección**, es decir,…

le duelen los oídos.

4. El señor Sánchez

Fuma constantemente y **tose**, por eso…

le duelen los pulmones.

5. El señor Pérez

Comió algo muy indigesto y ahora…

le duele el estómago.

6. Martita

Tiene fiebre y no puede tragar[1] bien porque…

le duele la garganta.

 9-4 Una cita con la doctora RECYCLES Expressions of time

Paso 1. Un paciente llama al consultorio médico para hacer una cita. Hagan los papeles de recepcionista y paciente. Incluyan: saludos, descripción de los síntomas, días y horas para la cita, confirmación de la cita, despedida.

MODELO

Paciente: *Buenos días, señorita. Soy Tom Smith.*

Recepcionista: *Buenos días, señor Smith. ¿En qué puedo servirle?*

Paciente: *Me duele mucho la garganta. Quiero hacer una cita con la doctora López.*

Recepcionista: *¿Esta tarde a las cinco, o mañana a las ocho de la mañana?*

Paciente: *Esta tarde a las cinco, por favor.*

Paso 2. Luego, el paciente pasa a ver a la doctora. Hagan los papeles de la doctora y del paciente.

MODELO

Doctora: *Buenos días. ¿Cómo está?*

Paciente: *No muy bien. Me duele mucho la garganta.*

Doctora: *¿Está congestionado?*

Paciente: *Sí, estoy muy, muy congestionado.*

Doctora: *A ver… Voy a tomarle la temperatura…*

(*Ideas:* La doctora le toma la presión, le da su diagnóstico y posiblemente, le pone una inyección.)

¿SABES QUE…?

When offering a toast at a celebration, Spanish speakers say **¡Salud!** *To your health! Cheers!* **¡Salud!** is also said when a person sneezes, as is **¡Jesús!**

9-4 Have one pair of students perform the telephone conversation in *Paso 1,* and have another pair role-play the visit to the doctor's office in *Paso 2.*

Palabras útiles

Abra la boca y diga «ah». *Open your mouth and say "ah."* **Respire hondo.** *Breathe deeply.*

¡A escuchar! En el consultorio médico

Paso 1. La recepcionista y una enfermera atienden[2] a los enfermos que llegan al consultorio médico mientras unos pacientes charlan en la sala de espera. Escucha la conversación.

PLUS Go to *WileyPLUS* to complete **Paso 2** of this listening activity.

The scripts and recordings for the **¡A escuchar!** sections are included on the Book Companion Site (BCS) for instructors and in *WileyPLUS.*

[1]swallow, [2]assist

Ernesto está en el consultorio médico porque tiene un dolor de estómago muy fuerte.

Me duele el estómago. Anoche fui a un restaurante y...

¿Qué **pidió**?

Pedí camarones con mayonesa.

¿Cómo **se sintió**? ¿Cómo **durmió**? ¿Tuvo vómitos?

Me sentí muy mal, no **dormí** nada y tuve vómitos toda la noche.

Bueno, por lo menos no **se murió**.

© John Wiley & Sons, Inc.

WILEY PLUS Go to *WileyPLUS* to review this grammar point with the help of the **Animated Grammar Tutorial** and **Verb Conjugator**. For more practice, go to the **Grammar Handbook**.

To introduce students to the preterit of stem-changing verbs used in context, have them take parts and read the **historieta** out loud. To check their comprehension and call their attention to the preterit forms, ask the following questions: 1. **¿Qué pidió Ernesto en el restaurante? 2. ¿Cómo se sintió la noche anterior?**

For additional practice on this grammar point, see PowerPoint slides on BCS and in *WileyPLUS*.

Familiarize students with the stem changes through examples: **Me divertí en la fiesta. (mis amigos, tú,...).**

Write the following activities on 3" x 5" cards and hand them to six students: **dormirse, vestirse, servir la comida, reírse, repetir las palabras del vocabulario, morir.** Students mime the actions. The class identifies what each student is doing, using the present progressive. Highlight the stem change. When students finish miming the actions, the rest of the class indicates what each classmate *did*, using the preterit: **(Sandra) se durmió.**

GRAMÁTICA

¡Manos a la obra!

Talking about what happened: The preterit of stem-changing verbs

1

Verbs ending in **-ar** and **-er** that undergo stem changes in the present (see page 164) *do not* do so in the preterit. Verbs ending in **-ir** *do* change in the preterit (**e → i, o → u**), but only in the third person singular and plural as seen in these examples based on Ernesto's visit to the doctor.

Ernesto y Mario **pidieron** camarones.   Ernesto no **durmió** nada.

pedir	**e → i**	**dormir**	**o → u**
pedí	pedimos	dormí	dormimos
pediste	pedisteis	dormiste	dormisteis
p**i**dió	p**i**dieron	d**u**rmió	d**u**rmieron

- Here are nine other common verbs with stem changes in the preterit.

divertirse (ie, i)	*to have a good time*	Ernesto y Mario se divirtieron en un restaurante.
servir (i, i)	*to serve*	Les sirvieron camarones.
reírse* (i, i)	*to laugh*	Ernesto se rió mucho con Mario.
sentirse (ie, i)	*to feel*	Por la noche, Ernesto se sintió muy mal.
morir(se) (ue, u)	*to die*	Se murió de dolor y llamó al consultorio.
repetir (i, i)	*to repeat*	Nervioso, le repitió los síntomas a la enfermera.
preferir (ie, i)	*to prefer*	El médico prefirió examinarlo inmediatamente.
seguir (i, i)	*to follow, continue*	La enfermera siguió las instrucciones del médico.
vestirse (i, i)	*to dress oneself, get dressed*	Al final, Ernesto, se vistió y se fue a casa más tranquilo.

When two stem changes are given in parentheses after an infinitive **(ie, i), (ue, u),** and **(i, i),** the first refers to the present tense, and the second to the preterit.

PRESENT **divertirse (ie):** me div**ie**rto, te div**ie**rtes, se div**ie**rte,... se div**ie**rten
PRETERIT **divertirse (i)** ... se div**i**rtió,... se div**i**rtieron

- The present participle of the above verbs undergoes the same stem change as in the preterit: **e → i, o → u.**

pedir → p**i**diendo: El médico le está **pidiendo** que le explique los síntomas.
dormir → d**u**rmiendo: Ernesto no está **durmiendo**.

*In the third person singular and plural, **reírse** drops the **e** in the infinitive before adding the preterit **ió, ieron** endings: **se rió, se rieron.**

¡En acción!

¡Oye! ¿Es bueno para la salud?

Escucha lo que hicieron o pidieron las personas y di si es bueno o malo para la salud.

9-5 ¿Qué hicieron y cómo les fue?

Paso 1. Primero, cada uno/a lee las siguientes descripciones y marca la letra del/de la paciente que le corresponde. Luego, para confirmar las respuestas, **E1** lee la descripción y **E2** identifica al/ a la paciente describiéndolo/la con sus propias palabras. Sigan el modelo. Túrnense.

MODELO

E1: *Cuando el médico terminó de examinarlo,* **se vistió** *y se fue a casa. Ese día no fue al trabajo.*

E2: *Es el hombre que no lleva camisa. Un doctor lo está examinando…*

1. _g._ Después de examinarlo el médico, **se vistió** y se fue a casa. Ese día no fue al trabajo.
2. _f._ **Siguió** varias semanas con la tos y decidió dejar de fumar para siempre.
3. _b._ Le **pidió** una receta al médico para la congestión y esa noche **durmió** mejor.
4. _h._ **Se murió** de miedo en el consultorio y le dijo a su mamá: "No vuelvo aquí más."
5. _d._ La enfermera le dio unas pastillas para el dolor de cabeza y se **sintió** mucho mejor.
6. _e._ Esa tarde **prefirió** quedarse en casa con el pie[1] en alto mirando la televisión.
7. _a._ La médica le dijo que estaba embarazada de gemelos[2] y ella **sonrió** muy feliz.
8. _c._ Ese día no **se divirtió** mucho porque no pudo ir a la escuela por estar enferma.

a.

b.

c.

d.

e.

f.
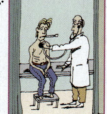

g.
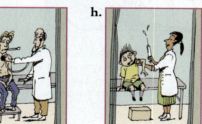

h.

All art © John Wiley & Sons, Inc.

Paso 2. Ahora, observa de nuevo a los pacientes del consultorio médico y comenta con tu compañero/a algunas de las cosas parecidas[3] que experimentaste o hiciste también en los últimos meses. Túrnense. Sigan el modelo.

MODELO

E1: *La semana pasada yo también tomé unas pastillas para el dolor de cabeza y después,* **me sentí** *mejor.*

E2: *Pues yo,…*

[1]foot, [2]twins, [3]similar

¡Oye! Read each statement slowly, emphasizing the verb. Then ask the follow-up question each time: **¿Es bueno o malo para la salud?**

Guión para ¡Oye!
1. Eva **durmió** tres horas anoche. ¿Es bueno o malo para la salud?
2. Tomás y su amigo Pedro vieron una película muy cómica y **se rieron** mucho.
3. El sábado, Paula y Ana jugaron al vólibol en el parque y **se divirtieron** mucho.
4. En el restaurante, José **pidió** una pizza con tres quesos, salchicha, tocino y jamón.
5. Sonia y Mónica **pidieron** pescado, vegetales y una ensalada.
6. El mesero les **sirvió** a todos jugos naturales.
7. De postre, Aurora **prefirió** comer fruta.
8. Eduardo **prefirió** comer pasteles, galletas, ¡y helado!

Palabras útiles
osito de peluche
teddy bear

9-6 Max y Nico en el hospital

RECYCLES regular and irregular verbs in the preterit.

Paso 1. Max y su hermano Nico tuvieron que pasar dos días en el hospital. Escucha a tu profesor/a que va a contar lo que hicieron, pero no en orden cronológico. Identifica el número del dibujo que corresponde a cada descripción.

1.

2.

3.

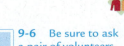

4.

6.

5.
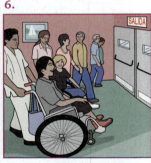

9-6 Script for *Paso 1*: —El médico les dijo "Chicos, descansen, por favor", pero Max y Nico no **siguieron** las instrucciones; ellos jugaron con las almohadas y saltaron (*act out*) en las camas sin parar. [2] —Max y Nico **se vistieron.** [5] —Max y Nico vieron la tele y **se rieron** mucho. [3] —La enfermera les dijo "Ya pronto regresan a su casa". Max y Nico **sonrieron.** [4] —Max **pidió** un helado de chocolate, y Nico **pidió** un helado de fresa, pero **les sirvieron** sopa de verduras. [1] —Al tercer día, salieron del hospital y se fueron muy contentos a casa con sus padres. [6]

Paso 2. Ahora, narren la historia en el pasado, pero en orden cronológico. Usen los siguientes verbos: **pedir, servirles, decir, no seguir, jugar, saltar, ver, reírse, decir, sonreír, vestirse, salir, irse.**

9-6 Be sure to ask a pair of volunteers to narrate the teenagers' story for the class. You may use the PowerPoint slide.

MODELO

E1: *Los dos* **pidieron** *helado. Max* **pidió**... *y Nico*...

9-7 ¡No me siento bien! RECYCLES regular and irregular verbs in the preterit.

Paso 1. Habla con tu compañero/a sobre la última vez que él/ella estuvo enfermo/a. Usa las preguntas de la primera columna. Él/Ella responde siguiendo los modelos de la segunda y tú apuntas la información en la tercera. Después, cambien de papel.

Preguntas	Respuestas	Información escrita
1. ¿Tuviste gripe? ¿Estuviste resfriado/a?	Sí (No, no) tuve...	... tuvo
2. ¿Te **sentiste** muy mal? Explica tu respuesta.		
3. ¿Qué hiciste para recuperarte?		
4. ¿Te quedaste en la cama?		
5. **¿Dormiste** durante el día? ¿Cuánto?		
6. ¿Qué comidas **pediste**?		
7. **¿Seguiste** las instrucciones de tu médico/a?		
8. ¿Qué comidas o bebidas te **sirvió** tu pareja (o tu madre o tu padre)?	Mi... me sirvió...	Su... le sirvió...

Paso 2. Comunícale la información obtenida a otro/a compañero/a o a la clase.

> ### . . . y algo más   *Hace...* to express "ago"
>
>
>
> **Hace...** to express *ago*
>
> To express how long *ago* something was done, you use **hace +** *a unit of time* (minutes, hours, days, months,...)
>
> —¿Cuánto tiempo hace que compraste tu carro? *How long ago did you buy your car?*
>
> —Lo compré **hace un mes**. *I bought it a month **ago**.*

9-8 ¿Cuánto tiempo hace?

Paso 1. Háganse preguntas para saber cuánto tiempo hace que hicieron lo siguiente. Respondan con **hace +** *cantidad de tiempo* y hagan preguntas adicionales según el modelo.

MODELO

cortarse el pelo

E1: *¿Cuánto tiempo hace que te cortaste el pelo?*

E2: *Me corté el pelo **hace un mes.***

E1: *¿Quién te lo cortó? o: ¿A qué peluquería fuiste?*

E2: *... me lo cortó. o: Fui a la peluquería... ¿Y tú?*

1. hacer un viaje
2. ir de compras
3. morirse de risa o de aburrimiento
4. comer un postre con muchas calorías
5. leer un libro
6. ver una película en el cine
7. comprar un carro nuevo
8. enfermarse

Paso 2. Ahora, contesten las preguntas de su profesor/a.

9-7 Poll students about their ailments (item 1) and also get feedback on item 3. Have a student write the suggestions for recovery on the board; the class determines which ones are the best to follow.

WILEY PLUS For more practice, see **Grammar Handbook** found in *WileyPLUS*.

For additional practice on this grammar point, see PowerPoint slides on BCS and in *WileyPLUS*.

Palabras útiles
morirse de risa
  to die laughing
morirse de
  aburrimiento *to die of boredom*

9-8 For *Paso 2*, instructor-led questions (supply names of students): **¿Cuánto tiempo hace que... hizo un viaje? ¿Cuánto tiempo hace que... fue de compras?** and so on.

Go to *WileyPLUS* to see the video related to this reading.

Meets ACTFL Standards
1.1, interpersonal speaking;
1.2, interpretive reading;
2.2, cultural products;
3.1, other disciplines, and
4.2, cultural comparisons.

For an additional activity related to this cultural theme, see the PowerPoint slides on BCS and in *WileyPLUS*.

Tu mundo cultural

La medicina natural en el mundo hispano

¿Te preocupa la salud y te gusta cuidar de tu cuerpo de forma natural? En ese caso, el mundo hispano te ofrece innumerables posibilidades.

Las plantas medicinales son los remedios para la salud más antiguos del mundo. Algunos estudios indican que un 80% de la población de América Latina usa plantas medicinales y métodos naturales para curarse, transmitidos de generación en generación. Además, las grandes compañías farmacéuticas usan plantas originarias de países hispanos para producir muchos medicamentos. La quinina, por ejemplo, que se usa para el tratamiento de la malaria, viene de un árbol de los Andes.

MÉXICO
PERÚ
BOLIVIA
PARAGUAY
ARGENTINA
URUGUAY

© John Wiley & Sons, Inc.

Una costumbre: el mate y sus propiedades preventivas

David R. Frazier Photolibrary, Inc./Alamy

Chica uruguaya bebiendo mate, una infusión o bebida caliente preparada con las hojas de la planta del mismo nombre. Generalmente, se sirve en una calabaza[1] seca y se bebe con una bombilla[2], que es un filtro de metal o bambú. Su uso está muy extendido entre los argentinos, uruguayos y paraguayos. Es antioxidante, diurético y digestivo, estimula la actividad muscular y pulmonar, regula los latidos del corazón[3] y produce una sensación de bienestar, vigor y lucidez intelectual. Ahora, se está poniendo de moda en EE. UU.

¿SABES QUE...?

Coca, a shrub that grows in the lower elevations of the Andes Mountains, produces leaves that can be chewed or brewed for tea for a mild stimulant effect that combats pain, fatigue, altitude sickness and hunger. The indigenous peoples of that region have valued coca leaves for their medicinal and ceremonial purposes for thousands of years. Although many continue to use the leaves to ease the physical symptoms of living in a harsh environment, the cultivation of coca is now controlled in many areas to reduce the production of cocaine, the illegal and much more powerful substance extracted from coca leaves.

Una ciencia: la medicina tradicional y las hierbas medicinales

Hugo Chang/iStockphoto

En Bolivia, las infusiones preparadas con guayaba se usan como remedio para múltiples enfermedades: úlceras, neuralgia, artritis, diarrea, soriasis y dolores de estómago. Allí se conocen unas 2.000 plantas medicinales.

La *uña de gato* crece en Perú. Se usa para combatir enfermedades inflamatorias. Además, se dice que tiene propiedades que estimulan la actividad inmunológica, razón por la que se utiliza para tratar el SIDA, aunque las investigaciones todavía no han confirmado si efectivamente puede tratarse con esta planta.

Mark Bowler/Photo Researchers, Inc.

[1]gourd, [2]straw for drinking mate, [3]**latidos...** heartbeat

Remedios caseros: sitios en la Red para intercambiar remedios

En el mundo hispano se usa un sinfín de remedios caseros. A continuación tienes algunos:

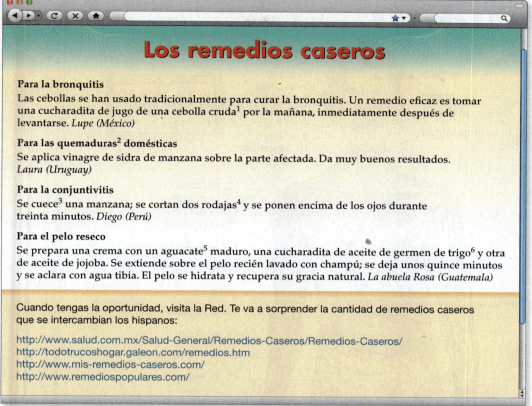

Los remedios caseros

Para la bronquitis
Las cebollas se han usado tradicionalmente para curar la bronquitis. Un remedio eficaz es tomar una cucharadita de jugo de una cebolla cruda[1] por la mañana, inmediatamente después de levantarse. *Lupe (México)*

Para las quemaduras[2] domésticas
Se aplica vinagre de sidra de manzana sobre la parte afectada. Da muy buenos resultados. *Laura (Uruguay)*

Para la conjuntivitis
Se cuece[3] una manzana; se cortan dos rodajas[4] y se ponen encima de los ojos durante treinta minutos. *Diego (Perú)*

Para el pelo reseco
Se prepara una crema con un aguacate[5] maduro, una cucharadita de aceite de germen de trigo[6] y otra de aceite de jojoba. Se extiende sobre el pelo recién lavado con champú; se deja unos quince minutos y se aclara con agua tibia. El pelo se hidrata y recupera su gracia natural. *La abuela Rosa (Guatemala)*

Cuando tengas la oportunidad, visita la Red. Te va a sorprender la cantidad de remedios caseros que se intercambian los hispanos:

http://www.salud.com.mx/Salud-General/Remedios-Caseros/Remedios-Caseros/
http://todotrucoshogar.galeon.com/remedios.htm
http://www.mis-remedios-caseros.com/
http://www.remediospopulares.com/

© John Wiley & Sons, Inc.

El uso tan extendido de remedios caseros en el mundo hispano explica por qué muchos hispanos se resisten a usar métodos curativos que no sean naturales. Es algo que, sin duda, debe conocer el personal médico de los consultorios, clínicas y hospitales de EE. UU., que cada vez cuentan con un mayor número de pacientes hispanos.

¿Qué aprendiste?

1. ¿A qué clase de medicina están acostumbrados los hispanos? Explica tu respuesta.
   A la medicina natural.
2. De las hierbas y medicinas naturales que se mencionan, ¿cuáles te interesan más? ¿Y de los remedios caseros? Explica tu respuesta.

3. ¿Qué debe saber el personal médico que trata con pacientes hispanos en EE. UU.?
   Que muchos prefieren el uso de remedios caseros a métodos no naturales.

Actividad cultural

La clase se divide en grupos de *cinco* con un/a secretario/a para cada grupo. Los secretarios hacen una encuesta entre los estudiantes de su grupo para saber cuántos prefieren la medicina natural y qué clase de remedios usan. Luego, informan a la clase de los resultados obtenidos.

Contraste cultural

En grupos de *cinco*, hablen de los médicos naturistas que conocen y de las tiendas de productos y medicinas naturales que hay en su pueblo o ciudad. Comenten también si piensan que es importante que las facultades de medicina de EE. UU. ofrezcan clases de medicina preventiva y natural. Den razones.

[1]raw, [2]burns, [3]boil, [4]slices, [5]avocado, [6]**germen...** wheat germ

¹El cuerpo humano

Pronunciación: Practice pronunciation of the chapter's new vocabulary in *WileyPLUS*.

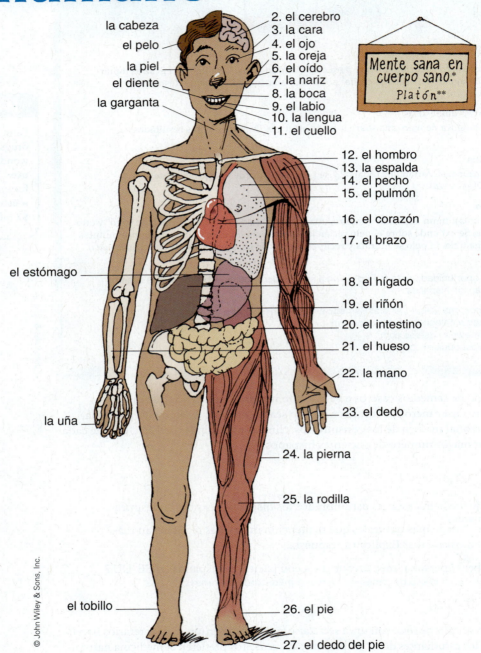

la cabeza
el pelo
la piel
el diente
la garganta

2. el cerebro
3. la cara
4. el ojo
5. la oreja
6. el oído
7. la nariz
8. la boca
9. el labio
10. la lengua
11. el cuello

Mente sana en cuerpo sano.
*Platón***

12. el hombro
13. la espalda
14. el pecho
15. el pulmón
16. el corazón
17. el brazo

el estómago

18. el hígado
19. el riñón
20. el intestino
21. el hueso
22. la mano
23. el dedo

la uña

24. la pierna

25. la rodilla

el tobillo

26. el pie

27. el dedo del pie

© John Wiley & Sons, Inc.

---

1. human body 2. brain 3. face 4. eye 5. ear 6. inner ear 7. nose 8. mouth 9. lip 10. tongue 11. neck 12. shoulder 13. back 14. chest, breast 15. lung 16. heart 17. arm 18. liver 19. kidney 20. intestine 21. bone 22. hand 23. finger 24. leg 25. knee 26. foot 27. toe

---

Mente sana en cuerpo sano. *A sound mind in a healthy body,* **Plato

¡En acción!

9-9   Un pediatra bilingüe

Eres pediatra y estás examinando a un niño para su chequeo anual. ¿Qué partes del cuerpo tienes que saber decir para comunicarte con él en español? Completa las oraciones. Luego, dos estudiantes hacen de pediatra y niño; el niño hace lo que le dice el/la pediatra.

A ver, voy a examinarte los __ojos__, para ver si ves bien; y los __oídos__ para ver si me puedes oír. A ver, ¿cómo se llama esto que tienes entre los ojos y la boca? Sí, muy bien, la __nariz__. Respira profundamente, por favor. A ver, ¿cuántos dientes tienes? Abre la __boca__ y di ¡ah! Ahora, con mi estetoscopio, voy a escuchar los latidos[1] de tu __corazón__. Respira profundamente otra vez, por favor. Muy bien; estoy escuchando tus __pulmones__ y no hacen ruidos raros. Ahora, muéstrame las __manos__; ábrelas y ciérralas. ¿Cuántos __dedos__ tienes en cada una? Cinco y cinco, diez. Muy bien. Y para terminar, levántate y camina sin zapatos. Quiero ver lo bien que lo haces con tus __pies__ tan pequeñitos. ¡Excelente! ¡Qué niño tan bueno eres!

9-10   El cuerpo humano

¿Qué saben de anatomía? Observen el dibujo de la página 304 y contesten las preguntas.

1. ¿Qué hay en la cara? ¿Este joven tiene la piel oscura o clara?
2. ¿Qué se ve dentro de la boca? ¿Y fuera?
3. ¿Qué parte del cuerpo sirve para proteger los oídos?
4. ¿Qué parte conecta la cabeza con el torso? ¿Qué conecta el cuello y los brazos? ¿Se ve la espalda?
5. ¿Qué partes forman la mano? ¿Y el pie?
6. ¿Qué parte del cuerpo sirve para doblar la pierna?
7. En la figura, ¿en qué extremidades se ven músculos?
8. ¿Cuáles son los siete órganos internos que se observan?
9. ¿De qué se compone el esqueleto humano?

9-11   Un juego: ¿Qué parte del cuerpo es?

El objetivo del juego es adivinar la parte del cuerpo que escoge el otro equipo, haciendo el mayor número de preguntas posible en un tiempo limitado de unos *dos* minutos.

1. Se ponen papelitos con los nombres de las partes del cuerpo en una bolsa.
2. La clase se divide en dos equipos (**A** y **B**), que se sientan uno enfrente del otro.
3. El/La profesor/a muestra un papelito de la bolsa a los miembros del equipo **A.**
4. Los miembros del equipo **B,** siguiendo un orden, le hacen preguntas al equipo **A.** El equipo **A** sólo puede responder **Sí** o **No.**
5. Después de 2 minutos, el equipo **B** tiene que decir qué parte del cuerpo es. Si es correcto, obtiene un punto. Ahora es el turno del equipo **A.**

(continúa)

[1]beats

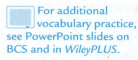
For additional vocabulary practice, see PowerPoint slides on BCS and in *WileyPLUS*.

9-9   Allow students a few minutes to complete the narration. After reviewing answers, have two students perform for the class: the pediatrician speaks and the child carries out the instructions.

Additional vocabulary, to present at your discretion: **la muela, el codo, la planta de la mano** and **la planta del pie.**

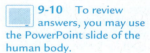
9-10   To review answers, you may use the PowerPoint slide of the human body.

9-10   PERSONALIZED QUESTIONS: ¿Quién se fracturó alguna vez una mano, un brazo o una pierna? Todos tenemos dolores de vez en cuando. ¿Qué les duele a Uds. con más frecuencia?

9-10   ANOTHER STEP: Write these verbs on the board: **respirar, nadar, manejar, comer, ver, oír, pintar, jugar al fútbol, tocar el piano.** Students in pairs jot down parts of the body they associate with each activity: **respirar → la nariz, el pulmón.**

9-11   To make the game simpler, ask students not to include the organs.

MODELO

los ojos

Equipo A, E1: *¿Hay uno? o: ¿Hay más de uno?*

Equipo B. E1: *Sí. o: No.*

Equipo A, E2: *¿Está en la cabeza? o: ¿Está en el tronco/ en las extremidades?*

Equipo B, E2: *Sí. o: No.*

Equipo A, E3: *¿Sirve para... (verbo)?*

Equipo B, E3: *Sí. o: No.*

Equipo A, E4: (Pregunta final) *¿Es el/la...? o: ¿Son los/las...?*

Palabras útiles

girar *to turn*
masticar *to chew*
respirar *to breathe*
tocar *to touch*

9-12 Prueba de Anatomía 101: ¿Para qué son los órganos?

Activities 9–12 and 9-13 introduce students interested in the health professions to useful medical terminology. As most of the words are cognates, they will be easy for students to recognize.

Paso 1. ¿Sabes para qué sirven los órganos y las partes del cuerpo que siguen? Haz la prueba. Empareja cada palabra de la columna **A** con la definición que le corresponde de la columna **B**.

MODELO

E1: *¿Para qué es el estómago?*

E2: *Es para hacer la digestión.*

You might want to point out to your students the use of the preposition **para** with the meaning "to be used for". Also remind them that when a verb follows a preposition it remains in the infinitive.

A. Órganos y más	B. Sus funciones
1. el estómago	__4__ a. filtrar la sangre y ayudar a formar la orina
2. el hígado	__5__ b. tomar oxígeno
3. el corazón	__7__ c. dar soporte a los órganos internos
4. los riñones	__2__ d. segregar la bilis
5. los pulmones	__3__ e. hacer circular la sangre
6. los intestinos	__1__ f. hacer la digestión
7. los huesos	__6__ g. absorber los alimentos y eliminar los residuos de la digestión

Paso 2. Ahora, comprueba con tu compañero/a si tienes la información correcta. Sigan el modelo.

9-13 Especialistas, enfermedades y más

Paso 1. Di a qué especialistas deben ir las siguientes personas.

9-13 ANOTHER STEP: Call out the following illnesses and disorders, and have students guess their meaning: *(-itis)* apendicitis, artritis, bronquitis, conjuntivitis, gastritis, hepatitis, sinusitis, tendonitis; *(-ión)* indigestión, intoxicación; *(-exia)* anorexia, dislexia; *(-ma)* glaucoma, melanoma, trauma, asma; *otros:* alergia, diabetes, epilepsia, leucemia, osteoporosis, tumor benigno/ maligno.

1. un señor con problemas de corazón	f.	a. dermatólogo/a	
2. un joven con cáncer de piel	a.	b. pediatra	
3. una mujer embarazada	e.	c. quiropráctico/a	
4. una persona con esquizofrenia	g.	d. oculista (*eye doctor*)	
5. un bebé con fiebre alta	b.	e. ginecólogo/a	
6. un adolescente con problemas en casa	h.	f. cardiólogo/a	
7. una persona que no ve bien	d.	g. psiquiatra	
8. una persona con dolor de cuello y de espalda	c.	h. psicólogo/a	

Paso 2. ¿A qué especialistas vas con más frecuencia? Explícaselo a un/a compañero/a.

🎧 ¡A escuchar! La Tienda Natural

Paso 1. Escucha el anuncio de *La Tienda Natural,* donde se puede encontrar todo lo necesario para el cuidado[1] del cuerpo.

PLUS Go to *WileyPLUS* to complete **Paso 2** of this listening activity.

En muchos países hispanos las farmacias se reconocen por una cruz verde o roja. Sus farmacéuticos pueden aconsejar al paciente, y a veces, incluso recetarle[2] medicamentos.

Clase de *zumba* en Salsa Touch, en Bettendorf, Iowa. El *zumba* es una forma de hacer ejercicio que está teniendo mucho éxito en EE. UU. y en muchos otros países del mundo. Hacer *zumba* es muy bueno para los glúteos, las piernas, los brazos, los abdominales y el corazón. También es un modo divertido de hacer ejercicio al mismo tiempo que se aprenden pasos de salsa, merengue, cumbia, hip hop, reggaetón, mambo, calypso, flamenco o rumba. Además, sirve para tonificar el cuerpo y quemar calorías.

🎧 **Yolanda quiere saber cómo era su abuelita de niña, cuando vivía en Puerto Rico.**

Abuelita, ¿cómo **eras** de niña?

Tenía los ojos, la nariz y la boca como tú.

¡Eso ya lo sé!

¿Y **tenías** el pelo negro como esta muñeca[3]?

Sí, y **hacía** siempre la tarea de la escuela y **ayudaba** a mi mamá.

¡Como yo! Lo **sabía**, abuelita. Tú y yo somos muy parecidas.[4]

¡Pero yo no **hablaba** ni **escribía** inglés tan bien como tú!

To introduce students to the imperfect tense used in context, have them take parts and read the **historieta** out loud. To check their comprehension and call their attention to the imperfect forms, ask the following questions: 1. **¿Cómo era de niña la abuela de Yolanda?** 2. **¿Qué no hacía la abuela tan bien como Yolanda?**

[1]care, [2]write a prescription for, [3]doll, [4]similar

Go to *WileyPLUS* to review this grammar point with the help of the **Animated Grammar Tutorial** and **Verb Conjugator.** For more practice, go to the **Grammar Handbook.**

For additional practice on this grammar point, see PowerPoint slides on BCS and in *WileyPLUS.*

To introduce the imperfect, write two model verbs on the board, with endings highlighted. In a side box, add the three irregular verbs. Also write on the board: **Cuando era niño/a...** Make statements about yourself: **Cuando era niño/a,** *jugaba* **con mis amigos todos los sábados.** Ask several students: **¿Y tú?** They each respond: **Sí, jugaba con mis amigos...** (or) **No, no jugaba con mis amigos...** Recap student answers: *... jugaba* **con sus amigos...;** *... y... jugaban* **con sus amigos... ; ... y yo** *jugába- mos* **con nuestros ami- gos...** In later examples, allow students to provide the recap. *More examples:* **Veía dibujos animados en la televisión. Comía pizza. Escuchaba música. Iba al cine con frecuencia.**

Introduce the imperfect by describing a poster or a magazine picture of your choice. Focus on *descrip- tions* and *actions in progress.*

¡Manos a la obra!

Describing in the past: The imperfect

2

Spanish uses both the preterit and the imperfect tenses to talk about the past, but each is used in different situations.

The *preterit,* as you know, is used to talk about actions in the past that the speaker views as *completed.* These are *one time only* actions—they have a definite ending.

The *imperfect* is used to talk about things in the past that do *not* have a definite or stated ending, because the speaker views them as in progress. Here are some examples based on Yolanda's conversation with her grandmother:

- Setting the stage: background description, including season, weather, date, and time.

Era verano y **hacía** sol; **eran** las cuatro de la tarde. **Era** el 3 de julio; el cumpleaños de Yolanda. **Había** dos personas en la cocina; **eran** Yolanda y su abuela. Encima de la mesa **había** un vaso de leche y unas galletas.

It was summer and it was sunny; it was four in the afternoon. It was the third of July, Yolanda's birthday. There were two people in the kitchen; they were Yolanda and her grandmother. On the table there was a glass of milk and some cookies.

- Description of characteristics (people, places, things), ongoing conditions, telling age

De bebé, Yolanda **era** bonita y tranquila. Siempre **estaba** muy contenta. Cuando **tenía** un año ya caminaba.

As a baby, Yolanda was pretty and calm. She was always happy. When she was a year old she was already walking.

- What *used to/ would happen* (actions that were ongoing, habitual, happening repeatedly)

Cuando Jennifer **tenía** clase, su madre **cuidaba** a Yolanda. **Ayudaba** mucho a su hija.

When Jennifer had class, her mother used to take care of Yolanda. She helped her daughter a lot.

- What *was happening* (actions in progress)

Yolanda **hablaba** con su abuela cuando Jennifer llegó de la universidad.

Yolanda was talking to her grandmother when Jennifer arrived from the university.

The imperfect tense is formed by dropping the infinitive ending (**-ar, -er, -ir**) and adding the endings below. The endings for **-er** verbs and **-ir** verbs are the same.

	tomar (-ar)	tener (-er)	pedir (-ir)
(yo)	tom**aba**	ten**ía**	ped**ía**
(tú)	tom**abas**	ten**ías**	ped**ías**
(Ud., él, ella)	tom**aba**	ten**ía**	ped**ía**
(nosotros/as)	tom**ábamos**	ten**íamos**	ped**íamos**
(vosotros/as)	tom**ábais**	ten**íais**	ped**íais**
(Uds., ellos, ellas)	tom**aban**	ten**ían**	ped**ían**

. . . y algo más   Irregular verbs in imperfect

There are three irregular verbs in the imperfect tense.

ser *to be*	**ver** *to see*	**ir** *to go*
era	veía	iba
eras	veías	ibas
era	veía	iba
éramos	veíamos	íbamos
érais	veíais	íbais
eran	veían	iban

. . . y algo más   The imperfect of *haber*

Hay means *there is* or *there are*.

Había (imperfect of **haber**) means *there was* or *there were*.

¡En acción!

¡Oye!   ¡A dibujar!

Escucha la siguiente descripción y, después de cada oración, dibuja lo que oyes. Al final, compara tu dibujo con el de tu compañero/a.

9-14   Nostalgia del pasado

Paso 1.   En grupos de *tres*, escojan la época de su niñez, juventud u otra con la que más se identifiquen o que mejor conozcan y escríbanla en el espacio en blanco: **años cincuenta, sesenta, setenta, ochenta o noventa.** Luego, piensen durante unos minutos para recordar lo que ocurría en aquellos años en las categorías 1–7 y apunten la información.

En los años _____ en EE. UU.

1. ¿Quién **era** presidente?	*Era…*
2. ¿Qué música se **escuchaba**?	
3. ¿Qué moda se **llevaba**?	
4. ¿Qué películas se **veían**?	
5. ¿Qué programas de televisión **daban**?	
6. ¿Qué carro **estaba** de moda?	
7. ¿Qué **ocurría** en el resto del mundo?	

Paso 2.   Ahora, Uds. le hacen preguntas a otro grupo que contesta usando los *siete* verbos en imperfecto, pero *sin nombrar la época*. Uds. tienen que adivinarla: (**Eran los años**...). Luego, le toca al otro grupo preguntarles a Uds. y adivinar la época que escogieron.

9-14   Helpful information on the presidents: **50s,** Truman, Eisenhower; **60s,** Kennedy, Johnson; **70s,** Nixon, Ford, Carter; **80s,** Reagan; **90s,** G. H. W. Bush, Clinton.

Go to WileyPLUS to review these grammar points with the help of the **Animated Grammar Tutorial** and **Verb Conjugator**. For more practice, go to the **Grammar Handbook.**

For additional practice on this grammar point, see PowerPoint slides on BCS and in *WileyPLUS*.

¡Oye! Pause after each sentence, allowing time for students to draw.

Guión para ¡Oye!
1. **Era** verano y **hacía** sol. (Dibujen el sol en el cielo.)
2. **Había** algunas nubes.
3. En el centro de la escena, se **veía** una casa pequeña.
4. A la derecha de la casa, **había** dos árboles.
5. A la izquierda, **había** un pequeño lago, con flores cerca.
6. Alguien **pescaba** en el lago.
7. Fuera de la casa, dos niños **jugaban** con una pelota.
8. Cerca de ellos, se **veía** un camino pequeño que cruzaba de este a oeste.
9. Por el camino, una niña **montaba** en bicicleta.
10. Detrás de ella, **corría** su perro.

Repeat the description so that students can check their drawings. Have students in pairs compare their drawings, and then try to describe what they have drawn using the imperfect.

9-14   *Option:* If your class is large, have one group ask another the questions; the first group guesses the period being described. The groups then switch roles.

9-16 You may want to project the PowerPoint slide of Alejandro, Eulalia, and Eduardo. After students complete the activity, ask them to share their comparisons with the class.

9-15 La vida sana[1]

Paso 1. Los hábitos de nutrición y cuidado del cuerpo cambian de una generación a otra. Primero, marca **Sí** o **No** para indicar si la generación de tus abuelos hacía o no lo siguiente. Luego, compárala con la de ahora. Usa el imperfecto y el presente según el modelo.

MODELO

Sí	No	
☐	☑	*comer* **tofu**

*Antes no se **comía** tofu. Ahora, mucha gente lo **come**.*

Sí	No	
☐	☐	**1.** *comer* mucha carne
☐	☐	**2.** *comprar* agua
☐	☐	**3.** *beber* leche descremada[2]
☐	☐	**4.** *tomar* leche de soja[3]
☐	☐	**5.** *contar* las calorías de cada ración[4]
☐	☐	**6.** *dar* importancia a las grasas saturadas de las comidas
☐	☐	**7.** *hacer* ejercicio en el gimnasio
☐	☐	**8.** *conocer* los efectos del estrés
☐	☐	**9.** *pedir* productos orgánicos
☐	☐	**10.** *fumar* mucho

Paso 2. En grupos de *tres*, comenten qué cosas poco saludables comían o bebían antes que ya no comen ni beben ahora.

9-16 Los años pasan para todos RECYCLES the present tense.

Paso 1. Comparen cómo eran antes y cómo son ahora Alejandro, Eulalia y Eduardo según las fotos. Para describirlos, escojan verbos y expresiones de las listas que acompañan las fotos. Anoten en la burbuja correspondiente como mínimo *tres* cosas para cada persona. Sigan el modelo.

1

© John Wiley & Sons, Inc.

Alejandro a los seis meses

... y a los ochenta años

¡Ja, ja, ja!

*Antes Alejandro **tenía** mucho pelo.*

*Ahora no **tiene** pelo. **Está** calvo.*

Antes Alejandro . . .

llevar, llorar, reírse, estar, tener

[1]healthy, [2]skim, [3]soy, [4]portion

2

Eulalia a los cinco años

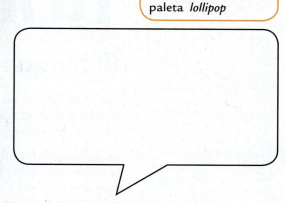

... y a los treinta

All art © John Wiley & Sons, Inc.

3

Eduardo a los diecinueve años

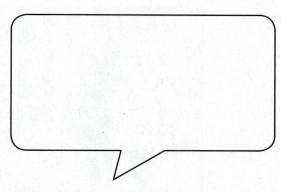

... y a los cincuenta

All art © John Wiley & Sons, Inc.

beber, comer, manejar, montar en bicicleta,
pintarse, salir con, ser, ir

afeitarse, escuchar, hacer ejercicio, leer,
peinarse, vestirse

Paso 2. Ahora, comparen sus observaciones con las de otra pareja.

9-17 Cuando tenía... años   RECYCLES home, food, activities, and clothing vocabulary.

Paso 1. Uds. son dos pacientes que comparten habitación en el hospital y están charlando de los siguientes aspectos de su vida cuando tenían... años (escojan su edad favorita):

- su casa o apartamento
- personas con quienes vivían
- quiénes eran sus amigos y a qué jugaban
- sus comidas favoritas

- qué programas veían en la televisión
- qué otras cosas les gustaba hacer
- adónde iban de vacaciones
- qué ropa se ponían

Paso 2. Tu hijo quiere saber acerca de tu vida cuando tenías... años y quiere que lo grabes[1] en un video, para poder compartirlo con toda la familia. Dilo en *ocho* oraciones. Incluye la misma información del *Paso 1.*

MODELO

Voy a hablarles acerca de mi niñez. Cuando tenía... años, vivía en...

[1]record

9-16 ANOTHER STEP: Students in groups take turns describing a member of their family, mentioning what the person *was* like and/or what he/she *used to do* (imperfect, two items) and what the person *is* like and/or *does* now (present, two items).

9-17 For *Paso 1,* have two students reenact their conversation for the class, followed by others volunteering information regarding their partner's childhood experiences.

Tu mundo cultural

Meets ACTFL Standards
1.1, interpersonal speaking;
1.2, interpretive reading;
2.1, cultural practices; and
4.2, cultural comparisons.

For an additional activity related to this cultural theme, see the PowerPoint slides on BCS and in *WileyPLUS*.

El lenguaje corporal[1]

Cada cultura tiene un lenguaje corporal y formas de comunicación no verbal que la caracterizan. ¿Cuáles son las de tu cultura? ¿Es el contacto físico frecuente y aceptable en la comunicación? ¿Qué gestos se usan?

En su mayoría, los hispanos son muy expresivos. Cuando hablan, mantienen una distancia pequeña entre ellos y las interrupciones son frecuentes y más toleradas en su cultura. Además, usan muchos gestos[2] con la cara y con las manos, y para ellos el contacto físico es un elemento importante de la comunicación. En privado y en los lugares públicos como calles, autobuses, filas de cines y bancos, se observa también gran proximidad entre las personas.

En los países hispanos, cuando dos amigas salen de paseo, es común ir del brazo.

En el caso de los hombres, cuando dos amigos salen de paseo, al hablar, es común poner el brazo por encima del hombro del otro. La proximidad física, en estos casos, es una forma de expresar afecto y amistad.

Saludos y despedidas

Si por razones profesionales tienes contacto frecuente con hispanos en EE. UU., o si eres un hombre o una mujer de negocios que va a viajar a países hispanos, te va a ser muy útil familiarizarte con las siguientes formas de saludarse.

Cuando dos hombres que se conocen se encuentran o se despiden, se dan un abrazo y unas palmaditas[3] en la espalda, incluso si se han visto hace poco tiempo.

Cuando dos mujeres o un hombre y una mujer se encuentran o se despiden, se saludan con un beso en la mejilla[4], o rozando[5] la mejilla. En algunos países como España, se dan dos besos. No importa si se vieron hace tiempo o el día anterior.

[1]**El...** Body language, [2]gestures, [3]little pats [4]cheek, [5]barely touching

Courtesy Conchita Lucas

En las situaciones de trabajo, el contacto físico también es frecuente, pero a veces, cuando dos hombres o mujeres no se conocen, y si es una situación de trabajo formal, se dan la mano para saludarse o despedirse.

¿Sabes interpretar los gestos hispanos?

Cada cultura tiene gestos que la diferencian de otras culturas. A veces, el mismo gesto en una, significa algo muy diferente en otra. Hay gestos comunes a muchos países, y otros exclusivos de unos pocos. A continuación vas a observar algunos gestos hispanos útiles.

Courtesy Conchita Lucas

En España se usa este gesto para indicar que hay mucha gente en un lugar. En otros países hispanos, como México, Chile y Argentina, significa tener miedo.

Courtesy Conchita Lucas

Courtesy Conchita Lucas

Besarse el dedo, como indica la foto, es un gesto para asegurar[1] a otra persona que es cierto lo que se dice.

Este gesto indica que la persona de quien se habla es tacaña, es decir, poco generosa. Se usa en México, América Central, el Caribe y Venezuela, entre otros. No se usa en España.

¿Qué aprendiste?

1. ¿En qué detalles se nota que el contacto físico entre los hispanos es importante?
   En los saludos, despedidas y en la comunicación en general.
2. Cuando dos amigas hispanas se encuentran, ¿cómo se saludan? ¿Y dos hombres hispanos que son amigos? ¿Y dos que no se conocen?
   Con dos besos. Con un abrazo. Se dan la mano.
3. ¿Para quiénes, en particular, es importante conocer los saludos y gestos hispanos?
   Para los profesionales que tienen contacto con hispanos.

Actividad cultural

1. Ahora, tu compañero/a y tú hacen los siguientes papeles: **(a)** una persona que saluda "*a la hispana*" a una amiga que encuentra por la calle; **(b)** una persona que saluda a un compañero de trabajo.

2. Usa gestos hispanos para decirle a tu compañero/a lo siguiente: **(a)** que alguien es tacaño/a; **(b)** que le aseguras que cierta persona es muy inteligente y **(c)** que hay mucha gente en un lugar. Túrnense.

Contraste cultural

Hablen de las maneras de saludarse y del contacto físico en su cultura. Incluyan saludos entre sólo mujeres, sólo hombres, hombres y mujeres y personas que se conocen bien o no. ¿Cuáles de los saludos son similares a los hispanos y cuáles son diferentes?

[1]assure

Situaciones de emergencia

WILEY **PLUS**

Pronunciación: Practice pronunciation of the chapter's new vocabulary in *WileyPLUS.*

VOCABULARIO

En ¹el lugar del accidente

²¡Socorro!

3. gritar

4. chocar

6. el paramédico

7. la camilla

¹¹*Está inconsciente.*

AMBULANCIA

5. lastimarse

9. el herido

10. tener cuidado

8. tener prisa

En ¹²la sala de emergencias

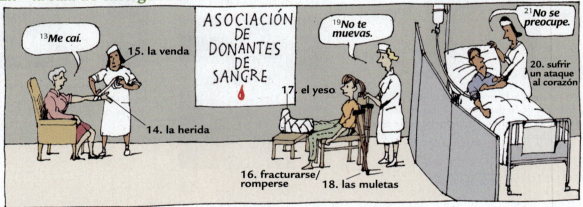

¹³*Me caí.*

15. la venda

ASOCIACIÓN DE DONANTES DE SANGRE

¹⁹*No te muevas.*

²¹*No se preocupe.*

17. el yeso

20. sufrir un ataque al corazón

14. la herida

16. fracturarse/ romperse

18. las muletas

En el quirófano*

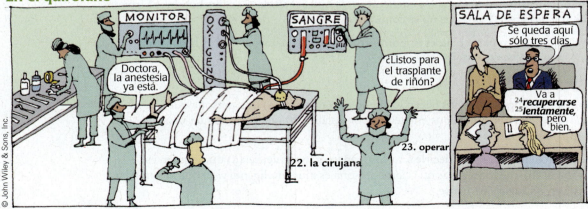

MONITOR

OXÍGENO

SANGRE

SALA DE ESPERA

Se queda aquí sólo tres días.

Doctora, la anestesia ya está.

¿Listos para el trasplante de riñón?

Va a ²⁴*recuperarse* ²⁵*lentamente,* pero bien.

23. operar

22. la cirujana

© John Wiley & Sons, Inc.

---

1. the scene/ place of the accident 2. Help! 3. to yell, scream 4. to crash 5. to hurt/ injure oneself 6. paramedic (*m.*); **la paramédica** (*f.*)
7. stretcher 8. to be in a hurry 9. injured/wounded person (*m.*); **la herida** (*f.*) 10. to be careful 11. He is unconscious. **estar inconsciente** to be unconscious 12. emergency room 13. I fell. **caer(se)** to fall 14. wound 15. bandage 16. to fracture, break 17. cast 18. crutches 19. Do not move. **mover(se)** to move (oneself) 20. to have a heart attack 21. Don't worry. **preocupar(se)** to worry 22. surgeon (*f.*) **el cirujano** (*m.*) 23. to operate
24. to recuperate 25. slowly

* En el quirófano *In the operating room*

¡En acción!

9-18 ¿Es así o no?

Observa las escenas de la página 314 e indica si las afirmaciones son ciertas o falsas. Si son falsas, da la oración correcta.

MODELO

C	F	
☐	☑	Alguien grita «¡Un accidente!». *Falso. Alguien grita «¡Socorro!».*

C	F	
☐	☑	**1.** En el lugar del accidente, un paramédico se lastimó.
☑	☐	**2.** El herido que llevan en la camilla a la ambulancia está inconsciente.
☐	☑	**3.** El señor que está en la sala de emergencias sufrió un ataque de nervios.
☑	☐	**4.** Las muletas de la chica le sirven de ayuda para caminar.
☐	☑	**5.** Una enfermera pone un yeso en la herida de una paciente.
☐	☑	**6.** En el quirófano, la cirujana está lista para poner la anestesia al paciente.
☐	☑	**7.** Según la persona de la sala de espera, el paciente va a recuperarse rápidamente.

9-19 Situaciones de emergencia

¿Qué pasó? ¿Hubo heridos? ¿Los llevaron al hospital? Para saberlo, observen las escenas de la página 314 y contesten las preguntas.

1. En el lugar del accidente, ¿cuántos carros chocaron? ¿Qué grita el señor que viene corriendo del otro lado de la carretera?

2. ¿Qué le pasó al señor de la corbata azul?

3. ¿Quiénes tienen prisa?

4. ¿Por qué tienen cuidado los paramédicos que ponen la camilla en la ambulancia?

5. En la sala de emergencias, ¿por qué está allí cada una de las tres personas?

6. ¿Qué hacen las tres enfermeras? ¿Qué dicen dos de ellas?

7. En el quirófano, ¿qué va a hacer la cirujana? ¿Qué clase de operación es? ¿Y qué dice el anestesista?

8. En la sala de espera, ¿qué pronostica una de las señoras? ¿Cuánto tiempo va a quedarse el paciente en el hospital?

9-20 Accidentes y emergencias

RECYCLES verbs in the preterit and **hace** + *time*.

Paso 1. ¿Qué les pasó a tus compañeros alguna vez[1]? Camina por la clase y hazles preguntas para saberlo. Apunta en el espacio en blanco (pág. 316) el nombre de cada estudiante que responda *afirmativamente*. Sigue el modelo. Tienes *cinco* minutos.

MODELO

E1: *Alguna vez, ¿tuviste que hacer rehabilitación o terapia física?*

E2: *Sí, tuve que hacer terapia física **hace dos años**.*

E1: (Apunta el nombre del/ de la estudiante. Si la respuesta es negativa, haz otra pregunta.)

(continúa)

[1]**alguna...** at some time

For additional vocabulary practice, see PowerPoint slides on BCS and in *WileyPLUS*.

9-18 ANSWERS: (for false responses) 1. F: Un señor (o una señora) se lastimó. 3. F: ... sufrió un ataque al corazón.
5. F: ... pone una venda...
6. F: ... para operar al paciente. (o) ... para el trasplante de riñón.
7. F: ... va a recuperarse lentamente.

9-19 You may want to project the PowerPoint slide of the "emergency" vignettes and have the class describe each one.

9-19 PERSONALIZED QUESTIONS: ¿Quién tuvo un accidente? (¿Cuándo? ¿Qué clase de accidente?) ¿Quiénes tuvieron una operación? (¿Cuándo?) ¿Quiénes se fracturaron la pierna o el brazo? (¿Cuándo?)

9-20 *Option*: Students complete the activity in groups of six.

9-20 Spot-check responses by asking **¿Quiénes se fracturaron la pierna o el brazo? ¿Quiénes tuvieron un accidente?** Elicit multiple responses, with students answering according to the names they noted: **Pedro tuvo una operación.**

Alguna vez,...

_____ 1. ... ¿tuviste una operación? ¿Te pusieron anestesia local o general?

_____ 2. ... ¿te caíste? ¿Te lastimaste?

_____ 3. ... ¿te fracturaste la pierna o el brazo? ¿Te pusieron un yeso?

_____ 4. ... ¿te torciste el tobillo?

_____ 5. ... ¿tuviste un accidente en bicicleta, en motocicleta o montando a caballo? ¿Tuviste heridas?

_____ 6. ... ¿estuviste inconsciente?

 Paso 2. Comparte la información obtenida con otro/a compañero/a: _... tuvo una operación._

¡A escuchar! Situaciones de emergencia

Paso 1. Escucha las conversaciones.

PLUS Go to _WileyPLUS_ to complete **Paso 2** of this listening activity.

For additional practice on this grammar point, see PowerPoint slides on BCS and in _WileyPLUS_.

De paso

The verb **haber**

Había (imperfect) _There was, there were_ (existing state or condition)

Hubo (preterit) _There was_ (occurred), _there were_ (completed action or event)

Había mucho tráfico y **hubo** un accidente.
There **was** a lot of traffic and there **was** an accident.

For additional practice on this grammar point, see PowerPoint slides on BCS and in _WileyPLUS_.

Mario está en la sala de emergencias. Allí se encuentra con Mabel, que es enfermera del hospital.

Mario, ¿qué haces aquí en la sala de emergencias?

Creo que **me rompí** el tobillo... **Estaba jugando** al fútbol en el parque y otro jugador **chocó** conmigo.

A ver... No te lo **fracturaste**, pero sí te lo **lastimaste**. Necesitas una venda y unas muletas.

TRAUMATOLOGÍA

No **quería** venir al hospital pero el tobillo **comenzó** a dolerme mucho.

¡Qué alivio! **Creí** que **era** más grave.

© John Wiley & Sons, Inc.

To introduce students to the uses of the preterit and the imperfect in context, have them take parts and read the **historieta** out loud. To check their comprehension and call their attention to these tenses, ask the following questions: **1. ¿Qué hacía Mario en el parque? 2. ¿Por qué fue al hospital?**

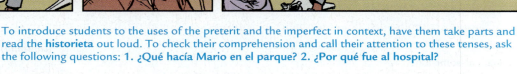

¡Manos a la obra!

GRAMÁTICA

3

Piecing together the past: The preterit and the imperfect

You have been using the preterit and the imperfect tenses to refer to the past. Study the contrasts in their meanings in the following chart, with examples based on Mario's accident.

IMPERFECT	Examples	PRETERIT	Examples
1. Describes a past action or condition that was *in progress*, with no emphasis on the beginning or end.	Mario **estaba** en la sala de emergencias. **Esperaba** pacientemente. Le **dolía** mucho el tobillo.	**1.** Indicates a single past action, generally quickly *completed*, or a series of actions in the past.	Mario **llegó** al hospital. Mabel le **examinó** el tobillo, le **puso** una venda y le **dio** unas muletas.
2. Describes a past action that was repeated or *habitual* over an indefinite period of time.	**Jugaba** al fútbol con sus amigos todos los domingos. Después de jugar, siempre **cenaban** pizza.	**2.** Focuses on a past action or condition with an evident *beginning, end, or time frame.*	Mario **se lastimó** esta tarde. El tobillo **comenzó** a dolerle mucho después del partido. **Pasó** dos horas en la sala de emergencias.
3. *Describes the background*, often setting the stage for other actions or events to take place. Includes: • the date or the season • the time • the weather • A description of the scene: Who and what was there;	**Era** el 8 de octubre. **Era** otoño. **Eran** las cinco de la tarde. **Hacía** fresco y **estaba** nublado. **Había** mucha gente en la sala de emergencias.	**3.** Indicates an action that *interrupts* an ongoing scene, action, or condition described in the imperfect.	Cuando Mario **se lastimó, estaba** en el parque. **Jugaba** al fútbol cuando otro jugador **chocó** con él. Mientras Mabel le **examinaba** el tobillo, Mario la **invitó** al cine.
4. Describes people: • age • physical and personality traits • mental or emotional states, conditions, or attitudes	El médico de Mario **tenía** 52 años. **Era** muy competente. **Estaba** muy ocupado porque tenía muchos pacientes.	**4.** Indicates a sudden, unexpected *change of condition or attitude.*	Los otros jugadores **tuvieron** miedo cuando Mario se cayó. Mabel **se preocupó** cuando lo vio.

ADVERBIOS ÚTILES

mientras *while*   mientras tanto *meanwhile*   por fin *finally*   de repente *suddenly*

For additional practice on this grammar point, see PowerPoint slides on BCS and in *WileyPLUS*.

Go to *WileyPLUS* to review this grammar point with the help of the **Animated Grammar** Tutorial and **Verb Conjugator**. For more practice, go to the **Grammar Handbook**.

You may introduce the preterit and the imperfect by projecting the PowerPoint slide of the opener scene for this chapter. Begin by describing the scene using the *imperfect*. Include **(a)** day, hour, date: **Era/n...;** **(b)** description of the setting: **Había...;** **(c)** description of various patients and their ailments; **(d)** description of ongoing actions: in the reception area, waiting room, examination rooms. Introduce an interrupting (*preterit*) action, such as **De repente, entraron cuatro policías al consultorio.** Follow with students providing a series of actions in the past: **La niña empezó a llorar...** Encourage students to use their imaginations!

Let students know that certain time-related expressions are often associated with either the imperfect or the preterit. For example, *Preterit*: **anoche, ayer, la semana pasada, una vez, de repente...** *Imperfect*: **todos los días, siempre, por lo general, normalmente, mientras,...**

Guión para ¡Oye!

Era sábado, el quince de marzo, y **llovía** mucho (*draw rain on the board*). **Eran** las cuatro de la tarde y Juan **estaba** en casa, aburrido. **Quería** ver a su novia Sofía, a quien **amaba** con pasión, y **decidió** ir a visitarla. **Se puso** la chaqueta y **salió** de casa. **Manejaba** por la calle San Martín y **hablaba** con ella por el celular, cuando... ¡Ay! No **vio** la señal de tráfico que **decía** ¡ALTO! y **chocó** con otro carro (*clap hands together to make a crashing sound*). Alguien **llamó** al 911, la ambulancia **llegó** inmediatamente y lo **llevaron** a la sala de emergencias. **Tuvo** mucha suerte—sus heridas no **fueron** graves y **se quedó** sólo unas horas en el hospital. Mientras tanto, Sofía **estaba** *muy* preocupada. Cuando Juan por fin **llegó** a casa y la **llamó**, ella **fue** inmediatamente a verlo. Le **llevó** un DVD de una comedia y **se rieron** mucho el resto de la noche. El día **terminó** mejor de lo que **empezó**.

Comprensión para ¡Oye!

1. ¿Era sábado o domingo? *Era sábado.*
2. ¿Llovía o hacía sol?
3. ¿Juan manejaba y escuchaba música, o manejaba y hablaba por el celular?
4. ¿Vio la señal de tráfico?
5. ¿Chocó?
6. ¿Llegó la ambulancia inmediatamente o media hora después?
7. ¿Tuvo heridas graves?
8. ¿Se quedó Juan en el hospital unos días o unas horas?
9. Mientras tanto, ¿estaba Sofía enojada o preocupada?
10. ¿Le llevó a Juan un DVD o un CD?
11. ¿Lo pasaron bien?
12. ¿Cómo terminó el día, mejor o peor de lo que empezó?

¡En acción!

¡Oye! Lo que le pasó a Juan

Escucha la narración, y luego contesta las preguntas.

9-21 Un mal día para Jorge y Zacarías

Paso 1. Un/a narrador/a lee el relato de forma dramática, haciendo pausas donde haya //, para que los actores sepan cuándo les toca actuar. Los actores siguen las instrucciones que escuchan y las representan con mímica.

Actores y actrices en orden de aparición:

Un/a narrador/a
Jorge y Zacarías
Dos paramédicos

En la sala de emergencias:
Unas personas que miran la televisión
Unas personas que leen revistas
Unas personas que charlan
Una persona que está resfriada
Una persona con dolor de estómago
Una persona con tos
Dos mujeres embarazadas, a punto de dar a luz[1]
Dos niños
Una médica

Narrador/a:
Todos los días, Jorge y su amigo Zacarías **jugaban** al vólibol // y **montaban** en bicicleta, // pero el sábado pasado, Jorge **se cayó** de la bicicleta // y **se fracturó** una pierna. Inmediatamente, Zacarías **llamó** al 911 por el celular, // y los paramédicos **llegaron** poco después. // Rápidamente, **pusieron** a Jorge en la camilla // y lo **llevaron** al hospital. //

En la sala de emergencias **había** mucha gente. Unas personas **miraban** la televisión, // otras **leían** revistas // y otras **hablaban.** // Una persona **estaba** resfriada; // otra **tenía** dolor de estómago; // y otra, mucha tos. // **Había** incluso, dos mujeres embarazadas a punto de dar a luz. Cada cinco minutos, **decían** «¡¡¡Ay!!!, ¡¡¡Ay!!!». // Dos niños **corrían** por todas partes, // y Jorge, en la silla de ruedas, no **estaba** nada contento.

Jorge **leía** una revista en la silla de ruedas, cuando de repente, uno de los niños que **corría** por la sala, **chocó** contra[2] su pierna rota. // «¡¡¡Ay!!! ¡Dios mío!» **gritó** Jorge. // Mientras Zacarías **consolaba** al pobre Jorge, **entró** la médica // y lo **llevó** a un cuarto. // Zacarías los **acompañó.** // La médica le **tomó** la temperatura // y la presión a Jorge, y luego le **sacó** unas radiografías. // Por último, le **puso** un yeso, // le **dio** unas pastillas para el dolor y unas muletas. //

Jorge y Zacarías **regresaron** a casa, caminando muy lentamente. // Al llegar, **estaban** bien cansados. **Fue** un mal día.

9-21 First, select the participants as listed. The narrator, Jorge, and Zacarías go to the front of the class. The other characters remain seated until their participation is required. If the first run-through is rough, call it a dress rehearsal and try it again, perhaps assigning students different roles.

> **Pregunta:** De los cuatro usos del pretérito que se explican en la página 317, ¿cuál es el uso en "Fue un mal día"? Especifica el número.
>
> (Véase la pág. 317, bajo el **PRETÉRIT 2**). Porque se refiere a una acción que ocurre dentro de un espacio de tiempo determinado: "ayer".

[1]give birth, [2]against

Paso 2. Contesten las siguientes preguntas. Al terminar de responder a todas, indiquen en el espacio en blanco qué uso del pretérito o del imperfecto se expresa en cada una de las preguntas y respuestas (A, B, C o D). Túrnense.

9-21 Before beginning *Paso 2*, have students review the four preterit and imperfect concepts. After students complete their work in pairs, they share answers to the questions with the class. Write on the board the verbs that are mentioned in the answers. Students then confirm the concept they selected.

___A___   **1.** ¿Qué **hacían** Jorge y Zacarías todos los días?

___C___   **2.** ¿Qué **pasó** después de fracturarse Jorge la pierna?

___B, B___   **3.** En la sala de emergencias, ¿cómo **estaban** algunas personas? ¿Qué **hacían** otras?

___D, D___   **4.** ¿Qué **ocurrió** cuando Jorge leía la revista? ¿Quién **entró** cuando Zacarías lo **consolaba**?

___C___   **5.** ¿Qué **hizo** la médica?

___B___   **6.** ¿Cómo **estaban** Jorge y Zacarías al regresar a casa?

Usos del imperfecto		Usos del pretérito	
A. Acción pasada que **se repite** o es **habitual** durante un periodo de tiempo indeterminado.	**B. Acción** o condición pasada **en progreso, sin** un **principio o fin**[1] determinado.	**C. Acción** o serie de **acciones** pasadas que se consideran **concluidas**.	**D. Acción** pasada que **interrumpe** otra acción o condición en progreso.

9-22 Malestares y remedios   RECYCLES the preterit along with the imperfect.

Primero, marca las casillas de los malestares que tuviste en alguna ocasión. Luego, descríbele a tu compañero/a **(a)** el malestar que **tenías** (imperfecto), **(b)** lo que **hiciste** (pretérito) para remediarlo y **(c)** cómo **estás** (presente) ahora. Sigan el modelo. Túrnense.

Malestares que tenías antes	Remedios
1 ☐ *tener* problemas digestivos	*Dejé de…*
2 ☐ *tener* dolores de cabeza frecuentes	*Tomé…*
3 ☐ *dolerme* la espalda/ los oídos/ el estómago/…	*Fui a un/a…*
4 ☐ *dormir* mal y *sentirme* cansado/a	*Empecé a…*
5 ☐ *estar* estresado/a	*Decidí…*
6 ☐ *tener* el colesterol alto	*…*
7 ☐ *toser* a causa de fumar	

MODELO

E1: *¿Qué problema **tenías** antes?*

E2: *Me **dolía** la espalda.*

E1: *¿Qué **hiciste** para remediarlo?*

E2: ***Fui** a una médica y me **dio** unas pastillas.*

E1: *¿Y cómo **estás** ahora?*

E2: ***Estoy** bien.*   **o:** *Todavía me duele la espalda.*

[1]**principio…** beginning or end

9-23   ¿Y qué pasó después?

Paso 1.   Veamos si son Uds. personas creativas. Su profesor/a le va a asignar a cada grupo de cuatro estudiantes una de las siguientes situaciones. Su tarea es completarlas con gran imaginación. Usen los verbos en pretérito o imperfecto.

> **Eran** las nueve de la noche, y después de un día largo, el cirujano **se iba** a casa. De repente, **sonó** su iPhone, y…

> **Era** una noche de verano y **hacía** muchísimo calor. Una mujer embarazada de más de nueve meses **empezó** a sentir contracciones. Inmediatamente,…

> **Era** invierno y **nevaba** mucho. Un esquiador que iba a toda velocidad, no **vio** un árbol y **chocó**. En ese momento,…

> Un día de verano, **nadábamos** tranquilamente en el agua azul turquesa de una playa del Caribe, cuando de repente vimos, ¡la aleta de un tiburón!…

aleta   tiburón

© John Wiley & Sons, Inc.

Paso 2.   Lean sus historias a la clase. ¿Cuál fue la más original?

9-24   Noticias de última hora

Paso 1.   ¿Sabes lo que pasó ayer? Lee el artículo. Luego, <u>subraya</u> los *diez* verbos que están en pretérito y haz un círculo alrededor del verbo que está en imperfecto.

9-24   In *Paso 1,* students are asked to underline verbs for the purpose of recognizing preterit and imperfect endings. Point out that in the newspaper article, the ten verbs in the preterit focus on a past actions with an evident beginning, end or time frame, while **pasaba** is in the imperfect because it is an *ongoing* action.

The *Preguntas* that follow the article serve to quickly confirm key elements of the story, prior to moving on to *Paso 2.*

Paso 2: When students have completed the activity, ask a volunteer to read the story aloud. The class confirms answers.

ANSWERS: For *Paso 2:* Eran, manejaba, nevaba, oí, estaba, dijo, Salí, vi, estaba, Saqué, limpié, dije, venía/vino, tomé, di, empezó, puse, dio, abrazamos, Fue

Noticias de última hora: Diario local

¡Un bebé <u>nació</u> en un taxi!

Ayer domingo, a las dos de la mañana, doña Eugenia Pérez <u>dio</u> a luz[1] en un taxi a un precioso bebé de 3 kilos y medio. El taxi no <u>pudo</u> llegar al hospital a tiempo a causa de la tormenta de nieve. Las personas que <u>estuvieron</u> con la embarazada en el parto[2] <u>fueron</u> su esposo José, el conductor del taxi y una enfermera. La enfermera, llamada Lola, casualmente pasaba por allí y al oír los gritos de socorro procedentes del taxi, <u>corrió</u> a ayudarles. Los bomberos y la ambulancia <u>llegaron</u> demasiado tarde, pero gracias a la eficacia de la enfermera y al valor de los dos hombres que la <u>ayudaron</u>, el evento <u>tuvo</u> un final muy feliz. Los padres del bebé ya tienen otros cinco hijos y <u>dijeron</u> que éste va a ser el último, y que lo van a llamar Benjamín, alias «el intrépido».

Preguntas: ¿Qué pasó ayer domingo a las dos de la mañana? ¿Por qué paró allí Lola, la enfermera? ¿Quiénes más ayudaron a la embarazada en el parto? ¿Cuántos hijos tienen ahora los padres?

Paso 2.   Ahora, escojan la forma correcta de cada verbo para narrar lo que Lola les contó a sus compañeros al llegar al hospital.

Eran/Fueron las dos de la mañana y yo **manejaba/manejé** al hospital con gran dificultad porque afuera **nevaba/nevó** mucho. De repente, **oí/oía** unos gritos procedentes de un taxi que **estaba/estuvo** estacionado cerca. Un hombre desde el taxi me **decía/dijo**: «¡¡Por favor, venga, necesitamos su ayuda!!». **Salía/Salí** inmediatamente y **veía/vi** a una mujer embarazada que **estaba/estuvo** dando a luz en ese momento. **Sacaba/Saqué** alcohol y unas toallas de mi bolsa, me **limpiaba/limpié** las manos y le **decía/dije** a la señora: «No se preocupe. Me llamo Lola, soy enfermera y todo va a salir bien.» El bebé **venía/vino** al mundo a gran velocidad. Lo **tomaba/tomé** por los pies, le **daba/di** suavemente unas palmaditas y el recién nacido **empezaba/empezó** a llorar. Lo **ponía/puse** en los brazos de su madre en una cobija[3] que me **daba/dio** el taxista y finalmente, los cuatro nos **abrazábamos/abrazamos** con gran alegría. **Era/Fue** un día que todos vamos a recordar[4].

---

[1]**dio…** gave birth, [2]birthing, [3]blanket, [4]remember

9-25 Un día en el parque

Paso 1. ¿Qué les pasó a una señora y a su perrita, Bolita, hace una semana? Para saberlo, primero, escucha la descripción de tu profesor/a e identifica la escena que le corresponde (del 1 al 6).

MODELO

Profesor/a: *La señora **tomó** a Bolita en sus brazos y **llamó** a un taxi.*

Tú: (marcas o dices) *Número 4.*

9-25 Read the script twice. The first time, students jot down their responses. The second, they call out answers.

· De repente, un perro enorme atacó a Bolita. [3]

· Pocos días después, Bolita se recuperó, y ella y la señora estaban contentas de nuevo. [6]

· Era primavera y hacía sol. Una señora muy elegante caminaba por el parque con su perrita. [1]

· El veterinario le puso una venda a Bolita. [5]

· A Bolita le encantaba caminar por el parque y en su cara se observaba su felicidad. [2]

1.

2.

3. ¡Socorro!

4. ¡Taxi!

5. CLÍNICA CANINA

6. BOLITA LA HEROÍNA

All art © John Wiley & Sons, Inc.

Paso 2. Ahora, cuenten la historia. Usen los verbos que siguen y otros, en imperfecto o pretérito según corresponda. Digan como mínimo *tres* cosas para cada escena.

9-25 After students complete *Paso 2,* you may want to project the PowerPoint slide of the scenes. Students volunteer their descriptions, one scene at a time.

atacar	encantar	haber	irse	llevar	sentirse	tomar	ver
caminar	gritar	hacer	llamar	ponerle	ser	venir	volver

MODELO

E1: ***Era** primavera y **hacía** sol.*

E2: *Una señora muy elegante **caminaba** por el parque con su perrita.*

9-26 Algo personal

Paso 1. ¿Tuviste un accidente o un incidente grave de niño o de joven? Cuéntaselo a tu compañero/a. Incluye lo siguiente:

- cuándo **ocurrió** (mes y año)
- cuántos años **tenías**
- qué hora **era**
- dónde **estabas**
- qué tiempo **hacía**
- qué **hacías** cuando **ocurrió**
- qué **pasó**
- cómo te **sentiste** después

Paso 2. En grupos de *cinco,* cuéntense lo que les pasó y decidan cuál es la historia más original. Luego, esa persona se lo cuenta a la clase.

![WileyPLUS] Go to *WileyPLUS* to see the video related to this reading.

Tu mundo cultural

La diversidad racial de los hispanos

Meets ACTFL Standards 1.1, interpersonal speaking; 1.2, interpretive reading; 2.1, cultural practices; and 4.2, cultural comparisons.

For an additional activity related to this cultural theme, see the PowerPoint slides on BCS and in *WileyPLUS*.

Have students turn to the map of the Hispanic world on the inside front cover of their books to locate each of the countries mentioned.

Cuando usamos el término *hispano*, ¿nos referimos a una raza?

El término *hispano* no denota la entidad racial, sino la entidad cultural de una persona. La composición racial de los hispanos es muy variada, tal como se ve en las siguientes fotografías. Esa misma diversidad racial se observa entre los hispanos que residen en EE. UU.

Con la conquista de América, los europeos se mezclaron[1] con los indígenas americanos y los esclavos africanos y surgieron[2] nuevas razas. Este proceso continuó con la emigración de europeos a Latinoamérica. En la décadas recientes, debido a la emigración de latinoamericanos a España, el fenómeno ha continuado.

Keith Dannemiller/©Corbis

Muchos mexicanos tienen antepasados[3] de los indígenas que habitaron su territorio.

Martin San/Riser/Getty Images, Inc.

Hay mexicanos descendientes de europeos que tienen la piel, los ojos y el pelo claros[4].

Jeanne Nakamaru.

Los descendientes de los mayas en la península de Yucatán y Guatemala tienen rasgos[5] muy característicos. Guatemala es el país hispano con más alto porcentaje de indígenas (41%).

Kevin O'Hara/Age Fotostock America, Inc.

Los países del Caribe, como[6] Cuba (10%), República Dominicana (11%), Panamá (14%) y Venezuela (9%) tienen población de raza negra. Hay también minorías de raza negra en Colombia y Ecuador.

[1]mixed, [2]emerged, [3]ancestors, [4]light colored, [5]features, [6]like

En los países andinos como Ecuador, Perú y Bolivia, gran parte de la población conserva los rasgos de sus antepasados incas. En Paraguay tienen rasgos de los nativos guaraníes.

Jean Phillippe Soule/Alamy Limited

Courtesy Conchita Lucas

Courtesy Conchita Lucas

Además de en España, en países como Costa Rica, Argentina, Uruguay y Chile, la población es de origen predominantemente europeo. Chile y Argentina tienen mucha población de origen alemán e italiano.

Henry Beeker/Age Fotostock America, Inc.

En países de la costa del Caribe como República Dominicana (73%), Cuba (51%) y Colombia (14%) hay población de raza mulata, resultado de la mezcla de los europeos con los esclavos procedentes de África.

Este joven es de Honduras, país donde un alto porcentaje de la población es mestiza (90%). Lo mismo ocurre en otros países de América Central y del Caribe, como por ejemplo: El Salvador (85%), Nicaragua (74%) y Panamá (70%).

¿SABES QUE...?

Spanish-speaking countries are not only racially diverse but also linguistically diverse. Although Spanish is the official language of 21 countries, in most of them other languages are also spoken, and some of these are official languages. For example, in **Bolivia,** Spanish, Quechua, and Aymara are all official languages. In **Mexico,** 62 indigenous languages and 100 dialects are spoken along with Spanish. In **Paraguay,** Spanish and Paraguayan Guaraní are official languages, but 20 indigenous languages are also spoken. In **Spain,** Castilian Spanish is the official language, with Basque, Galician, and Catalan each official in their respective regions.

¿Qué aprendiste?

1. ¿Qué denota el término *hispano*?
   La entidad cultural de una persona.
2. ¿Qué razas se mezclaron con la conquista?
   Los europeos, indígenas americanos y esclavos africanos.
3. En el mundo hispano, ¿dónde hay más población de raza indígena, mestiza, mulata, africana y blanca? Den ejemplos concretos.
   Indígena: Guatemala y península de Yucatán. Mestiza: Honduras. Mulata: Caribe. Africana: Caribe. Blanca: España, Costa Rica, Argentina, Uruguay y Chile.

Actividad cultural

En grupos de *tres*, entrevístense para obtener la siguiente información: el lugar de origen de sus antepasados y su composición racial.

Contraste cultural

Comenten la diversidad racial en su *college*, universidad o comunidad. Indiquen qué razas predominan y las razones que explican su presencia.

¿SABES QUE...?

Evo Morales, the president of Bolivia (elected 2006), is a native Aymara. He is the first indigenous president of his country.

For the *Actividad cultural*, students might find it helpful to refer to the list of countries and nationalities of the world found in the inside back cover of their textbooks.

Meets ACTFL Standards 1.2, interpretive listening; 2.1, cultural practices; 2.2, cultural products; 3.2, acquiring information; and 4.2, cultural comparisons.

For additional information on this cultural theme, see PowerPoint slides on BCS and in WileyPLUS.

Tu mundo en vivo

¡Videos en acción!

9.1   La medicina moderna y tradicional

1. Antes de ver el video

   a. ¿Te gusta ir al médico? Explica tu respuesta.

   b. ¿Usas la medicina alternativa? Explica tu respuesta.

PLUS Go to *WileyPLUS* to complete the **Mientras ves el video** activity.

2. Después de ver el video

   a. En tu pueblo o ciudad, ¿hay lugares donde venden hierbas medicinales?

   b. ¿Crees que hay mucha gente en EE. UU. que usa hierbas medicinales cuando está enferma?

9.2   ¿Qué significa ser hispano?

1. Antes de ver el video

   Para ti, ¿qué significan los términos «hispano» y «latinoamericano»?

PLUS Go to *WileyPLUS* to complete the **Mientras ves el video** activity.

2. Después de ver el video

   Al final del video, una señora mexicana dice que está orgullosa de ser:

   _____mestiza_____, ____latinoamericana____ y ____mexicana____.

Meets ACTFL Standards 1.1, interpersonal speaking; 1.2, interpretive listening; and 2.1, cultural practices.

Dialogue Tips: Play the dialogue once all the way through. Check comprehension by asking students to tell you everything they understood (English is OK). Then play it a second time, pausing after each sentence or phrase and asking students what was said.

You can also find the **transcripts** for the **Diálogos** in the PowerPoint slides, on the BCS and in *WileyPLUS*.

¡Diálogos en acción!

9.1   El accidente de María

María vuelve a casa con muletas[1] y se encuentra con Paula, su compañera de piso.

Paso 1.   Primero, mira las **Expresiones útiles** de la página A-9. Luego, escucha el diálogo dos veces y contesta las preguntas de tu profesor/a.

Paso 2.   Mira la transcripción del diálogo (pág. A-19) y represéntalo con tu compañero/a. Túrnense. Ahora, vete a la página A- 9 para completar los **Pasos 3** y **4**.

9.2   Los Picapiedra[2]

María le hace preguntas a Paula, su compañera de piso, acerca de su niñez.

PLUS Go to *WileyPLUS* to listen to and practice this dialogue.

Diálogo 9.1 models the functions of narrating a past event and soliciting and providing information about a past event. It also practices preterit and imperfect verbs and accident/emergency vocabulary.

Diálogo 9.2 models the function of describing habitual past events and soliciting/providing information about a past situation. It also practices imperfect and preterit verbs.

[1]crutches, [2]**Los...** The Flintstones

¡Lectura en acción!

¡Nunca es tarde para empezar!

Meets ACTFL Standards 1.2, interpretive reading, 3.2, acquiring information.

Si buscas en sitios de Internet como *Yahoo en español*, vas a encontrar mucha información sobre cómo llevar una vida saludable. Un ejemplo es el siguiente artículo, que trata de cómo prevenir las enfermedades cardiovasculares. Antes de leerlo, ¿puedes mencionar *tres* cosas que ayuden a tener un corazón sano?

Paso 1. Ahora, lee el artículo. Siguiendo la estrategia, después de cada sección describe lo que leíste con tus propias palabras. A ver cuánto recuerdas.

Según datos de la Organización Mundial de la Salud (OMS), cada dos segundos se produce una muerte por enfermedad cardiovascular. Por ser esta la causa principal de fallecimientos[1] en el mundo, cuidar el corazón debe convertirse en una prioridad.

Dos reglas[2] de oro para cuidar el corazón

1. Vigila tu dieta

Alimentarse[3] de forma adecuada beneficia no sólo al sistema cardiovascular, sino a todo el cuerpo.

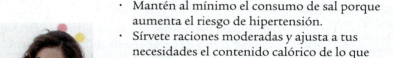

- Consume cinco o más raciones diarias de verduras y frutas.
- Come pescado al menos dos veces por semana.
- Escoge granos integrales[4] (pan, arroz, pasta y cereales).
- Reduce el consumo de proteínas de origen animal.
- Usa aceite de oliva para cocinar y condimentar tus comidas.

- Mantén al mínimo el consumo de sal porque aumenta el riesgo de hipertensión.
- Sírvete raciones moderadas y ajusta a tus necesidades el contenido calórico de lo que consumes.

2. Haz ejercicio con regularidad

La actividad física mejora los niveles de colesterol, ayuda a reducir la presión alta y mantiene niveles normales de glucosa en la sangre.

- Practica algún deporte, nada, baila, camina,... como mínimo, 30 minutos al día.

iStockphoto

Paso 2. Escribe aquí abajo tu interpretación de las siguientes secciones del texto.

En el anuncio se dice:	Tú dices:
• Alimentarse de forma adecuada beneficia... al sistema cardiovascular...	• *Comer bien ayuda al corazón.*
• Reduce el consumo de proteínas de origen animal.	•
• Sírvete raciones moderadas...	•
• ... ajusta a tus necesidades el contenido calórico de lo que consumes.	•
• Haz ejercicio con regularidad.	•

Paso 3. Ahora, sin mirar el artículo, responde a las siguientes preguntas.

1. ¿Por qué es importante cuidar el corazón?

2. Y tú, en tu dieta, ¿cuáles de las recomendaciones debes seguir con más atención?

3. ¿Por qué es importante hacer ejercicio con frecuencia? ¿Qué ejercicio haces tú?

[1]deaths, [2]rules, [3]To nourish oneself, [4]**granos...** whole grains

Reading Strategy

Read, Look up, and Describe

While actively reading a passage, frequently stop, look away from the text, and describe, in your own words, what you just read. This is a quick and effective way to check that you understand a reading and to identify sections that you don't fully understand. Additionally, it helps you remember more about what you've just read.

Meets ACTFL Standard
1.1, interpersonal speaking.

Speaking Strategy

Borrowing New Words

In **Capítulo 8**, you learned to listen actively to improve your comprehension of another person's speech. You can apply that same strategy to increase your vocabulary by borrowing words and phrases from your conversation partner. When you hear an interesting new word, request a repetition and an explanation if necessary, but don't stop there. Try incorporating the word into your part of the conversation by asking questions for more information. For example, if your friend uses the word **heridos** while describing the car accident he had last year, you could ask **¿Cuántos heridos había?** and **¿Fueron los heridos al hospital?** Active use of new words will help you retain the vocabulary in your memory.

¡A conversar!

Situaciones de emergencia

Pónganse en cada una de las situaciones de emergencia que siguen, basándose en la información provista. Un/a estudiante llama al 911 y pide ayuda de la forma más clara y expresiva posible. Otro/a estudiante hace el papel de operador/a. Antes de empezar, repasen el vocabulario para hacer llamadas de la página 188. Túrnense.

- *En tu casa:* tu bebé/ muy enfermo/ fiebre altísima...
- *En el parque:* tu mejor amiga/ jugar a.../ caerse/ fracturarse...
- *En el centro comercial:* otro cliente de una tienda/ inconsciente.../ un ataque al corazón
- *En la carretera:* dos carros/ chocar.../ los frenos.../ tres heridos.../ lastimarse...

¡A escribir!

Un accidente de carro

Ustedes son periodistas que colaboran para escribir una noticia en el periódico de su pueblo o ciudad acerca de un accidente de carro que ocurrió esta mañana. Usen el pretérito y el imperfecto. Incluyan lo siguiente:

• quién es	• el clima
• qué	• el estado físico y mental de los heridos antes y después del accidente
• cuándo	
• dónde	• la experiencia en el hospital
• cómo	

Meets ACTFL Standard
1.3, presentational writing.

You may want to assign a minimum number of words or sentences as appropriate for the **¡A ESCRIBIR!** task. Students can use the word count tool available in their word processing application to check the length of their work before and after the revising step of the writing process.

Writing Strategy

Drafting a Newspaper Article, from Catchy Title to Strong Conclusion

You will want to come up with a catchy title for your article, followed by a topic sentence that will grab the attention of the reader. When you describe the accident, remember to include details (supporting information). End with a concluding sentence that wraps up the content of the narration and/or leaves the reader anticipating what might happen next.

Steps:

1. *Prewriting:* Brainstorm with a classmate about the car accident you are going to describe.
2. *Writing:* Follow the steps outlined in the accompanying strategy.
3. *Revising:* Have you successfully conveyed the information but also kept your audience interested? Is your article to the point, but also descriptive? Have you included all the information requested and checked for correct spelling and punctuation? **¡Ojo!** Be sure to check all forms and uses of the preterit and the imperfect.
4. *Peer correction:* Exchange articles with another pair of students. With your partner, circle errors or areas where there are questions. As a foursome, review your articles and then make corrections as necessary.

¡A investigar!

El acceso a la información médica

Meets ACTFL Standards
1.2, interpretive reading;
1.3, presentational writing;
3.1, other disciplines; and
3.2, acquiring information.

Algunos hispanos en EE. UU., como muchos otros residentes del país, sufren de presión alta, de diabetes o de enfermedades del corazón. ¿Cuáles son los síntomas de esas enfermedades? ¿Cuáles son los tratamientos[1] que se usan más? ¿Qué se puede hacer para prevenirlas? Para los inmigrantes que acaban de llegar, es beneficioso tener acceso a esta información en español.

Paso 1.   Trabajen en grupos de *tres* y con la ayuda de su profesor/a, elijan una de las enfermedades mencionadas arriba. Un/a estudiante va a encargarse de los síntomas, otro/a de los tratamientos y el/la tercero/a de los métodos para prevenirlas.

You may assign the appropriate Pasos of **¡A investigar!** for pairs or small groups to complete outside of class.

Paso 2.   Usen los recursos indicados en la estrategia y otros que usaron en los capítulos anteriores e investiguen los tres aspectos de esa enfermedad. Colaboren para organizar, escribir y revisar un breve informe sobre lo que aprendieron. Publíquenlo en un blog o wiki para compartirlo con los otros estudiantes.

If your access to technology is limited, have the students create Word document reports.

Paso 3.   Después de leer todos los informes, hablen con sus compañeros de lo que sabían o no sabían de esas enfermedades antes de investigarlas. Mencionen las ventajas que tiene el que los inmigrantes puedan acceder a la información médica en su propia lengua.

Research Strategy

Identifying Healthcare Sources

In previous chapters you've used search engine language tools and Spanish search terms to find information on a number of topics. The same strategy will lead you to many healthcare sources from other countries and also from the US. Additionally, several health-related agencies of the federal government maintain Spanish-language versions of their websites for Hispanics in this country and their healthcare providers. These include the CDC or Centros para el Control y la Prevención de Enfermedades at www.cdc.gov/spanish, offices of the NIH or Institutos Nacionales de la Salud such as www.nlm.nih.gov/medlineplus/spanish/, and the Department of Health and Human Services at http://healthfinder.gov/espanol/.

Trivia

A ver cuánto sabes.

1. ¿Cuáles son las lenguas oficiales de Bolivia? ¿Y de Paraguay?
   a. el español, el quechua y el aymara   b. el español y el guaraní
2. ¿Qué porcentaje de blancos hay en México y en El Salvador? ¿Y en Argentina?
   a. 9%   b. 97%
3. ¿Qué país de América Central tiene el porcentaje más alto de indígenas? ¿Cuál es el porcentaje?
   a. Guatemala   b. 41%

If you don't know the answers, take a look at the front inside cover of the textbook. Try to respond in complete sentences.

You may want to tell your students that to express the percentage (%) in Spanish one says **por ciento**.

[1]treatments

Vocabulario: Capítulo 9

Escena 1

La salud *Health*
la cita *appointment, date*
el consultorio médico *doctor's office*
la cura *cure*
el/la discapacitado/a *disabled*
la enfermedad *illness, disease*
el/la paciente *patient*
la pastilla *pill*
la piel *skin*
la radiografía *X-ray*
la receta *prescription*
la sala de espera *waiting room*
el seguro médico *medical insurance*
el SIDA *AIDS*
la silla de ruedas *wheelchair*
el termómetro *thermometer*

Verbos y expresiones verbales
Verbs and verbal expressions
cuidarse *to take care of yourself/ oneself*
dejar de + *infinitivo* *to stop doing something*
doler (ue) *to hurt*
enfermarse *to get sick*
estar congestionado/a *to be congested*
estar embarazada *to be pregnant*
estar resfriado/a *to have a cold*
examinar *to examine*
fumar *to smoke*
morir(se) (ue, u) *to die*
poner una inyección *to give a shot*
quedarse *to stay, remain*
quejarse *to complain*
sacar sangre *to take blood*
tomar la presión *to take one's blood pressure*
tomar la temperatura *to take one's temperature*
torcerse (ue) el tobillo *to twist/sprain one's ankle*

tener dolor de cabeza *to have a headache*
tener dolor de estómago *to have a stomachache*
tener fiebre *to have a fever*
tener gripe *to have the flu*
tener miedo *to be afraid*
tener tos *to have a cough*
tener vómitos *to be vomiting*
Me duele la garganta. *My throat hurts.*

Escena 2

El cuerpo humano *The human body*
la boca *mouth*
el brazo *arm*
la cara *face*
el cerebro *brain*
el corazón *heart*
el cuello *neck*
el dedo *finger*
el dedo del pie *toe*
la espalda *back*
el hígado *liver*
el hombro *shoulder*
el hueso *bone*
el intestino *intestine*
el labio *lip*
la lengua *tongue*
la mano *hand*
la nariz *nose*
el oído *inner ear*
el ojo *eye*
la oreja *ear*
el pecho *chest, breast*
el pie *foot*
la pierna *leg*
el pulmón *lung*
el riñón *kidney*
la rodilla *knee*

Escena 3

Las emergencias *Emergencies*
la camilla *stretcher*
el/la cirujano/a *surgeon*
la herida *wound*
el/la herido/a *injured/wounded person (m./f.)*
el lugar del accidente *the scene/place of the accident*
las muletas *crutches*
el/la paramédico/a *paramedic*
la sala de emergencias *emergency room*
la venda *bandage*
el yeso *cast*
¡Socorro! *Help!*

Otras expresiones útiles
Other useful expressions
de repente *suddenly*
lentamente *slowly*
mientras *while*
mientras tanto *meanwhile*
por fin *finally*

Verbos y expresiones verbales
Verbs and verbal expressions
caerse *to fall*
chocar *to crash*
estar inconsciente *to be unconscious*
fracturarse/ romperse *to fracture, break*
gritar *to yell, scream*
lastimarse *to hurt/ injure oneself*
mover(se) *to move (oneself)*
operar *to operate*
preocuparse *to worry*
recuperarse *to recuperate*
sufrir un ataque al corazón *to have a heart attack*
tener cuidado *to be careful*
tener prisa *to be in a hurry*

Capítulo 10

El barrio

WILEY PLUS

Additional activities and **Autopruebas** for each **Escena** available online.

Danita Delimont/Alamy

Escena 1
La vida en el barrio
GRAMÁTICA:
· Present subjunctive: formation
· Present subjunctive: expressions of influence

CULTURA:
El barrio en EE. UU.

Escena 2
Actividades del barrio
GRAMÁTICA:
· Present subjunctive: expressions of emotion

CULTURA:
Voluntarios dentro y fuera de EE. UU.

Escena 3
Asuntos sociales, políticos y religiosos
GRAMÁTICA:
· Present subjunctive: expressions of doubt or negation

CULTURA:
Los murales de los barrios de EE. UU.

TU MUNDO EN VIVO
¡Videos en acción! CLUES ayuda a inmigrantes hispanos; Un muralista con conciencia

¡Diálogos en acción! Expressing Opinions and Disagreement; Requesting that Someone Change Behavior

¡Lectura en acción! Recognizing Word Families

¡A conversar! Confirming Comprehension

¡A escribir! Persuasive Business Letter

¡A investigar! Finding Opportunities for Service

LEARNING OBJECTIVES
By the end of the chapter you will be able to:
· Talk about life in the neighborhood and about various social, political and religious matters.
· Express wishes and requests.
· Express feelings and reactions.
· Express doubt and disbelief.
· Demonstrate familiarity with the Hispanic concept of neighborhood and contrast it with the American concept.
· Identify organizations in the US and abroad to volunteer with Latinos.

La vida en ¹el barrio

© John Wiley & Sons, Inc.

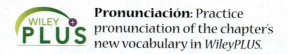

Pronunciación: Practice pronunciation of the chapter's new vocabulary in *WileyPLUS*.

You may use the PowerPoint slides of all scenes to present and practice the vocabulary.

1. neighborhood
2. neighbors
3. to hang
4. remember . . . ; **acordarse (ue) de** to remember
5. soap opera
6. I won't forget; **olvidarse de** to forget . . .
7. mail carrier; **la cartera**
8. to go down/ pass by . . .
9. sidewalk
10. doorman, concierge
11. to move (from house to house)
12. to pick up, gather
13. garbage truck
14. fire
15. to burn oneself, burn down
16. smoke
17. Fire!
18. *Don't jump!* **saltar** to jump
19. (pizzas) delivery person; **la repartidora** (*f.*)
20. to greet
21. to obey
22. They have just . . . ; **acabar de** + *inf.* to have just done something
23. owner (*m.*); **la dueña** (*f.*)
24. tow truck
25. vote; **votar** to vote
26. party (political)
27. prejudices
28. vendor (*f.*); **el vendedor** (*m.*)
29. sweets, candies (*m.*)
30. chewing gum
31. to relax
32. boys; **las muchachas** girls
33. citizen (*m.*); **la ciudadana** (*f.*)
34. town, people

***recoger** (presente): recojo, recoges,...

****obedecer** (presente): obedezco, obedeces...

¡La pronunciación!

Pay attention to the correct pronunciation of the Spanish **ch** (on page P-3 and in *WileyPLUS*.)

mu**ch**acho   **ch**icle

For additional vocabulary practice, see PowerPoint slides on BCS and in *WileyPLUS*.

¡En acción!

10-1 En el barrio

¿Qué pasa en el barrio? Empareja las dos columnas para describir lo que ocurre en la escena de las páginas 330–331.

1. Las dos vecinas que están en el balcón...	g.	**a.** ... se muda a dos cuadras de allí.
2. Una familia del barrio...	a.	**b.** ... quiere que su perro obedezca.
3. El camión del Servicio Municipal...	d.	**c.** ... acaba de llevarse un carro.
4. Una mujer grita «¡Socorro!»...	h.	**d.** ... acaba de recoger la basura.
5. El Servicio de Grúas...	c.	**e.** ... los ciudadanos voten.
6. La mujer que cruza la calle...	b.	**f.** ... dulces y chicles a los niños.
7. Los anuncios del barrio piden que...	e.	**g.** ... cuelgan la ropa.
8. La vendedora del parque les vende...	f.	**h.** ... porque hay un incendio en su edificio.

10-1 Review the **acabar de** + *infinitive* construction highlighted in items c. and d. Give several examples: **Acabo de hablar con mi vecina. Acabamos de terminar la *Actividad 10-1*.** Then ask if students have just done certain things: **¿Acabas de aprender el vocabulario?**

10-2 ¡Qué vitalidad hay en el barrio!

Observen el dibujo de las páginas 330–331 y usen el vocabulario de la escena y el presente progresivo para describir: **(a)** lo que hacen y dicen las personas en los siguientes lugares; **(b)** lo que pasa en cada lugar; **(c)** las tiendas, negocios o anuncios que hay allí.

- en la Calle Sol
- en la Calle Luna
- en la Calle Estrella
- en las esquinas y proximidades de la Calle Luna y la Calle Estrella
- en el parque y cerca de allí

10-2 You may project the PowerPoint slides of the opener scene. When pairs have completed the activity, have students volunteer statements for each area of the scene.

10-2 You may want to tell your students to go to page 173 to review the present progressive before doing this activity. To review the present progressive, students in pairs identify all actions in progress in the opener scene: **Dos señoras *están hablando* de telenovelas.**

10-2 PERSONALIZED QUESTIONS: ¿A quiénes les gustan sus vecinos? Expliquen. ¿Y a quiénes no les gustan? Expliquen. ¿Hay tiendas o negocios en su barrio? Expliquen.

10-3 Concurso de burbujas

Paso 1. Tú y tu compañero/a van a participar en un concurso para ver quién crea los mejores diálogos para las siguientes situaciones. Sigan el modelo y usen el vocabulario que acompaña a las burbujas. ¿Cuál es la más original?

MODELO

relajarse, divertirse

mudarse, olvidarse de

2.

muchachos, acordarse de, chicles.

3.

dueña, obedecer

4.

incendio, quemarse, el humo

Paso 2. Ahora, únanse a otra pareja; léanse los diálogos y voten por el mejor. Luego, compártanlo con el resto de la clase.

10-4 Algo personal: tú y tu barrio

Paso 1. Tu compañero/a y tú se hacen preguntas sobre su barrio para conocerse un poco mejor. Sigan el modelo.

Preguntas	Respuestas	Tu informe
1. ¿Eres el/la **dueño/a** de tu casa o apartamento? ¿O vives en una casa o apartamento alquilado o en una residencia de estudiantes?	*Sí/ No, (no) soy ...* *Sí/ No (no) vivo en ...*	*... (no) es ...* *.... (no) vive en...*
2. Donde tú vives, ¿sabes qué día pasa **el camión de la basura** por allí?		
3. ¿Hay un/a **cartero/a** que pase por tu casa, apartamento o edificio? ¿Lo/La conoces?		
4. **¿Obedeces** las señales de tráfico y las normas de tu barrio o calle? ¿Y tus vecinos?		
5. ¿Mantienes una buena relación con tus **vecinos** y los **saludas?** ¿Los ayudas cuando lo necesitan?		
6. Cuando estás en casa, ¿qué haces para **relajarte?** ¿**Te acuerdas** de ver tu telenovela o tus programas favoritos?		
7. Cuando lavas la ropa, ¿la **cuelgas** o la pones en la secadora?		
8. En caso de **incendio** o de una emergencia, ¿a quién debes llamar? ¿Qué debes gritar en español si tu vida está en peligro[1]?		
9. ¿**Te olvidas** a veces de cerrar con llave la puerta de tu carro o del lugar donde vives?		
10. ¿**Te mudas** con frecuencia de casa, apartamento o residencia?		

Paso 2. Informa a la clase de dos o tres cosas curiosas que sabes ahora de tu compañero/a.

¡A escuchar! Conversaciones de barrio

Paso 1. Escucha las conversaciones de varias personas en el barrio: el cartero y un portero; dos vecinas en la Calle Luna; el conductor de la grúa y el dueño del carro.

PLUS Go to *WileyPLUS* to complete **Paso 2** of this listening activity.

The scripts and recordings for the **¡A escuchar!** sections are included on the Book Companion Site (BCS) for instructors and in *WileyPLUS*.

After completing the *¡A escuchar!* activity, let students know that Spanish-speakers in the US and Mexico often use *se renta* instead of *se alquila*.

[1]danger

Mario y Ernesto se encuentran en el campus al salir de clase. Es ya de noche.

¿**Quieres que veamos** una película? ¿O **prefieres que cenemos** en un restaurante?

Esta noche es la fiesta de mi barrio para recoger fondos. ¡**Dudo**[1] **que sea** una fiesta aburrida! ¿**Quieres que vayamos**?

¿Una fiesta? ¡Tengo mucho que estudiar! No creo que sea una buena idea…

Quiero que vengas y conozcas a mis amigos de la asociación. Además, Mabel va a estar allí.

¿Mabel? Bueno, puedo estudiar más tarde. ¡Después de todo, es por una buena causa!

¡Vamos! ¡**No quiero que lleguemos** tarde!

¡Sin duda, Mario!

© John Wiley & Sons, Inc.

For additional practice on this grammar point, see PowerPoint slides on the BCS or in *WileyPLUS*.

To introduce students to the forms of the subjunctive used in context, have them take parts and read the **historieta** out loud. To check their comprehension and call their attention to the verb forms, ask the following questions:
1. ¿Qué piensa Ernesto de la fiesta de esta noche?
2. Con respecto a su amigo Mario, ¿qué quiere Ernesto? ¿Por qué?

Go to *WileyPLUS* to review this grammar point with the help of **the Animated Grammar Tutorial** and **Verb Conjugator**. For more practice, go to the Grammar Handbook.

Write a lead sentence on the board, such as **El/La profesor/a quiere que los estudiantes estudien**. Provide additional items that instructors want students to do: **aprender el vocabulario, hacer la tarea, llegar a clase a tiempo, hablar en español,**... Students restate the original sentences using the new items and changing the verbs to the present subjunctive.

¡Manos a la obra!

GRAMÁTICA

1

Expressing subjective reactions: The subjunctive mood and the formation of the present subjunctive

The tenses or verb forms you have studied to this point (the present, the preterit, and the imperfect) belong to the *indicative mood*. This mood is used to objectively convey information perceived as real or factual, or to ask questions.

Let's look at examples based on the conversation between Mario and Ernesto as they are leaving campus.

> Mis vecinos **organizan** una fiesta. *My neighbors are organizing a party.*
> ¿**Sabes** cuándo es? *Do you know when it is?*

The *subjunctive mood*, in contrast, is used to express the speaker's wishes, desires, hopes, doubts, fears, and, other emotional reactions to events and, in most cases to the actions of *others*.

> **Quiero** que **conozcas** a mis amigos. *I want **you** to meet my friends.*

The present subjunctive–formation of regular verbs

You have already used some present subjunctive forms—in the **Ud./Uds.** commands (**Vengan** a la fiesta) and in the **tú** negative commands (**No vayas** a casa).

To form the present subjunctive of regular verbs:

Take the **yo** form of the present tense; drop the **-o** ending and add the subjunctive endings, as shown below.

Note that the present subjunctive endings for **-er** and **-ir** verbs are the same.

infinitive	present (yo)	drop the -o	-ar endings	present subjunctive	
pasar	paso	pas-	**-e**	pas**e**	
			-es	pas**es**	
			-e	pas**e**	
			-emos	pas**emos**	
			-éis	pas**éis**	
			-en	pas**en**	
			-er/ir endings		
poner	pongo	pong-	**-a**	pong**a**	dig**a**
decir	digo	dig-	**-as**	pong**as**	dig**as**
			-a	pong**a**	dig**a**
			-amos	pong**amos**	dig**amos**
			-áis	pong**áis**	dig**áis**
			-an	pong**an**	dig**an**

[1] I doubt

For additional practice on these grammar points, see PowerPoint slides on BCS and in *WileyPLUS*.

Go to *WileyPLUS* to review these grammar points with the help of the **Verb Conjugator**. For more practice, go to the **Grammar Handbook**.

De paso

The present subjunctive and the present indicative have the same English equivalents, though the subjunctive can also express a future meaning.

   Dudo que Mario **estudie** esta noche.   *I doubt Mario **will study** tonight.*

Later in this chapter you will be introduced to several concepts and uses of the present subjunctive. First, you will practice its formation.

. . . y algo más   Spelling changes in the *yo* form in the present subjunctive

The spelling changes that some verbs undergo in the **yo** form in the preterit also take place in the present subjunctive:

-car   c → qu → to**car**   to**que**, to**ques**, to**que**, to**quemos**, to**quéis**, to**quen**

-gar   g → gu → lle**gar**   lle**gue**, lle**gues**, lle**gue**, lle**guemos**, lle**guéis**, lle**guen**

-zar   z → c → cru**zar**   cru**ce**, cru**ces**, cru**ce**, cru**cemos**, cru**céis**, cru**cen**

. . . y algo más   Wishes with ¡*Qué* + present subjunctive!

When saying good-bye or ending a conversation, people commonly express good wishes to the person with whom they are speaking. This is how to say it in Spanish: ¡**Que** + *present subjunctive*...!

Situation: Your neighbors are leaving on a trip.

You say: ¡**Que lo pasen bien!** *Have a good time!* (See *Actividad 10-5*)

¡En acción!

¡Oye!   En nuestro barrio

Imagínate que tu profesor/a y tú viven en el mismo barrio. Escucha lo que propone él/ella y responde **sí** o **no** para indicar si estás de acuerdo.

10-5   Lo que se dice en las despedidas

Paso 1.   En las despedidas es importante saber decir lo apropiado. Empareja cada situación con la burbuja correspondiente para indicar lo que les dices a las siguientes personas al despedirte.

MODELO

Tu vecino se va a la fiesta del barrio. ⟶

¿Qué dices al despedirte en estas situaciones?

1. Tu vecina tiene gripe.

2. Te encuentras con un vecino que se va a la estación de tren.

3. Dos de tus vecinos se mudan de casa.

4. Ves a tu sobrino en el cibercafé y al salir le deseas suerte en el examen.

¡Que lo pases bien!

© John Wiley & Sons, Inc.

Guión para ¡Oye!
1. Queremos que el camión de la basura **recoja** la basura una vez al mes. ¿Sí o no?
2. Queremos que la banda **toque** música en el parque toda la noche.
3. Queremos que todos **voten** en las elecciones.
4. Queremos que la panadería **abra** a las cinco de la mañana.
5. Queremos que la farmacia **esté abierta** las 24 horas del día.
6. Queremos que los repartidores de periódicos los **repartan** a mediodía.
7. Queremos que la heladería **venda** helado de cebolla.
8. Queremos que el cartero **deje** nuestros paquetes en la calle.
9. Queremos que los vecinos nos **inviten** a sus fiestas.

(continúa en la p. 336)

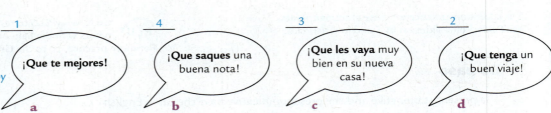

1 — **¡Que te mejores!** — **a**

4 — **¡Que saques** una buena nota! — **b**

3 — **¡Que les vaya** muy bien en su nueva casa! — **c**

2 — **¡Que tenga** un buen viaje! — **d**

 Paso 2. Ahora, inventa despedidas apropiadas para las siguientes situaciones. Primero, marca al lado de cada burbuja el número de la situación (1-5) que le corresponde. Luego, completa la burbuja usando la expresión apropiada.

1. Tu compañera de cuarto sale de casa por la mañana para irse al trabajo.

2. Es sábado y te despides del cartero hasta el lunes.

3. Tus amigos se van de excursión a las montañas.

4. Tu hermana menor se va a una fiesta y no quieres que vuelva tarde.

5. Unos amigos recién casados se van de luna de miel.

2 — 5 — 4 — 3 — 1 — **¡Que tengas** un buen día!

a. *pasar* un buen fin de semana   **b.** *ser* muy felices   **c.** *regresar* pronto   **d.** *divertirse*   **e.** *tener* un buen día

 ## 10-6 Lo quiere el presidente de la asociación

10-6 *Actividades 10-6 and 10-7 preview the use of the subjunctive with expressions of influence.*

10-6 ANSWERS:
1. Quiero que venga...
2. Quiero que limpie y barra... 3. No quiero que deje... 4. No quiero que invite... 5. Quiero que asista... 6. No quiero que le permita... 7. No quiero que ponga... 8. No quiero que tenga...

10-6 ANOTHER STEP:
Students write one thing they want a neighbor to do and one they do not, then share their thoughts with the class.

El presidente de la asociación de vecinos les comunica a ocho vecinos que no respetan las normas lo que **quiere** o **no quiere** que haga cada uno/a. Haz el papel de presidente.

MODELO
respetar las normas → **Quiero** que Ud. **respete** las normas.
fumar en la reunión → **No quiero** que **fume** en la reunión.

1. *venir* a las reuniones de la asociación con más frecuencia

2. *limpiar* y *barrer* su parte de la escalera

3. *dejar* el cubo de la basura delante de su casa toda la semana

4. *invitar* a grupos de *hard rock* a acampar en su jardín

5. *asistir* a la fiesta del barrio

6. *permitirle* a su perro hacer sus necesidades en los jardines de los vecinos

7. *poner* música por la noche a todo volumen

8. *tener* fiestas hasta las cuatro de la mañana

Go to *WileyPLUS* to review these grammar points with the help of the **Verb Conjugator.** For more practice, go to the **Grammar Handbook.**

 For additional practice on these grammar points, see PowerPoint slides on BCS and in *WileyPLUS.*

. . . **y algo más** Stem-changing verbs in the present subjunctive

Just as in the present indicative, stem-changing verbs ending in -**ar** and -**er** *do not* undergo a change in the stem in the **nosotros** and **vosotros** forms of the present subjunctive.

cerrar (e → ie)   cierre, cierres, cierre, cerremos, cerréis, cierren
volver (o → ue)   vuelva, vuelvas, vuelva, volvamos, volváis, vuelvan

Verbs ending in -**ir** *do* undergo a stem change in the **nosotros** and **vosotros** forms. The change (e → i, o → u) is the same as in the present participle (pidiendo, sintiendo, durmiendo), which you have already learned.

pedir (e → i, i)   pida, pidas, pida, pidamos, pidáis, pidan
sentir (e → ie, i)   sienta, sientas, sienta, sintamos, sintáis, sientan
dormir (o → ue, u)   duerma, duermas, duerma, durmamos, durmáis, duerman

Present the conjugations of stem-changing verbs through contextual examples: **Mi vecino quiere que *almuerce* con él. (tú, nosotros,...). El dueño de la pastelería quiere que *pruebes* sus pasteles. (ellos, nosotros,...) El mesero recomienda que Uds. *pidan* langosta. (yo, nosotros,...)**

Remind students that the stem change that verbs ending in –ir have in the ***nosotros*** and ***vosotros*** forms of the present subjunctive is the same change the verbs have in the third person singular and plural of the preterit, which they learned in Ch. 9, on page 298.

. . . **y algo más** Six irregular verbs in the present subjunctive

Only six verbs have irregular forms in the present subjunctive, and you have already used several of these in **Ud./Uds.** and negative **tú** commands (see pages 206 and 222).

dar   dé, des, dé, demos, deis, den
estar   esté, estés, esté, estemos, estéis, estén
ir   vaya, vayas, vaya, vayamos, vayáis, vayan
saber   sepa, sepas, sepa, sepamos, sepáis, sepan
ser   sea, seas, sea, seamos, seáis, sean

As you know, the present indicative of **haber** *to* indicate *there is/are* is **hay.** The present subjunctive is **haya.**

Let students know that the six irregular verbs presented in the chart are the same six verbs whose present indicative tense **yo** forms do not end in –**o.**

10-7   Todos queremos algo de los otros, ¿no?

Paso 1.   Un **novio** quiere tres cosas de su novia; una **madre** quiere tres cosas de sus hijos pequeños; y una **esposa,** otras tres para su marido o para los dos. Escriban en los espacios en blanco quién quiere cada cosa.

1. _madre_ *vestirse* más rápido por la mañana
2. _novio_ *ir* conmigo a bailar a la discoteca
3. _esposa_ *dormir* más; ya no somos jóvenes
4. _madre_ *probar* toda la comida que preparo
5. _novio_ *ser* la madre de mis hijos
6. _madre_ *acordarse* de cepillarse los dientes
7. _esposa_ *darnos* regalos por nuestro aniversario de 25 años de casados
8. _novio_ *saber* que ¡¡te quiero con pasión!!
9. _esposa_ *divertirnos* más y *trabajar* menos, como cuando éramos jóvenes

10-7   Review answers for **Paso 1.** Students may complete Paso 2 individually or in pairs, with answers reviewed by the instructor.

ANSWERS:
Novio: ... vayas... (provided), ... seas..., ...sepas...;
Madre: ... se vistan..., prueben..., se acuerden de...;
Esposa: ... durmamos..., ... nos demos..., ...nos divirtamos más y trabajemos...

Paso 2.   Ahora, hagan los tres papeles y completen las oraciones para expresar sus deseos. Sigan los ejemplos.

Novio: Mi amor, quiero que (tú) **vayas** *conmigo a bailar a la discoteca; quiero que…*

Madre: Niños, quiero que (Uds.)…

Esposa: Querido, quiero que a partir de ahora, (nosotros)…

Go to *WileyPLUS* to review this grammar point with the help of the **Animated Grammar Tutorial** and **Verb Conjugator**. For more practice, go to the **Grammar Handbook**.

Ysenia y Mabel visitan el barrio donde vivieron los abuelos de Ysenia.

Antes este barrio era muy bonito, pero ahora está muy mal. Mucha gente se está mudando a otra parte.

¡Qué lástima! **Es necesario que informemos** a los políticos. **Es importante que ayuden** a este barrio.

Sí, y **es mejor que** todos los vecinos **sepan** que es posible hacerlo. Voy a escribir un artículo acerca de este asunto.

¡Qué buena idea! **Te aconsejo que hables** con los vecinos y **les pidas** su opinión.

Sí, **es necesario que hagamos** algo por un barrio con tanta historia.

¡Que te vaya bien con el artículo! Yo voy a recoger firmas de apoyo.

© John Wiley & Sons, Inc.

For additional practice on this grammar point, see PowerPoint slides on BCS and in *WileyPLUS*.

To introduce students to the subjunctive with expressions of influence used in context, have them take parts and read the **historieta** out loud. To check their comprehension and call their attention to the verb forms, ask the following questions:
1. **Según Mabel, ¿qué es importante que hagan los políticos? ¿Por qué?**
2. **¿Qué le aconseja a Ysenia que haga antes de escribir el artículo?**

To contrast direct commands and the use of the subjunctive with expressions of influence, bring to class six items: a sentence written on a piece of paper, a dollar bill, a comb, a baseball cap, an apple, and a soda. Invite a student to the front to play the role of **el señor/ la señora Gómez**. Give the items to other students who, one by one, hand their item to **el señor/ la señora Gómez** and, using **Ud.** commands, tell him/her what to do with it: **Lea la oración. Gaste el dinero. Péinese. Póngase la gorra. Coma la manzana. Beba el refresco. El señor/ La señora Gómez** complies with their requests. The class, with your assistance, sums up what is happening: **Margaret quiere que el señor/ la señora Gómez lea la oración. Susana quiere que gaste el dinero. Jaime quiere que se peine…**

GRAMÁTICA

¡Manos a la obra!

2

Expressing wishes and requests: The subjunctive with expressions of influence

As you have noticed in the previous activities, the subjunctive mood is used with expressions of *influence*—when one person wishes to influence the actions of another. A sentence that expresses a desire to influence consists of two clauses joined by **que**.

expression of a desire to influence	+ que +	action influenced
(*present indicative*)		(*present subjunctive*)

Let's look at examples of the subjunctive based on the conversation between Ysenia and Mabel as they walk through Ysenia's grandparents' neighborhood.

• With the subjunctive, therefore, each sentence has *two* different subjects—the person influencing and the person influenced.

Quiero que **hables** con los vecinos. *I want **you** to speak with the neighbors.*
Mabel **desea** que los políticos **ayuden**. *Mabel wants **the politicians** to help.*

• If there is only one subject, the infinitive, not the subjunctive, is used.

Quiero recoger firmas de apoyo. *I want to collect signatures of support.*
Mucha gente **prefiere mudarse** a otro barrio. *Many people prefer to move to another neighborhood.*

• A number of verbs you already know (those in the first column) are commonly used to express the wish to influence. The other verbs and expressions are new.

querer (ie)	aconsejar	*to advise*	es necesario	*it is necessary*
desear	insistir (en)	*to insist (on)*	es importante	*it is important*
preferir (ie)	recomendar (ie)	*to recommend*	es mejor	*it is better*
pedir (i)				

• The indirect object pronouns (**me, te, le, nos, os, les**) are used with the verbs **pedir** and **aconsejar,** and commonly with **recomendar.** These precede the verb:

Me piden que escriba un artículo. *They are asking me to write an article.*
Les recomiendo que hagan algo. *I recommend that they do something.*

• **Le** and **les** are commonly used even when the person *to whom* one is asking, advising, or recommending is mentioned.

Les aconsejamos **a los vecinos** que den su opinión.
We advise the neighbors to give their opinion.

¡En acción!

¡Oye! Consejos de un padre

Dos hermanos de diez y doce años van a salir a la calle, pero antes su padre les da los *ocho* consejos que vas a escuchar. Di si son razonables o no.

PARA HABLAR DE TELENOVELAS

(no) llevarse bien con...	*to (not) get along well with*
enamorarse	*to fall in love*
comprometerse	*to get engaged*
casarse	*to get married*
divorciarse	*to get divorced*

¿SABES QUE...?

In Spanish-speaking countries and among Hispanics in the United States, **telenovelas** are very popular, especially those produced in Colombia. Venezuelan and Mexican soap operas also have a large following.

Guión para ¡Oye!
1. Les pido que tengan cuidado al cruzar las calles. ¿Es razonable o no?
2. Quiero que jueguen a la pelota en la calle.
3. Les recomiendo que prueben el helado de la heladería de la Calle Estrella.
4. Quiero que me traigan pan de la panadería de la Calle Luna.
5. Insisto en que compren todo el chicle que vende la vendedora del parque.
6. Les aconsejo que corran por las aceras cuando hay muchos peatones.
7. En el parque, es importante que pongan la basura en las papeleras.
8. Y es mejor que siempre me obedezcan.

10-8 Una telenovela: *El amor lo puede todo*

¡LA SENSACIÓN DEL AÑO! *El amor lo puede todo* se emite todos los jueves por televisión. Cuenta la vida de dos familias: una muy rica, los Castillo, y otra pobre, los Soto. Los ricos viven en una mansión en las afueras del pueblo, y los pobres, en un pequeño apartamento de un barrio humilde. Conozcan a los personajes principales:

LOS CASTILLO (LOS RICOS)

Don Aureliano Castillo
62 años
esposo de Josefina y padre de Víctor
director del banco
quiere divorciarse de su esposa

Josefina Castillo
61 años
esposa de don Aureliano y madre de Víctor
dominante y celosa[1]

Víctor Castillo
28 años
hijo de Aureliano y Josefina
guapo, inteligente y compasivo[2]
médico y voluntario
está muy enamorado de Angelita quiere comprometerse y casarse

LOS SOTO (LOS POBRES)

Angelita Soto
21 años
hija de Pascual y Rosa
bella
se lleva bien con todos
maestra en la guardería infantil
está muy enamorada de Víctor

Pascual Soto
41 años
esposo de Rosa y padre de Angelita
guapo, muy trabajador
buen padre y esposo
policía y bombero voluntario

Rosa Soto
39 años
esposa de Pascual y madre de Angelita
simpática e inteligente
trabaja en la farmacia

(tl) Ryan McVay/PhotoDisc/Getty Images, Inc.; (tc) Philip Lee Harvey/Riser/Getty Images, Inc.; (tr) MedioImages/Getty Images, Inc.; (bl) Javier Pierini/Jupiter Images Corp; (bc) Thinkstock/Royalty-Free/Index Stock Imagery; (br) MedioImages/Getty Images, Inc.

Paso 1. En grupos de *cinco*, hagan los papeles de **doña Josefina, Víctor, Angelita, Pascual** y **Rosa** como si fueran actores de telenovela. Pero antes de hacerlo, completen el guión[3] poniendo los verbos en presente de subjuntivo.

10-8 Introduce the activity by having one student read the introduction followed by six students reading the descriptions of the characters to the rest of the class.

[1]jealous, [2]kind-hearted, [3]script

(continúa en la p. 340)

1. *Primero, en la mansión de los Castillo...*

Dª Josefina: Víctor, tu padre y yo **insistimos** en que no (*ver*) ___veas___ a Angelita más. **Queremos** que (*conocer*) ___conozcas___ a personas de clase alta, como nosotros.

Víctor: ¡Pero, mamá! Para mí su clase social no es un problema, pero sí **es importante** que (*ser*) ___sea___ sincera y compasiva.

Dª Josefina: **No quiero** que me (*hablar*) ___hables___ de tus amores. Y **te aconsejo** que no (*olvidarse*) ___te___ ___olvides___ de algo muy importante: tu herencia.

Víctor: No seas tan fría y calculadora, mamá. ¿Cómo puedes **pedirme** que no (*pensar*) ___piense___ en el amor de mi vida? Me enamoré de ella en el momento en que la vi.

Dª Josefina: ¡Olvídate de ella! Y en cuanto a las personas sin hogar,[1] **prefiero** que no (*trabajar*) ___trabajes___ con ellas. Tenemos asuntos más importantes en que pensar.

Víctor: Mamá, sólo **quiero** que las personas sin hogar (*tener*) ___tengan___ lo suficiente para comer y que no (*morirse*) ___se___ ___mueran___ de hambre y frío.

2. *Más tarde, en el parque...*

Víctor: ¡Amor de mi vida! **¡Quiero** que (*casarse*) ___te___ ___cases___ conmigo! ¡No puedo esperar ni un día más!

Angelita: ¡Ay, cariño! Sabes que tus padres **no quieren** que nosotros (*casarse*) ___nos___ ___casemos___. Y **es mejor** que tú no (*perder*) ___pierdas___ el apoyo de tu familia.

Víctor, corazón mío, **te pido** que me (*olvidar*) ___olvides___. **Quiero** que (*tener*) ___tengas___ una vida sin problemas; en otras palabras, sin mí.

Víctor: ¡No digas eso! ¡Lo único que yo **deseo** es que tú (*estar*) ___estés___ siempre conmigo y que me (*besar*) ___beses___ y me (*abrazar*) ___abraces___!

3. *Luego, en la farmacia...*

Pascual: Rosa, vine para decirte algo. Mi amor, siempre estás tan cansada. **Te pido** que (*trabajar*) ___trabajes___ menos. **Deseo** que (*descansar*) ___descanses___ más.

Rosa: Querido, no te preocupes, sólo quiero ganar lo suficiente para comprar una casita algún día. (*En voz baja para que no la oigan*) ¡Mira quién viene! ¡Es doña Josefina!

Pascual: Bueno, nos vemos esta noche en la reunión.
(*Se va y llega doña Josefina.*)

Dª Josefina: Buenos días, Rosa. **Quiero** que me (*dar*) ___des/ dé___ algo para los nervios. La relación entre mi hijo Víctor y su hija Angelita no me deja dormir.

Rosa: Lo siento muchísimo, doña Josefina. **Le recomiendo** que (*tomar*) ___tome___ este medicamento para tranquilizarse. (*Le da uno demasiado fuerte, por error.*)

4. *En la guardería infantil... (Hay un pequeño incendio y llegan los bomberos.)*

Angelita: Niños, **les pido** que (*escuchar*) ___escuchen___ con atención a los bomberos y que (*obedecer*) ___obedezcan___ sus instrucciones.

Pascual: **Es importante** que todos (*salir*) ___salgan___ rápidamente del edificio. Vengan por aquí, niños, síganme, por favor. ¡Rápido! ¡Rápido!

5. *Poco después, a la entrada de la guardería, llega Víctor...*

Víctor: ¡Ay, mi amor! ¡Cuando oí lo del incendio vine corriendo!

Angelita: ¡Ay, Víctor! Tuvimos suerte. Los bomberos apagaron el fuego y los niños están bien. Pero **nos aconsejan** que no (*entrar*) ___entremos___ al edificio de momento.

6. *Esa noche, en una reunión de la asociación de vecinos...*

Pascual: **Queremos** que los pobres de este barrio (*tener*) ___tengan___ lo básico para vivir.

Rosa: Y para nuestros hijos deseamos paz y bienestar.

Víctor: Debemos **insistir en** que (*haber*) ___haya___ seguro médico no sólo para los ricos sino también para los pobres, y tenemos que decirle al alcalde que nos apoye.

---

[1]personas ... homeless people

Paso 2.   Ahora, cada grupo de *cinco* estudiantes va a darles consejos a los cinco personajes anteriores. Usen las expresiones que siguen. Luego compartan sus consejos con el resto de la clase. ¡A ver qué grupo tiene más!

Le recomiendo a... que...	**Le aconsejo a... que...**	**Le pido a... que...**	
Insisto en que...	**Es importante que...**	**Es mejor que...**	

10-8   At the conclusion of *Paso 1*, confirm answers by having 5 students perform for the class, playing the roles of Dª Josefina, Víctor, Angelita, Pascual, and Rosa.

10-9   ¡Expresa tus deseos!

Paso 1.   Expresa *tres* deseos o recomendaciones para **tu pareja, hijo/a, mejor amigo/a, madre** o **padre.** Pueden ser los tres para la misma persona o para personas distintas. Usa las expresiones de la lista.

Quiero/Prefiero que...	**Te aconsejo/pido que...**	**Te recomiendo que...**	**Es importante que...**

Paso 2.   Comparte con la clase *uno* de tus deseos o recomendaciones, a ver si ellos pueden adivinar para quién es.

MODELO

E1:   *Quiero que **pasemos** una semana romántica en una isla tropical.*

Clase: *Se lo dijiste a tu pareja.*

E1:   *¡Cierto!*

10-10   Preparativos para una visita

RECYCLES clothing and city vocabulary.

10-10   Have pairs team up with other pairs and recite their conversations to each other. Conclude with one pair of students performing for the class.

Un estudiante chileno que conociste en un viaje a Chile va a visitar tu pueblo o ciudad, y te llama por teléfono con varias preguntas. Dale tus recomendaciones. Hagan los dos papeles.

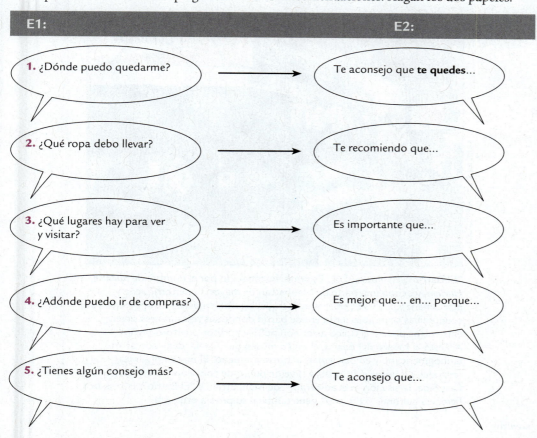

E1:   **E2:**

1. ¿Dónde puedo quedarme?   →   Te aconsejo que **te quedes**...

2. ¿Qué ropa debo llevar?   →   Te recomiendo que...

3. ¿Qué lugares hay para ver y visitar?   →   Es importante que...

4. ¿Adónde puedo ir de compras?   →   Es mejor que... en... porque...

5. ¿Tienes algún consejo más?   →   Te aconsejo que...

Meets ACTFL Standards
1.1, interpersonal speaking;
1.2, interpretive reading;
2.1, cultural practices;
2.2, cultural products; and
4.2, cultural comparisons.

Tu mundo cultural

El barrio en EE. UU.

¿Hay un barrio hispano en tu pueblo o ciudad? La existencia de barrios hispanos en casi todas las ciudades estadounidenses confirma la presencia, cada vez más evidente, de los hispanos en EE. UU. Algunos son como auténticos barrios mexicanos, cubanos, puertorriqueños o dominicanos; otros son ya historia. Y con la continua emigración de hispanos a EE. UU. están apareciendo nuevos barrios, algunos en lugares donde tradicionalmente no había hispanos.

For an additional activity related to this cultural theme, see PowerPoint slides on BCS and in *WileyPLUS*.

Jan Butchofsky/ © Corbis

Olvera Street (1700) está situada en *El Pueblo de Los Ángeles Historic Monument*, el barrio más antiguo de Los Ángeles. Fue territorio de México hasta que en 1848 pasó a formar parte de EE. UU. Muchos mexicanos y otros grupos étnicos emigraron allí en busca de oportunidades económicas. Pasear por Olvera Street recuerda a los barrios de México, con sus restaurantes y puestos de la calle donde sirven especialidades mexicanas. Los fines de semana, los mariachis tocan en la plaza, y durante el año se celebran allí El Día de los Muertos y Las Posadas.

¿SABES QUE...?

El Día de los Muertos is a Mexican celebration where families remember their dead by visiting the graves of their close kin. At home they decorate altars with flowers and at the cemetery, the gravesites. There they have elaborate picnics, often serving **pan de muerto** (egg-battered bread). It is their way of recognizing the cycle of life and death.

¿SABES QUE...?

Las Posadas is a Mexican celebration of nine consecutive days of candlelight processions and lively parties that takes place between December 16 and 24. In villages and urban neighborhoods throughout Mexico, youngsters gather each afternoon to reenact Joseph and Mary's quest for *shelter* in Bethlehem, which in Spanish translates as **posada.**

Gebhard/laif/Redux Pictures

"El Barrio", en Nueva York. Es también conocido por el nombre de *Spanish Harlem*, y ocupa una parte de Manhattan de mayoría puertorriqueña y afro-americana. Los puertorriqueños que llegaron en busca de oportunidades económicas se establecieron en ese barrio donde sus restaurantes sirven, entre otros platos, el típico arroz con pollo y burritos puertorriqueños. Allí está el Museo del Barrio, el único museo de EE. UU. dedicado al arte latinoamericano y en particular, al puertorriqueño. El museo organiza festivales y eventos culturales, y sirve de punto de conexión entre el Upper East Side, la sección más adinerada[1] de Manhattan, y "El Barrio", con su rica herencia cultural. "El Barrio" tiene también su propia orquesta.

[1]wealthy

Gerald Haene/laif/Redux Pictures

Alexander Tamargo/Getty Images, Inc.

La Calle Ocho, en *Little Havana*. En el corazón de Miami está el barrio conocido por el nombre de "Little Havana", donde se encuentran desde puros[1] enrollados a mano hasta fruterías, mercados, herbolarios y cafés al aire libre. Es el barrio donde residen muchos exiliados cubanos llegados después de la instauración del régimen comunista en Cuba, y también inmigrantes de otros países hispanos. El español es la lengua predominante y muchos de sus residentes no hablan inglés. Hay restaurantes con auténtica comida cubana y tiendas de toda clase. El Carnaval de la Calle Ocho tiene fama internacional.

 ## ¿Qué aprendiste?

1. ¿Qué indica la existencia de barrios hispanos en casi todos los pueblos y ciudades de EE. UU.? ¿Qué está ocurriendo actualmente? Answers may vary.

2. ¿Quiénes residen en cada unos de los tres barrios mencionados? Los mexicanos, los puertorriqueños y los cubanos.

3. ¿Qué cosas interesantes ofrece cada uno de ellos? Answers may vary.

 ## Actividad cultural

Un/a estudiante va a hacer de turista y otro/a, de residente de uno de los barrios mencionados. Túrnense para preguntar y dar información acerca del barrio: quiénes y por qué se establecieron en él; la cultura que representa; tiendas/ museos/ edificios que hay; y lo que se puede hacer allí.

Contraste cultural

Hablen de los barrios étnicos que Uds. conocen. ¿De dónde proceden sus residentes? ¿Qué los caracteriza? ¿Por qué se establecieron allí?

¿SABES QUE...?

Los Angeles, New York, Miami, and other US cities have long had large Hispanic populations due to their history, location, and employment opportunities. In the last few decades, other parts of the country have seen tremendous increases in the number of Spanish-speaking residents. Hispanic immigrants have moved to small towns and cities such as Lexington, Nebraska; Beaverton, Oregon; and Springdale, Arkansas, to work in agriculture, meat-packing, and other industries. In some states recent efforts to control illegal immigration have resulted in an exodus of Hispanic residents and negative economic consequences for the area.

---

[1]cigars

2 Actividades del barrio

WILEY PLUS

Pronunciación: Practice pronunciation of the chapter's new vocabulary in *WileyPLUS*.

VOCABULARIO

En la asociación de vecinos

1. reunirse
2. discutir
3. organizar
5. *ahorrar* tiempo.
¡Vamos a *tratar de* organizarnos!
6. resolver (ue)
¡Tenemos la solución! ¡Sí! ¡Sí!
No hay problema.
No hay problema.
7. estar de acuerdo
¡No! ¡Sí!

En la fiesta del barrio

Durante la fiesta…

8. la banda
9. el alcalde
Aplausos para la banda…
10. aplaudir
¡Quiero un globo!
HELADERÍA
11. *Te invito a* un helado.

Joyería Ortiz
12. la violencia
13. el crimen
16. robar
¡No me *mate*!
15. el arma
17. la víctima
18. el ladrón

En trabajos voluntarios

RESIDENCIA DE ANCIANOS
19. *Extraño* a mi familia.
20. atender (ie)

IGLESIA DE SANTA ANA
SOY POBRE, AYÚDEME, POR FAVOR.
21. donar

CAMPAÑA DE ALFABETIZACIÓN
bebe vive lee escribe
22. enseñar
23. la voluntaria

PARROQUIA DE SAN MIGUEL
24. dar de comer
25. las personas sin hogar

ALCOHÓLICOS ANÓNIMOS
26 *bebidas alcohólicas…*
27 *Emborracharse* es un error.

HÁBITAT PARA LA HUMANIDAD
28. construir*

© John Wiley & Sons, Inc.

1. to meet (get together) 2. to argue 3. to organize 4. to try to (do something); **tratar** + **de** + *infinitive* 5. to save (time, money) 6. to solve, resolve 7. to agree 8. the band 9. mayor; **la alcaldesa** (*f.*) 10. to applaud 11. I'll treat/ invite you to…; **invitar a** to invite… 12. violence 13. crime 14. kill; **matar** to kill 15. weapon (*f.*) 16. to rob 17. victim (*m./f.*); 18. thief, robber; **la ladrona** (*f.*) 19. to miss 20. to look after, tend 21. to donate 22. to teach, show 23. volunteer (*f.*); **el voluntario** (*m.*) 24. to feed 25. homeless people 26. alcoholic drinks 27. to get drunk 28. to build

*construir (presente): construyo, construyes, construye, construimos, construís, construyen
(pretérito): construí, construiste, construyó, construimos, construisteis, construyeron

¡En acción!

10-11   ¿Hay otra forma de decirlo?

Empareja los verbos o expresiones de la columna A con los que les corresponden de la columna B.

A.
1. resolver   d.
2. emborracharse e.
3. atender a alguien c.
4. discutir   g.
5. enseñar   f.
6. mudarse   b.
7. ahorrar   h.
8. estar de acuerdo   a.

B.
a. compartir la misma opinión
b. cambiarse de casa
c. cuidar a una persona
d. solucionar
e. beber alcohol en exceso
f. educar
g. manifestar opiniones contrarias
h. guardar parte de lo que se gana

10-12   ¡Qué barrio tan activo!

Observen las escenas de la página 344 y describan lo siguiente.

- En la asociación de vecinos: lo que hacen y dicen las personas
- En la fiesta del barrio: lo que pasa y lo que dicen las personas
- Durante la fiesta: lo que pasa en la joyería Ortiz
- En trabajos voluntarios: quiénes son y qué hacen esas personas

10-13   Para mejorar nuestro barrio o ciudad   RECYCLES subjunctive with expression of influence.

En grupos de *tres,* piensen en *tres* cosas que Uds. quieren, recomiendan o insisten que hagan algunas personas de su barrio o ciudad **(los vecinos, el alcalde, la policía...).** Un/a secretario/a apunta las ideas para luego informarle a la clase:

MODELO

E1:   *Recomendamos que los vecinos reciclen la basura. . . .*

¡A escuchar!   Voluntarios universitarios

Paso 1.   Escucha la conversación de cuatro miembros de una organización universitaria que hablan de la importancia de hacer trabajos voluntarios en su comunidad.

 Go to *WileyPLUS* to complete **Paso 2** of this listening activity.

¿SABES QUE...?

The word **alcalde** is of Arabic origin. Actually, most of the Spanish words that start with **al-** come from the Arabic language. Remember that about 5,000 Spanish words come directly from Arabic.

For additional vocabulary practice, see PowerPoint slides on BCS and in *WileyPLUS.*

You may want to tell your students that **enseñar + a + infinitive** means *to teach how to do something* and **invitar + a + infinitive** means *to invite to do something,* as in **La voluntaria les enseña a leer y a escribir; Te invito a comer un helado.** Remind them that they have already learned a similar construction in ch. 4, p. 115, with **aprender a + infinitive.**

10-12   You may want to project the PowerPoint slide of the scenes. Have four pairs of students each describe one scene, with the class providing additional input.

10-12   PERSONALIZED QUESTIONS: ¿Es la dependencia del alcohol o de las drogas un problema grave entre los estudiantes de este *college*/ esta universidad? ¿Se emborrachan frecuentemente? En este pueblo/ esta ciudad, ¿hay mucho crimen? ¿Y personas pobres o sin hogar? Expliquen.

10-13   A volunteer writes on the board, in abbreviated form, the ideas presented by the groups' secretaries. Each student then votes for his/her top three choices, to determine, by class consensus, the best plans for town or neighborhood improvements.

The scripts and recordings for the **¡A escuchar!** sections are included on the Book Companion Site (BCS) for instructors and in *WileyPLUS.*

Ysenia, Mabel y Jennifer están hablando en la cafetería del éxito¹ que tuvo el artículo de Ysenia.

¿Qué tal el artículo, Ysenia?

¡Muy bien! Se va a organizar una asociación de vecinos en el barrio. Muchos quieren hablar de sus problemas con el alcalde.

Entonces hiciste buenas entrevistas, ¿verdad?

Sí, y los jóvenes, especialmente, **se alegran mucho de que** la situación **se haga** pública; me dieron mucha información.

Espero que el alcalde **ayude** a las personas sin hogar y **termine** con la delincuencia en el barrio.

Yo también. ¿Saben? Me encantó esta experiencia. ¡Es posible que en el futuro sea reportera!

© John Wiley & Sons, Inc.

WILEY PLUS Go to *WileyPLUS* to review this grammar point with the help of the **Animated Grammar Tutorial** and **Verb Conjugator**. For more practice, go to the **Grammar Handbook**.

For additional practice on this grammar point, see PowerPoint slides on the BCS and in *WileyPLUS*.

To introduce students to the subjunctive with expressions of emotion used in context, have them take parts and read the **historieta** out loud. To check their comprehension and call their attention to the verb forms, ask the following questions:
1. **¿De qué se alegran los jóvenes que viven en el barrio de los abuelos de Ysenia?**
2. **¿Qué espera Jennifer que haga el alcalde?**

To introduce the subjunctive with expressions of emotion, draw three faces on the board, each representing an emotion: a smiling face (**alegrarse**), a face with large open eyes and a straight mouth (**esperar**), and a face with a frown and tears (**sentir/ es una lástima**). Write the corresponding expression/s under each face. Give personalized examples while referring to the faces: **Me alegro de que ustedes estén aquí. Es una lástima que John no esté aquí hoy. Siento que muchos estudiantes estén enfermos. Espero que todos saquen una «A» en el próximo examen.** Then make statements about yourself: **Estoy enfermo/a hoy. Estoy contento/a.**

(CONT.)

GRAMÁTICA

¡Manos a la obra!

Expressing emotional reactions and feelings: The subjunctive with expressions of emotion

3

Another common use of the subjunctive is with expressions of *emotion*—when a person expresses emotional reactions and feelings (joy, hope, sorrow,...) about the actions, state, or condition of another person or thing.

expression of emotion	+ que +	action, state, or condition of another person or thing
(*present indicative*)		(*present subjunctive*)

Let's look at examples based on the conversation between Ysenia, Mabel, and Jennifer in the cafetería.

You already know some verbs and expressions that convey feelings or emotions: **gustar, encantar, tener miedo.** Here are a few others:

alegrarse (de)	*to be glad/ happy (about)*	**es una lástima**	*it is a shame*
esperar	*to hope, expect*	**es ridículo**	*it is ridiculous*
sentir (ie, i)	*to be sorry, regret, feel*	**es increíble**	*it is incredible*

• As with expressions of influence (see page 338), each sentence contains *two* subjects: the person expressing the emotion and the person or thing that triggers the emotional reaction.

Los jóvenes del barrio **se alegran de** que la situación **se haga** pública.
The young people of the neighborhood are glad that the situation is becoming public.

Espero que el alcalde **termine** con la delincuencia en el barrio.
I hope the mayor ends the delinquency in the neighborhood.

• If no change of subject occurs after the expression of emotion, the infinitive is used.

| **Siento no poder** hacer más entrevistas. | *I regret not being able to do more interviews.* |
| **Me alegro de hablar** con los jóvenes. | *I am glad to talk with the young people.* |

• **Ojalá (que)...** also means *I hope . . .*, and when referring to a present or future action, is followed by the present subjunctive.

Ojalá que el alcalde **ayude** a los pobres. *I hope the mayor helps the poor.*

¹success

¡En acción!

¡Oye! Trabajos voluntarios

Un/a estudiante tiene una hoja con una sonrisa ☺ y otra con una cara triste ☹. Su profesor/a le hace preguntas. Cuando la respuesta debe ser positiva, el/la estudiante muestra la hoja con la sonrisa; cuando debe ser negativa, muestra la de la cara triste. Luego, la clase contesta las preguntas con «**Nos alegramos de que...**» o «**Sentimos que...**», según la cara que ve.

10-14 ¡Reacciona!

Piensa en un aspecto positivo y uno negativo de tu vida actual y comparte uno de ellos con la clase. Luego, otro/a estudiante reacciona diciendo **"Me alegro de que..."** o **"Siento que..."**.

MODELO

E1: ¡Tengo un carro nuevo!

o: Hoy estoy cansadísimo/a.

E2: **Me alegro de que tengas** un carro nuevo.

o: **Siento que estés** cansadísimo/a.

10-15 Observa la vida

Reaccionen ante las situaciones de los dibujos. Usen las expresiones y los verbos que siguen.

Me alegro de que...	Es una lástima que...	Me gusta que...
Espero que...	Es ridículo que...	Me encanta que...
Siento que...	Es increíble que...	Ojalá (que)...

MODELO

E1: **Siento que haya** pobres en el mundo.

E2: **Es una lástima que** el hombre **tenga** que pedir dinero.

E3: **Me alegro de que** muchos **donen** dinero.

haber, tener que, donar

1 estar en, atender, extrañar

2 construir, ayudar, haber voluntarios

3 haber analfabetos, enseñar, aprender

4 quemarse, saltar, venir los bomberos

5 relajarse, jugar, disfrutar de

(CONT.)

No hay examen final. Students react according to each face/ emotion: **Siento que esté enfermo/a hoy.**

¡Oye! After you read each sentence, the student reacts by raising the smiling or frowning face. The class then answers the question.

Guión para ¡Oye!
1. Los voluntarios les enseñan a los niños a leer y a escribir. ¿Nos alegramos o sentimos que les **enseñen** a leer y a escribir?
2. Los voluntarios se duermen constantemente. ¿Nos alegramos o sentimos que **se duerman** constantemente?
3. Las personas sin hogar no tienen comida. ¿Nos alegramos o sentimos que no **tengan** comida?
4. Los voluntarios construyen casas para Hábitat para la Humanidad. ¿Nos alegramos o sentimos que **construyan** casas?
5. ¡Hay un incendio en la residencia de ancianos! ¿Nos alegramos o sentimos que **haya** un incendio en la residencia de ancianos?
6. Los voluntarios atienden a los ancianos. ¿Nos alegramos o sentimos que **atiendan** a los ancianos?
7. Nadie dona dinero. ¿Nos alegramos o sentimos que nadie **done** dinero?

10-15 You may want to project the PowerPoint slide of the illustrations and elicit feedback on each item from a number of students.

10-15 Let students know that the expression **Ojalá (que)** comes from Arabic and means literally "May Allah grant…" In modern Spanish **Ojalá (que)** + *present subjunctive* is synonymous with *I hope*.

10-16 *El amor lo puede todo: continuación*

¿Qué personajes son nuevos en este episodio?

Don Aureliano Castillo,
el rico del pueblo

Dª Josefina Castillo,
su esposa

Víctor Castillo,
su hijo

Angelita Soto,
la novia de Víctor

Pascual Soto,
su padre

10-16 Before students begin *Actividad 10-16,* have them describe each soap opera character and recap the plot thus far. Refer to *Actividad 10-8,* on pages 339–341.

Rosa Soto,
su madre

El alcalde

Carlitos, huérfano[1]

(tfl) Ryan McVay/PhotoDisc/Getty Images, Inc.; (tl) Philip Lee Harvey/ Riser/Getty Images, Inc.; (tc) MedioImages/Getty Images, Inc.; (tr) Javier Pierini/Jupiter Images Corp; (tfr) Thinkstock/Royalty-Free/Index Stock Imagery; (bl) MedioImages/ Getty Images, Inc.; (bc) ThinkStock/ Jupiter Images Corp; (br) Anderson Ross/Getty Images, Inc.

RECYCLES subjunctive with verbs of influence.

Paso 1. Completen el guión para el nuevo episodio de la telenovela. Finalmente, *cinco* parejas representan las *cinco* escenas de la telenovela para la clase. ¿Quién gana el Óscar?

1. *Angelita visita a **doña Josefina**, que está muy mal a causa del medicamento tan fuerte que le dio Rosa por error.*

   Angelita: Buenas tardes, doña Josefina. **Siento** mucho que Ud. (*estar*) ___esté___ así. Mi madre está muy preocupada.

   Dª Josefina: Mira, Angelita, vamos a ser sinceras. **Es increíble** que (*decir*) ___digas___ eso, porque tu madre...

   Angelita: ¡Pero, doña Josefina! Ud. sabe que mi madre no...

   Dª Josefina: Bueno, eso no cambia nada; tú no eres de nuestra clase social y **queremos** que nuestro hijo (*casarse*) _se_ _case_ con alguien de su misma clase.

   Angelita: **Es una lástima** que Ud. no (*entender*) ___entienda___ que Víctor y yo nos amamos de verdad.

2. *Doña Josefina habla con **don Aureliano**, su esposo, que es el dueño del apartamento de los Soto.*

   Dª Josefina: Aureliano, **insisto en** que tú (*echar*)[2] ___eches___ a los Soto del apartamento inmediatamente.

   Don Aureliano: Josefina, **me preocupa** que (*haber*) ___haya___ leyes que lo prohíban, pero puedo hablar con mi amigo, el alcalde. Tiene que haber alguna manera de resolverlo.

   Dª Josefina: Pues, hazlo hoy. Y, otra cosa, **no me gusta** que tú (*salir*) ___salgas___ por las noches. ¿Adónde vas?

   Don Aureliano: Querida, **es mejor** que nosotros (*hablar*) ___hablemos___ de eso más tarde.

3. *Don Aureliano y el alcalde hablan por teléfono.*

   El alcalde: Buenas tardes, don Aureliano. ¿En qué puedo servirle?

   Don Aureliano: Ud. sabe lo de mi hijo Víctor y Angelita Soto, pues... mi esposa **insiste en** que yo (*echar*) ___eche___ a los Soto del apartamento.

   El alcalde: Vamos a ver, don Aureliano, seguro que hay alguna forma de hacerlo.

   Don Aureliano: Muchísimas gracias, sabía que podía contar con Ud., señor alcalde.

   El alcalde: Estoy a su disposición, don Aureliano, y **espero** que nosotros (*poder*) ___podamos___ solucionarlo pronto.

[1]orphan, [2]to evict

4. **Angelita** *es voluntaria con los niños de la Parroquia de San Miguel. Un día aparece* **Carlitos**, *un niño de siete años.*

Angelita: Carlitos, **me alegro** de que te (*gustar*) ___guste___ dibujar. ¡Qué lindo es este dibujo!

Carlitos: Gracias. Es mi papá, don Aureliano. A veces me visita... y dicen que tiene mucho dinero.

Angelita: (*Piensa: ¡Ay! ¡***Tengo miedo de** *que (*ser*)* ___sea___ *el Aureliano que yo conozco!*)

5. **Víctor** *y Angelita se encuentran en la fiesta del barrio.*

Víctor: ¡Angelita, me acaban de ofrecer un trabajo en un hospital, muy lejos de aquí! **Te pido** que (*venir*) ___vengas___ conmigo.

Angelita: Pero, Víctor, no puedo irme contigo. Mi madre acaba de decirme que tu padre los va a echar de su apartamento. **No quiero** que mis padres (*tener*) ___tengan___ que pasar por una situación tan difícil sin mí.

Víctor: ¡Ay, Angelita! **Siento** mucho que mi padre (*ser*) ___sea___ tan cruel. Voy a hablar con él inmediatamente.

Angelita: Gracias, mi amor. Víctor... ¿conoces a un niño que se llama Carlitos?

Paso 2. Ahora, cada pareja escribe *tres* reacciones acerca de lo que ocurre en este episodio. Usen las expresiones que siguen. Luego, comparen sus reacciones con las de otra pareja y compartan con la clase una que tengan en común o que sea todo lo contrario.

> **Me alegro de que...**   **Espero que...**   **Siento que...**
>
> **Es una lástima que...**   **Es ridículo que...**   **Es increíble que...**

For an additional activity, have students work in groups to create and present a new episode of *El amor lo puede todo* using the same characters.

10-17 Mis deseos y emociones

Paso 1. Expresa tus deseos y emociones respecto a las personas importantes de tu vida. Para hacerlo, completa las burbujas. Menciona a la persona en cuestión y usa el presente de subjuntivo.

LO POSITIVO   **LO NEGATIVO**   **DESEOS PARA EL FUTURO**

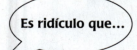

Me alegro de que *mi amiga Sandra...*

Siento que...

Espero que...

Me gusta que...

Es una lástima que...

Ojalá que...

Es ridículo que...

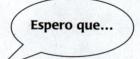

Palabras útiles

estar enfermo/a triste, deprimido/a, enamorado/a
hacer un viaje conmigo a...
(no) *tener* talento para los idiomas, la música, etc....
(no) *ser* bueno/a en deportes
sacar buenas/malas notas
salir con una/s persona/s (in)compatible/s
venir a verme

Paso 2. Comparte con tu compañero/a alguna de las cosas que mencionaste en el *Paso 1*. Túrnense. Finalmente, digan a la clase una de las cosas que dijo su compañero/a.

MODELO

E1: *Elena* **se alegra** *de que su amiga Sandra* **la visite** *este fin de semana.*

E2: *Juan* **siente** *que su novia no* **esté** *aquí.*

Tu mundo cultural

Voluntarios dentro y fuera de EE. UU.

Meets ACTFL Standards 1.1, interpersonal speaking; 1.2, interpretive reading; 5.1, within and beyond school; and 5.2, life-long learning.

For an additional activity related to this cultural theme, see PowerPoint slides on BCS and in *WileyPLUS*.

¿Quieres conocer a gente hispana y su cultura y al mismo tiempo practicar español? Hazte voluntario. Los trabajos voluntarios son además experiencias enriquecedoras[1]. A continuación, vas a informarte de varias opciones de voluntariado en EE. UU. y en países hispanos.

Trabajos voluntarios en las comunidades hispanas de EE. UU.

Cada vez son más las personas en este país que hacen trabajos voluntarios con hispanos. Y también son más los *colleges* y universidades estadounidenses que ofrecen a sus alumnos la oportunidad de obtener créditos mediante lo que se llama *service learning*, a cambio de trabajos voluntarios realizados en la comunidad.

Courtesy of Laila Dawson

Julia, una voluntaria, de excursión con dos niñas de la comunidad mexicana. Ella, como otros estudiantes de español de la Universidad de Richmond, en Virginia, trabaja con familias hispanas, haciendo de tutora e intérprete. De esta forma, practica español, conoce una cultura diferente y hace amigos.

¿SABES QUE...?

Depending on their college or university's service-learning program, students learning Spanish may find opportunities to volunteer with local schools, churches, clinics and hospitals, community centers, and organizations such as the American Red Cross, the YMCA, or the Boys and Girls Clubs of America. Students can develop their language and cultural skills and utilize their knowledge of other disciplines they are studying as they serve the Hispanic residents in their community.

Rachel, voluntaria de Loyola University Chicago Stritch School of Medicine, sacándole sangre a una paciente hispana. En esta facultad de medicina y en otras, los estudiantes voluntarios atienden a pacientes hispanos en clínicas que se dedican a ayudar a los que no tienen seguro médico.

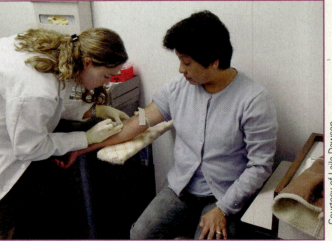

Courtesy of Laila Dawson

[1]enriching

Trabajos voluntarios en países hispanos

Si recuerdas los efectos devastadores del huracán Katrina en EE. UU. en el año 2005, puedes entender por qué en tantos países de América Central donde los huracanes, terremotos[1] e inundaciones[2] son muy frecuentes, es tan necesaria la labor de las organizaciones humanitarias.

GUATEMALA
EL SALVADOR
HONDURAS
NICARAGUA
PERÚ
BOLIVIA

© John Wiley & Sons, Inc.

Courtesy of Jeanne Nakamaru

Muchos voluntarios de EE. UU., Canadá y Europa trabajan para organizaciones humanitarias en países de América Central ayudando en el cuidado y educación de los niños huérfanos, abandonados o con discapacidades físicas o mentales. Jeanne, voluntaria estadounidense, trabaja como terapeuta del lenguaje con niños en el Centro Maya Xe´Kiyqasiiwaan de San Juan de la Laguna, en Guatemala. También, como se aprecia abajo en la fotografía, a los niños de la organización NPH se les ve felices en el rancho, donde son muy bien atendidos por los voluntarios.

 ## ¿Qué aprendiste?

1. ¿Cómo se benefician los estudiantes que hacen trabajos voluntarios con hispanos? ¿Qué ejemplos se mencionan? Pueden conocer la cultura hispana más de cerca y practicar el español. Además, pueden conseguir créditos por *service learning*.

2. ¿A qué niños ayudan muchos voluntarios extranjeros[3] en América Central?
A ayudar a los países a recuperarse de las catástrofes naturales.

3. ¿Qué ofrece la organización Nuestros Pequeños Hermanos para niños y voluntarios?
Answers may vary.

 ## Actividad cultural

Un/a estudiante hace el papel de director/a de una organización humanitaria y explica las cualidades que busca en los voluntarios. Otro/a estudiante hace de voluntario/a e indica las cualidades y talentos que le hacen buen/a candidato/a y qué clases de trabajos le gustaría hacer.

 ## Contraste cultural

Hablen de sus experiencias como voluntarios y de las oportunidades para hacer trabajos voluntarios que hay en su pueblo o ciudad.

[1]earthquakes, [2]floods, [3]foreign

Courtesy of Friends of the Orphans

FRIENDS OF THE ORPHANS
Bolivia, El Salvador, Guatemala, Haití, Honduras, México, Nicaragua, República Dominicana, Perú

Misión: Nuestra organización ayuda a niños huérfanos, abandonados o de bajos recursos apoyando a Nuestros Pequeños Hermanos (NPH), una red de orfanatos de América Latina y el Caribe. La misión es darles un hogar y proveerles de comida, ropa, cuidados médicos y educación. No se separa a los niños de sus hermanos y no se dan en adopción. Los niños están en un ambiente seguro y de amor, donde aprenden los valores del trabajo, responsabilidad y a compartir.

Voluntarios y sus responsabilidades: En los voluntarios se busca a personas trabajadoras, flexibles, con actitud positiva y sentido del humor, que quieren ayudar a los niños y compartir con ellos sus talentos y conocimientos. Se necesitan voluntarios para cuidar a los niños o darles clases de inglés. También se necesitan profesores de educación especial, coordinadores de voluntarios, médicos y bibliotecarios.

¿Cómo puede ayudarnos? Haga una donación, hágase padrino o madrina de un niño o niña, o sea voluntario.

Póngase en contacto con nosotros: www.friendsoftheorphans.org

Used by permission of Friends of the Orphans.

Escena

3

Pronunciación:
Practice pronunciation of the chapter's new vocabulary in *WileyPLUS*.

Asuntos* sociales, políticos y religiosos

VOCABULARIO

En ¹la manifestación

En ¹⁰la campaña electoral

En el templo

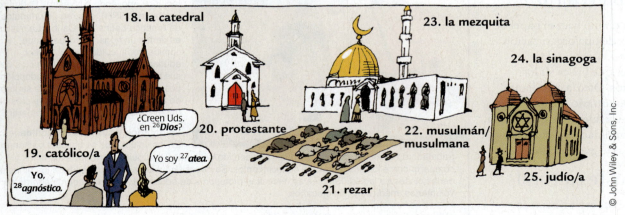

© John Wiley & Sons, Inc.

---

1. demonstration 2. justice 3. equality (*f.*) 4. laws (*f.*) 5. reporter (*m.*); **la reportera** (*f.*) 6. we fight for...; **luchar por** to fight for 7. human rights 8. war 9. peace (*f.*) 10. electoral campaign 11. taxes 12. liberals; **progresista** 13. the conservatives; **conservador/a** 14. Are you in favor...? **estar a favor de** to be in favor of 15. against 16. dangerous 17. national security 18. cathedral 19. Catholic 20. Protestant 21. to pray 22. Muslim 23. mosque 24. synagogue 25. Jewish 26. God 27. atheist 28. agnostic

****Asuntos** *matters*

¡En acción!

10-18   ¿Qué pasa en la calle?

Observa las escenas de la página 352 y di si es cierto o falso lo siguiente. Si es falso, da la información correcta.

C   F

- [x] [ ] **1.** En la manifestación hay mucha gente protestando.
- [x] [ ] **2.** Unas personas no quieren la guerra; están a favor de la paz.
- [ ] [x] **3.** Un vecino informa acerca de lo que pasa en la manifestación.
- [ ] [x] **4.** La candidata Mora está a favor de las centrales nucleares.
- [x] [ ] **5.** El candidato Trujillo quiere que los ciudadanos paguen menos impuestos.
- [ ] [x] **6.** Unos católicos rezan cerca de la mezquita mirando en dirección a La Meca.
- [x] [ ] **7.** Los judíos rezan en la sinagoga.
- [x] [ ] **8.** Los ateos no creen en Dios.

10-19   Asuntos sociales, políticos y religiosos

¿Todos hacen y piensan lo mismo? Para saberlo, observen las escenas de la página 352 y describan lo siguiente:

- lo que hace el reportero y sobre qué está informando
- por qué luchan y qué piden las personas que protestan en la manifestación
- qué prioridades tiene cada uno de los candidatos
- las religiones representadas por los tres edificios de la escena; y qué hacen o dicen las personas en ella

For additional vocabulary practice, see PowerPoint slides on BCS and in *WileyPLUS*.

10-18   ANSWERS: Corrections for false (F) responses: 3. Un reportero...; 4. Está en contra de...; 6. Unos musulmanes...

10-19   You may want to project the PowerPoint slide of the scenes and elicit responses from the class and/or have pairs of students describe each scene.

10-19   PERSONALIZED QUESTIONS: ¿Participan Uds. en manifestaciones? ¿Por qué? ¿Votaron en las últimas elecciones? ¿Qué organizaciones políticas, religiosas o humanitarias les interesan más?

Oaxaca, México. Festividad de la Virgen de Guadalupe, patrona de los mexicanos. En toda ciudad mexicana hay una iglesia dedicada a ella. El día antes de la festividad, el 12 de diciembre, los niños y bebés van a la catedral en procesión para hacerle ofrendas[1] a la virgen y pedirle protección.

[1]offerings, [2]**Semana...** Holy Week

Antigua, Guatemala. La Semana Santa[2] de Antigua es famosa por las magníficas alfombras florales con las que sus habitantes decoran las calles para la procesión religiosa. Las alfombras, como la que se observa en la fotografía, se hacen con pétalos de flores.

10-20 Write the numbers 1–8 on the board in a horizontal line. Invite a volunteer to come to the board to record the votes in favor of and against each item. As you call out the categories, ask for a show of hands: ¿Quién está a favor? ¿Quién está en contra?

10-20 Un sondeo

Paso 1. Camina por la clase y pregúntales a *ocho* personas diferentes si están *a favor* o *en contra de* lo siguiente. Marca la respuesta (**A favor** o **En contra**) y el nombre de cada persona que responde. Tienes *seis* minutos.

MODELO

E1: *Ana, ¿estás **a favor** o **en contra de** las leyes para proteger el medio ambiente?*

E2: *Estoy a favor.*

SONDEO	A favor de	En contra de	Nombre	
	☐	☐	_____	1. las leyes para proteger el medio ambiente[1]
	☐	☐	_____	2. los programas de «Acción afirmativa»
	☐	☐	_____	3. el seguro médico universal
	☐	☐	_____	4. el matrimonio entre personas del mismo sexo
	☐	☐	_____	5. la pena de muerte[2]
	☐	☐	_____	6. el derecho a llevar armas
	☐	☐	_____	7. subir los impuestos para reducir el déficit nacional
	☐	☐	_____	8. reducir la edad a la que se permite consumir bebidas alcohólicas

Paso 2. Al terminar, compartan con la clase algunas de las opiniones de sus compañeros. Luego, voten todos *a favor* o *en contra de* cada categoría. ¿Tienen opiniones similares?

PLUS For more practice, see **Grammar Handbook** found in *WileyPLUS*.

You might want to give your students a third option for the survey namely that they could abstain by saying **Me abstengo.**

Remind your students that both **estar a favor de** and **estar en contra de** require the preposition **de.** However, when both expressions go together as in the example in the Modelo, the first **de** is dropped to avoid repetition. Remind them also that de combination **de + el** as in questions 3, 4 and 6 of the **SONDEO** results in **del.**

For additional practice on this grammar point, see PowerPoint slides on the BCS and in *WileyPLUS*.

Explain your students that even though **ninguno/a** does not have a plural form, exceptionally, **ningunos/ as** can be used as an adjective accompanying plural nouns. For instance: **No he comprado ningunos zapatos. No tengo ningunas gafas de ese color.**

. . . y algo más   *Alguno/a/os/as* and *ninguno/a*

You have already learned two pairs of affirmative/ negative words: **algo/ nada** and **alguien/ nadie.** Here is another pair:

alguno/a/os/as *any, some, someone*   **ninguno/a** *no (not a single), none, not any*

· Just as **uno** shortens to **un** before a masculine singular noun, **alguno** and **ninguno** become **algún** and **ningún:**

Ningún ciudadano está a favor de esa ley. **Algún** día todos van a quejarse.
No *(not a single) citizen is in favor of that law.* **Some** *day they are all going to complain.*

· Because **ninguno/a** means *not a single (one)*, it does not have a plural form.

—¿Van a votar **algunos** estudiantes?   —No, **ninguno** va a votar.

[1]**medio...** environment, [2]**pena...** capital punishment

354 trescientos cincuenta y cuatro   CAPÍTULO 10   EL BARRIO

10-21 **¿A quién conoces y qué sabes de la vida política de tu país?** RECYCLES *saber* and *conocer*.

 Paso 1.   Marca la casilla que corresponde para indicar la información que tienes sobre personas destacadas[1] de la política de tu país.

Sí	No	¿Conoces a...
☐	☐	**1.** ... alguna mujer que sea senadora de un estado de EE. UU.? ¿A quién?
☐	☐	**2.** ... algún político estadounidense que luchó en la guerra de Vietnam? ¿A quién?
☐	☐	**3.** ... alguna jueza del Tribunal Supremo de EE. UU.? ¿A cuál?
☐	☐	**4.** ... algún ex-presidente o gobernador que fue antes actor de Hollywood? ¿A quién?
☐	☐	**5.** ... algún político que tenga como prioridad la defensa del medio ambiente? ¿A quién?

Sí	No	¿Sabes...
☐	☐	**6.** ... de algún grupo político que sea nuevo? ¿Qué sabes?
☐	☐	**7.** ... de un Jefe de Gabinete[2] de la Casa Blanca que es ahora alcalde de una gran ciudad? ¿Quién es?
☐	☐	**8.** ... de algunos de los candidatos que se presentaron a las últimas elecciones presidenciales de EE. UU.? ¿Qué sabes?
☐	☐	**9.** ... de algún estado que tenga una ley que permita llevar armas? ¿Qué sabes?
☐	☐	**10.** ... de algunos políticos que sean de derechas o de izquierdas? ¿Qué sabes?

 Paso 2.   Ahora, comparte la información diciendo a quién conoces y lo que sabes y no sabes con tu compañero/a. Usa alguno/a (s) y ninguno/a.

¡A escuchar!   Elecciones presidenciales

Paso 1.   Escucha las entrevistas[3] de una reportera.

WILEY PLUS   Go to *WileyPLUS* to complete **Paso 2** of this listening activity.

The scripts and recordings for the ¡**A escuchar!** sections are included on the Book Companion Site (BCS) for instructors and in *WileyPLUS*.

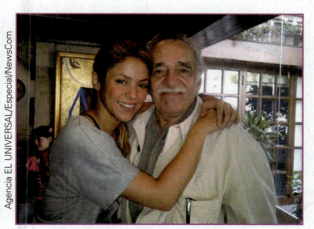

¿Conoces a Shakira, la famosa cantante? ¿Y a Gabriel García Márquez, el escritor que ganó el Premio Nobel de Literatura en 1982? Los dos son de Barranquilla, en Colombia. Los dos colaboran en la organización ALAS (América Latina en Acción Solidaria), que ayuda a los niños pobres. García Márquez es el presidente honorario de la organización y Shakira, una de sus activistas más conocidas. Para más información sobre ALAS, puedes ir a www.fundacionalas.org.

En el invierno del año 2011 (verano en EE. UU.) cientos de miles de estudiantes chilenos organizaron manifestaciones para pedir una reforma del sistema de educación chileno. La voz detrás del movimiento fue Camila Vallejo, una estudiante de geografía de 23 años y segunda mujer presidenta de la FECH (Federación de Estudiantes de la Universidad de Chile), una organización que tiene más de cien años. Muchos consideran que la carismática Vallejo, tiene un futuro prometedor en la política chilena.

[1]outstanding, [2]**Jefe...** Chief of Staff, [3]interviews

Al volver del supermercado, Ernesto y Fabio ven en su barrio un mural acerca de la tolerancia religiosa.

¡Qué mural tan interesante!

Sí. Se llama "Tolerancia religiosa". El artista es amigo mío.

¿**Crees que** eso es posible?

Sinceramente, no. **No creo que podamos** vivir en un mundo sin guerras.

Depende de las generaciones futuras, ¿no?

Sí. Yo le enseño a mi hija a ser tolerante. Si todos lo somos, sin duda la vida va a ser mejor.

No lo niego, pero **no estoy seguro de que sea** tan fácil.

© John Wiley & Sons, Inc.

PLUS Go to *WileyPLUS* to review this grammar point with the help of the **Animated Grammar Tutorial** and **Verb Conjugator**. For more practice, go to the **Grammar Handbook**.

For additional practice on this grammar point, see PowerPoint slides on BCS and in *WileyPLUS*.

To introduce students to the subjunctive with expressions of doubt or negation used in context, have them take parts and read the **historieta** out loud. To check their comprehension and call their attention to the verb forms, ask the following questions:
1. **¿Cree Fabio que podemos vivir en un mundo sin guerras?**
2. **¿Está seguro Ernesto de que es fácil hacerlo?**

Let students know that in questions like those in the annotation above, when the speaker expects a negative answer to the question, the verb after **creer** or **estar seguro/a de** could be in the subjunctive.

To introduce this structure, write **Dudo que** + *subjunctive* and **Creo que** + *indicative* on the board. Then make statements about yourself, some true and some obviously false (**Tengo 17 años. Hablo español.** etc.), and allow students to either doubt or believe your statements. Create other personalized statements to practice additional expressions of doubt.

GRAMÁTICA

¡Manos a la obra!

Expressing uncertainty or denial: The subjunctive with expressions of doubt or negation

4

Another common use of the subjunctive is with expressions of *doubt* or *negation*—when a person expresses doubt or disagreement about the actions, state, or condition of another person or thing. As before, each sentence has two clauses, with the subjunctive in the second clause.

expression of doubt or negation	+ que +	action, state, or condition of another person or thing
(present indicative)		*(present subjunctive)*

Some verbs and expressions that convey doubt, uncertainty, disbelief, or negation are:

Doubt and uncertainty		*Disbelief or negation*	
dudar	*to doubt*	**no creer**	*not to believe*
no estar seguro/a (de)	*not to be sure*	**no es verdad**	*it's not true*
es posible	*it is possible*	**es imposible**	*it's impossible*
es probable	*it is probable*	**es improbable**	*it's improbable*

Let's look at examples based on Ernesto and Fabio's discussion of the theme of the mural.

Sentences that begin with expressions of doubt or negation generally have two different subjects: the person expressing the doubt or negation and the person or thing towards which the doubt or negation is directed.

Fabio **no cree** que **podamos** vivir en un mundo sin guerras.
Fabio does not believe that we can live in a world without war.
Ernesto **duda** que **sea** fácil hacerlo.
Ernesto doubts that it is easy to do it.

Because expressions such as **ser verdad** and **estar seguro/a (de)** express certainty, they require the indicative. The verbs **creer** and **pensar** also express sufficient certainty to take the indicative.

Fabio **cree/ está seguro de** que la vida **va** a ser mejor si todos son tolerantes.
Fabio believes/ is sure that life is going to be better if everyone is tolerant.

¡En acción!

¡Oye! ¿Están de acuerdo o no?

Vas a escuchar ocho opiniones. Apunta si estás de acuerdo o no con cada una.

10-22 Opiniones opuestas

Paso 1. Lee las siguientes opiniones y marca tus reacciones.

1. En nuestro país hay justicia e igualdad para todos.

   ☐ Creo que **hay...**   ☐ Dudo que **haya...**

2. La mayoría de los ciudadanos de este país hacen trabajos voluntarios.

   ☐ Creo que muchos **hacen...**   ☐ No estoy seguro/a de que muchos **hagan...**

3. Las centrales nucleares son peligrosas.

   ☐ Estoy seguro/a de que **son...**   ☐ No creo que **sean...**

4. Hay suficiente trabajo y suficientes viviendas para las personas sin hogar.

   ☐ Sé que **hay...**   ☐ Dudo que **haya...**

5. El plan del presidente para resolver la crisis financiera es bueno.

   ☐ Creo que **es...**   ☐ Es improbable que **sea...**

6. En este país, muchos judíos, cristianos y musulmanes se entienden bien.

   ☐ Es verdad que **se entienden...**   ☐ Dudo que un gran número **se entiendan...**

Paso 2. Comparte tus reacciones con la clase. Usa oraciones completas. Luego, decidan entre todos si los estudiantes de la clase son, por lo general, optimistas, pesimistas o realistas.

P. Narayan/Age Fotostock America, Inc.

[1]pan... gold leaf

El catolicismo es todavía la religión predominante entre los hispanos. Las innumerables y magníficas iglesias y catedrales edificadas por todo el mundo hispano, como la catedral de Quito (siglo XVI) en Ecuador, dan testimonio de ello. Este altar es de pan de oro[1].

¿SABES QUE...?

"2011 Hours Against Hate" or "2011 **Horas Contra el Odio**" was a campaign launched by the US Department of State to promote respect among peoples of different religions and cultures. Using Facebook and Twitter, organizers hoped to encourage young people to volunteer 2011 hours to combat hatred by assisting those who are not like themselves. In early 2011, the US ambassador to Spain, Alan Solomont, presented the campaign to Spaniards in the city of **Córdoba** because of its history as a Muslim capital and a city where Christians, Jews, and Muslims coexisted.

¡Oye! Students jot down the numbers 1–8, and after each statement write: **Estoy de acuerdo** (or) **No estoy de acuerdo**. Write the two expressions on the board.

Guión para ¡Oye!
1. **Creo** que todos los ciudadanos **tienen** que pagar impuestos. ¿Están Uds. de acuerdo o no?
2. **Dudo** que **pueda** haber paz en el mundo.
3. **Es probable** que **haya** más ataques terroristas en este país.
4. **Estoy seguro/a** de que todos los políticos **respetan** las leyes.
5. **Es cierto** que el presidente de este país **es** siempre sincero.
6. **Es imposible** que una mujer **gane** las elecciones y **sea** presidenta de EE. UU.
7. **Dudo** que en el futuro **haya** más tolerancia entre judíos, cristianos y musulmanes.
8. **Es verdad** que **hay** que respetar todas las religiones.

10-22 For each item, ask several students to share their opinions with the class. Then ask for a show of hands to gauge the class's sentiments.

10-22 ANOTHER STEP: Have students tell the class something about themselves that is either true or false. The other students respond, indicating if they doubt what was said or not, using **dudar**, **(no) creer** and **(no) estar seguro/a**. *Example:*
E1: **Tengo tres novios.**
E2: **¡Eso no es verdad! Dudo que tengas tres novios.** (o) **Sí, creo que tienes tres novios.**

You may want to emphasize to students that expressions like **estar seguro/ es verdad/ creer/ pensar** require indicative in the affirmative, and subjunctive in the negative, while **dudar** shows the opposite pattern.

Hubert Stadler/Corbis Images

La sinagoga Gran Templo de Paso de Buenos Aires. Se calcula que en Argentina hay unos 395.000 judíos, la mayoría de los cuales residen en la capital, lo que constituye la comunidad judía más grande del continente americano después de las de EE. UU. y Canadá.

Rafael Marchante/Reuters/© Corbis

El Imán de la mezquita de Fuengirola, en Málaga, reza en memoria de las víctimas del ataque terrorista en la estación de Atocha de Madrid (11 de marzo de 2004). Se calcula que hay unos 400.000 musulmanes en España; y el número va en aumento.

10-23 Tres religiones: ¿Cuánto saben?

Vamos a ver qué saben Uds. sobre tres religiones que han tenido y todavía tienen gran influencia en el mundo hispano: la cristiana (católica y protestante), la judía y la musulmana.

Primero, cada uno/a marquen **Cierto** o **Falso** para indicar si las siguientes afirmaciones son ciertas o no. Luego, díganse si **creen** o **no** lo que se dice en ellas. Túrnense. Al terminar, verifiquen sus respuestas.

MODELO

E1: *La Biblia es un libro sagrado para los musulmanes.*

E2: *(E2 marcó la F.)* **No creo** *que la Biblia* **sea** *un libro sagrado para los musulmanes. ¿Y tú?*

E1: *Estoy de acuerdo.*

o: *(E2 marcó la C.)* **Yo creo** *que la Biblia* **es** *un libro sagrado para los musulmanes.*

C	F		
☐	☑	**1.**	Uno de los símbolos de la religión cristiana *es* la estrella de David.
☑	☐	**2.**	El nombre Cristo *viene* del griego y *significa* Mesías, Salvador.
☑	☐	**3.**	El cristianismo *es* la religión con más seguidores en el mundo.
☐	☑	**4.**	La religión judía y la musulmana *permiten* comer carne de cerdo.
☑	☐	**5.**	Casi la mitad[1] de los 14 millones de judíos del mundo *vive* en EE. UU.
☑	☐	**6.**	Las religiones judía y musulmana *prohíben* representar la imagen de Dios, o de figuras humanas o de animales en las sinagogas y mezquitas.
☑	☐	**7.**	El Islam *es* la segunda religión con más seguidores en el mundo.
☑	☐	**8.**	El Corán (612–632) *es* el libro sagrado de los musulmanes; *contiene* la revelación transmitida a Mahoma por Alá (Dios).
☐	☑	**9.**	Durante el Ramadán, los musulmanes adultos, incluso los enfermos y las mujeres embarazadas, no *comen* ni *beben* de sol a sol[2].
☑	☐	**10.**	Los musulmanes *rezan* mirando en dirección a La Meca.

[1]half, [2]**de...** from sunrise to sunset

10-24　Debate político

Paso 1. Son dos analistas políticos para *CNN en español*. Primero, decidan quién es el/la conservador/a y el/la progresista. Luego, reaccionen a las promesas del presidente de su país.

MODELO

E1: *(conservador/a)* **Dudo que** *el/la presidente/a reduzca el déficit.*

E2: *(progresista) ¡En absoluto![1]* **¡Es ridículo que** *mi colega diga eso!* Yo **creo que...**

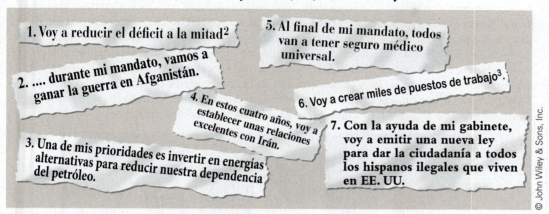

1. Voy a reducir el déficit a la mitad[2]

2. .... durante mi mandato, vamos a ganar la guerra en Afganistán.

3. Una de mis prioridades es invertir en energías alternativas para reducir nuestra dependencia del petróleo.

4. En estos cuatro años, voy a establecer unas relaciones excelentes con Irán.

5. Al final de mi mandato, todos van a tener seguro médico universal.

6. Voy a crear miles de puestos de trabajo[3].

7. Con la ayuda de mi gabinete, voy a emitir una nueva ley para dar la ciudadanía a todos los hispanos ilegales que viven en EE. UU.

© John Wiley & Sons, Inc.

Paso 2. Ahora, compartan algunas de sus reacciones con el resto de la clase.

10-25　Mensajes con deseos, emociones y dudas

RECYCLES subjunctive with expressions of influence and emotion.

Paso 1. Haz el papel de Julia. Lee los mensajes y escribe lo que vas a contestar a las personas que llamaron. Usa los verbos que siguen y otros en tus respuestas.

MODELO

Respuesta al mensaje nº 1: *Hola, Pili. Soy Julia. No te preocupes,* **dudo que haya** *un examen mañana.*

| aconsejarte | alegrarse de | sentir | esperar | dudar | creer | es una lástima | es probable |

3. Hija, soy mamá. No puedo ir a tu casa porque hay huelga[4] de transporte público y mi carro no funciona.

2. Julia, cariño, soy Paco. La entrevista acaba de terminar; tengo el trabajo que quería. ¡Soy el nuevo abogado del alcalde!

4. Señorita Julia Bravo, aquí Tecnología Siglo XXI. Su computadora ya está reparada. Díganos cuándo va a pasar a recogerla.

1. Julia, ¿sabes si hay examen de inglés mañana? Llámame. Soy Pili.

5. Julia, soy Fernando. Estoy muy deprimido. No encuentro mi billetera con el dinero, la tarjeta de crédito, la licencia de manejar...; no sé qué hacer.

Greeting　Voicemail (3)　Speaker

● **Mamá**　9/7/11
● **Paco**　9/7/11
II **Julia Bravo**　9/7/11
● **Fernando**　9/7/11
● **Pili**　9/7/11

0:05　-0:05

Call Back　　Delete

© John Wiley & Sons, Inc.

10-25 Remind students that they cannot use the present subjunctive to react about what happened in the past.

10-25 If time is short, have each student respond to only one message (items 1–5). Then read each of Julia's messages, and have all students who responded to a particular one read their replies.

Paso 2. Uno/a de Uds. hace el papel de la persona que deja el mensaje para Julia, y otro/a hace el papel de Julia que devuelve la llamada y deja otro mensaje. Túrnense.

[1]**En... Absolutely not!** [2]**half,** [3]**puestos ... jobs,** [4] **strike**

Tu mundo cultural

Los murales de los barrios de EE. UU.

¿Hay murales en las calles de tu pueblo o ciudad? ¿Son hispanos los artistas?

La pintura muralista tiene una larga tradición en México. En el pasado, los grandes maestros como Rivera (1886–1957), Orozco (1883–1949) y Siqueiros (1896–1974) promocionaron el arte mural para concienciar al pueblo de los problemas sociales y políticos. Esta tradición continúa en los barrios mexicanos de EE. UU. donde se pintan murales en las calles y edificios para concienciar a la comunidad de las preocupaciones sociales y políticas más urgentes. Son patrocinados[1] por compañías y organizaciones de la comunidad y en ellos participan jóvenes locales. A continuación, vas a observar primero, un mural de David Alfaro Siqueiros que se acaba de exponer al público después de haber estado censurado 80 años.

¿SABES QUE...?

The Mexican muralist **Diego Rivera** created murals in various locations in the United States. His mural in the Detroit Institute of Arts, "Detroit Industry or Man and Machine," painted in 1932 and 1933, appeared in a 2011 Superbowl commercial for Chrysler featuring the rapper Eminem. Rivera also designed a mural for Nelson Rockefeller in the RCA building in New York, but it was destroyed after a disagreement over the political content of the mural.

La América tropical: oprimida y destrozada por los imperialismos, del mexicano David Alfaro Siqueiros (1932), en Olvera Street, en Los Angeles. Al artista le encargaron un mural con el nombre de *América Tropical* y posiblemente, esperaban que pintara una escena exuberante e idílica. Sin embargo, Siqueiros cambió el título y su interpretación fue una dura crítica de la política opresiva de EE. UU. hacia los mexicanos, en los años treinta. En consecuencia, el mural fue censurado y cubierto de pintura blanca. Así ha permanecido casi 80 años hasta que por fin, desde el 2012 se puede contemplar en Olvera Street. La figura central representa a un campesino indígena colgado de una cruz; tiene encima un águila, símbolo de EE. UU. Desde la esquina, se observa a dos guerreros indígenas apuntando al águila.

A continuación, observa tres de los murales que se encuentran en El Paso, en Texas.

"AIDS" de Carlos Callejo y sus estudiantes (1988), situado detrás de la Clínica La Fe, en El Paso. Es una de las tres pinturas que forman un mural. Fue pintado para concienciar de los peligros[2] del SIDA. El tornado representa la epidemia que transmite la enfermedad y devasta la tierra. Una mujer expresa su dolor porque el hijo que espera va a nacer[3] con SIDA.

[1] sponsored, [2] dangers, [3] be born

"NUESTRA HERENCIA" de Carlos Flores (1992), El Paso. Las tres caras representan la herencia mexicana: la indígena, la española y la mestiza, combinación de las dos primeras. Este mural refleja la diversidad cultural que hay en la frontera entre México y EE. UU.

Mural sin título, pero que se conoce por el nombre de "LÁGRIMAS[1]". El mural expresa el malestar de los residentes de Chihuahuita en 1975, por la decisión del departamento de carreteras del estado de Texas de hacer pasar la autopista de la frontera por allí. A los residentes les preocupaban las consecuencias negativas que eso tendría para su pueblo.

James de la Vega es un joven muralista nuyorican que reside y trabaja en la ciudad de Nueva York. Graduado de la universidad de Cornell, su obra expresa la vida cotidiana del Barrio con referencias a personajes políticos y culturales del mundo hispano. De la Vega también es conocido por los dibujos en tiza[2] que hace sobre las aceras de la ciudad con mensajes dedicados a la juventud. Un paseo por las calles del Barrio facilita un acercamiento[3] a los murales de De la Vega. Estos reflejan las técnicas tanto del graffiti como del muralismo mexicano de los años 40 y sirven de introducción a la cultura dinámica del Barrio.

¿Qué aprendiste?

1. ¿Qué clase de pintura tiene larga tradición en México? Da ejemplos. Los murales.

2. ¿Dónde se pintan murales en EE. UU.? ¿Con qué propósito? ¿Quiénes los pintan y quiénes los patrocinan? Se pintan en los barrios mexicanos para concienciar a la comunidad de las preocupaciones sociales y políticas. Son patrocinados por compañías y organizaciones de la comunidad.

3. ¿Qué representa cada uno de los cinco murales? Explícalo.
   1. Crítica de la política opresiva de EE.UU. hacia los mexicanos, en los años treinta; 2. los peligros del SIDA; 3. la herencia mexicana; 4. crítica por la autopista de la frontera; 5. la vida cotidiana del barrio.

Actividad cultural

Uds. van a encargar[4] a un grupo de artistas un mural que represente un problema o una preocupación de su barrio, *college* o universidad. En grupos de *tres*, hagan una lista de los elementos e imágenes que Uds. quieren que aparezcan en el mural, y si quieren, hagan también un bosquejo[5] del mural.

Contraste cultural

Hablen de los murales y otras manifestaciones artísticas (monumentos, edificios, etc.) que representen la herencia histórica y cultural o las preocupaciones sociales de su ciudad. Digan de qué temas tratan y qué símbolos o imágenes usan.

[1]tears, [2]chalk, [3]understanding, [4]to commission, [5]sketch

WILEY PLUS Go to *WileyPLUS* to see these videos and to find more activities for **¡Diálogos en acción!**, **¡A conversar!**, **¡A escribir!** and **¡A investigar!**

Tu mundo en vivo

¡Videos en acción!

10.1 CLUES ayuda a inmigrantes hispanos

1. **Antes de ver el video**
   a. ¿Hay organizaciones en donde tú vives que ayudan a la comunidad hispana?
   b. ¿Cuáles crees que son las prioridades de esas organizaciones?

WILEY PLUS Go to *WileyPLUS* to complete the **Mientras ves el video** activity.

2. **Después de ver el video** Relaciona las fotos con lo que dice cada persona.

© John Wiley & Sons, Inc.

___C___ «Hoy tengo una cita con... que me va a ayudar a conseguir un trabajo.»

___A___ «Lo que le aconsejo a un latino es... clases de inglés.»

___B___ «Tenemos talleres que tratan de cómo tener una entrevista exitosa.»

10.2 Un muralista con conciencia

1. **Antes de ver el video** ¿Hay murales en tu barrio? ¿Dónde? ¿Qué representan?

WILEY PLUS Go to *WileyPLUS* to complete the **Mientras ves el video** activity.

2. **Después de ver el video** ¿Cuáles de los temas de los murales de Cortada te interesan más?

¡Diálogos en acción!

10.1 El proyecto para aumentar los impuestos

Santiago y Catalina, una pareja de jóvenes colombianos, discuten sobre el proyecto para aumentar los impuestos locales.

Paso 1. Primero, mira las **Expresiones útiles** de la página A-11. Luego, escucha el diálogo dos veces y contesta las preguntas de tu profesor/a.

Paso 2. Mira la transcripción del diálogo (pág. A-19) y represéntalo con tu compañero/a. Túrnense. Ahora, vete a la página A-11 para completar los **Pasos 3 y 4**.

10.2 Sola en casa

Santiago y Catalina son una joven pareja colombiana que acaba de mudarse a un nuevo barrio. Catalina se siente sola y por eso, le pide a su esposo que pase más tiempo con ella.

WILEY PLUS Go to *WileyPLUS* to listen to and practice this dialogue.

Diálogo 10.1 models the functions of expressing opinions and disagreeing in an informal situation. It also practices the present subjunctive with expressions of influence and emotion.

Diálogo 10.2 models the functions of complaining, expressing dissatisfaction, and requesting that someone change behavior. It also practices the present subjunctive with expressions of doubt.

¡Lectura en acción!

Empresa[1] modelo por sus servicios voluntarios

Reading Strategy

Recognizing Word Families

When presented With a reading passage with numerous unfamiliar words, pay attention to their prefixes, suffixes, and root words to help you clarify or decipher their meaning.

A continuación, vas a leer un artículo acerca de una empresa de Costa Rica que ha recibido varios premios por sus actividades en múltiples áreas de la comunidad.

Paso 1. Antes de leer el artículo, sigue los siguientes pasos para concentrarte en las palabras más difíciles.

1. Es posible que no conozcas las dos siguientes palabras: **promueve** y **reconocimiento**. Analiza los prefijos y la raíz[2] de cada una. ¿Puedes deducir su significado o identificar palabras con las que se relacionen?

2. ¿Puedes identificar palabras que se relacionen con las tres siguientes? Presta atención a la raíz y también a su terminación y escribe una palabra que se asocie con cada una.

voluntariado	
premió	
comunitarios	

Students may need your help to get started with this activity. Guide them toward identifying the parts of each word that they do recognize and help them to think of related words that they already know or are familiar with.

Meets ACTFL Standards 1.2, interpretive reading; and 3.2, acquiring information.

Paso 2. Ahora, lee el artículo. Piensa en las palabras que has asociado con las que están en negrita[3]. Luego, teniendo en cuenta el contexto, decide si tus asociaciones son correctas.

Reconocimiento al programa *Intel Activo en la Comunidad*

Intel Activo en la Comunidad es el programa a través del cual *Intel Costa Rica* **promueve** el **voluntariado** y la participación de sus empleados en programas y proyectos **comunitarios**.

La Cámara Costarricense - Norteamericana de Comercio (AMCHAM) **premió** a *Intel* con el mayor **reconocimiento** por su proyección comunitaria y sentido de responsabilidad social en varias ocasiones, siendo la última a finales del año 2009. Igualmente, *Intel Costa Rica* recibió en el año 2005 el *Premio de Responsabilidad Social Corporativa* otorgado por la Cámara Costarricense de Comercio.

Componentes Intel de Costa Rica recibió el premio que se otorga a empresas que de manera consistente desarrollan programas de proyección comunitaria en el área social, de educación y medio ambiente, en beneficio de su comunidad y del país. Ésta es la primera vez que AMCHAM otorga el premio, en todas las categorías, a una sola empresa.

El honor que le ha correspondido a *Intel Costa Rica* es el resultado de una clara filosofía y política de responsabilidad social, con respecto al papel que deben jugar las empresas privadas en el desarrollo de la sociedad moderna.

Used by permission of Intel.com, Costa Rica.

Paso 3. Ahora, responde las siguientes preguntas para ver si entendiste la información más importante.

1. ¿Quiénes participan en los programas y proyectos comunitarios?

2. ¿Qué organización ha premiado a *Intel* por su activismo ambiental y social?

3. ¿Por qué es notable el premio?

4. ¿Qué factores contribuyeron a que *Intel* ganara el premio?

[1]Company, [2]root, [3]boldface

¡A conversar!

Vamos a solucionar los problemas

Speaking Strategy

Confirming Comprehension

To verify that you've understood what another person is saying, summarize what you know and ask for a confirmation. For example, you could ask, **¿Dices que hay mucho crimen en el barrio?**

En grupos de *cuatro*, hablen de un barrio, pueblo o ciudad con problemas terribles (puede ser su barrio, pueblo o ciudad) y de cómo solucionarlos. Un/a secretario/a apunta la información para luego compartirla con la clase.

Paso 1.   Identifiquen tres o cuatro problemas del barrio, pueblo o ciudad.

Paso 2.   Expresen sus opiniones, preferencias y recomendaciones respecto a las soluciones para los problemas (*Es importante que..., Espero que..., Prefiero que..., Recomiendo que...*). Túrnense.

Paso 3.   Compartan su lista con la clase y compárenla con las listas de los otros grupos.

¡A escribir!

¡No cierre el parque!

En tu barrio hay un parque muy popular donde se reúnen con frecuencia los vecinos para hablar y divertirse. Acabas de leer un artículo del periódico en que el alcalde o la alcaldesa anuncia que se va a cerrar el parque porque la ciudad no tiene los fondos suficientes para mantenerlo abierto. Tu compañero/a y tú están muy interesados en la preservación del parque y le escriben una carta al alcalde o a la alcaldesa para pedirle que no lo cierre. (*Le pedimos / Preferimos / Es importante que...*)

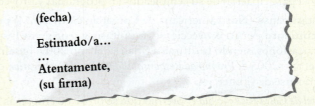

> (fecha)
>
> Estimado/a...
> ...
> Atentamente,
> (su firma)

Writing Strategy

Drafting a Persuasive Business Letter

In this instance, you and a classmate will be writing to the mayor. He/she is your audience, so you must keep that in mind. Address him/her formally, using the **Ud.** form, and be succinct yet convincing in stating your recommendations.

Steps:

1. *Prewriting:* Brainstorm with a classmate, jotting down and grouping your reasons for why the park should not be closed.

2. *Writing:* Write your letter (see strategy), beginning with the date and **Estimado/a...** Introduce yourselves and explain why you are writing. Provide your reasons and express your recommendations for the future of the park. End with a polite closing statement.

3. *Revising:* Have you been clear and to the point? Convincing? Be sure to check for correct spelling and punctuation. **¡Ojo!** Are your verbs in the **Ud.** form? In your recommendations and when making your request, have you used the subjunctive correctly?

4. *Peer correction:* Exchange letters with another pair of students. With your partner, circle errors or areas where there are questions. As a foursome, review your letters and then make corrections as necessary.

Meets ACTFL Standard 1.1, interpersonal speaking.

You may wish to assign certain steps of the **¡A escribir!** writing process for students to complete outside of class.

Meets ACTFL Standard 1.3, presentational writing.

You may want to assign a minimum number of words or sentences as appropriate for the **¡A escribir!** task. Students can use the word count tool available in their word processing application to check the length of their work before and after the revising step of the writing process.

¡A investigar!

En nuestra comunidad

You may assign the appropriate **Pasos** of ¡A investigar! for pairs or small groups to complete outside of class.

En su comunidad, ¿qué servicios se ofrecen para los inmigrantes hispanos?

Paso 1. En grupos de *tres*, investiguen los servicios disponibles. Tengan en cuenta los siguientes aspectos: la educación; el empleo; las agencias sociales; las iglesias, sinagogas y mezquitas; los servicios médicos. Es posible que su profesor/a prefiera asignarle a cada grupo un aspecto específico. Cada miembro del grupo va a investigar los servicios ofrecidos por una agencia u oficina.

Paso 2. Trabajen juntos para preparar una breve presentación oral para sus compañeros de clase que incluya lo siguiente:

- El nombre y la ubicación de las agencias u oficinas
- Qué servicios se ofrecen
- Dónde y cuándo se consiguen los servicios
- Cuánto cuestan los servicios

Paso 3. Creen un PowerPoint que les sirva de recurso visual mientras se turnen para hablar, o, creen una presentación que tenga un comentario grabado. Otra opción es poner las presentaciones grabadas en el blog o el wiki de la clase para que todos las puedan ver. Si quieren, ¡compártanlas con otros estudiantes de su *college* o universidad!

Paso 4. Después de escuchar todas las presentaciones, analicen si hay suficientes servicios en su comunidad. Si les parece que no hay suficientes, preparen una lista de recomendaciones (*Creemos que... / Recomendamos que... / Es mejor que...*)

Research Strategy

Finding Opportunities for Service

To research services available to Latinos and opportunities to volunteer in your community, consult local government and social service agencies, school districts, libraries, religious and charitable organizations, and chambers of commerce. Find out if there is a bilingual newspaper or radio station in your area. For volunteer opportunities in other countries, look for reputable organizations with clear expectations for program participants. Remember, your college or university may have a service learning or study abroad office that could assist you.

Meets ACTFL Standards 1.3, presentational speaking; 5.1, within and beyond school; and 5.2, life-long learning.

If your access to technology is limited, have the students create posters or transparencies to use as visual aids as they speak.

Trivia

A ver cuánto sabes.

1. ¿Es verdad que el dólar es la moneda oficial de El Salvador? ¿Cuál es la moneda oficial de Puerto Rico y Ecuador?   a. Sí   b. el dólar

2. ¿Es el analfabetismo un problema en Cuba? ¿Cuál es el porcentaje de personas que no saben leer y escribir allí?   a. No   b. 0,2%

3. ¿Cuál es el grupo étnico dominante en Uruguay? ¿Y en Nicaragua y Panamá?
   a. los blancos   b. Los mestizos

If you don't know the answers, take a look at the front inside cover of the textbook. Try to respond in complete sentences.

You may want to tell your students that to express the percentage (%) in Spanish one says **por ciento**.

Vocabulario: Capítulo 10

Escena 1

En el barrio   *In the neighborhood*
la acera *sidewalk*
el camión de la basura *garbage truck*
el/la cartero/a *mail carrier*
el chicle *chewing gum*
el/la ciudadano/a *citizen*
el/la dueño/a *owner*
el dulce *sweet, candy*
la grúa *tow truck*
la muchacha *girl*
el muchacho *boy*
el partido *party (political)*
el portero *doorman, concierge*
el prejuicio *prejudice*
el pueblo *town, people*
el/la repartidor/a (de pizzas)
    (pizzas) delivery person

el/la vecino/a *neighbor*
el/la vendedor/a *vendor*

El incendio   *The fire*
el fuego *fire*
el humo *smoke*

Las telenovelas   *Soap operas*
casarse *to get married*
comprometerse *to get engaged*
divorciarse *to get divorced*
enamorarse *to fall in love*
(no) llevarse bien con *to (not) get along
    well with*

Verbos y expresiones verbales
Verbs and verbal expressions
acabar de + *infinitivo to have just done
    something*
aconsejar *to advise*
acordarse (ue) de *to remember*
colgar (ue) *to hang*
insistir (en) *to insist (on)*
mudarse *to move (from house to house)*
obedecer *to obey*
olvidarse de *to forget...*
pasar por *to go down/ pass by*
quemarse *to burn oneself, burn down*
recoger *to pick up, gather*
recomendar (ie) *to recommend*
relajarse *to relax*
saltar *to jump*
saludarse *to greet*
votar *to vote*
es importante *it is important*
es mejor *it is better*
es necesario *it is necessary*

Escena 2

Actividades del barrio
Neighborhood activities
el alcalde/ la alcaldesa *mayor*
el arma (f.) *weapon*
la banda *the band*
la bebida alcohólica *alcoholic drink*
el crimen *crime*
el ladrón/ la ladrona *thief, robber*
la persona sin hogar *homeless person*
la víctima *victim*
la violencia *violence*
el/la voluntario/a *volunteer*

Verbos y expresiones verbales
Verbs and verbal expressions
ahorrar *to save (time, money)*
alegrarse (de) *to be glad/ happy (about)*
aplaudir *to applaud*
atender (ie) *to look after, tend*
construir *to construct*
dar de comer *to feed*
discutir *to argue*
donar *to donate*
emborracharse *to get drunk*
enseñar *to teach, show*
esperar *to hope, expect*
estar de acuerdo *to agree*
extrañar *to miss*
invitar a *to invite*
matar *to kill*
organizar *to organize*
robar *to rob, steal*
resolver (ue) *to solve, resolve*
reunirse *to meet (get together)*
sentir (ie, i) *to be sorry, regret, feel*
tratar de + *infinitive to try to (do something)*

es increíble *it is incredible*
es ridículo *it is ridiculous*
es una lástima *it is a shame*

ojalá (que) + *present subjunctive I hope...*
te invito a... *I'll treat/invite you to*

Escena 3

Los asuntos sociales y políticos
Social and political matters
la campaña electoral *electoral campaign*
los derechos humanos *human rights*
la guerra *war*
la igualdad *equality*
los impuestos *taxes*
la justicia *justice*
la ley *law*
la manifestación *demonstration*
la paz *peace*
el/la progresista *liberal*
el/la reportero/a *reporter*
la seguridad nacional *national security*

el/la conservador/a *conservative*
peligroso/a *dangerous*

Los asuntos religiosos
Religious matters
la catedral *cathedral*
la mezquita *mosque*
la sinagoga *synagogue*

Dios *God*
agnóstico/a *agnostic*
ateo/a *atheist*
católico/a *Catholic*
judío/a *Jewish*
musulmán/ musulmana *Muslim*
protestante *Protestant*

Palabras afirmativas y negativas
Affirmative and negative words
alguno/a/os/as *any, some, someone*
ninguno/a *no (not a single), none, not any*

Verbos y expresiones verbales
Verbs and verbal expressions
dudar *to doubt*
estar a favor de/ en contra de *to be in favor
    of/ against*
luchar por *to fight for*
no creer *not to believe*
no estar seguro/a (de) *not to be sure*
rezar *to pray*

es imposible *it is impossible*
es improbable *it is improbable*
es posible *it is possible*
es probable *it is probable, likely*
no es verdad *it is not true*

WILEY **PLUS**
Additional activities and **Autopruebas** for each **Escena** available online.

Capítulo 11

En el trabajo

© Tom Merton/Age Fotostock America, Inc.

Escena 1
En la oficina

GRAMÁTICA:
· The present perfect

CULTURA:
La etiqueta en los negocios

Escena 2
En la empresa

GRAMÁTICA:
· The future tense

CULTURA:
Dos empresas modelo de éxito

Escena 3
En la fábrica

GRAMÁTICA:
· *Por* and *para*, a summary

CULTURA:
Las maquiladoras de la frontera mexicana

TU MUNDO EN VIVO

¡Videos en acción! La jornada laboral en dos países diferentes; Fábrica que protege el medio ambiente

¡Diálogos en acción! Interacting in an Interview; Describing a Future Situation

¡Lectura en acción! Making Predictions About a Text

¡A conversar! Reformulating Your Speech

¡A escribir! Reviewing a Cover Letter

¡A investigar! Using Business-Related Search Terms

LEARNING OBJECTIVES

By the end of the chapter you will be able to:

· Talk about what has happened.
· Talk about what will happen.
· Express destination, deadline, purpose, and motive.
· Describe business etiquette in the Hispanic world.
· Talk about successful Hispanic business.

En la oficina

© John Wiley & Sons, Inc.

You may use the PowerPoint slides of all scenes to present and practice the vocabulary.

WILEY PLUS

Pronunciación: Practice pronunciation of the chapter's new vocabulary in *WileyPLUS*.

1. letters of recommendation
2. sales manager (*m.*) **la gerente...** (*f.*)
3. position, job
4. executives
5. briefcase
6. Hello?
7. to save
8. to reply, answer
9. *By when?*
10. cubicle
11. boss (*m.*) **la jefa** (*f.*)
12. part time
13. full time
14. long distance call
15. area code
16. to dial
17. telephone book
18. files
19. job applications
20. résumés
21. to send
22. to copy
23. to delete, erase
24. @
25. subject
26. attachment
27. Dear... (*formal, m.*) **Estimada...** (*f.*)
28. Sincerely
29. director of human resources
30. envelope
31. address
32. printer
33. scissors
34. to photocopy
35. photocopier
36. *I'm not going to be bored* **aburrirse** to get bored

¡La pronunciación!
Pay attention to the correct pronunciation of the Spanish **je** and **ge** combinations (see P-3).

jefe   e**je**cutivo   **ge**rente

For additional vocabulary practice, see PowerPoint slides on BCS and in *WileyPLUS*.

Present alternatives to vocabulary at your discretion: **solicitud/ aplicación**.

11-1 As the "winners" call out their answers, a student writes them on the board, with the class providing additional items.

¡En acción!

11-1 ¿Qué hay y qué se hace en la oficina?

Escriban una lista de los aparatos y objetos que hay en la oficina (págs. 368–369) y las acciones que asocien con cada uno. Tienen *cuatro* minutos. Luego, la pareja con la lista más larga de objetos y acciones se la lee a la clase.

Aparatos y objetos	Acciones
el contestador automático ⟶	*dejar mensajes*

For additional practice on this grammar point, see PowerPoint slides on BCS and in *WileyPLUS*.

De paso

Here are two uses of **para** that are helpful in the workplace:

- **trabajar para** *to work for* (a company, a person, etc.)

  Trabaja **para** una compañía multinacional.

- **para** + *deadline* *by, for* (a specified future time)

  Téngalo listo **para** mañana.

11-2 En la oficina

11-2 You may want to project the PowerPoint slide of the opener scene. Have five students come to the front of the class and ask each to describe one of the areas indicated, with the class providing additional input.

¿Cómo es un día típico allí? Observen con mucha atención la escena de las páginas 368–369. Luego, digan: **(a)** lo que están haciendo y diciendo las siguientes personas, y **(b)** los objetos y aparatos que hay cerca de ellas. Usen todas las palabras del vocabulario.

- la secretaria que lleva lentes
- los dos ejecutivos
- el empleado de la camisa azul
- la empleada de la blusa verde
- el empleado que está delante de la fotocopiadora
- la señorita Ana López Roca, secretaria del jefe de personal (mencionen lo que vean en el escritorio, en la pantalla y en el resto del cubículo)

11-2 PERSONALIZED QUESTIONS: ¿Quiénes de Uds. trabajan? ¿Qué puesto de trabajo es? ¿Dónde trabajan? ¿Es un trabajo de tiempo parcial o de tiempo completo? ¿Qué tal es su jefe o jefa?

MODELO

La secretaria que lleva lentes **está hablando por teléfono** *sobre…*

11-3 Mi primer día de trabajo

RECYCLES **estar** and prepositions of location.

Es tu primer día en la oficina. Como eres nuevo/a, cada vez que quieres saber dónde está algo se lo preguntas a tu colega Juana. Ella está en el cubículo de al lado y te contesta detalladamente, usando varias preposiciones. Usen el plano de la oficina que sigue. Hagan los dos papeles y túrnense.

MODELO

hablar con el director

Yo: *Quiero hablar con el director. ¿Dónde está su oficina?*

Juana: *Está **en** la esquina, **al lado de** la oficina de la jefa de personal, **enfrente del** cubo de reciclaje.*

Yo: *¡Ah, sí! ¡Ahí está!*

Quiero...

1. hablar con la jefa de personal
2. imprimir un documento de 20 páginas
3. reciclar unas hojas de papel usado
4. prepararme un café
5. ir al baño
6. buscar un número de teléfono
7. escanear el plano de la oficina
8. poner cartas en los sobres
9. mandar un fax
10. hacer fotocopias
11. ... (uno de tu elección)
12. ... (uno de tu elección)

> **Palabras útiles**
> entre
> enfrente de
> al lado de
> encima de/ debajo de
> delante de/ detrás de
> cerca de/ lejos de
> a la derecha (de)/
>   a la izquierda (de)
> pared norte, sur,
>   este, oeste

You might want to remind your students that after most prepositions **mí** and **ti** follow, not **yo** or **tú**. As in: **Eso es para mí, no es para ti.** [Exceptions: **conmigo/contigo, según yo/tú, entre tú/yo.**]

11-3 Mention that vocabulary related to technology is highly influenced by English. Thus, words like *escanear* are common in Spanish-speaking workplaces.

11-3 You may want to review answers using the PowerPoint slide of the illustration.

The scripts and recordings for the **¡A escuchar!** sections are included on the Book Companion Site (BCS) for instructors and in *WileyPLUS*.

© John Wiley & Sons, Inc.

¡A escuchar!   En la oficina

Paso 1.   Escucha la conversación entre dos secretarias en una oficina.

WILEY **PLUS**   Go to *WileyPLUS* to complete **Paso 2** of this listening activity.

Jennifer tiene una entrevista con la jefa de personal para un puesto en una compañía.

Dígame, ¿por qué quiere ser recepcionista?

He solicitado un puesto de recepcionista de tiempo parcial porque me gusta el contacto directo con la gente.

¿Por qué cree que puede hacerlo bien?

Ya **he trabajado** antes en puestos similares y mis jefes siempre **han estado** muy satisfechos con mi trabajo. ¿**Ha leído** las cartas de recomendación?

Sí, son excelentes. ¿Sabe usar distintos programas?

Sí, **he tomado** varios cursos de computación.

¿**Ha estudiado** idiomas?

Hablo español e inglés y **he aprendido** un poco de chino.

© John Wiley & Sons, Inc.

WILEY PLUS Go to *WileyPLUS* to review this grammar point with the help of the **Animated Grammar Tutorial** and **Verb Conjugator**. For more practice, go to the **Grammar Handbook**.

To introduce students to the present perfect used in context, have them take parts and read the historieta out loud. Ask the following questions: 1. ¿Por qué cree Jennifer que puede hacer el trabajo? 2. ¿Qué ha estudiado Jennifer?

For additional practice on this grammar point, see PowerPoint slides on BCS and in *WileyPLUS*.

Point out that in this construction, the Spanish equivalent of *to have* is **haber**, not **tener**.

Draw up a list of verbs with regular past participles. Have students first provide the **yo** form of the present perfect, then add words or phrases to create a context. Examples: **comprar → He comprado... He comprado una computadora portátil. hablar → He hablado... He hablado con mi amiga.** After practicing the **yo** form, shift to other subjects.

Ud. ha comido una manzana, se ha levantado, ha cerrado su libro,...

GRAMÁTICA

¡Manos a la obra!

1

Talking about what has happened: The present perfect

In Spanish, as in English, the present perfect describes an action that *has happened*, often in the recent past, and with its consequences still felt in the present. For example, observe the following conversation based on Jennifer's interview, with more information possibly yet to come:

—¿**Ha tomado** cursos de idiomas?   ***Have*** *you taken foreign language courses?*
—Sí, **he aprendido** varios.   *Yes, I **have learned** several languages.*

The present perfect is formed by combining the present tense of the verb **haber** (*to have*) and a past participle:

present tense of haber + *past participle*				
(yo)	**he**		*I have*	
(tú)	**has**		*you have*	
(Ud., él, ella)	**ha**	**+ llegado**	*you/ he/ she has*	*+ arrived*
(nosotros/as)	**hemos**	**+ comido**	*we have*	*+ eaten*
(vosotros/as)	**habéis**	**+ salido**	*you have*	*+ left*
(Uds., ellos, ellas)	**han**		*you/they have*	

To form the past participle in Spanish, **-ado** is added to the stem of **-ar** verbs and **-ido** is added to the stem of **-er** and **-ir** verbs.

infinitive	stem	add ending	past participle*
reserv**ar**	reserv-	**ado**	**reservado**
respond**er**	respond-	**ido**	**respondido**
dorm**ir**	dorm-	**ido**	**dormido**

- Pronouns (direct, indirect, and reflexive) precede **he, has, ha,...**

  (*direct*)   ¿Las cartas de recomendación? Sí, **las he** recibido.
  (*indirect*)   La compañía **le ha** dado el puesto de recepcionista.
  (*reflexive*)   Jennifer **se ha** reunido con la jefa de personal.

- In a negative statement, **no** precedes **he, has, ha...** and a pronoun, if included.

  No he solicitado ese puesto. **No lo he** solicitado porque es de tiempo completo.

*The past participles of **caer(se), leer,** and **oír** have an accent on the **í**: **caído, leído, oído.**

Go to *WileyPLUS* to review this grammar point with the help of the **Verb Conjugator**. For more practice, go to the **Grammar Handbook**.

. . . y algo más   Verbs with irregular past participles

The verbs below have irregular past participles (**imprimir** and **romper** are new to you).

abrir	**abierto**	*opened, open*	poner	**puesto**	*put, placed*
decir	**dicho**	*said, told*	romper[2]	**roto**	*broken*
escribir	**escrito**	*written*	ver	**visto**	*seen*
hacer	**hecho**	*done, made*	volver	**vuelto**	*returned*
imprimir[1]	**impreso***	*printed*	devolver	**devuelto**	*returned (something)*
morir	**muerto**	*died, dead*	resolver	**resuelto**	*resolved*

*also **imprimido**

For additional practice on this grammar point, see PowerPoint slides on BCS and in *WileyPLUS*.

¡En acción!

¡Oye! ¿Es bueno el jefe o no?

Escucha lo que ha hecho tu jefe y reacciona diciendo si es algo **buenísimo** o **malísimo.**

11-4   Un día en la compañía ¡Con brío!

Paso 1.   Hoy la presidenta (**P**) está preparando la reunión[3] que tiene anualmente con los ejecutivos de la compañía *¡Con brío!* Hoy también, el jefe de personal (**J**) está organizando un almuerzo para celebrar el día de la secretaria. Identifiquen lo que ha hecho cada uno marcando la casilla correspondiente.

P   J

☑ ☐ 1. **He decidido** lo que voy a incluir en la agenda de la reunión.

☐ ☑ 2. **He ido** al restaurante para ver cómo es y dónde está exactamente.

☑ ☐ 3. **He escrito** un cuestionario para todos los ejecutivos.

☐ ☑ 4. **He invitado** a las secretarias al almuerzo.

☑ ☐ 5. **He planeado** mi presentación sobre el futuro de la compañía.

☐ ☑ 6. **He comprado** flores para las secretarias.

☑ ☐ 7. Le **he dicho** a mi secretaria que reserve el salón de conferencias.

☐ ☑ 8. **He visto** el menú y **he pedido** platos vegetarianos y no vegetarianos.

☐ ☑ 9. **He resuelto** el problema de cómo estacionar todos cerca del restaurante.

Paso 2.   Ahora, comenten lo que han hecho el resto de los empleados de la compañía (págs. 368–369). Usen la imaginación. Túrnense.

MODELO

E1:   ¿Qué **ha hecho** la secretaria que se llama Ana López Roca?

E2:   **Ha escrito** un e-mail, **ha...** ¿Y qué **ha hecho** el empleado rubio?

[1]to print, [2]to break, [3]meeting

Guión para ¡Oye!
1. **He cancelado** las vacaciones de todos Uds.
2. **He comprado** computadoras nuevas para todos.
3. **He reducido** el personal, así que Uds. van a tener que trabajar más horas.
4. **He cambiado** la hora del almuerzo; ahora pueden pasar hora y media en la cafetería.
5. **He fotocopiado** sus datos personales y los he puesto en la recepción.
6. **He decidido** que los viernes no es necesario venir a la oficina.
7. **He escuchado** todas sus conversaciones telefónicas.
8. **He decidido** hacerles pagar 200 dólares al mes por usar el estacionamiento.
9. Me **he comido** casi todos los pasteles que Uds. trajeron a la oficina y tengo un dolor de estómago terrible.
10. **He dado** mi aprobación para que vengan a la oficina con *jeans*, camisetas y zapatillas de tenis.

11-4   After students complete their work in pairs, ask nine students to each read aloud one of the items listed, with the class identifying the person that has completed the task:
la presidenta or **el jefe de personal.**

11-5 En busca de trabajo RECYCLES subjunctive with expressions of influence in *Paso 2*.

11-5 Before beginning the activity, give student **A** a moment to mark the **Sí/No** columns and student **B** a moment to familiarize him/herself with the questions to be asked.

11-5 Review answers by playing the role of student **B**, asking the questions. Students play the role of student **A** and respond as follows: 1. … las he mirado. 2. … los he buscado. 3. … lo he revisado. 4. … las he completado. 5. … las he pedido. 6. … la he solicitado. 7. … la he leído. 8. … lo he enviado.

Paso 1. Un/a estudiante que busca trabajo de tiempo completo **(A)** marca **Sí** o **No** en su lista para ver lo que ha hecho ya. Luego su compañero/a **(B)**, para confirmarlo, le pregunta cada cosa de la lista. **A** responde usando **lo/la/los/las**. Hagan los dos papeles. Sigan el modelo.

El estudiante A marca…

Sí	No	
☐	☐	1. *mirar* en Internet las ofertas de trabajo
☐	☐	2. *buscar* puestos de trabajo en el periódico
☐	☐	3. *revisar* el currículo
☐	☐	4. *completar* las solicitudes de empleo
☐	☐	5. *pedir* cartas de recomendación
☐	☐	6. *solicitar* información acerca de los lugares de empleo
☐	☐	7. *leer* toda la información con cuidado
☐	☐	8. *enviar* el currículo en un archivo adjunto[1]

MODELO

Estudiante B: *¿Has mirado en Internet las ofertas de trabajo?*

Estudiante A: *Sí, (No, no) las he mirado.*

Paso 2. Según las respuestas, ¿se ha organizado bien el/la estudiante **A**? ¿Qué le recomienda el/la estudiante **B**?: *Te recomiendo que revises el currículo; que…*

11-6 ¿Qué ha hecho ya? RECYCLES reflexive verbs.

11-6 You may want to project the PowerPoint slide and have students volunteer all that **el señor Pérez** has done, stating the evidence: **Se ha cepillado los dientes. Están muy blancos.**

11-6 Prior to begin activity 11-6 you may want to refer your students to page 196 to review the reflexive verbs.

11-7 Prior to beginning *Actividad 11-7*, review the irregular past participles on p. 373, and then as a class, have students convert the verbs in items 1 through 10 of the activity into regular or irregular past participles as appropriate.

El señor Pérez ya está listo para empezar un nuevo día de trabajo en la oficina. Basándose en los dibujos, digan como mínimo *ocho* cosas que ha hecho ya entre las 6:30 y las 7:30 de la mañana: *El señor Pérez **se ha levantado.***

A las 6:30 de la mañana

¡Adiós, cariño!

A las 7:30 de la mañana

[1]attached

11-7 Recientemente, en tu trabajo, *college* o universidad RECYCLES interrogatives.

Paso 1.   En la columna que dice **Yo**, cada estudiante marca lo que ha hecho o no *recientemente*. Luego, háganse preguntas para saber qué ha hecho el/la otro/a. Apunten las respuestas de su compañero/a en la segunda columna. Túrnense.

MODELO

E1: *Recientemente, ¿**has solicitado** trabajo?*

E2: *Sí, (No, no) **he solicitado** trabajo recientemente. ¿Y tú?*

Yo				Mi compañero/a	
Sí	**No**			**Sí**	**No**
☐	☐	**1.**	¿... *solicitar* trabajo?	☐	☐ *ha solicitado...*
☐	☐	**2.**	¿... *hacer* una cita para una entrevista? ¿Con quién?	☐	☐ ...
☐	☐	**3.**	¿... *devolver* una llamada a un/a cliente/a o compañero/a? ¿Para qué?	☐	☐ ...
☐	☐	**4.**	¿... *decirle* algo divertido a tu colega o compañero/a? ¿Qué?	☐	☐ ...
☐	☐	**5.**	¿... *ir* a la oficina de tu jefe/a o profesor/a? ¿Por qué? ¿Para qué?	☐	☐ ...
☐	☐	**6.**	¿... *imprimir* algo en el trabajo, en la universidad o en el *college*? ¿Qué?	☐	☐ ...
☐	☐	**7.**	¿... *abrir* una nueva cuenta de correo electrónico? ¿Dónde?	☐	☐ ...
☐	☐	**8.**	¿... *aburrirse* en el trabajo o en clase? ¿Por qué?	☐	☐ ...
☐	☐	**9.**	¿... *resolver* un problema con tu jefe/a o profesor/a? ¿Cuál?	☐	☐ ...
☐	☐	**10.**	¿... *escribir* en Twitter o en un *blog* sobre tu trabajo o clases? ¿Qué?	☐	☐ ...

Paso 2.   Ahora, compartan con la clase varias cosas que Uds. dos han hecho o no: *Mi compañero/a y yo **hemos solicitado** trabajo.* o: *Ni mi compañero/a ni yo **hemos solicitado** trabajo.*

> **Palabras útiles**
> **ni... ni** *neither... nor*

11-8 ¿Qué han hecho los empleados?

Paso 1.   La jefa no ha venido a la oficina esta semana y en su ausencia han pasado muchas cosas. En grupos de *tres*, digan *ocho* cosas que han hecho los empleados. Usen los verbos que siguen y la imaginación.

> **11-8** Before beginning the activity, have students identify and circle verbs in the list that have irregular past participles: **abrir, escribir, poner, romper, ver.**

abrir	cancelar	comprar	encontrar	escribir	escuchar	fotocopiar
hablar	jugar	navegar	pedir	poner	romper	ver

MODELO

*Han **cancelado** todas las citas con los clientes.*

Paso 2.   Al final, mencionen sus ideas a la clase. ¿Qué grupo tiene las ideas más originales?

11-9 ¿Dices la verdad? RECYCLES subjunctive with expressions of doubt.

Di *tres* cosas que has hecho en el trabajo y *tres* más que has hecho cuando estabas de vacaciones. En cada categoría, incluye por lo menos una cosa que no sea verdad. Túrnense.

MODELO

E1: *He **vendido** cien carros y **he hecho** surf en Hawái.*   **E2:** *Creo que es verdad.* o: *Dudo que sea verdad.*

Go to *WileyPLUS* to see the video related to this reading.

Tu mundo cultural

La etiqueta en los negocios

Meets ACTFL Standards 1.2, interpretive reading; 1.3, presentational speaking; 2.1, cultural practices; and 4.2, cultural comparisons.

For an additional activity related to this cultural theme, see PowerPoint slides on BCS and in *WileyPLUS*.

Nunca se sabe. Quizás en un futuro próximo tengas que ir de viaje de negocios a un país hispano. Si eso ocurre, ¿estás preparado/a? Lee lo que sigue. Tal vez un día te pueda ser muy útil[1].

Hacer negocios en un país extranjero es siempre un reto[2] porque requiere conocer un idioma[3], una cultura y un sistema legal diferentes. Para tener éxito[4] en las relaciones comerciales con los países hispanos, conviene conocer la etiqueta o protocolo que siguen en los negocios. Es cuestión de estar preparado.

Las relaciones personales son la base del éxito en los negocios con los hispanos. Lo primero que hay que hacer es crear una relación personal y amistosa, y luego vienen los negocios.

Suedhang/Cultura/Getty Images, Inc.

I love images/Cultura/Getty Images, Inc.

En los negocios, como en el resto de la vida hispana, la proximidad física es algo normal, tanto en los saludos como durante la conversación y negociación.

El almuerzo es para los hispanos una ocasión para entablar[5] relaciones personales y conocerse, y no necesariamente para hacer negocios. En ocasiones, el almuerzo puede durar de 1:30 a 3:00 de la tarde o incluso más.

Allan Danahar/Digital Vision/Getty Images, Inc.

[1]useful, [2]challenge, [3]language, [4]**tener...** to be successful, [5]to strike up

Guía práctica para hacer negocios en los países hispanos

You may want to tell your students that these guidelines are to be taken only as a general rule, as some variations apply according to area and country.

Saludos y presentaciones

Acuérdese siempre de saludar a cada persona (Buenas tardes, etc.) y preguntarle cómo está.

Nombres y títulos

Use el título de la persona (ingeniero/a, licenciado/a, doctor/a) o señor, señora, señorita y el apellido, excepto cuando le digan lo contrario. Use Ud., no tú.

La puntualidad

Por lo general, en el mundo hispano el concepto del tiempo es menos rígido que en el mundo anglosajón. En muchos casos, llegar media hora tarde puede ser aceptable, pero en el mundo de los negocios, o cuando se dice "*Nos vemos a las 8, hora inglesa*", lo que se quiere decir es que la cita es a las ocho en punto, y no más tarde.

La ropa

Los hispanos en general ponen mucha atención a la ropa. Ese es también el caso cuando se trata del mundo de los negocios.

Lo que se debe evitar:

- Llamar por el nombre de pila[1] a la otra persona.

- Hablar de negocios durante el almuerzo, a menos[2] que lo haga el anfitrión[3].

- Tomar el café durante el almuerzo; se toma al final.

- Insistir en pagar el almuerzo de negocios a medias[4]; no es costumbre. Generalmente lo paga la persona que hace la venta.

- Hacer el gesto de "OK" con los dedos; puede considerarse vulgar.

- Llevar pantalones cortos o zapatillas de tenis a reuniones de negocios.

- Pedir leche o refrescos en un almuerzo de negocios. Pida agua o una buena botella de vino.

¿Qué aprendiste?

1. ¿Qué es importante conocer cuando se hacen negocios en países extranjeros? Y con los hispanos, en particular, ¿qué se recomienda hacer primero?
   El idioma, la cultura y el sistema legal. Con los hispanos, lo primero que hay que hacer es crear una relación personal.
2. En tu opinión, ¿cuáles son las tres cosas más importantes para tener éxito en los negocios con hispanos? ¿Y cuáles son las tres que más se deben evitar?
   Answers will vary.
3. ¿Cuáles de las normas de etiqueta hispanas encuentras más extrañas? ¿Y a cuáles te va a costar más trabajo adaptarte? Explica.
   Answers will vary.

Actividad cultural

Paso 1. Uds. están preparando un DVD para educar a los hombres y mujeres de negocios de su país sobre las normas de etiqueta cuando se hacen negocios con hispanos. En grupos de *tres,* escriban un guion de la conversación entre un hombre o una mujer de negocios estadounidense y dos ejecutivos de una compañía latinoamericana. Decidan:

- dónde va a ser (oficina, restaurante,...)

- de qué van a hablar (productos, ventas,...)

- los errores de etiqueta que van a hacer

Paso 2. Represéntenlo para la clase. Luego, los otros estudiantes comentan lo que *se debe hacer o no,* según lo que vieron.

Contraste cultural

Tomando como inspiración la guía anterior, escriban una lista de consejos prácticos para las personas extranjeras que vayan de negocios a su país.

[1]first name, [2]unless, [3]host, [4]**pagar...** to split the bill

En ¹la empresa

WILEY PLUS

Pronunciación: Practice pronunciation of the chapter's new vocabulary in *WileyPLUS*.

1. corporation 2. to succeed, be successful 3. budget 4. ready 5. colleague (*m.*) **la colega** (*f.*) 6. employee (*f.*) **el empleado** (*m.*) 7. interview 8. experience
9. promotion 10. to earn 11. economy 12. profits 13. stock market 14. investments 15. shares 16. to invest 17. bull (up) and bear (down) markets
18. We weren't mistaken; **equivocarse** to be mistaken, make a mistake 19. debts 20. We are lucky; **tener suerte** to be lucky 21. You are right; **tener**
razón to be right

¡En acción!

11-10 ¿Hay otra forma de decirlo?

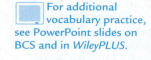For additional vocabulary practice, see PowerPoint slides on BCS and in *WileyPLUS*.

Empareja cada palabra o expresión de la columna **A** con la que le corresponde de la columna **B**.

A.
1. la solicitud — f.
2. el presupuesto — g.
3. el/la colega — e.
4. tener éxito — h.
5. la entrevista — i.
6. tener razón — d.
7. quejarse — a.
8. deuda — c.
9. equivocarse — b.

B.
a. expresar dolor o resentimiento
b. cometer un error
c. débito
d. estar en lo cierto
e. compañero/a de trabajo
f. papel que se completa para solicitar un trabajo
g. gastos que se anticipan
h. triunfar, obtener lo que se busca
i. conferencia entre dos o más personas

11-10 Students may complete the activity individually or in pairs, with answers reviewed by the instructor.

Present alternatives to vocabulary at your discretion: **promoción/ ascenso**

11-11 En la empresa

¿Es un día muy activo? Observen las escenas de la página 378 y digan **(a)** qué hay, **(b)** qué pasa y **(c)** de qué se habla en los siguientes lugares. Usen todas las palabras del vocabulario.

MODELO

En la oficina del gerente hay una ventana grande por donde se ven unos rascacielos,...

- En la oficina del gerente
- En la oficina de al lado
- En la sala de conferencias: las estadísticas, las preocupaciones de los empleados,...

11-11 You may want to project the PowerPoint slide of the scenes and have students describe each one. As a follow-up, have them describe each worker, including apparel.

11-11 PERSONALIZED QUESTIONS: ¿Quiénes de Uds. trabajan o van a trabajar en una empresa? Expliquen. ¿Quiénes han tenido una entrevista de trabajo o una promoción recientemente? Expliquen.

11-12 Cómo "meter la pata"[1] y quedarse sin el puesto de trabajo

Paso 1. La compañía ¡*Con brío!* tiene tal prestigio que puede permitirse el lujo de poder escoger entre los mejores candidatos que solicitan trabajar en ella. Por eso, el más mínimo error deja descalificado/a a un/a candidato/a. Miren los errores de los candidatos que han solicitado trabajo recientemente y marquen los *cuatro* que, en su opinión, son los más graves.

1. ☐ *insistir* en que la empresa no va a tener éxito si no le dan el puesto
2. ☐ durante la entrevista, *preguntarle a la jefa de personal cuánto gana ella*
3. ☐ *escribir la carta de presentación y* el currículo en papel de color fucsia
4. ☐ durante la entrevista, *decirle* al jefe de personal que no tiene razón
5. ☐ *equivocarse* y llamar al gerente por un nombre que no es el suyo
7. ☐ *decirle* al jefe de personal que la empresa *tiene suerte* de tener un candidato/a como él/ella
6. ☐ *regalarle* una botella de champán al jefe de personal antes de la entrevista
8. ☐ *hacer* errores ortográficos[2] en la carta que acompaña al currículo (Vean un ejemplo en el margen.)

> **Errores inaceptables:**
>
> (Ej.: "*Estoy* el candidato que *buscan*. No *ay* otro como yo.")

Paso 2. Ahora, teniendo en cuenta lo que han marcado, hagan de **jefe/a de personal** que llama al/ a la **candidato/a** para darle la mala noticia, mencionando dos de los errores que ha cometido. Sigan el modelo. Túrnense.

MODELO

Jefe/a de personal:	*Le llamo para informarle que Ud. no ha obtenido el puesto.*
Candidato/a:	*¿Pero cómo? ¡No es posible! ¿Qué he hecho mal?*
Jefe/a de personal:	*A ver, primero, Ud. ha…*

[1]to put your foot in your mouth, [2]spelling

11-13 Una entrevista RECYCLES descriptive adjectives and work-related vocabulary.

La jefa de personal de la empresa donde tú solicitas un puesto quiere saber cómo es tu personalidad antes de ofrecerte el trabajo. Hagan los papeles de jefa de personal y candidato/a durante una entrevista. Usen la forma de **Ud.** e incluyan lo siguiente:

11-13 If time allows, students switch roles. Walk around the classroom listening to the interviews. If one pair stands out, ask them to conduct their interview in front of the class. The class then votes on whether to offer the job to the interviewee or not, explaining why.

11-13 ANOTHER STEP: Students jot down the characteristics of their ideal job. They then form groups of three and share the descriptions with each other. The group decides who described the best job. That student shares the description with the class.

Jefa de personal	Candidato/a
1a. Saluda al/ a la candidato/a →	**1b.** Saluda a la jefa de personal
2a. Quiere saber: • de dónde es y cuál es su especialización • los tres adjetivos que mejor lo/la describen • su experiencia en trabajos previos • si se considera líder o seguidor/a, y por qué • si trabaja bien o no en equipo	**2b.** Quiere información acerca de: • el horario de trabajo • sus responsabilidades en el puesto • los beneficios y las vacaciones • el sueldo y las promociones • la frecuencia de los viajes de negocios
3a. Se despide del/ de la candidato/a	**3b.** Se despide de la jefa de personal

LOS NÚMEROS ORDINALES

primer, primero/a	*first*	sexto/a	*sixth*
segundo/a	*second*	séptimo/a	*seventh*
tercer, tercero/a	*third*	octavo/a	*eighth*
cuarto/a	*fourth*	noveno/a	*ninth*
quinto/a	*fifth*	décimo/a	*tenth*

PLUS For more practice, see **Grammar Handbook** found in *WileyPLUS*.

For additional practice on this grammar point, see PowerPoint slides on BCS and in *WileyPLUS*.

. . . y algo más Ordinal numbers

- Ordinal numbers are adjectives, and like other adjectives in Spanish, they agree in gender and number with the nouns they modify.

    Las **primeras** candidatas para este puesto fueron Elena y Marisa.
    The first candidates for this job were Elena and Marisa.
- **Primero** and **tercero** become **primer** and **tercer** when they immediately precede a masculine singular noun.

    El ascensor está en el **tercer** piso. *The elevator is on the third floor.*
- In Spanish, ordinal numbers can be abbreviated as follows: 1°, 2°, 3°,... or 1ª, 2ª, 3ª,... when referring to a feminine noun.

11-14 ¿En qué piso está?

Hoy es el primer día de trabajo para muchos empleados de la empresa *Tecnomundo*. Por eso quieren saber en qué piso están los distintos lugares o servicios de la empresa y se lo preguntan a los recepcionistas. Tu profesor/a asigna a *cinco* estudiantes el papel de recepcionistas y al resto, el de empleados que hacen fila para preguntar. Después de *tres* minutos, cambien de papel.

11-14 Read aloud, in random order, each of the floors in *Empresa Tecnomundo* and ask students to say what is there. You say «En la planta baja del edificio...» and students complete the statement by adding «... están la una recepción y la guardería infantil».

11-14 *Option:* This activity may be completed by students in pairs.

11-14 Mention that ordinal numbers are commonly used only from 1 to 10, and that cardinal numbers are used above 10 (e.g., el piso **veinte** *the 20th floor*).

You may want to project the PowerPoint slide of **Empresa Tecnomundo** as students complete this activity.

EMPRESA TECNOMUNDO

Terraza de descanso – Piscina[1]	10º
Peluquería	9º
Cafetería – Restaurante	8º
Salas de reuniones	7º
Oficina del gerente	6º
Departamento de contabilidad[2]	5º
Departamento de ventas	4º
Recursos humanos[3]	3º
Biblioteca	2º
Gimnasio	1º
Recepción – Guardería infantil	Planta baja
Garaje	Sótano

© John Wiley & Sons, Inc.

MODELO
desayunar

Empleado: *Perdón. Quisiera desayunar. ¿En qué piso está la cafetería?*
Recepcionista: *Está en el **octavo** piso. Allí está el ascensor.*

El/La empleado/a quiere:

1. dejar a los hijos en la guardería
2. hablar con el jefe de personal
3. asistir a una reunión
4. nadar
5. hablar con el gerente
6. almorzar
7. consultar libros técnicos
8. hacer ejercicio
9. cortarse el pelo
10. estacionar el carro
11. descansar al aire libre
12. confirmar unos precios

¿SABES QUE...?

In most Spanish-speaking countries, the main floor of a building is called **la planta baja**, and the floor above it is called **el primer piso**. Therefore, what in the United States is the second floor, is the first floor in Spanish-speaking countries.

Note that in general, the words **piso** and **planta** are synonymous. The word **piso** is preferred when referring to a residential building, while **planta** is used when referring to buildings for businesses or hotels.

Palabras útiles
el ascensor *elevator*

¡A escuchar! En la empresa: una entrevista

Paso 1. Escucha la entrevista que tiene lugar en una empresa.

WILEY PLUS Go to *WileyPLUS* to complete **Paso 2** of this listening activity.

---

[1]Swimming pool, [2]**Departamento...** Accounting department, [3]**Recursos...** Human resources

Es el primer día de trabajo de Jennifer y ahora habla con su jefa y con un compañero de trabajo.

Jennifer, como hoy es su primer día de trabajo, le **mostraremos** la empresa y le **presentaremos** a sus colegas.

Tengo mucha suerte de trabajar aquí. Estoy segura de que **tendré** oportunidades de aprender muchísimo.

No lo dudo. También **tendrá** muchas oportunidades de promoción.

Así lo espero. Hoy **celebraré** mi primer día de trabajo.

© John Wiley & Sons, Inc.

Go to *WileyPLUS* to review this grammar point with the help of the **Animated Grammar Tutorial** and **Verb Conjugator**. For more practice, go to the **Grammar Handbook**.

To introduce students to the future tense used in context, have them take parts and read the **historieta** out loud. Ask the following questions: 1. ¿De qué está segura Jennifer? 2. ¿Qué celebrará hoy?

For additional practice on this grammar point, see PowerPoint slides on BCS and in *WileyPLUS*.

Additional information, to present at your discretion: **Ir + a...** commonly relates the future to the present moment, conveying an intentional plan or prediction. For example: **El sábado voy a salir con mis amigos.** The future tense is used to talk about future actions, situations, or events that are seen as more detached from the present, often not fully planned, and commonly taking place in the more distant future. For example: **En el futuro, haré un viaje por todo el mundo.** Point out that there are many variations and exceptions to these uses.

(cont. in next page)

GRAMÁTICA

¡Manos a la obra!

2

Talking about what will happen: The future tense

You have been using **ir + a + *infinitive*** to talk about actions that are *going to happen*.

Voy a hablar con mi jefa hoy.   *I am going to speak to my boss today.*

The future tense tells what *will happen*, commonly when the action or event is to occur in the more distant future. As in these examples from Jennifer's first day, it is formed by adding the same set of endings to the infinitive of all **-ar**, **-er**, and **-ir** verbs: ***Infinitive* + -é, -ás, -á, -emos, -éis, -án**.

—¿**Tendrás** oportunidades de promoción?   *Will you have opportunities for promotion?*
—Sí, y **aprenderé** muchísimo.   *Yes, and I will learn a lot.*

	llamar	volver	ir
(yo)	llamaré	volveré	iré
(tú)	llamarás	volverás	irás
(Ud., él, ella)	llamará	volverá	irá
(nosotros/as)	llamaremos	volveremos	iremos
(vosotros/as)	llamaréis	volveréis	iréis
(Uds., ellos, ellas)	llamarán	volverán	irán

Irregular verbs

Some verbs add the future endings to irregular stems, not to the infinitive.

infinitive	*irregular stem*	*future forms*
decir	**dir-**	dir**é**, dir**ás**, dir**á**, dir**emos**, dir**éis**, dir**án**
hacer	**har-**	haré, harás,...
poder	**podr-**	podré, podrás,...
poner	**pondr-**	pondré, pondrás,...
querer	**querr-**	querré, querrás,...
saber	**sabr-**	sabré, sabrás,...
salir	**saldr-**	saldré, saldrás,...
tener	**tendr-**	tendré, tendrás,...
venir	**vendr-**	vendré, vendrás,...

. . . y algo más   The future of *haber*

The future of **hay** (*there is, there are*) is **habrá** (*there will be*). Both are only used in singular.

¿**Habrá** una reunión esta tarde?   *Will there be a meeting this afternoon?*
Habrá tres reuniones esta tarde.   *There will be three meetings this afternoon.*

De paso

The future of **haber** is used to form the *future perfect* tense.

Habrán terminado el proyecto   *They will have completed the project by*
antes del martes.   *Tuesday.*

Likewise, the imperfect of **haber** is used to form the *past perfect* tense.

No tenía dinero porque había   *I did not have any money because I had lost*
perdido mi billetera.   *my wallet.*

. . . y algo más   The future of probability

The future tense may also be used to express wondering, guessing, or probability.
—¿A qué hora **será** la entrevista?   *I wonder what time the interview is?*
—No sé; **será** a las tres.   *I don't know; it will probably be at three.*

¡En acción!

¡Oye! El trabajo del futuro

¿Cómo serán los trabajos dentro de diez años? Escucha las predicciones y responde diciendo: «**¡Es probable!**» o «**¡Es improbable!**».

11-15   ¿Quieres saber qué clase de inversor/a eres?

Paso 1.   En la Bolsa, ¿eres conservador/a o te gusta el riesgo[1]? Recientemente han ocurrido ciertas cosas con tus finanzas. Marca la casilla ☐ apropiada para indicar lo que harás en cada caso.

1. **Has ganado 50.000 dólares en la lotería. ¿Qué harás con el dinero?**

    ☐ a. Iré al casino más cercano para triplicar mi capital.

    ☐ b. Lo invertiré en la Bolsa.

    ☐ c. Los guardaré debajo del colchón[2] de mi cama.

2. **Estás en un casino de Las Vegas jugando al *black jack*. Empezaste con 1.000 dólares y has perdido 400. ¿Cuánto arriesgarás[3] para recuperar los 600?**

    ☐ a. Jugaré más de 400 dólares.

    ☐ b. Jugaré 200 dólares.

    ☐ c. Nada, me iré a casa con los 600 dólares.

3. **Has decidido aprender a invertir tu dinero. ¿Cómo lo harás?**

    ☐ a. Investigaré y leeré antes de hacer la inversión.

    ☐ b. Lo consultaré con un amigo.

    ☐ c. Buscaré el consejo de un corredor de Bolsa[4].   *(continúa)*

[1]risk, [2]mattress, [3]will you risk, [4]**corredor...** stockbroker

---

(Cont. from p. 382.)

To familiarize students with the future endings, make statements about yourself such as: **En el futuro, ganaré mucho dinero.** Ask several students, **¿Y tú?** They each respond **Sí, ganaré...** (or) **No, no ganaré...** Recap student responses: **... ganará mucho dinero; ... y... ganarán...; ... y yo ganaremos...** In subsequent examples, allow students to provide the recap.

For additional practice on these grammar points, see PowerPoint slides on BCS and in *WileyPLUS*.

PLUS For more practice, see **Grammar Handbook** found in *WileyPLUS*.

Guión para ¡Oye!
Predicciones:
1. Los hombres y las mujeres llevarán ropa unisexo al trabajo. ¿Es probable o es improbable?
2. Todos los empleados tendrán ocho semanas de vacaciones.
3. La mayoría de la gente trabajará en casa.
4. Los empleados no tendrán que usar teclados; las computadoras escribirán lo que se dicte.
5. Las impresoras imprimirán diez páginas por segundo.
6. El padre y la madre podrán quedarse en casa con su nuevo bebé sin ir a trabajar durante seis meses.
7. En el almuerzo, los empleados tomarán la comida en cápsulas.
8. Habrá menos estrés en el trabajo.

4. Te han dicho que tus acciones han bajado un 20%. ¿Qué harás?

☐ a. Invertiré más si los precios son bajos.

☐ b. Esperaré antes de vender.

☐ c. Venderé todo, guardaré el dinero en el banco y dormiré tranquilo/a.

5. El mercado está en baja, pero milagrosamente tus acciones han aumentado un 50%. ¿Qué harás?

☐ a. Compraré más acciones.

☐ b. Seguiré como estoy.

☐ c. Venderé todo y depositaré el dinero en el banco.

11-15 At the conclusion of *Paso 2,* take a survey to find out how many students consider themselves conservative investors, and how many are risk-takers.

 Paso 2. Háganse las preguntas y digan las respuestas en voz alta para ver los resultados. Finalmente, evalúen la clase de inversor/a que es la otra persona según los resultados. Si ha marcado cuatro veces o más la opción **(a)**, le gusta el riesgo; **(b)**, es un/a inversor/a medio/a; **(c)** es conservador/a.

WILEY PLUS For more practice, see **Grammar Handbook** found in *WileyPLUS.*

For additional practice on this grammar point, see PowerPoint slides on BCS and in *WileyPLUS.*

> **. . . y algo más** *Cuando* + present subjunctive
>
> Observe the examples below and note that when **cuando** introduces an action or condition that has not taken place yet the verb that follows it is in the **present subjunctive.**
>
> Antes, cuando llegaba tarde a una reunión, mi jefe se enojaba conmigo.
>
> Ahora, cuando tengo una reunión, soy muy puntual.
>
> En el futuro, **cuando sea** jefe, mis empleados **tendrán** que ser puntuales también. Y **cuando lleguen** tarde, me **enojaré.**

11-16 ¿Qué harás?

 Paso 1. Eres una persona curiosa y quieres saber lo que hará tu compañero/a después de este cuatrimestre/ semestre. Hazle las preguntas de la primera columna. Luego él/ella responde siguiendo el ejemplo de la segunda y te pregunta "¿Y tú?". Tú respondes y los dos apuntan las respuestas en la tercera columna.

You might want to point out to your students the **cuando** followed by the present subjunctive in **Cuando termine** el cuatrimestre/semestre,...

Preguntas	Respuestas	Información escrita
Cuando termine el cuatrimestre / semestre,...		
1. ... **¿tomarás** más clases? ¿Cuáles?	*... tomaré...*	*... tomará...*
2. ... **¿podrás** dormir y descansar más?		
3. ... **¿saldrás** más por la noche?		
4. ... **¿trabajarás?** ¿Dónde? ¿Cuánto ganarás?		
5. ... **¿tendrás** vacaciones? ¿Cuántos días serán?		
6. ... **¿harás** un viaje? ¿Adónde irás?		
7. ... **¿te mudarás** de casa/ apartamento...?		
8. ... (una de tu elección)		

 Paso 2. Dile a otro/a compañero/a o a la clase una cosa interesante o curiosa que hará la persona a quien entrevistaste y otra que Uds. dos harán: *... hará un viaje a Francia. Él/Ella y yo trabajaremos.*

11-17 ¡Se busca trabajo en un crucero!

Paso 1. Uds. son unos amigos que ha decidido buscar trabajo en un crucero, para así poder viajar juntos y gratis a lugares exóticos. En este momento, Uds. están preparándose para la entrevista que tienen la semana próxima. Usen el futuro para indicar lo que harán o pasará, según la siguiente lista. Apunten la información.

Cuando vayamos a la entrevista...

1. *llevar* (qué cosas) _Llevaremos los currículos._ _____
2. *ponerse* (qué ropa) _____
3. *salir* (a qué hora) _____
4. *solicitar* (qué puesto de trabajo) _____
5. *hablar* (de qué) _____
6. *hacer* la entrevista (con quién) _____
7. *poder* preguntar (acerca de qué) _____
8. *saber* más (acerca de qué) _____

Paso 2. Una pareja **(A)** se reúne con otra **(B)** que también busca empleo en un crucero. La pareja **A** pregunta a la pareja **B,** y viceversa.

MODELO

Uno/a de la pareja A: *¿Qué cosas **llevarán** Uds. a la entrevista?*
Uno/a de la pareja B: *Llevaremos los currículos y…*

11-18 La transformación de Casimiro

Paso 1. La semana que viene, Casimiro tiene una entrevista con una compañía de gran prestigio. Ahora, está pensando en cómo cambiar su imagen para conseguir el puesto. Según el dibujo, digan que **hará** antes de la entrevista. Trabajen en grupos de *tres* y túrnense.

MODELO

E1: *Primero, **se duchará.*** **E2:** *Luego,...* **E3:** *Después,...*

Paso 2. ¿Y tú qué **harás cuando tengas** una entrevista?

11-19 La bola de cristal

Paso 1. ¿Quieres saber tu futuro? Un/a estudiante hace el papel de adivino/a[1] que predice tu futuro usando la información que sigue y tú reaccionas a lo que te dice. Luego, cambien de papel.

MODELO

Adivino/a: *Dentro de cinco años **trabajarás** para una compañía de pasta de dientes...*
Tú: *¡No! Dentro de cinco años **trabajaré** para MTV.*

- **Dentro de cinco años:** para qué compañía o dónde trabajará
- **Dentro de diez años:** la clase de trabajo que hará
- **Dentro de veinte años:** dónde vivirá y cómo será su vida

Paso 2. Ahora, dile a la clase una predicción que el/la adivino/a ha hecho acerca de ti: *El/La adivino/a dice que dentro de cinco años **trabajaré** para una compañía de pasta de dientes pero yo creo que **trabajaré** para MTV.*

[1] fortune-teller

11-17 Prior to beginning this activity, have students identify the verbs that are irregular in the future tenses (numbers 2, 3, 6, 7, and 8).

You might want to point out to your students that **cuando** is followed by the present subjunctive in **Cuando vayamos a la entrevista.**

Palabras útiles

ayudante, *assistant*
bailarín/bailarina, *dancer*
cantante, *singer*
cocinero/a, *cook*
masajista, *masseuse*
peluquero/a, *hairstylist*
socorrista, *lifesaver*

© John Wiley & Sons, Inc.

11-18 When students complete the activity, you may want to project the PowerPoint slide of Casimiro and ask students to give their creative feedback.

Casimiro

© John Wiley & Sons, Inc.

For an additional activity related to this cultural theme, see PowerPoint slides on BCS and in *WileyPLUS*.

Meets ACTFL Standards
1.1, interpersonal speaking
1.2, interpretive reading;
2.2, cultural products and
4.2, cultural comparisons.

Tu mundo cultural

Dos empresas modelo de éxito

Una empresa otavaleña

¿Has visto a los indígenas otavaleños vendiendo suéteres de lana y otra clase de mercancía en las calles o en los centros comerciales de tu pueblo o ciudad? Si todavía no los has visto, algún día tendrás la ocasión de hacerlo, ya que estos hombres y mujeres de negocios indígenas se mueven por todo el mundo.

Otavalo, situado en Ecuador, en un valle rodeado de volcanes, es famoso por sus productos textiles desde la época preincaica. Su industria textil floreció durante la ocupación española y es ahora la base de la economía de la región. En la actualidad, hay unas 6.000 empresas familiares en la región de Otavalo que se dedican con éxito a la manufacturación de productos textiles que luego se venden por todo el mundo.

A Coruña
ESPAÑA

Otavalo,
ECUADOR

© John Wiley & Sons, Inc.

Pep Roig/Alamy Images

El mercado de Otavalo, Ecuador, en plena actividad. La comunidad indígena de Otavalo ha sabido usar su habilidad para tejer[1] y su sentido de los negocios para crear una industria familiar que ha dado a sus miembros solvencia económica. Además, lo ha hecho sin renunciar a su tradición, algo que no muchas comunidades indígenas han conseguido. Los otavaleños están orgullosos[2] de su cultura y la promueven con éxito.

Nigel Pavitt/AWL Images/Getty Images, Inc.

Los otavaleños son conocidos por su iniciativa, inteligencia y sentido del negocio. Son además personas muy dedicadas a sus hijos; y tanto los hombres como las mujeres administran las empresas familiares. Lo común es que mientras la mayor parte de la familia permanece en Otavalo produciendo prendas[3], uno de los miembros viaja al exterior con la mercancía para venderla.

[1]weave, [2]proud, [3]articles of clothing

Una empresa gallega

Incluso en tiempos de crisis económica, la empresa española de tiendas de ropa Zara es la líder mundial en ventas del sector textil. Su sede central[1] está en La Coruña (Galicia) y su fundador es Amancio Ortega Gaona. El modelo de hacer negocios de Zara es ahora objeto de estudio en muchas escuelas de negocios.

El éxito de Zara reside en tener control total de todos los aspectos de su negocio. No sólo diseña su ropa, sino que la produce, la vende y la distribuye en las 1.516 tiendas que tiene en 77 países. En sus tiendas se ofrecen cosas nuevas cada dos semanas.

Zara sigue una política de respeto al medioambiente. Sus tiendas son ecoeficientes (usan tejidos[2] ecológicos, algodón orgánico y zapatos sin PVC). Usa bolsas de papel, y en las rebajas, bolsas de plástico biodegradables. Para el transporte, usa combustible biodiesel. Curiosamente, en su catálogo en la Red se anuncia en múltiples idiomas, entre otros, en gallego.

Manuel J. Prieto

Una de las tiendas Zara, en Salamanca, está ubicada en el edificio restaurado de San Antonio el Real, un antiguo convento franciscano del siglo XVIII. A los habitantes de Salamanca probablemente no les sorprende[3], ya que en su ciudad abundan los edificios antiguos, pero, ¿cuántas tiendas de ropa de moda conoces tú que estén en el edificio de un convento del siglo XVIII?

Europa Press/Getty Images, Inc.

Entrada a una tienda Zara en Nueva York. Hay también tiendas en Chicago, Miami y Los Ángeles.

¿Qué aprendiste?

1. ¿Dónde está Otavalo? ¿Cuántas familias tienen empresas textiles allí? ¿Dónde venden sus productos? En Ecuador. Unas 6.000 familias que venden por todo el mundo.

2. ¿Dónde está la sede central de Zara? ¿En cuántos países tiene tiendas? En Galicia, España; en 77.

3. ¿Por qué tienen tanto éxito las empresas otavaleñas? ¿Y la empresa gallega? Answers may vary.

Actividad cultural

En grupos de *cuatro,* imagínense que Uds. son una familia o un grupo de vecinos que desea iniciar un negocio. Teniendo en cuenta sus habilidades, talento y experiencia, formulen un plan para el negocio. Luego compártanlo con la clase.

Contraste cultural

¿Conocen empresas familiares en su comunidad? En grupos de *cuatro,* digan de qué tamaño[4] son, si trabajan muchas horas a la semana y si tienen éxito.

[1]**sede...** headquarters, [2]**fabrics,** [3]**les...** surprises them, [4]**size**

En ¹la fábrica

Pronunciación: Practice pronunciation of the chapter's new vocabulary in *WileyPLUS*.

VOCABULARIO

© John Wiley & Sons, Inc.

1. factory 2. worker (*m.*) **la obrera** (*f.*) 3. to punch in 4. day and night shifts 5. supervisor (*f.*) **el supervisor** (*m.*) 6. to operate the machine 7. I don't feel like... **tener ganas de** + *infinitive* to feel like doing something 8. Will you retire...? **jubilarse** to retire 9. break, rest 10. sick leave 11. maternity leave 12. there are strikes; **hacer huelga** to go on strike 13. layoffs 14. union 15. salaries 16. holidays 17. workdays 18. benefits 19. unemployment 20. (a) raise, increase (in salary, production, etc.)

¡En acción!

11-20 ¿Qué pasa en la fábrica de pan?

Observa las escenas de la página 388 y di si es cierto o falso lo siguiente. Si es falso, da la información correcta.

C **F**

- ☑ ☐ **1.** Una obrera marca tarjeta al entrar.
- ☐ ☑ **2.** Hay varios supervisores en la línea de producción.
- ☑ ☐ **3.** Los obreros tienen turnos de día y de noche.
- ☐ ☑ **4.** No hay nadie en el área de descanso de la fábrica.
- ☑ ☐ **5.** Un obrero tiene permiso por enfermedad y una obrera, permiso por maternidad.
- ☑ ☐ **6.** En la huelga hay representantes del sindicato de obreros.
- ☐ ☑ **7.** Los obreros piden más días de trabajo.
- ☐ ☑ **8.** Los obreros piensan que sus sueldos son buenos.
- ☐ ☑ **9.** Los obreros que hacen huelga dicen que el salario mínimo es suficiente.

11-21 Dos días muy diferentes en la fábrica

Observen las escenas de la página 388 y comenten **(a)** lo que pasa allí y **(b)** las preocupaciones de los obreros. Usen todas las palabras del vocabulario.

- al entrar a la fábrica
- en la fábrica
- en el área de descanso
- fuera de la fábrica

11-22 ¡A escoger trabajo!

Paso 1. Indica el grado de importancia (A, B, C) que tienen para ti los siguientes aspectos a la hora de elegir un trabajo.

A. muy importante	B. importante	C. menos importante

___ sueldo

___ aumento de sueldo anual

___ un buen seguro médico

___ compensación por accidente de trabajo[1]

___ guardería infantil en el lugar de trabajo

___ turnos flexibles

___ fondos para la jubilación[2]

___ vacaciones de tres semanas como mínimo

___ permiso por maternidad o paternidad

___ permiso por enfermedad y accidente

Paso 2. Habla con un/a compañero/a para comparar respuestas. ¿Coinciden Uds.? Luego, digan en cuáles han puesto una **A** y expliquen por qué.

MODELO

Para mí, el sueldo es muy importante porque tengo muchos gastos[3].

[1]**accidente...** workman's compensation, [2]**fondos...** retirement funds/pension, [3]expenses

¿SABES QUE...?

In the offices of the Spanish prime minister (president of the government of Spain), "fair trade" coffee is served. By doing so, the Spanish government supports the consumption of products from co-ops where fair salaries and working conditions prevail. In this case, the coffee comes from a co-op in Nicaragua formed by 1,900 families. Do you purchase "fair trade" products?

¡A escuchar! En la fábrica

Paso 1. Escucha el reportaje de un reportero a la entrada de la fábrica de galletas *Buensabor*.

Go to *WileyPLUS* to complete **Paso 2** of this listening activity.

Jennifer y Fabio pasean por la calle y hablan del primer día de trabajo de Jennifer.

¿Cómo te fue hoy **por** la mañana?

Muy bien. Seré recepcionista. Trabajaré **por** las mañanas y me pagarán **por** semana.

© John Wiley & Sons, Inc.

¿Cuántos días festivos tendrás?

Tendré quince días festivos y dos semanas de vacaciones. ¡Me encanta trabajar **para** esta compañía!

Ese sueldo te servirá **para** pagar parte de tus estudios.

Sí, y tendré permiso **por** enfermedad y seguro médico. Y el trabajo me dará más experiencia **para** mi futuro profesional.

Bueno, con ese sueldo, y **para** celebrarlo, ¿pagarás tú la cena?... ¡Es un chiste!

To introduce students to the prepositions **por** and **para** used in context, have them take parts and read the **historieta** out loud. To check their comprehension and call their attention to these prepositions, ask the following questions: 1. **¿Cuándo trabajará Jennifer?** 2. **¿Qué le dará el trabajo?**

Go to *WileyPLUS* to review this grammar point with the help of the **Animated Grammar Tutorial**. For more practice, go to the **Grammar Handbook**.

For additional practice on this grammar point, see PowerPoint slides on BCS and in *WileyPLUS*.

GRAMÁTICA

¡Manos a la obra!

3

Por and para, a summary

You have been using **por** and **para** throughout *¡Con brío!* Most of the uses below, with examples based on Jennifer's new job, are already familiar to you.

POR:

a. **Cause, reason:** *because (of), for*
—**¿Por** qué* solicitaste el puesto, Jennifer?
—Lo hice **por** mi hija y **por** no perder una oportunidad como esta.

b. **Duration of time:** *in, during, for*
Está en la oficina **por** la mañana y **por** la tarde, asiste a clase.
Trabaja y estudia (**por**)** muchas horas.

c. **Exchange:** *for, in exchange for*
La compañía le va a pagar bastante **por** las horas que trabaja.
Jennifer le ha dicho a su jefa "Gracias **por** darme esta oportunidad".

d. **Movement:** *by, through, around, alongside*
Jennifer pasó **por** las oficinas para conocer a sus compañeros.
Luego fue **por** el pasillo para ver el área de descanso.

PARA:

e. **Purpose or goal**: *in order to + infinitive*
El sueldo le servirá **para** pagar parte de sus estudios.
Para tener un aumento, tendrá que negociar.

f. **Recipient:** *for (destined for, to be given to)*
Los beneficios **para** los empleados son excelentes.
Hay una guardería **para** sus hijos.

g. **Deadline:** *for, by (a specified future time)*
¿**Para** cuándo quiere el documento?
¿**Para** el lunes?

h. **New! Destination:** *for, toward, to...*
La jefa de Jennifer sale **para** el aeropuerto.
Se va **para** Panamá.

i. **Employment:** *for...*
Le encanta trabajar **para** esta compañía.

*Note that ¿**Por** qué? and **por**que both contain the preposition **por**, as each relates back to the cause of or reason for an action or condition.

Por is often omitted when the amount of time (minutes, hours, days, months, years) is stated.

¡En acción!

¡Oye! El dolor de cabeza de Sebastián

Escucha la historia de Sebastián. Luego, di si la información es cierta o falsa. Si es falsa, corrígela.

11-23 Lo que se oye por la fábrica

Para saber de qué se habla en la fábrica, completen los espacios en blanco con **por** o **para**. Luego, escriban la letra (a-i de la pág. 390) para indicar a cuál de los nueve usos de **por** o **para** corresponde.

MODELO

1.
_d_ Oye, ¿ha pasado ya el supervisor _por_ la línea de producción?

2.
_f_ ¿Sabes _para_ quiénes es la reunión de esta tarde?

3.
_e_ Dicen que habrá huelga _para_ protestar por los despidos.

4.
_g_ ¿ _Para_ cuándo es la huelga?

5.
_b_ El sindicato se reunirá hoy _por_ la tarde.

6.
_a_ Ayer despidieron a cien compañeros; dicen que es _por_ la crisis económica.

7.
_h_ Los directivos de la fábrica saldrán _para_ Washington mañana.

8.
_c_ ¿Cuánto van a pagar _por_ hora en el turno de noche?

9.
_i_ Trabajar _para_ una fábrica como esta no siempre es fácil.

11-24 La vida académica y laboral

Paso 1. Hablen de la vida académica y laboral de cada uno/a. Háganse las siguientes preguntas.

1. ¿Trabajas? ¿**Por** qué? ¿Cuántas horas **por** semana? ¿**Para** quién trabajas?
2. ¿**Por** qué estudias? ¿Cuántas clases tienes **por** semana?
3. ¿Cuánto pagas **por** tus libros y matrícula?
4. ¿**Para** qué título académico, especialidad o profesión te preparas?
5. ¿**Para** cuándo piensas realizar tus planes académicos y profesionales?

Paso 2. Ahora, cuéntale a otra persona lo que sabes de tu compañero/a.

Guión para ¡Oye!
Sebastián trabaja **para** una compañía de computadoras. Una tarde, según dijo, tuvo que irse del trabajo temprano, **por** el dolor de cabeza tan horrible que tenía. Al salir, su jefe le recordó: «¡Tienes que terminar este proyecto **para** mañana!» ¡Pobre Sebastián! Salió **para** su casa. Caminó **por** la calle hasta llegar a una floristería y allí compró rosas **para** su novia. Luego, en vez de ir a su casa, fue al apartamento de su novia y ella, al ver las rosas, dijo: «¿**Para** mí? ¡Gracias **por** las rosas, mi amor! ¡Me encantan!» Esa noche los dos cenaron en un restaurante, y después, fueron a una discoteca **para** bailar. ¿Y el dolor de cabeza?

Comprensión para ¡Oye!
¿Cierto o falso?
1. Sebastián trabaja **para** una compañía de celulares. F
2. Salió de la oficina temprano **por** el dolor de estómago tan horrible que tenía. F.
3. Tiene que terminar su proyecto **para** el miércoles. F
4. Salió de la oficina **para** su casa pero no fue allí. C
5. Compró rosas **para** su novia. C
6. A ella le encantaron, y dijo: "¡Gracias **por** las rosas, mi amor!" C
7. Luego se fue a casa **para** descansar. F

11-23 After students complete their work in pairs, check answers by asking nine students to read each of the speech bubbles. As a follow-up, ask students what working in a factory might be like.

Go to *WileyPLUS* to see the video related to this reading.

For an additional activity related to this cultural theme, see PowerPoint slides on BCS and in *WileyPLUS*.

Meets ACTFL Standards 1.1, interpersonal speaking; 1.2, interpretive reading; 2.2, cultural products; 3.1, other disciplines; and 4.2, cultural comparisons.

Tu mundo cultural

Las maquiladoras de la frontera mexicana

Como sabes, el problema de la inmigración ilegal mexicana crea constante tensión en las relaciones entre México y EE. UU. Las maquiladoras, tal como se menciona a continuación, son un ejemplo de lo que se ha tratado de hacer para buscar una solución al problema. Desafortunadamente, también ha creado otros.

Las maquiladoras son fábricas de manufacturación situadas en el norte de México y en América Central. Por lo general, usan materia prima que se importa a México, sin pagar impuestos, para fabricar productos que luego se exportan a EE. UU. Muchas compañías estadounidenses son dueñas de maquiladoras, de las que obtienen grandes beneficios. Las razones para ello son el bajo costo de la mano de obra[1] mexicana y la casi inexistencia de impuestos o tarifas, resultado del TLC, Tratado de Libre Comercio (NAFTA). Actualmente hay unas 3.800 maquiladoras en México, donde trabajan más de un millón de mexicanos.

¿SABES QUE...?

Maquiladora comes from **maquila**, the name of the tax charged by millers in colonial Mexico who processed other people's corn. Most maquiladoras are owned by U.S. companies, more than 26,000 of which supply the factories with raw materials and components. The **maquiladoras** are the Mexican equivalent of outsourcing or off-shore production.

¿SABES QUE...?

NAFTA (North American Free Trade Agreement), implemented in 1994, is a trade agreement between Canada, Mexico, and the United States that calls for the eventual elimination of tariffs through their gradual reduction, and the liberalization of other trade barriers.

Dave Rudkin/Dorling Kindersley/Getty Images, Inc.; Thomas Northcut/ Getty Images, Inc.; Andy Crawford/Dorling Kindersley/Getty Images, Inc.; Liam Bailey/Photographer's Choice/Getty Images, Inc.

Las maquiladoras se originaron en los años sesenta y aumentaron rápidamente por toda la frontera. Producen sobre todo equipo electrónico, ropa, plásticos, muebles, aparatos y partes de automóvil. El 80% de lo que se produce en las maquiladoras se exporta a EE. UU.

[1]**mano...** labor

Trabajadoras de una maquiladora de México cosiendo[1] pantalones para exportarlos a EE. UU. Las maquiladoras ofrecen muchas ganancias a las compañías extranjeras y a la economía mexicana. Sin embargo, en muchas de ellas las condiciones de trabajo son malas, con sueldos bajos y pocos beneficios.

Vista de El Paso tomada desde Ciudad Juárez, al otro lado de la frontera. El Paso se ha beneficiado enormemente de los intercambios comerciales con México, y en particular, de las maquiladoras situadas en la vecina Ciudad Juárez. Allí, llegan inmigrantes procedentes del sur de México para trabajar en esas fábricas.

¿Qué aprendiste?

1. ¿Por qué han comprado maquiladoras muchas compañías estadounidenses? ¿Qué acuerdo ha favorecido el negocio de las maquiladoras?
   Por el bajo costo de la mano de obra mexicana y la casi inexistencia de impuestos; NAFTA.
2. ¿Cuándo se originaron las maquiladoras? ¿Qué producen? ¿Adónde mandan sus productos?
   En los años sesenta; producen sobre todo equipo electrónico, ropa, plásticos, muebles, aparatos y
3. ¿Cómo son las condiciones de trabajo en muchas de ellas?   partes de automóvil; a EE. UU.
   Malas, con sueldos bajos y pocos beneficios.

Actividad cultural

Una reportera (**E1**) entrevista al gerente de una maquiladora (**E2**). La reportera le pregunta sobre las condiciones laborales en la maquiladora, y las ventajas y desventajas que tienen estas fábricas fronterizas para México y EE. UU.

Contraste cultural

En grupos de *cuatro,* hablen de compañías de su país que, en su opinión, se beneficien del trabajo de las maquiladoras de México o de fábricas similares en China. Digan qué productos venden.

[1]sewing

¿SABES QUE...?

In **maquiladoras** the minimum wage for Mexican workers, the majority of whom are women, is 25% of the minimum wage for U.S. workers. The average work week is 48 hours and there is no overtime pay. Many **maquiladoras** are known for not respecting workers' rights.

¿SABES QUE...?

César Chávez (1927–1993) was a Mexican-American labor leader who used nonviolent methods to fight for the rights of migrant farm workers in the southwestern USA. In 1962, together with **Dolores Huerta** (see p. 355) and **Gilbert Padilla**, he founded a union that would later become the *United Farm Workers* (the UFW). His life was devoted to a quest for social justice, reflected in his motto, **"Sí, se puede"** (*Yes, we can*). His work for the fair treatment of farm workers improved the lives of millions of people.

¿SABES QUE...?

Since 2000, as a result of the economic downturn in the United States and competition from China, the **maquiladoras** have experienced economic losses. Unemployment in the border towns of Mexico has increased 20 percent.

Tu mundo en vivo

¡Videos en acción!

11.1 La jornada laboral¹ en dos países diferentes

1. **Antes de ver el video**
¿Crees que es muy diferente la jornada laboral en una compañía mexicana que en una de EE. UU.? Explica tu respuesta.

PLUS Go to *WileyPLUS* to complete the **Mientras ves el video** activity.

2. **Después de ver el video**
Según lo que has observado, ¿hay diferencias entre el trabajo de un empleado de esta compañía y el de una compañía estadounidense? Explica tu respuesta.

11.2 Fábrica que protege el medio ambiente

1. **Antes de ver el video**

¿Conoces alguna compañía que haga productos que no dañen el medio ambiente? Explica.

PLUS Go to *WileyPLUS* to complete the **Mientras ves el video** activity.

2. **Después de ver el video**
   a. ¿Qué tipo de productos hace Freezetone?
   b. ¿Por qué crees que es una compañía con éxito?
   c. ¿Qué mensaje tiene el dueño de esa compañía para los líderes hispanos?

¡Diálogos en acción!

11.1 La entrevista de trabajo
Briseida Pagador, una joven peruana, se entrevista con la directora de una escuela de Lima, en Perú, para un puesto de maestra de inglés.

Paso 1. Primero, mira las **Expresiones útiles** de la página A-12. Luego, escucha el diálogo dos veces y contesta las preguntas de tu profesor/a.

Paso 2. Mira la transcripción del diálogo (pág. A-19) y represéntalo con tu compañero/a. Túrnense. Ahora vete a la página A-12 para completar los **Pasos 3** y **4**.

11.2 El trabajo de mis sueños
Pedro y Soledad son una joven pareja mexicana. Hoy, al llegar a casa, Soledad tiene muy buenas noticias para su esposo.

PLUS Go to *WileyPLUS* to listen to and practice this dialogue.

Diálogo 11.1 models the function of interacting in an interview situation (formal greetings/leave-taking, soliciting and providing information, and expressing thanks). It also practices present perfect and future tenses.
Diálogo 11.2 models the functions of recounting a past event, describing a future situation, congratulating, and making plans in an informal context. It also practices the future tense.

¹**jornada...** workday

¡Lectura en acción!

El consumidor hispano

A continuación, vas a leer un artículo sobre la publicidad dirigida a la población hispana de EE. UU.

Paso 1. Antes de leerlo, piensa en un anuncio publicitario que te parezca particularmente eficaz o divertido y descríbeselo a tu compañero/a. En la descripción, indica qué producto se anuncia, a quién va dirigido y por qué es eficaz. ¿Sabes qué otras cosas sobre el consumidor hispano se van a mencionar en este artículo?

Paso 2. Ahora, lee el artículo:

Seduciendo al consumidor hispano

Por: **Cristina F. Pereda** | 9 de agosto de 2010
(Blog adaptado de elpaís.com)

Una mujer camina por la calle. Podría[1] ser hispana. Sus rasgos[2] no permiten adivinarlo[3]. Lleva un café en la mano. La voz en off habla en inglés. El fondo de la imagen adquiere un color rojo y aparecen dos arcos amarillos. Es el anuncio de café de McDonald's. El slogan "I'm loving it" se convierte en "Me encanta".

Se trata de una de las campañas de publicidad más efectivas, según nos explica Juan Tornoe, especialista en estrategias de márketing que buscan consumidores hispanos. "Para el americano, sigue diciendo[4] "I'm loving it". Y al latino, le estás diciendo que entiendes que vive dos mundos en uno". La heterogeneidad de este grupo de consumidores es una de las dificultades más grandes a las que se enfrentan las empresas de Estados Unidos.

Según Felipe Korzenny, director del Centro de Márketing y Comunicación Hispanos de la Universidad del Estado de Florida: "Entender la cultura hace posible establecer conexiones más fuertes y aprovechar[5] otras oportunidades". La cultura, según Korzenny, es la clave. Los anuncios están dirigidos siempre a subgrupos, ya sean adolescentes, mujeres trabajadoras, padres o deportistas. Y todos ellos tienen características culturales distintas.

Tornoe, autor de la página especializada *Hispanic Trending*, coincide en que es necesario conocer el origen de los consumidores que residen en Estados Unidos. Aunque sean de América Latina, recomienda que los anunciantes no caigan[6] en el error de considerar a brasileños y mexicanos en el mismo grupo. "Tienen mucho en común, pero son diferentes también en su forma de ver el mundo", explica. Entre los factores que "complican la vida" a las agencias de publicidad, afirma Tornoe, están el país de origen de los consumidores, el estado en el que viven, y si son inmigrantes de primera o segunda generación. Hay que recordar que un tercio[7] de los hispanos son menores de 18 años que han crecido bajo la presión de la cultura estadounidense en las escuelas, donde también han estudiado en inglés. Todo esto les convertirá en consumidores distintos a sus padres.

El crecimiento de la población hispana en Estados Unidos debe inspirar a las empresas y agencias de publicidad a dirigirse a este grupo de consumidores.

¡El mercado hispano sigue siendo una mina por explotar!

Paso 3. Contesta las preguntas que siguen para comprobar si has entendido bien y si tus predicciones eran acertadas.

1. ¿Por qué es tan efectivo el anuncio publicitario de McDonald's?

2. ¿Cuál es el gran reto al que se enfrentan las agencias de Estados Unidos que hacen campañas de publicidad dirigidas a los hispanos?

3. Nombra los tres factores que deberían tener en cuenta las agencias de publicidad de EE. UU. a la hora de hacer una campaña publicitaria dirigida a los americanos de origen hispano.

Paso 4. En grupos de *cuatro*, inventen su propio anuncio publicitario dirigido a un público específico hispano de EE. UU.

---

[1]could, [2]features, [3]guess, [4]**sigue...** it still says, [5]to take advantage of, [6]**caer...** to fall, [7]third

Meets ACTFL Standard 1.1, interpersonal speaking.

Meets ACTFL Standard 1.3, presentational writing.

You may wish to assign certain steps of the **¡A escribir!** writing process for students to complete outside of class.

You may want to assign a minimum number of words or sentences as appropriate for the **¡A escribir!** task. Students can use the word count tool available in their word processing application to check the length of their work before and after the revising step of the writing process.

¡A conversar!

Las experiencias laborales

En grupos de *cuatro*, hablen de sus experiencias laborales, las del presente y las del pasado. Incluyan:

- El trabajo que tienen ahora: si es de tiempo parcial o completo, la descripción de un día típico en su puesto de trabajo, los aspectos positivos y negativos del trabajo;

- Los trabajos previos: si fueron de tiempo parcial o completo, la descripción de un día típico en su puesto de trabajo, los aspectos positivos y negativos del trabajo;

- Los trabajos que les han gustado más y por qué.

Túrnense.

¡A escribir!

Una carta de presentación

Después de leer muchos anuncios clasificados, has encontrado algo que te gusta. Escribe una carta de presentación para el puesto de... En la carta, explica las razones por las que te interesa y por las que consideras que eres un/a buen/a candidato/a.

(fecha)

Estimado/a señor/ señora/ señorita...:

Le escribo para...

Atentamente,
(su firma)

Writing Strategy

Reviewing a Cover Letter

If you are writing a cover letter when applying for a job, you need to put your best foot forward. After composing your letter, it's helpful to ask someone with an objective eye to review it and make suggestions regarding its organization, clarity, convincing information, spelling, and punctuation.

Steps:

1. *Prewriting*: Make an outline of what you want to cover.
2. *Writing*: Use formal forms of address (**Ud.**). Your letter would include: a short introductory statement, a sincere expression of interest in the job, and your ample qualifications for it. In your concluding statement, thank the individual for his/her attention.
3. *Revising*: Do you describe your attributes in a positive and enthusiastic way, without sounding like a braggart? Have you checked your letter for the points listed at the end of the accompanying strategy? **¡Ojo!** In your description of your attributes, do your adjectives agree with you, the subject?
4. *Peer correction*: Check each other's letters for the points listed at the end of the strategy, being as objective and critical as possible. Circle and discuss areas that are in question, and then make corrections accordingly.

¡A investigar!

Los líderes empresariales hispanos de EE. UU.

Meets ACTFL Standards 1.2, interpretive reading; 1.3, presentational speaking; and 3.2, acquiring information.

Ya saben que la población hispanohablante de EE. UU. ha crecido mucho y que algunas empresas reconocen los beneficios de usar campañas de publicidad para atraer a los consumidores hispanos. ¿Tienen esas empresas líderes hispanos? ¿Quiénes son?

Paso 1.   Trabajen en grupos de *tres*, usen las estrategias de investigación que ya conocen e identifiquen a un/a líder hispano/a de una empresa estadounidense.

You may assign the appropriate **Pasos** of ¡**A investigar!** for pairs or small groups to complete outside of class.

Paso 2.   Investiguen la biografía y carrera profesional del individuo. Luego, colaboren para preparar una breve presentación oral sobre él o ella. Incluyan:

- Su nombre

- Sus datos biográficos (de dónde es, sus estudios, edad, experiencia previa, etc.)

- El nombre de la empresa donde trabaja

- El puesto que ocupa en la empresa, sus responsabilidades

- El URL de la Web donde encontraron la información

Creen un *PowerPoint* que les sirva de recurso visual mientras se turnen para hablar, o creen una presentación que tenga un comentario grabado. Otra opción es poner las presentaciones grabadas en el blog o el wiki de la clase para que todos las puedan ver.

If your access to technology is limited, have the students create posters or transparencies to use as visual aids as they speak.

Paso 3.   Después de las presentaciones de sus compañeros, comparen las características personales y profesionales de los individuos sobre quienes se ha investigado. ¿Qué han hecho para tener éxito? En su opinión, ¿qué harán en el futuro?

Research Strategy

Using Business-Related Search Terms

As you've seen in previous chapters, using search terms specific to your research task will help you find appropriate online resources more quickly. Two useful terms for business and employment are **cámara de comercio** (chamber of commerce) and **portal de empleo** (job search website). Many cities in Spanish-speaking countries have chambers of commerce and sites for job seekers, just as in the US. The United States Hispanic Chamber of Commerce or USHCC (www.ushcc.com), has information about its programs and members and links to local Hispanic chambers of commerce. For additional search terms, review your vocabulary and, for better results, combine words into phrases such as **economía de México** or **empresas tecnológicas**.

Trivia

A ver cuánto sabes.

If you don't know the answers, take a look at the front inside cover of the textbook. Try to respond in complete sentences.

1. ¿Cuál es el país hispanohablante con mayor extensión? ¿Y el país hispanohablante con menor extensión?   a. Argentina b. Puerto Rico

2. ¿Cuál es el país hispanohablante con mayor número de habitantes? ¿Y el país hispanohablante con menor número de habitantes?   a. México b. Guinea Ecuatorial

3. ¿Qué tres países hispanohablantes tienen frontera con cinco países?
   Argentina, Colombia y Bolivia

Vocabulario: Capítulo 11

Escena 1

En la oficina   *At the office*
el archivo *file*
el cubículo *cubicle*
la fotocopiadora *photocopier*
la impresora *printer*
el maletín *briefcase*
las tijeras *scissors*

Buscando empleo   *Looking for a job*
el (trabajo) de tiempo parcial/de tiempo completo *part time/ full time (job/work)*
el currículo *résumé*
el/la ejecutivo/a *executive*
el/la gerente de ventas *sales manager*
el jefe/ la jefa *boss*
el jefe/ la jefa de personal *director of human resources*
el puesto de trabajo *position, job*
la solicitud de empleo *job application*

Cartas y documentos   *Letters and documents*
el anexo *attachment*
(la) arroba *@*
el asunto *subject*
la carta de recomendación *letter of recommendation*
la dirección *address*
el sobre *envelope*

Estimado/a... *Dear...*
Atentamente *Truly yours*

Por teléfono   *On the phone*
el código de área *area code*
la guía telefónica *telephone book*
la llamada de larga distancia *long distance call*
¿Aló? *Hello?*
¿Para cuándo? *By when?*

Verbos y expresiones verbales   *Verbs and verbal expressions*
aburrirse *to get bored*
borrar *to delete, erase*
copiar *to copy*
enviar *to send*
fotocopiar *to photocopy*
guardar *to save*
imprimir *to print*
marcar *to dial*
responder *to reply, answer*
romper *to break*

Escena 2

En la empresa   *At the corporation*
la acción *share*
la Bolsa *stock market*
el/la colega *colleague*
la deuda *debt*
la economía *economy*
el/la empleado/a *employee*
la entrevista *interview*
la experiencia *experience*
la ganancia *profit*
la inversión *investment*
listo/a *ready*
el mercado en alza y en baja *bull (up) and bear (down) markets*
el presupuesto *budget*
la promoción *promotion*

Verbos y expresiones verbales   *Verbs and verbal expressions*
equivocarse *to be mistaken, make a mistake*
ganar *to earn*
invertir (ie, i) *to invest*
tener éxito *to succeed, be successful*
tener razón *to be right*
tener suerte *to be lucky*

Números ordinales   *Ordinal numbers*
primer, primero/a *first*
segundo/a *second*
tercer, tercero/a *third*
cuarto/a *fourth*
quinto/a *fifth*
sexto/a *sixth*
séptimo/a *seventh*
octavo/a *eighth*
noveno/a *ninth*
décimo/a *tenth*

Escena 3

En la fábrica   *At the factory*
el aumento *raise, increase (in salary, production, etc.)*
los beneficios *benefits*
el descanso *break, rest*
el desempleo *unemployment*
los despidos *layoffs*
el día festivo *holiday*
el día laboral *workday*
el/la obrero/a *worker*
el permiso por enfermedad *sick leave*
el permiso por maternidad *maternity leave*
el sindicato *union*
el sueldo *salary*
el supervisor/ la supervisora *supervisor*
el turno de día/ noche *day/ night shift*

Verbos y expresiones verbales   *Verbs and verbal expressions*
hacer huelga *to go on strike*
jubilarse *to retire*
marcar tarjeta *to punch in*
operar la máquina *to operate the machine*
tener ganas de + *infinitivo* *to feel like doing something*

12 Nuevos horizontes

To introduce the theme, you may want to play one of the videos from this chapter, with or without the audio, and then ask students what they think the chapter is about. You may also want to use the video to motivate cultural discussion in Spanish. At the end of the chapter, ask students if their predictions about its content and culture were accurate.

WILEY **PLUS**

Additional activities and **Autopruebas** for each **Escena** available online.

Travelstock44/Juergen Held/The Image Bank/Getty Images, Inc.

Escena 1
De viaje por el mundo hispano

GRAMÁTICA:
· The conditional

CULTURA:
El ecoturismo

Escena 2
La ciencia y la tecnología

GRAMÁTICA:
· The imperfect (past) subjunctive

CULTURA:
Los desastres ecológicos

Escena 3
En busca de una vida mejor

GRAMÁTICA:
· Relative pronouns

CULTURA:
Inmigrantes en busca de una vida mejor

TU MUNDO EN VIVO

¡Videos en acción! La contaminación: no todo está perdido; Inmigrantes: aprende de ellos
¡Diálogos en acción! Requesting a Favor; Apologizing
¡Lectura en acción! Inferring Meaning from Text
¡A conversar! Asking Clarifying Questions
¡A escribir! Reading Aloud
¡A investigar! Following Current Events

LEARNING OBJECTIVES

By the end of the chapter you will be able to:
· Talk about hypothetical situations.
· React to past actions and events.
· Form more complex sentences by combining clauses.
· Talk about travels.
· Talk about the environment.
· Talk about immigration.

VOCABULARIO

De viaje por el mundo hispano

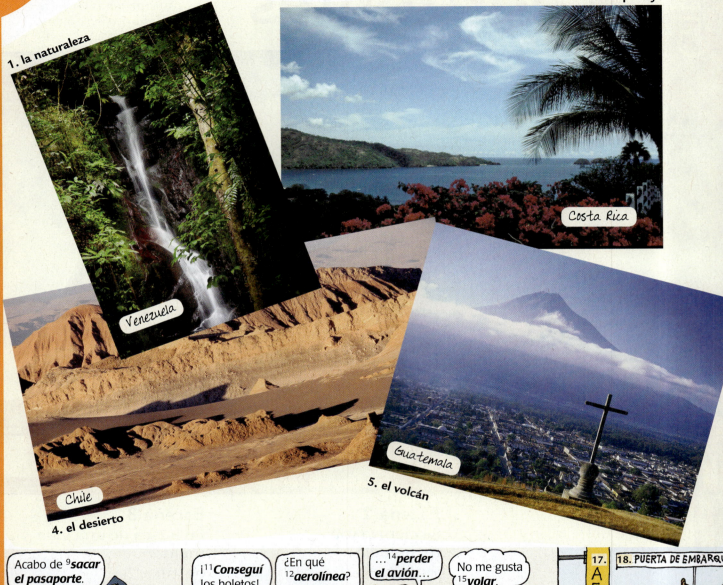

2. el paisaje

1. la naturaleza

Costa Rica

Venezuela

Chile

4. el desierto

Guatemala

5. el volcán

Acabo de ⁹**sacar** el pasaporte.

Pues, vamos a ¹⁰**reservar** los boletos.

¡¹¹**Conseguí** los boletos!

¿En qué ¹²**aerolínea**? ¿Y en qué ¹³**vuelo**?

…¹⁴**perder el avión**…

No me gusta ¹⁵**volar**.

16. hacer la maleta

17. AEROPUERTO

18. PUERTA DE EMBARQUE

19. la tarjeta de embarque

20. facturar el equipaje

3. la cordillera

7. la selva

Perú

Ecuador

Honduras

6. la cascada/catarata

Photos: TL; Ted Kerasote/Photo Researchers; CR: Nature's Image/Photo Researchers, Inc; CL: Courtesy of Liz Dougherty; BR: Courtesy of Laila Dawson

Panamá

8. las plantas tropicales

Pronunciación: Practice pronunciation of the chapter's new vocabulary in *WileyPLUS*.

1. nature
2. landscape
3. mountain range
4. desert
5. volcano
6. waterfall
7. jungle
8. tropical plants
9. to get a passport
10. to reserve
11. I got; **conseguir (i, i)** to get, obtain
12. airline
13. flight
14. to miss the plane
15. to fly; **volar (ue)**
16. to pack
17. airport
18. boarding gate
19. boarding pass
20. to check the luggage/baggage
21. window seat
22. aisle seat
23. flight attendant (female)
24. passenger
25. flight attendant (male)
26. customs
27. pilot
28. elevator
29. to check in
30. bellhop
31. room service
32. sheet
33. pillow
34. swimming pool
35. heating
36. air conditioner
37. blanket
38. double room; **... sencilla** single room

¡La pronunciación!

Pay attention to the correct pronunciation of the Spanish **tr** combination (see P-5).

tropical ex**tr**anjero

regis**tr**arse

21. el asiento de ventanilla 22. el asiento de pasillo

26. ADUANA SALIDA

¡Bienvenidos! ¡Gracias! ¿hay piscina? 30. el botones

28. ASCENSOR

29. registrarse

27. el piloto

23. la azafata 24. el pasajero

25. el auxiliar de vuelo

31 ¡Servicio de habitación! 34. la piscina 35. la calefacción

36. el aire acondicionado

32. la sábana 37. la cobija

38. la habitación doble

33. la almohada

© John Wiley & Sons, Inc.

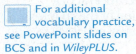

¡En acción!

 12-1 Preparativos para un viaje RECYCLES regular and irregular verbs in the preterit.

 Paso 1. Los señores Solís encuentran una lista escrita por su hijo para su viaje a Lima. Es un chico organizado, pero como nunca ha volado, ni ha estado en el extranjero, la lista tiene errores. Hagan el papel de los señores Solís y pongan la lista en orden cronológico.

A. Antes de llegar al aeropuerto (del 1 al 4):

   __3__ *hacer* la maleta
   __4__ *ir* al aeropuerto
   __2__ *conseguir* el boleto por Internet
   __1__ *sacar* el pasaporte

B. En el aeropuerto y en el avión (del 5 al 12):

   __6__ *pasar* por el control de seguridad
   __8__ *darle* la tarjeta de embarque al empleado de la aerolínea
   __5__ *facturar* el equipaje y *recibir* la tarjeta de embarque
   __11__ *sentarse* y *abrocharse* el cinturón
   __7__ *ir* a la puerta de embarque
   __12__ *tomar* una bebida, *relajarse* y *ver* una película
   __9__ *subir* al avión
   __10__ *poner* el equipaje de mano en el compartimento de equipaje

Paso 2. Hagan el papel del hijo, que cuenta lo que hizo siguiendo el orden cronológico anterior. Usen el pretérito y palabras como **primero, luego, después, finalmente.** Cambien de papel después de completar del 1 al 6.

1. *Primero, saqué el pasaporte.*   7.
2.   8.
3.   9.
4.   10.
5.   11.
6.   12.

Hint: Before completing *Paso 2*, review the preterit of regular verbs (page 226) and irregular verbs (pages 237 and 262). Can you identify the irregular verbs in the list in *Paso 1?*

12-1 *Option:* Students write the answers for *Paso 2*.
ANSWERS: 1. (provided)
2. Luego, conseguí...
3. hice... 4. fui...
5. facturé... y recibí...
6. pasé... 7. fui... 8. le di...
9. subí... 10. puse...
11. me senté y me abroché... 12. Finalmente, tomé..., me relajé y vi...

12-2 ¡De viaje!

¿Adónde van y qué hacen los viajeros? Para saberlo, observen la escena de las páginas 400–401 y describan:

 • las fotos de la naturaleza

 • lo que hace la pareja antes de llegar al aeropuerto

 • las preocupaciones que tiene cada uno

 • lo que pasa en el aeropuerto, en el avión y después

12-2 You may want to project the PowerPoint slide of the opener scene and ask students to describe each area or item of the illustration as indicated.

PERSONALIZED QUESTIONS: ¿Quiénes tienen pasaporte? ¿A qué países han viajado? ¿A quiénes les gusta volar y a quiénes no?

12-3 En el hotel Caribe

12-3 You may want to project the PowerPoint slide as students describe the people and items in the two scenes.

Paso 1. A ver si tienen buena memoria. Primero, escriban el número de la persona o cosa que corresponde a cada descripción (a–g) en los espacios en blanco que están debajo de las ilustraciones. Luego, tu compañero/a lee una descripción y tú la identificas con el número que le corresponde y dices lo que es. Sigan el modelo. Túrnense.

MODELO

E1: ___8___ *Es lo que usamos para calentar la habitación cuando hace frío.*   **E2:** *¡Ya sé! ¡El número 8! Es la calefacción.* **o:** *No sé. ¿Y tú?*

© John Wiley & Sons, Inc.

EN EL HOTEL CARIBE

a. _7_ Es el empleado del hotel que ayuda con el equipaje.

b. _4_ Es el lugar del hotel donde se puede nadar.

c. _6_ Es lo que se usa para cubrirse en la cama cuando se tiene frío.

d. _2_ Es lo que se usa para subir y bajar las escaleras de un piso a otro.

e. _5_ Es lo que se usa para enfriar la habitación cuando se tiene calor.

f. _1_ Es lo que se usa para apoyar la cabeza cuando se duerme.

g. _3_ Es lo que se usa para hacer la cama. Hay dos. Nos acostamos sobre una y nos cubrimos con la otra.

Paso 2. Ahora, túrnense para describir **a)** lo que pasa en la recepción y **b)** lo que hay y lo que ocurre en la habitación.

12-4 Un vuelo «inolvidable»   RECYCLES Ud./Uds. commands.

Viajan en un vuelo procedente de Nueva York que hace escala[1] en Miami y tiene por destino Caracas, la capital de Venezuela. Para resolver cada uno de los siguientes problemas que ocurren en el viaje, hablen con las personas indicadas. Tienes *un* minuto para cada conversación. Túrnense para hacer el papel de pasajero/a.

Hint: Before starting activity 12-4, review the formation of **Ud./Uds.** commands (page 222).

Problemas:

1. Tienes reservado un asiento de ventanilla, pero encuentras a **otro pasajero** sentado en tu asiento. Habla con él.

2. **La azafata** te sirve una cena que no puedes comer porque eres vegetariano/a. Habla con ella.

3. Llegas a Caracas, recoges el equipaje y sólo encuentras dos de las tres maletas que facturaste. Habla con **el empleado de la aerolínea.**

4. En el momento de pasar la aduana, no encuentras el pasaporte. Habla con **el agente de la aduana.**

5. Llegas al hotel con maletas grandes y pesadas[2] y necesitas ayuda. Habla con **el botones.**

12-4 Remind students to use the **Ud.** form, and be sure to time their conversations. *Option:* Students change partners after each conversation. When students have finished the activity, ask five pairs to perform for the class.

The scripts and recordings for the ¡A escuchar! sections are included on the Book Companion Site (BCS) for instructors and in *WileyPLUS.*

¡A escuchar! Siempre corriendo

Paso 1. Escucha la conversación entre dos amigas, Belén y Pepa, en el aeropuerto.

PLUS Go to *WileyPLUS* to complete **Paso 2** of this listening activity.

[1]stopover, [2]heavy

Ysenia se encuentra con Ernesto y él le cuenta que se va a Florida a visitar a sus tíos.

¡Hola Ernesto! ¿Adónde vas con tanta prisa?

Voy a casa para hacer la maleta. Me voy a Florida a ver a mis tíos y no me **gustaría** perder el avión.

No sabía que tenías familia allí. ¿Conseguiste un boleto barato?

Sí, en una aerolínea nueva. Mi vuelo sale a las tres y ya tengo la tarjeta de embarque.

Me gusta viajar en avión, pero **preferiría** no tener que hacer fila para facturar el equipaje.

Y a mí no me gusta pasar por controles de seguridad.

Pero sabes, Ernesto, **me encantaría** ir contigo. Florida debe de ser precioso. ¡Que tengas buen viaje!

© John Wiley & Sons, Inc.

WILEY PLUS Go to *WileyPLUS* to review this grammar point with the help of the **Animated Grammar Tutorial** and **Verb Conjugator**. For more practice, go to the **Grammar Handbook**.

To introduce students to the conditional used in context, have them take parts and read the **historieta** out loud. To check their comprehension and call their attention to the forms of the conditional, ask the following questions: 1. **¿Qué no le gustaría a Ernesto? 2. ¿Qué preferiría no hacer Ysenia? ¿Y Ernesto?**

For additional practice on this grammar point, see PowerPoint slides on BCS and in *WileyPLUS*.

Write the conditional endings oh the board or on a transparency. Then ask several students questions, such as: **¿Viajarías a otro planeta?** Recap responses: ... viajaría a otro planeta; ... y... viajarían a otro planeta; ... y yo viajaríamos a otro planeta. Additional questions: **¿Harías un viaje solo/a por todo el mundo? ¿Te gustaría aprender a pilotar un avión?**

You might want to point out to your students that the endings for conditional are the same as the imperfect indicative tense endings for **-er** and **-ir** verbs.

¡Manos a la obra!

GRAMÁTICA

1

Talking about what would happen: The conditional

In our daily lives, we often express what *would potentially happen* in certain circumstances. The conditional tense conveys this concept.

As with the future tense, the conditional of all regular **-ar, -er,** and **-ir** verbs, and most irregular verbs, is formed by adding the following endings to the infinitive. Let's look at examples based on Ysenia's encounter with Ernesto.

Infinitive + -ía, -ías, -ía, -íamos, -íais, -ían			
	volar	**volver**	**ir**
(yo)	volar**ía**	volver**ía**	ir**ía**
(tú)	volar**ías**	volver**ías**	ir**ías**
(Ud., él, ella)	volar**ía**	volver**ía**	ir**ía**
(nosotros/as)	volar**íamos**	volver**íamos**	ir**íamos**
(vosotros/as)	volar**íais**	volver**íais**	ir**íais**
(Uds., ellos, ellas)	volar**ían**	volver**ían**	ir**ían**

—**¿Viajarías** a Florida en carro?   *Would you travel to Florida by car?*
—No, **iría** en avión.   *No, I would go by plane.*

With some irregular verbs, the conditional endings are added not to the infinitive but to an irregular stem. These irregular stems are the same as those of the future.

infinitive	*irregular stem*	*conditional forms*
decir	**dir-**	dir**ía**, dir**ías**, dir**ía**, dir**íamos**, dir**íais**, dir**ían**
hacer	**har-**	har**ía**, har**ías**,...
poder	**podr-**	podr**ía**, podr**ías**,...
poner	**pondr-**	pondr**ía**, pondr**ías**,...
querer	**querr-**	querr**ía**, querr**ías**,...
saber	**sabr-**	sabr**ía**, sabr**ías**,...
salir	**saldr-**	saldr**ía**, saldr**ías**,...
tener	**tendr-**	tendr**ía**, tendr**ías**,...
venir	**vendr-**	vendr**ía**, vendr**ías**,...

¿Harías un viaje a la selva?   *Would you take a trip to the rain forest?*
Sí. Y tú **podrías** venir conmigo.   *Yes. And you **could** come with me.*

. . . y algo más   The conditional of *haber*

The conditional of **hay** (*there is, there are*) is **habría** (*there would be*). Remember: there is no plural for **habría.**

En un mundo ideal no **habría** ni pobreza ni guerras.
In an ideal world there would be neither poverty nor wars.

De paso

The conditional is also used to make polite requests:

Me gustaría...; Querría un...; Preferiría...; Podría Ud. darme un...

Me gustaría una habitación con dos camas.   *I would like a room with two beds.*
Preferiría tomar el ascensor.   *I would prefer to take the elevator.*
¿Podría Ud. ayudarme con el equipaje?   *Could you help me with the luggage?*

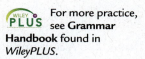

For more practice, see **Grammar Handbook** found in *WileyPLUS.*

For additional practice on these grammar points, see PowerPoint slides on BCS and in *WileyPLUS.*

¡En acción!

¡Oye!   ¿Lo harías o no?

A ver si eres aventurero/a. Escucha las *ocho* preguntas de tu profesor/a y responde, apuntando **sí** o **no** en una hoja de papel.

12-5   El vuelo ideal

Paso 1.   Marquen con un símbolo de más (+) las características de lo que en su opinión sería un vuelo ideal y con un símbolo de menos, (−) las de un vuelo desastroso.

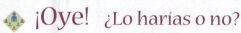

 _+_ **1.**   Los auxiliares de vuelo **servirían** comida a la carta y unos postres deliciosos.

 _−_ **2.**   Los bebés **llorarían** constantemente y no **dormirían** durante todo el vuelo.

 _+_ **3.**   En el avión **habría** peluquería y una sala para hacer ejercicio y yoga.

 _−_ **4.**   Los auxiliares de vuelo **se enojarían** con los pasajeros y les **gritarían**.

 _+_ **5.**   Todas las azafatas **serían** simpatiquísimas y extremadamente corteses[1].

 _+_ **6.**   Los baños **estarían** limpísimos y **tendrían** duchas e incluso sauna.

 _−_ **7.**   **Habría** turbulencias y mucho ruido durante todo el vuelo.

 _−_ **8.**   El vuelo **saldría** y **llegaría** tarde.

 _+_ **9.**   Durante el vuelo **pondrían** películas recientes y **habría** wifi para los pasajeros.

 _+_ **10.**   Se **ofrecerían** masajes gratis.

Paso 2.   Ahora, mencionen otras *cuatro* características de un vuelo ideal y *cuatro* más de un vuelo desastroso. Usen el condicional. Luego, compártanlas con la clase para ver cuáles son las más originales de cada categoría.

[1]polite

¡**Oye!** Before you read the questions, have students write the numbers 1–8 on a sheet of paper. After completing the activity, students share their responses with the class.

Guión para ¡Oye!
1. **¿Comerías** insectos para no morirte de hambre?
2. **¿Caminarías** por una densa selva solo/a?
3. **¿Acamparías** en un desierto?
4. **¿Pasarías** una noche en un bosque solo/a?
5. **¿Nadarías** en un río con pirañas?
6. **¿Vivirías** cerca de un volcán activo?
7. **¿Subirías** el pico Aconcagua, el más alto de Sudamérica?
8. **¿Viajarías** en un barco pequeño a las islas Galápagos?

12-6 El avión del futuro   RECYCLES the future, the preposition **para** and verbs like **gustar**.

Paso 1.   A continuación, hay una serie de oraciones que resumen lo que anunció la compañía Airbus en la reciente presentación de su prototipo de avión del futuro. Primero, escriban en los espacios en blanco de la primera columna las letras de la segunda columna que mejor completan cada oración. Luego, tú dices la oración completa y tu compañero/a hace lo siguiente: **a)** la confirma si es correcta; **b)** identifica a cuál de las cuatro categorías en azul corresponde la innovación, y **c)** dice si le gustaría o no. Túrnense. Sigan el modelo y usen el condicional.

> ocio[1]   salud   comunicación   medioambiente

Palabras útiles
interesar, importar
(se usan como **gustar**
y **encantar**)

MODELO

E1: _d_ _La cabina del avión tendrá el techo transparente para poder admirar las vistas._

E2: _Sí. Es una innovación para el ocio. Eso **me encantaría**._ (Si tu compañero/a escoge la oración incorrecta, corrígela antes de continuar.)

12-6 You may want to show the PowerPoint slide of the photo of the prototype plane as students complete this activity.

1. _d_ La cabina del avión tendrá el techo transparente...
2. _c_ Los asientos serán...
3. _g_ El avión del futuro contará con tecnología para reducir...
4. _f_ Los pasajeros podrán comunicarse con el exterior...
5. _a_ En el avión se les ofrecerán a los viajeros...
6. _b_ El material de la cabina será...
7. _h_ Habrá una zona revitalizante para recibir aire enriquecido...
8. _e_ Habrá un espacio de realidad virtual para...

a. ... juegos interactivos.
b. ... biodegradable.
c. ... ergonómicos.
d. ... para poder admirar las vistas.
e. ... poder jugar al golf o hacer las compras.
f. ... por videoconferencia.
g. ... las emisiones de CO^2 y la contaminación acústica.
h. ... con antioxidantes y vitaminas, aromaterapia y servicios de acupuntura.

Xinhua/eyevine/Redux Pictures

Paso 2.   Ahora, compartan con otra pareja otras innovaciones que preferirían para su vuelo en el avión del futuro.

[1]leisure

12-7   El hotel del futuro

Paso 1. Primero, lean el siguiente artículo. Luego, háganse preguntas para saber cuáles de las *siete* características que se mencionan en la segunda columna escogería cada uno/a de Uds. para su habitación *a la carta*. Usen los siguientes verbos en el condicional.

> escoger   gustar   pedir   poner   preferir   ser   tener   usar

MODELO

E1: ¿De qué color **te gustarían** las paredes y cortinas?

E2: **Pondría** paredes azules y cortinas verdes. ¿Y tú?

E1: Yo **escogería** paredes verdes y cortinas rojas.

La habitación de hotel del futuro, *a la carta*

Una cadena de hoteles estadounidense quiere crear la habitación de hotel *a la carta*. Se calcula que dentro de 50 años el cliente será una persona con más estrés que ahora. Por eso, los ingredientes fundamentales serán: el *relax* y la ergonomía.

© John Wiley & Sons, Inc.

¡Estimula los cinco sentidos!

Los sentidos de la vista y el tacto

- *Las paredes y cortinas* serán transparentes. El cliente podrá escoger los colores y texturas.
- *El techo*: con cielo estrellado, luna o soleado,...
- *La pantalla de la televisión* proyectará el paisaje deseado: mar, montañas, desierto,...

El sentido del oído

- *Sonidos de la naturaleza*: pájaros, olas,...
- *Música de fondo*: clásica, rock, pop,...

El sentido del olfato

- *Olores o perfumes deseados*: suaves para relajarse y estimulantes para despertarse.

El sentido del gusto

- *El mini-bar* tendrá las bebidas favoritas del cliente.

Paso 2. Ahora, comparte con el resto de la clase lo que[1] escogiste para tu habitación.

12-8   Entrevista sobre un viaje   RECYCLES travel vocabulary and weather.

Paso 1. Entrevista a tu compañero/a para obtener información acerca de un viaje que **le encantaría** hacer y apunta lo que dice en la segunda columna. Luego, cambien de papel.

Preguntas	Información de tu compañero/a
1. ¿Adónde **irías** y con quién?	... **iría** a Chile con su pareja.
2. ¿Cuándo **irías** y cuánto tiempo te **quedarías**?	
3. ¿Cómo **irías** (en carro, en avión,...)?	
4. ¿Dónde te **quedarías** y **cómo sería** el lugar?	
5. ¿Qué atracciones históricas, culturales o naturales **habría** allí?	
6. ¿Qué tal el clima de allí (**haría** calor, frío,...)?	
7. ¿Qué **harías** por la mañana, por la tarde,...?	
8. ¿Qué cosas especiales **te gustaría** hacer?	

Paso 2. Luego, cuéntale a otro/a compañero/a acerca del viaje que **haría** la persona que entrevistaste.

[1]what

12-9 You may want to project the PowerPoint slides of the photos and maps of the two countries in this activity.

12-9   De turismo por España y Argentina

Paso 1.   Tus amigos y tú quieren presentarse a un concurso[1] cuyo[2] premio es un viaje a España o a Argentina. Primero, observen las fotos y los mapas y lean la información. Luego, para recordar lo que han aprendido, marquen lo que se les pide en la siguiente tabla:

¿España o Argentina?   Identifica con una **E** lo que corresponde a España y con una **A** lo que corresponde a Argentina.

1. _A_ ver 275 cataratas espectaculares
2. _E_ visitar un museo modernísimo
3. _A_ observar el hielo azul y hacer senderismo
4. _E_ admirar la arquitectura árabe
5. _E_ ver una obra en un teatro romano
6. _A_ visitar un Parque Nacional de interés científico
7. _E_ ver o jugar partidos de pelota vasca (jai-alai)

8. _E_ hacer surf y esquiar en las montañas
9. _A_ hacer turismo alternativo
10. _E_ visitar una pequeña Roma
11. _A_ montar en los mejores caballos
12. _A_ comer carne de res y empanadas exquisitas
13. _A_ admirar la increíble variedad de fauna y flora
14. _E_ probar tapas, paella, gazpacho y chocolate con churros

ESPAÑA: Arquitectura de tres épocas

Roderick Chen/Age Fotostock America, Inc.

12-9   ANOTHER STEP: Divide the class into four groups, two of which promote Argentina and the other two, Spain. Groups present a travel plan, including itinerary, means of transportation, duration of stay, cultural visits, activities and sports, gastronomy, and so on. Half of the class then votes to determine which of the two presentations on a particular country was the best.

El museo Guggenheim de Bilbao (1997), uno de los más modernos del mundo, diseñado por F. Gehry. Después de visitarlo, pruebe la exquisita gastronomía vasca[3], asista a un partido de pelota vasca (jai-alai) y recorra la costa en cuyas playas se practica el surf.

Gastronomía

Pruebe...
las tapas
el gazpacho
la rica paella
la tortilla española
el pescadito frito
la empanada gallega
los vinos, quesos y dulces
el chocolate con churros

© John Wiley & Sons, Inc.

Bilbao
ESPAÑA
★ Madrid
Mérida
Granada

Linh Hassel/Age Fotostock America, Inc.

Mérida, pequeña Roma (año 25 antes de Cristo). Su teatro de más de 2.000 años sigue siendo escenario de obras teatrales. Allí hay también un circo, un anfiteatro, un acueducto, un templo, casas romanas y un museo donde se exhiben joyas y piezas de esa época.

El Palacio de la Alhambra (1338–1390), en Granada, ejemplo de la magnífica arquitectura árabe. Los jardines, con sus fuentes[4], son prueba de la fascinación que sentían esas gentes del desierto por el agua. Allí residieron los reyes moros hasta su expulsión en 1492. Desde la Alhambra (véase la foto →) se ve Sierra Nevada, donde se puede esquiar hasta el mes de abril.

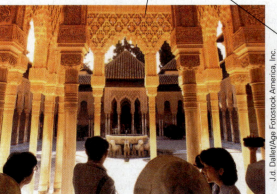

J.d. Dallet/Age Fotostock America, Inc.

Mark Sunderland/Age Fotostock America, Inc.

[1]contest, [2]which, [3]Basque, [4]fountains

ARGENTINA: Paisajes espectaculares

Las espectaculares Cataratas del Iguazú, en la frontera entre Argentina y Brasil, y cerca de la frontera con Paraguay. Hay 275 cataratas diferentes y allí también hay más de 21.000 variedades de plantas, 450 especies de aves, así como[1] reptiles, anfibios, peces y mariposas[2].

Parque Nacional Los Glaciares, en la Patagonia argentina. Ha sido declarado Patrimonio de la Humanidad por la UNESCO por su belleza espectacular y el interés científico que despierta. Las personas aventureras pueden disfrutar caminando por el glaciar Perito Moreno, navegando por el lago para observar el hielo azul o haciendo senderismo[3] por los montes Fitzroy y Torre.

La pampa argentina, tierra del gaucho. Allí el visitante puede disfrutar de los atractivos del turismo alternativo: hospedarse en una hacienda rural, respirar el aire puro, apreciar la variada flora y fauna, y montar en los mejores caballos.

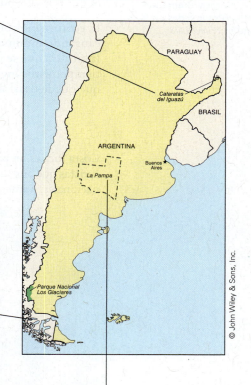

Gastronomía

Pruebe...
la carne de res más rica del mundo
el vino tinto de la región de Mendoza
la trucha y el salmón de los lagos y ríos
las empanadas
el pan y el queso de las regiones rurales
los alfajores
el dulce de leche

Paso 2. Ahora, hablen con su compañeros y **a)** decidan cuál de los dos viajes escogerían y por qué; **(b)** indiquen qué harían allí y, finalmente, **(c)** díganle a la clase qué viaje escogieron, por qué lo prefieren y qué harían allí.

[1]as well as, [2]butterflies, [3]trekking

Tu mundo cultural

Meets ACTFL Standards
1.1, interpersonal speaking;
1.2, interpretive reading;
2.1, cultural practices; 3.1,
other disciplines; and 4.2,
cultural comparisons.

For an additional
activity related to
this cultural theme, see the
PowerPoint slides on BCS
and in *WileyPLUS*.

El ecoturismo

COSTA RICA

© John Wiley & Sons, Inc.

¿Te gustaría viajar a un lugar exótico donde hay conciencia del medio ambiente? ¿Te interesaría practicar toda clase de deportes y descansar en medio de la naturaleza?

Si eso es lo que buscas, el ecoturismo es para ti.

El ecoturismo consiste en viajar por áreas naturales causando mínimo impacto en el medio ambiente y en la cultura que se visita, generando ingresos[1] al mismo tiempo. Estos ingresos benefician a la población local, que puede usarlos para conservar sus recursos[2] locales.

Costa Rica: modelo de ecoturismo

Costa Rica es un país pionero en ecoturismo y modelo para aquellos países que quieran atraer a turistas que busquen reencontrarse con la naturaleza y escapar del estrés urbano. Tiene 30 parques nacionales, numerosas reservas biológicas y forestales, y una variedad increíble de flora y fauna.

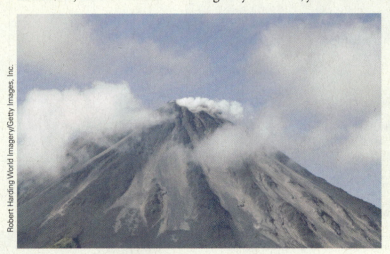

Robert Harding World Imagery/Getty Images, Inc.

El volcán Arenal, uno de los muchos volcanes activos de Costa Rica. Sus emisiones de lava incandescente son un gran espectáculo.

Roy Toft/Danita Delimont

Jardín de mariposas. Costa Rica tiene 12.000 especies de mariposas diurnas y unas 4.000 nocturnas. Los jardines de mariposas y sus flores son espectaculares.

[1]income, [2]resources

Art Wolfe, Inc.

Costa Rica tiene 850 especies de aves, como el quetzal (arriba), y el programa de conservación medioambiental más avanzado de América. Por eso no sorprende que la Universidad de Costa Rica ofrezca una especialidad de estudios en Turismo Ecológico.

Michael Brinson/Iconica/Getty Images

En las costas del Caribe y del Pacífico, Costa Rica ofrece sus playas a los amantes del surf y de otros deportes acuáticos. En el interior del país se puede practicar el balsismo[1], el piragüismo[2], el ciclismo, el montañismo, el camping y la equitación[3].

HOTEL CONSTRUIDO CON CONCIENCIA MEDIOAMBIENTAL

Costa Rica. En la localidad de Punta Uva se construyen alojamientos para turistas respetando el medio ambiente. En su construcción no se cortan árboles sino que se usan árboles caídos[4], y para su transporte se utilizan bueyes[5] en vez de vehículos, para no alterar el medio ambiente. Son alojamientos con vistas magníficas de los jardines botánicos y de la playa con sus palmeras y arena blanca. Uno de ellos es una casa que está en un árbol (véase la foto).

Courtesy of Laila Dawson

¿Qué aprendiste?

1. ¿Cuál es una de las diferencias entre el turismo tradicional y el ecoturismo?
   El segundo causa un impacto mínimo en el medio ambiente.
2. ¿Cómo se sabe que en Costa Rica se da mucha importancia al medio ambiente? Den ejemplos.
   Tiene muchos parques y reservas naturales, y el programa de conservación más avanzado de América.
3. En el artículo de periódico sobre Punta Uva, ¿en qué se nota la conciencia del medio ambiente que existe en Costa Rica?
   En el tipo de transporte y alojamiento que usan.

Actividad cultural

Imaginen que a Uds. les ofrecen la oportunidad de hacer ecoturismo en Costa Rica. Hagan una lista de lo que les gustaría ver y de las actividades que preferirían hacer allí. Luego, compártanla con otra pareja.

Contraste cultural

Hablen de las medidas que ya se han tomado, o que en su opinión, se deben tomar en su país o región para proteger la naturaleza y sus especies, y atraer al ecoturista.

[1]rafting, [2]canoeing, [3]horseback riding, [4]fallen, [5]oxen

¿SABES QUE...?

Words related to sports, as well as those related to technology, are often borrowed from English (**hacer surf, escribir** *e-mails*, etc.). In this chapter you were introduced to **el senderismo** (p. 409), also referred to as **el** *trekking*. **El balsismo** (this page), is also called **el** *rafting*. In magazines and in on-line advertising, you will often see the English variations of these words.

Pronunciación: Practice pronunciation of the chapter's new vocabulary in *WileyPLUS*.

VOCABULARIO

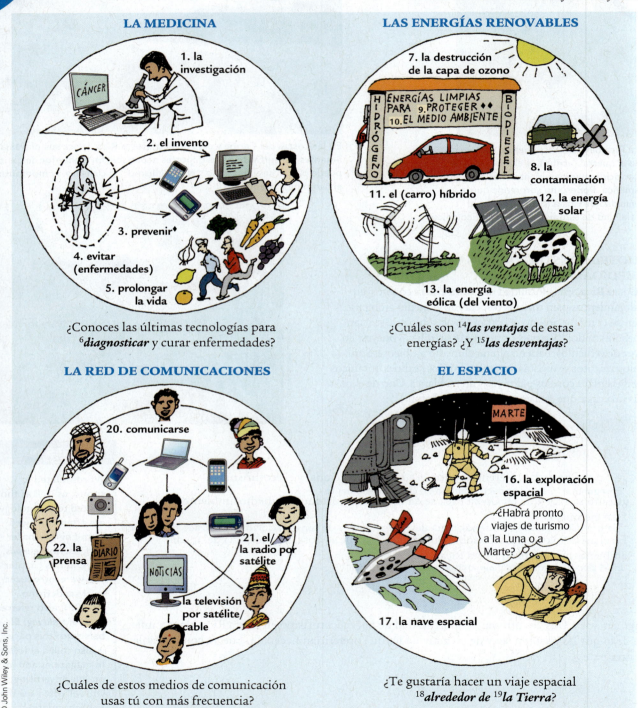

LA MEDICINA

1. la investigación

CÁNCER

2. el invento

3. prevenir◆

4. evitar (enfermedades)

5. prolongar la vida

¿Conoces las últimas tecnologías para ⁶*diagnosticar* y curar enfermedades?

LAS ENERGÍAS RENOVABLES

7. la destrucción de la capa de ozono

ENERGÍAS LIMPIAS PARA 9. PROTEGER◆◆ 10. EL MEDIO AMBIENTE

HIDRÓGENO

BIODIESEL

8. la contaminación

11. el (carro) híbrido

12. la energía solar

13. la energía eólica (del viento)

¿Cuáles son ¹⁴*las ventajas* de estas energías? ¿Y ¹⁵*las desventajas*?

LA RED DE COMUNICACIONES

20. comunicarse

EL DIARIO

NOTICIAS

22. la prensa

21. el/la radio por satélite

la televisión por satélite/cable

¿Cuáles de estos medios de comunicación usas tú con más frecuencia?

EL ESPACIO

MARTE

16. la exploración espacial

¿Habrá pronto viajes de turismo a la Luna o a Marte?

17. la nave espacial

¿Te gustaría hacer un viaje espacial ¹⁸*alrededor de* ¹⁹*la Tierra*?

© John Wiley & Sons, Inc.

1. research 2. invention 3. to prevent 4. to avoid (illnesses) 5. to prolong life 6. to diagnose 7. destruction of the ozone layer 8. pollution 9. to protect 10. environment 11. hybrid (car) 12. solar energy 13. aeolic (wind) energy 14. advantages 15. disadvantages 16. space exploration 17. spaceship 18. around 19. Earth 20. to communicate 21. satellite radio 22. press

◆ **Prevenir** is conjugated like **venir**. ◆◆ **Proteger** (presente): protejo, proteges, protege...

¡En acción!

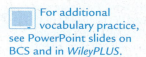 For additional vocabulary practice, see PowerPoint slides on BCS and in *WileyPLUS*.

 12-10 Asociaciones

¿Por qué se relacionan? Combina las dos palabras que se asocian en cada serie y explica por qué.

MODELO

el síntoma, la investigación, el diagnóstico

El síntoma y el diagnóstico. El síntoma ayuda a determinar el diagnóstico de una enfermedad.

1. curar, prevenir, evitar
2. cortar, extender, prolongar
3. la prensa, las noticias, el invento
4. la energía eólica, el sol, el viento
5. la contaminación, la capa de ozono, la deforestación
6. la ventaja, el planeta, la nave espacial

12-10 Students may complete the activity individually or in pairs, followed by feedback to the class.

ANSWERS:
1. prevenir, evitar
2. extender, prolongar
3. la prensa, las noticias
4. la energía eólica, el viento 5. la contaminación, la capa de ozono 6. el planeta, la nave espacial

 12-11 Los avances científicos y tecnológicos

¿Están Uds. bien informados? Observen las escenas de la página 412 y comenten lo siguiente.

La medicina:
- clase de investigaciones e inventos que para Uds. serían importantes
- lo que se puede hacer para prevenir o evitar enfermedades
- ventajas y desventajas de prolongar la vida

Las energías renovables:
- ventajas y desventajas
- las que se usan en la región donde viven

El espacio:
- la exploración espacial
- sus respuestas a las preguntas que se hacen en la escena

La red de comunicaciones:
- para qué sirve cada medio de comunicación que se observa
- cuáles usan Uds. con más frecuencia y para qué

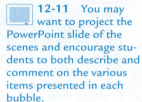 **12-11** You may want to project the PowerPoint slide of the scenes and encourage students to both describe and comment on the various items presented in each bubble.

12-11 PERSONALIZED QUESTIONS: ¿Hasta qué edad les gustaría vivir? ¿Qué hacen Uds. para mantenerse sanos, evitar enfermedades y prolongar la vida?

12-12 Un mundo ideal

 Paso 1. En grupos de *cuatro,* reflexionen unos minutos y después anoten sus ideas. Luego, describan en qué tipo de mundo les gustaría vivir a Uds. Usen las siguientes preguntas como guía.

- ¿Qué avances médicos y científicos habría? ¿Y qué nuevos inventos?
- ¿Qué métodos de transporte se usarían? ¿Y qué energías alternativas?
- ¿Cómo se comunicaría la gente?
- ¿Se podría vivir en otros planetas?
- ¿Habría paz?

Paso 2. Compartan con la clase lo que dijeron. Luego, todos deciden qué grupo tiene la descripción más interesante.

¡A escuchar! Nuevos inventos

Paso 1.   Escucha las noticias acerca de algunos de los nuevos inventos.

PLUS   Go to *WileyPLUS* to complete **Paso 2** of this listening activity.

Mabel convence a Mario para que se haga voluntario de su organización ecológica.

¿Cómo te va de voluntaria?

Regular. Quería que **hubiera** más voluntarios, pero muchos no pueden en este momento.

© John Wiley & Sons, Inc.

Esperaba que todos **organizáramos** una gran campaña de prensa para informar a la gente y enseñarle a prevenir y evitar tanta contaminación.

Es verdad. **Si trabajara** contigo, convenceríamos a muchos de las ventajas de usar carros híbridos.

¿Estás tratando de decirme algo?

Sí, que acabas de conseguir otro voluntario. Vamos a hacer grandes cosas juntos.

GRAMÁTICA

¡Manos a la obra!

Reacting to past actions, conditions or events: The imperfect (past) subjunctive

For additional practice on this grammar point, see PowerPoint slides on BCS and in *WileyPLUS*.

The imperfect subjunctive of **_all_** verbs is formed by dropping the **-ron** from the *ellos* form of the preterit and adding the endings **-ra, -ras, -ra, -ramos -rais, -ran.***

	reciclar recicla~~ron~~	**hacer** hicie~~ron~~	**ir** fue~~ron~~
(yo)	recicla**ra**	hicie**ra**	fue**ra**
(tú)	recicla**ras**	hicie**ras**	fue**ras**
(Ud., él, ella)	recicla**ra**	hicie**ra**	fue**ra**
(nosotros/as)	reciclá**ramos**	hicié**ramos**	fué**ramos**
(vosotros/as)	recicla**rais**	hicie**rais**	fue**rais**
(Uds., ellos, ellas)	recicla**ran**	hicie**ran**	fue**ran**

The imperfect subjunctive is used following the same types of expressions as the present subjunctive (see Chapter 10, pages 338, 346, and 356), but refers to actions, conditions, or events that took place *in the past*, as we see in these examples based on Mabel's conversation with Mario.

PAST TENSE: IMPERFECT/ PRETERIT + QUE + IMPERFECT SUBJUNCTIVE

Mabel **quería** que los voluntarios **organizaran** una gran campaña de prensa.
Mabel wanted the volunteers to organize a great press campaign.

Mario **recomendó** que **usaran** carros híbridos.
Mario recommended that they use hybrid cars.

The imperfect subjunctive of **hay** (*there is, there are*) is **hubiera** (*there was, there were*).
Ojalá que no **hubiera** tanta contaminación. *I wish there weren't so much pollution.*

*In Spain, the endings **-se, -ses, -se, -semos, -seis, -sen** are often preferred.

¡En acción!

¡Oye! ¿En cuál de las dos décadas?

Escucha lo que va a decir tu profesor/a y luego, di a cuál de las dos décadas se refiere cada afirmación: a **los años cincuenta** o a **los años noventa**.

12-13 En aquellos años…

Tu compañero/a lee una de las siguientes afirmaciones (1–5) y tú respondes con la época (cuadro azul) que corresponde a cada una para indicar cuándo ocurría. Sigue el modelo.

MODELO

E1: *Se **temía** que Hitler **ocupara** gran parte de Europa.*

E2: *En los años cuarenta, **se temía** que Hitler **ocupara** gran parte de Europa.*

a. En los años cuarenta…	**d.** Durante las primeras horas del ataque a las Torres Gemelas…
b. Antes de la invasión de Irak,…	**e.** Cuando EE. UU. invadió Irak…
c. Antes de la llegada de Cristóbal Colón a América…	**f.** Hasta hace poco, en ningún estado de EE. UU…

1. ..f.. se **permitía** que las personas del mismo sexo **se casaran**.
2. .b. se **temía** que allí **hubiera** un arsenal de armas nucleares.
3. .d. no se **creyó** que **fuera** un ataque terrorista.
4. .c. **no** se **creía** que la **tierra** fuera redonda.
5. .e. se **esperaba** que EE. UU. **ganara** la guerra en poco tiempo.

> **Palabras útiles**
> dudar, no creer

12-14 Los avances tecnológicos

Paso 1. Lean la lista de los inventos que, según el científico y futurólogo de California, Michio Kaku, veremos en los próximos 20 años.

1. carros que **circulan** solos	5. mundos virtuales que nos **permiten** tocar y sentir los objetos
2. lentes de contacto que **tienen** la capacidad de navegar por internet	6. carros que **llaman** a la ambulancia y **dan** nuestro historial médico después de un accidente
3. paredes que **pueden** hablar y darnos información	7. ropa que **detecta** la condición física: tensión alta, irregularidades en el corazón, etc.
4. computadoras y celulares de papel electrónico flexible que se **pueden** doblar y guardar en el bolsillo	

Paso 2. Ahora, imagínense que Uds. viven en el año 2030 y que están comentando el pasado. Reaccionen con expresiones de duda seguidas del imperfecto de subjuntivo de los verbos en negrita. Sigan el modelo.

MODELO   **12-14. ANSWERS:** 1. (provided); 2. … que… los lentes de contacto **tuvieran**… ; 3. … que… **fueran**… que… **pudieran**… ; 4. … que… **se pudieran**… ; 5. … que… **permitieran**… ; 6. … que… **llamaran**… **dieran** ; 7. … que… **detectara**…
*¡Es increíble! Antes la gente **dudaba** que un día los carros **circularan** solos.*

12-15 Para prolongar la vida

Cuando sus abuelos se jubilaron y se mudaron a Florida, Uds. estaban muy contentos con la idea y deseaban lo mejor para ellos. Según las ilustraciones, digan lo que Uds. **querían** o **no querían** que hicieran ellos para mantenerse con buena salud y poder vivir muchos años.

MODELO

No queríamos que fumaran.

All art © John Wiley & Sons, Inc.

12-16 ¿Qué te gustaría?

Paso 1. Camina por la clase y pregunta a tres compañeros qué les gustaría que inventaran en un futuro próximo para alguna de las siguientes categorías:

para viajar	para trabajar	para cocinar	para divertirte	para curar enfermedades

MODELO

E1: *¿Qué **te gustaría que inventaran** para viajar?*

E2: *Me gustaría que inventaran un carro autodirigido. ¿Y a ti?*

E1: *A mí, **me gustaría que** / Yo **preferiría que**…*

Enfermedades

el Alzheimer
el cáncer
la diabetes
la esclerosis múltiple
el glaucoma
la leucemia
el Parkinson
el SIDA

Paso 2. Ahora, comparte con la clase lo que les gustaría que inventaran a tus compañeros.

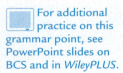

For more practice, see **Grammar Handbook** found in *WileyPLUS*.

For additional practice on this grammar point, see PowerPoint slides on BCS and in *WileyPLUS*.

> ### . . . y algo más   If clauses
>
> To express what *would happen* in a hypothetical or contrary-to-fact situation (*If I were a billionaire…*) you use:
>
> **Si** (*If*) + **imperfect subjunctive** + **conditional**
>
> or
>
> **Conditional** + **si** + **imperfect subjunctive**
>
> **Si fuera** presidente/a, **protegería** los parques nacionales.
> **Protegería** los parques nacionales **si fuera** presidente/a.

12-17 Preguntas para conversar

En grupos de *cuatro*, usen las siguientes preguntas para iniciar la conversación.

1. Si **pudieras** prolongar tu vida hasta los 150 años, ¿lo **harías**? ¿Cuáles **serían** dos ventajas y dos desventajas?

2. Si **fuera** posible encontrar la cura para sólo dos enfermedades, ¿cuáles **escogerías**?

3. Si **fueras** presidente/a, ¿**apoyarías** la investigación de las células madre[1]?

4. Si el precio de la gasolina **subiera** a diez dólares el galón, ¿qué **harías**?

5. Si **pudieras** hacer un viaje a la Luna en una nave espacial, ¿te **gustaría** hacerlo? ¿Por qué?

6. Si te **encontraras** con un extraterrestre, ¿qué dos preguntas le **harías**?

7. Si **tuvieras** que pasar un mes completamente solo/a, ¿qué tres cosas te **llevarías**? ¿Por qué?

8. Si **pudieras** reencarnarte en otra persona, ¿en quién te **reencarnarías**? ¿Por qué?

12-17 *Additional questions:* Si tuvieras un hijo o una hija que quisiera casarse con una persona de su mismo género, ¿lo/la apoyarías? Si vieras al novio de tu mejor amiga con otra mujer, ¿qué harías? Si tu madre saliera con tu mejor amigo, ¿cómo reaccionarías? Si pudieras cambiar algo de tu familia, ¿qué cambiarías?

 ## 12-18 Una cadena de posibilidades

Primero, divídanse en grupos de *cinco*. Después, su profesor/a les asigna uno de los siguientes temas y Uds. crean una cadena larga según el modelo. Al final, lean sus "creaciones" a la clase.

MODELO

*Si tuviera un mes de vacaciones, **iría** a Argentina.* (Usen **Si** + el verbo **ir** en la siguiente oración.)

*Si fuera a Argentina, **visitaría** La Patagonia.* (Usen **Si** + el verbo **visitar** →)

*Si visitara La Patagonia, **vería**...* (Usen **Si** + el verbo **ver** →)

1. **Si fuera** a la Luna...
2. **Si viviera** en la selva amazónica...
3. **Si estuviera** en la Ciudad de México...
4. **Si no tuviera** computadora ni celular...
5. **Si hablara** perfectamente español...
6. **Si tuviera** una varita[2] mágica...

12-19 La tecnología también ayuda a las personas ciegas[3]

 Paso 1. Lee lo siguiente para conocer los inventos gracias a los cuales las personas discapacitadas, como los ciegos, pueden tener una mejor calidad de vida. Escoge los dos que, en tu opinión, serían más útiles si fueras ciego/a.

Aparatos disponibles en el mercado para las personas ciegas: Con ellos, una persona ciega puede hacer la rutina diaria: levantarse, desayunar, vestirse, orientarse, caminar por las calles, trabajar, cocinar y comunicarse por correo electrónico.

- **Despertador parlante:** Se aprieta un botón y una voz indica la hora.
- **Colorímetro:** Se pone al lado de la ropa, indica su color y ayuda a combinar los colores.
- **Microondas y estufa en Braille:** Cocinar es ya posible para una persona ciega.
- **Reloj en Braille:** Se levanta la cubierta y se pueden tocar las agujas[4] para saber la hora.
- **Agenda electrónica en Braille:** Para anotar fechas y citas.
- **Computadora con teclado en Braille y programa JAWS:** Lee lo escrito en voz alta y escribe lo que se dice.
- **Ojo electrónico:** Se pone en las gafas o lentes, y antes de cruzar la calle, una mini-cámara con computadora y sistema de voz indica el color del semáforo, la distancia entre las dos aceras y la presencia de peatones.
- **Bastones[5] telescópicos láser y con sensor:** Se usan para orientarse más fácilmente.

12-19 *Option:* Have students complete *Paso 2* in pairs, then poll the class to find out which inventions they found most useful and why.

12-19 ANOTHER STEP: To heighten awareness, have students write down three things in their daily routine that they would have great difficulty doing, or would not be able to do, if they were blind: **Si fuera ciego/a,...** Students share their ideas with the class.

 Paso 2. Ahora, dile a la clase los dos inventos que has elegido y explícale cómo te ayudarían en tu rutina diaria si fueras una persona ciega.

MODELO

*Si fuera ciego/a, **tendría** un colorímetro porque me gusta combinar bien los colores de mi ropa.*

---

[1]**investigación...** stem-cell research [2]wand, [3]blind *also* **invidentes**, [4]hands of the clock, [5]canes, walking sticks

Go to *WileyPLUS* to see the video related to this reading.

Tu mundo cultural

Los desastres ecológicos

¿Qué sabes sobre la contaminación y los desastres ecológicos de tu país? A continuación siguen unos ejemplos de problemas de Latinoamérica relacionados con el medio ambiente.

© John Wiley & Sons, Inc.

La contaminación en México

La Ciudad de México tiene graves problemas de contaminación. El tráfico de los cuatro millones de vehículos que circulan diariamente por ella, unido a su ubicación en un valle rodeado de montañas, hacen de esta capital una de las ciudades más contaminadas del planeta. Entre su población, cada vez son más las personas que sufren enfermedades respiratorias. En el norte del país, la industria de las maquiladoras y el tráfico entre México y EE. UU., resultado del TLC, Tratado de Libre Comercio (NAFTA), son la causa principal de la contaminación en las ciudades de los dos lados de la frontera.

En la Ciudad de México el gobierno está creando soluciones innovadoras para combatir la contaminación. Las principales son: hacer obligatorio el uso de conversores catalíticos en los carros; reducir la cantidad de plomo[1] en la gasolina y el sulfuro en el diésel; modernizar el sistema de transporte de autobuses; y promover las energías renovables como la energía hidroeléctrica y la solar, que tienen gran potencial en México.

Daniel Aguilar/NewsCom

La deforestación del Amazonas

Hay seis países que comparten la cuenca[2] del Amazonas y todos, excepto Brasil, son hispanos: Venezuela, Colombia, Ecuador, Perú y Bolivia. Este grupo de países, llamado «el pulmón del mundo», cuenta con uno de los ecosistemas más diversos del planeta. Sin embargo, la deforestación está teniendo consecuencias tan graves en su medio ambiente, que muchas especies ya han desaparecido y otras están en peligro de extinción.

[1]lead, [2]basin

Visum/The Image Works

El exceso de población en la cuenca del Amazonas es una de las causas de los 19.000 km^2 de deforestación anual. Se eliminan bosques para obtener tierras cultivables y beneficios para la industria maderera[1]. El potencial económico de la cuenca del Amazonas reside en las plantas, de las que se hacen medicamentos; en la madera, que se usa para muebles y construcción; y en la diversidad de especies terrestres y acuáticas. El gran reto al que se enfrentan estos países es mantener el crecimiento[2] económico, pero sin dañar[3] el medio ambiente.

Iquitos es una de las ciudades peruanas situadas en la cuenca del Amazonas. Esta ciudad, como tantas otras de esta región, ha experimentado gran crecimiento económico gracias a las riquezas naturales de la zona. Allí, como en el resto de los países del Amazonas, finalmente se está empezando a tomar conciencia de la situación y a crear políticas para frenar la deforestación, preservar las especies y restituir la capa de ozono de la atmósfera.

Andoni Canela/Age Fotostock America, Inc.

¿Qué aprendiste?

1. ¿En qué áreas de México hay graves problemas de contaminación?
   En la Ciudad de México y en la frontera con EE.UU.
2. ¿Qué problema ecológico existe en los países de la cuenca del Amazonas?
   La deforestación.

Actividad cultural

Completen el formulario según la información presentada.

lugar	problema	causas	posibles repercusiones	posibles soluciones
México				
Amazonas				

Contraste cultural

Hablen de lugares de su país o región que estén sufriendo daños medioambientales. Describan los daños, y hablen de las causas y de lo que se está haciendo para solucionarlos.

[1]lumber, [2]growth, [3]damaging

En busca de* una vida mejor

Pronunciación:
Practice pronunciation
of the chapter's
new vocabulary in
WileyPLUS.

VOCABULARIO

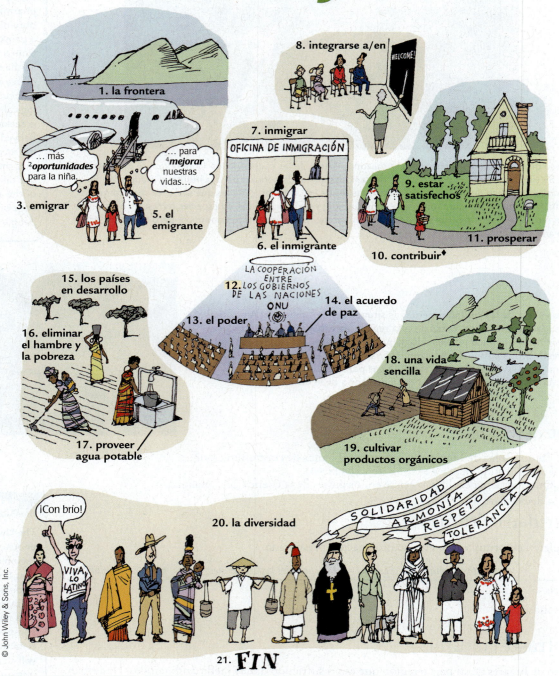

1. la frontera

8. integrarse a/en

7. inmigrar

OFICINA DE INMIGRACIÓN

… más ²*oportunidades* para la niña.

… para ⁴*mejorar* nuestras vidas…

3. emigrar

5. el emigrante

6. el inmigrante

9. estar satisfechos

10. contribuir♦

11. prosperar

15. los países en desarrollo

16. eliminar el hambre y la pobreza

12. LA COOPERACIÓN ENTRE LOS GOBIERNOS DE LAS NACIONES ONU

13. el poder

14. el acuerdo de paz

18. una vida sencilla

17. proveer agua potable

19. cultivar productos orgánicos

¡Con brío!

VIVA LO LATINO

20. la diversidad

SOLIDARIDAD ARMONÍA RESPETO TOLERANCIA

© John Wiley & Sons, Inc.

21. **FIN**

---

1. border 2. opportunities 3. to emigrate 4. to improve 5. emigrant (*m.*) **la emigrante** (*f.*) 6. immigrant (*m.*) **la inmigrante** (*f.*) 7. to immigrate 8. to adjust, integrate oneself 9. to be satisfied 10. to contribute 11. to prosper 12. governments 13. power 14. peace treaty 15. developing countries 16. to eliminate poverty and hunger 17. to provide potable water 18. a simple life 19. to grow organic produce 20. diversity 21. The end (*m.*)

---

* **En busca de** *In search of*
♦ **Contribuir** has the same irregularities as **construir**. See *Apéndice 1*, p. A-4.

¡En acción!

12-20 ¡A emparejar!

A ver si los reconoces. Empareja los términos de la primera columna con los que mejor les corresponden de la segunda.

1. el acuerdo de paz	e.	a. línea divisoria	
2. la diversidad	h.	b. prosperar, progresar	
3. la pobreza	i.	c. entrar a formar parte, unirse a	
4. la frontera	a.	d. estar contento	
5. el fin	f.	e. pacto para terminar la guerra	
6. el poder	g.	f. conclusión	
7. estar satisfecho	d.	g. dominio, supremacía	
8. integrarse	c.	h. variedad	
9. mejorar	b.	i. no tener lo necesario para vivir	

12-21 En busca de una vida mejor

Describan y comenten las escenas de la página 420. Usen todo el vocabulario de la escena para hablar de:

- la familia que emigra
- la vida de la familia de inmigrantes en el nuevo país
- la reunión de las naciones del mundo y cómo piensan Uds. que deben ejercer su poder
- la escena rural de los países en desarrollo
- la pareja que busca una vida sencilla y cómo piensan Uds. que será su vida
- las personas que representan la diversidad

12-22 ¿Quién lo ha hecho? RECYCLES the present perfect.

Paso 1. Camina por la clase y pregúntales a tus compañeros si han hecho lo siguiente. Apunta en el espacio en blanco el nombre de la primera persona que responda afirmativamente a la pregunta. Luego pasa a la siguiente pregunta.

Nombre

_____ 1. ¿Has cruzado la frontera entre EE. UU. y México? ¿Cuándo?

_____ 2. ¿Has experimentado alguna vez un «choque cultural»? ¿Cómo te sentiste?

_____ 3. ¿Has vivido en otro país? ¿En qué país? ¿Cuándo? ¿Te gustó?

_____ 4. ¿Hay personas de tu familia que sean inmigrantes? ¿De dónde son/eran?

_____ 5. Si trabajaras en el gobierno de tu país, ¿votarías por leyes a favor de los inmigrantes?

_____ 6. ¿Estás satisfecho/a con tu vida?

_____ 7. ¿Te gustaría vivir de forma más sencilla?

_____ 8. ¿Te gustaría ser voluntario/a en un país en desarrollo?

Paso 2. Ahora, según los nombres que tienes, dile a la clase quién ha hecho las cosas indicadas.

¹slogan

Niña boliviana bebiendo agua. ¿Será potable? La Asamblea General de las Naciones Unidas ha declarado el 22 de marzo el Día Mundial del Agua. Su lema¹ es: *El agua es fuente de vida*. Cada día mueren cerca de 4.000 niños por beber agua no potable.

PictureNet/Alamy Images

For additional vocabulary practice, see PowerPoint slides on BCS and in *WileyPLUS*.

You may want to tell your students that feminine words that begin with a stressed **a** or **ha** such as **agua, arma** o **hambre** use the masculine article **el/un** in the singular (to avoid a double "a" sound), but in the plural they use the feminine article **las/unas**. As in **El agua/Las aguas**.

12-21 You may want to project the PowerPoint slide of the scenes. Students describe each area as indicated, adding personal input.

12-21 PERSONALIZED QUESTIONS: ¿Conocen Uds. a personas de esta universidad/ *college* que sean inmigrantes? ¿De qué países son? ¿Hay mucha diversidad en esta universidad/ en este *college*? Expliquen sus respuestas.

12-22 Ask the class ¿Quiénes han cruzado la frontera...? and elicit answers from several students, asking them to elaborate according to the follow-up questions.

¡A escuchar! Los inmigrantes

Paso 1. Escucha a Olivia y a Julio mientras charlan durante el almuerzo. Los dos son maestros de origen mexicano que trabajan en una escuela de Estados Unidos.

PLUS Go to *WileyPLUS* to complete **Paso 2** of this listening activity.

Después de la cena, Fabio acompaña a Jennifer a su casa. Hablan del futuro y...

A veces, cuando se es inmigrante, es difícil mejorar en la vida.

Claro, pero tanto tú como yo tenemos familias **que** han sabido integrarse perfectamente en la vida de este país.

Sí, somos muy trabajadores, contribuimos mucho y vivimos sencillamente, pero bien.

O sea,... **lo que** quieres decir es que estás satisfecha con tu vida.

Sí, pero estaría más contenta si pudiera compartirla con alguien.

Jennifer, creo que es hora de hablar claro.

Hace tiempo que quiero decirte **con quién** quiero compartir mi vida...

© John Wiley & Sons, Inc.

FIN

Go to *WileyPLUS* to review this grammar point with the help of the **Animated Grammar Tutorial**. For more practice, go to the **Grammar Handbook**.

To introduce students to the relative pronouns used in context, have them take parts and read the **historieta** out loud. To check their comprehension and call their attention to the relative pronouns, ask the following questions: 1. **¿Cómo son las familias de Jennifer y Fabio?** 2. **¿Con quién quiere Fabio compartir su vida?**

The *¡Con brío!* comic strips have ended. Ask students to recall elements of the plot. If time allows, ask students to review all of the vignettes and write a plot summary.

GRAMÁTICA

¡Manos a la obra!

Referring to people, objects, and situations: Relative pronouns

In *Capítulo 10* (page 338), you learned that **que** can act as a conjunction connecting two clauses. Let's review examples based on Jennifer and Fabio's conversation.

Dice **que** está satisfecha con su vida. — *She says that she is satisfied with her life.*
Quiere **que** hablen del futuro. — *He wants them to talk about the future.*

Now you will learn to use **que** as a relative pronoun to refer back to previously mentioned persons or things. In English, relative pronouns are **that, which, who** and **whom.** In Spanish, some of the more common relatives are **que, quien(es)** and **lo que.**

- **Que** can refer to objects, places, and people. In English, the corresponding relative pronoun may be omitted, but Spanish requires the use of the relative to connect the clauses.

  La vida **que** llevan es sencilla, pero buena. — *The life they live is simple but good.*
  Es una mujer **que** contribuye mucho. — *She is a woman **who** contributes a lot.*

- **Quien** and its plural **quienes** refer to a person or persons and are used in combination with short prepositions such as **a, con** or **de.** If there is no preposition, use **que.**

  Fabio es el hombre **con quien** Jennifer quiere compartir su vida.
  *Fabio is the man **with whom** Jennifer wants to share her life.*

  Muchas de las personas **a quienes** admiro son inmigrantes.
  *Many of the people **whom** I admire are immigrants.*

  Son personas **que** se han integrado en la vida de este país.
  *They are people **who** have adjusted to life in this country.*

- **Lo que** refers to abstract concepts such as situations, ideas and actions.

  A Jennifer le gusta **lo que** le dice Fabio. — *Jennifer likes **what** Fabio tells her.*
  Lo que él quiere es compartir su vida con ella. — ***What** he wants is to share his life with her.*

¡En acción!

¡Oye!   ¿A quién se refiere?

Escucha lo que va a decir tu profesor/a y luego di si es cierto o falso lo que oyes.

12-23   ¿A quiénes admiras?

Paso 1.   Primero, en grupos de *tres*, túrnense para leer en voz alta las descripciones de las contribuciones de ocho hispanos muy conocidos. Luego, cada uno/a identifica a las *dos* personas de la lista a quienes más admira.

MODELO

*Admiro a Roberto Clemente, el beisbolista **que** quería ayudar a la gente de Nicaragua.*

1. Roberto Clemente es el beisbolista **que** murió al estrellarse el avión donde volaba para llevar ayuda humanitaria a las víctimas de un terremoto de Nicaragua.

2. Shakira es la cantante colombiana **que** ha fundado dos organizaciones **que** ayudan a niños pobres de América Latina.

3. Óscar Arias fue el presidente de Costa Rica **a quien** le dieron el Premio Nobel de la Paz en 1987 por promover la democracia en Centroamérica.

4. Jaime Escalante es el maestro boliviano **que** enseñaba cálculo a los estudiantes de una escuela de Los Ángeles. La película **que** se hizo sobre su vida se llama "Stand and Deliver".

5. Ellen Ochoa es una astronauta mexicana-americana **que** realizó cuatro viajes en naves espaciales, **lo que** le permitió investigar sobre el clima de la Tierra y la energía solar.

6. Julia Álvarez es una poeta y novelista dominicana-americana **a quien** le interesan los temas de inmigración, cultura e identidad.

7. Óscar Romero es el arzobispo salvadoreño **que** luchó por los derechos humanos. Fue asesinado en 1980, **lo que** fue una tragedia.

8. Sonia Sotomayor, de padres puertorriqueños, es la juez del Tribunal Supremo de EE. UU. **a quien**, de niña, le gustaban los libros de la detective Nancy Drew.

Paso 2.   Ahora, en grupos de *tres*, hablen de *tres de* sus "héroes personales". Escojan entre *tres de* las siguientes categorías y expliquen **lo que** hacen esas personas. Sigan el modelo y túrnense.

> **Categorías:**
> **a.** Personas **con quienes** vives
> **b.** Personas **que** conoces bien
> **c.** Personas **que** ves en el *college* o universidad
> **d.** Personas **sobre quienes** lees en los periódicos o en Internet
> **e.** Personas **para quienes** trabajas

MODELO

E1: *Entre las personas **con quienes** vives, ¿a quién admiras?*

E2: *Entre las personas **con quienes** vivo, admiro a mi madre.* **o:** *No admiro a nadie/ninguna.*

E3: *¡Dinos **lo que** hace!* (Dilo con entusiasmo)

E2: *Es una persona **que** contribuye mucho a su comunidad. Enseña en una escuela y es una maestra excelente.*

¡Oye! Before you read the statements, have students write the numbers 1-6 on a sheet of paper. After completing the activity, students share their responses with the class.

Guión para ¡Oye!
1. Prosperar y mejorar sus vidas no es **lo que** motiva a muchas personas a emigrar a otro país. (F)
2. Las personas **a quienes** les gusta comer productos orgánicos, probablemente vivirán más años. (C)
3. Una vida sencilla es una vida **que** generalmente produce bastante estrés. (F)
4. Hábitat para la Humanidad es una organización **que** tiene como objetivo proveer agua potable a los países en desarrollo. (F)
5. Un acuerdo de paz es **lo que** se firma al terminar una guerra. (C)
6. Normalmente, las personas **que** prosperan están satisfechas con sus vidas. (C)

12-24 En busca de una vida mejor

Paso 1. Lee el siguiente artículo del periódico *El Mercurio* para saber lo que están haciendo en una ciudad argentina que busca una vida mejor.

Prohibido apurarse

La pequeña localidad de Mar de las Pampas quiere ser la primera "ciudad lenta" de América Latina.

RODRIGO LARA

¿Se imagina vivir en una ciudad sin celulares ni carteles en las calles, y donde la velocidad máxima sea de 30 kilómetros por hora? Eso es lo que pretende la ciudad argentina de Mar de las Pampas.

Este pequeño balneario, a 380 kilómetros al sur de Buenos Aires, intenta conciliar lo moderno con la calidad de vida. Sus habitantes quieren que en la ciudad no se conozcan las alarmas ni las bocinas de los autos, que no haya torres de comunicación y que la policía patrulle las calles a caballo.

"Tiene que ver con darse tiempo para vivir", dice Luis Mazzoni, la cara pública del proyecto.

Vivir sin prisa

El concepto de "ciudad lenta" es primo del de "comida lenta", donde "comer no son 30 minutos, es una hora y media".

En el caso de las "ciudades lentas", la idea es promover la calidad del espacio urbano, la restauración y protección de las zonas típicas, la ecología, una atmósfera amigable y la promoción de los productos de la región.

"Prohibido apurarse" and "Vivir sin prisa," *El Mercurio* (Santiago de Chile), 11 de Febrero de 2006. Used by permission.

Palabras útiles

apurarse	*to hurry*
lento/a	*slow*
calidad de vida	*quality of life*

Paso 2. En grupos de *cuatro*, **(a)** digan cuáles son, según el artículo, las características de esta "ciudad lenta". **(b)** Digan también lo que más y lo que menos les gustaría de vivir en una ciudad así. **(c)** Para concluir, hablen de los aspectos que consideren esenciales para una "vida ideal".

12-24 Write the characteritics of the "slow city" on the board, then have students give their positive or negative reactions (or both) to each item. As students provide feedback on their concept of the "ideal life," a student writes those characteristics on the board. The class then talks about each, stating their priorities. Is there a class consensus?

NOTE! The remainder of this chapter is devoted to activities that encourage both guided conversation and free expression, most commonly springing from readings based on current topics. Students thus recycle what they have learned through-out the course.

12-25 Historia de un inmigrante que ha triunfado

Paso 1. Lee acerca de Jesse Treviño y observa su mural.

Jesse Treviño (1946–) es un pintor y muralista estadounidense de origen mexicano. Estudió en el *Art Students League* en Nueva York. Perdió el brazo derecho en la guerra de Vietnam, pero volvió a pintar, y aprendió a hacerlo con la mano izquierda. Más tarde, obtuvo su Máster de la Universidad de Texas. Tiene una obra dedicada a las víctimas del ataque terrorista del 11 de septiembre. Ahora está trabajando en un monumento que se dedicará a los veteranos de guerra.

Courtesy of Alfonzo Fernandez

El famoso mural de Treviño, *Spirit of Healing*, se encuentra en *Santa Rosa Children's Hospital* en San Antonio, Texas. Este mural, compuesto de 150.000 azulejos[1] cortados a mano, tiene 90 pies de altura y es el mural más grande de América del Norte.

Paso 2. Conversen acerca de:

- la descripción e interpretación del mural
- lo que más les impresiona de la vida de Jesse Treviño
- dos obstáculos o retos[2] que Uds. o personas que conocen han experimentado y lo que hicieron para superarlos[3]

Palabras útiles
el ángel
la paloma *dove*

[1]tiles, [2]challenges, [3]overcome them

12-26 Para mejorar la vida de los demás[1]

 Paso 1.   A continuación, vas a conocer una de las múltiples facetas de una mujer extraordinaria: Laila Dawson. Para ello, lee el artículo y observa las fotografías.

Es evidente, que para Laila una de las prioridades de la vida es ayudar a los demás. Desde hace diez años, es voluntaria en Leadville, un pueblecito situado en las montañas de Colorado. Allí, entre otras muchas actividades, da clases de inglés a un grupo de mujeres inmigrantes de México y Honduras, a quienes también les enseña la cultura y las costumbres de EE. UU. Gracias a Laila, esas mujeres podrán integrarse más fácilmente a la vida de este país. Además, Laila les da consejos sobre nutrición y aspectos relacionados con la salud, la drogadicción y el maltrato[2]. Y para completarlo, organiza actividades que desafían[3] al grupo (escalar precipicios[4], trepar por cuerdas[5]) y las ayudan a desarrollar su carácter y autoestima a la vez que crean fuertes lazos[6] entre ellas. La organización patrocinadora Full Circle les proporciona el local donde se reúnen y los materiales que necesitan.

Sin embargo, la dedicación de Laila a los demás no termina ahí. Desde hace 15 años, es madrina de cuatro niñas de la organización Nuestros Pequeños Hermanos (mira en la pág. 351) que tienen entre 13 y 20 años. Algunas de las niñas tienen discapacidades físicas o emocionales y otras han sido maltratadas o abandonadas por sus padres. Laila las visita todos los años en Honduras y mantiene correspondencia con ellas durante el resto del año.

En fin, no se sabe de dónde saca tiempo para hacer tantas cosas esta mujer increíble. La única explicación es que es una mujer *¡Con brío!* ☺

 Paso 2.   Ahora, hablen de lo siguiente:

- El tipo de actividades voluntarias que hace Laila, dentro y fuera de EE. UU. y cómo se beneficia el grupo de mujeres a quienes ayuda.

- Una o dos personas que Uds. conocen que ayudan a los demás a tener una vida mejor.

- Una o más personas que hayan contribuido a mejorar la vida de Uds. e indiquen cómo.

12-27 La comunicación: algo esencial en el mundo de hoy

 RECYCLES vocabulary from chapter themes.

La clase se divide en dos grupos. El primer grupo se sienta en un círculo, y el segundo, en otro círculo alrededor del primero. Cada estudiante de un círculo se sitúa mirando a un/a estudiante del otro. Las parejas hablan durante *un minuto* del primer tema. Luego, el círculo exterior gira[7] hacia la izquierda para efectuar el cambio de parejas y cada pareja habla del siguiente tema y así, hasta hablar de todos. ¡Adelante!

1. Las personas más importantes de tu vida. Explica por qué. (El círculo exterior gira hacia la izquierda.)

2. Los pasatiempos y deportes que más te gustan y por qué.

3. Las comidas que más te gustan, dónde las comes y con quién.

4. De todos los trabajos que has tenido, el que te gustó más y por qué.

5. Viajes interesantes que has hecho—adónde, cuándo y con quién.

6. Un incidente interesante que ocurrió en tu vida hace unos años o recientemente.

7. Los efectos de la tecnología en tu vida—los positivos y los negativos.

8. Las prioridades que, en tu opinión, debe tener un gobierno.

12-26   Remind students that they don't need to understand every word they read in order to understand the meaning of the text. Encourage them to focus on cognates, and to guess meaning by context.

12-26   Tell students that Laila Dawson is one of the authors of this book. Ask them to go to the Dedication page at the beginning of their books to find out more about her.

12-27   If possible, move tables and desks to make room for the circles. Students may either sit on the floor, if space allows, or stand. The activity can also be carried out with students standing in two rows (A and B), facing each other. If you have an uneven number of students, take part in the activity. At the end of each conversation, the first student in row A moves to the end of the line, with the line moving up one person; students in row B remain in their positions.

[1]others, [2]abuse, [3]challenges, [4]cliffs, [5]**trepar...** rope climbing, [6]ties, [7]turns

Go to *WileyPLUS* to see the video related to this reading.

Meets ACTFL Standards
1.1, interpersonal speaking;
1.2, interpretive reading;
2.1, cultural practices; and
4.2, cultural comparisons.

For an additional activity related to this cultural theme, see the PowerPoint slides on BCS and in *WileyPLUS*.

Tu mundo cultural

Inmigrantes en busca de una vida mejor

¿Dejarías a tu familia, a tus amigos y tu país para ir en busca de una vida mejor?

Por razones diversas, no todo el mundo encuentra trabajo y condiciones de vida aceptables en su país, y para muchos, la única forma de sobrevivir es emigrar. Estados Unidos ha sido tradicionalmente el destino más frecuente de los emigrantes latinoamericanos, pero en las últimas décadas un elevado número de latinoamericanos ha emigrado a España. En ambos casos, los emigrantes han tomado la decisión difícil y dolorosa de dejar su tierra, su cultura, su familia y sus amigos en busca de una vida mejor.

Los efectos de la inmigración hispana en EE. UU.

La inmigración de hispanos en EE. UU. ha disminuido, pero sus efectos son evidentes. Según el censo de 2010, EE. UU. ha experimentado un crecimiento sin precedentes en su historia con respecto a los hispanos. Solamente en la década anterior, la población hispana ha aumentado en un 43%, superando los 50 millones. Se calcula que la tendencia continuará y que para el año 2025, la mitad de las familias estadounidenses serán multiculturales. Para el año 2050, EE. UU. será el país con mayor número de hispanohablantes del mundo y los hispanos, que son ahora minoría, constituirán la mayoría.

John Nordell/The Image Works

Los Ángeles, en California. Muchos latinoamericanos que emigran a Estados Unidos no están familiarizados con su lengua y su cultura. Sin embargo, la proximidad, el fácil acceso, las oportunidades de trabajo y la existencia de comunidades de sus países que ya están establecidas allí sirven de incentivo para emigrar.

Courtesy of Alfonzo Fernandez

El restaurante Mi Tierra, en San Antonio, Texas. Excepto en el caso de Cuba y algún otro país, de donde emigraron principalmente por razones políticas, los latinoamericanos generalmente emigran por motivos económicos. Muchos tienen éxito y abren negocios o restaurantes que llegan a formar parte de la cultura de EE. UU. Tal es el caso del restaurante Mi Tierra, que se abrió en 1941 con tres mesas y ahora tiene capacidad para más de 500 personas.

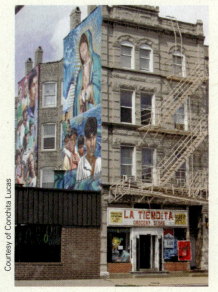
Courtesy of Conchita Lucas

El *Mexican Fine Arts Center Museum* de Chicago. La presencia hispana en EE. UU. y la continua llegada de nuevos inmigrantes está cambiando el paisaje demográfico, la composición étnica y la cultura de EE. UU. Este museo, situado en el barrio mexicano de Pilsen, revela la importancia que están adquiriendo los hispanos en este país. Cuenta con la colección de arte mexicano más grande de EE. UU.

Courtesy of Conchita Lucas

El barrio mexicano de Pilsen, en Chicago. Antes, los latinoamericanos comúnmente se establecían en los estados del sudoeste de Estados Unidos, en Florida y en Nueva York. En la actualidad, los estados de Carolina del Norte y Carolina del Sur, Arkansas, Georgia, Tennessee, Nevada, Alabama y el Medio Oeste son los lugares que atraen a mayor número de estos emigrantes.

La emigración de latinoamericanos a España

En el pasado, los españoles emigraron a países como México, Venezuela, Argentina y Chile en busca de fortuna o como exiliados políticos. En las últimas décadas, gracias al desarrollo económico que tuvo lugar en España y a ser miembro de la Unión Europea, el fenómeno se invirtió[1]. La inmigración de México, República Dominicana, Colombia, Venezuela, Ecuador, Perú, Argentina y de otros países latinoamericanos es ya una realidad en España. Allí la lengua y la cultura no suponían un obstáculo para los inmigrantes latinoamericanos y además, tenían otros incentivos como el seguro médico para todos, un mes de vacaciones y recibir el sueldo en euros, que entonces era una moneda fuerte. Muchos inmigrantes, una vez regularizada su situación en España, tuvieron incluso la oportunidad de trabajar en otros países de la Unión Europea. Con la reciente crisis económica todo ha cambiado y ahora, muchos inmigrantes han comenzado a regresar a sus países de origen.

La crisis económica ha afectado en gran medida a la economía española y del mismo modo que en EE. UU., muchos emigrantes que fueron allí están teniendo que regresar a su país de origen. En cualquier caso, España es ya el lugar de residencia de gran número de inmigrantes latinoamericanos que han decidido quedarse y echar raíces[2] allí.

La bandera española (roja, amarilla y roja) ondea[3] junto al resto de las veintisiete banderas de los países miembros de la Unión Europea.

Emigrantes latinoamericanos haciendo fila en una oficina de inmigración de Madrid. La llegada de latinoamericanos a España, con su alto índice de natalidad[4], ha contribuido a mejorar la demografía española que empezaba a alcanzar niveles muy bajos. Además, como en el caso de EE. UU., los inmigrantes están contribuyendo a su economía, cambiando la composición étnica de su población e influenciando la cultura de los españoles.

 ## ¿Qué aprendiste?

1. ¿A qué lugares de EE. UU. emigraban antes los latinoamericanos y adónde lo hacen al actualidad? Antes al sudoeste, Florida y Nueva York. Ahora a Carolina del Norte y del Sur, Arkansas, Georgia, Tennessee, Nevada, Alabama y al Medio Oeste.
2. ¿Por qué emigran? ¿Es una decisión fácil? Explica tu respuesta. Para mejorar sus condiciones de vida. Las respuestas pueden variar.
3. ¿Qué incentivos ofrece EE. UU. a los inmigrantes latinoamericanos? ¿Y qué ofrecía España? EE. UU.: la proximidad, el fácil acceso, las oportunidades de trabajo y la presencia de comunidades de sus países España: el seguro médico, un mes de vacaciones y recibir el sueldo en euros.
4. ¿Cuáles son los efectos de la inmigración hispanoamericana en EE. UU. y en España? Las respuestas pueden variar.

Actividad cultural

Imagínense que Uds. tuvieran que emigrar de su país por razones políticas, religiosas o económicas. Digan a qué país emigrarían, cómo y por qué. Mencionen los incentivos que en su opinión ofrece el país de su elección, los obstáculos y la clase de trabajo que van a encontrar allí.

Contraste cultural

En grupos de *cuatro*, hablen de los inmigrantes de su familia. Indiquen el país de procedencia, las razones por las que emigraron, los obstáculos que encontraron y su contribución a la comunidad.

¿SABES QUE...?

The European Union (EU), formerly known as the European Community, includes twenty-seven Member States and is an institutional framework for the construction of a united Europe.

¿SABES QUE...?

Prior to the current economic crisis, Spain experienced an economic boom that attracted immigrants from many countries, including **1,426.490** Latin Americans. The biggest number of immigrants from Latin America was from Ecuador (about 400,000), followed by Colombia, Bolivia and Peru.

[1]reversed, [2]set roots, [3]waves, [4]**índice...** birth rate

Tu mundo en vivo

¡Videos en acción!

12.1   La contaminación: no todo está perdido

1. Antes de ver el video

En tu opinión, ¿cuáles son las causas de la contaminación del aire en la Ciudad de México?

Go to *WileyPLUS* to complete the **Mientras ves el video** activity.

2. Después de ver el video

   a. ¿Qué medidas se están tomando en la Ciudad de México para reducir la contaminación del aire?

   b. ¿Qué medida recomienda el ingeniero civil entrevistado?

12.2   Inmigrantes: aprende de ellos

1. Antes de ver el video

   a. ¿Conoces a alguien de Latinoamérica que haya dejado su país para vivir en EE. UU.? ¿Por qué se fue de su país?

   b. ¿Cuáles son algunas de las razones por las que muchas personas emigran?

Go to *WileyPLUS* to complete the **Mientras ves el video** activity.

2. Después de ver el video

   Comenta las razones por las que emigraron las personas entrevistadas y comparte tus impresiones.

¡Diálogos en acción!

12.1   El Cuerpo de Paz

Ana, una estudiante peruana que solicita un puesto en el Cuerpo de Paz, le pide una carta de recomendación a la profesora Lozada, también peruana.

Paso 1.   Primero, mira las **Expresiones útiles** de la página A-13. Luego, escucha el diálogo dos veces y contesta las preguntas de tu profesor/a.

Paso 2.   Mira la transcripción del diálogo (pág. A-20) y represéntalo con tu compañero/a. Túrnense. Ahora vete a la página A-13 para completar los **Pasos 3** y **4**.

12.2   Planes de viaje

María y Briseida son dos amigas peruanas que piensan hacer un viaje juntas. María le pregunta a Briseida, que prometió reservar el hotel y los billetes de avión, cómo van los planes.

Go to *WileyPLUS* to listen to and practice this dialogue.

Diálogo 12.1 models the function of requesting a favor, agreeing to do the favor, expressing thanks, and leave-taking in a formal situation. It also practices conditional and imperfect subjunctive verbs.

Diálogo 12.2 models the functions of expressing reproach, apologizing, and accepting an apology. It also practices travel vocabulary and recycles the present perfect tense and present subjunctive.

¡Lectura en acción!

Cada vez menos ecuatorianos emigran a España

El siguiente artículo es una versión adaptada del artículo escrito por J. Barreno que apareció en el periódico español *El Mundo*, el 5 de diciembre de 2011.

Paso 1. Basándote en el título del artículo, ¿puedes predecir las razones por las que los inmigrantes latinoamericanos de España están regresando a sus países de origen?

Paso 2. Ahora, lee el artículo.

Jessica mira a su padre por la 'webcam' de un cibercafé. Le pregunta: "¿Cuándo vas a volver, papá?". "Pronto, hija, la cosa no está muy bien por aquí", contesta su progenitor. Walter es uno de los más 400.000 ecuatorianos que viven en España.

Cruzó el océano hace seis años para buscar un futuro mejor. Por aquel entonces el país europeo experimentaba un fuerte crecimiento[1] económico y necesitaba una importante cantidad de mano de obra[2], principalmente en el sector de la construcción.

Los tiempos han cambiado y los países latinoamericanos crecen ahora a más del cinco por ciento, mientras que España se ha estancado[3]. "Ya tengo ganas de que venga", confiesa Julia, la mujer de Walter.

"La idea era que mi marido fuera unos años para ahorrar platita[4] y así comprarnos una buena casa y un buen carro. Yo creo que ya es hora de que venga, lo de la construcción se acabó y ahora Walter trabaja en un supermercado. Con lo que gana le llega justo para pasar el mes, ya no manda nada a Ecuador", manifiesta Julia.

Walter es uno de los miles de ecuatorianos que están pensando en volver a su país. Hace tres años que la llegada de inmigrantes comenzó a disminuir en España. Pasó de los 480.974 en 2009 a 465.169 en 2010. Este año, según el informe 'Extranjeros residentes en España', llevado a cabo por la Secretaría de Estado de Inmigración y Emigración, las llegadas de extranjeros disminuirán hasta los 450.000. Por primera vez desde la Guerra Civil española la emigración superará a la inmigración.

El descenso del número de inmigrantes ocurre por tres factores: el retorno de los inmigrantes a su país, la obtención de la nacionalidad española y el incumplimiento del trámite de renovación de la inscripción padronal[5] cada dos años. La segunda nacionalidad extracomunitaria con más residentes en España, la ecuatoriana, por detrás de la marroquí, se redujo en 2011 en 3.234 personas.

Ecuador sigue siendo el primer país latinoamericano emisor de emigrantes a España, seguido de Colombia, Bolivia y Perú. En total, los inmigrantes latinoamericanos suman 1.426.490 personas, un 28,22% del total, por debajo de los 2.064.404 ciudadanos de la Unión Europea (UE). Los lazos entre Ecuador y España son considerables. No hay ni un ecuatoriano que no tenga a algún familiar o a algún amigo viviendo en el país europeo.

Pero no todos los ecuatorianos quieren volver porque no les ha afectado tanto lo de la crisis. Algunos ya volvieron, pero por otros motivos distintos de la crisis como Jorge Díaz, que tiene muy buenos recuerdos de España: "Fueron los mejores años de mi vida. Estuve allí once años. Todo lo que tengo se lo debo a ese país".

Jorge regresó a Ecuador por amor: "En España trabajaba para una empresa de leche. Con los años ascendí hasta ser gerente de planta. Pero mi mujer quería criar a nuestras hijas en Quito, así que nos volvimos. Me arrepiento".

"En España podía viajar, fui a Italia, a Inglaterra, hice amigos de Marruecos que me invitaron a sus casas. Mi relación aquí está mal ahora, así que de aquí a un tiempo me vuelvo a España; lo pasaba mejor allí", dice Jorge, que se compró una casa y su taxi con el dinero que ahorró al otro lado del océano. Sin embargo, muchos de sus compatriotas opinan que en Ecuador cada vez se vive mejor. Los centros comerciales y las terminales de autobús ultramodernas se reproducen como setas[6].

Jorge Barreno, "Emigración: La economía del país andino mejora", *El Mundo*, lunes, el 12 de mayo de 2011. Used by permission of Unidad Editorial Información General, S.L.U.

Paso 3. Ahora contesta las siguientes preguntas para comprobar si has entendido bien el texto.

1. Según el artículo, ¿en qué sector de la economía española se necesitaba más mano de obra de inmigrantes?
   a) en la construcción X   b) en la informática   c) en servicios

2. ¿Cuál es el factor que más influyó en que tantos latinoamericanos quisieran trabajar en España?
   a) razones económicas X   b) razones políticas   c) razones personales

3. Entre los inmigrantes residentes en España, ¿de qué país latinoamericano hay más?
   a) Colombia   b) Perú   c) Ecuador X   d) Bolivia

4. En el caso de Jorge, ¿cuál fue la razón principal por la que regresó a Ecuador?
   a) ya no hay trabajo en España   b) por nostalgia de su país   c) su mujer quería criar a sus hijas en Ecuador X

Paso 4. En grupos de *tres*, hablen de las razones por las que ha dejado de crecer la economía española. ¿Ha ocurrido lo mismo en EE. UU.? Actualmente, ¿está creciendo o disminuyendo el número de inmigrantes que llegan a EE. UU.? ¿En qué se basan sus opiniones?

[1]growth, [2]labor, [3]has stagnated, [4]to save money, [5]failure to renew residency documents, [6]mushrooms

When you need help with more than individual words to understand what another person is saying, request a clarification by asking for an example or an explanation. For instance, if you can't follow a description of environmental issues, you could ask, **"¿Podrías darme un ejemplo?"**. If a rephrased or simplified description would help, you could ask **"¿Podrías explicármelo otra vez?"**.

¡A conversar!
Meets ACTFL Standard 1.1, interpersonal speaking.

Todos somos responsables

Cualquier persona puede ayudar a mejorar el mundo en que vivimos. En grupos de *tres*, hablen de lo siguiente:

- Lo que haces tú para contribuir a tu comunidad, lo que hiciste en el pasado o lo que harás en el futuro.
- Lo que hacen tus amigos o parientes, lo que hicieron en el pasado o lo que harán en el futuro.
- Lo que hacen las organizaciones, escuelas o empresas que conoces, lo que hicieron en el pasado o lo que harán en el futuro. Túrnense.

¡A escribir!
Meets ACTFL Standard 1.3, presentational writing and speaking.

Minidramas: Escenas del mundo hispano

La clase se divide en grupos de *tres* a *cinco* estudiantes. Cada grupo escoge un tema diferente de la lista que sigue y escribe un minidrama siguiendo las instrucciones que se dan más abajo.

• En la playa	• En el hotel
• En el centro de la ciudad	• En la oficina de inmigración
• En el museo	• En... (un lugar del mundo hispano de su elección)

Instrucciones

- Escriban un minidrama con el vocabulario y las estructuras que han aprendido. Usen distintos tiempos verbales y ¡no traduzcan del inglés!
- El minidrama debe incluir un problema o complicación que hay que resolver.
- Cada minidrama debe tener una duración máxima de cinco minutos.
- Aprendan sus papeles de memoria.
- Al representar el minidrama, pronuncien y hablen claramente. ¡Sean muy expresivos!

You may want to assign a minimum number of words or sentences as appropriate for the **¡A escribir!** task. Students can use the word count tool available in their word processing application to check the length of their work before and after the revising step of the writing process.

Writing Strategy

Reading Aloud

Before finalizing and then memorizing your part in the mini-drama, get together with your group and read your parts aloud. Pause to critique areas that might require clarification or revision. Repeat the process a second time, critiquing only at the end.

Steps:

1. *Prewriting:* Work as a group to brainstorm and narrow your ideas. Develop a list **¡en español!** of the roles each one of you will play, actions that will take place, the problem or complication that is to be resolved, and the ending. At this stage you might even want to decide upon props and costumes/apparel to be worn.

2. *Writing:* Be sure to write directly in Spanish (don't translate from English) and use only Spanish that you have studied! If the skit is divided into subsections, each subgroup is responsible for writing their portion. Another option is for the entire group to work together, with each one providing and jotting down what he or she will say. One student is responsible for getting copies of the first draft to everyone.

3. *Revising:* Each student revises the script and refines his or her role, but also checks the scripts of others. Be sure to check for correct grammar, spelling, and punctuation. Then follow the procedure outlined in the accompanying strategy.

4. *Practicing:* Memorization and ample practice are keys to a successful performance.

¡A investigar!

Los asuntos de interés para las comunidades hispanas de EE. UU.

¿Cuáles son los asuntos que les interesan a los hispanos que viven en EE. UU.? ¿Qué eventos culturales se organizan en sus comunidades?

Paso 1. Con la ayuda de su profesor/a, la clase se divide en *cinco* equipos. Cada equipo se encarga de una región de este país: el noreste, el sureste, el noroeste, el suroeste o el centro.

Paso 2. Primero, busquen en Internet por lo menos uno de los periódicos bilingües que se publican en la región. Colaboren para escoger los artículos más interesantes y divídanlos entre los estudiantes del equipo. Lean los artículos y preparen un resumen. Apunten el URL del periódico y cualquier otra información que requiera su profesor/a.

Paso 3. Después, trabajen juntos para escribir y revisar un guión[1] basado en la información que encontraron. Hagan un *podcast* en el que hablen de los asuntos y eventos de interés para los hispanos de esa región de EE. UU. Publíquenlo para que lo puedan compartir no sólo con sus compañeros de clase, sino también con los otros estudiantes de español de su *college* o universidad.

Paso 4. Después de escuchar todos los *podcasts*, los estudiantes pueden hablar de las semejanzas y diferencias que existen entre las regiones del país con respeto a las comunidades hispanas. ¿Cuáles son las comunidades hispanas que les gustaría conocer y por qué?

Research Strategy

Following Current Events

To follow current events in the Hispanic world, use online news services such as **¡Yahoo! en español**, **CNN en español**, and **BBC Mundo** and Spanish-language television networks for an overview of important issues. Your favorite search engine will help you find directories with links to online newspapers so that you can learn about events in specific countries. Many cities in the US have bilingual or Spanish-language newspapers with online versions that will allow you to see the city from the perspective of its Hispanic community. As you use these sources, remember to apply the reading strategies that you've learned in each chapter of *¡Con brío!*.

Trivia

A ver cuánto sabes.

1. ¿Cuáles son los dos países hispanos más próximos a EE. UU.?
   1. México y Cuba
2. ¿Cómo se llama un país que exporta esmeraldas y flores y lleva el nombre de Cristóbal Colón?
   2. Colombia
3. ¿En cuántos continentes hay países que tienen por lengua oficial el español? ¿Qué continentes son?
   3. En tres. América, África y Europa

If you don't know the answers, take a look at the front inside cover of the textbook. Try to respond in complete sentences.

[1]script

Vocabulario: Capítulo 12

Escena 1

La naturaleza   *Nature*
la cascada/ catarata   *waterfall*
la cordillera   *mountain range*
el desierto   *desert*
el paisaje   *landscape*
la planta tropical   *tropical plant*
la selva   *jungle*
el volcán   *volcano*

En el aeropuerto   *At the airport*
la aduana   *customs*
la aerolínea   *airline*
el/la pasajero/a   *passenger*
la puerta de embarque   *boarding gate*
la tarjeta de embarque   *boarding pass*
el vuelo   *flight*

En el avión   *On the plane*
el asiento   *seat*
 de pasillo   *aisle...*
 de ventanilla   *window...*
el auxiliar de vuelo   *flight attendant (male)*
la azafata   *flight attendant (female)*
el/la piloto   *pilot*

En el hotel   *At the hotel*
el aire acondicionado   *air conditioning*
el ascensor   *elevator*
el botones   *bellhop*
la calefacción   *heating*
la habitación doble/ sencilla
    double/ single room
la piscina   *swimming pool*
el servicio de habitación   *room service*

Para la cama   *For the bed*
la almohada   *pillow*
la cobija   *blanket*
la sábana   *sheet*

Verbos y expresiones verbales
   Verbs and verbal expressions
conseguir (i, i)   *to get, obtain*
hacer la maleta   *to pack*
facturar el equipaje   *to check the luggage/ baggage*
perder el avión   *to miss the plane*
registrarse   *to check in*
reservar   *to reserve*
sacar el pasaporte   *to get a passport*
volar (ue)   *to fly*

Escena 2

La ciencia y la tecnología
   Science and technology
el (carro) híbrido   *hybrid (car)*
la contaminación   *pollution*
la destrucción de la capa de ozono
   destruction of the ozone layer
la energía eólica (del viento)   *aeolic (wind) energy*
la energía solar   *solar energy*
la exploración espacial   *space exploration*
el invento   *invention*
la investigación   *research*
el medio ambiente   *environment*
la nave espacial   *spaceship*
la prensa   *press*
el/la radio por satélite   *satellite radio*
la Tierra   *Earth*
la ventaja/ la desventaja   *advantage/ disadvantage*

Preposición   *Preposition*
alrededor de   *around*

Verbos y expresiones verbales
   Verbs and verbal expressions
comunicarse   *to communicate*
diagnosticar   *to diagnose*
evitar (enfermedades)   *to avoid (illnesses)*
prevenir   *to prevent*
prolongar la vida   *to prolong life*
proteger   *to protect*

Escena 3

En busca de una vida mejor
   In search of a better life
el acuerdo de paz   *peace treaty*
el agua potable   *potable water*
la diversidad   *diversity*
el/la emigrante   *emigrant*
el fin   *end*
la frontera   *border*
el gobierno   *government*
el hambre   *hunger*
el/la inmigrante   *immigrant*
la oportunidad   *opportunity*
el país en desarrollo   *developing country*
la pobreza   *poverty*
el poder   *power*
el producto orgánico   *organic produce*
la vida sencilla   *simple life*

Verbos y expresiones verbales
   Verbs and verbal expressions
contribuir   *to contribute*
cultivar   *to grow (produce)*
eliminar   *to eliminate*
emigrar   *to emigrate*
estar satisfecho/a   *to be satisfied*
inmigrar   *to immigrate*
integrarse a/en   *to adjust, integrate oneself*
mejorar   *to improve*
prosperar   *to prosper*
proveer   *to provide*

Apéndice 1: ¡Diálogos en acción!

Chapter 1

1.1 Saludos y presentaciones informales

> **EXPRESIONES ÚTILES**
>
> | | |
> |---|---|
> | Muchos exámenes | *A lot of exams* |
> | Tengo un examen | *I have an exam* |
> | Mira | *Hey (literally: Look)* |
> | ¡Qué coincidencia! | *What a coincidence!* |

Paso 3. Which of the Spanish expressions at right is most appropriate in the situations described at left? More than one answer may apply.

1. You want to say you're pleased to meet someone to whom you've just been introduced. g	a. ¿Cómo estás?
	b. Muy bien, gracias.
2. You want to ask someone where s/he is from. d	c. ¡Ay! ¡Las dos! Tengo un examen. ¡Adiós!
3. I t turns out that your new acquaintance is from the same place as you. Express your surprise and explain you're also from that place. h	d. ¿De dónde eres?
	e. Mira, te presento a...
4. You want to say that you're fine, thanks, when someone asks how you are. b	f. ¿Qué tal?
	g. ¡Mucho gusto!
5. You want to ask how someone is doing. a, f	h. ¡Qué coincidencia! Yo también soy de...
6. You want to introduce someone. e	
7. You need to end the conversation abruptly because it's two o'clock and you have an exam. c	

Paso 4. Now create your own dialogue following the instructions given below. Incorporate as many expressions from **Paso 3** as possible.

E1: Greet **E2** and ask how s/he is.

E2: Return the greeting and ask how **E1** is.

E1: Say that you have a lot of exams but are fine.

E2: Introduce your partner to **E3**.

E1: Say you're pleased to meet **E3.**

E3: Say you're also pleased to meet **E1**, and ask where s/he is from.

E1: Say where you're from.

E3: Say you're also from that place and express surprise at the coincidence.

E2: You notice the time and realize that you have an exam right now. Say good-bye.

E1 and E3: Say good-bye.

Chapter 2

2.1 ¿Dónde está?

EXPRESIONES ÚTILES	
Oye	*Listen*
Claro, dime	*Sure, go ahead (literally: tell me)*
¿Sabes...?	*Do you know...?*
Mira	*Look*
Entonces	*So*
Disculpa	*I'm sorry / Excuse me*
Mil gracias	*Thank you so much (literally: a thousand thanks)*
Cuando quieras	*No problem (literally: whenever you want)*

Paso 3. Rank the following expressions in logical order (from 1-8).

   2   Claro, dime.

   8   Cuando quieras, hasta luego.

   1   Oye, tengo una pregunta.

   4   Sí. La facultad de derecho está enfrente del estadio de deportes, a un lado de la secretaría.

   7   Mil gracias.

   5   Muchísimas gracias. Otra pregunta, disculpa. Eh, ¿sabes si hay una librería aquí, en la universidad?

   3   Eh, ¿sabes dónde está la facultad de derecho?

   6   Sí, claro. Eh... la librería está a un lado de la residencia estudiantil.

Paso 4. Now create your own dialogue following the instructions given below. Incorporate as many expressions from **Paso 3** as possible.

E1: Greet your partner.

E2: Return the greeting and ask how your partner is.

E1: Say you're fine and say you have a question to ask.

E2: Invite your partner to go ahead and ask the question.

E1: Ask about the location of a building on campus.

E2: Explain where that building is located, using prepositions.

E1: Thank your partner and say you have another question. Ask your partner if s/he knows if some other type of building can be found on campus.

E2: Say sure and explain where that building is located, using prepositions.

E1: Thank your partner.

E2: Respond graciously to the thanks and say good-bye.

E1: Say good-bye.

Chapter 3

3.1 El novio de Graciela

EXPRESIONES ÚTILES

Tanto tiempo sin vernos	*Long time no see*
¿Qué hay de nuevo en tu vida?	*What's new in your life?*
Noticias	*News*
A ver, cuéntame	*Let's see, tell me*
Pues	*Well*
Fíjate que	*(literally: Notice that) Expression used to signal that speaker is about to explain something*
Estoy saliendo con	*I'm going out with*
¡No me digas!	*Wow! (literally: Don't tell me!)*
Háblame sobre él	*Tell me about him*
Lo que más me gusta es	*What I like best is*
Caballeroso	*Gentlemanly*
No era	*He wasn't*
Ya no hay	*There are no longer any*
Está estudiando un doctorado	*He is studying for a doctorate*
Quiero que lo conozcas	*I want you to meet him*
Me parece bien	*That sounds good (to me)*

Paso 3.   Rank the following expressions in logical order (from 1-10).

___4___   Pues, fíjate que estoy saliendo con un chico maravilloso.

___7___   Bueno, quiero conocerlo.

___2___   ¡Uy! Bueno, tengo muchas noticias ahora.

___9___   Sí, me parece bien.

___5___   ¡Ay! ¡No me digas! A ver, háblame sobre él. ¿Cómo es?

___3___   A ver, cuéntame.

__10__   ¡Ok! ¡Nos vemos!

___1___   Bueno, ¡tanto tiempo sin vernos! Dime, ¿qué hay de nuevo en tu vida?

___8___   ¡Sí, sí! ¡Quiero que lo conozcas! ¿La próxima semana salimos?

___6___   ¡Ah! Pues, bueno, para mí es guapísimo porque es muy alto, es rubio, tiene los ojos azules...

Paso 4.   Now create your own dialogue following the instructions given below. Incorporate as many expressions from **Paso 3** as possible.

E1: Greet your partner and ask how s/he is.

E2: Return the greeting and say you're fine. Say it's been a long time since you've seen each other and ask what's new in your partner's life.

E1: Say you've got a lot of news right now.

E2: Ask your partner to tell you the news.

E1: Say you're going out with someone really great.

E2: Express enthusiasm and ask your partner to tell you about him/her.

E1: Describe your new significant other's appearance and personality.

E2: Ask other details (where s/he is from, what his/her name is, how old s/he is, etc.).

E1: Answer your partner's questions.

E2: Say you want to meet this new person.

E1: Agree enthusiastically that you want your partner to meet him/her, and suggest you all go out next week.

E2: Say that sounds good to you and say good-bye.

E1: Say good-bye.

Chapter 4

4.1 La fiesta cubana

EXPRESIONES ÚTILES

¡Qué alegría verte!	How nice to see you! (literally: What joy to see you)
¡Claro que sí!	Sure
Llevar	To take/bring
Quizás	Maybe
Los pastelitos de guayaba	Guava pastries
El postre	Dessert
Ropa vieja	Cuban dish consisting of shredded flank steak in a tomato sauce base (literally: Old clothes)
Dentro de dos sábados	Two Saturdays from now
Déjame chequear mi calendario	Let me check my calendar ("chequear" is an anglicism commonly heard in the Caribbean and Mexico)
Enseguida	Right away
¡Qué lástima!	What a shame!
Ya planificado	Already planned
Contaba con tu buen ritmo	I was counting on your good (sense of) rhythm
Seguro, será la próxima	For sure, (it will be) next time

Paso 3. Match each expression on the left with the most appropriate answer on the right.

1. Hola. ¿Cómo estás? c	a. ¡Ah! ¿Sí? ¡Qué lástima, porque contaba con tu buen ritmo!
2. ¿Sabes? Voy a dar una fiesta. ¿Puedes venir? f	b. Seguro, será la próxima.
3. ¿Qué debo llevar? e	c. Eh, ¡qué alegría verte!
4. ¿Tú crees que puedas venir dentro de dos sábados? d	d. Déjame chequear mi calendario... te digo enseguida...
5. ¡Oh! ¡Qué lástima! Ese día tengo algo ya planificado. No voy a poder ir. a	e. Quizás puedas traer...
6. Bueno... La próxima vez. b	f. ¡Oh! ¡Una fiesta! ¡Sí! ¡Claro que sí!

Paso 4. Now create your own dialogue following the instructions given below. Incorporate as many expressions from **Paso 3** as possible.

E1: Greet your partner and invite him/her to a party you are having. Don't mention when yet.

E2: Accept the invitation gladly and ask what you can bring.

E1: Suggest something for your partner to bring. Describe what activities you will do at the party. Ask if s/he can make it on such-and-such date.

E2: Say you'll check your calendar and will let your partner know right away. You discover you have something planned that day and can't make it. Decline the invitation with regret.

E1: Express regret that your partner can't come and end the conversation.

E2: Say good-bye.

Chapter 5

5.1 En el Café Ibérico

<table>
<tr><td colspan="2">EXPRESIONES ÚTILES</td></tr>
<tr><td>Se la podemos servir</td><td>We can serve it (=la) to you (=se)</td></tr>
<tr><td>Término medio</td><td>Medium (in describing how one prefers one's meat to be cooked)</td></tr>
<tr><td>Tinto/a</td><td>Red (in describing wine or sangría)</td></tr>
<tr><td>Ya</td><td>Right away</td></tr>
</table>

Paso 3. Pon en orden lógico las expresiones que siguen (de 1 a 13).

_3_ OK. ¿Le gusta esta mesa?

_13_ Ah, muy bien. Ya vuelvo con su orden.

_1_ Bienvenido al Café Ibérico. ¿Quiere almorzar?

_10_ Término medio, por favor.

_6_ Gracias. Mira, creo que sé lo que quiero pedir.

_4_ Sí, esta mesa está muy bien.

_11_ Ah, está bien. Y, ¿quiere tomar algo? ¿Quiere algo de beber?

_9_ Ah, muy bien. Eh, ¿cómo prefiere la carne?

_7_ ¡Ah, sí! ¿Qué prefiere comer?

_12_ Una tinta, por favor.

_5_ Mire, tome el menú.

_2_ Sí, por favor.

_8_ Voy a empezar con pulpo a la gallega, y después, voy a pedir un pincho de solomillo.

Paso 4. Ahora, inventen su propio diálogo siguiendo las instrucciones que hay a continuación. Incluyan el mayor número posible de expresiones del **Paso 3.** Usen el menú del *Café Ibérico* de la página 167.

E1: You are a server. Greet your customer and welcome him/her to your restaurant.

E2: You are a customer. Return the greeting and thank the server.

E1: Ask the customer if s/he wants to have lunch (or dinner).

E2: Say yes, please.

E1: Show him/her to a table and ask if it's OK.

E2: Say the table is fine.

E1: Offer the menu to the customer.

E2: Say you think you know what you want to order.

E1: Ask him/her what s/he'd like to have.

E2: Order two dishes from the menu.

E1: Say that's fine and ask what s/he would like to drink.

E2: Order something to drink.

E1: Say that's fine and that you'll be right back with his/her order.

Chapter 6

6.1 En busca de compañera de piso

EXPRESIONES ÚTILES

Un anuncio	*An ad*	Será mejor si	*It will be better if*
En alquiler	*For rent*	¿Te va bien?	*Is that OK with you?*
Un piso	*Apartment (Spain)*	De acuerdo	*OK*
Me/te parece bien	*It is fine with me/you*	A partir de	*After*

Paso 3.

A. Pon en orden lógico las expresiones que siguen (de 1 a 7).

___5___ Sí. La habitación es para ti, eh, lo que sí es que tenemos que compartir baño. No sé si te parece bien eso.

___3___ Sí, es aquí. Mmm, a ver, es un piso pequeño. No sé si buscas un espacio muy grande, pero este es un piso pequeño.

___6___ Sí, ningún problema. Si el baño está limpio, no me importa compartir baño. En todo caso, si no tenemos problemas de horarios, no hay ningún problema.

___4___ No, está bien. Yo busco una habitación para mí sola, así que si tengo una habitación para mí, está bien. Es perfecto, ningún problema.

___2___ ¡Hola! Buenas tardes. Mira, te llamo por el anuncio de Craigslist, que... ¿hay una habitación en alquiler?

___7___ Bueno, yo me despierto a las seis cada mañana. Necesito usar el baño de seis a siete. Me ducho, me maquillo y todo esto. Necesito una hora por las mañanas, de seis a siete.

___1___ Sí, ¿dígame?

B. Ahora, pon en orden lógico las demás expresiones para terminar la conversación (de 8 a 14).

___9___ Muy bien. Bueno, ¿puedes venir a ver el piso? Será mejor si nos conocemos, y así podemos decidir. ¿Te va bien mañana?

___14___ Venga. ¡Hasta mañana! ¡Adiós!

___8___ De acuerdo. Yo entro a trabajar a las ocho, así que normalmente me levanto a las siete, me ducho, y desayuno a esa hora. Así que para mí, tener el baño de siete a siete y media, está perfecto.

11	Bueno, yo llego a casa a las cinco. ¿Te parece bien a las cinco?
12	Sin ningún problema. Nos vemos a las cinco, en la dirección que hay *online*, ¿sí?
13	Bueno, muy bien. Pues, ¡nos vemos mañana!
10	Perfecto. Mañana, a partir de las tres, estoy libre.

Paso 4. Finalmente, inventen su propio diálogo siguiendo las instrucciones que hay a continuación. Incluyan el mayor número posible de expresiones del **Paso 3.**

E1: Answer the phone.

E2: Say hello and explain that you are calling about an ad for a room to rent.

E1: Say that yes, you have a room for rent. Explain that the apartment is small and ask if that's OK.

E2: Say that's fine. Add that you're looking for a room just for yourself, so as long as you have your own room, it's not a problem.

E1: Say that the room is the renter's own, but that you'll have to share the bathroom, and you're not sure if the caller is OK with that.

E2: Say that it's no problem, that if the bathroom is clean and there are no scheduling conflicts you don't mind sharing.

E1: Describe your morning routine, including what time you get up, need the bathroom, and leave for work.

E2: Describe your own routine. (Your schedules don't overlap.)

E1: Since there is no scheduling conflict, suggest that the caller come to see the apartment in person so that you both can decide what to do. Suggest tomorrow.

E2: Say that's great and say what time you're free tomorrow.

E1: Say what time you get home from work and suggest a time after that.

E2: Agree, verify the address, and say good-bye.

E1: Confirm the address is correct and say good-bye.

Chapter 7

7.1 ¿Cómo se llega al Museo Botero?

EXPRESIONES ÚTILES

La moda	*Fashion*
La actualidad	*Current events*
No hay de qué	*Don't mention it/ You're welcome*

Paso 3.

A. Pon en orden lógico las expresiones que siguen (de 1 a 7).

3	Sí, señorita. Le recomiendo el periódico *El Universal*.
6	¡Ay! ¡Qué bien! ¿Me da uno por favor?
1	Buenos días, señorita. ¿Puedo ayudarla con algo?
5	Sí, tiene todas las secciones: de deportes, de moda, de actualidad. De todo.

__2__	Sí. Buenos días, señor. Mire, no conozco bien la ciudad y quisiera comprar un periódico. ¿Me recomienda alguno?
__4__	¡Ah! ¡Qué bien! Y, ¿tiene una sección de arte y cultura en el periódico *El Universal*?
__7__	Sí, señorita. Aquí tiene. Son dos pesos.

B. Ahora, pon en orden lógico el resto de la conversación (de 8 a 14).

__9__	Dígame.
__12__	¡Muy bien! Bueno, ¡muchísimas gracias por su ayuda!
__14__	¡Hasta luego!
__10__	¿Dónde está el museo Botero?
__13__	No hay de qué. Hasta luego, señorita.
__8__	Ah, muy bien. ¡Oiga! Y tengo otra pregunta.
__11__	Mire, el museo Botero está cerca de aquí. Mire, estamos en la calle José Martí. Entonces siga derecho y cruce la plaza de la Hispanidad. Y entonces [...] doble a la derecha. Y siga derecho hasta llegar [...] al museo Botero que está a una cuadra.

Paso 4. Finalmente, inventen su propio diálogo siguiendo las instrucciones que hay a continuación. Incluyan el mayor número posible de expresiones del **Paso 3**.

E1: You are a newspaper vendor. Greet your customer and ask if you can be of help.

E2: Return the greeting. Explain that you don't know the city well and would like to buy a newspaper. Ask the vendor if s/he recommends one.

E1: Say yes and recommend your favorite paper.

E2: React appropriately and ask if that paper has your favorite section (arts, sports, fashion, etc.).

E1: Say, yes, it has all kinds of sections (name some).

E2: React with enthusiasm and ask the vendor to give you a copy.

E1: Hand the customer the paper and say how much it costs.

E2: Hand the vendor the money and say you have another question.

E1: React appropriately.

E2: Ask where a particular tourist attraction is located.

E1: Give directions.

E2: Thank the vendor and say good-bye.

E1: Say s/he is welcome and say good-bye.

Chapter 8

8.1 En la zapatería

EXPRESIONES ÚTILES

¿En qué puedo servirle?	*How can I help you?*
Me gustaría que me enseñen	*I'd like you (plural) to show me...*
El tamaño	*Size*
Se ven preciosos	*They look beautiful*
Tal vez	*Maybe*
Ningún problema	*No problem*

Paso 3. Empareja las preguntas o peticiones de la izquierda con la respuestas apropiadas de la derecha. En algunos casos, es posible más de una respuesta.

1. Buenos días, señora. ¿En qué puedo servirle? d	a. Me quedan perfectos, gracias, son muy cómodos, me encantan. Creo que me voy a llevar los dos pares.
2. ¿Y en qué tamaño los traigo, señora? g	b. OK, aquí se los traigo. Pruébese estos rojos.
3. Ahora se los traigo... Pruébese estos. a, f	c. Ahora se los traigo. Aquí le traje un número más grande. Pruébeselos.
4. ¿Quisiera tal vez probarme los rojos, por favor? b	d. Buenos días. Quisiera comprar unos zapatos, y me gustaría que me enseñen unos en negro y otros en blanco...
5. ¿Me podría traer un número más grande, por favor? c	e. Hoy no voy a usar la tarjeta de crédito, voy a pagar en efectivo.
6. ¿Y con qué va a pagar, señora? e	f. Ah, me encantan, se ven preciosos... Ay no. Me quedan súper incómodos, no me gustan...
	g. Eh, en 39 por favor.

Paso 4. Finalmente, inventen su propio diálogo con las instrucciones que hay a continuación Incluyan el mayor número posible de expresiones del **Paso 3.**

E1: You're a shoe salesperson. Greet your customer and ask if you can be of help.

E2: Return the greeting, and explain that you would like the salesperson to show you two pairs of shoes in different colors.

E1: Ask what size you should bring your customer.

E2: Tell the salesperson what size you need.

E1: Say you'll bring them right away. After you bring both pairs, invite the customer to try the first pair on.

E2: Say you love the way the shoes look. After trying them on, though, say you don't like them because they are uncomfortable. Ask the salesperson to bring you a larger size.

E1: Bring the larger size and invite the customer to try them on.

E2: The larger pair size fits perfectly. Say so and add that you love them.

E1: Ask if the customer wants to try the 2nd pair.

E2: Say you do since the other pair looks comfortable. Say that these also fit perfectly and that you like them as much as the first pair. Say you'll take them both.

E1: Ask how your customer wants to pay.

E2: Say that you want to pay with cash, not a credit card. Ask if that's all right.

E1: Say of course.

E2: Thank the salesperson.

Chapter 9

9.1 El accidente de María

EXPRESIONES ÚTILES

Conducir	*To drive (Esp.)*
Iba distraída	*I was (going along) distracted*
Resbalar	*To slip, to be slippery*
Así que	*So*
Atropellar	*To run over*
Dar un volantazo	*To turn the steering wheel (el volante) violently*
Avisar	*To notify, to let someone know*

Paso 3.   ¿Cuál de las siguientes expresiones es más apropiada en las situaciones que se describen a continuación?

You want to...

1.	...express surprise to see your friend on crutches. g	a.	Ya...
2.	...indicate that you have a dramatic story to tell. d	b.	Mira...
3.	...invite your friend to tell you what happened. f	c.	¿Cuántas veces te dije que no se puede...?
4.	...signal you're about to explain something a bit complicated. b	d.	¡No sabes lo que me pasó anoche!
5.	...scold your friend for doing something dumb. c	e.	Por eso...
6.	...acknowledge your friend is right, but start to explain. i	f.	¡Cuéntame!
7.	...acknowledge you've heard and understood what your friend just said. a	g.	¿Qué haces con muletas?
8.	...explain the reason for something e	h.	Bueno, espero que te recuperes pronto.
9.	...express the hope that your friend gets better soon. h	i.	Tienes razón, pero...

Paso 4.   Ahora, inventen su propio diálogo siguiendo las instrucciones que hay a continuación. Incluyan el mayor número posible de expresiones del **Paso 3.**

E1: Greet your partner.

E2: Express surprise to see your partner on crutches.

E1: Tell your partner s/he won't believe what happened to you last night.

E2: Ask your partner to tell you what happened.

E1: Explain that you were driving while talking on your cellphone with someone...

E2: Gently scold your partner for doing something so foolish.

E1: Agree but explain that it was an important conversation and that it was why you were distracted. Say that it was raining and the freeway was slippery. There was a curve, and you almost ran over someone. To avoid hitting the person you turned the steering wheel hard but ran into a tree. Say that you were very worried in that moment because your leg was hurting and your nose would not stop bleeding.

E2: Ask your partner if s/he went to see a doctor and if someone called an ambulance.

E1: Explain that the person you almost ran over called an ambulance. The ambulance came and took you to the hospital. Add that the doctor took some X-rays and gave you a cast. Say that you have to wear the cast and walk on crutches for 3 weeks.

E2: Express well-wishes for your partner's quick recovery.

Chapter 10

10.1 El proyecto para aumentar los impuestos

EXPRESIONES ÚTILES

Aprobar	*To approve*	Los recursos	*Resources*
Recaudar fondos	*To gather funds*	Confiar en	*To trust in*
Despedir	*To fire*	Seguir soñando	*To keep dreaming*
Medio ridículo	*Pretty ridiculous*	Igual	*Maybe*
Recoger	*To collect*		

Paso 3.   ¿Cuál de las siguientes expresiones es apropiada en las situaciones que se describen a continuación? En algunos casos, es posible más de una respuesta.

You want to...

1. ...stop debating. e	a. ¡Ay, no! A mí me parece...
2. ...say you're really happy about something. f	b. Me parece medio ridículo. ¿Tú crees que...?
3. ...disagree without being too aggressive. a, d	c. ¡Sigue soñando!
4. ...disagree forcefully and keep debating. b	d. No creo.
5. ...end the discussion while still signaling your strong disagreement. c	e. Bueno, de todas maneras, no sigamos discutiendo...
	f. Me alegro enormemente.

Paso 4.   Ahora, inventen su propio diálogo siguiendo las instrucciones que hay a continuación. Incluyan el mayor número posible de expresiones del **Paso 3** y expresiones que requieren subjuntivo.

E1: Express your opinion about something.

E2: Disagree and explain why.

E1: Explain your position.

E2: Provide a counter-argument.

E1: Rebut the counter-argument.

E2: Suggest that you stop arguing and end the discussion.

Chapter 11

11.1   La entrevista de trabajo

EXPRESIONES ÚTILES

Gracias por haber venido a	*Thanks for having come to (past infinitive)*
Con respecto a	*With respect to*
Un par de	*A few*
El bachillerato	*Bachelor's degree (in Peru; in other countries it means high school diploma)*
De hecho	*Actually*
Un refuerzo	*Reinforcement*

Paso 3.   ¿Cuáles son las expresiones que corresponden a las situaciones que se describen a continuación? En algunos casos, es posible más de una respuesta.

You want to...

1.	...thank the person you're about to interview for coming. d	a.	Muchas gracias por la entrevista y fue un gusto conocerla.
2.	...signal that you are about to ask one or more questions. c, e, j	b.	¡Qué interesante!
3.	...ask if the position is full or part-time. f	c.	Otra pregunta más...
4.	...express interest in what the other person just said. b	d.	Gracias por haber venido a esta entrevista.
5.	...signal that you've heard, understood and approve of what the other person has just said. g, i	e.	Y bueno, una última pregunta...
6.	...ask when the interviewer will make a final decision about the job. h	f.	¿Quería saber si el puesto es a tiempo completo o a tiempo parcial?
7.	...thank the interviewer and say it was a pleasure to meet her. a	g.	Muy bien.
		h.	¿Cuándo tomará su decisión final sobre el puesto?
		i.	Bueno, me parece perfecto.
		j.	Quería hacerle un par de preguntas.

Paso 4.   Finalmente, inventen su propio diálogo siguiendo las instrucciones que hay a continuación. Incluyan el mayor número posible de expresiones del **Paso 3.**

E1:   You are interviewing a candidate for a job. Greet the candidate, thank him/her for coming, and say you'd like to ask a few questions. Start by asking about the candidate's educational background.

E2:   Explain your educational background to the interviewer.

E1:   Respond politely and ask about the candidate's previous work experience.

E2:   Talk about your prior work experience.

E1:   Respond appropriately and ask why the candidate is interested in the job.

E2:   Explain your interest.

E1:   Respond politely and ask the candidate if s/he has any questions for you.

E2: Say you do have a few questions as a matter of fact. Ask several questions about the job (e.g., whether it is full or part-time, whether there are benefits, when the interviewer will make a final decision, etc.).

E1: Answer the candidate's questions.

E2: Respond appropriately. Then thank the interviewer and say it was a pleasure to meet him/her.

E1: Respond appropriately.

Chapter 12

12.1 El Cuerpo de Paz

> **EXPRESIONES ÚTILES**
>
> | | |
> |---|---|
> | ¿Qué te trae por mi oficina? | *What brings you to my office?* |
> | Una posta médica | *Health clinic/medical center* |
> | Una hoja de vida | *Resumé /CV* |
> | Agradecer | *To thank* |

Paso 3. Pon en orden lógico las expresiones que siguen (de 1 a 7).

___5___ Ya. Sí, te voy a pedir que me mandes la copia de tu hoja de vida para que pueda escribir una carta.

___2___ Buenos días, profesora. Mire, venía para preguntarle si Ud. pudiera escribirme una recomendación para...

___7___ Con todo gusto.

___4___ Creo que no, pero yo podría mandársela si Ud. la requiere.

___1___ Buenos días. ¿Qué te trae por mi oficina?

___3___ Con todo gusto... Dime: ¿tengo tu hoja de vida más reciente?

___6___ Bien, muchas gracias. Le agradecería mucho su ayuda.

Paso 4. Ahora, inventen su propio diálogo siguiendo las instrucciones que hay a continuación. Incluyan el mayor número posible de expresiones del **Paso 3.**

E1: You need a recommendation letter for something (e.g., an internship/grad school/etc.). Go to your boss/professor's office and say hello.

E2: Your employee/student shows up at your door and says hello. Return the greeting and ask what brings him/her to your office.

E1: Ask politely if s/he could write you a recommendation and explain why you need it.

E2: Say you're happy to write the letter. Ask for more details about what the employee/student would do if s/he got the position s/he is applying for.

E1: Answer your boss/professor's questions.

E2: Ask if you have the employee/student's most recent CV.

E1: Say that you don't think so but could send it if need be.

E2: Say that yes, you need him/her to send it to you.

E1: Agree to do so and thank your boss/professor for his/her help.

Apéndice 2: Transcripts for ¡Diálogos en acción!

1.1 Saludos y presentaciones informales

Olivia: Hola Claudio. ¿Qué tal?

Claudio: ¿Cómo estás, Olivia?

Olivia: Muy bien, gracias. Muchos exámenes, pero bien. Y tú, ¿qué tal?

Claudio: Muy bien, gracias.

Olivia: Mira, Claudio, te presento a una amiga: Marta Serrano.

Claudio: Hola, Marta. ¡Mucho gusto!

Marta: Mucho gusto, Claudio.

Claudio: ¿De dónde eres, Marta?

Marta: Yo soy de Ecuador. ¿Y tú?

Claudio: ¡Qué coincidencia! Yo también soy de Ecuador.

Marta: ¡Ay! ¡Fabuloso!

Olivia: ¡Ay, las dos! Tengo un examen. ¡Adiós!

Claudio: ¡Hasta luego!

Marta: ¡Chao!

2.1 ¿Dónde está?

Jorge: ¡Hola!

Estudiante: Hola. ¿Qué tal?

Jorge: Bien, gracias. Oye, tengo una pregunta.

Estudiante: Claro. ¡Dime!

Jorge: Eh... ¿Sabes dónde está la... facultad de derecho?

Estudiante: Sí, la facultad de derecho... Mira, aquí estamos en el gimnasio, entonces la facultad de derecho está en frente del estadio de deportes, a un lado de la secretaría.

Jorge: Muchísimas gracias. Otra pregunta, disculpa. Eh, ¿sabes si hay una librería aquí, en la universidad?

Estudiante: Sí, claro. Eh... La librería está a un lado de la residencia estudiantil San Carlos, y también, cerca de la librería vas a encontrar la cafetería Oaxaca.

Jorge: Mil gracias.

Estudiante: Cuando quieras. Hasta luego.

Jorge: Hasta luego.

Estudiante: *Bye*!

3.1 El novio de Graciela

Alberto: Hola, Graciela. ¿Cómo estás?

Graciela: Hola, muy bien. ¿Y tú?

Alberto: Bien, gracias. Bueno, tanto tiempo sin vernos.

Graciela: Sí...

Alberto: Dime, ¿qué hay de nuevo en tu vida?

Graciela: ¡Uy! Bueno, tengo muchas noticias ahora.

Alberto: A ver, cuéntame.

Graciela: Pues, fíjate que estoy saliendo con un chico maravilloso.

Alberto: ¡Ay! ¡No me digas!

Graciela: ¡Sí!

Alberto: A ver, háblame sobre él. ¿Cómo es?

Graciela: Ah, pues, bueno para mí es guapísimo porque es muy alto, es rubio, tiene los ojos azules...

Alberto: Y, ¿de dónde es?

Graciela: Sí. Bueno, él es norteamericano, y eh... Bueno, y... lo que más me gusta es que es muy sensible.

Alberto: ¿Es muy sensible?

Graciela: Sí, sí.

Alberto: Muy bien. ¿Y es romántico?

Graciela: Es romántico, y es muy caballeroso.

Alberto: Muy caballeroso...

Graciela: Sí.

Alberto: Eso es bueno, ¿no?

Graciela: Ajá.

Alberto: Porque tu último novio... ¡*Bleeehh*! Era...

Graciela: Sí.

Alberto: No era bueno.

Graciela: No. Y ya no hay caballeros en este mundo.

Alberto: Exacto, muy bien. Y es... ¿es inteligente?

Graciela: Sí, es muy inteligente. Está estudiando un doctorado.

Alberto: Muy bien. Bueno, entonces, muy trabajador también.

Graciela: ¡También, sí! Muy trabajador y también es muy creativo.

Alberto: Sí. Bueno y... Bueno, quiero conocerlo.

Graciela: Sí, sí. ¡Quiero que lo conozcas!

Alberto: ¿Cuándo?

Graciela: ¿La próxima semana salimos?

Alberto: Sí, me parece bien.

Graciela: ¡Ok!

Alberto: Nos vemos.

Graciela: Nos vemos.

4.1 La fiesta cubana

Magali: ¡Hola William! ¿Cómo estás?

William: ¡Eh, Magali! ¡Qué alegría verte!

Magali: Ah… ¿Sabes? Voy a dar una fiesta, eh… ¿Puedes venir?

William: ¡Oh! Una fiesta. Sí, claro que sí. ¿Qué debo llevar?

Magali: Quizás puedes traer pastelitos de guayaba porque no tengo postre. Eh… Es una fiesta cubana con mucha comida cubana. Eh… Voy a hacer ropa vieja. Eh… Tú, ¿crees que puedas venir dentro de dos sábados?

William: ¿Dentro de dos sábados? Déjame chequear mi calendario. Te digo enseguida. ¡Oh, qué lástima, Magali! Ese día tengo algo ya planificado. No voy a poder ir.

Magali: ¡Ah! ¿Sí? ¡Qué lástima! Porque contaba con tu buen ritmo. Bueno, la próxima vez.

William: Seguro, será la próxima.

Magali: ¡Chao!

William: ¡Hasta luego!

5.1 En el Café Ibérico

Mujer: Buenas tardes, señor. ¿Cómo está?

Hombre: Buenas tardes.

Mujer: Bienvenido al Café Ibérico.

Hombre: ¡Gracias!

Mujer: Eh… ¿Quiere almorzar?

Hombre: Sí, por favor.

Mujer: Ok. ¿Le gusta esta mesa?

Hombre: Sí, esta mesa está muy bien.

Mujer: Mire, tome el menú.

Hombre: Mira, creo que sé lo que quiero pedir.

Mujer: ¿Ah sí? ¿Qué… qué prefiere comer?

Hombre: Voy a empezar con pulpo a la gallega.

Mujer: ¡Ah! Muy rico el pulpo aquí.

Hombre: Y después voy a pedir un pincho de solomillo.

Mujer: Ah… Muy bien. Eh… ¿Cómo prefiere la carne?

Hombre: Término medio, por favor.

Mujer: Ah, está bien, y… ¿Quiere tomar algo? ¿Quiere algo de beber?

Hombre: ¿Tiene sangría?

Mujer: Sí, la sangría es muy buena… Ah, se la podemos servir, eh… blanca o tinta.

Hombre: Una tinta, por favor.

Mujer: Ah… Muy bien, y ¿va a tomar agua?

Hombre: Sí, también. ¡Gracias!

Mujer: Ya vuelvo con su orden.

6.1 En busca de compañera de piso

Paula: Sí, ¿dígame?

María: Hola, buenas tardes. Mira, te llamo por el anuncio de Craigslist, que... ¿hay una habitación en alquiler?

Paula: Sí, es aquí. Mmm... A ver, es un piso pequeño. No sé si buscas un espacio muy grande, pero éste es un piso pequeño.

María: No, eh, está bien. Yo busco una, una habitación para mí sola, así que si... si tengo una habitación para mí, está, está bien. Es perfecto, ningún problema.

Paula: Sí. La habitación es para ti, eh, lo que sí es que tenemos que compartir baño. No sé si te parece bien eso.

María: Sí, ningún problema. Si... Si el baño está limpio, no, no me importa compartir baño. En todo caso, si no tenemos problemas de, de horarios, no hay ningún problema.

Paula: Bueno, yo me despierto a las seis cada mañana. Uh, y necesito usar el baño de seis a siete. Me ducho, me maquillo, y todo esto, necesito una hora por las mañanas, de seis a siete.

María: Mmm. De acuerdo. Yo entro a trabajar a las ocho, así que normalmente me levanto a las siete, me ducho, y desayuno a esa hora, así que para mí tener el baño de siete a siete y media, está, está perfecto.

Paula: Muy bien. Bueno, ¿puedes venir a ver el piso? Será mejor si nos conocemos, y así podemos decidir. ¿Te va bien mañana?

María: Mmm. Perfecto. Mañana, a partir de las tres, estoy libre.

Paula: Bueno, yo llego a casa a las cinco. ¿Te parece bien a las cinco?

María: Mmm. Sin ningún problema. Nos vemos a las cinco, en la dirección que hay online, ¿sí?

Paula: Mmm. Bueno, muy bien. Pues, ¡nos vemos mañana!

María: Venga, hasta mañana, ¡adiós!

Paula: ¡Adiós!

7.1 ¿Cómo se llega al Museo Botero?

Vendedor: Buenos días señorita, ¿puedo ayudarla con algo?

Verónica: Sí. Buenos días, señor. Mire, ah, no conozco bien la ciudad y quisiera comprar un periódico. ¿Me recomienda alguno?

Vendedor: Sí, señorita, le recomiendo el periódico *El Universal*.

Verónica: Ah, qué bien. Y... ¿Tiene una sección de arte y cultura en el periódico *El Universal*?

Vendedor: Sí, tiene todas las secciones: de deportes, de moda, de actualidad. De todo.

Verónica: ¡Ay! ¡Qué bien! ¿Me da uno por favor?

Vendedor: Sí, señorita. Aquí tiene. Ah, son dos pesos.

Verónica: Ah, muy bien. ¡Oiga! Y tengo otra pregunta.

Vendedor: Dígame.

Verónica: ¿Dónde está el Museo Botero?

Vendedor: Mire, el Museo Botero está cerca de aquí. El... ah... Mire, estamos en la Calle José Martí. Entonces siga derecho y cruce la Plaza de la Hispanidad, y entonces en la Avenida Emiliano Zapata, doble a la derecha, ¿no? Y siga derecho hasta llegar al Banco Hispano. Entonces, en el Banco Hispano doble a la izquierda y siga derecho hasta el Museo Botero que está a una cuadra...

Verónica: Ah...

Vendedor: ...enfrente de la Tienda Gómez.

Verónica: ¡Muy bien! Bueno, ¡muchísimas gracias por su ayuda!

Vendedor: No hay de qué. Hasta luego, señorita.

Verónica: ¡Hasta luego!

8.1   En la zapatería

Hombre: Buenos días, señora. ¿En qué puedo servirle?

Mujer: Buenos días. Quisiera comprar unos zapatos y me gustaría... que me enseñe unos en negro, otro en rojo y otro en blanco.

Hombre: ¿En qué tamaño los traigo, señora?

Mujer: En 39, por favor.

Hombre: Ahora se los traigo. ¡Pruébese estos negros!

Mujer: Ah, me encantan, se ven preciosos. ¡Ay no! , me quedan súper incómodos. No me gustan, quisiera tal vez... probarme los rojos, por favor.

Hombre: ¡Ok! Aquí se los traigo. ¡Pruébese estos rojos!

Mujer: Me quedan perfectos, gracias. Son muy cómodos. Me encantan.

Hombre: ¿Quiere probarse los blancos?

Mujer: Sí, porque parece que, que son buenos también, que son cómodos. Mmm. ¿Me podría traer un número más grande, por favor?

Hombre: Ahora se los traigo. Aquí le traje un número más grande, ¡pruébeselos!

Mujer: Ay, estos me quedan perfectos, gracias. Me gustan los... eh, rojos tanto como los blancos, así que creo que me voy a llevar los dos pares.

Hombre: ¿Con qué va a pagar, señora?

Mujer: Hoy no voy a utilizar la tarjeta de crédito. Hoy voy a pagar en efectivo, ¿está bien?

Hombre: Muy bien, no hay ningún problema.

Mujer: Gracias.

9.1   El accidente de María

María: Hola, Paula.

Paula: ¡María! ¿Qué haces con muletas?

María: ¡No sabes lo que me pasó anoche!

Paula: ¡Cuéntame!

María: Mira, iba conduciendo mientras hablaba por teléfono con mi novio.

Paula: ¿Cuántas veces te dije que no se puede conducir y hablar por teléfono?

María: Tienes razón, pero era una conversación muy importante.

Paula: Ya...

María: Por eso iba distraída, y además llovía, y la carretera resbalaba. Así que había una curva, y había... iba un chico caminando, que casi le atropellé, di un volantazo para no atropellar al chico, y me choqué contra un árbol. Estaba muy preocupada en aquel momento porque me dolía mucho la pierna y la nariz no paraba de sangrar.

Paula: ¿Fuiste al médico? ¿Alguien avisó a la ambulancia?

María: El chico llamó a la ambulancia. Vino la ambulancia y me llevaron al hospital. Y en el hospital el..., el doctor me hizo unas radiografías, me pusieron un yeso, y ahora... Mmm, tengo que llevar el yeso durante tres semanas y caminar con muletas.

Paula: Bueno, espero que te recuperes pronto.

María: Mmm. Sí. Yo también.

10.1 El proyecto para aumentar los impuestos

Catalina: Dudo que aprueben el proyecto para aumentar los impuestos.

Santiago: Yo también, y me alegro enormemente.

Catalina: ¡Ay, no! A mí sí me parece una lástima. Yo creo que, que necesitan recaudar muchos más fondos.

Santiago: Pero si suben los impuestos, las empresas van a tener que despedir una cantidad de gente.

Catalina: No creo. Es probable que, que tengan menos ganancias, pero lo que el gobierno recoja va a ayudar a..., a estimular muchos programas públicos, y yo creo que eso es muy bueno.

Santiago: Me parece medio ridículo. ¿Tú crees que el gobierno realmente va a hacer buen uso de los recursos?

Catalina: Es posible, es... Es en lo que tenemos que confiar en este momento.

Santiago: Bueno, de todas maneras, no sigamos discutiendo porque igual el proyecto no va a ser aprobado.

Catalina: Pues hay una probabilidad, y yo quiero confiar en ella.

Santiago: ¡Sigue soñando!

11.1 La entrevista de trabajo

Entrevistadora: Buenos días, señorita Pagador. Gracias por haber venido a nuestra entrevista. Quería hacerle un par de preguntas. ¿Dónde ha estudiado inglés usted?

Señorita Pagador: He estudiado inglés en la universidad de Chicago en los EE. UU., eh... De hecho, de ahí conseguí mi bachillerato en lingüística.

Entrevistadora: Ah, muy bien, y ¿ha tenido oportunidad de enseñar inglés?

Señorita Pagador: De hecho que sí. Durante 2 años enseñé inglés a emigrantes hispanos.

Entrevistadora: ¡Ah! ¡Qué interesante! Y... otra pregunta más: ¿por qué quisiera venir al Perú?

Señorita Pagador: Creo que para mí es una gran oportunidad de usar los conocimientos que pude adoptar mientras enseñaba inglés hace... hace 2 años.

Entrevistadora: Muy bien, y ¿quizás tenga algunas preguntas con respecto al puesto?

Señorita Pagador: De hecho que sí, eh..., quería saber si... ¿el puesto es a tiempo completo o a tiempo parcial?

Entrevistadora: Éste es un puesto a tiempo completo, es decir, que va a trabajar más o menos 8 horas por día.

Señorita Pagador: Y, ¿cómo son los estudiantes aquí?

Entrevistadora: Bueno, eh... Usted va a trabajar con ellos en la parte escrita. Los estudiantes hablan el inglés más o menos bien, pero pienso que necesitan un refuerzo con... Ah, la parte de redacción. El grupo de estudiantes no es muy grande, va a tener unos catorce estudiantes.

Señorita Pagador: Ah, muy bien. Ah... Bueno, una última pregunta: ¿cuándo tomará su decisión final sobre el puesto?

Entrevistadora: Bueno, eh, yo la voy a estar llamando... eh, probablemente a fines de esta semana. Tendré, creo, una respuesta el viernes, porque tengo que reunirme con mis colegas.

Señorita Pagador: Bueno, me parece perfecto. Muchas gracias por la entrevista y fue un gusto conocerla.

Entrevistadora: Por nada, señorita Pagador.

12.1   El Cuerpo de Paz

Doctora Losada: Buenos días, Ana. ¿Qué te trae por mi oficina?

Ana: Buenos días, Doctora Losada. Eh, mire, venía para preguntarle ¿si usted pudiera escribirme una recomendación para el cuerpo de paz?

Doctora Losada: Con todo gusto Ana, eh... Dime, ¿a dónde te gustaría viajar?

Ana: Me gustaría viajar a Argentina o tal vez Chile.

Doctora Losada: ¿Y me puedes decir que harías si te dieran, eh, la oportunidad de viajar?

Ana: Si me dieran la oportunidad, me gustaría trabajar en una posta médica, con niños.

Doctora Losada: Y dime, ¿ya tuviste experiencia eh... con ese tipo de trabajo en el pasado?

Ana: Sí, hace un par de años trabajé en un país de desarrollo, eh... con niños.

Doctora Losada: Ah, gracias. Y dime, eh.. ¿tengo tu ah... hoja de vida más reciente?

Ana: Creo que no, pero yo, yo podría mandársela si usted la requiere.

Doctora Losada: Ya sí, te voy a pedir que me mandes la copia de tu ah... hoja de vida, para que pueda escribir una carta eh... para el Cuerpo de Paz.

Ana: Bien, muchas gracias, le agradecería mucho su ayuda.

Doctora Losada: Con todo gusto Ana.

Apéndice 3: Verbos

Regular Verbs: Simple Tenses

Infinitive Present Participle Past Participle	Indicative					Subjunctive		Imperative (commands)
	Present	Imperfect	Preterit	Future	Conditional	Present	Imperfect	
hablar *to speak* hablando hablado	hablo hablas habla hablamos habláis hablan	hablaba hablabas hablaba hablábamos hablabais hablaban	hablé hablaste habló hablamos hablasteis hablaron	hablaré hablarás hablará hablaremos hablaréis hablarán	hablaría hablarías hablaría hablaríamos hablaríais hablarían	hable hables hable hablemos habléis hablen	hablara hablaras hablara habláramos hablarais hablaran	habla tú no hables hable Ud. hablen Uds. hablemos hablad no habléis
comer *to eat* comiendo comido	como comes come comemos coméis comen	comía comías comía comíamos comíais comían	comí comiste comió comimos comisteis comieron	comeré comerás comerá comeremos comeréis comerán	comería comerías comería comeríamos comeríais comerían	coma comas coma comamos comáis coman	comiera comieras comiera comiéramos comierais comieran	come tú no comas coma Ud. coman Uds. comamos comed no comáis
vivir *to live* viviendo vivido	vivo vives vive vivimos vivís viven	vivía vivías vivía vivíamos vivíais vivían	viví viviste vivió vivimos vivisteis vivieron	viviré vivirás vivirá viviremos viviréis vivirán	viviría vivirías viviría viviríamos viviríais vivirían	viva vivas viva vivamos viváis vivan	viviera vivieras viviera viviéramos vivierais vivieran	vive tú no vivas viva Ud. vivan Uds. vivamos vivid no viváis

Regular Verbs: Perfect Tenses

Indicative								Subjunctive			
Present Perfect		Past Perfect		Future Perfect		Conditional Perfect		Present Perfect		Past Perfect	
he has ha hemos habéis han	hablado comido vivido	había habías había habíamos habíais habían	hablado comido vivido	habré habrás habrá habremos habréis habrán	hablado comido vivido	habría habrías habría habríamos habríais habrían	hablado comido vivido	haya hayas haya hayamos hayáis hayan	hablado comido vivido	hubiera hubieras hubiera hubiéramos hubierais hubieran	hablado comido vivido

Stem-changing -ar and -er Verbs: e → ie; o → ue

Infinitive Present Participle Past Participle	Indicative					Subjunctive		Imperative (commands)
	Present	Imperfect	Preterit	Future	Conditional	Present	Imperfect	
pensar (ie) *to think* pensando pensado	**pienso** **piensas** **piensa** pensamos pensáis **piensan**	pensaba pensabas pensaba pensábamos pensabais pensaban	pensé pensaste pensó pensamos pensasteis pensaron	pensaré pensarás pensará pensaremos pensaréis pensarán	pensaría pensarías pensaría pensaríamos pensaríais pensarían	**piense** **pienses** **piense** pensemos penséis **piensen**	pensara pensaras pensara pensáramos pensarais pensaran	**piensa** tú no **pienses** **piense** Ud. **piensen** Uds. pensemos pensad no penséis
volver (ue) *to return* volviendo vuelto (irreg.)	**vuelvo** **vuelves** **vuelve** volvemos volvéis **vuelven**	volvía volvías volvía volvíamos volvíais volvían	volví volviste volvió volvimos volvisteis volvieron	volveré volverás volverá volveremos volveréis volverán	volvería volverías volvería volveríamos volveríais volverían	**vuelva** **vuelvas** **vuelva** volvamos volváis **vuelvan**	volviera volvieras volviera volviéramos volvierais volvieran	**vuelve** tú no **vuelvas** **vuelva** Ud. **vuelvan** Uds. volvamos volved no volváis

Other verbs of this type are:

e → ie: **atender, cerrar, despertarse, empezar, entender, nevar, pensar, perder, preferir, querer, recomendar, regar, sentarse**

o → ue: **acordarse de, acostarse, almorzar, colgar, costar, encontrar, jugar, mostrar, poder, probar, recordar, resolver, sonar, volar, volver**

Stem-changing -ir Verbs: e → ie, i; e → i, i; o → ue, u

Infinitive Present Participle Past Participle	Indicative					Subjunctive		Imperative (commands)
	Present	Imperfect	Preterit	Future	Conditional	Present	Imperfect	
sentir (ie, i) *to feel, regret* **sintiendo** sentido	**siento** **sientes** **siente** sentimos sentís **sienten**	sentía sentías sentía sentíamos sentíais sentían	sentí sentiste **sintió** sentimos sentisteis **sintieron**	sentiré sentirás sentirá sentiremos sentiréis sentirán	sentiría sentirías sentiría sentiríamos sentiríais sentirían	**sienta** **sientas** **sienta** **sintamos** **sintáis** **sientan**	**sintiera** **sintieras** **sintiera** **sintiéramos** **sintierais** **sintieran**	**siente** tú no **sientas** **sienta** Ud. **sientan** Uds. **sintamos** sentid no **sintáis**
pedir (i, i) *to ask (for)* **pidiendo** pedido	**pido** **pides** **pide** pedimos pedís **piden**	pedía pedías pedía pedíamos pedíais pedían	pedí pediste **pidió** pedimos pedisteis **pidieron**	pediré pedirás pedirá pediremos pediréis pedirán	pediría pedirías pediría pediríamos pediríais pedirían	**pida** **pidas** **pida** **pidamos** **pidáis** **pidan**	**pidiera** **pidieras** **pidiera** **pidiéramos** **pidierais** **pidieran**	**pide** tú no **pidas** **pida** Ud. **pidan** Uds. **pidamos** pedid no **pidáis**
dormir (ue, u) *to sleep* **durmiendo** dormido	**duermo** **duermes** **duerme** dormimos dormís **duermen**	dormía dormías dormía dormíamos dormíais dormían	dormí dormiste **durmió** dormimos dormisteis **durmieron**	dormiré dormirás dormirá dormiremos dormiréis dormirán	dormiría dormirías dormiría dormiríamos dormiríais dormirían	**duerma** **duermas** **duerma** **durmamos** **durmáis** **duerman**	**durmiera** **durmieras** **durmiera** **durmiéramos** **durmierais** **durmieran**	**duerme** tú no **duermas** **duerma** Ud. **duerman** Uds. **durmamos** dormid no **durmáis**

Other verbs of this type are:

e → ie, i: **divertirse, invertir, preferir, sentirse**

e → i, i: **conseguir, despedirse de, reírse, repetir, seguir, servir, teñirse, vestirse**

o → ue, u: **morir(se)**

Verbs with Spelling Changes

1. c → qu: tocar (model); also buscar, explicar, pescar, sacar

Infinitive / Present Participle / Past Participle	Indicative					Subjunctive		Imperative (commands)
	Present	Imperfect	Preterit	Future	Conditional	Present	Imperfect	
tocar *to play (musical instrument), touch* tocando tocado	toco tocas toca tocamos tocáis tocan	tocaba tocabas tocaba tocábamos tocabais tocaban	**toqué** tocaste tocó tocamos tocasteis tocaron	tocaré tocarás tocará tocaremos tocaréis tocarán	tocaría tocarías tocaría tocaríamos tocaríais tocarían	**toque** **toques** **toque** **toquemos** **toquéis** **toquen**	tocara tocaras tocara tocáramos tocarais tocaran	toca tú no **toques** **toque** Ud. **toquen** Uds. **toquemos** tocad no **toquéis**

2. z → c: abrazar; also almorzar, cruzar, empezar (ie)

Infinitive / Present Participle / Past Participle	Indicative					Subjunctive		Imperative (commands)
	Present	Imperfect	Preterit	Future	Conditional	Present	Imperfect	
abrazar *to hug* abrazando abrazado	abrazo abrazas abraza abrazamos abrazáis abrazan	abrazaba abrazabas abrazaba abrazábamos abrazabais abrazaban	**abracé** abrazaste abrazó abrazamos abrazasteis abrazaron	abrazaré abrazarás abrazará abrazaremos abrazaréis abrazarán	abrazaría abrazarías abrazaría abrazaríamos abrazaríais abrazarían	**abrace** **abraces** **abrace** **abracemos** **abracéis** **abracen**	abrazara abrazaras abrazara abrazáramos abrazarais abrazaran	abraza tú no **abraces** **abrace** Ud. **abracen** Uds. **abracemos** abrazad no **abracéis**

3. g → gu: pagar; also apagar, jugar (ue), llegar

Infinitive / Present Participle / Past Participle	Indicative					Subjunctive		Imperative (commands)
	Present	Imperfect	Preterit	Future	Conditional	Present	Imperfect	
pagar *to pay (for)* pagando pagado	pago pagas paga pagamos pagáis pagan	pagaba pagabas pagaba pagábamos pagabais pagaban	**pagué** pagaste pagó pagamos pagasteis pagaron	pagaré pagarás pagará pagaremos pagaréis pagarán	pagaría pagarías pagaría pagaríamos pagaríais pagarían	**pague** **pagues** **pague** **paguemos** **paguéis** **paguen**	pagara pagaras pagara pagáramos pagarais pagaran	paga tú no **pagues** **pague** Ud. **paguen** Uds. **paguemos** pagad no **paguéis**

4. gu → g: seguir (i, i); also conseguir

Infinitive / Present Participle / Past Participle	Indicative					Subjunctive		Imperative (commands)
	Present	Imperfect	Preterit	Future	Conditional	Present	Imperfect	
seguir (i, i) *to follow* siguiendo seguido	**sigo** sigues sigue seguimos seguís siguen	seguía seguías seguía seguíamos seguíais seguían	seguí seguiste siguió seguimos seguisteis siguieron	seguiré seguirás seguirá seguiremos seguiréis seguirán	seguiría seguirías seguiría seguiríamos seguiríais seguirían	**siga** **sigas** **siga** **sigamos** **sigáis** **sigan**	siguiera siguieras siguiera siguiéramos siguierais siguieran	sigue tú no **sigas** **siga** Ud. **sigan** Uds. **sigamos** seguid no **sigáis**

5. g → j: recoger; also escoger, proteger

Infinitive / Present Participle / Past Participle	Present	Imperfect	Preterit	Future	Conditional	Present (Subj.)	Imperfect (Subj.)	Imperative
recoger *to pick up* recogiendo recogido	recojo recoges recoge recogemos recogéis recogen	recogía recogías recogía recogíamos recogíais recogían	recogí recogiste recogió recogimos recogisteis recogieron	recogeré recogerás recogerá recogeremos recogeréis recogerán	recogería recogerías recogería recogeríamos recogeríais recogerían	recoja recojas recoja recojamos recojáis recojan	recogiera recogieras recogiera recogiéramos recogierais recogieran	recoge tú no recojas recoja Ud. recojan Uds. recojamos recoged no recojáis

6. i → y: leer; also caer, oír. Verbs with additional i → y changes: construir; also destruir, contribuir

Infinitive / Present Participle / Past Participle	Present	Imperfect	Preterit	Future	Conditional	Present (Subj.)	Imperfect (Subj.)	Imperative
leer *to read* leyendo leído	leo lees lee leemos leéis leen	leía leías leía leíamos leíais leían	leí leíste leyó leímos leísteis leyeron	leeré leerás leerá leeremos leeréis leerán	leería leerías leería leeríamos leeríais leerían	lea leas lea leamos leáis lean	leyera leyeras leyera leyéramos leyerais leyeran	lee tú no leas lea Ud. lean Uds. leamos leed no leáis
construir *to construct, build* construyendo construido	construyo construyes construye construimos construís construyen	construía construías construía construíamos construíais construían	construí construiste construyó construimos construisteis construyeron	construiré construirás construirá construiremos construiréis construirán	construiría construirías construiría construiríamos construiríais construirían	construya construyas construya construyamos construyáis construyan	construyera construyeras construyera construyéramos construyerais construyeran	construye tú no construyas construya Ud. construyan Uds. construyamos construid no construyáis

Irregular Verbs

Infinitive Present Participle Past Participle	Indicative					Subjunctive		Imperative
	Present	Imperfect	Preterit	Future	Conditional	Present	Imperfect	
caer *to fall* cayendo caído	caigo caes cae caemos caéis caen	caía caías caía caíamos caíais caían	caí caíste cayó caímos caísteis cayeron	caeré caerás caerá caeremos caeréis caerán	caería caerías caería caeríamos caeríais caerían	caiga caigas caiga caigamos caigáis caigan	cayera cayeras cayera cayéramos cayerais cayeran	cae tú no caigas caiga Ud. caigan Uds. caigamos caed no caigáis

Infinitive / Participles	Present	Imperfect	Preterite	Future	Conditional	Present Subjunctive	Imperfect Subjunctive	Commands
conocer *to know, to be acquainted with* conociendo conocido	conozco conoces conoce conocemos conocéis conocen	conocía conocías conocía conocíamos conocíais conocían	conocí conociste conoció conocimos conocisteis conocieron	conoceré conocerás conocerá conoceremos conoceréis conocerán	conocería conocerías conocería conoceríamos conoceríais conocerían	conozca conozcas conozca conozcamos conozcáis conozcan	conociera conocieras conociera conociéramos conocierais conocieran	conoce tú, no conozcas conozca Ud. conozcan Uds. conozcamos conoced no conozcáis
dar *to give* dando dado	doy das da damos dais dan	daba dabas daba dábamos dabais daban	di diste dio dimos disteis dieron	daré darás dará daremos daréis darán	daría darías daría daríamos daríais darían	dé des dé demos deis den	diera dieras diera diéramos dierais dieran	da tú, no des dé Ud. den Uds. demos dad no déis
decir *to say, tell* diciendo dicho	digo dices dice decimos decís dicen	decía decías decía decíamos decíais decían	dije dijiste dijo dijimos dijisteis dijeron	diré dirás dirá diremos diréis dirán	diría dirías diría diríamos diríais dirían	diga digas diga digamos digáis digan	dijera dijeras dijera dijéramos dijerais dijeran	di tú, no digas diga Ud. digan Uds. digamos decid no digáis
estar *to be* estando estado	estoy estás está estamos estáis están	estaba estabas estaba estábamos estabais estaban	estuve estuviste estuvo estuvimos estuvisteis estuvieron	estaré estarás estará estaremos estaréis estarán	estaría estarías estaría estaríamos estaríais estarían	esté estés esté estemos estéis estén	estuviera estuvieras estuviera estuviéramos estuvierais estuvieran	estés tú, no estés esté Ud. estén Uds. estemos estad no estéis
haber *to have* habiendo habido	he has ha hemos habéis han	había habías había habíamos habíais habían	hube hubiste hubo hubimos hubisteis hubieron	habré habrás habrá habremos habréis habrán	habría habrías habría habríamos habríais habrían	haya hayas haya hayamos hayáis hayan	hubiera hubieras hubiera hubiéramos hubierais hubieran	
hacer *to do, make* haciendo hecho	hago haces hace hacemos hacéis hacen	hacía hacías hacía hacíamos hacíais hacían	hice hiciste hizo hicimos hicisteis hicieron	haré harás hará haremos haréis harán	haría harías haría haríamos haríais harían	haga hagas haga hagamos hagáis hagan	hiciera hicieras hiciera hiciéramos hicierais hicieran	haz tú, no hagas haga Ud. hagan Uds. hagamos haced no hagáis

Infinitive	Present	Imperfect	Preterite	Future	Conditional	Present Subjunctive	Imperfect Subjunctive	Commands
ir *to go* **yendo** ido	voy / vas / va / vamos / vais / van	iba / ibas / iba / íbamos / ibais / iban	fui / fuiste / fue / fuimos / fuisteis / fueron	iré / irás / irá / iremos / iréis / irán	iría / irías / iría / iríamos / iríais / irían	vaya / vayas / vaya / vayamos / vayáis / vayan	fuera / fueras / fuera / fuéramos / fuerais / fueran	ve tú, no vayas / vaya Ud. / vayan Uds. / vayamos / id, no vayáis
oír *to hear* **oyendo** **oído**	oigo / oyes / oye / oímos / oís / oyen	oía / oías / oía / oíamos / oíais / oían	oí / oíste / oyó / oímos / oísteis / oyeron	oiré / oirás / oirá / oiremos / oiréis / oirán	oiría / oirías / oiría / oiríamos / oiríais / oirían	oiga / oigas / oiga / oigamos / oigáis / oigan	oyera / oyeras / oyera / oyéramos / oyerais / oyeran	oye tú, no oigas / oiga Ud. / oigan Uds. / oigamos / oíd, no oigáis
poder (ue) *to be able, can* pudiendo podido	**puedo** / **puedes** / **puede** / podemos / podéis / **pueden**	podía / podías / podía / podíamos / podíais / podían	**pude** / **pudiste** / **pudo** / **pudimos** / **pudisteis** / **pudieron**	**podré** / **podrás** / **podrá** / **podremos** / **podréis** / **podrán**	**podría** / **podrías** / **podría** / **podríamos** / **podríais** / **podrían**	**pueda** / **puedas** / **pueda** / podamos / podáis / puedan	pudiera / pudieras / pudiera / pudiéramos / pudierais / pudieran	
poner *to put, place* poniendo **puesto**	**pongo** / pones / pone / ponemos / ponéis / ponen	ponía / ponías / ponía / poníamos / poníais / ponían	**puse** / **pusiste** / **puso** / **pusimos** / **pusisteis** / **pusieron**	**pondré** / **pondrás** / **pondrá** / **pondremos** / **pondréis** / **pondrán**	**pondría** / **pondrías** / **pondría** / **pondríamos** / **pondríais** / **pondrían**	ponga / pongas / ponga / pongamos / pongáis / pongan	pusiera / pusieras / pusiera / pusiéramos / pusierais / pusieran	**pon tú**, no pongas / ponga Ud. / pongan Uds. / pongamos / poned, no pongáis
querer (ie) *to wish, want, love* queriendo querido	**quiero** / **quieres** / **quiere** / queremos / queréis / **quieren**	quería / querías / quería / queríamos / queríais / querían	**quise** / **quisiste** / **quiso** / **quisimos** / **quisisteis** / **quisieron**	**querré** / **querrás** / **querrá** / **querremos** / **querréis** / **querrán**	**querría** / **querrías** / **querría** / **querríamos** / **querríais** / **querrían**	quiera / quieras / quiera / queramos / queráis / quieran	quisiera / quisieras / quisiera / quisiéramos / quisierais / quisieran	quiere tú, no quieras / quiera Ud. / quieran Uds. / queramos / quered, no queráis

Infinitive Present Participle Past Participle	Present	Imperfect	Preterite	Future	Conditional	Present Subjunctive	Imperfect Subjunctive	Commands
saber *to know* sabiendo sabido	sé sabes sabe sabemos sabéis saben	sabía sabías sabía sabíamos sabíais sabían	supe supiste supo supimos supisteis supieron	sabré sabrás sabrá sabremos sabréis sabrán	sabría sabrías sabría sabríamos sabríais sabrían	sepa sepas sepa sepamos sepáis sepan	supiera supieras supiera supiéramos supierais supieran	sabe tú, no sepas sepa Ud. sepan Uds. sepamos sabed, no sepáis
salir *to leave, go out* saliendo salido	salgo sales sale salimos salís salen	salía salías salía salíamos salíais salían	salí saliste salió salimos salisteis salieron	saldré saldrás saldrá saldremos saldréis saldrán	saldría saldrías saldría saldríamos saldríais saldrían	salga salgas salga salgamos salgáis salgan	saliera salieras saliera saliéramos salierais salieran	sal tú, no salgas salga Ud. salgan Uds. salgamos salid, no salgáis
ser *to be* siendo sido	soy eres es somos sois son	era eras era éramos erais eran	fui fuiste fue fuimos fuisteis fueron	seré serás será seremos seréis serán	sería serías sería seríamos seríais serían	sea seas sea seamos seáis sean	fuera fueras fuera fuéramos fuerais fueran	sé tú, no seas sea Ud. sean Uds. seamos sed, no seáis
tener *to have* teniendo tenido	tengo tienes tiene tenemos tenéis tienen	tenía tenías tenía teníamos teníais tenían	tuve tuviste tuvo tuvimos tuvisteis tuvieron	tendré tendrás tendrá tendremos tendréis tendrán	tendría tendrías tendría tendríamos tendríais tendrían	tenga tengas tenga tengamos tengáis tengan	tuviera tuvieras tuviera tuviéramos tuvierais tuvieran	ten tú, no tengas tenga Ud. tengan Uds. tengamos tened, no tengáis
traer *to bring* trayendo traído	traigo traes trae traemos traéis traen	traía traías traía traíamos traíais traían	traje trajiste trajo trajimos trajisteis trajeron	traeré traerás traerá traeremos traeréis traerán	traería traerías traería traeríamos traeríais traerían	traiga traigas traiga traigamos traigáis traigan	trajera trajeras trajera trajéramos trajerais trajeran	trae tú, no traigas traiga Ud. traigan Uds. traigamos traed, no traigáis

Infinitive	Present	Imperfect	Preterite	Future	Conditional	Present Subjunctive	Imperfect Subjunctive	Commands
venir *to come* **viendo** venido (also **prevenir**)	**vengo** **vienes** **viene** venimos venís **vienen**	venía venías venía veníamos veníais venían	**vine** **viniste** **vino** **vinimos** **vinisteis** **vinieron**	**vendré** **vendrás** **vendrá** **vendremos** **vendréis** **vendrán**	**vendría** **vendrías** **vendría** **vendríamos** **vendríais** **vendrían**	venga vengas venga vengamos vengáis vengan	viniera vinieras viniera viniéramos vinierais vinieran	**ven** tú no vengas venga Ud. vengan Uds. vengamos venid no vengáis
ver *to see* viendo **visto**	**veo** ves ve vemos veis ven	**veía** **veías** **veía** **veíamos** **veíais** **veían**	**vi** viste **vio** vimos visteis vieron	veré verás verá veremos veréis verán	vería verías vería veríamos veríais verían	vea veas vea veamos veáis vean	viera vieras viera viéramos vierais vieran	ve tú no veas vea Ud. vean Uds. veamos ved no veáis

Glosario: español-inglés

Note: The glossary that follows is not a dictionary. It only contains words and expressions presented as active vocabulary in *¡Con brío!*

Gender of nouns is indicated except for masculine nouns ending in **-o** and feminine nouns ending in **-a.** Verbs appear in the infinitive form. The number following the entries refers to the chapter in which the word or phrase first appears. The following abbreviations are used in this glossary:

adj.	adjective	*form.*	formal	*pl.*	plural
adv.	adverb	*inform.*	informal	*prep.*	preposition
conj.	conjunction	*m.*	masculine	*pron.*	pronoun
f.	feminine	*n.*	noun	*s.*	singular

A

a *prep.* at, to 2
abierto/a open 2
abogado/a *m./f.* lawyer 2
abrazar to hug 3
abrigo coat 8
abril April 1
abrir to open 7
abrocharse el cinturón to fasten one's seatbelt 7
abuela grandmother 3
abuelo grandfather 3
aburrido/a bored 2
aburrirse to get bored 11
acabar de + *infinitivo* to have just done something 10
acampar to camp 4
acción *f.* share (stock) 11
aceite *m.* oil 5
aceituna olive 5
acera sidewalk 10
acerca de *prep.* about (a topic) 6
aconsejar to advise 10
acordarse (ue) de to remember 10
acostarse (ue) to go to bed 6
acuerdo de paz peace treaty 12
acuerdo: estar de acuerdo to agree 10
adiós good-bye 1
aduana customs 12
adultos *m. pl.* adults 3
aerolínea airline 12
aeropuerto airport 12
afeitarse to shave 6
agnóstico/a agnostic 10
agosto August 1
agua *f.* (*but* **el agua**) water 5; **agua potable** potable water 12
ahora now 2
ahorrar to save (time, money) 10
aire *m.* **acondicionado** air conditioning 12
ajo garlic 5
al + *infinitivo* upon (doing something) 6; **al lado de** beside *prep.* 2
alcalde/ alcaldesa mayor 10
alegrarse (de) to be glad/ happy (about) 10
alemán (alemana) *n. adj.* German 2
alfombra rug, carpet 6
álgebra *f.* (*but* **el álgebra**) algebra 2
algo something 6
algodón *m.* cotton 8
alguien someone 6

algún (alguno/a/os/as) any, some 10; **algún día** someday, sometime 4
allí there 2
almohada pillow 12
almorzar (ue) to have lunch 5
almuerzo lunch 5
¿Aló? Hello? 11
alquilar to rent 6; **se alquila** for rent 6
alrededor de around 12
alto stop (road sign) 7
alto/a *adj.* tall 3
altoparlantes *m. pl.* loudspeakers 8
alumno/a student 1
ama de casa *f.* (but **el ama...**) homemaker 2
amable kind, pleasant 5
amar to love 3
amarillo/a yellow 2
amigo/a friend 1; **mejor amigo/a** best friend 3
amistad *f.* friendship 3
amor *m.* love 3
anaranjado/a orange 2
ancianos *n. pl.* elderly 3
anexo attachment 11
anillo (de diamante) (diamond) ring 8
anoche *adv.* last night 7
anteayer *adv.* day before yesterday 7
antes de *conj.* before 6
antipático/a disagreeable, unpleasant 3
anuncio ad 8
año year 1; **Año Nuevo** New Year's 1; **año pasado** last year 7; **año que viene** next year 4
apagar to turn off 8
aparato electrónico electronic device/ equipment 8
aplaudir to applaud 10
apoyar to support 8
apoyo support 8
aprender (a) to learn (to) 4
aquí *adv.* here 2
árabe *n. adj.* Arabic 2
árbol *m.* tree 4
archivo file 11
arena sand 4
arete *m.* earring 8
arma *f.* (*but* **el arma**) weapon 10
arquitectura architecture 2
arroba @ 11
arroz *m.* rice 5
arte *m.* art 2

arveja pea 5
ascensor *m.* elevator 12
asiento seat 12; **asiento de pasillo/ de ventanilla** aisle/ window seat 12
asistir a to attend 4
aspiradora vacuum cleaner 6; **pasar la aspiradora** to vacuum 6
asunto subject 11
ataque: sufrir un ataque al corazón to have a heart attack 9
atender (ie) to look after, tend 10
atentamente truly yours 11
ateo/a atheist 10
atún *m.* tuna 5
audífonos headphones 8
aumento raise, increase (in salary, production, etc.) 11
autobús *m.* bus 2
autopista freeway 7
auxiliar de vuelo *m.* flight attendant 12
avenida avenue 2
avión *m.* airplane 12; **perder el avión** to miss the plane 12
ayer *adv.* yesterday 7
ayudar to help 3
azafata *f.* flight attendant 12
azúcar *m.* sugar 5
azul blue 2

B

bailar to dance 4
bajar to go down 6
bajo/a short 3
banana banana 5
banco bank, bench 7
banda band 10
bañarse to take a bath 6
bañera bathtub 6
baño restroom 7; **cuarto de baño** bathroom 6
barato/a cheap, inexpensive 8
barrer to sweep 6
barrio neighborhood 10
basura garbage 6; **cubo de la basura** garbage can 6; **sacar la basura** to take out the trash 6
bebé *m./f.* baby 3
beber to drink 4
bebida drink 5
beige beige 2
beneficio benefit 11
besar to kiss 3
biblioteca library 2
bicicleta bicycle 2
Bien. Fine. Okay. 1; **Muy bien, gracias.** Very well, thanks. 1
bikini *m.* bikini 8
billetera wallet 8
biología biology 2
bistec *m.* steak 5
blanco/a white 2
blusa blouse 8
boca mouth 9
boda wedding 3
boleto ticket (movie/ theater/ bus/ plane/ train) 7
bolígrafo pen 1
bolsa bag; purse, handbag 8
Bolsa stock market 11
bombero/a *m./f.* firefighter 2
bonito/a pretty 3
borrador *m.* eraser 2

borrar to delete, erase 11
bosque *m.* forest 4
bota boot 8
botones *m. s.* bellhop 12
brazo arm 9
brócoli *m.* broccoli 5
bucear to snorkel 4
bueno/a good 3
bufanda scarf 8
buscar to look for 5
buzón *m.* mailbox 7

C

cabeza head 9; **tener dolor de cabeza** to have a headache 9
cadena chain 8
caerse to fall 9
café *m.* coffee 5; **(color) café** brown 2
cafetería cafeteria 2
cajero/a *m./f.* cashier 2
cajero automático ATM 7
calcetín *m.* sock 8
cálculo calculus 2
calefacción *f.* heating 12
calle *f.* street 2
calor: Hace (mucho) calor. It is (very) hot. 4; **tener calor** to be hot 8
calvo/a bald 3
cama bed 6; **hacer la cama** to make the bed 6
cámara digital digital camera 8
camarón *m.* shrimp 5
cambiar to change; to exchange 7
camilla stretcher 9
caminar to walk 4
camino: Estoy en camino. I'm on my way. 7
camión *m.* truck 10; **camión de la basura** garbage truck 10
camisa shirt 8
camiseta t-shirt 8
campaña electoral electoral campaign 10
campo field, countryside 4
cansado/a tired 2
cantar to sing 4
cara face 9
cariñoso/a affectionate 3
carne *f.* **de res** beef 5
caro/a expensive 8
carretera highway, road 7
carro car 2; **carro híbrido** hybrid car 12; **Mi carro se descompuso.** My car broke down. 7
carta letter 11; **carta de recomendación** letter of recommendation 11
cartera purse, handbag 8
cartero/a mail carrier 10
casa house 6; **en casa** at home 2
casado: estar casado/a to be married 3; **recién casados** newlyweds 3
casarse to get married 10
cascada waterfall 12
casi *adv.* almost 3
catarata waterfall 12
catedral *f.* cathedral 10
católico/a Catholic 10
catorce fourteen 1
cebolla onion 5
celular *m.* cell phone 8

cena dinner 5

cenar to have dinner 3

centro downtown 7; **centro comercial** mall 8; **centro estudiantil** student center 2

cepillarse (los dientes) to brush (one's teeth) 6

cepillo de dientes toothbrush 6

cerca de *prep.* near 2

cereal *m.* cereal 5

cerebro brain 9

cereza cherry 5

cero zero 1

cerrado/a closed 2

cerrar (ie) to close 7

cerveza beer 5

champú *m.* shampoo 6

Chao. Bye. 1

chaqueta jacket 8

charlar (con) to chat (with) 3

cheque *m.* check 7

chica child, girl 3

chícharo pea 5

chicle *m.* chewing gum 10

chico child, boy 3

chimenea fireplace, chimney 6

chino/a *n. adj.* Chinese 2

chocar to crash 9

chuleta de cerdo pork chop 5

cielo sky 4

cien mil one hundred thousand 5

cien one hundred 3, 5

ciencia science 12; **ciencias políticas** political science 2

ciento uno one hundred one 5

cinco five 1

cincuenta fifty 1

cine *m.* movie theater 7

cinturón *m.* belt 8

cirujano/a surgeon 9

cita appointment, date 9

ciudad *f.* city 4

ciudadano/a citizen 10

clase *f.* class 1

clima *m.* weather 4

cobija blanket 12

cobrar to cash; to charge 7

cocina kitchen 5, 6

código de área area code 11

colega *m./f.* colleague 11

colgar (ue) to hang 10

collar *m.* necklace 8

comedor *m.* dining room 6

comer to eat 4

comida food, meal 5

cómo how 2; **¿Cómo está usted?** *form.* How are you? 1; **¿Cómo estás?** *inform.* How are you? 1; **¿Cómo se llama usted?** *form.* What is your name? 1; **¿Cómo te llamas?** *inform.* What is your name? 1

cómoda dresser 6

cómodo/a comfortable 8

compañero/a de clase classmate 2

compartir to share 4

comprar to buy 3

compras: hacer las compras to buy groceries, run errands 6

comprometerse to get engaged 10

comprometido: estar comprometido/a to be engaged 3

computadora computer 1; **computadora portátil** laptop 8

comunicarse to communicate 12

con *prep.* with 5; **con frecuencia** *adv.* frequently 3; **Con permiso.** Excuse me (to ask permission to pass by someone or to leave). 1

congestionado: estar congestionado/a to be congested 9

conocer to know, be acquainted with 4

conseguir (i, i) to get, obtain 12

conservador/a conservative 10

construir to construct 10

consultorio médico doctor's office 9

contabilidad *f.* accounting 2

contador/a *m./f.* accountant 2

contaminación *f.* pollution 12

contar (ue) to count 5; to tell, narrate (a story or incident) 5

contento/a happy 2

contestador automático *m.* answering machine 8

contestar to answer 6

contribuir to contribute 12

control remoto *m.* remote control 8

copa wine glass, goblet 5

copiar to copy 11

corazón *m.* heart 9; **sufrir un ataque al corazón** to have a heart attack 9

corbata tie 8

cordillera mountain range 12

correr to run 4

correo: oficina de correos post office 7

cortar to cut 5; **cortar el césped** to mow the lawn 6; **cortarse el pelo** to get a haircut, to cut one's hair 7

cortina curtain 6

corto/a short 8

costar (ue) to cost 5

creer (que) to believe, think (that) 4; **no creer** not to believe 10

crema cream 5

crimen *m.* crime 10

cruzar to cross 7

cuaderno notebook 1

cuadra block 7; **a una cuadra** a block away 7

cuándo when 2

¿cuánto/a? how much? 2

¿cuántos/as? How many? 1, 2

cuarenta forty 1

cuarenta y uno forty one 1

cuarto room 6; **y cuarto** fifteen past/ quarter after (the hour) 1

cuarto/a fourth 11

cuatro four 1

cuatrocientos/as four hundred 5

cubículo cubicle 11

cubo de la basura garbage can 6

cuchara spoon 5

cuchillo knife 5

cuello neck 9

cuenta account 7; bill 5

cuerpo humano the human body 9

cuidado: tener cuidado to be careful 9

cuidar(se) to take care of (yourself/oneself) 3, 9

cultivar to grow (crops) 12

cumpleaños *m. s.* birthday 1

cuñado/a brother-in-law/ sister-in-law 3

cura cure 9

currículo résumé 11

D

dar to give 4; **dar de comer** to feed 10; **dar fiestas** to give/ throw parties 4; **dar un paseo** to take a walk/stroll 4

de from, of 1; **De nada.** You're welcome. 1; **de repente** suddenly 9

debajo de *adv.* beneath, below, under 6
deber (+ *infinitivo*) should/ must/ ought to (*do something*) 4
décimo/a tenth 11
decir to say, tell 4
dedo finger 9; **dedo del pie** toe 9
dejar to leave (behind) 5; **dejar de** + *infinitivo* to stop (*doing something*) 9
delante de *prep.* in front of 2
delgado/a thin, slender 3
demasiado *adv.* too (much) 8
dentro de *adv.* within, inside (of) 6
dependiente/a *m./f.* salesclerk 2
deporte *m.* sport 4; **practicar deportes** to play, go out for sports 4
derecha: a la derecha to the right, on the right 7
derecho law 2, straight ahead 7; **derechos humanos** human rights 10
desayunar to have breakfast 3
desayuno breakfast 5
descansar to rest 4
descanso break, rest 11
desear to want, wish, desire 5
desierto desert 12
desordenado/a disorganized, messy 3
despedirse (i) (de) to say good-bye (to) 6
despertador *m.* alarm clock 6
despertarse (ie) to wake up 6
despido layoff 11
después de *prep.* after 2, 6
destrucción *f.* **de la capa de ozono** destruction of the ozone layer 12
desventaja disadvantage 12
detrás de *prep.* behind 2
deuda debt 11
devolver (ue) to return (something) 7
día *m.* day 1; **Buenos días.** Good morning. 1; **día festivo** holiday 11; **día laboral** workday 11; **todo el día** all day 3; **todos los días** every day 3
diagnosticar to diagnose 12
dibujar to draw 4
diciembre December 1
diecinueve nineteen 1
dieciocho eighteen 1
dieciséis sixteen 1
diecisiete seventeen 1
diente tooth 6; **cepillarse los dientes** to brush one's teeth 6
diez ten 1
difícil difficult 3
dinero money 5
Dios *m.* God 10
dirección *f.* address 11
discapacitado/a disabled 9
discutir to argue 10
disfrutar de to enjoy 4
diversidad *f.* diversity 12
divertido/a funny, fun 3
divertirse (ie) to have fun/ a good time 6
divorciarse to get divorced 10; **estar divorciado/a** to be divorced 3
doblar to turn 7; **doblar la ropa** to fold the clothes 6
doce twelve 1
documento document 11
doler (ue) to hurt 9
dolor *m.* pain; **tener dolor de cabeza/ estómago** to have a headache/ stomachache 9
domingo Sunday 1
donar to donate 10
dónde where 2; **¿De dónde eres?/¿De dónde es usted?** *inform./form.* Where are you from? 1
dormir (ue) to sleep 5; **dormirse (ue)** to fall asleep 6

dormitorio bedroom 6
dos mil two thousand 5
dos millones two million 5
dos two 1
doscientos mil two hundred thousand 5
doscientos/as two hundred 5
ducha shower 6
ducharse to take a shower 6
dudar to doubt 10
dueño/a owner 10
dulce *m.* sweet, candy 10
durante during 6
durazno peach 5

E

economía economy 11; economics 2
edificio building 2
efectivo: en efectivo cash 8
ejecutivo/a executive 11
ejercicio: hacer ejercicio to exercise 4
eliminar to eliminate 12
embarazada: estar embarazada to be pregnant 9
emergencia emergency 9; **sala de emergencias** emergency room 9
emigrante *m./f.* emigrant 12
emigrar to emigrate 12
empezar (ie) to begin, start 7
empleado/a employee 11
empleo: solicitar empleo to look for a job 11; **solicitud** *f.* **de empleo** job application 11
empresa corporation 11
en in, at 2
enamorarse to fall in love 10; **estar enamorado/a** to be in love 3
Encantado/a. I'm delighted to meet you. 1
encantar to like a lot, love 4
encima de *adv.* on top of, above 6
encontrar (ue) to find 7; **encontrarse (ue) (con)** to meet up (with) (by chance) 7
energía: energía eólica (del viento) aeolic (wind energy) 12; **energía solar** solar energy 12
enero January 1
enfermarse to get sick 9
enfermedad *f.* illness, disease 9, 12
enfermería nursing 2
enfermero/a *m./f.* nurse 2
enfermo/a sick 2
enfrente de *adv.* opposite, facing 2
enojado/a angry 2
ensalada salad 5
enseñar to teach, show 10
entender (ie) to understand 5
entrada entrance 7
entrar (a/en) to enter 7
entre *prep.* between 2
entrevista interview 11
enviar to send 11
equipaje luggage, baggage 12; **facturar el equipaje** to check the luggage/ baggage 12
equipo team 4; **equipo de DVD y video** DVD/VCR player 8
equivocarse to be mistaken, make a mistake 11
escalera stairs 6
escribir to write 4
escritorio desk 1
escuchar (música) to listen to (music) 4

escuela school 2; **en la escuela** at school 2
espalda back 9
español (española) *n. adj.* Spanish 2
espejo mirror 6
espera: sala de espera waiting room 9
esperar to hope, expect 10; to wait for 7
esposa wife 3
esposo husband 3
esquiar to ski 4
esquina corner 7
estación *f.* season 4; **estación de tren** train station 7
estacionamiento parking 2
estacionar to park 7
estadio de deportes stadium 2
estadística statistics 4
estante *m.* bookcase, shelf 6
estar to be 2; **estar a favor de/ en contra de** to be in favor of/against 10
estatua statue 2
estimado/a dear 11
estómago stomach 9; **tener dolor de estómago** to have a stomachache 9
estrella star 4
estresado/a stressed 2
estudiante *m./f.* student 1
estudiar to study 3
estufa stove 6
evitar to avoid 12
examen *m.* exam 2
examinar to examine 9
éxito: tener éxito to succeed, be successful 11
experiencia experience 11
explicar to explain 7
exploración *f.* **espacial** space exploration 12
extrañar to miss 10

F

fábrica factory 11
fácil easy 3
facturar el equipaje to check the luggage/ baggage 12
facultad *f.* school (of a university) 2; **Facultad de Administración de Empresas** Business School 2; **Facultad de Ciencias** School of Sciences 2; **Facultad de Derecho** Law School 2; **Facultad de Filosofía y Letras** School of Arts 2; **Facultad de Medicina** Medical School 2
falda skirt 8
familia family 3
febrero February 1
fecha date 1; **¿Qué fecha es hoy?** What is today's date? 1
feo/a (un poco) ugly (a little bit) 3
fiebre: tener fiebre to have a fever 9
fila: hacer fila to wait in line 7
filosofía philosophy 2
fin *m.* end 12; **este fin de semana** this weekend 2; **fin de semana pasado** last weekend 7; **los fines de semana** on weekends 3
firmar to sign 7
física physics 2
flan *m.* caramel custard 5
flor *f.* flower 4
foto: tomar fotos to take photos 8
fotocopiadora photocopier 11
fotocopiar to photocopy 11
fracturarse to fracture 9

francés (francesa) *n. adj.* French 2
fregadero kitchen sink 6
freno brake
fresa strawberry 5
fresco: Hace fresco. It is cool. 4
frijol *m.* bean 5
frío cold 4; **Hace (mucho) frío.** It is (very) cold. 4; **tener frío** to be cold 8
frito/a fried 5
frontera border 12
fruta fruit 5
fuego fire 10
fuente *f.* fountain 7
fuera de *adv.* outside (of) 6
fuerte strong 3
fumar to smoke 9
funcionar to work (machinery) 7

G

gafas de sol sunglasses 8
galleta cookie 5
ganancia profit 11
ganar to earn 11; to win 4
ganas: tener ganas de + *infinitivo* to feel like (*doing something*) 11
garaje *m.* garage 6
garganta throat 9; **Me duele la garganta.** My throat hurts. 9
gasolinera gas station 7
gastar to spend 8
gato cat 3
gente *f.* people 7
geografía geography 2
geometría geometry 2
gerente *m./f.* **de ventas** sales manager 11
gimnasio gym 2
gobierno government 12
gordo/a (un poco) fat (a little bit) 3
gorra de béisbol baseball cap 8
gorro de lana wool cap 8
Gracias. Thanks. 1
grande large, big 3
granja farm 4
gripe: tener gripe to have the flu 9
gris gray 2
gritar to scream, yell 9
grúa tow truck 10
guante *m.* glove 8
guapo/a good-looking 3
guardar to save 11; **guardar (la ropa)** to put away (clothes) 6
guardería infantil child care center 2
guerra war 10
guía telefónica telephone book 11
gustar to like 4; **me gustaría** I would like/ love to 8
gusto: Mucho gusto. Nice/Pleased to meet you. 1

H

habitación *f.* room 12; **habitación doble** double room 12; **habitación sencilla** single room 12; **servicio de habitación** room service 12
hablar to speak 3
hacer to make, do 4; **hacer la maleta** to pack a suitcase 12; **hacer un viaje (al campo/ a la ciudad)** to take a trip (to the country/ city) 4

hambre *f.* hunger 12; **tener hambre** to be hungry 5

hamburguesa hamburger 5

harina flour 5

hasta *adv.* until 7; **hasta llegar a...** until you arrive at . . . 7; **Hasta luego.** See you later. 1; **Hasta mañana.** See you tomorrow. 1

hay there is, there are 1; **hay que...** one must/ should . . . 7

helado (de vainilla) (vanilla) ice cream 5

herida wound 9

herido/a injured/ wounded person 9

hermano/a brother/ sister 3

hielo ice 5

hígado liver 9

hija daughter 3

hijo son 3

historia history 2

hoja leaf 4; **hoja de papel** sheet of paper 2

Hola. Hello. Hi. 1

hombre *m.* man 1

hombre/ mujer de negocios *m./f.* business executive 2

hombro shoulder 9

hora hour 1; **¿Qué hora es?** What time is it? 1

hotel hotel 12

hotelería hotel management 2

hoy *adv.* today 2

huelga: hacer huelga to go on strike 11

hueso bone 9

huevo (frito) (fried) egg 5

humo smoke 10

I

idioma *m.* language 1

iglesia church 7

igualdad *f.* equality 10

impermeable *m.* raincoat 8

importante important 10

imposible impossible 10

imprimir to print 11

improbable improbable 10

impuestos taxes 10

incendio fire 10

inconsciente: estar inconsciente to be unconscious 9

increíble incredible 10

informática computer science 2

ingeniería engineering 2

inglés (inglesa) *n. adj.* English 2

inmigrante *m./f.* immigrant 12

inmigrar to immigrate 12

inodoro toilet 6

insistir (en) to insist (on) 10

integrarse a/en to adjust, integrate oneself 12

intestino intestine 9

invento invention 12

inversión *f.* investment 11

invertir (ie, i) to invest 11

investigación *f.* research 12

invierno winter 4

invitar to invite 10; **Te invito a...** I'll treat/ invite you to...

inyección: poner una inyección to give a shot 9

ir to go 2; **ir a...** to go to . . . 2; **irse** to go away 6; **ir de compras** to go shopping 4; **ir en barco** to go by boat/ ship 4

isla island 4

italiano/a *n. adj.* Italian 2

izquierda left 7; **a la izquierda** to the left, on the left 7

J

jabón *m.* soap 6

jamón *m.* ham 5

japonés (japonesa) *n. adj.* Japanese 2

jardín *m.* garden 6

jeans *m. pl.* jeans 8

jefe/a de personal director of human resources 11

jefe/a boss 11

joven *adj.* young 3

jóvenes *n. m./f.* young people 3

joyas jewelry 8

joyería jewelry store 7

jubilarse to retire 11

judío/a Jewish 10

jueves *m.* Thursday 1

jugar (ue) al vólibol to play volleyball 4

jugo (de naranja) (orange) juice 5

julio July 1

junio June 1

justicia justice 10

L

labio lip 9

ladrón (ladrona) thief, robber 10

lago lake 4

lámpara lamp 6

lana wool 8

langosta lobster 5

lápiz *m.* pencil 1

largo/a long 8

lástima: es una lástima it is a shame 10

lastimarse to hurt oneself, injure oneself 9

lavabo sink (bathroom) 6

lavadora washing machine 6

lavaplatos *m. s.* dishwasher 6

lavar (los platos) to wash (the dishes) 6; **lavarse (el pelo)** to wash (one's hair) 6

leche *f.* milk 5

lechuga lettuce 5

leer to read 4

legumbre *f.* vegetable 5

lejos de *prep.* far from 2

lengua tongue 9

lentamente slowly 9

lentes *m.* glasses 8; **lentes de contacto** contact lenses 8

levantar: levantar pesas to lift weights 4; **levantarse** to get up 6

ley *f.* law 10

librería bookstore 2

libro book 1

licencia de manejar driver's license 7

limón *m.* lemon 5

limpiar to clean 3; **limpiar el polvo** to dust 6

limpio/a clean 8

listo/a smart 3; ready 11

literatura literature 2

llamada de larga distancia long distance call 11

llamar to call 3; **Me llamo...** My name is ... 1

llanta pinchada flat tire 7

llave *f.* key 7

llegar to arrive 2

llenar el tanque to fill the tank 7

llevar to wear, carry 8; to carry, take 7; **(no) llevarse bien con** to (not) get along well with 10

llorar to cry 3
llover (ue) to rain 4
lluvia rain 4
luchar por to fight for 10
lugar *m.* place 1; **lugar del accidente** scene/ place of the accident 9
luna moon 4
lunes *m.* Monday 1
luz *f.* light, electricity 6

M

madre *f.* mother 3
maestro/a *m./f.* teacher 2
maíz *m.* corn 5
maleta suitcase 12; **hacer la maleta** to pack a suitcase 12
malo/a bad 3
mamá mother 3
mañana morning, tomorrow 2; **de la mañana** in the morning 1; **esta mañana** this morning 2; **mañana por la mañana** tomorrow morning 4; **por la mañana** in the morning 2; **todas las mañanas** every morning 3
mandar to send 4; **mandar una carta** to mail/ send a letter 7
manejar to drive 4; **licencia de manejar** driver's license 7
manifestación *f.* demonstration 10
mano *f.* hand 9
mantel *m.* tablecloth 5
mantequilla butter 5
manzana apple 5
mapa *m.* map 2
maquillarse to put on makeup 6
mar *m./f.* sea 4
marca brand 8
marcador *m.* marker 2
marcar to dial 11; **marcar tarjeta** to punch in 11
mariscos seafood/ shellfish 5
martes *m.* Tuesday 1
marzo March 1
más more 5
matar to kill 10
matemáticas mathematics 2
mayo May 1
mayonesa mayonnaise 5
mayor older 3
media naranja soulmate 3
medianoche *f.* midnight 1
medicina medicine 2
médico/a *m./f.* doctor 2
medio ambiente *m.* environment 12
mediodía *m.* noon 1
mejor better 8; **es mejor** it is better 10; **mejor amigo/a** best friend 3
mejorar to improve 12
menor younger 3
menos less 1, 5; **menos cuarto** quarter to (hour) 1
mensaje electrónico e-mail 4
mercado market 5; **mercado en alza y en baja** bull (up) and bear (down) stock markets 11
merienda afternoon snack 5
mermelada jam 5
mes *m.* month 1; **mes que viene** next month 4
mesa table 2; **poner la mesa** to set the table 6
mesero/a *m./f.* server 2
mezquita mosque 10
microondas *m. s.* microwave 6
miedo: tener miedo to be afraid 9

mientras *conj.* while 9; **mientras tanto** meanwhile 9
miércoles *m.* Wednesday 1
mil one thousand 5
millón million 5
mirar to look at, watch 4
mochila backpack 1
moda fashion 8
montaña mountain 4
montar: montar a caballo to ride horseback, go horseback riding 4; **montar en bicicleta** to ride a bicycle 4
morado/a purple 2
moreno/a dark-haired, dark-skinned 3
morir (ue, u) to die 9
mostrar (ue) to show 7
moto(cicleta) *f.* motorcycle 7
mover(se) to move (oneself) 9
muchacho/a boy/ girl 10
mucho *adv.* much, a lot 2, 4
mucho/a/os/as *adj.* much, many, a lot 2
mudarse to move (from house to house) 10
muebles *m. pl.* furniture 6
mujer *f.* woman 1; **mujer de negocios** business executive *f.* 2; **mujer policía** police woman 2
muleta crutch 9
museo museum 7
música music 2
musulmán (musulmana) *n. adj.* Muslim 10
muy very 1

N

nada nothing 6; **De nada.** You're welcome. 1
nadar to swim 4
nadie no one, not anyone, nobody 6
naranja orange 5
nariz *f.* nose 9
naturaleza nature 12
nave espacial *f.* spaceship 12
navegar por la Red to surf the Web 4
Navidad *f.* Christmas 1
necesario/a necessary 10
necesitar to need 3
negocios business 2
negro/a black 2
nevar (ie) to snow 4
nervioso/a nervous 2
nieta granddaughter 3
nieto grandson 3
nieve *f.* snow 4
niña child, girl 3
niñera nanny 3
ningún, ninguno/a no (not a single); none, not any 10
niño child, boy 3
noche *f.* night 3; **Buenas noches.** Good evening./ Good night. 1; **de la noche** in the evening 1; **esta noche** tonight 2; **por la noche** at night 2; **todas las noches** every night 3
nota grade 2
noticias news 7
novecientos/as nine hundred 5
noveno/a ninth 11
noventa ninety 3
novia girlfriend 3
noviembre November 1
novio boyfriend 3

nube *f.* cloud 4

nublado: Está nublado./Está muy nublado. It is cloudy./ it is very cloudy. 4

nueve nine 1

nuevo/a new 3

número number 1

nunca: (casi) nunca *adv.* (almost) never 3

O

o or 1

obedecer to obey 10

obrero/a worker 11

ochenta eighty 3

ocho eight 1

ochocientos/as eight hundred 5

octavo/a eighth 11

octubre October 1

ocupado/a busy 2

oficina office 11

oído inner ear 9

oír to hear 4

Ojalá (que) + *present subjunctive* I hope . . . 10

ojo eye 9

ola wave 4

olvidarse de to forget 10

once eleven 1

operar to operate 9; **operar la máquina** to operate the machine 11

oportunidad *f.* opportunity 12

oratoria speech 2

ordenar (el cuarto) to straighten up (the room) 6

oreja ear 9

organizar to organize 10

oro gold 8

otoño fall (season), autumn 4

otro/a *adj.* other, another 5

P

paciente *m./f.* patient 9

padre *m.* father 3

padres *m. pl.* parents 3

pagar to pay (for) 5

país *m.* country 7; **país en desarrollo** developing country 12; **país extranjero** foreign country 7

paisaje *m.* landscape 12

pájaro bird 4

pan *m.* bread 5; **pan tostado** toast 5

pantalones *m. pl.* **cortos/ largos** shorts/ long pants 8

pantimedias panty hose 8

papa *f.* potato 5; **papas fritas** French fries 5; **puré** *m.* **de papas** mashed potatoes 5

papá *m.* father 3

papelera wastebasket 2

paquete *m.* package 7

para *prep.* for 6; **para** + *infinitivo* in order to (*do something*) 6

parada de autobús bus stop 7

paraguas *m. s.* umbrella 8

paramédico/a paramedic 9

parar to stop 7

pared *f.* wall 2

pareja couple 3; **mi pareja** significant other 3

¡Paren! Stop! 7

pariente *m./f.* relative 3

parque *m.* park 7

parrilla: a la parrilla grilled 5

partido party (political) 10; game 4; **partido de fútbol** soccer game 4

pasado *n.* past 7

pasajero/a passenger 12

pasaporte: sacar el pasaporte to get a passport 12

pasar: pasar por to go down; to go, pass by 7, 10; **pasar el tiempo (con la familia)** to spend time (with the family) 4; **¡Que lo pases bien!** Have a good time! 7

pasillo hallway 2; aisle 12

pasta de dientes toothpaste 6

pastel *m.* **(de chocolate)** (chocolate) cake 5

pastelería pastry shop 7

pastilla pill 9

patinar to skate 4

pavo turkey 5

paz *f.* peace 10

peatón *m.* pedestrian 7

pecho chest, breast 9

pedir (i) to order, ask for 5

peinarse to comb one's hair 6

peine *m.* comb 6

película film 7

peligroso/a dangerous 10

pelirrojo/a red-headed 3

pelo hair 6; **lavarse el pelo** to wash one's hair 6

pelota ball 4

peluquería hair salon 7

pensar (ie) (+ *infinitivo*) to think, plan/ intend (*to do something*) 5

peor worse 8

pequeño/a small 3

pera pear 5

perder (ie) to lose 7

Perdón. Pardon me./ Excuseme (*to get someone's attention*). 1

perezoso/a lazy 3

periódico newspaper 7

permiso por enfermedad sick leave 11; **permiso por maternidad** maternity leave 11

pero *conj.* but 1

perro dog 3

persona mayor older/eldery person 3

persona sin hogar homeless person 10

pescado fish (caught) 5

pescar to fish 4

pez *m.* fish (live) 4

pie *m.* foot 9

piel *f.* skin 9

pierna leg 9

pijama pajamas 8

piloto *m./f.* pilot 12

pimienta pepper (spice) 5

pimiento verde/ rojo green/ red bell pepper 5

pintar (un cuadro) to paint (a painting) 4

pintarse las uñas to have one's nails painted, to paint one's nails 7

piña pineapple 5

piscina swimming pool 12

piso floor 6; **primer piso** first floor 6; **segundo piso** second floor 6

pizarra chalkboard 2

planchar to iron 6

planta tropical tropical plant 12

plata silver 8

plato plate, dish 5

playa beach 4

plaza square, plaza 2

pobre poor 3

pobreza poverty 12

poco: un poco a little 1, 4

poder *m.* power 12; **poder (ue)** to be able 5

policía/ mujer policía *m./f.* police officer 2

pollo chicken 5

poner to put 4; **poner la mesa** to set the table 6; **poner una inyección** to give a shot 9; **ponerse (los zapatos)** to put on (one's shoes, etc.) 6

por by, through, around, alongside 6; **por fin** *adv.* finally 9

portero porter, concierge 10

portugués (portuguesa) *n. adj.* Portuguese 2

posible possible 10

postre *m.* dessert 5

practicar deportes to play, go out for sports 4

precio price 8

preferir (ie) to prefer 5

preguntar to ask 7

prejuicio prejudice 10

prender to turn on 8

prensa press 12

preocupado/a worried 2

preocuparse to worry 9

preparar to prepare 5

presentar: Le/ Te presento a... Let me introduce you to . . . 1

presión: tomar la presión to take one's blood pressure 9

prestar to lend 7

presupuesto budget 11

prevenir (enfermedades) to prevent (illnesses) 12

primo a cousin 3

primavera spring 4

primer, primero/a first 11; **primer piso** first floor 6

prisa: tener prisa to be in a hurry 9

probable probable 10

probar (ue) to taste, try 5; **probarse** to try on 8

producto orgánico organic produce 12

profesor/a professor 1

programador/a programmer 2

progresista *m./f.* liberal 10

prolongar la vida to prolong life 12

promoción *f.* promotion 11

propina tip 5

prosperar to prosper 12

proteger to protect 12

protestante *m./f.* Protestant 10

proveer to provide 12

próximo mes/ año/ verano next month/ year/ summer 4

(p)sicología psychology 2

prueba quiz, test 2

pueblo town, people 10

puente *m.* bridge 7

puerta door 2; **puerta de embarque** boarding gate 12

puesto de trabajo position, job 11

pulmón *m.* lung 9

pulsera bracelet 8

punto: en punto on the dot, sharp (time) 1

pupitre *m.* desk (student's) 2

puré *m.* **de papas** mashed potatoes 5

Q

qué what 2; **¿Qué tal el clima?** What is the weather like? 4; **¿Qué tal?** How are you (doing)? 1; **¿Qué tiempo hace?** What is the weather like? 4

quedarse to stay, remain 9; **quedar bien/ mal** to fit/ not fit 8

quehaceres *m. pl.* **domésticos** household chores 6

quejarse to complain 9

quemarse to burn oneself, burn down 10

querer (ie) to want, wish, love 1, 5

queso cheese 5

química chemistry 2

quince fifteen 1

quinientos/as five hundred 5

quinto/a fifth 11

quiosco newsstand 7

quitar: quitar la mesa to clear the table 6; **quitarse (la ropa)** to take off (one's clothes, etc.) 6

R

radio por satélite *m./f.* satellite radio 12

radiografía X-ray 9

rascacielos *m. s.* skyscraper 7

ratón (óptico USB) *m.* (wireless USB) mouse 8

razón: tener razón to be right 11

rebaja sale 8

recepcionista *m./f.* receptionist 2

receta prescription 9

recibir to receive 4

reciclar to recycle 6

recoger to pick up, gather 10

recomendar (ie) to recommend 10

recto straight ahead 7

recuperarse to recuperate 9

refresco soft drink, soda 5

refrigerador *m.* refrigerator 6

regalar to give (as a gift) 7

regalo gift 5

regar (ie) (las plantas) to water (the plants) 6

registrarse to check in 12

regresar to return 3

Regular. Okay./ So, so. 1

reírse (i) to laugh 6

relajarse to relax 10

religión *f.* religion 2

reloj *m.* clock, watch 1

reparar to repair, to fix 7

repartidor/a (de pizzas) *m./f.* (pizzas) delivery person 10

repente: de repente suddenly 9

repetir (i) to repeat 5

reportero/a reporter 10

reservar to reserve 12

resfriado: estar resfriado/a to have a cold 9

residencia estudiantil dormitory, residence hall 2

resolver (ue) to solve, resolve 10

responder to reply, answer 11

reunirse to meet (get together) 10

revisar (el aceite) to check (the oil) 7

revista magazine 7

rezar to pray 10

rico/a rich 3

ridículo/a ridiculous 10

riñón *m.* kidney 9

río river 4

robar to rob, steal 10

rodilla knee 9

rojo/a red 2

romper(se) to break 9, 11

ropa clothing 6, 8

ropa interior underwear 8
ropero closet 6
rosado/a pink 2
rubio/a blond(e) 3
ruido noise 7
ruso/a *n. adj.* Russian 2

S

sábado Saturday 1
sábana sheet 12
saber to know (facts, information), to know how (skills) 4
sacar to take out 7; **sacar la basura** to take out the trash 6; **sacar sangre** to take blood 9
sal *f.* salt 5
sala living room 6; **sala de espera** waiting room 9
salchicha sausage 5
salida exit 7
salir to leave, go out 4; **salir de paseo** to take a walk/ stroll 4
saltar to jump 10
salud *f.* health 2, 9
saludarse to greet 10
sandalia sandal 8
sandía watermelon 5
sándwich *m.* sandwich 5
satisfecho: estar satisfecho/a to be satisfied 12
secador *m.* hairdryer 6
secadora dryer 6
secar (los platos) to dry (the dishes) 6; **secarse** to dry oneself 6
secretario/a *m./f.* secretary 2
Secretaría Registrar's Office 2
sed: tener sed to be thirsty 5
seguir (i) to continue, to follow 7
segundo/a second 11
seguridad nacional *f.* national security 10
seguro (médico) (medical) insurance 9; **(no) estar seguro/a (de)** to (not) be sure 10
seis six 1
seiscientos/as six hundred 5
selva jungle 12
semáforo traffic light 7
semana week 1; **próxima semana** next week 4; **semana pasada** last week 7; **semana que viene** next week 4
sentarse (ie) to sit down 6
sentir (ie, i) to be sorry, regret, feel 10; **sentirse (ie) mal/ bien** to feel bad, sick/ well 6
señal *f.* **de tráfico** road sign 7
señor (Sr.) Mr., sir 1
señora (Sra.) Mrs., ma'am 1
señorita (Srta.) Miss 1
separado/a separated 3
septiembre September 1
séptimo/a seventh 11
ser to be 1
servicio de habitación room service 12
servilleta napkin 5
servir (i) to serve 5
sesenta sixty 3
setecientos/as seven hundred 5
setenta seventy 3
sexto/a sixth 11
sí yes 1
SIDA *m.* AIDS 9
siempre: (casi) siempre *adv.* (almost) always 3

siete seven 1
silla chair 2; **silla de ruedas** wheelchair 9
sillón *m.* easy chair 6
simpático/a nice, likeable 3
sin *prep.* without 5
sinagoga synagogue 10
sindicato union 11
sobre *m.* envelope 11
sobre *prep.* on, above 6; about (a topic) 6
sobrino/a nephew/ niece 3
sociología sociology 2
¡Socorro! Help! 9
sofá *m.* sofa 6
sol *m.* sun 4; **Hace sol./Hace mucho sol.** It is sunny./ It is very sunny.; **tomar el sol** to sunbathe 4
soldado/ la soldado *m./f.* soldier 2
solicitar empleo to look for a job 11
solicitud *f.* **de empleo** job application 11
soltero: ser soltero/a to be single 3
sombrero hat 8
sonar (ue) to ring (phone); to go off (alarm clock) 6
sopa soup 5
sótano basement 6
subir to go up 6
sucio/a dirty 8
sudadera sweatshirt 8
suegro/a father-in-law/ mother-in-law 3
sueldo salary 11
suelo floor 6
sueño: tener sueño to be sleepy 6
suerte luck 7; **¡Qué mala suerte!** What bad luck! 7; **tener suerte** to be lucky 11
suéter *m.* sweater 8
sufrir un ataque al corazón to have a heart attack 9
supervisor/a supervisor 11

T

talla size 8
taller *m.* **mecánico** auto repair shop 7
también *adv.* also 1
tampoco *adv.* not either 1
tanque: llenar el tanque to fill the tank 7
tarde *adv.* late 3; *n. f.* afternoon 1; **Buenas tardes.** Good afternoon. 1; **de la tarde** in the afternoon (p.m.) 1; **esta tarde** this afternoon 2; **más tarde** later 2; **por la tarde** in the afternoon 2; **todas las tardes** every afternoon 3
tarea homework 2
tarjeta: tarjeta de crédito/tarjeta de débito credit card/debit card 8; **tarjeta de embarque** boarding pass 12; **tarjeta postal** postcard 7
taza cup 5
té *m.* **(caliente/ helado)** (hot/ iced) tea 5
teatro theater 2
techo roof, ceiling 6
teclado keyboard 8
teléfono telephone 8; **teléfono inalámbrico** cordless phone 8
telenovela soap opera 10
televisor *m.* television 2 **de pantalla plana** flat-screen TV 8
temperatura: tomar la temperatura to take one's temperature 9
temprano *adv.* early 3
tenedor *m.* fork 5
tener to have 3; **tener que** + *infinitivo* to have to (*do something*) 6
teñirse (i) el pelo to have one's hair colored, to color one's hair 7

terapia física physical therapy 2; **terapia del lenguaje** speech therapy 2

tercer, tercero/a third 11

terminar to finish 7

termómetro thermometer 9

tía aunt 3

tío uncle 3

tiempo weather 4; **a tiempo** on time 3; **Hace buen tiempo./ Hace muy buen tiempo./Hace mal tiempo./Hace muy mal tiempo.** The weather is nice./The weather is very nice. /The weather is bad./The weather is very bad. 4

tienda store 7; **tienda por departamentos** department store 7

Tierra Earth 12

tijeras scissors 11

tiza chalk 2

toalla towel 6

tocar (la guitarra) to play (the guitar) 4

tocino bacon 5

tomar to drink, take 5

tomate *m.* tomato 5

tonto/a silly, dumb 3

tobillo ankle 9; **torcerse (ue) el tobillo** to twist/ sprain one's ankle 9

torta (de chocolate) (chocolate) cake 5

tos: tener tos to have a cough 9

trabajador/a hard-working 3

trabajador/a social *m./f.* social worker 2

trabajar to work 3

trabajo work, job 2; **puesto de trabajo** position, job 11; **trabajo social** social work 2; **trabajo de tiempo parcial/ completo** part-time/ full-time work/ job 11

traer to bring 4

tráfico traffic 7

traje *m.* suit 8; **traje de baño** bathing suit 8

tratar de + *infinitivo* to try to (*do something*) 10

trece thirteen 1

treinta y uno thirty-one 1

treinta thirty 1

tres three 1

trescientos/as three hundred 5

triste *adj.* sad 2

turno de día/ noche day/ night shift 11

U

uña finger/ toenail 7; **pintarse las uñas** to paint one's finger/ toenails 7

universidad *f.* university 2

uno one 1

usar to use 3

uva grape 5

V

valle *m.* valley 4

vaso glass 5

veces: a veces sometimes 3

vecino/a neighbor 10

veinte twenty 1

veinticinco twenty-five 1

veinticuatro twenty-four 1

veintidós twenty-two 1

veintinueve twenty-nine 1

veintiocho twenty-eight 1

veintiséis twenty-six 1

veintisiete twenty-seven 1

veintitrés twenty-three 1

veintiuno twenty-one 1

velocidad *f.* **máxima** maximum speed 7

venda bandage 9

vendedor/a vendor 10

vender to sell 5; **se vende** for sale 5

venir to come 4

ventaja advantage 12

ventana window 2

verano summer 4

ver to see, look at 4; **ver la televisión** to watch TV 4

verdad true 10

verde green 2

verdura vegetable 5

vez: en vez de in place of, instead of 6; **una vez/ dos veces por semana** once/ twice per week 3

verano summer 4; **verano que viene** next summer 4

vestido dress 8

vestirse (i) to get dressed 6

viajar to travel 4; **hacer un viaje (al campo/a la ciudad)** to take a trip (to the country/ city) 4

víctima *f.* victim 10

vida life 6; **vida diaria** daily life 6; **vida sencilla** simple life 12

viejo/a old 3

viento wind 4; **Hace viento./Hace mucho viento.** It is windy./ It is very windy. 4

viernes *m.* Friday 1; **viernes pasado** *m.* last Friday 7

vinagre *m.* vinegar 5

vino wine 5

violencia violence 10

visitar to visit 3

viudo/a widower/ widow 3

vivir to live 4

volar (ue) to fly 12

volcán *m.* volcano 12

voluntario/a volunteer 10

volver (ue) to return 5

vómitos: tener vómitos to be vomiting 9

votar to vote 10

vuelo flight 12

Y

y and 1; **y cuarto** fifteen past/ quarter after 1; **y media** half past (the hour)/ thirty 1

ya *adv.* already 7

yeso cast 9

Z

zanahoria carrot 5

zapatería shoe store 7

zapato shoe 6; **zapatos de tenis** sneakers 8

Glosario: inglés-español

A

about (a topic) acerca de 6; sobre *prep.* 6
above encima de 6; sobre *adv.* 6
account cuenta 7
accountant contador/a *m./f.* 2
accounting contabilidad *f.* 2
ad anuncio 8
address dirección 11
adjust oneself integrarse a/en 12
adults adultos *m. pl.* 3
advantage ventaja 12
advise aconsejar 10
affectionate cariñoso/a 3
afraid: to be afraid tener miedo 9
after después (de) 6
afternoon tarde *f.* 1; **every afternoon** todas las tardes 3; **Good afternoon.** Buenas tardes. 1; **in the afternoon** de la tarde 1, por la tarde 2; **this afternoon** esta tarde 2; **afternoon snack** merienda 5
agnostic agnóstico/a 10
agree estar de acuerdo 10
AIDS SIDA *m.* 9
air conditioning aire *m.* acondicionado 12
airline aerolínea 12
airport aeropuerto 12
alarm clock despertador *m.* 6
algebra álgebra *m.* 2
almost casi *adv.* 3
alongside por *adv.* 6
already ya *adv.* 7
also también *adv.* 1
always siempre *adv.* 3
and y 1
angry enojado/a 2
another otro/a 5
answer contestar 6; responder 11
answering machine contestador *m.* automático 8
any algún, alguno/a/os/as 10
applaud aplaudir 10
apple manzana 5
appointment cita 9
April abril 1
Arabic árabe *adj.* 2
architecture arquitectura 2
area code código de área 11
argue discutir 10
arm brazo 9
around alrededor de 12; por 6
arrive llegar 3
art arte *m.* 2
ask preguntar 7; **to ask for** pedir (i) 5
asleep: to fall asleep dormirse (ue) 6
at a; en *prep.* 2; **at home** en casa 2
atheist ateo/a 10
ATM cajero automático 7
attachment anexo 11
attend asistir a 4
August agosto 1

B

aunt tía 3
auto repair shop taller *m.* mecánico 7
autumn otoño 4
avenue avenida 2
avoid evitar 12

baby bebé *m./f.* 3
back espalda 9
backpack mochila 1
bacon tocino 5
bad malo/a 3
bag bolsa 8
bald calvo/a 3
ball pelota 4
banana banana 5
band banda 10
bandage venda 9
bank banco 7
basement sótano 6
bathe, to take a bath bañarse 6
bathing suit traje *m.* de baño 8
bathroom (cuarto de) baño 6
bathtub bañera 6
be able poder (ue) 5
be in a hurry tener prisa 9
be in favor of/ against estar a favor de/ en contra de 10
be estar, ser 1, 2
beach playa 4
bean frijol *m.* 5
bed cama 6; **to go to bed** acostarse (ue) 6
bedroom dormitorio 6
beef carne de res *f.* 5
beer cerveza 5
before antes de *conj.* 6
begin empezar (ie) 7
behind detrás de 2
beige beige 2
believe (that) creer (que) 4
bellhop botones *m.* 12
below debajo de *adv.* 6
belt cinturón *m.* 8
bench banco 7
beneath debajo de *adv.* 6
benefit beneficio 11
beside al lado de *prep.* 2
better mejor 8, 10
between entre *prep.* 2
bicycle bicicleta 2
big grande 3
bill cuenta 5
bikini bikini *m.* 8
biology biología 2
bird pájaro 4
birthday cumpleaños *m.* 1
black negro/a 2
blanket cobija 12
block cuadra 7; **a block away** a una cuadra 7

blond(e) rubio/a 3

blood: to take blood sacar sangre 9; **to take one's blood pressure** tomar la presión 9

blouse blusa 8

blue azul 2

boarding gate puerta de embarque 12

boarding pass tarjeta de embarque 12

body: human body cuerpo humano 9

bone hueso 9

book libro 1

bookcase estante *m.* 6

bookstore librería 2

boot bota 8

border frontera 12

bored aburrido/a 2; **to get bored** aburrirse 11

boss jefe/a 11

boy chico 3; niño 3; muchacho 10

boyfriend novio 3

bracelet pulsera 8

brain cerebro 9

brake freno 7

brand marca 8

bread pan *m.* 5

break/ rest descanso 11

break romper(se) 9, 11; fracturarse 9; **My car broke down.** Mi carro se decompuso. 7

breakfast desayuno 5; **to have breakfast** desayunar 3

breast pecho 9

bridge puente *m.* 7

bring traer 4

broccoli brócoli *m.* 5

brother hermano 3

brother-in-law cuñado 3

brown (color) café 2

brush (one's teeth) cepillarse (los dientes) 6

budget presupuesto 11

building edificio 2

burn oneself, burn down quemarse 10

bus autobús *m.* 2

bus stop parada de autobús 7

business school Facultad *f.* de Administración de Empresas 2

business negocios 2; **business executive** hombre/ mujer de negocios *m./f.* 2

busy ocupado/a 2

but pero *conj.* 1

butter mantequilla 5

buy comprar 3; **to buy groceries** hacer las compras 6

by por *prep.* 6

Bye. Chao. 1

C

cafeteria cafetería 2

cake pastel *m.* 5; **(chocolate) cake** torta (de chocolate) 5

calculus cálculo 2

call llamar 3; **long distance call** llamada de larga distancia 11

camera: digital camera cámara digital 8

camp acampar 4

campaign: electoral campaign campaña electoral 10

candy dulce *f.* 10

cap: baseball cap gorra de béisbol 8; **wool cap** gorro de lana 8

car carro 2

caramel custard flan *m.* 5

care: to take care of (yourself/oneself) cuidar(se) 3, 9

careful: to be careful tener cuidado 9

carpet alfombra 6

carrot zanahoria 5

carry llevar 7, 8

cash en efectivo 8; cobrar 7

cashier cajero/a *m./f.* 2

cast yeso 9

cat gato 3

cathedral catedral *f.* 10

Catholic católico/a 10

ceiling techo 6

cell phone celular *m.* 8

cereal cereal *m.* 5

chain cadena 8

chair silla 2; **easy chair** sillón *m.* 6

chalk tiza 2

chalkboard pizarra 2

change cambiar 7

charge cobrar 7

chat (with) charlar (con) 3

cheap barato/a 8

check cheque *m.* 7

check in registrarse 12; **check the luggage/ baggage** facturar el equipaje 12; **check (the oil)** revisar (el aceite) 7

cheese queso 5

chemistry química 2

cherry cereza 5

chest pecho 9

chewing gum chicle *m.* 10

chicken pollo 5

child niño/a 3

child care center guardería infantil 2

chimney chimenea 6

Chinese chino/a *n. adj.* 2

Christmas Navidad *f.* 1

church iglesia 7

citizen ciudadano/a 10

city ciudad *f.* 4

class clase 1

classmate compañero/a de clase 2

clean limpio/a 8; limpiar 3

clear the table quitar la mesa 6

clock reloj *m.* 1

close cerrar (ie) 7

closed cerrado/a 2

closet ropero 6

clothing ropa 6, 8

cloud nube *f.* 4

cloudy: It is cloudy./It is very cloudy. Está nublado./ Está muy nublado. 4

coat abrigo 8

coffee café *m.* 5

cold frío/a 4; **to be cold** tener frío 8; **to have a cold** estar resfriado/a 9; **It is (very) cold.** Hace (mucho) frío. 4

colleague colega *m./f.* 11

color one's hair, to have one's hair colored teñirse (i) el pelo 7

comb peine *m.* 6; **to comb one's hair** peinarse 6

come venir 4

comfortable cómodo/a 8

communicate comunicarse 12

complain quejarse 9

computer science informática 2

computer computadora 1

concierge portero 10

congested: to be congested estar congestionado/a 9
conservative conservador/a 10
construct construir 10
contact lenses lentes *m.* de contacto 8
continue seguir (i) 7
contribute contribuir 12
cookie galleta 5
cool: It is cool. Hace fresco. 4
copy copiar 11
corn maíz *m.* 5
corner esquina 7
corporation empresa 11
cost costar (ue) 5
cotton algodón *m.* 8
cough tos *f.*; **to have a cough** tener tos 9
count contar (ue) 5
country país *m.* 7; **foreign country** país extranjero 7
countryside campo 4
couple pareja 3
cousin primo/a 3
crash chocar 9
cream crema 5
credit card/debit card tarjeta de crédito/tarjeta de débito 8
crime crimen *m.* 10
cross cruzar 7
crutch muleta 9
cry llorar 3
cubicle cubículo 11
cup taza 5
cure cura 9
curtain cortina 6
customs aduana 12
cut cortar 5

D

dance bailar 4
dangerous peligroso/a 10
dark-haired/ dark-skinned moreno/a 3
date cita 9; fecha 1; **What is today's date?** ¿Qué fecha es hoy? 1
daughter hija 3
day día *m.* 1; **all day** toda el día 3; **day before yesterday** anteayer *adv.* 7; **day shift** el turno de día 11; **every day** todos los días 3
dear estimado/a 11
debt deuda 11
December diciembre 1
delete borrar 11
Delighted to meet you. Encantado/a. 1
demonstration manifestación *f.* 10
department store tienda por departamentos 7
desert desierto 12
desire desear 5
desk escritorio 1; **desk (student's)** pupitre *m.* 2
dessert postre *m.* 5
destruction of the ozone layer destrucción *f.* de la capa de ozono 12
developing country país *m.* en desarrollo 12
diagnose diagnosticar 12
dial marcar 11
die morir (ue, u) 9
difficult difícil 3
dining room comedor *m.* 6
dinner cena 5; **to have dinner** cenar 3
director of human resources jefe/a de personal 11

dirty sucio/a 8
disabled discapacitado/a 9
disadvantage desventaja 12
disagreeable antipático/a 3
disease enfermedad *f.* 9
dish plato 5
dishwasher lavaplatos *m.* 6
disorganized desordenado/a 3
diversity diversidad *f.* 12
divorced: to be divorced estar divorciado/a 3; **to get divorced** divorciarse 10
do hacer 4
doctor médico/a *m./f.* 2
doctor's office consultorio médico 9
document documento 11
dog perro 3
donate donar 10
dormitory/ residence hall residencia estudiantil 2
door puerta 2
doubt dudar
downtown centro 7
draw dibujar 4
dress vestido 8; **to dress, get dressed** vestirse (i) 6
dresser cómoda 6
drink bebida 5; beber 4; tomar 5
drive manejar 4
driver's license licencia de manejar 7
dry (the dishes) secar (los platos) 6; **to dry oneself** secarse 6
dryer secadora 6
dumb tonto/a 3
during durante 6
dust limpiar el polvo 6
DVD/VCR player equipo de DVD y video 8

E

ear oreja 9; **inner ear** oído 9
early temprano *adv.* 3
earn ganar 11
earring arete *m.* 8
Earth Tierra 12
easy fácil 3
eat comer 4
economics economía 2
economy economía 11
egg (fried) huevo (frito) 5
eight hundred ochocientos/as 5
eight ocho 1
eighteen dieciocho 1
eighth octavo/a 11
eighty ochenta 3
elderly ancianos 3
electricity luz *f.* 6
elevator ascensor *m.* 12
eleven once 1
eliminate eliminar 12
e-mail messages mensajes *m.* electrónicos/ e-mails 4
emergency emergencia 9; **emergency room** sala de emergencias 9
emigrant emigrante *m./f.* 12
emigrate emigrar 12
employee empleado/a 11
end fin *m.* 12
energy: aeolic (wind) energy energía eólica (del viento) 12

engaged: to be engaged estar comprometido/a/os/as 3; **to get engaged** comprometerse 10
engineering ingeniería 2
English inglés (inglesa) *n. adj.* 2
enjoy disfrutar de 4
enter entrar (a/en) 7
entrance entrada 7
envelope sobre *m* 11
environment medio ambiente *m.* 12
equality igualdad *f.* 10
erase borrar 11
eraser borrador *m.* 2
evening: Good evening./Good night. Buenas noches. 1; **in the evening** de la noche 1
exam examen *m.* 2
examine examinar 9
exchange cambiar 7
Excuse me. Perdón.; Con permiso. 1
executive ejecutivo/a 11
exercise hacer ejercicio 4
exit salida 7
expect esperar 10
expensive caro/a 8
experience experiencia 11
explain explicar 7
eye ojo 9

F

face cara 9
facing enfrente de *adv.* 2
factory fábrica 11
fall caerse 9
fall (season) otoño 4
family familia 3
far from lejos de *prep.* 2
farm granja 4
fashion moda 8
fasten one's seatbelt abrocharse el cinturón 7
fat gordo/a 3
father papá; padre *m.* 3
father-in-law suegro 3
February febrero 1
feed dar de comer 10
feel sentir (ie, i) 10; **to feel bad, sick/well** sentirse (ie) mal/bien 6; **to feel like doing something** tener ganas de + *infinitivo* 11
fever: to have a fever tener fiebre 9
field campo 4
fifteen quince 1
fifth quinto/a 11
fifty cincuenta 1
fight for luchar por 10
file archivo 11
fill the tank llenar el tanque 7
film película 7
finally por fin *adv.* 9
find encontrar (ue) 7
Fine. Bien. 1
finger dedo 9
fingernail uña 7
finish terminar 7
fire fuego 10; incendio 10
firefighter bombero/a *m./f.* 2

fireplace chimenea 6
first primer, primero/a 11
fish pescar 4; *n.* **(caught)** pescado 5; **(live)** pez *m.* (peces *pl.*) 4
fit quedar 8
five hundred quinientos/as 5
five cinco 1
fix reparar 7
flight attendant (female) azafata 12; **(male)** auxiliar *m.* de vuelo 12
flight vuelo 12
floor suelo, piso 6; **first floor** primer piso 6
flour harina 5
flower flor *f.* 4
flu: to have the flu tener gripe 9
fly volar (ue) 12
follow seguir (i) 7
food comida 5
foot pie *m.* 9
footwear calzado 8
for para *prep.* 6
foreign country país *m.* extranjero 7
forest bosque *m.* 4
forget olvidarse de 10
fork tenedor *m.* 5
forty cuarenta 1
forty one cuarenta y uno 1
fountain fuente *f.* 7
four hundred cuatrocientos/as 5
four cuatro 1
fourteen catorce 1
fourth cuarto/a 11
fracture fracturarse 9
freeway autopista 7
French francés (francesa) *n. adj.* 2
French fries papas fritas 5
frequently con frecuencia *adv.* 3
Friday el viernes 1; **last Friday** el viernes pasado 7
fried frito/a 5
friend amigo/a 1; **best friend** mejor amigo/a 3
friendship amistad *f.* 3
from de 1
front: in front of delante de *prep.* 2
fruit fruta 5
funny, fun divertido/a 3
furniture muebles *m.* 6

G

game partido 4; **partido de fútbol** soccer game 4
garage garaje *m.* 6
garbage can cubo de la basura 6
garbage truck camión *m.* de la basura 9
garden jardín *m.* 6
garlic ajo 5
gas station gasolinera 7
gather recoger 10
geography geografía 2
geometry geometría 2
German alemán (alemana) *n. adj.* 2
get conseguir (i, i) 12; **to get along well with** llevarse bien con 10; **to get together** reunirse 10; **to get up** levantarse 6
gift regalo 5
girl chica 3; niña 3; muchacha 10
girlfriend novia 3

give (as a gift) regalar 7

give dar 4; **to give a party** dar una fiesta 4

glad: to be glad (about) alegrarse (de) 10

glass vaso 5

glasses (eye) lentes *m.* 8

glove guante *m.* 8

go ir 2; **to go away** irse 6; **to go by boat/ ship** ir en barco 4; **to go by** pasar por 7, 10; **to go down** bajar 6; **to go down/ pass by** pasar por 10; **to go horseback riding** montar a caballo 4; **to go out** salir 4; **to go shopping** ir de compras 4; **to go to bed** acostarse (ue); **to go up** subir 6

goblet copa 5

God Dios *m.* 10

gold oro 8

good bueno/a 3

Good-bye. Adiós. 1

good-looking guapo/a 3

government gobierno 12

grade nota 2

granddaughter nieta 3

grandfather abuelo 3

grandmother abuela 3

grandson nieto 3

grape uva 5

gray gris 2

green verde 2

greet saludarse 10

grilled a la parrilla 5

grow (crops) cultivar 12

gym gimnasio 2

H

hallway pasillo 2

hair pelo 6; **to wash one's hair** lavarse el pelo 6

hair salon peluquería 7

haircut: to get a haircut, cut one's hair cortarse el pelo 7

hairdryer secador *m.* 6

half past (the hour) y media 1

hallway pasillo 2

ham jamón *m.* 5

hamburger hamburguesa 5

hand mano *f.* 9

handbag bolsa 8; cartera 8

hang colgar (ue) 10

happy contento/a 2; **to be happy (about)** alegrarse (de) 10

hard-working trabajador/a 3

hat sombrero 8

have tener 3; **to have fun/ a good time** divertirse (ie) 6; **to have just done something** acabar de + *infinitivo* 10; **to have to do something** tener que + *infinitivo* 6; **to have a headache** tener dolor de cabeza 9

head cabeza 9; **tener dolor de cabeza** to have a headache 9

headphones audífonos 8

health salud *f.* 2, 9

hear oír 4

heart corazón *m.* 9; **to have a heart attack** sufrir un ataque al corazón 9

heating calefacción *f.* 12

Hello./ Hi. Hola. 1; **Hello?** ¿Aló? 11

help ayudar 3; **Help!** ¡Socorro! 9

here aquí *adv.* 2

highway carretera 7

history historia 2

holiday día *m.* festivo 11

homeless person persona sin hogar 10

homemaker ama de casa *f.* (*but* el ama...) 2

homework tarea 2

hope esperar 10, Ojalá (que)+ *present subjunctive* 10

hot: It is (very) hot. Hace (mucho) calor. 4; **to be hot** tener calor 8

hotel hotel *m.* 12; **hotel management** hotelería 2

house casa 6

household chores quehaceres *m.* domésticos 6

how cómo 2; **How are you (doing)?** ¿Qué tal?/ ¿Cómo estás? *inform.* 1; ¿Cómo está usted? *form.* 1; **How many?** ¿Cuántos/ as? 1, 2; **How often?** ¿Con qué frecuencia? 3

hug abrazar 2

human humano/a; **human body** cuerpo humano 9; **human rights** derechos humanos 10

hunger hambre *m.* 12; **to be hungry** tener hambre 5

hurt doler (ue) 9; **to hurt oneself** lastimarse 9

husband esposo 3

hybrid car carro híbrido 12

I

ice cream (vanilla) el helado (de vainilla) 5

ice hielo 5

illness enfermedad *f.* 9

immigrant inmigrante *m./f.* 12

immigrate inmigrar 12

important importante 10

impossible imposible 10

improbable improbable 10

improve mejorar 12

in en 2; **in order to (do something)** para + *infinitivo* 6; **in place of** en vez de 6

increase (in salary, production, etc.) aumento 11

incredible increíble 10

inexpensive barato/a 8

injure oneself lastimarse 9

injured (person) herido/a 9

inside (of) dentro de *prep.* 6

insist (on) insistir (en) 10

instead of en vez de 6

integrate oneself integrarse a/en 12

intend (to do something) pensar (ie) (+ *infinitivo*) 5

interview entrevista 11

intestine intestino 9

introduce: Let me introduce you to . . . Le presento a.../ Te presento a... 1

invention invento 12

invest invertir (ie, i) 11

investment inversión *f.* 11

invite invitar 10; **I'll treat/invite you to . . .** te invito a 10

iron planchar 6

island isla 4

Italian italiano/a *n. adj.* 2

J

jacket chaqueta 8

jam mermelada 5

January enero 1

Japanese japonés (japonesa) *n. adj.* 2

jeans jeans *m.* 8

jewelry store joyería 7
jewelry joyas 8
Jewish judío/a 10
job trabajo 2; puesto de trabajo 11; **job application** solicitud
f. de empleo 11; **to look for a job** solicitar empleo 11; **part/
full-time job** trabajo de tiempo parcial/ completo 11
juice (orange) jugo (de naranja) 5
July julio 1
jump saltar 10
June junio 1
jungle selva 12
justice justicia 10

K

key llave f. 7
keyboard teclado 8
kidney riñón m. 9
kill matar 10
kind amable 5
kiss besar 3
kitchen sink fregadero 6
kitchen cocina 5, 6
knee rodilla 9
knife cuchillo 5
know saber, conocer 4; **to know how to** saber 4

L

lamp lámpara 6
landscape paisaje m. 12
language idioma m. 2
laptop computadora portátil 8
large grande 3
late tarde adv. 3
later más tarde 2
laugh reírse (i) 6
law school Facultad f. de Derecho 2
law derecho 2; ley f. 10
lawyer abogado/a m./f. 2
layoff despido 11
lazy perezoso/a 3
leaf hoja 4
learn (to) aprender (a) 4
leather goods artículos de cuero 8
leave salir 4; **to leave (behind)** dejar 5
left: on/to the left a la izquierda 7
leg pierna 9
lemon limón m. 5
lend prestar 7
less menos 1, 5
letter carta 11; **letter of recommendation** carta de
recomendación 11
lettuce lechuga 5
liberal progresista m./f. 10
library biblioteca 2
life vida 6; **daily life** vida diaria 6; **simple life** vida sencilla 12
lift weights levantar pesas 4
light luz f. 6
like gustar 4; **like a lot** encantar 4
likeable simpático/a 3
lip labio 9
listen to (music) escuchar (música) 4

literature literatura 2
little: a little un poco 1, 4
live vivir 4
liver hígado 9
living room sala 6
lobster langosta 5
long largo/a 8
look after atender (ie) 10
look at mirar 4
look for buscar 5
lose perder (ie) 7
loudspeakers altoparlantes m. pl. 8
love amor m. 3; **to love** amar 3; querer (ie) 5; encantarle a
uno/a 4; **to be in love** estar enamorado/a 3; **to fall in love**
enamorarse 10
lucky: to be lucky tener suerte 11; **What bad luck!** ¡Qué mala
suerte! 7
lunch almuerzo 5; **to have lunch** almorzar (ue) 5
lung pulmón m. 9

M

magazine revista 7
mail a letter mandar una carta 7
mail carrier cartero/a 10
mailbox buzón m. 7
make hacer 4; **to make a mistake** equivocarse 11; **to make
the bed** hacer la cama 6
mall centro comercial 8
man hombre m. 1
many muchos/as 2
map mapa m. 2
March marzo 1
marker marcador m. 2
market mercado 5
marry, to get married casarse 10; **to be married** estar casado/a 3
maternity leave permiso por maternidad 11
mathematics matemáticas 2
May mayo 1
mayonnaise mayonesa 5
mayor alcalde/ alcaldesa 10
meal comida 5
meanwhile mientras tanto 9
meat carne f. 5
medical insurance seguro médico 9; **Medical School** Facultad de
Medicina 2
medicine medicina 2
meet reunirse 10; **to meet up (with) (by chance)** encontrarse (ue)
(com) 7
message: e-mail messages mensajes m. electrónicos/ e-mails 4
messy desordenado/a 3
microwave microondas m. 6
midnight medianoche f. 1
milk leche f. 5
million millón m. 5
mirror espejo 6
miss extrañar 10; **to miss the plane** perder el avión 12
Miss señorita (Srta.) 1
mistaken: to be mistaken equivocarse 11
Monday lunes m. 1
money dinero 5
month mes m. 1; **next month** mes que viene 4; próximo mes 4
moon luna 4

more más 4, 5

morning mañana 1; **every morning** todas las mañanas 3; **Good morning.** Buenos días. 1; **in the morning** de la mañana 1, por la mañana 2; **this morning** esta mañana 2

mother mamá, madre *f.* 3

mother-in-law suegra 3

motorcycle moto(cicleta) *f.* 6

mountain range cordillera 12

mountain montaña 4

mouse (wireless USB) ratón *m.* (óptico USB) 8

mouth boca 9

move (from house to house) mudarse 10; **to move (oneself)** mover(se) 9

movie theater cine *m.* 6

mow the lawn cortar el césped 6

Mr., sir señor (Sr.) 1

Mrs., ma'am señora (Sra.) 1

much, a lot mucho *adv.* 2, 4; mucho/a *adj.* 2

museum museo 7

music música 2

Muslim musulmán (musulmana) *n. adj.* 10

must (do something) deber (+ *infinitivo*) 4; **one must/ should** hay que 7

N

nail (finger/toe) uña 7; **to have one's nails painted, to paint one's nails** pintarse las uñas 7

name: My name is . . . Me llamo... 1; **What is your name?** ¿Cómo se llama usted?/ ¿Cómo te llamas? 1

nanny niñera 3

napkin servilleta 5

narrate (a story or incident) contar (ue) 7

national security seguridad *f.* nacional 10

near cerca de *prep.* 2

necessary necesario/a 10

neck cuello 9

necklace collar *m.* 8

necktie corbata 8

need necesitar 3

neighbor vecino/a 10

neighborhood barrio 10

nephew sobrino 3

nervous nervioso/a 2

never nunca *adv.* 3

New Year's Año Nuevo 1

new nuevo/a 3

newlyweds recién casados *m.* 3

news noticias 7

newspaper periódico 7

newsstand quiosco 7

nice simpático/a 3

niece sobrina 3

night noche *f.* 3; **at night** por la noche 2; **every night** todas las noches 3; **last night** anoche *adv.* 7; **night shift** turno de noche 11

nine hundred novecientos/as 5

nine nueve 1

nineteen diecinueve 1

ninety noventa 3

ninth noveno/a 11

no (not a single); none, not any ningún, ninguno/a 10

no one, not anyone, nobody nadie 6

no no 1

noise ruido 7

noon mediodía *m.* 1

nose nariz *f.* 9

not either tampoco *adv.* 1

notebook cuaderno 1

nothing nada 6

November noviembre 1

now ahora 2

number número 1

nurse enfermero/a *m./f.* 2

nursing enfermería 2

O

obey obedecer 10

obtain conseguir (i, i) 12

October octubre 1

of de 1

office oficina 11

oil aceite *m.* 5

Okay. Regular. Bien. 1

old viejo/a 3

older mayor 3

older/eldery person persona mayor 3

olive aceituna 5

on sobre 6; **on the dot (time)** en punto 1

once una vez 3

one uno 1

one hundred cien 3, 5

one hundred one ciento uno 5

one hundred thousand cien mil 5

one thousand mil *m.* 5

onion cebolla 5

open abrir 7; abierto/a *adj.* 2

operate operar 9; **operate the machine** operar la máquina 11

opportunity oportunidad *f.* 12

opposite enfrente de *adv.* 2

or o 1

orange naranja 5; anaranjado/a (color) 2

order pedir (i) 5

organic produce producto orgánico 12

organize organizar 10

other otro/a 5

ought to (do something) deber (+ *infinitivo*) 4

outside (of) fuera (de) *adv.* 6

owner dueño/a 9

P

pack a suitcase hacer la maleta 12

package paquete *m.* 7

paint (a painting) pintar (un cuadro) 4

pajamas pijama *m.* 8

pants: long pants pantalones *m.* largos 8

panty hose pantimedias 8

paramedic paramédico/a 9

Pardon me. Perdón. 1

parents padres *m.* 3

park parque *m.* 7; estacionar 7

parking estacionamiento 2

party (political) partido 10

pass (through, by) pasar por 7
passenger pasajero/a 12
passport: to get a passport sacar el pasaporte 12
past: in the past en el pasado 7
pastry shop pastelería 7
patient paciente 9
pay (for) pagar 5
pea arveja, chícharo 5
peace treaty acuerdo de paz 12
peace paz *f.* 10
peach durazno 5
pear pera 5
pedestrian peatón *m.* 7
pen bolígrafo 1
pencil lápiz *m.* 1
people gente *f.* 7; pueblo 10
pepper (spice) pimienta 5; **green / red bell pepper** pimiento verde/ rojo 5
philosophy filosofía 2
phone: cordless phone teléfono inalámbrico 8
photograph, take photos tomar fotos 8
photocopier fotocopiadora 11
photocopy fotocopiar 11
physical therapy terapia física 2
physics física 2
pick up recoger 10
pill pastilla 9
pillow almohada 12
pilot piloto *m./f.* 12
pineapple piña 5
pink rosado/a 2
pizzas delivery person repartidor/a de pizzas 10
place of the accident lugar *m.* del accidente 9
plan (to do something) pensar (ie) (+ *infinitivo*) 5
plane avión *m.* 12
plate plato 5
play, go out for sports practicar deportes 4; **to play (the guitar)** tocar (la guitarra) 4; **to play volleyball** jugar (ue) al vólibol 4
pleasant amable 5
Pleased/Nice to meet you. Mucho gusto. 1
police officer policía/ mujer policía *m./f.* 2
political science ciencias políticas 2
pollution contaminación *f.* 12
poor pobre 3
pork chop chuleta de cerdo 5
porter portero 10
Portugese portugués (portuguesa) *n. adj.* 2
position (work) puesto de trabajo 11
possible posible 10
post office oficina de correos 7
postcard tarjeta postal 7
potato papa 5; **mashed potatoes** puré *m.* de papas 5
poverty pobreza 12
power poder *m.* 12
pray rezar 10
prefer preferir (ie) 5
pregnant: to be pregnant estar embarazada 9
prejudice prejuicio 10
prepare preparar 5
prescription receta 9
press prensa 12
pretty bonito/a 3
prevent (illness) prevenir (enfermedades) 12
price precio 8

print imprimir 11
probable probable 10
professor profesor/a 1
profit ganancia 11
programmer programador/a *m./f.* 2
prolong life prolongar la vida 12
promotion promoción *f.* 11
prosper prosperar 12
protect proteger 12
Protestant protestante *m./f. n. adj.* 10
provide proveer 12
psychology (p)sicología 2
punch in marcar tarjeta 11
purple morado/a 2
purse bolsa, cartera 8
put poner 4; **to put away (clothes)** guardar (la ropa) 6; **to put on (one's shoes, etc.)** ponerse (los zapatos) 6; **to put on makeup** maquillarse 6

Q

quarter past/to (hour) y/menos cuarto 1
quiz prueba 2

R

radio: satellite radio radio *m./f.* por satélite 12
rain lluvia 4; llover (ue) 4
raincoat impermeable *m.* 8
raise (in salary, production, etc.) aumento 11
read leer 4
ready listo/a 11
receive e-mail messages recibir mensajes electrónicos/ e-mails 4
recommend recomendar (ie) 10
receptionist recepcionista *m./f.* 2
recuperate recuperarse 9
recycle reciclar 6
red rojo/a 2
red-headed pelirrojo/a 3
refrigerator refrigerador *m.* 6
Registrar's Office Secretaría 2
regret sentir (ie, i) 10
relative pariente *m./f.* 3
relax relajarse 10
religion religión *f.* 2
remain quedarse 9
remember acordarse (ue) de 10
remote control control *m.* remoto 8
rent alquilar 6; **for rent** se alquila 6
repair reparar 7
repeat repetir (i) 5
reply responder 11
reporter reportero/a 10
research investigación *f.* 12
reserve reservar 12
resolve resolver (ue) 10
rest descanso 11; descansar 4
restroom baño 7
résumé currículo 11
retire jubilarse 11
return (something) devolver (ue) 7
return regresar 3; volver (ue) 5

rice arroz *m.* 5
rich rico/a 3
ride: to ride a bicycle montar en bicicleta 4; to ride
  horseback montar a caballo 4
ridiculous ridículo/a 10
right: human rights derechos humanos 10; on/to the right
  a la derecha 7; to be right tener razón 11
ring anillo 8; diamond ring anillo de diamante 8; to ring
  (phone), go off (alarm clock) sonar (ue) 6
river río 4
road carretera 7
road sign señal *f.* de tráfico 7
rob robar 10
robber ladrón (ladrona) 10
roof techo 6
room cuarto 6; habitación *f.* 12; double room habitación
  doble 12; room service servicio de habitación 12; single
  room habitación sencilla 12
rug alfombra 6
run correr 4; to run errands hacer las compras 6
Russian ruso/a 2

S

sad triste *adj.* 2
salad ensalada 5
salary sueldo 11
sale rebaja 8; for sale se vende 5
salesclerk dependiente/a *m./f.* 2
sales manager gerente *m./f.* de ventas 11
salt sal *f.* 5
sand arena 4
sandal sandalia 8
sandwich sándwich *m.* 5
satisfied: to be satisfied estar satisfecho/a 12
Saturday sábado 1
sausage salchicha 5
save guardar 11; save (time, money) ahorrar 10
say good-bye (to) despedirse (i) (de) 6
say decir 4
scarf bufanda 8
scene of the accident lugar *m.* del accidente 9
school escuela 2; at school en la escuela 2; (of a university)
  facultad 2; School of Arts Facultad *f.* de Filosofía y Letras 2;
  School of Sciences Facultad de Ciencias 2
science ciencia 12
scissors tijeras 10
scream gritar 9
screen: flat screen TV televisor *m.* de pantalla plana 8
sea mar *m./f.* 4
seafood/ shellfish mariscos 5
season estación *f.* 4
seat asiento 12; aisle/ window seat asiento de pasillo/
  ventanilla 12
second segundo/a 11; second floor segundo piso 6
secretary secretario/a *m./f.* 2
see ver 4; See you later. Hasta luego. 1; See you
  tomorrow. Hasta mañana. 1
sell vender 5
send enviar 11; to send a letter mandar una carta; to send e-mail
  messages mandar mensajes electrónicos/ e-mails 4
separated: to be separated estar separado/a 3
September septiembre 1
serve servir (i) 5

server mesero/a *m./f.* 2
set the table poner la mesa 6
seven hundred setecientos/as 5
seven siete 1
seventeen diecisiete 1
seventh séptimo/a 11
seventy setenta 3
shame: It is a shame. Es una lástima. 10
shampoo champú *m.* 6
share (of stock) acción *f.* 11
share compartir 4
sharp (time) en punto 1
shave afeitarse 6
sheet sábana 12; sheet of paper hoja de papel 2
shelf estante *m.* 6
shirt camisa 8
shoe store zapatería 7
shoe zapato 6; ponerse (los zapatos) to put on (one's shoes) 6
shopping: to go shopping ir de compras 4
short bajo/a 3; corto/a 8
shorts pantalones *m.* cortos 8
shot: give a shot poner una inyección 9
should (do something) deber (+ *infinitivo*) 4
shoulder hombro 9
show enseñar 10; mostrar (ue) 7
shower ducha 6; to take a shower ducharse 6
shrimp camarón *f.* 5
sick enfermo/a 2; to get sick enfermarse 9
sick leave permiso por enfermedad 11
sidewalk acera 9
sign firmar 7
significant other pareja 3
silly tonto/a 3
silver plata 8
simple life vida sencilla 12
sing cantar 4
single: to be single ser soltero/a 3
sink (bathroom) lavabo 6
sister hermana 3
sister-in-law cuñada 3
sit down sentarse (ie) 6
six hundred seiscientos/as 5
six seis 1
sixteen dieciséis 1
sixth sexto/a 11
sixty sesenta 3
size talla 8
skate patinar 4
ski esquiar 4
skin piel *f.* 9
skirt falda 8
sky cielo 4
skyscraper rascacielos *m. s.* 7
sleep dormir (ue) 5
sleepy: to be sleepy tener sueño 6
slender delgado/a 3
slowly lentamente 9
small pequeño/a 3
smart listo/a 3
smoke humo 10; fumar 9
snack: afternoon snack merienda 5
sneakers zapatos de tenis 8
snorkel bucear 4
snow nieve *f.* 4; nevar (ie) 4
So so. Regular. 1

soap opera telenovela 10

soap jabón *m.* 6

soccer game partido de fútbol 4

social work trabajo social 2

social worker trabajador/a social *m./f.* 2

sociology sociología 2

sock calcetín *m.* 8

sofa sofá *m.* 6

soft drink, soda refresco 5

solar energy energía solar 12

soldier soldado *m./* la soldado *f.* 2

solve resolver (ue) 10

some algún, alguno/a/os/as 10

someday, sometime algún día 4

someone alguien 6

something algo 6

sometimes a veces 3

son hijo 3

sorry: to be sorry sentir (ie, i) 10

soulmate media naranja 3

soup sopa 5

space exploration exploración *f.* espacial 12

spaceship nave *f.* espacial 12

Spanish español (española) *n. adj.* 2

speak hablar 3

speech oratoria 2; **speech therapy** terapia del lenguaje 2

speed: maximum speed velocidad *f.* máxima 7

spend gastar 8; **to spend time (with the family)** pasar el tiempo (con la familia) 4

spoon cuchara 5

sport deporte *m.* 4; **to play, go out for sports** practicar deportes 4

sprain one's ankle torcerse (ue) el tobillo 9

spring primavera 4

square, plaza plaza 1

stadium estadio de deportes 2

stairs escalera 6

star estrella 4

start empezar (ie) 7

statistics estadística 2

statue estatua 1

stay quedarse 9

steak bistec *m.* 5

steal robar 10

stock market la Bolsa 11; **bull (up) and bear (down)market** el mercado en alza y en baja 11

stomach estómago 9; **to have a stomachache** tener dolor de estómago 9

stop parar 7; **to stop doing something** dejar de + *infinitivo* 9; **stop (road sign)** alto 7; **Stop!** ¡Paren! 7

store tienda 7

stove estufa 6

straight: straight ahead recto/a, derecho 7

straighten up (the room) ordenar (el cuarto) 6

strawberry fresa 5

street calle *f.* 2

stressed estresado/a 2

stretcher camilla 9

strike (to go on) hacer huelga 11

strong fuerte 3

student alumno/a, estudiante *m./f.* 1

student center centro estudiantil 2

study estudiar 3

subject asunto 11

succeed, be successful tener éxito 11

suddenly de repente 9

sugar azúcar *m.* 5

suit traje *m.* 8

suitcase maleta 12; **to pack a suitcase** hacer la maleta 12

summer verano 4; **next summer** verano que viene 4; próximo verano 4

sun sol *m.* 4; **It is sunny./It is very sunny.** Hace sol./ Hace mucho sol. 4

sunbathe tomar el sol 4

Sunday domingo 1

sunglasses gafas de sol 8

supervisor supervisor/a 11

support apoyo 8; apoyar 8

sure: to (not) be sure (no) estar seguro/a (de)

surf the Web navegar por la Red 4

surgeon cirujano/a 9

sweater suéter *m.* 8

sweatshirt sudadera 8

sweep barrer 6

sweet dulce *n. adj.* 10

swim nadar 4

swimming pool piscina 12

synagogue sinagoga 10

T

table mesa 2

tablecloth mantel *m.* 5

take llevar 7, 8; tomar 5; **to take a trip** hacer un viaje 4; **to take off (one's clothes, etc.)** quitarse (la ropa) 6; **to take out (the trash)** sacar (la basura) 6, 7

tall alto/a 3

taste probar (ue) 5

taxes impuestos 10

tea (hot/iced) tea té *m.* (caliente/helado) 5

teach enseñar 10

teacher maestro/a *m./f.* 2

team equipo 4

telephone: telephone book guía telefónica 11; **cell phone (with camera)** celular *m.* (con cámara) 8; **cordless phone** teléfono inalámbrico 8

television televisor *m.* 2; **flat-screen TV** televisor de pantalla plana 8

tell decir 4; **to tell (a story or incident)** contar (ue) 7

temperature: to take one's temperature tomar la temperatura 9

ten diez 1

tend atender (ie) 10

tenth décimo/a 11

test prueba 2

Thanks. Gracias. 1

theater teatro 2

there is, there are hay 1

there allí 2

thermometer termómetro 9

thief ladrón (ladrona) 10

thin delgado/a 3

think (that) creer (que) 4; **to think (to do something)** pensar (ie) (+ *infinitivo*) 5

third tercer, tercero/a 11

thirsty: to be thirsty tener sed 5

thirteen trece 1

thirty treinta 1

thirty-one treinta y uno 1

three hundred trescientos/as 5

three tres 1
throat garganta 9; **My throat hurts.** Me duele la garganta. 9
through por 6
throw parties dar fiestas 4
Thursday jueves *m.* 1
ticket (movie/ theater/ bus/ plane/ train) boleto 7
time hora 1; **on time** a tiempo 3; **What time is it?** ¿Qué hora es? 1
tip propina 5
tire: flat tire llanta pinchada 7
tired cansado/a 2
toast pan *m.* tostado 5
to a *prep.* 2
toast pan *m.* tostado 5
today hoy *adv.* 2
toe dedo del pie 9
toilet inodoro 6
tomato tomate *m.* 5
tomorrow mañana 2; **tomorrow morning** mañana por la mañana 4
tongue lengua 9
tonight esta noche 2
too (much) demasiado *adv.* 8
tooth diente 6; **to brush one's teeth** cepillarse los dientes 6
toothbrush cepillo de dientes 6
toothpaste pasta de dientes 6
top: on top of encima de *adv.* 6
tow truck grúa 10
towel toalla 6
town pueblo 10
traffic light semáforo 7
traffic tráfico 7
train station estación *f.* de tren 7
travel viajar 4
tree árbol *m.* 4
trip: to take a trip (to the country/city) hacer un viaje (al campo/a la ciudad) 4
tropical plant planta tropical 12
true verdad
truly yours atentamente 11
try probar (ue) 5; **to try on** probarse 8; **to try to (do something)** tratar de + *infinitivo* 10
t-shirt camiseta 8
Tuesday martes *m.* 1
tuna atún *m.* 5
turkey pavo 5
turn off apagar 8
turn on prender 8
turn doblar 7
TV: flat-screen TV televisor *m.* 2; de pantalla plana 8
twelve doce 1
twenty veinte 1
twenty-eight veintiocho 1
twenty-five veinticinco 1
twenty-four veinticuatro 1
twenty-nine veintinueve 1
twenty-one veintiuno 1
twenty-seven veintisiete 1
twenty-six veintiséis 1
twenty-three veintitrés 1
twenty-two veintidós 1
twice dos veces 3
twist one's ankle torcerse (ue) el tobillo 9
two hundred thousand doscientos mil 5

two hundred doscientos/as 5
two million dos millones 5
two thousand dos mil 5
two dos 1

U

ugly (a little bit) feo/a (un poco) 3
umbrella paraguas *m. s.* 8
uncle tío 3
unconscious: to be unconscious estar inconsciente 9
under debajo de *adv.* 6
understand entender (ie) 5
underwear ropa interior 8
union sindicato 11
university universidad *f.* 2
unpleasant antipático/a 3
until you arrive at . . . hasta llegar a... 7
upon (doing something) al + *infinitivo* 6
use usar 3

V

vacuum pasar la aspiradora 6
valley valle *m.* 4
vegetable legumbre *m.* 5; verdura 5
vendor vendedor/a 10
very muy 1
victim víctima *f.* 10
vinegar vinagre *m.* 5
violence violencia 10
visit visitar 3
volcano volcán *m.* 12
volunteer voluntario/a 10
vomiting: to be vomiting tener vómitos 9

W

wait for esperar 7
wait in line hacer fila 7
waiting room sala de espera 9
wake up despertarse (ie) 6
walk caminar 4; **to take a walk/ stroll** salir de paseo/dar un paseo 4
wall pared *f.* 2
wallet billetera 8
want desear 5; querer (ie) 5
war guerra 10
wash (the dishes) lavar (los platos) 6; **(one's hair)** lavarse (el pelo) 6
washing machine lavadora 6
wastebasket papelera 2
watch reloj *m.* 1; mirar 4; **to watch TV** ver la televisión 4
water (the plants) regar (ie) (las plantas) 6
water agua *f.* (*but* el agua) 5; **potable water** agua potable 12
waterfall cascada, catarata 12
watermelon sandía 5
wave ola 4
weapon arma *f.* (*but* el arma) 10
wear llevar 8

weather clima *m.* 4; **The weather is nice./The weather is very nice. /The weather is bad./The weather is very bad.** Hace buen tiempo./Hace muy buen tiempo./Hace mal tiempo./Hace muy mal tiempo. 4; **What is the weather like?** ¿Qué tal el clima?/ ¿Qué tiempo hace? 4

wedding boda 3

Wednesday miércoles *m.* 1

week semana 1; **last week** semana pasada 7; **next week** próxima semana 4; semana que viene 4; **once/ twice per week** una vez/ dos veces por semana 3

weekend: last weekend fin *m.* de semana pasado 7; **on weekends** los fines de semana 3; **this weekend** este fin de semana 2

welcome: You're welcome. De nada. 1

well bien 1; **Very well, thanks.** Muy bien, gracias. 1

wheelchair silla de ruedas 9

when cuándo 2

where dónde 2; **Where are you from?** ¿De dónde es usted?/ ¿De dónde eres? 1

while mientras *conj.* 9

white blanco/a 2

widower/ widow viudo/a 3

wife esposa 3

win ganar 4

wind viento 4; **It is windy./It is very windy.** Hace viento./ Hace mucho viento. 4

window ventana 2

wine glass copa 5

wine vino 5

winter invierno 4

wish desear 5

with con *prep.* 5

within dentro de *prep.* 6

without sin *prep.* 5

woman mujer *f.* 1

wool de lana 8

work trabajar 3; trabajo 2; **to work, function (machinery)** funcionar 7; **part-time/ full-time work/job** trabajo de tiempo parcial/ completo 11

workday día *m.* laboral 11

worker obrero/a 11

worried preocupado/a 2

worry preocuparse 9

worse peor 8

wound herida 9

wounded person herido/a 9

write escribir 4

X

x-ray radiografía 9

Y

year año 1; **last year** año pasado 7; **next year** próximo año 4; año que viene 4

yell gritar 9

yellow amarillo/a 2

yes sí 1

yesterday ayer *adv.* 7

young joven 3

young people jóvenes *m./f.* 3

younger menor 3

Z

zero cero 1

Índice

A

A
+ **el,** 2-58
personal, 3-87
Accents
for commands, 6-207
with interrogatives, 2-61
Address, forms of, 1-5
Adjectives
agreement with nouns, 1-11, 3-89
changes of meaning of, 3-90
demonstrative, 6-191
descriptive, 3-86, 3-89
ending in **-e, -ista** or consonant, 1-11, 3-89
ending in **-o,** 3-89
irregular comparative forms of, 8-272
+ **ísimo,** 5-156
of nationality, 1-9
placement, 3-90
plural forms, 2-51
position of, 3-90
possessive, 3-77, 8-283
preceding nouns, 3-89, 3-90
and their opposites, 3-89
Adverbs, 6-198
irregular comparative forms of, 8-272
Alguno, 10-354
Alphabet and pronunciation, P-3
Amenábar, Alejandro, 7-221
Aprender a, 4-116
Argentina, 3-85, 4-118, 5-149, 5-158, 5-163, 5-169, 6-188, 6-195,
6-210, 6-211, 7-243, 8-267, 8-287, 9-302, 9-313, 9-323,
9-327, 10-358, 12-409, 12-424, 12-427
Articles
definite, 1-16, 2-39
indefinite, 2-39, 2-57
with professions/vocations, 2-57

B

Bardem, Javier, 2-36
Blades, Rubén, 3-76
Bolívar, Simón, 7-220
Bolivia, 4-119, 5-169, 9-302, 9-323, 9-327, 12-418, 12-421
Borrowed words, 12-411
Botero, Fernando, 3-84
Buscar versus **mirar,** 5-148

C

Calendar, 1-23
California, 12-426
Canadá, 11-392
Castro, Julián, 2-55
Cervantes, Miguel de, 2-36
Chávez, César E., 11-393
Chile, 2-36, 4-118, 4-138, 4-143, 5-149, 5-151, 5-158, 5-159, 5-169,
6-210, 6-211, 7-225, 7-251, 8-286, 8-287, 9-313, 9-323, 10-355,
12-400, 12-427
Cognates, 1-11, 2-39
Colombia, 1-10, 2-54, 2-55, 3-84, 3-85, 3-105, 4-119, 5-149, 5-158,
5-159, 5-169, 7-229, 8-286, 8-287, 9-322–323, 10-339, 10-355,
12-418–419, 12-427

Colón, Cristóbal, 1-26, 2-36, 12-431
Colors, 2-48
Commands
accents for, 6-207
estar, 7-222
formal, 7-222
informal (**tú**), 3-83, 6-206, 6-207
formation, 4-115
irregular verbs, 4-123
ir, 7-222
let's, 4-134, 7-222
negative, 7-222
nosotros, 7-222
pronouns and, 7-222, 8-281
ser, 7-222
spelling changes, 7-222
Comparisons
of equality, 8-270
of inequality, 8-272
superlatives, 8-274
Conditional
in *if* clauses, 12-416
of irregular verbs, 12-404
of regular verbs, 12-404
uses of, 12-404, 12-405
Conocer versus **saber,** 4-131
Costa Rica, 2-287, 5-158, 5-163, 6-210, 6-211, 8-267, 8-279, 8-291,
9-323, 12-400, 12-410, 12-411
Courtesy, expressions of, 1-9
Creer que, 4-116
Cruz, Penélope, 2-55
Cuando, verb use with, 11-384
¿Cuántos?/¿cuántas?, 1-16
Cuba, 2-54, 2-69, 5-149, 5-158, 5-168–169, 7-220, 7-246, 8-276,
8-277, 9-322, 9-323, 10-343, 10-365, 12-426

D

Dalmau, Custo and David, 8-277
Dates, 1-22
Days of the week, 1-20, 1-21
De
+ adjectives, 5-161
+ **el,** 2-43
+ **ser,** 3-97
to express possession, 3-76
+ noun, 2-37
possession with, 2-49
Deber, 4-116
Definite articles, 2-39
Del Toro, Guillermo, 2-55
Demonstratives, 6-191, 6-192
Descriptive adjectives, 3-89
Diphthongs, P-2
Directions, giving, 7-225
Dormir, 5-164, 9-298

E

Ebrard, Marcelo, 3-84
Ecuador, 1-10, 2-54, 3-85, 4-139, 4-143, 5-149, 5-159, 5-169, 7-229,
8-260, 8-286, 9-323, 10-365, 11-386, 12-401, 12-418–419,
12-427, 12-429

El Salvador, 8-260, 8-286, 8-289, 9-323, 9-327, 10-365

Encantar, 4-113

España, 1-6, 1-7, 1-10, 1-25, 1-26, 1-27, 1-30, 2-36, 2-37, 2-45, 2-54, 2-55, 2-65, 2-69, 3-85, 3-93, 3-101, 3-103, 4-110, 4-118, 4-126, 4-133, 4-141, 5-149, 5-159, 5-162, 5-163, 5-167, 5-169, 6-188, 6-194, 6-195, 6-210, 7-220, 7-221, 8-267, 8-277, 8-286, 8-287, 9-312, 9-313, 9-316, 9-322–323, 9-323, 10-357, 10-358, 11-386, 11-387, 11-389, 12-408, 12-414, 12-427

Estados Unidos, 1-10, 1-22, 1-24, 2-54, 2-64, 3-85, 3-101, 5-158, 5-162, 5-167, 5-171, 6-194, 6-210, 7-228, 7-231, 7-241, 8-266, 8-267, 8-269, 8-276, 8-286, 8-287, 9-302, 9-307, 9-312, 10-339, 10-342, 10-343, 10-350–351, 10-355, 10-360–361, 11-392, 11-393, 12-424, 12-426

Estar
command form, 7-222
to express conditions, feelings, 2-51
+ location, 2-41
with marital status, 3-95
in present progressive, 5-173
preterit, 8-262
ser versus, 2-41, 3-95, 3-97

Exclamations, punctuation of, 1-3

F

Formal commands, 7-222
Frequency, expressions of, 1-13, 3-82
Future
with **ir + a +** infinitive, 4-134
of irregular verbs, 11-382
of probability, 11-383
of regular verbs, 11-382
time expressions, 4-136
uses of, 11-382, 11-383
perfect, 11-383

G

García Bernal, Gael, 2-36
Gender
cognates, 1-11
of nouns, 2-39
Gestures, 1-5, 1-6
González Iñárritu, Alejandro, 2-36
Good-bye, saying, 1-4
Goya Foods, Inc., 11-387
Greetings
formal, 1-4, 1-5
informal, 1-2, 1-5
Guatemala, 5-158, 5-159, 5-168, 7-244, 9-303, 9-322, 10-351, 10-353, 11-386, 12-400
Gustar, 4-112
verbs similar to, 4-112, 4-113, 9-296, 10-346

H

Haber, 10-337, 11-372 (*See also* **Hay**)
Había/hubo, 9-316
Hace... (*ago*), 9-301
Hacer
conditional, 12-404
future, 11-382
imperfect subjunctive, 12-414
preterite, 7-237, 8-262
Hay, 9-309, 9-316, 11-383, 12-405, 12-414 (*See also* **Haber**)
Herrera, Carolina, 8-276
Holidays, 1-22, 1-23, 1-24, 2-36
Honduras, 3-105, 4-118, 5-149, 5-158, 5-159, 9-323, 12-401, 12-425

I

If clauses, 12-416
Imperfect indicative
of irregular verbs, 9-309
preterit versus, 9-308, 9-317, 9-319
of regular verbs, 9-308
Imperfect subjunctive
formation, 12-414
in *if* clauses, 12-416
uses, 12-414, 12-415
Impersonal **se,** 5-149
Indefinite articles, 2-39, 2-57
Indefinite/negative words, 10-354
Indicative versus subjunctive, 10-334, 10-335
Indirect object pronouns, 8-281 (*See also* Pronouns)
Infinitives
with expressions of emotion, 10-346
ir + a +, 4-134
prepositions used with, 6-189
Interrogative words, 2-61
Introductions
formal, 1-4
gestures with, 1-6
informal, 1-2, 1-3
Ir, 9-309
+ a + destination, 2-58
+ a + infinitive, 4-134
command form, 7-222
present indicative, 2-58
Ir + a +
destination, 2-58
infinitive, 4-134

J

Jugar, 4-111

K

Kahlo, Frida, 2-36, 5-149

L

Linking words, P-6
Llevar, 8-260
Location
adverbs and prepositions expressing, 2-43
estar +, 2-41
Lo que, 12-422

M

Maps
Hispanic influence in the United States, 2-54
Mexico City subway, 7-250
northern and southern hemispheres, 4-130
Spain, Roman conquest of, 1-25
Spaniards arrive in America, 1-26, 1-27
Martí, José, 7-220
–mente, 6-198
México, 1-10, 1-30, 2-36, 2-44, 2-55, 2-69, 3-84, 3-85, 3-87, 3-101, 4-118, 4-119, 4-126, 4-138, 5-149, 5-158, 5-159, 5-163, 5-168, 5-171, 6-188, 6-194, 6-202, 7-220, 7-228, 7-238–239, 7-250, 7-251, 8-269, 8-286, 8-287, 9-303, 9-313, 9-322, 9-323, 9-327, 10-339, 10-342, 10-353, 10-360, 11-387, 11-392, 11-393, 12-418, 12-427
Months, 1-22

N

Nationalities, 1-9
Negatives
 commands, 6-206, 7-222
 statements, 1-13
 statements, questions, 5-154
 words, 6-186, 10-354
Neruda, Pablo, 2-36
Nicaragua, 6-210, 6-211, 9-323, 10-365, 11-389
Nicknames, 6-197
Ninguno, 10-354
Ni...ni, 11-375
Nouns
 gender of, 2-39
 masculine that end in **-a,** 2-39
 plural, 1-11, 1-17, 2-39
Numbers
 0 to 59, 1-14
 from 60 to 100, 3-76
 100 and up, 5-150
 ordinal, 11-380

O

O (*or*) changed to **u,** 1-13
Object of preposition pronouns, 6-189
Ojalá (que)..., 10-346

P

Panamá, 3-105, 4-119, 6-210, 9-322, 9-323, 10-365, 12-401
Para
 + deadline, by/for, 11-370
 + infinitive, 6-189
 por versus, 8-280, 11-390
 trabajar para, 11-370
Paraguay, 4-118, 5-158, 5-169, 6-211, 7-255, 8-291, 9-302, 9-323, 9-327
Pasabán, Edurne, 4-141
Past participles
 with **haber,** 11-372
 irregular, 11-373
 regular, 11-372
Past perfect, 11-383
Pedir, 5-164, 9-298
Pensar, 5-165
Personal **a,** 3-87
Perú, 1-10, 2-54, 5-149, 5-159, 5-169, 5-179, 6-211, 7-230, 7-240,
 7-241, 9-302, 9-323, 12-401, 12-418–419, 12-427
Poder, 5-164, 8-262
Por, 4-110, 8-280
 para versus, 8-280, 11-390
 to express spatial relationships, 4-110, 6-189
Possession
 adjectives of, 3-77
 to clarify, 8-283
 with **de,** 2-49
 emphatic adjectives of, 8-283
 possessive adjectives, 3-77
Prepositions
 directional, 11-371
 expressing location, 2-43
 pronouns as objects of, 6-189
 used with infinitives, 6-189 (*See also specific prepositions*)
 verbs following, 6-189
Present indicative
 irregular **yo** form in, 4-123
 present subjunctive versus, 10-334, 10-335
 regular **-ar** verbs, 3-80

regular **-er** verbs, 4-115–116
regular **-ir** verbs, 4-115–116
of stem-changing verbs, 4-111, 5-164
Present participles
 irregular, 5-173
 in present progressive, 5-173
 regular, 5-173
 stem-changing verbs, 5-173
Present perfect, 11-372, 11-373
Present progressive, 5-173
Present subjunctive
 in expressing good wishes, 10-335
 formation of irregular verbs, 10-337
 formation of regular verbs, 10-334
 formation of spelling-change verbs, 10-335
 formation of stem-changing verbs, 10-337
 present indicative versus, 10-334, 10-335
 usage, 10-334
Preterit
 dar, 7-237
 hacer, 7-237
 imperfect versus, 9-308, 317, 319
 ir, 7-237
 irregular verbs, 7-237, 8-262
 leer, 7-234
 oír, 7-234
 of regular **-ar** verbs, 7-226
 of regular **-er** verbs, 7-234
 of regular **-ir** verbs, 7-234
 ser, 7-237
 spelling-change verbs, 7-226
 stem-changing verbs, 9-298
Pronouns
 with commands, 6-206, 7-222
 demonstrative, 6-192
 direct and indirect together, 8-281
 direct object, 5-154, 7-245
  in present progressive, 5-173
 indirect object, 7-245, 246, 9-296, 10-338
 indirect objects with **gustar,** 4-112, 4-113
 objects of prepositions, 6-189
 possessive, 8-283
 in present progressive, 5-173
 relative, 12-422
 subject, 1-7
Pronunciation, P-1
Puerto Rico, 1-10, 2-54, 2-55, 2-69, 3-93, 4-119, 4-127, 5-149,
 5-168, 7-230, 10-342, 10-365

Q

¡Qué...!, 10-335
Que, 12-422
Querer, 5-164, 8-262
Questions
 punctuation of, 1-3
 yes/no, 1-13
Quien(es), 12-422

R

Reading strategies
 guessing meaning from context, 3-103
 identifying target audience and point of view, 7-253
 inferring meaning from text, 12-429
 making lists as you read, 6-213
 making predictions about a text, 11-395
 reading for main idea, 8-289

read, look up, describe, 9-325
recognizing word families, 10-363
scanning for specific information, 4-141
skimming for cognates, familiar words, 1-29
summarizing, 5-179
using images to understand context, 1-29
utilizing background knowledge, 2-67
Recipes, 5-176–177
Reflexive pronouns, 6-199, 6-207, 7-222
Reflexive verbs, 6-199
Relative pronouns, 12-422
República Dominicana, 2-54, 4-114, 4-119, 4-143, 5-149, 5-168, 8-277, 8-287, 9-322–323, 10-342, 12-427
Research strategies
    applying reading strategies to research, 3-105
    exploring cities online, 7-255
    finding opportunities for service, 10-365
    finding Spanish-language sources, 2-69
    following current events, 12-431
    identifying healthcare sources, 9-327
    including photo and video sources, 1-30, 6-215
    participating in language communities, 8-291
    using bilingual dictionaries, 5-181
    using business-related search terms, 11-397
    using geography and climate resources online, 4-143
Rivera, Diego, 2-36
Rodríguez, Narciso, 8-276

S

Saber
    conocer versus, 4-131
    preterit, 8-262
Santana, Johan, 2-55
Se, 5-149, 6-199, 7-222, 8-281
Seasons, 4-128
Ser, 9-309
    adjectives used with, 1-11
    command form, 7-222
    + de, 2-49, 3-97
    plus descriptive adjectives, 3-89
    estar versus, 2-41
    to express origins, 1-8
    with location, 2-63
    subject pronouns with, 1-7
    telling time with, 1-18
Shakira, 2-55
Sotomayor, Sonia, 2-55
Spanish words used in English, 1-13
Speaking strategies
    active listening, 8-290
    asking clarifying questions, 12-430
    borrowing new words, 9-326
    confirming comprehension, 1-30, 10-364
    handling unknown words, 4-142
    increasing participation through questions, 3-104
    using nonverbal cues, 6-214
    reformulating your speech, 11-396
    requesting repetitions, 2-68
    using descriptions to avoid lapses, 5-180
    using strategic pauses, 7-254
Stress and written accent, P-2
Subject pronouns
    omission of, 1-7
    with **ser,** 1-7
Subjunctive
    expressing subjective reactions, 10-334
        with expressions of doubt or negation, 10-356
        with expressions of emotion, 10-346
        with expressions of influence, 10-338
        if clauses, 12-416
        with meaning of *will,* 10-335
Superlatives, 5-156, 8-274

T

Tan/tanto, 8-270
Telephone greetings, 6-188
Tener, 3-75
    + años, 3-76
    to express age, 3-76
    to express symptoms, 9-296
    to indicate possession, 3-75, 3-77
    + que, 6-204
Time
    telling, 1-18
    24-hour clock, 1-20
    at what time, 2-38
Time expressions, 1-18, 2-59
    future, 4-136
    past, 7-228
Titles of persons, 1-5, 3-74
Toledo, Isabel, 8-276
Treviño, Jesse, 12-424

U

Uruguay, 3-85, 4-118, 5-149, 5-158, 7-243, 7-255, 9-302, 9-303, 9-323, 10-365

V

Venezuela, 1-10, 2-54, 2-55, 3-93, 4-119, 4-138, 5-149, 5-163, 7-220, 8-276, 9-313, 9-322, 10-339, 12-400, 12-418–419, 12-427
Ver, 9-309
Vosotros/as, 1-7
Vowels, P-1

W

Weather, 4-128, 4-130, 9-308
Wishes, expressing, 1-21
Writing strategies
    developing a good topic sentence, 6-214
    drafting a newspaper article, 9-326
    drafting a persuasive business letter, 10-364
    gathering information, 4-142
    letting the first draft flow, 5-180
    listing information, 1-30, 2-68
    providing supporting information, 8-290
    reading aloud, 12-430
    reviewing a cover letter, 11-396
    thinking about your audience, 3-104
    using sequencing words to connect sentences, 7-254

Y

Years, expressing, 5-150
Yes/no questions, 1-13

Z

Zapata, Emiliano, 7-220
Zodiac, 1-23

Países y Gentilicios

Abisinia abisinio/a
Afganistán (el) afgano/a
Albania albanés, albanesa
Alemania alemán, alemana
Andorra andorrano/a
Angola angoleño/a
Antigua y Barbuda antiguano/a
Arabia Saudí o Arabia Saudita saudí
Argelia argelino/a
Argentina (la) argentino/a
Armenia armenio/a
Australia australiano/a
Austria austriaco/a
Azerbaiyán azerbaiyano/a

Bahamas (las) bahameño/a
Bahréin bahreiní
Bangladesh bengalí
Barbados barbadense
Bélgica belga
Belice beliceño/a
Benín beninés, beninesa
Bielorrusia bielorruso/a
Bolivia boliviano/a
Bosnia-Herzegovina bosnio/a
Botsuana botsuano/a
Brasil (el) brasileño/a
Brunéi Darussalam bruneano/a
Bulgaria búlgaro/a
Burkina Faso burkinés, burkinesa
Burundi burundés, burundesa
Bután butanés, butanesa

Cabo Verde caboverdiano/a
Camboya camboyano/a
Camerún (el) camerunés, camerunesa
Canadá (el) canadiense
Chad (el) chadiano/a
Chile chileno/a
China chino/a
Chipre chipriota
Ciudad del Vaticano vaticano/a
Colombia colombiano/a
Comoras (las) comorense/a
Congo (el) congoleño/a
Corea del Norte norcoreano/a
Corea del Sur surcoreano/a
Costa Rica costarricense
Costa de Marfil marfileño/a
Croacia croata
Cuba cubano/a

Dinamarca danés, danesa
Dominica dominiqués/ dominiquesa

Ecuador (el) ecuatoriano/a
Egipto egipcio/a

Emiratos Árabes Unidos (los) emiratense
Eritrea eritreo/a
Eslovaquia eslovaco/a
Eslovenia esloveno/a
España español/a
Estados Unidos de América (los) estadounidense
Estonia estonio/a
Etiopía etíope

Filipinas filipino/a
Finlandia finlandés, finlandesa
Francia francés, francesa
Fiyi fiyiano/a

Gabón (el) gabonés, gabonesa
Gambia gambiano/a
Georgia georgiano/a
Ghana ghanés, ghanesa
Granada granadino/a
Grecia griego/a
Guatemala guatemalteco/a
Guinea guineano/a
Guinea-Bissáu guineano/a
Guinea Ecuatorial (la) guineano, ecuatoguineano/a
Guyana guyanés, guyanesa

Haití haitiano/a
Honduras hondureño/a
Hungría húngaro/a

India (la) indio/a
Indonesia indonesio/a
Irán iraní
Iraq iraquí
Irlanda irlandés, irlandesa
Islandia islandés, islandesa
Islas Cook (las) cookiano/a
Islas Marshall (las) marshalés, marshalesa
Islas Salomón (las) salomonense
Israel israelí
Italia italiano/a

Jamaica jamaicano/a
Japón (el) japonés, japonesa
Jordania jordano/a

Kazajistán kazako/a, kazajo/a
Kenia keniata
Kirguistán kirguís
Kiribati kiribatiano/a
Kuwait kuwaití

Laos laosiano/a
Lesotho lesothense
Letonia letón, letona